TORTS AND PERSONAL INJURY LAW

FOURTH EDITION

DELMAR CENGAGE Learning

Options.
Over 300 products in every area of the law: textbooks, online courses, CD-ROMs, reference books, companion websites, and more – helping you succeed in the classroom and on the job.

Support.
We offer unparalleled, practical support: robust instructor and student supplements to ensure the best learning experience, custom publishing to meet your unique needs, and other benefits such as Delmar Cengage Learning's Student Achievement Award. And our sales representatives are always ready to provide you with dependable service.

Feedback.
As always, we want to hear from you! Your feedback is our best resource for improving the quality of our products. Contact your sales representative or write us at the address below if you have any comments about our materials or if you have a product proposal.

Accounting and Financials for the Law Office • Administrative Law • Alternative Dispute Resolution • Bankruptcy Business Organizations/Corporations • Careers and Employment • Civil Litigation and Procedure • CLA Exam Preparation • Computer Applications in the Law Office • Constitutional Law • Contract Law • Court Reporting Criminal Law and Procedure • Document Preparation • Elder Law • Employment Law • Environmental Law • Ethics Evidence Law • Family Law • Health Care Law • Immigration Law • Intellectual Property • Internships Interviewing and Investigation • Introduction to Law • Introduction to Paralegalism • Juvenile Law • Law Office Management • Law Office Procedures • Legal Nurse Consulting • Legal Research, Writing, and Analysis • Legal Terminology • Legal Transcription • Media and Entertainment Law • Medical Malpractice Law Product Liability • Real Estate Law • Reference Materials • Social Security • Sports Law • Torts and Personal Injury Law • Wills, Trusts, and Estate Administration • Workers' Compensation Law

---

DELMAR CENGAGE Learning
5 Maxwell Drive
Clifton Park, New York 12065-2919

For additional information, find us online at:
www.delmar.cengage.com

TORTS AND PERSONAL INJURY LAW

FOURTH EDITION

Cathy J. Okrent

DELMAR
CENGAGE Learning™

Australia • Brazil • Japan • Korea • Mexico • Singapore • Spain • United Kingdom • United States

DELMAR
CENGAGE Learning™

Torts and Personal Injury Law, Fourth Edition
Cathy J. Okrent

Vice President, Career and Professional
    Editorial: Dave Garza
Director of Learning Solutions:
    Sandy Clark
Senior Acquisitions Editor: Shelley Esposito
Managing Editor: Larry Main
Senior Product Manager: Melissa Riveglia
Vice President, Career and Professional
    Marketing: Jennifer McAvey
Marketing Director: Deborah Yarnell
Marketing Manager: Erin Brennan
Marketing Coordinator: Jonathan Sheehan
Production Director: Wendy Troeger
Production Manager: Mark Bernard
Senior Content Project Manager:
    Betty Dickson
Senior Art Director: Joy Kocsis
Senior Director of Product Management for
    Career, Professional, and Languages:
    Tom Smith
Production Technology Analyst: Thomas Stover

For product information and technology assistance, contact us at
Cengage Learning Customer & Sales Support, 1-800-354-9706

For permission to use material from this text or product,
submit all requests online at **www.cengage.com/permissions.**
Further permissions questions can be e-mailed to
permissionrequest@cengage.com

Library of Congress Control Number: 2009923597

ISBN-13: 978-1-4283-2076-5
ISBN-10: 1-4283-2076-8

Delmar
5 Maxwell Drive
Clifton Park, NY 12065-2919
USA

Cengage Learning is a leading provider of customized learning solutions with office locations around the globe, including Singapore, the United Kingdom, Australia, Mexico, Brazil, and Japan. Locate your local office at:
international.cengage.com/region

Cengage Learning products are represented in Canada by Nelson Education, Ltd.

To learn more about Delmar, visit **www.cengage.com/delmar**

Purchase any of our products at your local college store or at our preferred online store **www.ichapters.com**

NOTICE TO THE READER
Publisher does not warrant or guarantee any of the products described herein or perform any independent analysis in connection with any of the product information contained herein. Publisher does not assume, and expressly disclaims, any obligation to obtain and include information other than that provided to it by the manufacturer. The reader is expressly warned to consider and adopt all safety precautions that might be indicated by the activities described herein and to avoid all potential hazards. By following the instructions contained herein, the reader willingly assumes all risks in connection with such instructions. The publisher makes no representations or warranties of any kind, including but not limited to, the warranties of fitness for particular purpose or merchantability, nor are any such representations implied with respect to the material set forth herein, and the publisher takes no responsibility with respect to such material. The publisher shall not be liable for any special, consequential, or exemplary damages resulting, in whole or part, from the readers' use of, or reliance upon, this material.

Printed in the United States of America
3 4 5 6 7 12 11

Dedication

This book is dedicated to my nieces Rachel, Rebecca, Madelynn, and my nephew Joseph.

Cathy J. Okrent

Contents

chapter 4
Defenses to Negligence   90

chapter 5
Intentional Torts: Injuries to Persons   110

chapter 10
Products Liability

chapter 11
Special Tort Actions

chapter 12
Tort Immunities
346

chapter 13
Tort Investigation
365

Appendices

Preface

WHAT IS NEW IN THE FOURTH EDITION?

As *Torts and Personal Injury Law* approaches two decades in publication, the fourth edition adds 30 new cases that include the following hot-button issues: malicious prosecution of the Duke lacrosse players, toxic mass torts, patient dumping, spoliation of evidence, sexual abuse by clergy, theft of donor eggs, spam e-mail fraud, and obesity caused by trans fats in fast food. Now the book contains a total of 66 annotated cases that were carefully selected for examination of various tort claims. We have also added a new and exciting feature that opens each chapter, "The Biggest Mistakes Paralegals Make and How to Avoid Them." Each illustrates a dilemma, an ethical lapse, or other unfortunate experience that actually happened to workers I have known. While I wish these mistakes had never occurred to the many hardworking individuals featured, the point of sharing them is learning how to avoid such errors. Avoiding similar mistakes should keep the reader on a solid career path to success.

OVERVIEW

This text is an overview of tort law for the personal injury paralegal. Chapter 1 discusses tort law generally and historically; it also provides an overview of a civil case and alternate dispute resolution (ADR). Chapter 2 summarizes negligence. Chapter 3 discusses special negligence actions, including premises liability, vicarious liability, and negligent infliction of emotional distress. Chapter 4 focuses on the defenses to negligence actions. Chapters 5 and 6 consider intentional torts and injuries to persons. Chapter 7 is devoted to intentional torts and injuries to property. Chapter 8 addresses defenses to intentional torts. Chapter 9 covers strict, or absolute, liability. Chapter 10 illustrates product liability cases. Chapter 11 features special tort actions. Chapter 12 discusses tort immunities. Chapter 13 focuses on tort investigation.

CHAPTER FEATURES

Of course, favorite elements have all been retained. Chapters begin with an outlined introduction. Chapters end with a summary, review questions, additional problems, and a list of key terms that were used throughout the chapter, in addition to chapter-specific Internet resources. Many recent cases have been added.

The running glossary features some standard definitions from *Oran's Dictionary of the Law*, © 2008, Delmar Cengage Learning, to help students learn or refresh their knowledge regarding these terms.

The text combines theoretical and practical applications. Accompanying each tort topic are hypothetical examples to illustrate how the abstract rules pertain to real life. Illustrative cases are included to portray the actual application of legal principles in appellate court opinions, legal encyclopedia summaries, and the *Restatement (Second) of Torts*.

All cases included are for educational purposes, as examples. The cases have been heavily edited, and most citations omitted, so as to include as many cases in the text as possible. The reader should always refer to original sources and verify that there have been no recent changes in the law in a particular jurisdiction. Sample letters, forms, and reports are included for illustrative purposes. The people named in the exhibits and hypotheticals are all fictional; any resemblance to known people is purely coincidental.

▌ SUPPLEMENTAL TEACHING MATERIALS

Instructor's Manual

▶ An Instructor's Manual and TestBank by the author of the text accompanies this edition and has been greatly expanded to incorporate all changes in the text and to provide comprehensive teaching support. It includes chapter summaries, chapter outlines, lecture hints, problems, and projects.

▶ **Student CD-ROM**—The new accompanying CD-ROM provides additional material to help students master the important concepts in the course. This CD-ROM includes a chapter on ethics, supplementary cases, and additional forms.

▶ **Spend Less Time Planning and More Time Teaching**—With Delmar Cengage Learning's Instructor Resources to Accompany Torts and Personal Injury Law, preparing for class and evaluating students has never been easier!

This invaluable instructor CD-ROM allows you anywhere, anytime access to all of your resources:

- The **Instructor's Manual** contains various resources and answers for each chapter of the book and is easily customizable in Microsoft Word.
- The **Computerized Testbank** in ExamView makes generating tests and quizzes a snap. With many questions and different styles to choose from, you can create customized assessments for your students with the click of a button. Add your own unique questions and print rationales for easy class preparation.
- Customizable **PowerPoint® Presentations** focus on key points for each chapter.

PowerPoint® is a registered trademark of the Microsoft Corporation.

All of these Instructor materials are also posted on our Website, in the Online Resources section.

Online Companion™

The Online Companion™ contains Torts Trends features, an additional chapter covering paralegal ethics, additional cases, and some sample forms, projects, and Web links. The Online Companion™ can be found at **www.paralegal.delmar. cengage.com** in the Online Companion™ section of the Website.

Web Page

Come visit our Web site at **www.paralegal.delmar.cengage.com**, where you will find valuable information such as hot links and sample materials to download, as well as other Delmar Cengage Learning products.

Please note that the Internet resources are of a time-sensitive nature and URL addresses may often change or be deleted.

Acknowledgments

Torts and Personal Injury Law could not have been produced without the dedication of many people. I thank my editors at Delmar (in particular, Shelley Esposito, Melissa Riveglia, and Lyss Zaza) and the American Law Institute, the *National Law Journal*, and the *Rutgers Computer & Technology Law Journal*, for allowing use of reprinted portions of their materials.

Special thanks to S4Carlisle Publishing Services and Tiffany Timmerman, project editor, for managing the production of this book in a timely, thorough, and professional manner. I truly appreciate your assistance.

Additionally, I would like to acknowledge the invaluable contributions of the following reviewers for their suggestions and attention to detail:

Hank Arnold
Aiken Technical College
Aiken, SC

Constance Herinkova
South College
Knoxville, TN

S. Whittington Brown
Pulaski Technical College
Little Rock, AR

Linda Hibbs
Community College of Philadelphia
Philadelphia, PA

John DeLeo
Central Pennsylvania College
Summerdale, PA

Jane Jacobs
Community College of Philadelphia
Philadelphia, PA

Karl Durand
McIntosh College
Dover, NH

Deborah Keene
Lansing Community College
Lansing, MI

Thank you one and all.

Table of Cases

chapter 1

Introduction to Torts and Legal Analysis

chapter outline

- The Biggest Mistakes Paralegals Make and How to Avoid Them
- Introduction
- Torts Defined
- History of Tort Law

- Public Policy Objectives in Tort Law
- Analyzing Hypothetical Problems
- Solving Tort Problems
- Overview of a Civil Case
- Case Resolution

THE BIGGEST MISTAKES PARALEGALS MAKE & HOW TO AVOID THEM

It Isn't All About You!

I loved everything about working as a paralegal at a prestigious downtown law firm, except time billing and expense reports. It really sapped my energy and distracted me from the really important work I do, so I tended to procrastinate about completing those financials. Typically I saved it all up and did it one Saturday morning every month or so. It worked out great until we went to a system that required contemporaneous billing throughout the day. Well, not only was I distracted, I was demoralized by how much it slowed me down! The managing attorney even threatened to put me on a performance improvement plan (PIP) if I couldn't improve my billable time. I was really mad about that after five years of service and good performance reviews. I was so close to quitting I could have screamed! Why do they want to micromanage me?

(continues)

LESSON LEARNED: Billing as you go is good work ethic because it is a tool to manage your time and ascertain how productive you really are each day.

Law firms are a business and need to budget and staff according to their revenue stream. If everyone haphazardly filed billable hours and expense reports, there would be economic chaos and possible bankruptcy from making uninformed forecasts and budgets. Most important of all, clients deserve to know on a timely basis exactly what their costs of legal services are. You are there to serve the firm, and by extension the client employs you. Rationalizing what works for you and feeling micromanaged contradict the fact that you are part of a team that needs to play as one. It is your firm's bat and ball and they determine who gets to play for them. Once I realized all these factors, it made sense.

▌ INTRODUCTION

This chapter covers the definition of a tort, the three broad categories of torts, the history of tort law, the public policy objectives behind tort law, and the analytical processes used both to understand appellate court opinions and to solve hypothetical problems.

This chapter includes:

- ▸ Definitions of torts
- ▸ An initial description of negligence
- ▸ The elements of strict (absolute) liability
- ▸ The historical roots of tort law
- ▸ The public policy objectives of tort law in terms of compensating injured parties, holding wrongdoers liable, and allocating losses across society
- ▸ Development of an analytical framework to understand appellate court opinions
- ▸ Construction of an analytical formula to solve hypothetical problems by applying the legal principles to the facts of the case
- ▸ Assembly of an analytical formula that allows any tort law problem or question to be continuously narrowed to reveal the answer (IRAC)
- ▸ Demonstration of how tort law analysis goes from the general to the specific
- ▸ An overview of a civil case
- ▸ A discussion of alternate dispute resolution.

▌ TORTS DEFINED

tort | A civil (as opposed to a criminal) wrong, other than a breach of contract. For an act to be a tort, there must be: a legal duty owed by one person to another, a breach (breaking) of that duty, and harm done as a direct result of the action.

tortfeasor | A person who commits a tort.

A **tort** is a wrongful injury to a person or his or her property. The person inflicting the harm is called the **tortfeasor** (*feasor* meaning "doer"). The word *tort* is French, taken from the Latin *torquere* (meaning "to twist") and characterizes behavior that warps or bends society's rules about avoiding causing harm to others. The French phrase *de son tort demesne* (meaning "in his own wrong") was used to describe grievous misconduct between individuals and to assign blame to the responsible party.

Sources of Tort Law

Tort law is derived from both **common law** and statutory law. Legislatures often enact statutes to supplement, modify, or supersede common law tort principles. Courts may turn the tables on the legislature by issuing new common law rulings interpreting the meaning of statutes. In this way the law matures, with both courts and legislatures adjusting the law to meet the changing needs of society.

common law | Either all case-law or the caselaw that is made by judges in the absence of relevant statutes.

Broad Categories of Tort Law

Tort law considers the rights and remedies available to persons injured through other people's carelessness or intentional misconduct. Tort law also holds persons in certain circumstances responsible for other people's injuries regardless of blame. Torts are commonly subdivided into three broad categories: negligence, intentional torts, and strict (or absolute) liability.

Negligence. **Negligence** is the failure of an ordinary, reasonable, and prudent person to exercise due care in a given set of circumstances. It is distinguishable from *intentional torts* in that negligence does not require an *intent* to commit a wrongful action; rather, the wrongful action itself is sufficient to constitute negligence. Intentional torts, as the name indicates, require the tortfeasor to intend to commit the wrongful act. What makes misconduct negligent is that the behavior was not reasonably careful and someone was injured as a result of this unreasonable carelessness; for example, failing to watch the road ahead when driving a car.

negligence | The failure to exercise a reasonable amount of care in a situation that causes harm to someone or something.

Intentional Torts. **Intentional torts** are actions expressly designed with purpose or intent to injure another person or that person's property, and not in the criminal sense. The tortfeasor intends a particular harm to result from the misconduct. There are several different types of intentional torts: intentional, reckless, or negligent. Examples of specific intentional torts are assault and battery, each of which is discussed in detail in later chapters. These are in contrast to injuries caused by negligence or accidents.

intentional tort | An injury *designed* to injure a person or that person's property.

Strict (Absolute) Liability. **Strict (absolute) liability** is the tortfeasor's responsibility for injuring another regardless of intent, negligence, or fault. The most important type of strict liability is *products liability,* a theory under which the manufacturer or other seller of an unreasonably dangerous or defective product

strict (absolute) liability | The legal responsibility for damage or injury, even if you are not at fault or negligent.

is held liable for injuries the product causes. Strict liability is different from intentional torts in that intent to commit an absolute liability tort is irrelevant. Likewise, strict liability is distinguishable from negligence, because the tortfeasor is responsible under absolute liability regardless of how careful he or she might have been.

These concepts are presented here only to establish basic terminology. Subsequent chapters explore each of these topics in greater detail.

The Unique Elements of Each Tort. Each type of tort contains its own unique elements, which are needed to bring a lawsuit. While the elements of each are unique, tort analysis in general is the same. In a tort case, one must always ask whether the following exist:

1. Duty
2. Breach of duty
3. Causation
4. Damages.

For instance, battery, an intentional tort, may be readily distinguished from defamation because it carries its own definition and rules. Likewise, the elements of negligence are different from strict liability's components, and so on. The key to understanding tort law is to identify the type of broad tort category involved in the case. Ask whether the problem contains intentional torts (and, if so, which particular one(s)), negligence, or strict liability. Next, apply the appropriate rules of law to the specific facts of the case.

Like all forms of law, torts have undergone a long and interesting period of growth and development. The next section briefly examines the history of tort law.

▐ HISTORY OF TORT LAW

Tort law, like all American law, traces its origins to English and Western European history. After the Norman conquest of England in 1066, William the Conqueror brought Norman law (which was heavily influenced by Roman law) to intermingle with Anglo-Saxon and Celtic legal traditions. The result was the common law, which at the time consisted of the underlying legal principles and social attitudes gleaned from generations of judicial decisions by local tribunals. Even today, the bulk of tort law has been derived from our common law heritage.

The King's Writs

During the Middle Ages, much of this common law was passed on orally. As a result, common law often varied widely among localities. To unify these divergent ideas, the king established formal procedures *(king's writs)* by which crown subjects could petition the king's courts for redress.

Evolution of Modern Tort Law

During the eighteenth and nineteenth centuries, English tort law began to shift from the old writs system to torts involving intent and fault, known today as intentional torts and negligence. This evolution was copied in the United States. Gradually, the common law grew to include the modern torts discussed throughout this text. Today's tort law is a combination of English and American common law plus statutory law.

What does tort law seek to accomplish? Next, we examine the social and economic purposes that influence, and are influenced by, tort law.

▌ PUBLIC POLICY OBJECTIVES IN TORT LAW

Like every aspect of our legal system, there are several purposes underlying tort principles. These include (1) protecting persons and property from unjust injury by providing legally enforceable rights; (2) compensating victims by holding accountable those persons responsible for causing such harms; (3) encouraging minimum standards of social conduct among society's members; (4) deterring violations of those standards of conduct; and (5) allocating losses among different participants in the social arena.

Protecting Persons and Property: Accountability

Like the king's writs, modern tort law strives to prevent unjustified harm to innocent victims. Tort law enables private citizens to use the legal system to resolve disputes in which one party claims that the other has acted improperly, resulting in harm.

Compensating the Victim

The system compels the tortfeasor to compensate the injured party for his or her losses. This *accountability* (or *culpability*) factor is crucial to our legal sense of fair play and equity. People should be held responsible for their actions, especially when they wreak havoc on others. Redress should be available for innocent victims of carelessness, recklessness, or intentional injury.

Minimum Standards of Social Conduct: Deterrence

To function meaningfully in American society, citizens must understand society's norms and values. One extremely important norm encourages the public to behave in such a manner as to avoid hurting others or their belongings. Tort law is largely composed of *minimum standards of conduct*. Persons functioning below such thresholds are defined as tortfeasors; individuals acting at or above such criteria are acceptable to the community. However, the intent is not to ensure conformity; rather, the ideal is to inspire people to respect the dignity and integrity each individual possesses.

Deterring Violations of Those Standards

Persons should not infringe heedlessly upon others' activities unless society is willing to accept such interference with its members' lives. Tort law discourages abuses by establishing a clear system of legal rights and remedies enforceable in court proceedings. We know that we can go to court when someone strikes us, invades our privacy, creates a nuisance, or acts negligently toward us. Likewise, we know that we might be hauled into court if we do these things to others. By establishing minimum standards of conduct, tort law sets the rules for living—those "rules of thumb" by which we try to get along with other people.

Allocating Losses among Different Individuals or Groups

It is easy to grasp the idea that an individual tortfeasor should compensate the victim for the tortfeasor's wrongdoing. However, in modern society there are often many different participants in virtually any activity, making it less clear who should be labeled as tortfeasor or victim. For example, at the time of the American Revolution, most Americans were fairly self-sufficient and dealt directly with other individuals for goods or services. If a colonist bought a broken plow or a poorly shod horse from the local blacksmith, he or she knew who to hold responsible. However, as the United States became more industrialized, commercial transactions ceased to be one-on-one interactions. Today, people buy canned fruit from a local grocery that bought it from a wholesaler that bought it from a manufacturer that bought it from a grower. If the fruit is spoiled, perhaps the purchaser's spouse or child, rather than the purchaser, will suffer the injury. The lines of culpability become less clear as the producer of the defective item becomes more removed from the ultimate user.

Tort law has evolved *products liability* to determine who is in the best position to bear the costs of defective products—the innocent user or the sellers and manufacturers. It is an economic decision that courts and legislatures have made by stating that industry can best afford the costs of injuries caused by dangerously made goods. In other words, the burden of shouldering the economic loss is placed upon commercial business instead of the individual suffering the harm.

Likewise, Workers' Compensation Statutes have been enacted by state law to address whether the employee or employer will bear the cost of workplace accidents. In most instances, it is the employer and not the employee who bears this cost, regardless of fault. With automobile accidents, state insurance laws, called no-fault statutes, have been enacted setting out in which instances an insurance company will be responsible for a collision regardless of fault. Insurance companies are sometimes referred to as "deep pockets," as they are thought to have the most money when an injured person looks for someone to sue for his or her injuries.

Thus, tort law can be used to assign the expenses associated with misfortune, even when fault is hazy at best. More commonly, though, a single tortfeasor can be identified and saddled with the financial obligation.

▌ ANALYZING HYPOTHETICAL PROBLEMS

This book poses many hypothetical fact problems (hypotheticals) to help develop analytical talents. Perhaps the most popular analytical framework is discussed here.

Analytical Framework for Hypotheticals: *IRAC*

The analytical framework for hypotheticals sequentially investigates four general elements of a problem: the **i**ssue, **r**ules of law, **a**pplication of the rules to the facts, and **c**onclusions (IRAC). With this approach, legal principles are applied to specific factual scenarios. When analyzing a hypothetical, first decide which *issues* are presented. To accomplish this, one must identify the general area of law involved in the problem. For instance, if John takes Jose's bicycle without permission, then John has committed some type of tort. This identifies the broad area of law (torts).

Next, the different parts of the general legal area must be explored to see which specific tort applies. The particular tort John appears to have engaged in is called conversion. So the issue would be whether or not John converted Jose's property. This question can be answered by referring to the appropriate *rule of law*. To generalize, the rule of law for conversion defines it as the wrongful deprivation of another's property without consent.

This rule must now be *applied* to the facts. John took Jose's property without permission. This means John wrongfully deprived Jose of the use and enjoyment of his property. This constitutes conversion.

The *conclusion* would be that Jose may successfully sue John to recover possession of the bicycle, plus damages, because these legal remedies are appropriate for conversion (as chapter 7 explains).

This analytical formula is a useful tool in applying abstract legal principles to different factual situations.

Factual Distinctions Result in Different Conclusions

A rule of law may be applied to various factual situations to reach different results. This is exactly what appellate courts do when deciding cases dealing with similar legal issues. It is also what attorneys and paralegals do when applying rules of law to the particular facts of a client's case. In the following hypothetical, if the puddle of water was there for just two minutes, instead of two hours, Raj's lawsuit would probably not be successful. A single variation in a factual situation can change the legal outcome.

---

hypothetical

Raj visited the Gym Dandy Fitness Center to use its weight and steam rooms. As he walked from the locker room into the weight room, he slipped on a puddle of water on the floor and fell. The puddle was caused by leaking water pipes along the wall leading to the steam room. Raj broke his left arm as a result of the fall. Mary Perrington, another patron, mentioned that she had seen the puddle when she first arrived at the center approximately two hours before Raj's accident.

LEGAL ANALYSIS IN ACTION

Issue: Would Raj's negligence lawsuit against Gym Dandy Fitness Center succeed?

Rule: Applying the rules of law established in other negligence cases, Raj (the plaintiff) must prove that Gym Dandy (the defendant) either created the hazardous condition or had actual or constructive notice of the danger.

Application: The puddle was caused by Gym Dandy's leaking water pipes, so Gym Dandy created the danger that hurt Raj. Further, Mary testified that the puddle had been visible on the floor for two hours. That was sufficient time for Gym Dandy's employees to observe and correct the problem. Thus, Gym Dandy had constructive notice of the puddle and the danger it posed to customers.

Conclusion: Gym Dandy was negligent in creating the puddle upon which Raj fell and was injured. Accordingly, Raj's negligence lawsuit against Gym Dandy should be successful.

▌ SOLVING TORT PROBLEMS

Another approach to tort problem solving is moving from broad subject areas to specific types of torts. This method identifies the exact issues, rules of law, and conclusions in a problem by helping the reader to narrow the analytical focus.

Tort Analysis: From General to Specific

Tort analysis should go from the general to the specific as depicted in Exhibit 1-1. For example, how can one tell if infliction of emotional distress has occurred unless one is aware that some type of tort law was involved in the problem? Experienced paralegals may appear to readily know the answer. In reality, that paralegal has streamlined the analytical process, but still has moved from the general to the specific. The paralegal recognized a general negligence problem and then narrowed it to the specific defense—assumption of risk—necessary to excuse the negligent conduct.

Hypothetical

The following hypothetical should more clearly illustrate tort analysis.

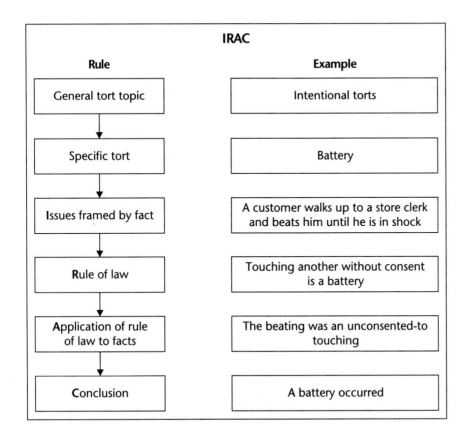

EXHIBIT 1-1
Sequence of tort analysis
from general to specific
(IRAC)

hypothetical

Jerry lives next to a vacant lot owned by Steven. Jerry dumps his grass clippings onto Steven's lot after mowing his lawn. Eventually, these grass clippings begin to smell and attract rats. Steven never gave Jerry permission to dump grass (or anything else) on Steven's lot. What legal rights does Steven have, if any?

Jerry's actions appear to fall within the intentional torts category, as Jerry is deliberately discarding his grass clippings onto Steven's lot.

Issue: Did Jerry trespass against Steven by dumping grass on Steven's lot without permission?

Rule: The elements of trespass are, generally, unlawful interference with another person's use of his or her property.

Application: Jerry's actions (1) were unlawful, in that he did not have Steven's permission to dump grass onto Steven's lot, and (2) interfered with Steven's use of his property, because Steven could not use his lot freely without having to contend with the grass and vermin.

Conclusion: Jerry is liable to Steven for the intentional tort of trespass.

▌ OVERVIEW OF A CIVIL CASE

Several basic steps occur in civil cases. However, it is important to note that at any point in the litigation process a plaintiff may decide to drop his or her lawsuit or settle with the defendant out of court. In some instances a plaintiff may not even need to institute a lawsuit to recover damages. Sometimes a simple letter from a law office can promote the necessary exchange, thus settling the claim. However, a civil case generally proceeds in the following manner:

- ▶ Complaint
- ▶ Answer
- ▶ Discovery
- ▶ Pretrial procedures
- ▶ Trial
- ▶ Post-trial procedures

Complaint

After being injured or harmed in some manner, a plaintiff might seek out legal representation. The attorney will have the client sign a *retainer*, a written agreement authorizing the attorney to represent him or her. The paralegal and/or attorney will conduct an interview of the client. As the interview progresses, the facts must be compared with the particular elements needed for the specific type of action alleged. Even though the facts might seem similar to those of a prior case, each case will have slightly different details that could change the results of the case. Accordingly, it is important to get *all* the facts.

Either the paralegal or the attorney will then draft a written **complaint** based upon the information provided. The exact procedural steps as to when the complaint must be filed with the court vary by jurisdiction, as do the time limits and rules for the **service of process.** Accordingly, it is very important to consult local court rules.

Answer

The defendant's response **(answer)** to the complaint must be filed with the court and served upon the opposing party. The defendant's response must either admit to or deny the allegations and, if denying, must explain the reason for the denial. This is also the opportunity for a defendant to bring counter-claims against the plaintiff.

Discovery

Discovery—the exchange of information and narrowing of the issues in dispute in a case—can be either a simple process or a long and drawn-out one that takes years and involves millions of documents. The nature of discovery depends on the

complaint | The first pleading filed in a civil lawsuit. It includes a statement of the wrong or harm done to the plaintiff by the defendant.

service of process | The delivery (or its legal equivalent, such as publication in a newspaper in some cases) of a legal paper by an authorized person.

answer | The first pleading by the defendant in a lawsuit. This pleading responds to the charges and demands of the plaintiff's complaint.

discovery | The formal and informal exchange of information between two sides in a lawsuit. Two types of discovery are interrogatories and depositions.

type of claim involved. If a case is clear-cut and there are witness statements and photographs of the scene, it is possible that not much discovery will be needed. In a complex case involving, for example, exposure to toxic chemicals, the discovery of information can go on for years.

Paralegals are typically involved in preparing discovery requests or gathering information to respond to discovery requests. This might involve the request for documents, setting up a time to question witnesses and parties in a case, or summarizing the contents of documents received in response to a request. Discovery is the point in the case at which a paralegal's communication skills come into play. Clients can become frustrated or confused, not understanding why a court date has not been scheduled immediately after the complaint was filed. The paralegal will need to explain the discovery required for the particular case and the anticipated time frame. It may be that the defendant has asked for additional time to respond to requests, thus delaying the progress of a case.

Pretrial Procedures

Depending on the kind of case and your local jurisdiction, various **pretrial procedures** might be scheduled. Generally there is a pretrial conference during which the judge who is to preside over the case will encourage the parties to settle the case pretrial. Alternatively, a court date is set and the parties must commence final preparation for trial.

pretrial procedures | Any procedure that immediately precedes trial; for example, the settlement conference.

Trial

The **trial** is your client's "day in court." This is the client's chance to be heard and explain his or her side of an incident. Few cases actually go to trial; the majority are settled at some point in the litigation proceedings. Because of the time and expense usually required to wait for and actually go to trial, other methods have been sought to streamline or avoid this process.

trial | The process of deciding a case (giving evidence, making arguments, deciding by a judge and jury, etc.).

Release-Settlement Agreement. If the case should settle, the client will need to sign a settlement agreement, outlining the terms of the settlement.

Post-Trial Procedures

Post-trial procedures are those that occur after a trial, such as an appeal or the steps necessary to collect on an award.

post-trial procedures | The procedures that occur after a trial, such as an appeal or the steps taken to collect on an award.

▌ CASE RESOLUTION

Not all lawsuits go to trial; in fact, the majority of cases are informally settled by the parties out of court. A very tiny percentage of cases are actually tried before a judge or jury. When you are initially analyzing a case, you should consider

alternate dispute resolution | Ways to resolve a legal problem without a court decision.

whether the particular case can be resolved early on through **alternate dispute resolution.**

Alternate Dispute Resolution (ADR)

Alternate dispute resolution is a way to resolve a legal problem without a court decision. This avenue of case resolution is becoming more and more popular as parties wish to avoid costly public court proceedings. Alternate dispute resolution is also a means of avoiding lengthy waits for a case to reach trial—in some jurisdictions the wait can be as long as three to five years. Many plaintiffs, particularly businesses, would prefer to have a lawsuit resolved quickly, rather than waiting years for closure. ADR also avoids the possibility of negative publicity.

There are a variety of different ways to resolve a legal dispute without the formality of a trial; for example, arbitration, mediation, minitrial, rent-a-judge, and a summary jury trial.

Arbitration

arbitration | Resolution of a dispute by a person whose decision is binding. This person is called an *arbitrator*. Submission of the dispute for decision is often the result of an agreement (an *arbitration clause*) in a contract.

Arbitration is a resolution of a dispute by a person other than a judge. This person's decision is binding and not a matter of public record. The person deciding the case is called the *arbitrator*. Sometimes parties agree through a written contract that, in the event of a potential dispute, they will resort to arbitration. Some companies routinely include an arbitration clause in their contracts. Arbitration was frequently used in the past for labor and construction disputes.

Mediation

mediation | Outside help in settling a dispute. The person who does this is called a *mediator*. This is different from arbitration in that a mediator can only persuade people into a settlement.

In **mediation** the parties use outside help in settling a dispute. Mediation differs from arbitration in that the mediator can only persuade the parties to reach a settlement. The mediator does not dictate an actual decision. Through a mediator's intervention and assistance the parties reach a mutually agreeable resolution. Mediation is less formal than arbitration, but like arbitration, it is not a matter of public record.

Minitrial

minitrial | Alternate dispute resolution by a panel of executives from two companies engaged in a complex dispute. A neutral moderator helps the two sides reach a settlement.

A **minitrial** is a means of alternate dispute resolution by a panel of executives from two companies engaged in a complex dispute. A neutral moderator helps the two sides sort out factual and legal issues to reach a settlement.

Rent-a-Judge

rent-a-judge | Alternate dispute resolution in which two sides in a dispute choose a person to decide the dispute. The two sides may agree to make the procedure informal or formal.

Rent-a-judge allows the parties to choose a person to decide their dispute. Retired judges often are willing to act in this capacity. The parties can decide the degree of formality of the procedure and whether the decision will be binding or merely advisory.

Summary Jury Trial

In complex cases, the two sides may present important facts and evidence to a small jury, an action referred to as a **summary jury trial.** Either the parties will agree in advance to be bound by the decision or, based on their interview with the jury, to use the jury's advice to aid in settlement negotiations.

Parties can save a lot of time and money if they are willing to consider and abide by one of the many forms of alternate dispute resolution. However, it is to be noted that, despite the many advantages, some claimants will insist on their day in court and their right to be heard by a jury. Accordingly, when alternate dispute resolution is elected, it is very important to obtain the client's consent in writing, having him or her acknowledge that this choice has been knowingly and freely made.

summary jury trial | Alternate dispute resolution in which the judge orders the two sides in a complex case to present their case to a small jury. The parties may agree in advance not to be bound by the verdict.

▋ SUMMARY

Tort law involves the study of wrongful conduct. Torts are wrongful injury to another's person or property. The wrongdoer is called the tortfeasor, and tort law provides the injured party with legal rights and remedies that may be enforced in a court of law. Torts may be divided into three general categories: negligence, intentional torts, and strict (absolute) liability. Negligence is the failure to exercise reasonable care to avoid injuring others. Intentional torts consist of misconduct designed to injure another person or that person's property. Strict (absolute) liability holds the tortfeasor liable for injuring another regardless of intent, negligence, or fault.

Much of tort law comes from ancient English and early American court decisions. In medieval England, there were primarily two torts. Both involved breaches of the king's peace. Today, there are many more tort actions because society is much more complicated than it was during the Middle Ages. Tort law has become correspondingly more sophisticated so as to deal with modern legal problems.

Tort law seeks to accomplish several goals. It serves to protect innocent persons and their property from careless or intentional injury at the hands of tortfeasors. It also attempts to hold tortfeasors responsible for their misconduct. Tort law encourages minimum standards of conduct among the public to avoid injuring others through heedless, reckless, or intentional behavior. It also deters persons from injuring other people and their property by holding tortfeasors liable for such mischief. Tort law allocates losses among different groups or individuals, based upon society's decision (as expressed through its legislatures and courts) as to who is best able to bear such losses.

To apply the rules of law to different hypothetical problems, one method breaks down the factual scenario in terms of the **i**ssues, the **r**ules of law that must then be **a**pplied to each case's specific facts, and the **c**onclusions regarding the probable outcome of the hypothetical case. When analyzing tort law problems, one decides on the general tort topic area, the specific tort involved, the issues framed by the facts, the rules of law for the particular tort involved, and how to apply those rules of law to the facts. Finally, one draws conclusions regarding the hypothetical or problem.

A civil case generally proceeds in the following manner: complaint, answer, discovery, pretrial procedures, trial, and post-trial procedures. Parties often look for alternative means to resolve a dispute. These alternatives to trial are referred to as *alternate dispute resolution.* A few of the means of resolving a case without a trial are the use of arbitration, mediation, a minitrial, rent-a-judge, or summary jury trials.

▌ KEY TERMS

alternate dispute resolution	mediation	strict (absolute) liability
answer	minitrial	summary jury trial
arbitration	negligence	tort
common law	post-trial procedures	tortfeasor
complaint	pretrial procedures	trial
discovery	rent-a-judge	
intentional tort	service of process	

▌ PROBLEMS

Using the definitions of specific torts discussed in this chapter, answer the following hypotheticals using the analytical approaches discussed earlier.

1. Tom Caster is a 12-year-old boy who enjoys climbing trees. The Caster family just moved into a new house. The electrical wires to Tom's house run from an electrical pole through the high branches of an oak tree in his backyard. While the rest of the family was moving into the home, Tom ran to the backyard to climb the tree. As he neared the top, he grabbed the electrical wires with his right hand. The wires were not insulated and Tom was severely burned from the resulting electrical shock. He also broke both his legs when he fell, unconscious, from the tree. Tom's father wishes to know if he might successfully sue the utility company for negligence.

2. Shady Acres is a subdivision being developed by Bartholomew Real Estate Management, Inc. (BREM). While bulldozing the lots and streets, BREM's crews created huge piles of dirt. BREM did not erect any barriers to keep these dirt piles in place. Pamela Jovanco owns a house at the bottom of a hill upon which BREM placed several earth piles. During heavy rains, mud would slide down the hill and cover Pamela's entire yard. Some mud even seeped through her basement windows, damaging her basement carpet and furniture. Pamela wonders if trespass has occurred.

3. Samantha Billingsly stood outside her downtown hotel hailing a cab. The driver screeched to a halt alongside the curb. Samantha opened the rear door of the automobile and began to climb inside. In doing so, she placed her right hand on the roof of the car where the top of the door would close. Suddenly, the cab driver accelerated the automobile, causing the rear door to slam shut onto Samantha's hand. Samantha suffered lacerations and several broken bones in her right hand and wrist. She also suffered a neck injury as she was thrown against the back seat as the taxi lurched forward. The cab driver later explained that he had accelerated suddenly to avoid being struck by a shuttle bus, which he thought was about to collide with his taxi when he saw it approaching very rapidly in his rearview mirror. Using negligence theory, Samantha would like to sue the cab driver who owns the taxi.

4. Ed Peterson owned a coyote, which he captured while hunting the previous summer in the mountains. The coyote had become quite tame and at parties, to entertain guests, Ed would routinely allow the animal to eat out of his hand. One day Ed's next-door neighbor, Angela Starlight, a seven-year-old girl, visited Ed's backyard to play with the coyote. Angela's parents had warned her several times to avoid approaching the coyote, although neither they nor Angela had ever seen the animal bite or growl at anyone. When Angela

reached out to pet the coyote, it bared its teeth and snapped at her hand, biting and cutting her severely. Angela's parents sued Ed under a theory of absolute liability. Under most states' common law, owners are strictly liable for injuries caused by wild animals kept as pets.

▌ REVIEW QUESTIONS

1. How is a tort best defined? What are the three broad categories of torts? How might you define each variety?

2. What is negligence? How might you distinguish it from intentional torts?

3. What are intentional torts? What are examples of intentional torts?

4. How might you define strict (absolute) liability? What is the most important type of strict liability?

5. Discuss the historical roots of tort law. From what country or countries did torts originate? How have torts changed since their inception?

6. What are the purposes that tort law attempts to accomplish? Do these objectives sometimes conflict? Do they sometimes complement one another?

7. Suggest an analytical formula you might use to answer a hypothetical fact problem. In what order are these steps taken? Why do you think this order is appropriate? Is each step of the technique necessary to reach the next phase?

8. Tort analysis moves from the general to the specific. Why is this best suited to answering tort hypotheticals?

9. Describe the stages of a civil lawsuit.

10. What is the difference between arbitration and mediation?

▌ HELPFUL WEBSITES

This chapter provides an introduction to torts and legal analysis. To learn about torts, the following sites can be accessed:

General Legal Information

http://www.law.emory.edu

http://www.law.cornell.edu

http://www.findlaw.com

http://law.harvard.edu

http://www.library.kentlaw.edu

http://www.law.indiana.edu

http://www.lawlibrary.rutgers.edu

Links to State Courts

http://vls.law.vill.edu

http://www.courts.net

http://www.lawidea.com

Links to Federal Courts

http://www.uscourts.gov

http://www.lawsource.com

Information for Paralegals

http://www.nala.org

http://www.paralegals.org

http://www.paralegalgateway.com

http://www.bls.gov

Link to Legal Newspapers

http://www.netlawlibrary.com

STUDENT CD-ROM™

For additional materials, please go to the CD in this book.

ONLINE COMPANION™

For additional resources, please go to
www.paralegal.delmar.cengage.com

chapter 2

Negligence

THE BIGGEST MISTAKES PARALEGALS MAKE & HOW TO AVOID THEM

Open Mouth/Insert Foot: We'll Have a Gay Time in the Ole Town Tonight!

Most of the paralegals in my firm are white women, but recently Human Resources embarked on a diversity campaign to recruit more men and minority candidates from other firms. Finally another man started working for us on product liability cases, but nobody knows him very well because he does not go out to lunch with the rest of us or socialize after work. A rumor even circulated that he is a homosexual because he doesn't wear a wedding ring. On Fridays, as usual, we sent an e-mail to everyone inviting one and all to Legal Eagles, a bar by the courthouse. After a few rounds, we were laughing and joking and someone asked where the "new guy" was. "Oh, he's probably at a gay bar cruising instead of joining us," I said. Just then, everyone went silent because suddenly he was standing right behind me and heard my every word.

(continues)

17

LESSON LEARNED: Sexual harassment and inappropriate humor often go hand in hand in the workplace. While technically the comments made in a bar after hours are not the same as comments made in an office, this event was planned using office e-mail. Unkind words made at the expense of a co-worker do contribute to a hostile work environment when expressed to all who work together. Law firms, the government, the military, corporations, and small businesses are faced with rising claims of sexual harassment each year. It is in no one's interest to be the source of unnecessary gossip that saps the productivity and esprit de corps of an office, to say nothing of fueling grounds for a lawsuit.

INTRODUCTION

The field of negligence is the most complex of the torts. What makes negligence challenging is its conceptual ambiguity. The **elements** of negligence appear to be so broadly defined that it is difficult to discern clear lines for negligent behavior. Negligence is not a mathematical equation. Instead, negligence resembles probability theory, in which specific conduct is more likely than not to be considered negligent under a particular set of circumstances. In this chapter, the following aspects of negligence are discussed:

elements | The essential parts or components of something.

> The elements of negligence
> The tortfeasor's duty of reasonable care
> The breach of duty, the reasonable person standard, and foreseeability
> Causation, substantial factor analysis, joint and several liability, and proximate cause
> Damages available in negligence actions.

NEGLIGENCE

Most people equate negligence with carelessness. The phrase conjures up images of actions that are slovenly, haphazard, heedless, or foolhardy. As a legal concept, negligence is much more precise, but it embodies all of these characteristics.

Negligence Defined: Reasonable Care

negligence | The failure to exercise a reasonable amount of care in a situation that causes harm to someone or something. It can involve doing something carelessly or failing to do something that should have been done.

Negligence may be broadly defined as the failure to exercise reasonable care to avoid injuring others or their property. Reasonable care depends upon the exact circumstances of each case. This is the "shifting sands" aspect of negligence with which legal students—and the legal system—struggle. The key term is *reasonableness*. In any tort case in which negligence might exist, ask the threshold question: Did the tortfeasor act unreasonably under the circumstances? This is essentially all that negligence entails.

Acts or Omissions

A tortfeasor can be negligent either by doing or by not doing something. When courts speak of *negligent acts* or *omissions* by the tortfeasor, they mean that the tortfeasor behaved unreasonably either by doing a specific careless activity or by failing to do something that the tortfeasor should have done.

Negligent actions are positive events; something is done. For instance, if Nick lit a fire in high winds that carried sparks onto a neighbor's roof and set the house ablaze, Nick's action (careless burning) would be deemed unreasonable. Negligent omissions are usually phrased negatively; the tortfeasor failed to do a reasonable act. For example, suppose Briana's front porch has a rotten step that she has failed to repair. A salesperson visiting her home falls through the step and breaks a leg. Briana's omission (failure to repair the step) would be considered unreasonable.

Like all areas of law, negligence has developed discernible elements that can be enumerated and outlined more clearly. The next section outlines the elements of negligence.

ELEMENTS OF NEGLIGENCE

Negligence can be specifically defined as a tortfeasor's failure to exercise reasonable care, thus causing a **foreseeable injury** to another person or that person's property. Negligence includes the following elements:

foreseeable injury | An injury that a reasonably prudent person should have anticipated.

1. Duty of care
2. Breach of the duty by the tortfeasor (unreasonable conduct)
3. Causation of injury to the victim
4. Damages to the victim (actual harm).

Each of these elements is required for negligence to exist, so each element is a threshold question. If "no" answers any single element, negligence does not exist. For example, the first question is: Did the tortfeasor owe a duty of reasonable care to the injured party? If not, then the analysis stops, with the conclusion that no negligence has occurred. If yes, then one must ask: Did the tortfeasor breach the duty of reasonable care? If not, the inquiry is finished, and once again the analyst concludes that there was no negligence. If yes, then one continues querying through causation, and damages. Each element must be satisfied for negligence to exist.

Each of the elements of negligence receives detailed treatment in the following sections.

SCOPE OF DUTY AND STANDARD OF REASONABLE CARE

Negligence analysis begins with the duty of reasonable care. First, the scope of the duty must be determined. This focuses on the **foreseeability** of the victim.

foreseeability | The notion that a specific action, under particular circumstances, would produce an anticipated result.

Duty Defined

duty | 1. An obligation to obey
a law. 2. A legal obligation to
another person, who has a corresponding right.

due (reasonable) care | That
degree of care a person of ordinary prudence (the so-called
reasonable person) would exercise
in similar circumstances.

In tort law, **duty** is the obligation either to do or not to do something. In negligence, the duty of **due (reasonable) care** is the responsibility to act reasonably so as to avoid injuring others. This may also be stated negatively: the duty of reasonable care is the obligation *not* to behave *un*reasonably so as to avoid injuring others.

For example, motor vehicle operators owe a duty of reasonable care to drive carefully and avoid injuring other drivers, their vehicles, or pedestrians. Suppose Parker is driving on a four-lane highway and chooses to pass the truck in front of him. He fails to look in the rearview mirror before pulling into the left lane. Unbeknownst to Parker, another vehicle is attempting to pass him, and he pulls directly in front of that driver. This action forces that driver to swerve and collide with a telephone pole. Did Parker violate any duty of reasonable care?

In analyzing this duty hypothetical, the first question is: Did Parker owe the other driver a duty of reasonable care? Parker owed anyone driving or walking upon the street a duty to drive safely. By failing to check his rearview mirror to see if any traffic was approaching from behind in the left lane, Parker breached his duty to the other driver. He acted imprudently by not looking for other traffic before he switched lanes. He failed to see that which was there to be seen.

Scope of Duty

scope of duty | In negligence
law, defined in terms of those
individuals who might foreseeably be injured as a result of the
tortfeasor's actions.

Clearly, one does not owe a duty of reasonable care to everyone else in the universe. **Scope of duty** is a limitation on the persons to whom one owes the duty.

For example, while driving on the four-lane highway in her city, Carri owes no duty of reasonable care to someone driving in another city hundreds of miles away. Carri's actions (i.e., driving her car) could not possibly have any effect on such a person. Carri's scope of duty does not extend to individuals who cannot directly be affected by her carelessness. Scope of duty is often described in terms of reasonable foreseeability.

THE CASE OF DRUNKEN DUTY

In negligence litigation, an injured plaintiff always tries to argue that the defendant's scope of duty extends to the plaintiff, the injured party. Plaintiffs attempt to avoid responsibility for their own injuries by claiming that the defendant breached a duty of care. In the following case, the defendant owner of the bar (Wesco, Inc.), referred to as the "licensee," is accused of furnishing liquor to the minor plaintiff Gregory Colby. Plaintiff Colby argues that his injuries are directly linked to the bar. A careful reading of the liquor law determines how far the defendant's duty extends.

Gregory A. COLBY, Plaintiff-Appellant,

v.

Rodney NOAH, Defendant, and Wesco, Inc., Defendant-Appellee.

Docket No. 275154.
Court of Appeals of Michigan
May 22, 2007

Under the liquor control code of 1998, MCL 436.1101 *et seq.*, also referred to as the dramshop act, it is unlawful for a retail licensee to "directly, individually, or by a clerk, agent, or servant sell, furnish, or give alcoholic liquor to a minor" and to "directly or indirectly, individually or by a clerk, agent, or servant sell, furnish, or give alcoholic liquor to a person who is visibly intoxicated." MCL 436.1801(2). An individual who is "personally injured by a minor or a visibly intoxicated person by reason of the unlawful selling, giving, or furnishing of alcoholic liquor to the minor or visibly intoxicated person" has a cause of action against the licensee "if the unlawful sale is proven to be a proximate cause of the . . . injury" and the licensee has "caused or contributed to the intoxication of the person or who has caused or contributed to the . . . injury. . . ." MCL 436.1801(3).

The elements of a claim predicated upon an unlawful sale to a visibly intoxicated person are: (1) the plaintiff was injured by the wrongful or tortious conduct of an intoxicated person, (2) the intoxication of that person was the sole or contributing cause of the plaintiff's injuries, and (3) the defendant sold, gave, or furnished to the alleged intoxicated person the alcoholic beverage which caused or contributed to that person's intoxication.

Defendant Rodney Noah purchased a 15-pack of 22-ounce cans of beer from defendant while allegedly visibly intoxicated. He took them home for a party to which plaintiff, a minor, had been invited by another guest. Noah offered the beer to plaintiff, who consumed four full cans and part of a fifth during the next hour to hour and a half. Plaintiff also smoked marijuana. Plaintiff thereafter went outside and dove into Noah's backyard pool and broke his neck.

Plaintiff failed to show that Noah's intoxication proximately caused plaintiff's injuries. To the extent plaintiff seeks to hold defendant liable on an agency theory of liability, his claim must fail. If plaintiff contends that defendant illegally furnished beer to a minor (himself) through Noah as his agent, defendant cannot be held liable because the statute only precludes direct sales to minors. Further, a minor or intoxicated person who becomes intoxicated and injures himself cannot recover damages from the licensee for his own injuries. Thus, where the injured minor seeks to hold the licensee liable for furnishing him alcohol through an intermediary, his claim must fail.

CASE QUESTIONS
1. What was the court's justification for its decision?
2. Suppose defendant Rodney Noah was a minor, and purchased the liquor for himself. If it had been Noah who dived into the pool, would the court's decision have been different?

▌ BREACH OF DUTY: FORESEEABILITY

In tort law, foreseeability is the notion that a specific action, under particular circumstances, would produce an anticipated result. If an injury were foreseeable, then one could take precautions to avoid the behavior that might be expected to cause harm. If a tortfeasor failed to take such precautions, he or she breached the duty of reasonable care. Breach of duty balances the foreseeability of harm against the probability of harm and the magnitude of harm.

For instance, in the preceding driving example, Parker did not check his rearview mirror before attempting to pass on a four-lane highway. Is it foreseeable that another vehicle might be passing Parker in the lane he was trying to enter, and that his failure to look behind him could result in a collision? This consequence is clearly foreseeable. Suppose, however, that it is late at night, and that the other driver trying to pass Parker did not have headlights on. Thus, Parker could not see the car approaching as he moved into the left lane to pass the truck. Was it reasonably foreseeable that another driver would come up from behind without headlights? No. So the result (the other driver swerving to avoid hitting Parker's car) was not foreseeable under these facts. A slight difference in the circumstances changes the answer.

THE CASE OF THE OBVIOUS HAZARD

Shopkeepers have a duty to warn shoppers of known hidden dangers. The plaintiff in this case stated that Lowe's Home Centers should have warned her about a pallet of boxed merchandise sitting on the floor. Yet, in her deposition, plaintiff testified that she saw the pallet when she entered the hedge trimmer aisle. This case demonstrates the importance of preparing witnesses for hearings.

Kathy B. WILLIAMS, et al., Appellants
v.
LOWE'S HOME CENTERS, INC., et al., Appellees.
No. L-06-1267.
2007 WL 1452892
Court of Appeals of Ohio, Sixth District,
Lucas County
Decided May 18, 2007

On May 29, 2003, J. H. Peter Jones was engaged by appellant to perform various lawn maintenance tasks, such as cutting grass and trimming hedges. Appellant furnished Jones with a hedge trimmer. During the course of performing the requested yard work, the hedge trimmer failed and was no longer useable. Jones was unable to repair it.

Jones instructed appellant that her hedge trimmer broke. Appellant asked Jones to accompany her to a new Lowe's Home Improvement store to assist her in selecting a replacement hedge trimmer.

Appellant selected a trimmer to purchase in her desired price range and informed Jones which trimmer she wanted. Jones reached up to the shelf where the trimmer was located and attempted to secure the box. Jones lost his grip on the box and it fell downwards towards appellant. The box knocked appellant into the adjacent pallet of stacked merchandise. Appellant fell to the floor next to the pallet.

Jones managed to catch the box before it struck the ground. Appellant refused medical treatment, completed her purchase, and left the store with her new trimmer.

On May 27, 2005, appellant filed a complaint alleging negligence against both Lowe's and Jones. Jones was later voluntarily dismissed from the case. On January 25, 2006, Lowe's filed a motion for summary judgment, asserting it owed no duty to appellant to warn her of an open and obvious condition such as a pallet of boxed merchandise plainly sitting in the aisle of a home improvement store. Lowe's argued that that the open and obvious nature of the condition complained of barred appellant from recovery against Lowe's for failure to warn her of such a condition.

We first note that appellant was a business invitee on Lowe's premises. As the premises' owner, Lowe's owed appellant a "duty of ordinary care in maintaining the premises in a reasonably safe condition and has the duty to warn its invitees of latent or hidden dangers."

The determinative issue is whether the condition was open and obvious or latent. The conclusion to this underlying question dictates whether or not Lowe's owed appellant a duty to warn.

The open and obvious doctrine is uniformly recognized and adhered to by courts in the state of Ohio. The open and obvious doctrine establishes that a premises' owner has no duty to warn invitees of conditions deemed to be open and obvious.

The underlying rationale justifying the liability consequences of the open and obvious doctrine is that the obvious nature of the hazard itself serves as an adequate warning. When the trier-of-fact concludes that the open and obvious doctrine is applicable to a particular case, the doctrine operates as a total bar to negligence recovery.

In her complaint, appellant specifically complains that Lowe's was negligent in failing to warn plaintiff of the pallets of boxed merchandise on the floor or in exposing her to the condition. Appellant's deposition transcript unambiguously establishes that appellant directly observed the pallet of boxes when she entered the hedge trimmer aisle.

We find that an objectively reasonable person would have observed and understood the condition. We find that a pallet of boxed merchandise plainly situated in the aisle constituted an open and obvious condition extinguishing any duty to warn.

Appellant has failed to establish a genuine issue of material fact as to negligence by Lowe's. Summary judgment was appropriate.

CASE QUESTIONS

1. Did defendant Lowe's have a duty to warn Williams about the pallet of merchandise in the aisle?
2. What would the reasonable person have done in this case?

Foreseeable Plaintiffs Theory

Foreseeability limits the scope (extent) of the duty owed to others. One asks the threshold question: Was it reasonably foreseeable that the person injured would be harmed as a consequence of the tortfeasor's actions? If so, the scope of the duty of reasonable care includes the individual hurt. This is sometimes called the **foreseeable plaintiffs theory,** because it was reasonably foreseeable that the **plaintiff** (who is suing the tortfeasor **(defendant)** for negligence) would be damaged because of the tortious conduct. It is the foreseeability of injury or damage that is of concern, not the degree or amount of injury or damage involved.

Persons outside this range of duty are considered **unforeseeable plaintiffs,** because the tortfeasor could not reasonably have anticipated that they would be harmed by the tortfeasor's actions. People driving several hundred feet in front of Parker would not likely be influenced by either Parker or the swerving other driver. They would be beyond Parker's scope of duty, and so he would not

foreseeable plaintiffs theory | Under this theory, if it were reasonably foreseeable that the injured victim would be harmed as a consequence of the tortfeasor's actions, then the tortfeasor's scope of duty includes the victim.

plaintiff | A person who brings a lawsuit.

defendant | A person against whom an action is brought.

unforeseeable plaintiffs | Persons whose injuries the tortfeasor could not reasonably have anticipated as a result of the tortfeasor's actions.

be required to exercise reasonable care toward them. However, persons driving close behind Parker and the swerving driver could reasonably be expected to become involved in the accident. These individuals would be within Parker's scope of duty. His failure to use reasonable care (by not looking in the rearview mirror, which caused him to cut off the swerving driver) violated his duty to them as well as to the swerving driver.

Table 2-1 outlines scope of duty and the foreseeable plaintiffs theory.

Scope of Duty	Foreseeable Plaintiffs Theory
The tortfeasor owes a duty of reasonable care to avoid injuring others or their property.	The plaintiff may recover from the defendant only if it was reasonably foreseeable that the defendant's actions would injure the plaintiff.
Duty includes persons for whom it is reasonably foreseeable that injury will occur as a result of the torfeasor's actions.	Persons outside the defendant's scope of duty are considered unforeseeable plaintiffs.

Standard of Reasonable Care

Reasonable care is a very difficult concept to define in negligence law. It depends upon the particular facts of each problem. Still, tort law has developed an abstract measure of reasonable care, called the **reasonable person test (standard)**.

reasonable person test (standard) | A means of determining negligence based on what a reasonable person would have done in the same or similar circumstances.

The Reasonable Person Standard. The *reasonable person* is an imaginary individual who is expected to behave reasonably under a given set of circumstances to avoid harming others. The tortfeasor is alleged to have done something, or have failed to do something, that was unreasonable and that caused the victim's injuries. The tortfeasor's conduct is measured under the reasonable person standard in this fashion: In the same or similar circumstances, would the reasonable person have acted as the tortfeasor behaved? If so, then the tortfeasor did not violate his or her duty of reasonable care. If not, then the tortfeasor breached the duty.

In our previous driving hypothetical, would the reasonable person have looked in his or her rearview mirror before entering the left lane to pass a truck on a four-lane highway, when it was reasonably foreseeable that another vehicle might already be occupying that lane while attempting to pass the reasonable person's car? Checking the rearview mirror when changing lanes seems reasonable, and so the reasonable person could be expected to do so under these conditions. Parker did not, however. Therefore, Parker acted unreasonably in this case. He violated his duty of care to the swerving driver because he did not act as the reasonable person would have behaved in the same situation.

The mythical reasonable person may seem too intangible to compare to real-life persons. Nevertheless, American and English courts have relied on the concept in over 200 years of court decisions (though older opinions refer to the *reasonable man*).

Who Decides How the Reasonable Person Would Have Acted.

The trier-of-fact in a negligence lawsuit determines whether the defendant did not act as the reasonable person would have behaved in a specific case. This is usually a jury, but it could be the judge in a bench trial. In effect, the jurors decide what was reasonable by investigating how they, and others they know, would have behaved. Suddenly, the reasonable person standard becomes clear: it is what the jurors conclude was reasonable under the circumstances. This settles the question of whether the defendant breached the duty of reasonable care to the plaintiff.

At first glance, the reasonable person standard seems arbitrary, as each juror determines the defendant's negligence based upon his or her own personal, gut-level response. However, sociologists would remind us that this is precisely how each individual views the world—through the eyes of his or her own experience. The judicial system safeguards against one capricious definition of reasonableness by offering the option of a jury trial, which forces several persons to agree upon an appropriate measure of due care. Although a judge in a bench trial is the sole trier-of-fact, the judge's legal training is presumed to compensate for any bias in defining reasonableness.

Matching Skills and Disabilities.

The reasonable person is supposed to resemble the defendant as closely as possible in terms of special abilities. This enables the trier-of-fact to assess reasonableness more precisely in a specific case. For example, if the defendant were a teacher and was alleged to have negligently supervised students, the reasonable person would also possess the same training and knowledge as teachers employed in the defendant's geographical area. This is sometimes called the **professional community standard of care,** which is based on the custom and practice among professionals working in the defendant's community. This measure is determined through expert testimony from members of the defendant's **profession.** The standard for experts is now a **national standard** in most jurisdictions.

The defendant's limitations are also important in shaping the reasonable person standard. For instance, if the defendant were physically disabled, then the reasonable person would likewise share identical disabilities. One could hardly decide how a blind defendant should have behaved by comparison with a reasonable person who has normal vision. This forces the trier-of-fact to empathize with the defendant's situation to understand more clearly how the defendant acted.

professional community standard of care | The standard of reasonable care used in negligence cases involving defendants with special skills and knowledge.

profession | An occupation that requires specialized advanced education, training, and knowledge. The skill involved is mostly intellectual rather than manual.

national standard | A standard applied throughout the nation.

In effect, the jury must conceptualize how the reasonable person would have behaved in a wheelchair or with a hearing disability. The result of this should be a more accurate definition of reasonableness that best fits the defendant and the circumstances of the case. The result, ideally, is a just and equitable outcome in the litigation. Generally, people who are mentally ill or insane are held to the reasonable person standard, an objective standard, even if they cannot appreciate the danger of their action.

Table 2-2 summarizes the reasonable person standard.

TABLE 2-2
Reasonable person standard

1. Ask: Would the reasonable person have acted as the defendant did, under the same or similar circumstances?

2. Match the skills or abilities of the reasonable person to those of the defendant (e.g., plumber, rodeo rider) if these abilities were involved in the alleged negligent actions (community or national standard).

3. Trier-of-fact decides how the reasonable person would have acted in a particular situation.

Professional Malpractice

A professional's negligent failure to observe the appropriate standard of care in providing services to a client or patient, or misconduct while engaging in the practice of a profession, is considered malpractice. Failure to exercise the degree of care and skill reasonably required of like professionals in similar circumstances, if that failure causes damage or injury, is malpractice. Originally, the precise degree of skill used to judge a professional's actions was the care and skill of other professionals practicing in the same community. Many jurisdictions expanded this to include the same community *or* a similar locality. Likewise, a specialist must possess the degree of skill and competence that a specialist in the same or similar community would exercise.

Now, many jurisdictions have taken this a step further and hold specialists to a national standard, without regard to their location. Some jurisdictions are applying the national standard to general practitioners as well. Professional malpractice cases have been brought against doctors, lawyers, accountants, travel agents, and even priests, depending on the jurisdiction.

Medical Malpractice. To prove a medical malpractice case, generally one or more expert witnesses will be needed for trial. This major expense prevents attorneys from bringing suit for anything but serious and permanent injury cases.

Typically, medical malpractice cases involve one or more of the following:

▶ Advanced skin ulcers (bedsores)

▶ Abandonment (failure to attend to a patient)

▶ Improper diagnosis

▶ Medical instruments, sponges, needles, or other foreign objects left in patient after surgery

▶ Lack of informed consent

▶ Errors in prenatal diagnostic and genetic testing

▶ Failure of hospital to supervise employees

▶ Failure to diagnose

▶ Failure to advise of diagnosis

▶ Medication errors

▶ Death/disability from restraints

▶ Sexual assault on patient

▶ Death after induction of anesthesia

▶ Death from a fall

▶ Surgery performed on wrong body part

▶ Death or disability from labor/delivery/post-delivery.

THE CASE OF THE LATE DIAGNOSIS

A physician's negligent failure to observe the appropriate standard of care in providing services to a patient is malpractice. In this case, a medical malpractice action was brought against a gynecologist for failure to diagnose breast cancer.

MEZRAH
v.
BEVIS
District Court of Appeal of Florida,
Second District
593 So. 2d 1215
(Fla. Dist. Ct. App. 1992)
February 21, 1992
Lehan, Acting Chief Judge

In this medical malpractice action the defendants, a gynecologist and his professional association, appeal a final judgment entered on a jury verdict finding them liable to plaintiff for failing to diagnose breast cancer. We affirm.

As to defendants' first argument that the trial court erred in allowing expert testimony from a pathologist that defendants breached the standard of care, we conclude that there was no error. Also, there was additional competent testimony from another expert to that effect.

As to defendants' second argument, we do not agree that the evidence on the issue of causation was merely speculative. There was competent expert testimony which, as we have said, was

(continues)

not improperly allowed that had defendants not breached the standard of care, plaintiff's breast cancer "more likely than not" would have been completely cured.

Noor v. Continental Casualty Co., in which this court affirmed a judgment for defendants in a medical malpractice case based upon the alleged failure to timely diagnose breast cancer, is distinguishable. Damages were sought in that case on the alleged basis that Mrs. Noor's life expectancy had been shortened due to a delay of several months in failing to diagnose her cancer. This court pointed out that her life expectancy had been shortened as a result of the disease even if the disease had been correctly diagnosed by defendant doctor at the first opportunity. The plaintiffs in that case did not prove causation because they did not produce any "nonspeculative evidence as to what extent, if any, [defendant doctor's] failure to immediately diagnose her disease added to Mrs. Noor's decreased life expectancy." On the other hand, plaintiff in this case apparently sought damages on a different basis, i.e., that had the breast cancer been timely diagnosed, she more likely than not would have been cured. As noted above, she produced sufficient evidence in that regard.

Affirmed.

CASE QUESTIONS

1. How is the *Noor* case distinguishable from the instant case?
2. Can you put a dollar value on a patient's claim of having lost the chance to be cured?

practical **application**

As a practical note, it is important to remember that the mere fact that there is an injury, or the occurrence of a bad result in medicine, does not necessarily mean that there has been malpractice.

The following hypothetical examines another situation in which the standard of care is at issue. Note how scope of duty, foreseeability, and the reasonable person standard are established.

hypothetical

Jamal makes an appointment to see his family physician. Jamal's throat has been hurting him for the past week. The doctor takes a throat culture. Jamal has strep throat, a condition that requires antibiotics. Jamal's doctor calls Jamal with the results and advises that he will call the pharmacy and order medication. Unbeknownst to Jamal, the drug that the doctor orders is one in a category of drugs to which Jamal is highly allergic and should never take. The doctor failed to check Jamal's chart for known allergies before ordering the prescription. Because the drug has a different name than the drug Jamal previously had a reaction to, Jamal assumes that the drug is a different drug that is safe for him to take. Minutes after taking the prescription, Jamal goes into shock and dies. Did the doctor owe Jamal a duty of reasonable care? If so, did the doctor breach that duty?

To establish negligence by a physician, it must be shown that the injury complained of was caused by the physician's failing to act as a family physician would have acted under like circumstances. Failing to check a chart for allergies falls below the standard of care that a family physician of ordinary skill would have used under similar circumstances. The physician did not follow professional practices and failed to comply with the reasonable standard of care owed to Jamal. It was foreseeable that Jamal would be hurt.

Special Duty Based upon Special Relationship

The majority of negligence actions are based upon an affirmative duty or act owed to another that is improperly performed. In contrast, if a person fails to act there generally is no liability in negligence, except under certain limited exceptions. An example of a failure to act would be when you are walking down the street and see a stranger about to trip and do not try to prevent the accident. In this example, you would have no duty to stop and warn the stranger. Only if the plaintiff and the defendant have a special relationship between them will the defendant's failure to act lead to a cause of action in negligence.

Just a few of the many special relationships that might create a duty to act are those between an employer and employee, a parent and child, a teacher and student, an innkeeper and guest, and common carriers and passengers. The law imposes a special relationship between these parties and also a duty to act based upon this relationship. For example, if one student injures another student or is about to hurt another student, their teacher has an obligation to intervene and try to help, even though the teacher was not negligent and did not cause the incident. Likewise, employers may be responsible for workers injured on the job even if the employer did not harm the employee (see chapter 8 for more information on workplace injuries).

THE CASE OF RESTRAINT

A patient enters a hospital and leaves in a worse condition than when admitted. Malpractice does not always involve problems with the actual surgery or medication; it could also involve issues such as failure to order appropriate restraints or to properly monitor a patient following surgery.

(continues)

DOUGLAS
v.
GIBSON

Supreme Court, Appellate Division,
Third Department
630 N.Y.S.2d 401 (App. Div. 1995)
August 3, 1995
Cardona, Presiding Justice

On December 1, 1988, defendant Mark D. Gibson surgically removed a previously placed fixation device from plaintiff's left hip. Following the surgery, plaintiff was placed in a vest restraint. Although no doctor ordered that plaintiff be restrained, his wife requested restraints during plaintiff's admission procedures because he had become confused in the past after surgery. Plaintiff was 64 years old at the time and suffering from Parkinson's disease. On the day after the surgery, plaintiff was examined by Gibson's partner, defendant William C. Bishop, who found him to be in stable condition. In the early morning hours of December 3, 1988, it was discovered that plaintiff had fallen between the side rails of his bed and suffered a fracture of his left distal femur.

Plaintiff commenced this medical malpractice action against Gibson and Bishop (hereinafter collectively referred to as defendants) alleging, *inter alia*, that they were negligent in failing to order that plaintiff be appropriately restrained, in failing to provide him with an adequate restraint and in failing to adequately monitor him. The bill of particulars further alleged that defendants failed to properly supervise staff personnel. Following joinder of issue and examinations before trial, defendants moved for summary judgment dismissing the complaint against them. Supreme Court granted the motion and plaintiff now appeals.

Initially, we are of the view that defendants made a prima facie showing that no material issues of fact exist as to the alleged malpractice asserted against them in the complaint as amplified by the bill of particulars. In support of their motion, defendants submitted, *inter alia*, their own affidavits, the affidavits of their attorney and Donald Douglas, a physician, as well as hospital records and transcripts of examinations before trial of staff personnel. Through this and other evidence in the record, defendants established that although they did not order plaintiff to be restrained, the vest restraint placed on him was appropriate and would have been the same device they would have ordered postoperatively. Douglas averred that the vest restraint used was the standard restraint and was not a departure from accepted medical standards of care. Defendants also established that no additional or further restraint prior to the incident was medically indicated. Finally, defendants sufficiently rebutted plaintiff's claim of improper supervision.

Given this evidence, the burden shifted to plaintiff to come forward with evidentiary proof sufficient to raise a question of fact. His evidence, in opposition to defendants' motion, consisted of the affidavits of Patricia Newland, a registered nurse, and Miles St. John, a surgeon. These averments, however, lacked the requisite level of proof necessary to defeat defendants' motion. These affidavits state that based on plaintiff's prior medical history, he was a "high risk" patient who needed more secure restraints than those provided and that defendants' failure to do so constituted a deviation from accepted medical practice. They claim that on previous occasions plaintiff had attempted to get out of bed and had fallen or injured himself. Notably absent from the record, however, is any evidence of any such prior incidents to support these allegations. Therefore, the allegations are conclusory, unsupported by competent evidence and fail to raise a question of fact. The affidavits also claim malpractice due to the lack of a physician's order to use a restraint. Defendants, however, averred that, had they ordered a restraining device, it would have been the vest restraint actually used. Thus, insofar as a restraint was in fact used and was the same one that would have been ordered, the failure to so order does not raise an issue of fact.

Plaintiff also failed to offer any competent proof that another physician would have ordered anything other than a vest restraint. Although

Newland's affidavit claimed that a more secure device was required, she was giving her professional opinion as to what a physician should have ordered which, in our view, went beyond her professional and educational experience and cannot be considered "competent medical opinion" on this issue. As to St. John's averment that a more secure restraint was warranted, this was based only on his unsupported assertion that plaintiff was a high risk patient. . . . There were no medical records submitted to support the specifically disputed factual assertion that there were prior falls, which was the basis for St. John's conclusion that plaintiff was a high risk patient.

We also note that plaintiff failed to offer any proof that the type of security restraint he claims should have been used would have prevented him from falling. He thus failed to establish the requisite nexus between the alleged malpractice and his injury. Finally, plaintiff submitted no adequate proof on the issue of sufficient oversight of plaintiff's case or of staff personnel. We therefore conclude that summary judgment was properly awarded to defendants. Plaintiff's remaining arguments are rejected as unpersuasive.

CASE QUESTIONS

1. What was the court's reason for denying the plaintiff's medical malpractice claim?
2. What specific kinds of proof did Justice Cardona suggest could have been introduced at trial to prove malpractice that were not offered as proof by this plaintiff's attorneys?
3. If you were the plaintiff in this case, how would you feel upon reading an appellate decision in which numerous suggestions are made to counsel as to what could have been offered at trial?

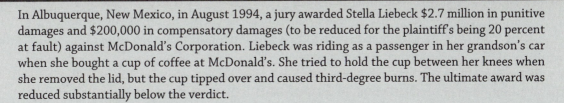

McDONALD'S COFFEE, A BURNING ISSUE

In Albuquerque, New Mexico, in August 1994, a jury awarded Stella Liebeck $2.7 million in punitive damages and $200,000 in compensatory damages (to be reduced for the plaintiff's being 20 percent at fault) against McDonald's Corporation. Liebeck was riding as a passenger in her grandson's car when she bought a cup of coffee at McDonald's. She tried to hold the cup between her knees when she removed the lid, but the cup tipped over and caused third-degree burns. The ultimate award was reduced substantially below the verdict.

This case caused a sensation when the jury award was first reported. Few people were privy to all the facts. Most people were aware that a woman was burnt while drinking coffee from McDonald's, but few could understand why the woman was suing McDonald's if it was she who spilled the coffee. More puzzling was why a jury would award almost $3 million in punitive damages against McDonald's when the plaintiff was either careless enough or foolish enough to be drinking hot coffee in a car.

The details put a different slant on the case. As a company policy, McDonald's sold coffee at between 180 and 190 degrees Fahrenheit. It takes two to seven seconds for coffee at this temperature to cause third-degree burns, which require skin grafts and debridement. The burns can leave a person in pain and disabled for many months or years, and can result in permanent and disfiguring injuries. Liebeck ended up in the hospital for a week and was disabled for more than two years.

(continues)

During trial, McDonald's acknowledged having been aware of the risk of serious burn injuries from its coffee for over 10 years. In fact, more than 700 people reported being burnt by McDonald's steaming coffee prior to Liebeck's incident. Witnesses who appeared for McDonald's admitted that consumers were unaware of the risk of serious burns from the coffee and that customers were never warned. Most incredible, witnesses for McDonald's stated that the company had no plans to reduce the temperature of the coffee sold, despite the fact that the coffee was "not fit for consumption" when sold because it could cause scalding burns.

CASE QUESTIONS

1. Taking the case from McDonald's perspective, are there any possible reasons for selling such hot coffee?
2. Balancing McDonald's need to sell hot coffee versus the possible risk of serious injury posed, could there be any reason that McDonald's did not have a plan to reduce the coffee's temperature in the future, despite the prior incidents?

Proving Breach of Duty

Proof is an essential aspect of all litigation. A cynic might suggest that what is true or false is irrelevant; rather, what can be proven during a lawsuit is all that matters. Negligence claims are normally proven through the typical evidentiary processes. These include oral testimony, written transcripts of discovery depositions, documentary evidence, and demonstrative evidence (such as photographs or computer simulations).

Affirmative defenses must be alleged or proven by the defendant. Unless alleged and proven, the law will presume that no defense exists. These defenses are covered in chapter 4.

Burdens of Proof and Rejoinder

preponderance of the evidence | The greater weight of the evidence. This is a standard of proof generally used in civil lawsuits. It is not as high a standard as *clear and convincing evidence* or *beyond a reasonable doubt.*

prima facie case | A case that will be won unless the other side comes forward with evidence to disprove it.

burden of rejoinder | The defendant's burden of proof to refute the plaintiff's evidence in a lawsuit.

The plaintiff has the burden of proving that the defendant was negligent. This forces the plaintiff to prove by a **preponderance of the evidence** that all negligence elements existed (duty, breach, causation, and injury). The evidence must establish that the defendant's actions were negligent and caused the plaintiff's injuries. Burden of proof is sometimes referred to as *burden of production.*

Once the plaintiff has made a **prima facie case** (meaning that proof has been established by or beyond a preponderance), the burden shifts to the defendant, who must then counter the plaintiff's evidence with proof of his or her own. This is sometimes called the defendant's **burden of rejoinder,** persuasion, or rebuttal. The defendant must refute the plaintiff's case against him or her.

In some cases, however, the burden of proof is different. What if the plaintiff cannot prove the defendant's negligence? Consider an example. Suppose a patient was unconscious during an operation. Suppose the surgical nurse failed to remove all the sponges from the patient, and later the patient contracted peritonitis. How could the plaintiff prove that the defendants (nurse, surgeon, and hospital) were negligent in leaving the sponge inside the plaintiff? What witnesses could the plaintiff call to testify, other than the surgical team? The plaintiff was unconscious and unaware of the entire procedure. How could the plaintiff meet the burden of proof in such circumstances? Such unusual cases require a special burden of proof, which is called *res ipsa loquitur.*

Res Ipsa Loquitur

Res ipsa loquitur is Latin meaning "the thing [*res*] speaks [*loquitur*] for itself [*ipsa*]." It is used in negligence cases in which the plaintiff is in a disadvantaged position for proving the defendant's negligence because the evidence is unavailable to the plaintiff, but is or should be available to the defendant. Under the doctrine of res ipsa loquitur, the defendant's negligence is presumed as a result of his or her actions. This shifts the burden of proof to the defendant. In other words, the defendant must disprove his or her negligence from the outset of litigation. The plaintiff's burden of proof is converted into the defendant's burden of rejoinder.

res ipsa loquitur | (Latin) "The thing speaks for itself." A rebuttable presumption (a conclusion that can be changed if contrary evidence is introduced) that a person is negligent.

Elements of Res Ipsa Loquitur

The plaintiff must prove only certain essential facts, such as what injury occurred, what the defendant was doing, and how the defendant's action (or inaction) related to the plaintiff's harm. To use res ipsa loquitur, whatever occurred must not ordinarily occur without someone acting negligently. Court opinions often quote the following elements:

1. The defendant (or his or her employee[s]) must have been in exclusive control of the object or action that produced the plaintiff's injury.
2. The plaintiff's injury must be of a type that ordinarily would not have happened unless negligence were involved.
3. The defendant must be in a better position to prove his or her lack of negligence than the plaintiff is to prove the defendant's negligence.

Certain courts and legal scholars add a fourth element, which states that the plaintiff cannot have contributed to his or her own injuries. This, however, simply states contributory and comparative negligence, which are two similar defenses to negligence.

Defendant's Exclusive Control. For res ipsa loquitur to apply, the events that led to the plaintiff's injury must have been under the defendant's exclusive control. This includes the defendant's employees. For example, suppose the plaintiff was walking through the defendant's warehouse. Suppose the defendant's employees had stacked many crates of merchandise, and the stacks rose thirty feet high. If a top crate fell upon and injured the plaintiff, but nobody except the plaintiff was present in that part of the building, who could the plaintiff point the finger toward as having been negligent? Using res ipsa loquitur, the plaintiff would shift the burden of proof to the defendant (warehouse owner) to show that the crates had been safely stowed. Because the crates were under the defendant's exclusive control, and one crate fell and hurt the plaintiff, the first element of res ipsa loquitur would be satisfied.

Presumption of Negligence. Res ipsa loquitur insists that the plaintiff's injury be one that normally would not have happened unless negligence were involved. Consider the preceding illustration. Crates usually do not fall over in warehouses unless they are improperly stacked. Negligence may be presumed in this case because the box fell. This would not normally occur if ordinary, reasonable care were used to store the crates. Because the box did fall on the plaintiff, then the defendant must not have exercised reasonable care in stacking the crates. At least the court will make this presumption and allow the defendant to refute it by proving that reasonable care was used when storing the boxes. Note, also see "Negligence Per Se" in chapter 3, as this is another method of proving breach of duty.

THE CASE OF THE FALLING PARALEGAL

Imagine this paralegal's fright being trapped alone in a falling elevator, while en route back from an attorney's office on another floor of a high-rise office building where she worked. After the ordeal, the paralegal brought an action for her injuries against both the elevator maintenance company, referred to as Schindler, and against the property manager of the building, referred to as Hines. The issues of alleged negligent response by Schindler and Hines, and failure to warn by Schindler, are the focus of this case.

Joan T. SANT et al., Plaintiffs-Appellants,
v.
HINES INTERESTS LIMITED PARTNERSHIP
et al., Defendants-Appellees.

No. 05AP-586.
Court of Appeals of Ohio, Tenth District,
Franklin County
Decided Dec. 15, 2005

Mrs. Sant is employed as a paralegal with a law firm that occupies six floors at the top of the Huntington Center building in downtown Columbus. Mrs. Sant's office is located on the 30th floor. As part of her job, Mrs. Sant regularly travels from one floor to another within the firm by way of elevators servicing the upper floors.

On October 16, 2001, Mrs. Sant took an elevator from the 30th floor to the 32nd floor, intending to speak with an attorney in her firm. The attorney was not in his office, so Mrs. Sant went back to the elevator bank to return to her office.

Mrs. Sant pressed the button to go to the 30th floor; however, instead of descending the elevator ascended to the 34th floor, where the doors remained closed. Mrs. Sant again pushed the button for the 30th floor. This time, the elevator moved downward, until it stopped at the 25th floor. Again, the doors remained closed. Mrs. Sant testified that the elevator began to drop intermittently from that point, falling approximately 20 times.

As these events unfolded, Mrs. Sant used the intercom system to inform the building courtesy staff that the elevator was malfunctioning. Carl Grubb and Chris Rogers were on duty that evening and informed her that they would check on the situation. Rogers then went to investigate whether he could see the position of the elevator. At one point, Rogers visually determined that the elevator was stuck about one inch below the 32nd floor, although the indicator registered its location as being at level 33. Approximately 20 minutes later, Rogers noted that the indicator showed that the elevator was at the 22nd level; however, visually, Rogers located the elevator in the blind hoistway, somewhere between the gallery level and what would be the 20th floor.

When Rogers first spotted the elevator, he informed Grubb of the situation. Grubb then used the intercom to tell Mrs. Sant that he was calling Schindler, the elevator maintenance company, to assist her. Grubb called Schindler's dispatch number at 6:40 p.m.

Mrs. Sant was trapped in the elevator for about two hours. At approximately 8:40 p.m., the elevator descended to the ground floor. The descent occurred at normal speed; however, Mrs. Sant testified that the landing was harder than usual. Mrs. Sant testified that she was not injured as the elevator dropped intermittently. Instead, she believes she was injured during the irregular landing.

On October 9, 2003, Mrs. Sant and her husband filed a complaint naming Schindler and Hines as defendants.

Appellants assert Defendant Schindler was aware, or should have been aware, of the dangers associated with the elevator located in the Huntington Center Building at the time it left Defendant Schindler's control, and Defendant Schindler failed to adequately warn or instruct consumers about the hazards associated with the elevators it designed and/or installed, as a manufacturer exercising reasonable care would have done, considering the risks and likelihood of the product causing harm.

The trial court correctly analyzed appellants' assertion of failure to warn pursuant to R.C. 2307.76. Under the statute, only the product's manufacturer is responsible for failing to adequately warn consumers of potential harm. Sean Walsh, Schindler's branch manager in Columbus, testified in an affidavit that Westinghouse Elevator Company designed and installed the elevator that malfunctioned. Appellants provide no evidence to the contrary.

Regarding appellants' claim of negligent response, we begin our analysis by determining whether Schindler owed appellants any duty.

Liability in such instance is not based upon any contractual relation between the person injured and the offending contractor, but upon the failure of such contractor to exercise due care in the performance of his assumed obligations.

The scope of Schindler's duty to appellant is limited by the maintenance agreement between Schindler and Huntington Center Associates. Thus, appellant must demonstrate that Schindler failed to exercise ordinary care in its obligations under the agreement in order to successfully establish her negligence claim.

Schindler represented that it would maintain the specified elevators and equipment in first class operating condition by conducting weekly examinations of the elevators and adjusting, lubricating, cleaning and repairing the equipment as necessary. Schindler also contracted to provide "24 Hour Emergency/After Hour Minor Adjustment Callback Service."

Appellants submit that Schindler could have and should have instructed the courtesy staff at the Huntington Center to shut off the power to the elevator, thereby preventing Mrs. Sant's ultimate descent.

(continues)

Appellants present the testimony of their expert, William Daley, to support their position.

All parties agree that it is not safe to shut off power to an elevator when it is moving. Yet, the record is replete with testimony that there was no absolute way to determine the elevator's true location in the hoistway, let alone whether the elevator was moving.

With no way to ensure that the elevator was not moving, there was no way for the Schindler technician to safely tell the Hines staff to shut off power to the elevator without his actual presence at the building.

Accordingly, appellants cannot show that Schindler breached its duty of ordinary care.

Appellants also assert that Hines was negligent in its response to Mrs. Sant's entrapment.

Appellants assert that Hines' staff should have done more to resolve Mrs. Sant's entrapment. Yet, Mrs. Sant provides no legal basis for this position. The Hines' courtesy staff acted in a reasonably prudent manner. They contacted Schindler, the party that had assumed the duty to respond to and work to resolve elevator entrapments. Accordingly, appellants cannot prove Hines breached any duty it may have owed.

CASE QUESTIONS

1. Who else could the Sants have brought an action against?
2. What did the Sants need to show to be successful with their claim?

Defendant's Superior Proof Position. Under res ipsa loquitur, the defendant must be in a better position to prove that he or she was not negligent than the plaintiff is to establish the defendant's negligence. In the warehouse example, the plaintiff did not see how the crate fell. None of the defendant's employees were present or nearby when the accident occurred. No witnesses actually saw why the crate fell. But the defendant originally stacked the crates. This makes it easier for the defendant to prove that reasonable care was used in stacking the boxes. The plaintiff is at a disadvantage to prove the defendant's negligence. However, the defendant can more easily show that safeguards were used in stacking the crates (such as ropes tied to support beams and crates, or walls and doors surrounding the stacked boxes). In this fashion, the defendant could prove that reasonable care was used when stacking the crates and therefore no negligence occurred.

Res ipsa loquitur cases often involve medical malpractice, particularly surgery. However, the doctrine is not restricted to such negligence cases, as the following hypothetical illustrates.

Table 2-3 summarizes proof of negligence and res ipsa loquitur.

hypothetical

Eugene supervises a road-repair crew employed by Pavement Plus, Inc. The county contracts road construction and renovation to Pavement Plus. Eugene's crew was filling potholes on Elm Avenue one spring day. One of Eugene's employees, Everest, improperly mixed the asphalt so that it would not harden adequately. This bad asphalt was used to fill the Elm Avenue holes. Rutherford, who lives on Elm Avenue, drove over the patched potholes a few days later. The asphalt collapsed and the front right tire of Rutherford's automobile wedged in a hole, bending the front axle. Rutherford discovered that Pavement Plus had repaired the street, but had kept no record of the asphalt mixtures used.

Could Rutherford use res ipsa loquitur to shift the burden of proof? Evaluate the elements under these facts. Pavement Plus's foreman, Eugene, and an employee were under exclusive control of the weak asphalt used to fix the street. Asphalt does not normally collapse under vehicular weight unless it is improperly prepared or applied. The defendant is in the best position to prove that the mixture was suitable, as its employees prepared and applied the asphalt. Thus, res ipsa loquitur applies in this case, and the plaintiff need only prove what happened (i.e., his car was damaged when it fell through an asphalted hole that the defendant repaired). The defendant must now establish that its employees used reasonable care in preparing and applying the asphalt. As an aside, this problem also illustrates the value of retaining written records (in this case, of asphalt mixture) to document reasonable care.

BURDENS OF PROOF AND REJOINDER (REBUTTAL)	RES IPSA LOQUITUR
Plaintiff must generally prove the defendant's negligence beyond a preponderance of the evidence.	"The thing speaks for itself." This doctrine shifts the burden of proof to the defendant, who must disprove the presumed negligence.
	Elements: (1) the defendant's exclusive control over acts or objects that injured the plaintiff; (2) the plaintiff's injury must be one that ordinarily does not occur without negligence; and (3) the defendant is in the best position to prove that he or she was not negligent.

TABLE 2-3
Burden of proof, burden of rejoinder (rebuttal), and res ipsa loquitur

Violation of a Statute

Sometimes there will be an allegation in a negligence claim that the defendant also violated a particular statute. For example, there might be a local ordinance requiring all outdoor swimming pools to be fenced. A couple in the area affected by the statute had a pool party for their child and the neighbors. The homeowners had taken down the fence when they bought the house and had not yet decided the kind of fence they would replace it with. One of the children dove into the pool, struck the bottom, and was severely injured. The question then arises as to what effect the possible violation of the statute might have upon the negligence action. In analyzing the case, you must look to see if the statute was in fact violated and, if so, whether this caused the accident or played a significant role in the accident. It is also important to see if the person injured was the kind of person the statute was designed to protect and whether the statute covers the kind of harm suffered by the plaintiff. In this example, the fact that there was no fence had nothing whatsoever to do with the accident.

However, if the facts had been different and a neighbor's child wandered into the unfenced backyard, fell into the pool, and drowned, this statute would have a direct bearing on the negligence case. In most states, the violation of such a statute would be considered *negligence per se*. This would mean that the proof of the violation of the statute would be sufficient to show that there was negligence; the defendant would thus be prevented from introducing evidence as to the degree of care or reasonableness used. This subject is also covered in chapter 3 under "Negligence Per Se."

▌ CAUSATION OF INJURY

Even if the defendant breaches his or her duty of care owed to the plaintiff, the defendant will not be legally negligent, nor liable for the plaintiff's injuries, unless the defendant's actions proximately caused the harm. To have causation, both "cause-in-fact" and "proximate cause" must be present.

Cause-in-Fact

cause-in-fact | Cause of injury in negligence cases. If the tortfeasor's actions resulted in the victim's injuries, then the tortfeasor was the cause-in-fact of the victim's harm.

Causation is a critical component of negligence. To be liable, the tortfeasor must have caused the victim's injuries. *Causation of injury* relates to the tortfeasor's actions that result in harm to the injured party. Courts frequently refer to this as **cause-in-fact,** meaning that, in negligence litigation, the defendant's misconduct produced the plaintiff's injuries.

The defendant's acts must be the *actual* and *factual* cause of the plaintiff's injuries. The formula is straightforward: but for the tortfeasor's (defendant's) actions, the victim (plaintiff) would not have been harmed. The tortfeasor's behavior is usually the immediate, direct, and dominant cause of the victim's injuries. For example, if Samantha spills a beverage on a stairway and does not clean it up, and Daniel slips on the slick spot and falls down the stairs, Samantha has caused Daniel's injuries. The causation is direct: but for Samantha's failure to clean the drink spill on the stairs, Daniel would not have slipped and fallen.

Consider another illustration. Suppose an automobile mechanic changes the tires on Zach's car but neglects to tighten the lug nuts properly. While the vehicle is moving, the left rear tire comes loose and flies off. The car skids out of control and crashes into a telephone pole, hurting Zach. Again, there is causation: but for the mechanic's failure to tighten the nuts sufficiently, the tire would not have come off and Zach would not have collided with the pole.

Sometimes several forces combine to produce injuries. For example, in the loose tire example, suppose the tire had not come completely off the automobile but was wobbling loosely. However, as Zach was driving, he encountered broken glass on the highway, which punctured his left rear tire. Because of the flat tire and the looseness of all the tires, Zach lost control of the car and crashed. Here, two factors resulted in Zach's injuries: the glass that ruptured his tire and the loose nuts that lessened his control of the vehicle.

Substantial Factor Analysis

Substantial factor analysis states that the tortfeasor is liable for injuries to the victim when the tortfeasor's misconduct was a *substantial factor* in producing the harm. In the preceding tire illustration, the broken glass flattened Zach's tire and made the car difficult to handle. However, had the lug nuts not also been loose, the tires would not have been wobbling. Zach probably would have been able to control the vehicle better and might not have crashed at all. The mechanic's failure to tighten the nuts was a substantial factor in Zach's losing control and colliding with the pole. Thus, the mechanic would be liable, even though the broken glass and punctured tire also influenced the accident.

A classic substantial factor analysis case is *Summers v. Tice*, 33 Cal. 2d 80, 199 P.2d 1 (1948). In this case, the plaintiff was hunting quail with two defendants. When the birds were flushed out, the defendants aimed and fired their shotguns in the plaintiff's direction, striking the plaintiff and causing severe physical injuries. It was unclear which defendant's shot hit the plaintiff, because both defendants used the same gauge shotgun and size of shot. The California Supreme Court applied the substantial factor test in determining causation and liability. Although it could not be conclusively established which defendant's weapon caused the plaintiff's injuries, either defendant's action was sufficient to produce the resulting harm. Quoting a Mississippi Supreme Court case, Justice Carter stated: "We think that . . . each is liable for the resulting injury . . . , although no one can say definitely who actually shot [the plaintiff]. To hold otherwise would be to exonerate both from liability, although each was negligent, and the injury resulted from such negligence."

substantial factor analysis | A test for indirect causation in negligence cases. The tortfeasor is liable for injuries to the victim when the tortfeasor's conduct was a substantial factor in producing the harm.

THE CASE OF THE QUARTER-SIZED PUDDLE

One of the more common negligence actions you will encounter is the slip-and-fall case. If the plaintiff is to be successful, causation must be established.

ADGER
v.
DILLARD DEPARTMENT STORES

Court of Appeal of Louisiana
662 So. 2d 864 (La. Ct. App. 1995)
November 1, 1995
Williams, Judge

On the evening of May 11, 1993, the plaintiff and a companion, Beverly Franklin, visited Dillard's Department Store at Pierre Bossier Mall. . . . Ms. Franklin was walking slightly ahead of the plaintiff and did not see her slip, but turned and saw her falling to the floor.

Margaret P. Stinson, area sales manager for Dillard's, was notified of the incident. When Ms. Stinson arrived at the young-men's section, plaintiff was standing with Ms. Franklin and David Piazza, a security guard. They helped plaintiff walk to a nearby chair. The security officer questioned the plaintiff and filled out an accident report.

* * *

[P]laintiff testified that she did not know what caused her fall and had not noticed anything on the floor before or immediately after she fell. She apparently did not examine her clothing for dampness or staining, which would have indicated that she slipped in liquid. She testified that her foot slid along the floor, but defense counsel pointed out that plaintiff had not made that claim during a prior deposition.

Ms. Franklin also testified that she did not notice any water on the floor before plaintiff fell, or immediately after the fall, when her attention centered on helping the plaintiff. Ms. Franklin asserted that a short time later, she returned to the place where the plaintiff fell and found a quarter-sized puddle of water. Ms. Franklin maintained that she told someone standing nearby that plaintiff had slipped in water. However, Ms. Stinson testified that she inspected the area where the accident occurred and found the floor clean and dry.

* * *

Here, the plaintiff has failed to establish that her fall was caused by the quarter-sized puddle of water observed by Ms. Franklin. Moreover, another witness contested the presence of any water in the area of the accident. Even if we were to assume that the small puddle of water was present at the time of the accident, there is no evidence, other than Ms. Franklin's hypothesis, that the water contributed to the plaintiff's fall. After reviewing the record and the trial transcript, we cannot find that the trial court was clearly wrong in granting the defendant's motion for involuntary dismissal.

* * *

AFFIRMED.

CASE QUESTIONS

1. Do you think the trial court believed the plaintiff's version of the facts? Explain.
2. What kinds of facts would have had to be presented to hold the defendant department store liable for the slip and fall?

Summers v. Tice resembles another type of case in which multiple forces combine to produce harm. When two or more defendants act together to produce the plaintiff's injury, the courts consider them to have *acted in concert.* All defendants are held liable for their combined conduct in such cases. This is called **joint and several liability,** another form of causation. This case can be found on-line.

Joint and Several Liability

Multiple tortfeasors are each held individually accountable to the victim for the combined negligent behavior of all the tortfeasors. For instance, suppose that a surgical team, composed of two surgeons, three nurses, and an anesthesiologist, loses count of surgical sponges and leaves one in the patient's abdomen. The patient contracts peritonitis as a consequence. Because all of the medical personnel acted together in the operation, they are said to have functioned in concert. Their collective conduct produced harm to the patient. Thus, each individual would be personally liable for the patient's injuries. In other words, all of the personnel would be jointly and severally liable.

Multiple tortfeasors may injure a victim by acting in sequence, rather than simultaneously as in the medical malpractice example. The sequence of combined events produces the harmful results. For example, assume that a shipping company does not refrigerate a shipment of perishable food. As a result, the items spoil in transit. The shipment arrives at a supermarket, which fails to notice the spoiled condition of the products and stocks them on its shelves. Jerome's roommate buys some of the goods but does not check them for freshness, despite obvious odors and discoloration. After his roommate cooks dinner, Jerome eats the bad food and becomes seriously ill.

Who does Jerome sue? Several tortfeasors combined negligent behavior to produce his injury. First the shipper failed to refrigerate the food, and it turned rotten. Next the grocery store failed to notice the spoiled food and stocked it. Then Jerome's roommate failed to notice the spoilage and prepared the food for him to eat. All these tortfeasors—the shipping company, the supermarket, and Jerome's roommate—contributed to a sequence of events that resulted in his illness. Jerome would not have become sick had any of these tortfeasors identified the threat (spoiled food) and taken reasonable precautions to avoid injuring customers. **But for** the concerted conduct of these tortfeasors, Jerome would not have been hurt. Therefore, they are all jointly and severally liable to him for the harm caused.

Table 2-4 outlines the causation-of-injury theories.

TABLE 2-4
Causation-of-injury
theories

CAUSE-IN-FACT (BUT-FOR CAUSATION)	SUBSTANTIAL FACTOR ANALYSIS	JOINT AND SEVERAL LIABILITY
But for the defendant's actions, the plaintiff's injury would not have happened.	When multiple defendants combine to injure the plaintiff, a single defendant is liable if his or her actions were a substantial factor in producing the harm.	When multiple defendants act together to injure the plaintiff, all defendants are liable for the harm.

SHARE AND SHARE ALIKE?

In this case, a physician repeatedly prescribes a corticosteroid to his injured patient for pain relief. On one prescription the physician circles "PRN" (refill as needed), instead of inserting a "0" in the refill box to indicate there are zero, or no more, refills permitted. The patient repeatedly refills the prescription and ends up with a serious disease from the accumulation of the drug in his system. Between the patient, the pharmacy, and the prescribing physician, who should bear the cost of this error?

William C. SULLIVAN, D.O.
v.
ROBERTSON DRUG CO., INC., et al.
Record No. 060647
Supreme Court of Virginia
639 S.E.2d 250
Jan. 12, 2007

This case is an appeal of a judgment entered in a contribution action involving joint tortfeasors. We consider whether the circuit court erred in instructing the jury that it could apportion damages based on the jury's assessment of the degree to which a defendant's negligence contributed to the injuries that were the subject of the underlying tort action.

David M. Hopper filed a complaint in the United States District Court for the Western District of Virginia against his physician, William C. Sullivan, D.O., alleging that Dr. Sullivan improperly prescribed excess amounts of Triamcinolone, a corticosteroid, which caused him to develop severe medical conditions including Cushing's Syndrome and osteoporosis.

Hopper sought $1 million in compensatory damages and $350,000 in punitive damages from Dr. Sullivan. Hopper and Dr. Sullivan later entered

into an agreement settling the federal court action for the amount of $735,000. In the agreement, Hopper released all claims he may have had against Dr. Sullivan and against Robertson Drug and its employees.

After the settlement, Dr. Sullivan filed the present motion for judgment against Michael S. Robertson, a pharmacist, and Robertson's employer, Robertson Drug Co., Inc. (Robertson Drug), seeking contribution for Dr. Sullivan's payment in settlement of Hopper's claim. Dr. Sullivan alleged that Robertson, in his individual capacity and as owner of Robertson Drug, negligently "refilled" Hopper's Triamcinolone prescriptions, thereby contributing to Hopper's injuries.

Dr. Sullivan asserted that Robertson and Robertson Drug were indebted to Dr. Sullivan for "their share of the total settlement paid by Sullivan for their release."

At trial, the evidence showed that Hopper initially sought medical treatment from Dr. Sullivan for multiple injuries he sustained in an automobile accident. Dr. Sullivan provided Hopper with his first dose of Triamcinolone for "pain management." Thereafter,

Dr. Sullivan gave Hopper two or three additional Triamcinolone injections.

Dr. Sullivan also wrote Hopper a prescription for Triamcinolone. Instead of writing "0" as the number of refills permitted, Dr. Sullivan circled "PRN," which allowed Hopper to receive unlimited "refills" for 24 months. According to Dr. Sullivan, he did not intend to allow unlimited "refills" of the drug because its long-term use can cause suppression of the immune system.

Based on the prescription written by Dr. Sullivan, Hopper obtained Triamcinolone on five occasions from Westover Pharmacy. After Westover Pharmacy permanently closed its business Hopper obtained "refills" of his prescription at Robertson Drug three times between early August and the middle of September. Robertson was the pharmacist who provided these last three "refills" and, at that time, he had access to Westover Pharmacy's prescription records.

In the middle of September, Hopper became ill, was admitted to a hospital for 20 days, and was diagnosed as having Cushing's Syndrome.

Dr. Barrett began treating Hopper for Cushing's Syndrome, osteoporosis, and several other related problems. Dr. Barrett attributed these conditions to Hopper's overuse of corticosteroids.

Dr. Sullivan contends that Robertson was a joint tortfeasor who was equally liable for half the damages caused by his concurrent negligence.

Robertson asserts that the evidence showed that Hopper suffered multiple divisible injuries, some of which were caused solely by Dr. Sullivan.

The right of contribution is based on the equitable principle that when two or more persons are subject to a common burden, their responsibility shall be borne equally.

If separate and independent acts of negligence of two parties directly cause a single indivisible injury to a third person, either or both wrongdoers are responsible for the whole injury.

Accordingly, each such wrongdoer is responsible for an equal share of the amount paid in damages for a single injury. Only when there are multiple, divisible injuries covered by a compromise settlement is the finder of fact required to attempt an allocation of the amount in contribution a wrongdoer must pay for his negligent act or acts causing one or more of those divisible injuries.

CASE QUESTIONS

1. In what instance would Dr. Sullivan have had to pay more than 50 percent of the settlement?
2. Who do you feel was primarily responsible for Hopper's injuries?

Contribution

Contribution is another issue that comes up when multiple defendants are involved in a negligence action. Most jurisdictions permit one tortfeasor to seek contribution from the others. Contribution means that one tortfeasor pays all or part of the liability for a wrong and is then allowed to recover all or part of this amount from the other tortfeasors. Some jurisdictions allow parties to seek contribution only when there was no concert of action, when the wrong was not an intentional one, or when the person seeking contribution was not primarily liable. For example, Marie sues Adam, Bobby, and Cindy and is awarded a judgment for $12,000. Each defendant's share is one-third of $12,000, or $4,000. If Adam pays the entire $12,000 judgment, he can seek contribution of $4,000 from Bobby and $4,000 from Cindy.

contribution | 1. The sharing of payment for a debt (or judgment) among persons who are all liable for the debt. 2. The right of a person who has paid an entire debt (or judgment) to get back a fair share of the payment from another person who is also responsible for the debt.

Indemnity

Sometimes there is an **indemnity** policy of insurance involved, which would change the outcome of a claim. Indemnity insurance specifically provides for reimbursing a party for actual losses or damages sustained. This is in contrast to liability insurance, which provides for payment of a specified sum upon the occurrence of a specific event regardless of the amount of actual losses or damages.

Courts and Causation

American Jurisprudence 2d, a legal encyclopedia, provides an excellent and accurate summary of causation analysis.

57A AMERICAN JURISPRUDENCE 2D *Negligence* §§ 431, 434, 436, 464, 471, 474-75, 478 (1989)
[All footnotes omitted.]

[§ 431] Cause in fact as an element of proximate cause means that the wrongful act was a substantial factor in bringing about the injury and without which no harm would have been incurred. . . .

[§ 464] In all cases where proximate cause is in issue, the first step is to determine whether the defendant's conduct, in point of fact, was a factor in causing plaintiff's damage. . . . If the inquiry as to cause in fact shows that the defendant's conduct, in point of fact, was not a factor in causing plaintiff's damage, the matter ends there. But if it shows that his conduct was a factor in causing such damage, then the further question is whether his conduct played such a part in causing the damage as makes him the author of such damage and liable therefor in the eyes of the law. . . .

[§ 471] Most jurisdictions have historically followed this so-called "**but-for**" **causation-in-fact test**. It has proven to be a fair, easily understood and serviceable test of actual causation in negligence actions. . . . Where the "but for" test is recognized, it is useful for the purpose of determining whether specific conduct actually caused the harmful result in question. It cannot be indiscriminately used as an unqualified measure of the defendant's liability. . . .

[§ 474] The "but-for" test, while it explains the greater number of cases, does not in all instances serve as an adequate test. If two causes concur to bring about an event, and either one of them, operating alone, would have been sufficient to cause the identical result, some other test is needed. . . . The response of many courts to this problem has been to apply the "substantial factor" test, either in addition to or in place of the "but for" test. . . .

[§ 475] The substantial factor test . . . makes the question of proximate or legal cause depend upon the answer to the question, "was defendant's conduct a substantial factor in producing plaintiff's injuries?"

Causation becomes clearer through an example. The following illustration should lend substance to the analytical formula.

hypothetical

Angel runs a beauty salon. Aspen is one of her regular customers. Angel received a shipment of hair coloring products in unlabeled bottles. Rather than return the shipment, Angel placed the bottles in a storeroom for future use. She applied one bottle to Aspen's hair without carefully checking its contents beforehand. Because of unusually high pH levels in Aspen's hair, the product turned Aspen's hair bright blue. Did Angel cause Aspen's injury?

But for Angel's failure to inspect the bottle's contents prior to treating Aspen's hair, Aspen would not have suffered hair discoloration. Direct causation functions easily and clearly to conclude that Angel caused Aspen's injury.

Suppose instead that Angie, one of Angel's employees, had taken the bottle from the storeroom and applied it to Aspen. Would both Angel and Angie be liable for Aspen's harm and damage? Angel failed to identify the unlabeled bottles before storing them. Angie failed to check the bottle's contents before applying them to Aspen's hair. Both combined in their unreasonable actions to produce the harmful result. Accordingly, Angel and Angie are jointly and severally liable to Aspen.

Suppose the bottles had been mislabeled by the manufacturer. Angel unknowingly stocked the bottles, assuming the labels to be correct. Angie then applied the contents of one bottle to Aspen's hair without observing that the contents were the wrong color and texture (a point that an experienced beautician should reasonably have known). The but-for test does not produce clear results in this case. One cannot say that, but for the manufacturer's mislabeling, Aspen would not have been hurt, because Angie actually misapplied the product to Aspen's hair. Neither may one contend that, but for Angie's use of the improperly labelled product, Aspen would not have been harmed, because Angie was not responsible for the mislabeling. Substantial factor analysis, however, helps to reach an acceptable answer. Angie's failure to inspect the bottle's contents and determine the error before applying the mixture to Aspen's hair was a substantial factor in producing Aspen's injury. Accordingly, Angie would be liable to Aspen.

Proximate Cause

In order to establish liability for negligence, the tortfeasor must be the legal or proximate cause of injury. However, the tortfeasor is not liable for *all* injuries. When a plaintiff suffers unusual injuries or the tortfeasor has started a chain of events causing injury, at some point the tortfeasor's liability might be cut off and limited to those injuries that were foreseeable.

Foreseeability of Injury

Duty is governed by foreseeability. **Proximate cause,** or *legal cause* as it is sometimes called, exists when the tortfeasor's actions cause a foreseeable injury to the victim. If foreseeability is not present, then no duty is owed. Court opinions often refer to the plaintiff's injuries as the natural and probable consequence of the defendant's misconduct. The key to proximate cause is foreseeable injury. Was the victim's injury the reasonably foreseeable result of what the tortfeasor did? If so, then the tortfeasor's actions proximately caused the plaintiff's harm and a duty is owed. If not, then proximate cause did not exist, and the defendant will not be liable to the plaintiff under negligence theory.

Proximate cause is a subcategory of causation. *Causation* is the chain of events linking the tortfeasor's conduct to the victim's injury. *Proximate cause* is the zone within which the plaintiff's injury was reasonably foreseeable as a consequence of the defendant's behavior. Think of proximate cause as a circle. Actions inside the circle cause foreseeable injuries to victims. Actions outside the circle are beyond the zone of danger. Exhibit 2-1 illustrates this concept.

Consider a hypothetical. Patrick is building an additional garage and workshop in his backyard. As he is excavating to install the foundation, he hits an underground natural gas pipeline that services his neighborhood. The pipe ruptures and disrupts gas supplies to the other houses in the area. As a result, those houses with gas heat cannot use their furnaces. It is January, and outside temperatures fall well below freezing at night. With no heat, the water pipes in the neighbors' homes freeze and burst, causing substantial water damage to the structures and furnishings. Did Patrick proximately cause the harm to the neighbors' houses?

Exhibit 2-1
Proximate cause zone of danger

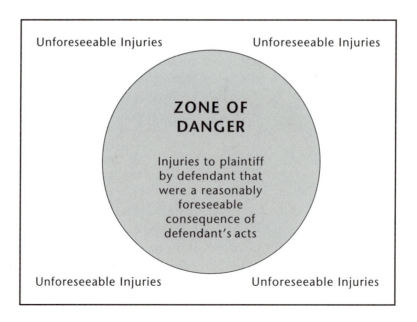

ZONE OF DANGER

Injuries to plaintiff by defendant that were a reasonably foreseeable consequence of defendant's acts

Unforeseeable Injuries   Unforeseeable Injuries

Unforeseeable Injuries   Unforeseeable Injuries

It was reasonably foreseeable that an underground utility line might be severed. If this line were carrying a heating source, such as natural gas, it would likewise be reasonably foreseeable that neighboring homes would lose their heat service. Because it was winter, it was also reasonably foreseeable that temperatures could go below freezing and cause water pipes in unheated buildings to freeze and burst. Water damage to structures and furnishings is a natural and inevitable consequence of broken pipes. Clearly, Patrick's actions proximately caused the injury to his neighbors' homes, because the harm was reasonably foreseeable as a result of Patrick's breaking the natural gas pipeline.

Proximate Cause and Scope of Duty Combined

Some legal scholars have included scope of duty as an aspect of proximate cause. This seems logical, as both include the element of foreseeability, but there is a subtle distinction. Scope of duty examines whether it was reasonably foreseeable that the plaintiff would be injured as a result of the defendant's actions. Proximate cause focuses upon whether the injury itself was reasonably foreseeable.

THE CASE OF THE SCALE THAT SHOOK TORT LAW

In this landmark case, a man waiting for a train was carrying a package wrapped in newspaper with fireworks inside. The railroad guards were unaware of the contents of the parcel and helped the man board the moving train. As the guards tried to help, the package was dislodged, fell to the tracks, and exploded. This caused the platform to shake, which in turn caused a scale to fall. The scale seriously injured Helen Palsgraf, who was waiting on the platform. Was a duty owed to the plaintiff?

PALSGRAF
v.
LONG ISLAND RAILROAD
Court of Appeals of New York
162 N.E. 99 (N.Y. Ct. App. 1928)
May 29, 1928
Cardozo, C.J.

Plaintiff was standing on a platform of defendant's railroad after buying a ticket to go to Rockaway Beach. A train stopped at the station, bound for another place. Two men ran forward to catch it. One of the men reached the platform of the car without mishap, though the train was already moving. The other man, carrying a package, jumped aboard the car, but seemed unsteady as if about to fall. A guard on the car, who had held the door open, reached forward to help him in, and another guard on the platform pushed him from behind. In this act, the package was dislodged, and fell upon the rails. It was a package of small size, about fifteen inches long, and was covered by a newspaper. In fact it contained fireworks, but there was nothing in its appearance to give notice of its contents. The fireworks when they fell exploded. The shock of the explosion threw down some scales at the other end of the platform many feet away. The scales struck the plaintiff, causing injuries for which she sues.

The conduct of the defendant's guard, if a wrong in its relation to the holder of the package, was not a wrong in its relation to the plaintiff, standing far away. Relatively to her it was not negligence at all.

(continues)

Nothing in the situation gave notice that the falling package had in it the potency of peril to persons thus removed. Negligence is not actionable unless it involves the invasion of a legally protected interest, the violation of a right. "Proof of negligence in the air, so to speak, will not do." "Negligence is the absence of care, according to the circumstances." . . . If no hazard was apparent to the eye of ordinary vigilance, an act innocent and harmless, at least to outward seeming, with reference to her, did not take to itself the quality of a tort because it happened to be a wrong, though apparently not one involving the risk of bodily insecurity, with reference to some one else.

* * *

One who jostles one's neighbor in a crowd does not invade the rights of others standing at the outer fringe when the unintended contact casts a bomb upon the ground. The wrongdoer as to them is the man who carries the bomb, not the one who explodes it without suspicion of the danger. . . . What the plaintiff must show is "a wrong" to herself; i.e., a violation of her own right, and not merely a wrong to some one else, nor conduct "wrongful" because unsocial, but not "a wrong" to any one. . . . The risk reasonably to be perceived defines the duty to be obeyed, and risk imports relation; it is risk to another or to others within the range of apprehension. This does not mean, of course, that one who launches a destructive force is always relieved of liability, if the force, though known to be destructive, pursues an unexpected path. "It was not necessary that the defendant should have had notice of the particular method in which an accident would occur, if the possibility of an accident was clear to the ordinarily prudent eye." Some acts, such as shooting, are so imminently dangerous to any one who may come within reach of the missile, however unexpectedly, as to impose a duty of prevision not far from that of an insurer. Even to-day, and much oftener in earlier stages of the law, one acts sometimes at one's peril. Under this head, it may be, fall certain cases of what is known as transferred intent, an act willfully dangerous to A resulting in injury to B. These cases aside, wrong is defined in terms of the natural or probable, at least when unintentional. The range of reasonable apprehension is at times a question for the court, and at times, if varying inferences are possible, a question for the jury. Here, by concession, there was nothing in the situation to suggest to the most cautious mind that the parcel wrapped in newspaper would spread wrekage through the station. If the guard had thrown it down knowingly and willfully, he would not have threatened the plaintiff's safety, so far as appearances could warn him. His conduct would not have involved, even then, an unreasonable probability of invasion of her bodily security. Liability can be no greater where the act is inadvertent.

* * *

One who seeks redress at law does not make out a cause of action by showing without more that there has been damage to his person. If the harm was not willful, he must show that the act as to him had possibilities of danger so many and apparent as to entitle him to be protected against the doing of it though the harm was unintended.

* * *

The law of causation, remote or proximate, is thus foreign to the case before us. The question of liability is always anterior to the question of the measure of the consequences that go with liability. If there is no tort to be redressed, there is no occasion to consider what damage might be recovered if there were a finding of a tort. We may assume, without deciding, that negligence, not at large or in the abstract, but in relation to the plaintiff, would entail liability for any and all consequences, however novel or extraordinary. There is room for argument that a distinction is to be drawn according to the diversity of interests invaded by the act, as where conduct negligent in that it threatens an insignificant invasion of an interest in property results in an unforeseeable invasion of an interest of another order, as, e.g., one of bodily security. Perhaps other distinctions may be necessary. We do not go into the question now. The consequences to be followed must first be rooted in a wrong.

The judgment of the Appellate Division and that of the Trial Term should be reversed, and the complaint dismissed, with costs in all courts.

ANDREWS, J. (dissenting). Assisting a passenger to board a train, the defendant's servant negligently knocked a package from his arms. It fell between the platform and the cars. Of its contents the servant knew and could know nothing. A violent explosion followed. The concussion broke some scales standing a considerable distance away. In falling, they injured the plaintiff, an intending passenger.

Upon these facts, may she recover the damages she has suffered in an action brought against the master? The result we shall reach depends upon our theory as to the nature of negligence. Is it a relative concept—the breach of some duty owing to a particular person or to particular persons? Or, where there is an act which unreasonably threatens the safety of others, is the doer liable for all its proximate consequences, even where they result in injury to one who would generally be thought to be outside the radius of danger?

* * *

Negligence may be defined roughly as an act or omission which unreasonably does or may affect the rights of others, or which unreasonably fails to protect one's self from the dangers resulting from such acts.

* * *

Where there is the unreasonable act, and some right that may be affected there is negligence whether damage does or does not result. That is immaterial.

* * *

The proposition is this: Every one owes to the world at large the duty of refraining from those acts that may unreasonably threaten the safety of others. Such an act occurs. Not only is he wronged to whom harm might reasonably be expected to result, but he also who is in fact injured, even if he be outside what would generally be thought the danger zone.

* * *

But, when injuries do result from our unlawful act, we are liable for the consequences. It does not matter that they are unusual, unexpected, unforeseen, and unforeseeable. But there is one limitation. The damages must be so connected with the negligence that the latter may be said to be the proximate cause of the former.

* * *

The proximate cause, involved as it may be with many other causes, must be, at the least, something without which the event would not happen. The court must ask itself whether there was a natural and continuous sequence between cause and effect. Was the one a substantial factor in producing the other? Was there a direct connection between them, without too many intervening causes?

* * *

When a lantern is overturned, the firing of a shed is a fairly direct consequence. Many things contribute to the spread of the conflagration—the force of the wind, the direction and width of streets, the character of intervening structures, other factors. We draw an uncertain and wavering line, but draw it we must as best we can.

* * *

The act upon which defendant's liability rests is knocking an apparently harmless package onto the platform. The act was negligent. For its proximate consequences the defendant is liable.

CASE QUESTIONS

1. Was a duty owed to the passenger with the package?
2. Was Helen Palsgraf owed a duty? Explain.
3. How does the dissenting opinion explain proximate cause?

It is possible for the tortfeasor to owe a duty of reasonable care to the victim but not proximately cause the injury if the harm was unforeseeable. For instance, suppose that Shannon, who manages a shoe store, gave away free helium balloons to families as a promotional gimmick. One of her customers, Addison, suffered from a rare allergy to helium, but was unaware of this condition. Addison inhaled some helium from the balloon to make himself talk in a high-pitched, funny voice, which is a common side effect of helium inhalation. Instead, Addison went into anaphylactic shock, suffered cardiac arrest, and died. Did Shannon proximately cause Addison's death?

Definitely, Shannon owed a duty of reasonable care to all of her patrons to maintain reasonably safe premises. But Addison's uncommon sensitivity to helium (of which even he was unaware) was not something that Shannon could reasonably have been expected to anticipate. The injury simply was not reasonably foreseeable. The vast majority of the population would not possess this allergy and would suffer no ill effects. Accordingly, Shannon did not proximately cause Addison's injury.

THE CASE OF THE LOST LIGHTER

A sixteen-year-old throws a party for his friends at his home while his parents are away. A seemingly common occurrence, students having a party when parents are not around, goes horribly wrong. One friend ends up seriously injured because another friend has lost a cigarette lighter. The sixteen-year-old thinks he's being really careful, he instructs his friends where to park their cars, he does not let his friends party in the house, only outside, and he does not supply any alcohol. Yet, the injured partygoer claims the sixteen-year-old host is the cause of his injuries.

Juan OTERO
v.
Tim FAZIO et al.

No. 200401841
Superior Court of Massachusetts
Worcester County
Aug. 22, 2007

This is a civil action brought by the plaintiff to recover damages for personal injuries he suffered while in attendance at a party at the home of defendant Tim Fazio on September 21, 2001. The party occurred while Tim's parents, Kathleen and Michael Fazio, were away and without their knowledge or permission. The plaintiff, a 16-year-old minor at the time

who had consumed a quantity of alcohol before arriving at the party, was asleep near a tree that abutted the unpaved driveway of the Fazios' property when he was run over and injured by another person, Jennifer Wright, who also was in attendance at the party.

Tim Fazio let it be known that a party would take place at his parent's home on the evening of September 21, 2001. There were between seven and ten guests present outside the Fazio home. Defendant Tim Fazio did not serve any alcohol to anyone on the night in question, although he was aware that people at the party were drinking alcohol that they brought with them. As guests arrived, he instructed them that no one was allowed inside the home, that vehicles were to be parked on an unpaved driveway adjoining the home, and that guests were to remain outside the home on the Fazios' property. Due to the natural darkness, defendant Tim Fazio also set up some spotlights on a tripod stand to illuminate the backyard. During the party, the plaintiff went over near a tree on the Fazio property to lie down and fell asleep. The injury occurred when Jennifer Wright backed up her motor vehicle in an apparent effort to illuminate an area to find a cigarette lighter lost by her friend and ran over the sleeping plaintiff.

Even if there was negligence on the part of defendant Tim Fazio not to illuminate all areas of the property to which guests had access, the evidence produced by the plaintiff would not support a finding that the defendant's negligence was a causal factor in bringing about the harm suffered by the plaintiff. Massachusetts law provides that a negligent defendant is not liable where "the causal connection between the original wrong of a defendant and the ultimate harm...has been broken and...something so distinct...has thereafter happened as to constitute an intervening efficient, independent and dominant cause." Although causation questions are usually reserved for the fact-finder, this court may properly decide, as a matter of law, that the harm suffered is sufficiently remote from the defendant's negligence that no reasonable jury could find that the injury was a reasonably foreseeable consequence.

The parents, who were not home at the time of the incident, did not give their permission for the party hosted by their son, and had no knowledge of such parties taking place in the past. On such facts, they did not owe a duty of care to the plaintiff.

CASE QUESTIONS

1. Was there any negligence on the part of Tim Fazio?
2. What act broke the causal connection between Tim Fazio's alleged negligence and the ultimate harm that occurred here?

hypothetical

Colleen operates a laundromat. Geoffrey often washes and dries his clothes there. One day, while Geoffrey was loading his laundry into the washer, the machine unexpectedly began agitating and injured his arms and hands. Did Colleen proximately cause Geoffrey's injuries?

Foreseeability of injury is the starting point. Was it reasonably foreseeable that the washer Geoffrey used would short-circuit and suddenly begin operating while Geoffrey was loading his clothes? It is not uncommon for electrical, mechanical devices to jump to life by themselves unexpectedly. This often occurs when electrical wiring short-circuits after the wires' insulation has frayed. Because people must insert their hands and arms inside the washing machine drum to load clothing, it is reasonably foreseeable that a shorted machine might start itself while a patron's arms are inside. Thus, Geoffrey's injuries were reasonably foreseeable and Colleen proximately caused the harm suffered.

(continues)

Suppose, however, that Geoffrey's arms and hands were not trapped inside the machine when it suddenly began agitating. Suppose, instead, that the surprise simply frightened Geoffrey, who was unusually susceptible to sudden, loud noises and suffered a heart attack as a consequence of the shock. Could Colleen have reasonably anticipated this tragedy? Most courts would reverse the reasonable person standard (applying it to the plaintiff) and say that a reasonable person would not be so easily alarmed (to the point of heart failure) by an upstart washing machine. However, a few courts would employ taking-the-victim analysis and say that even this remote and unexpected injury was foreseeable.

▎ DAMAGES

damages | Money that a court orders paid to a person who has suffered damage (a loss or harm) by the person who caused the injury.

Damages are the injury that the plaintiff suffered as a result of the defendant's tortious conduct. As in all torts, damages must be proven for negligence. Courts will not compensate a victim unless some documentable harm has been done.

With certain intentional torts, such as battery, assault, or trespass, no physical harm is required. With a technical trespass, it is sufficient that the tortfeasor engaged in the unauthorized act. Battery can be achieved merely by unconsented touching. In negligence law, however, some determinable injury must be proven for the tortfeasor to be held liable to the injured party. Normally, this involves monetary losses as a result of harm to a person or the person's property. For instance, if someone loses muscular control in the legs after an automobile accident with a careless driver, then the injured party could demonstrate economic loss as a consequence of the harm. The plaintiff could determine the losses sustained through lost wages, inability to continue an occupation, loss of bodily function, emotional impairment, and related damages.

This vital element of liability is often glossed over by legal scholars and courts. Following such reasoning, damage is often assumed from the fact that the plaintiff sued the defendant for negligence. Of course, it is always a mistake to assume anything in legal study. The plaintiff must prove actual injury to recover in a negligence action. This harm may be physical or emotional or both, but it must exist.

Compensatory Damages

compensatory damages | Damages awarded for the actual loss suffered by a plaintiff.

Compensatory or actual damages are most common in negligence cases. They consist of general and special damages. As the name suggests, **compensatory damages** are designed to compensate the victim for the tortfeasor's negligence. Normally, the plaintiff proves monetary losses, such as out-of-pocket expenses (e.g., medical bills, cost of property repair), lost income, pain and suffering, and loss of property value. The policy behind compensatory damages in tort law is to make the plaintiff whole.

Hedonic Damages. Damages for the loss of enjoyment of life, or value of life, are called hedonic damages (*Daubert v. Merrell Dow Pharmaceuticals Inc.,* 113 S.Ct. 2786). Examples of this are seeing your children married, enjoying the sunshine, and being able to play with your grandchildren. Some jurisdictions feel this kind of damages is similar to pain and suffering and do not allow it. This form of damages has caused a lot of controversy. Not everyone feels that you can place a value on human life, or define enjoyment of life. There is also a concern that the award of this kind of damages will raise the cost of obtaining insurance.

General Damages. General damages are those compensatory damages that naturally result from the harm caused by the defendant's actions. For example, in a slip-and-fall action anyone who is injured in this manner might suffer some degree of pain and suffering.

Special Damages. Special damages, unlike general damages, are compensatory damages that are specific to a particular plaintiff. In the slip-and-fall example discussed earlier in the chapter, the special damages might include a dry-cleaning bill for a stained suit, lost wages, and (depending on the severity of the fall) medical expenses, and **loss of consortium.** Usually special damages must specifically be pleaded and proved. In contrast, general damages need not be pleaded with specificity, as they are presumed by law. Another name used for special damages is *consequential damages*.

> **loss of consortium** | The loss of a spouse's services (i.e., companionship, or ability to have sexual relations).

Economic and Non-Economic Damages. Compensatory damages are divided into economic and non-economic losses. Economic losses are the out-of-pocket expenses a plaintiff incurs, such as medical expenses and lost earnings. Conversely, non-economic losses, such as pain or humiliation, have no particular objective dollar amount that can be placed on them.

Verdict. The trial judge will give the jury instructions in awarding damages in the event a verdict is awarded for the plaintiff. It is often difficult to place an exact dollar figure on pain and suffering. In some states, as a result of recent tort reform, the legislatures have enacted caps on the amount of damages that can be awarded in particular types of cases, such as medical malpractice claims.

Nominal Damages

Nominal damages are not recoverable in actions for ordinary negligence when damages are an element of the cause of action. Nominal damages are awarded in situations in which no actual damages have occurred, or the amount of injury has not been proven even though a right has been violated in an intentional tort action. The court might then award a dollar to a winning party as a symbolic gesture.

> **nominal damages** | Small or symbolic damages awarded in situations in which no actual damages have occurred, or the right has not been proven even though a right has been violated in an intentional tort action.

Punitive Damages

Punitive (exemplary) damages, which are often awarded for intentional torts such as fraud or intentional infliction of emotional distress, are almost nonexistent in negligence cases, because negligence involves carelessness rather than wanton or intentionally tortious behavior. The punishment component of punitive damages would be excessive in most negligence cases, although exemplary damages are occasionally used in gross negligence cases. **Gross negligence** involves carelessness that exceeds ordinary, reasonable care standards and approaches willful and wanton misconduct. If the negligence is sufficiently excessive, the court might allow punitive damages for the injured party. For instance, if a surgeon were drunk and left a scalpel inside a patient during an operation, this might be considered gross negligence by the medical community. Such misconduct exceeds that degree of reasonable care ordinarily expected of doctors. Physicians simply are expected to avoid harming patients.

Table 2-5 summarizes types of damages.

Table 2-6 summarizes proving damages in negligence actions.

See Chapter 1 for methods of resolving cases other than by trial.

"Taking the Victim as You Find Him"

Many appellate courts speak of a tortfeasor's **"taking the victim as you find him."** This means that peculiar health conditions are considered to be reasonably

TABLE 2-5
Types of damages

Compensatory	Damages awarded for actual loss suffered (e.g., medical bills, property repair, lost income, pain and suffering and hedonic damages).
General	Compensatory damages that naturally result from the harm. These are expected from this type of harm (e.g., pain and suffering, property repair).
Special or Consequential	Compensatory damages that are specific to a particular plaintiff. (For example, as a result of a slip and fall, the plaintiff dropped a valuable vase, and also couldn't work for weeks.)
Nominal	When no actual damages occur. A right has been violated but the amount of injuries has not been proven. (For example, the court awards $1 symbolically to show that plaintiff is the victor.)
Punitive or Exemplary	Awarded for intentional torts. Used for wanton or reckless conduct. On occasion used for gross negligence, not for ordinary negligence.

Plaintiff must suffer actual loss as a result of injury.
Loss is usually gauged in monetary terms.
Compensatory damages provide the plaintiff with recovery for losses that resulted from the defendant's actions (out-of-pocket expenses, pain and suffering, lost income, lost property value, loss of bodily function).

TABLE 2-6
Proving damages in negligence cases

foreseeable, as one must always assume that a victim could suffer from an odd affliction such as the helium allergy example discussed earlier. Most of these cases, however, involve more deliberate actions (such as striking the head of a person with "a thin skull" or an "eggshell skull" and killing him or her). Such cases involve more intentional torts than negligence (battery, in the eggshell-skull cases), as is typical with the taking-the-victim cases. Still, taking-the-victim analysis surfaces in pure negligence cases as well.

Taking-the-victim cases make almost any physical injury reasonably foreseeable. However it still must be proved that it was foreseeable that an injury would occur from the defendant's actions.

▌ SUMMARY

Negligence is the failure to use reasonable care to avoid injuring others or their property. Reasonable care is dependent upon the particular facts of each case. The key is the reasonableness or unreasonableness of the tortfeasor's actions under the circumstances.

There are four elements of negligence: duty of reasonable care, breach of duty, causation, and injury. The elements are considered sequentially. If any one is missing, then no negligence occurred.

The duty of reasonable care is the tortfeasor's obligation to act reasonably to avoid injuring others. The tortfeasor does not owe this duty to everyone in the world; however, the injured party must fall within the scope of the tortfeasor's duty. This means that it must have been reasonably foreseeable that the plaintiff would be harmed as a consequence of the defendant's actions. This is called the *reasonable plaintiffs theory*. Only foreseeable plaintiffs (who were actually injured as a result of the defendant's conduct) may recover damages in a negligence lawsuit. Reasonable care is defined by the standard of the mythical reasonable person. Would a reasonable person have acted in the same way the defendant did, under the same or similar circumstances? The trier-of-fact decides how the reasonable person would have behaved. The reasonable person standard is adjusted to reflect the defendant's special skills or limitations.

In professional malpractice actions, professionals such as physicians are held to exercise the degree of care and skill reasonably required of like professionals in similar circumstances. Depending on the jurisdiction, the professional will be judged by the skills of professionals in the same community, a similar locality, or (as is the trend) nationally.

The tortfeasor's actions must cause the victim's injuries. Causation under negligence is usually shown through cause-in-fact. But for the defendant's misconduct, the plaintiff would not have been harmed. When multiple tortfeasors are involved in producing the victim's injuries, however, but-for causation does not function well. An alternative causation theory, substantial factor analysis, states that each defendant is liable for the plaintiff's injuries if that defendant was a substantial factor in producing the harm. Joint and several liability holds multiple defendants liable for a plaintiff's injuries when those defendants combine to create the harm.

Proximate cause is an element of causation. Proximate cause declares the line at which injuries are reasonably foreseeable. Inside the boundary are tortfeasors' actions that could reasonably have been anticipated to produce the victim's harm. Outside the perimeter are injuries that were not reasonably foreseeable as a consequence of the tortfeasor's behavior. This circle is sometimes called the *zone of danger*. Some courts speak of proximate cause in terms of foreseeability and scope of duty. Other courts state that tortfeasors take their victims as they find them, which means that the particular injury the plaintiff suffered (usually due to some peculiar physical condition) is always considered foreseeable. While a person failing to act to stop a harm from happening to another is often not held liable for the inaction, under certain specific relationships, such as employer/employee or teacher/student, a person might have an obligation or special duty to act and may be held liable if he or she does not.

Damages must be proven in every negligence case. The plaintiff must prove that he or she suffered some actual loss as a result of the defendant's actions, whether physical injury, emotional injury, or harm to property. This loss is normally quantified in monetary terms as compensatory damages.

Most often, the plaintiff must prove that the defendant was negligent in causing the plaintiff's injuries. This burden of proof calls for a preponderance of the evidence. Once established, the defendant has the burden of rejoinder, or rebuttal, to counter the plaintiff's prima facie case. In certain cases, however, the plaintiff is at a disadvantage in proving the defendant's negligence. Res ipsa loquitur allows the plaintiff to shift the burden of proof to the defendant. Thus, the defendant must disprove the plaintiff's allegations of negligence. Res ipsa loquitur applies in cases in which the defendant exclusively controlled the object or action that hurt the plaintiff; that the plaintiff's injury was one that ordinarily would not happen without negligence; and the defendant is in the better position to prove that he or she was not negligent.

A defendant's violation of a statute might have an effect on the outcome of a negligence case. This is especially true where the statute was designed to prevent the kind of accident that occurred.

▌ KEY TERMS

burden of rejoinder
but-for causation
cause-in-fact
compensatory damages
contribution
damages
defendant
due (reasonable) care
duty
elements
foreseeability
foreseeable injury

foreseeable plaintiffs theory
gross negligence
indemnity
joint and several liability
loss of consortium
national standard
negligence
nominal damages
plaintiff
preponderance of the evidence
prima facie case
profession

professional community standard
  of care
proximate cause
punitive (exemplary) damages
reasonable person test (standard)
res ipsa loquitur
scope of duty
substantial factor analysis
taking the victim as you
  find him
unforeseeable plaintiffs

PROBLEMS

In the following hypotheticals, determine if negligence exists and if the tortfeasor will be liable to the injured party. Identify the plaintiff(s) and the defendant(s).

1. Carl operates a tanning salon. Meg is one of his customers. The salon uses tanning beds that are equipped with ultraviolet lights above and below the customer. These lights are automatically regulated to control radiation exposure. Meg visited the salon and, while lying upon one of the tanning beds, fell asleep. The automatic regulator became stuck at maximum intensity. Meg was severely burned by the radiation.

2. Dan operates a backhoe for a construction company. Doug hired the company to excavate a swimming pool in his backyard. Dan dug the hole using the backhoe. Unbeknownst to Doug, Dan, or the neighbors, the United States Army had used the area during World War II as an undercover training facility for minesweepers and several unexploded land mines remained buried in the ground. Dan hit one with the backhoe shovel, which detonated the explosive. The shovel was blasted away from the machine, flew several feet into the air, and crashed into Doug's new truck. The impact pushed the truck into the street, causing Debbie, a neighbor who was driving a van down the street, to swerve into Doug's front yard, hitting and felling an oak tree (that had been weakened by termites), which crashed into Mia Farlow's house next door to Doug's home.

3. Brad is a professional painter. He bought exterior latex paint to apply to Matt's barn. The paint store incorrectly labeled the paint as oil-based when in fact it was water-based. Brad painted the barn without noticing the difference. After several severe summer thunderstorms, the paint wore off.

4. Sam is a chemical dependency counselor. One of her clients, Trevor, has been addicted to alcohol and tobacco for years. He has suffered severe liver damage. Sam recommended hypnotherapy as a possible cure. Hypnosis is frequently used to treat chemical addiction, and Sam is a state-certified hypnotherapist. After hypnotizing Trevor, she discovered through regression that he had had a traumatic experience involving alcohol at age seven. She felt certain that this memory was the key to his current addiction. When Sam attempted to bring Trevor out of his hypnotized state, however, she discovered, much to her dismay, that he had fixated and would not return to consciousness. As a result, Trevor remained regressed at seven years of age. Psychiatrists indicated that this condition occurs in only 1 in every 10,000 hypnosis cases.

5. Dwanita plays guitar and sings in a rock-and-roll band at a local tavern, The Whiskey Slick. One of her songs, "Death to Phone Solicitors," contains certain explicit and graphically descriptive details. Josie, a bartender at the Slick, suffers from paranoid delusions. She found Dwanita's lyrics overwhelmingly absorbing, and she took them literally. After hearing Dwanita's "Death" song at work one night, Josie returned to her apartment, loaded her revolver, drove downtown to a local telephone solicitation business, entered, and shot six operators.

REVIEW QUESTIONS

1. Provide a broad definition of negligence. What key factors are involved in analyzing negligence problems?

2. List the elements of negligence. How do they fit together? How do you apply each part to a particular problem?

3. What is duty? How does it relate to reasonable care? How do you define the scope of duty? What role does foreseeability play in scope of duty? What is the foreseeable plaintiffs theory? What is reasonable care? Who

is the reasonable person, and why is he or she important in negligence analysis? Who defines this standard and how? How does the standard vary in different cases?

4. Define *causation*. What is cause-in-fact? But-for causation? What is substantial factor analysis, and when is it used? How does it differ from joint and several liability? How is it similar?

5. Define *proximate cause*. What role does foreseeability play? What is the zone of danger? How is scope of duty involved? What is taking the victim as you find him? How is it applied?

6. How are damages determined in negligence cases? What are consequential damages?

7. How is negligence normally proven? Who generally bears the burden of proof? The burden of rejoinder or rebuttal? When is negligence presumed? What Latin phrase is used to describe this presumption? What are this doctrine's elements, and how are they used?

8. What is medical malpractice? If a needle is left in a patient after surgery, can the doctrine of res ipsa loquitur be used to prove the plaintiff's case? Explain your answer.

9. What effect does the special relationship between a teacher and a student have on a student's claim of negligence?

10. How can the violation of a statute affect the outcome of a negligence case?

▌ HELPFUL WEBSITES

This chapter deals with the field of negligence. To learn more about negligence, the following sites can be accessed:

General Legal Information

http://findlaw.com

http://law.emory.edu

http://www.hg.org

http://www.dri.org

http://www.law.com

http://www.martindale.com

http://www.law.georgetown.edu

STUDENT CD-ROM™   For additional materials, please go to the CD in this book.

ONLINE COMPANION™   For additional resources, please go to
http://www.paralegal.delmar.cengage.com

chapter 3
Special Negligence Actions

THE BIGGEST MISTAKES PARALEGALS MAKE & HOW TO AVOID THEM

A Fate Worse than Missing the Trojans/Irish Game

The trial was on the docket for this coming Monday, but our legal team needed it adjourned to a later date due to the sudden illness of one client. The lead attorney asked me to call the judge's law clerk and request an adjournment. When I called I received the clerk's voice mail, where I recorded my request.

Just before the weekend started on Friday, around 4:30, I read an e-mail from the law clerk that said his judge's current trial was running longer than expected and that our trial was still scheduled for Monday because it had been transferred to another judge. It seems that the new judge required a personal appearance of our attorney who was requesting an adjournment. Usually an adjournment could be handled over the telephone, but not with this judge. Each court, judge, or jurisdiction may handle matters of procedure at his or her discretion. It was my responsibility to follow up with the law clerk earlier that week

(continues)

when I did not receive confirmation of an adjournment with a new date. I rushed to explain to our attorney but found his assistant gone and a note on his door: "At USC/Notre Dame game in L.A. all weekend. Go Trojans!"

I had no luck reaching the attorney on his cell phone because he was flying to LAX. He was unhappy when he reached his hotel and heard my message. Hearing my phone ring at midnight, I knew it was him. I spent the rest of the night worrying and trying to book an earlier flight back for him, all of which ruined his weekend too.

LESSON LEARNED: I needed to check local procedure and advise the attorney before his trip.

▋ INTRODUCTION

Negligence theory has evolved special legal concepts to apply, in certain circumstances, to particular types of activities.

Special negligence actions are cases involving certain well-defined activities. Special rules of negligence apply in these instances. The most common special negligence actions involve property ownership, employer/employee activities, and motor vehicle use. Theories of vicarious liability, in which someone is held accountable for the negligence of another person, and negligent infliction of emotional distress add unique and recognizable elements to the study of torts.

The basic negligence formula applies to all special actions discussed in this chapter. Negligence includes the following elements: duty of reasonable care, breach of duty, causation, and damages. Always keep this approach in mind when examining any negligence problem. However, each special action has its own peculiar analytical twists and turns that distinguish it from the other torts. This chapter covers the following:

- ▶ Vicarious liability and respondeat superior
- ▶ Premises liability
- ▶ Distinctions between trespassers, licensees, and invitees
- ▶ Attractive nuisance
- ▶ Negligent infliction of emotional distress
- ▶ Negligence per se.

▋ VICARIOUS LIABILITY

Previous chapters have presented hypotheticals in which someone acting on behalf of the defendant actually caused harm to the plaintiff. These have been employees of defendant businesses, in most problems. This illustrates one aspect of vicarious liability.

Vicarious Liability Defined

Vicarious liability is the liability of one person, called the *principal,* for the tortious conduct of another, subordinate individual, called the *agent,* who was acting on the principal's behalf. In negligence law, principal/agent relationships most often involve employers and employees. The situation is simple. The principal is the employer, who hires the agent (employee) to work on the employer's behalf.

Employment Not an Essential Element. The principal/agent relationship, however, need not be that of employer and employee. Nineteenth- and early twentieth-century cases spoke of *master and servant.* This older classification suggested that the servant could work for the master without being paid. Thus, whether the agent is compensated for acting upon the principal's behalf is largely irrelevant to the issue of vicarious liability. Instead, focus upon this inquiry: Was one person acting on behalf of another? If so, a principal/agent relationship is present, and vicarious liability can exist.

Respondeat Superior

The employer is responsible for the negligence (or, for that matter, any torts) that his or her employees commit while working. This doctrine of vicarious liability is called **respondeat superior,** a Latin phrase meaning, "Let the master answer."

Liability within Scope of Employment. Not every employee activity triggers the respondeat superior doctrine, however. An employer is responsible for an employee's actions that fall within the scope of employment. **Scope of employment** can be described as the range of conduct that the employer expects the employee to perform as part of his or her job. For example, a truck driver is expected to make deliveries and pickups for the employer; these actions fall within the scope of employment. But the driver is not expected to rob a liquor store while driving the company truck; this action falls outside the scope of employment.

Outside Scope of Employment: Examples. Employers are not liable for torts committed by employees that fall outside the scope of employment. Thus, in the preceding example, the employer would be responsible if the truck driver negligently crashed into another vehicle while making deliveries. However, the employer would not be accountable for the robbery (which actually involves criminal behavior but illustrates the scope concept).

Suppose the driver used the truck for personal purposes while not working, thereby going against company policy. Assume that the driver then negligently collided with another vehicle. Would the employer be responsible? No. The driver was acting outside the scope of employment by using the truck, not for the employer's business, but for unauthorized personal use.

vicarious liability | Legal responsibility for the acts of another person because of some special relationship with that person; for example, the liability of an employer for certain acts of an employee.

respondeat superior | (Latin) "Let the master answer." Describes the principle that an employer is responsible for most harm caused by an employee acting within the scope of employment. In such a case, the employer is said to have vicarious liability.

scope of employment | The range of actions within which an employee is considered to be doing work for the employer.

Frolic and Detour Rule

Employers are not vicariously liable for the negligence of their employees when employees go off on their own to handle personal matters, even though they might be performing work otherwise. For instance, suppose that, while making deliveries for the employer, the truck driver decided to drive 180 miles to stop by and visit a friend in the next state. The employer probably did not authorize this sidetrack from the employee's assigned duties. Visits to socialize with friends fall outside the employee's scope of employment. Thus, if the driver were negligent while pursuing activities unrelated to employment during ordinary working hours, this would be considered **frolic and detour,** and the employer would not be vicariously liable. Under the more modern view, an employee whose deviation is slight in terms of distance and time is considered to be acting within the scope of employment.

Coming and Going Rule

Employers are usually not vicariously liable for the negligence of their employees while the employees are coming to or going from work. This is called the **coming and going rule.** A situation in which an employer would be liable in such circumstances is if the employee were performing work-related activities while on the way to or from the job, such as picking up office supplies at the employer's request.

Independent Contractors

An **independent contractor** is someone who has entered into a contract with another person to perform a specific task. The independent contractor controls how he or she accomplishes the job. The individual hiring the independent contractor simply agrees to pay him or her for doing the chore. Independent contractors are distinguishable from employees in that the employer does not control how an independent contractor does the job. In contrast, employers do control how their employees perform their tasks. While an employer must deduct Social Security and withholding taxes from an employee's pay, this is not required for an independent contractor. (See Internal Revenue Ruling 87-41.) A housepainter is an example of an independent contractor.

No Vicarious Liability for Independent Contractors. Persons hiring independent contractors are not vicariously liable for the independent contractors' negligence. The reasoning is that the independent contractor is engaging in his or her own work and should be responsible for his or her own negligence. The hirer is simply buying the independent contractor's finished service, and has nothing to do with how the independent contractor achieves the desired results.

frolic and detour rule | Conduct of an employee that falls outside of the scope of employment that is purely for the benefit of said employee. An employer is not responsible for the negligence of an employee on a "frolic of his/her own."

coming and going rule | Rule used when employees commit torts while coming to or going from work. In respondeat superior cases, this rule helps decide whether an employee's actions fall outside the scope of employment.

independent contractor | A person who contracts with an "employer" to do a particular piece of work by his or her own methods and under his or her own control.

For example, suppose Manuel hires a plumber to install a new shower in his house. Manuel has nothing to do with the actual job; in fact, he only lets the plumber in to go to work. The plumber negligently installs the water lines so that the hot faucet is connected to the cold water line and vice versa. After the shower is completed, Manuel's visiting friend is the first to use it and shockingly discovers the mistake, suffering severe burns. Is Manuel vicariously liable to his friend for the plumber's negligence? No. The plumber was an independent contractor. Manuel had no say in how the plumber completed the job. Manuel merely paid the final price after the plumber did the work. Thus, Manuel cannot be vicariously liable for the plumber's negligence. Instead of suing Manuel, his friend should sue the plumber.

Motor Vehicle Vicarious Liability

Since the first half of the twentieth century, courts have ruled that passengers in automobiles could be held vicariously liable for the driver's negligence. Using this analysis, if the automobile occupants were involved in a joint enterprise, such as a family traveling to a single destination, then the driver's negligence could be imputed to the passengers. This outcome may seem unfair, because a passenger has no actual control over how the driver operates the vehicle. Legal commentators have long criticized this type of vicarious liability. The better principle, long employed by the courts, holds the vehicle owner vicariously liable for the negligence of a driver other than the owner. For instance, suppose Britney's younger brother is driving her car negligently. He crashes into a motorcyclist, injuring her. Under vicarious liability, Britney would be accountable for her brother's negligence, because he was carelessly using her vehicle and injured another person as a result.

Many state legislatures have enacted statutes imposing vicarious liability on owners for the negligence of others who drive their vehicles. These are sometimes called *motor vehicle consent statutes.* An example of this is California's Vehicle Code § 17150 *et seq.*

Table 3-1 outlines vicarious liability. Table 3-2 shows some states where the owner of the car has vicarious liability for the driver.

TABLE 3-1 Vicarious liability summary

Vicarious Liability	Liability of principal for negligent actions of agent serving on principal's behalf. Commonly involves employer/employee relationships.
Respondeat Superior	"Let the master answer." Doctrine through which employers may be held vicariously liable for employees' negligent actions committed within the scope of employment.
Scope of Employment	Range of conduct that employer expects of employee during performance of assigned employment responsibilities.

(continues)

TABLE 3-1 *(continued)*

Frolic and Detour Rule	Employers are not vicariously liable for employees' negligence when employees deviate from assigned tasks within scope of employment, unless the deviation is minor. Usually this involves employees going off on their own to pursue personal needs.
Coming and Going Rule	Employers are not vicariously liable for employees' negligence while employees are coming to and going from work, unless employer has specifically requested employee to carry out a specific work-related task during such times.
Independent Contractors	Employers are not liable for independent contractors' negligence, because independent contractors act independently and are responsible for their own conduct.
Motor Vehicle Vicarious Liability	Motor vehicle owners may be held vicariously liable for the driver's negligence. Liability may also be established in motor vehicle consent statutes.

TABLE 3-2
States in which owner of car has vicarious liability for driver

STATE	VICARIOUS LIABILITY OF OWNER FOR DRIVER
Arizona	Yes
California	Yes
Connecticut	Yes
Delaware	Yes
Florida	Yes
Idaho	Yes
Iowa	Yes
Maine	Yes
Michigan	Yes
Minnesota	Yes
Nevada	Yes
New York	Yes
Oklahoma	Yes
Pennsylvania	Yes
Rhode Island	Yes
Wisconsin	Yes

hypotheticals

Sarah is a physician. Her nurse's aide, Gladys, draws blood from patients as part of her responsibilities on the job. One day, Gladys used a contaminated needle and thus infected a patient when she drew blood for testing. Would Sarah be vicariously liable for Gladys's negligence?

Gladys was performing a specific job assignment on Sarah's behalf. Drawing blood falls within Gladys's scope of employment. Under respondeat superior, Sarah would be accountable for Gladys's negligent act of using a contaminated needle and infecting a patient.

Suppose Gladys worked for a blood bank that routinely did blood draws and tests for area physicians. Under this scenario, Sarah would not have control over how Gladys acted. Gladys's employer is the blood bank, which would be an independent contractor in relation to Sarah. Accordingly, Sarah would not be accountable for Gladys's negligence.

* * *

Fargo is a fast-food restaurant manager. Mitchell is one of his employees. Fargo asked Mitchell to drive across town to a soft-drink supplier and pick up additional carbonated water. While on this errand, Mitchell stopped by the post office to check his mail. As he was leaving the post office parking lot, he failed to look both ways and collided with another vehicle. Would Fargo be vicariously liable for Mitchell's negligent driving?

Although Mitchell was running a business-related errand on Fargo's behalf, stopping by the post office to check personal mail falls outside Mitchell's scope of employment. However, as this is only a slight deviation, frolic and detour would not apply here. Thus, Fargo would be responsible for Mitchell's negligent conduct.

Suppose Fargo had been a passenger in Mitchell's car during this incident. Fargo (as the boss) could have controlled his employee, Mitchell, and instructed him not to stop at the post office. By permitting Mitchell to check his mail, Fargo implicitly consented to Mitchell's detour. This would place the detour within the scope of Mitchell's employment. Assuming that no statutes stated differently, Fargo would be vicariously liable.

▋ PREMISES LIABILITY

Special negligence rules apply to owners and occupiers of land. **Occupiers** are individuals who do not own but who do use real estate; this includes tenants (lessees). For simplicity's sake, we will speak in terms of the owner. The term *occupier* may always be substituted for *owner,* because negligence theories apply to both.

occupier | An individual who does not own but who uses real estate; includes tenants (lessees).

Land Owner's Different Duties of Reasonable Care

As negligence law developed in the late nineteenth and early twentieth centuries, American courts devised different standards of reasonable care for land owners or land users. The distinctions depended upon who the injured party (plaintiff) was, in terms of the victim's purpose for being on the land where the owner's negligence was alleged to have occurred.

Victim's Status on Land Defines Scope of Duty

For example, under old common law, the land owner owed a different duty of reasonable care to the injured party depending upon whether the victim was a trespasser, a licensee, or an invitee. (These terms are explained later in this section.) Thus, the plaintiff's status as a trespasser, licensee, or invitee determined the scope of duty that the owner owed. These distinctions affect the balance of risk of injury from the tort in question, versus the possible benefits that might be received. Intentional torts involve intentional acts, and as such carry a high degree of risk and usually a low degree of social benefit. That is, the risk greatly outweighs the benefit. Therefore, the duty not to intentionally injure someone or something is great.

Modern Judicial Trends

For decades courts and legal scholars have complained that this three-tier analytical approach is arbitrary and unnecessary. After all, ordinary negligence theory appears adequately equipped to establish the land owner's duty of reasonable care. If an owner acted unreasonably in maintaining his or her realty, and as a result a victim was harmed, then the owner should be liable. Regular negligence theory works well to produce a just result, say these critics.

Many courts have in fact abolished the three-tier land owner standards of care. The landmark case was *Rowland v. Christian,* 69 Cal. 2d 108, 443 P.2d 561, 70 Cal. Rptr. 97 (1968) (superseded by statute, as explained in *Perez v. Southern Pacific Transport Co.,* 218 Cal. App. 3d 462, 267 Cal. Rptr. 100 (1990)), in which the distinctions were eliminated in favor of traditional negligence theory. Many states have followed the California Supreme Court's lead. Still, many courts continue to apply the three-tier system.

Table 3-3 shows duty of care owed by the land owner to others by state.

Land Owner's "Zero Duty" toward Trespassers

Land owners owe no duty of reasonable care toward trespassers. The risk to a trespasser should be essentially nonexistent compared to the benefit of keeping the trespasser away. Owners may not intentionally injure trespassers upon their real estate, but they need not search their realty and safeguard it for trespassers'

State	Duty Owed
Alaska	Standard of reasonableness
California	Standard of reasonableness
Florida	Depends on status: invitee, licensee, trespasser, child trespasser
New York	Standard of reasonableness
Ohio	Depends on status: invitee, licensee, trespasser, child trespasser
Pennsylvania	Depends on status: invitee, licensee, trespasser, child trespasser, recreational guest
Texas	Depends on status: invitee, licensee, trespasser, infant trespasser, recreational guest

Table 3-3
Duty of care owed by land owner to others by state

unauthorized uses (*Katko v. Briney*, 183 N.W.2d 657). Courts favoring this policy reason that a land owner should not be required to exercise ordinary reasonable care to protect a tortfeasor (i.e., trespasser) from harm. Because the trespasser is committing an intentional tort, negligence law insists only that real estate owners avoid intentionally injuring trespassers. Otherwise, the trespasser *assumes the risk* of entering someone else's land without permission.

Special Rule for Trespassing Children: Attractive Nuisance

However, land owners owe a higher duty of reasonable care to trespassing children. The reasoning behind this special rule states that children, especially when young, are so inexperienced and naive that they may not fully appreciate dangers lurking upon the land. Therefore, owners must exercise ordinary, reasonable care to safeguard their realty for trespassing children who are enticed onto the land to investigate the dangerous condition that injured them. Young children are often attracted, out of curiosity, to investigate dangerous conditions on realty, such as abandoned wells, railroad tracks, swimming pools, or unused machinery. These alluring items are often hazardous, a fact that the trespassing child may not understand. The attraction element has given this special rule its name of the **attractive nuisance doctrine** or, more commonly, **attractive nuisance.**

Currently, a four-part test is employed to hold the land owner liable under the attractive nuisance doctrine.

1. The owner must know or have reason to know of the artificial condition on the premises.
2. The structure, instrumentality, or condition must be alluring to children and endanger them. They cannot know or appreciate the danger.

attractive nuisance doctrine | A legal principle, used in some states, that if a person keeps dangerous property in a way that children might be attracted to it, then that person is responsible when they get hurt.

attractive nuisance | Any item that is dangerous to young children but that is so interesting and alluring as to attract them.

3. The presence of children must reasonably have been anticipated.

4. The danger posed to the children outweighs the cost of making the condition safe.

If a trespassing child is injured as a result of having been enticed onto the land to investigate some dangerous condition, then the land owner is liable for such harm.

Table 3-4 shows states that follow a form of attractive nuisance doctrine.

TABLE 3-4
States that follow a form of attractive nuisance doctrine

STATE	ATTRACTIVE NUISANCE DOCTRINE
California	No—legislates against specific dangers instead (i.e., must fence pools).
Florida	Yes
New York	Yes
Ohio	Yes
Pennsylvania	Yes
Texas	Yes

THE CASE OF THE INVITING POOL

Pool accidents are a tragedy waiting to happen. Adults are keenly aware of the dangers of open pools. Here, even with adult supervision, a drowning could not be prevented. While an adult might find a cloudy pool unappealing, a child might not recognize that anything is amiss and even find the pool more attractive.

UDDIN, Admr., Appellee,
v.
EMBASSY SUITES HOTEL et al., Appellants.
No. 2006-0189.
Supreme Court of Ohio.
Submitted Feb. 13, 2007
Decided May 2, 2007

A ten-year-old girl, Shayla Uddin, drowned in an indoor pool at a hotel while under adult supervision and while other children played around her. A witness stated that it was not possible to see the bottom of the pool, even though it was no more than five feet deep at its greatest depth. According to that witness,

"when a child went underwater . . . you lost sight of them because the water was so murky." Shayla was located by someone feeling along the bottom of the pool for her body.

Shayla and her family were invitees of the hotel, and accordingly the hotel was required to exercise reasonable care for their safety and protection, and to advise them of latent dangers on the premises.

The hotel, however, owed no duty to Shayla and her family regarding dangers on the premises that were open and obvious. The rationale for the open-and-obvious doctrine is that " 'the open and obvious nature of the hazard itself serves as a warning. Thus, the owner or occupier may reasonably expect that persons entering the premises will discover those dangers and take appropriate measures to protect themselves.'"

Ohio's appellate courts generally have held that a swimming pool constitutes an open and obvious danger. Our courts also have suggested generally, based on law from other jurisdictions, that the doctrine applies to both adults and minors.

Ohio's appellate courts have been reluctant to apply the open-and-obvious doctrine to children of tender years. ("We decline to determine whether a swimming pool is an open-and-obvious danger to a child under seven years of age.") Nevertheless, the trial court here held, without citation of authority, that the hotel's "indoor swimming pool was an open and obvious danger of which even a child of ten years old . . . should have been aware."

Given the importance of the issue presented here and the unique issues presented by children in Ohio tort law, I believe that this court should answer the question of whether the hotel owed a duty to Shayla, or whether no duty existed because the open-and-obvious doctrine applied to young children like her.

This court should also address whether the increased peril of drowning associated with opaque or murky water in a swimming pool, is sufficiently apparent to a child of tender years to warrant the application of the open-and-obvious-danger doctrine to her. On the facts presented by this case, I would hold that the open-and-obvious doctrine is not applicable to children of tender years.

An adult may instantly recognize that cloudy water increases his or her risk of drowning because the diminished clarity impairs the vision of those supervising, thereby hindering potential rescue efforts. To a ten-year-old child, however, the danger may not be as readily apparent. I agree with the court of appeals that the trial court erred by finding that the open-and-obvious doctrine applied to a ten-year-old child on the facts presented here, and in granting summary judgment in favor of the hotel. Accordingly, I would affirm.

CASE QUESTIONS

1. Was it foreseeable that children might be hurt as a result of the pool being poorly maintained?
2. What conditions must be found for the court to hold that an attractive nuisance exists?
3. Would the case have been decided differently if the pool was not cloudy?

The *Restatement (Second) of Torts*

For decades, the American Law Institute has assembled Restatements of the Law, which summarize the legal principles discussed in common law decisions. These include the *Restatement of Torts* and its successor, the *Restatement (Second) of Torts*.

Restatement (Second) of Torts § 339. Many courts now follow § 339 of the *Restatement (Second) of Torts* and hence have discarded the attraction element of the theory. For these courts, it is sufficient that (1) the injury to the trespassing child was reasonably foreseeable; (2) the danger on the land presented an unreasonable risk of harm to trespassing children; (3) the danger on the land was artificial, meaning manmade rather than natural; (4) because of the child's youth, he or she could not appreciate the risks involved or did not discover (and understand) the threat; (5) the threatening condition was located at a place across which children were likely to trespass; and (6) the land owner failed to exercise reasonable care to protect trespassing children from the danger that caused the harm. Under this version of attractive nuisance, the danger did not have to entice the child onto the land. It is adequate that the child encountered and was hurt by a danger that he or she did not fully discern.

Beneath all its trimmings, *Restatement* § 339 is simply negligence theory applied to trespassing children. The basic negligence elements are there, and the reasoning is identical.

A number of jurisdictions depart from the *Restatement*'s artificial condition element. These courts would include natural dangers, such as streams, quicksand,

hypothetical

Belle is a student attending the local community college. She occasionally tres-passes across Farmer Bob's cattle pasture when she walks from her apartment to campus. One day, while cutting across the land, Belle encountered Bob's prize bull, which was in a particularly agitated frame of mind. The bull charged and knocked Belle to the ground, injuring her. Is Bob liable?

Because Belle was a trespasser, Bob owed her no duty of reasonable care. Accordingly, she took her chances by walking across the pasture without per-mission. Bob would not be liable for her injuries.

Suppose that Belle were five years old and came upon Bob's farm to play on the swing set. The set is rickety and old. Attractive nuisance theory would hold Bob liable when Belle cuts her hand on a broken, jagged edge of the swing. Belle was enticed onto the realty by the swing set, which, due to her youth, she did not notice was old and in disrepair. Bob failed to exercise reasonable care to protect trespass-ing children such as Belle from the risk of being cut by a sharp edge on the swing. The threat of being hurt on the swing was unreasonable, as a child of Belle's age could not be expected to realize that the set was too old to be used safely. Young children are likely to be lured onto land to play on playground equipment. The dangerous condition was artificial because Bob installed the swing set on his prop-erty and then failed to repair the set or take it down. Any of the attractive nuisance theories discussed previously would hold Bob accountable under these facts.

Suppose, instead, that Belle were a cat burglar who was breaking into Bob's barn late one night. Unbeknownst to Belle, Bob had wired a shotgun to the windows inside the barn; anyone raising the window frame would instantly be shot. Belle tried to enter through the window and was seriously hurt by the gun blast. Would Bob be liable?

Although Bob owes Belle (who was trespassing) no duty of reasonable care, he may not set a lethal trap for would-be burglars. Land owners cannot cre-ate an unreasonable danger to injure trespassers. Bob would be liable for Belle's injuries in this factual scenario.

or rock formations, as risks against which the land owner must take precautions to protect trespassing children.

Licensees Defined. Licensees are persons who have permission to be upon another's land. They are distinguishable from trespassers in that the land owner has consented to their presence upon his or her realty. This consent may be expressed or implied. Examples of licensees include social guests, such as friends who gather at a person's house to study or neighbors coming over to borrow tools; door-to-door salespersons or charitable solicitors (when the land owner has not prohibited their entry by posting warning signs); and frequent trespassers to whose incursions the land owner implicitly consents (such as when trespassers frequently use shortcuts that the land owner does not discourage through fencing or sign-posting).

licensee | A person who is on property with permission, but without any enticement by the owner and with no financial advantage to the owner.

Land Owner's Duty of Reasonable Care toward Licensees

Owners owe licensees a duty of reasonable care in using the real estate, because the risk and the benefit are equal. This includes the owner's obligation to correct known dangers (both artificial and natural) on the land. In other words, if the owner knows (or reasonably should know) that a hazardous condition exists on the realty, then he or she must exercise reasonable care in safeguarding licensees from these risks. For example, if an abandoned well has not been covered, and a travelling salesperson visits and falls into the well (which cannot be seen because of overgrown grass), then the land owner has breached his or her duty of reasonable care to the salesperson, assuming that the owner knew (or should have known) that the well was there and could not be detected.

For licensees, the owner is not required to discover and correct unknown threats on the land. For invitees, however, the owner is obligated to do this, as we shall see later.

Invitees Defined. Invitees, or *business invitees* as older court opinions call them, are persons invited upon the land owner's premises. Originally, the common law restricted the term to individuals invited onto premises for business purposes, such as customers to a grocery, clothing store, amusement park, or tavern. Modern cases, however, state that an invitee need not be involved in any business-related purposes when he or she enters another's real estate. It is sufficient that the land owner encourage the invitee to visit.

invitee | A person who is at a place by invitation.

Usually, invitees are persons coming onto the land for some purpose that the owner wishes to serve. Commonly, this includes any business, but could also include nonprofit organizations, such as churches, soup kitchens, charitable hospitals, or even colleges.

hypothetical

Ben owns an apartment building. Fundraisers for a local charity frequently solicit contributions from his tenants. Ben does not object to this solicitation, although he does not encourage it. Alex is one of the charity's fundraisers. While visiting Ben's apartment complex, Alex broke his leg when he fell through a rotten wooden stairway. Alex could not see the rotting from the top of the steps, but the damage was evident if one looked up from below the stairway. Is Ben liable to Alex?

Alex is a licensee, because Ben permitted him to come onto the apartment premises. The key in this case is whether the rotten steps were a known hazard. Perhaps Ben did not know that the steps were rotten. However, Ben reasonably should have known that his apartment steps were dangerous. A building owner is expected to be aware of such easily discoverable risks, as it is easily foreseeable that a stairway user might be hurt if rotten steps collapse. Thus, Ben would be liable for Alex's injuries.

Suppose, instead, that Ben had posted signs clearly warning, "NO SOLICITORS ALLOWED! ALL TRESPASSERS WILL BE PROSECUTED!" Would he be liable for Alex's injuries? In this version of the facts, Alex would be a trespasser, and so Ben would not owe a duty of reasonable care to Alex. Accordingly, Ben would not be liable for the harm to Alex.

Suppose that Ben had posted such signs but did nothing further to discourage solicitors from coming onto his premises. Suppose that door-to-door salespersons and charitable solicitors, including Alex, regularly visited the apartments with impunity. Under this set of facts, Ben has implicitly consented to the solicitors' presence, including Alex's. Thus, Alex would be a licensee.

Land Owner's Highest Duty of Reasonable Care toward Invitees

Land owners owe the highest duty of reasonable care to invitees, because the risk of injury is greater and the benefit is more personal than social. Owners must not only repair known dangers on the property but also must discover and correct unknown risks. This is a broader standard, requiring the land owner to take extra efforts to render his or her premises reasonably safe for invitees.

The logic underlying this stiffer standard of care suggests that owners who invite someone onto realty should be expected to exercise greater caution to ensure that the premises are reasonably danger-free. After all, the invitee would not be on the land to begin with had it not been for the owners' invitation.

Invitees and Licensees Distinguished. *Invitee* is a subcategory of *licensee,* yet the terms are distinguishable. All licensees have the owner's implied or expressed permission to be on the land, but the land owner does not have to invite or encourage licensees to visit; rather, the owner may just passively tolerate the licensees' presence. With invitees, however, the owner either implies an invitation or expressly invites them onto the real estate. This reflects the owner's active role in getting the invitees onto his or her land. Usually, the owner seeks customers for business; hence, courts often speak of business invitees.

Implicit or Express Invitation. The land owner's invitation to others to enter the premises may be expressed (e.g., a welcome sign outside a church or a business posting its hours on its door) or implied (e.g., a business leaving its doors open during business hours).

Limited Areas of Invitation. Obviously, most land owners do not invite people into every nook and cranny of their property. Certain regions are off-limits. For example, most businesses have storage rooms, manager's offices, or machinery rooms that patrons are specifically discouraged from entering. Virtually any business has door signs warning "private," "authorized personnel only," "keep out," and similar prohibitions. The owner's invitation to invitees does not include such areas. If an individual were injured while visiting an off-limits zone, then that person would be considered merely a licensee, or perhaps even a trespasser (depending upon how sternly the warning was phrased—such as "no trespassing—keep out!"), rather than an invitee.

From a plaintiff's standpoint, being included as an invitee spells maximum tort relief, at least in terms of monetary damages. The following hypotheticals explore invitee cases.

Using Traditional Negligence Theory in Land Owner Cases

As noted earlier, many courts have eliminated the trespasser/licensee/invitee approach in favor of regular negligence theory. Instead of forcing the injured party into one of these three categories, many courts simply ask the routine negligence questions: Was the injury reasonably foreseeable? Did the land owner's scope of

hypotheticals

Mike operates a shelter for homeless persons. Anyone forced to live on the streets is welcome at the facility. Liz frequently visits the shelter for free meals and a bed for the night. While sleeping one evening, Liz was stabbed by a loose, rusty wire through the mattress upon which she was lying. She had to undergo precautionary medical treatment for tetanus. Would Mike be liable for Liz's injury?

Liz was an invitee, because she was homeless and Mike expressly encouraged persons such as her to use his premises. Liz was injured as a result of a hidden danger (the loose wire) that could have been discovered if Mike had inspected the mattresses for wear and tear. Thus, Mike failed to exercise reasonable care to make the shelter reasonably safe for his patrons. As a result, one of his customers, Liz, was harmed, so Mike is liable to her.

* * *

Karla manages a local appliance store. Wade came in one day to look for a new washer and dryer. Karla showed Wade a popular model. Wade wished to see the units operate, but there were no electrical outlets nearby. Karla went to her office to get an extension cord. Meanwhile, Wade wandered through a set of swinging doors labeled "warehouse—employees only," hoping that he might find another salesperson who could locate an extension cord. Instead, he found a fork-loading truck that swerved around a wall and knocked Wade to the ground, severely injuring him. The truck driver did not expect anyone to be in the area. Is Karla liable to Wade?

Wade was an invitee when he visited the store to look for new appliances. However, he ceased to be an invitee when he entered the restricted area (the warehouse) without permission. Because he had been invited into the store originally, most courts would say that Wade became a licensee once he entered the storeroom, as it is reasonably foreseeable that customers might mistakenly trespass into such a limited-access area. Karla owed Wade a duty of reasonable care to discover and correct known dangers on the premises. In this case, the fork truck was not threatening in and of itself, as a rotten stairway or improperly stacked boxes would be. The danger would be considered unknown, as it was not reasonably foreseeable that a patron would be hurt by a truck moving around a restricted-access warehouse. Accordingly, Karla would not be liable for Wade's injury.

Arguably, though, the threat of the fork truck harming a wayward customer *was* foreseeable, because the truck driver reasonably should have anticipated that patrons might enter the warehouse from time to time, looking for salespersons or restrooms. This would make the risk known and, arguably, Karla breached her duty of reasonable care when her employee failed to watch for patrons while driving the truck through the warehouse. This reasoning is equally sound and persuasive. This case points out the artificial distinctions in classifying people by the reason they are on land. The traditional negligence approach would be much simpler.

duty include the victim? Did the owner cause the victim's injury? and so forth. Many courts, however, cling tenaciously to the older three-tier analysis. This demonstrates how entrenched precedent becomes; once a rule of law becomes settled, it is difficult to change precedent. The law changes at a snail's pace. More often than not, this provides valuable stability and predictability in legal problem solving. Nonetheless, it also makes legal principles slow to adapt to the rapid changes of our dynamic society. Table 3-5 summarizes the special negligence analysis for land owners and occupiers.

Duty to Trespasser	Land owner/occupier owes no duty of reasonable care; is required only to avoid intentional (or willful and wanton) injury.
Duty to Licensee	Land owner/occupier owes duty of reasonable care to correct known dangers on premises.
Duty to Invitee	Land owner/occupier owes duty of reasonable care to discover and correct unknown dangers on premises.
Traditional Negligence Theory	Applies regular negligence standards to determine land owner/occupier liability.
Duty to Trespassing Children (Attractive Nuisance Theory)	Land owner/occupier owes duty of reasonable care to protect trespassing children from artificial dangers on premises, when (1) owner knows or has reason to know of the dangerous condition on the premises; (2) the structure, instrumentality, or condition is alluring to children and endangers them; (3) the presence of children can reasonably be anticipated; and (4) the danger posed to the children outweighs the cost of making the condition safe.

TABLE 3-5
Land owners'/occupiers' negligence liability

THE CASE OF THE ICY RECEPTION

At first blush, this case might seem like a plaintiff's attorney's perfect case. There is an extremely sympathetic fact pattern to present to a jury: A veteran, who is discharged from the military to care for his blind wife, slips and falls at a motel where they were staying to attend a funeral the next morning. However, judging the appearance of clients and the kind of impact they will later have on a jury is just one consideration in evaluating a negligence case. The elements of negligence must still be proved.

(continues)

Donald G. DEMO, et al., Plaintiffs,

v.

RED ROOF INNS, INC., Defendant.

No. 4:06-CV-54.

United States District Court, W.D.
Michigan, Southern Division

April 13, 2007

About three weeks before the incident in question, just before his unit was shipped to Iraq, Plaintiff Donald Demo was administratively discharged from military duty in order to care for his wife, who had become totally blind as a result of her diabetes. At approximately 11:00 p.m. on February 4, 2005, Plaintiffs Donald and Melony Demo, who were on their way to a family funeral, checked into a room at the Defendant's Red Roof Inn in Kalamazoo, Michigan. Because the motel had no rooms on the first floor, Plaintiffs were given a room on the second floor. The hotel had no elevator, so Plaintiffs were required to reach their room by way of one of the exterior stairways. Those stairways were made of wood, though the floors of the hotel and sides of the stairway were made of concrete. A metal edge connected the concrete floor to the first wooden riser of the steps. The stairwells were covered and partially enclosed by a roof. According to Plaintiffs, the stairwell was open to the elements, and not well lighted. No signs were posted to warn residents of possible wet, slippery or icy conditions. In addition, the stairs were not coated with a non-skid material.

On the night of February 4, 2005, Plaintiff Donald Demo made the trip from the car to the room at least twice, escorting his wife and carrying in their possessions.

At approximately 4:30 a.m. on February 5, Plaintiff Donald Demo left his room to go to the Denny's Restaurant. Both when he left the building and when he returned to the building with the breakfast, he used the same stairway he had used the night before. He had no difficulty with the stairs. Once he returned, he realized that he had forgotten to get his wife anything to drink. Donald Demo remembered when he first entered the motel he saw a vending machine.

Because he knew there was ice in the parking lot, he thought it would be safer to take the stairway at the front of the building rather than take the middle stairway and walk through the lot.

At the top of the stairway, just as he was stepping off the landing, Plaintiff's feet went out from under him and he fell down the stairway. Donald Demo was unable to identify the cause of his slip, though he speculated that a sheet of ice must have covered the step area. He testified that he never saw ice and he did not return to the area to see if there was anything there. At another point in his deposition, however, he stated more generally, "I would say that the surface on the steps were slippery and that's basically why I came down the steps the way I did."

Plaintiff suffered significant injuries, including herniations of two spinal disks requiring multiple surgeries. Plaintiff's injuries have resulted in total employment disability and the necessity of hiring replacement services for the performance of daily tasks. Plaintiff Melony Demo alleges loss of consortium and loss of Donald's ability to care for her.

Under Michigan law, possessors of land owe business invitees the duty to exercise ordinary care and prudence to keep their premises in reasonably safe condition for the invitees' use.

In the context of snow and ice, however, the Michigan Supreme Court recently has held that a premises holder does not have a duty to diminish the hazards of snow and ice if the accumulation is open and obvious. If an accumulation of snow or ice is open and obvious, the landlord must take reasonable measures within a reasonable period of accumulation to diminish the risk of injury, but only if there exists some "special aspects" that makes the accumulation "unreasonably dangerous."

In the instant case, Plaintiffs fail to demonstrate either that Defendant owed a duty to protect Donald Demo on February 5, 2005, or that it breached that duty. First, Donald Demo testified that he was aware that the weather was chilly, that some ice and snow was present, and that the stairs were open to the elements. However, Plaintiffs fail entirely to explain why, knowing those conditions and knowing that he was exiting by way of an exterior staircase, the danger of an icy stairway was not obvious to Donald Demo. Michigan law places an obligation upon invitees to avoid the open and obvious danger caused by winter weather. Plaintiff has suggested no special aspects warranting the imposition of a duty on Defendant.

Second, even were the potential danger of an icy external stairway not ordinarily an open and obvious danger, Plaintiff fails to present more than rank speculation about the cause of his fall. Donald Demo clearly and repeatedly indicated that he could only assume the stair was icy. He expressly testified that he did not see the ice and never examined the area after his fall. Michigan courts repeatedly have rejected claims of landowner negligence where the plaintiff cannot demonstrate the cause of the fall.

Moreover, even if the icy stairway was not deemed to be open and obvious, and even if Plaintiff Donald Demo could testify with certainty that ice caused his fall, Plaintiffs have provided no evidence as to how long the condition existed that could or should have made Defendant aware of the hazard. In order to demonstrate constructive notice, Plaintiffs must show that the condition existed for a sufficient period of time for the premises owner to discover and correct it.

Plaintiffs have presented absolutely no evidence of how long ice may have been present on the stairway.

For the foregoing reasons, the Court will grant Defendant's motion for summary judgment.

CASE QUESTIONS

1. If Plaintiff Donald Demo had testified that he was certain he fell on ice, would this have changed the outcome of the case?
2. If the Plaintiff Donald Demo had fallen closer to 8:00 a.m., instead of some time after 4:30 a.m., would this have changed the outcome of the case?

▌ NEGLIGENT INFLICTION OF EMOTIONAL DISTRESS

Emotional distress consists of mental anguish caused by a tortfeasor. This condition includes fright, anxiety, shock, grief, mental suffering, shame, embarrassment, and emotional disturbance. The tort exists when the tortfeasor inflicts psychological injury on the victim. **Negligent infliction of emotional distress** consists of: (1) Outrageous conduct by the tortfeasor, which (2) the tortfeasor reasonably should have anticipated would produce (3) significant and reasonably foreseeable emotional injury to the victim; when (4) the tortfeasor breached his or her duty of reasonable care to avoid causing such emotional harm to the victim; and (5) the victim was a reasonably foreseeable plaintiff.

Extra Elements in the Common Law

These generalized elements of negligent infliction of emotional distress are synthesized from those of many jurisdictions. Different courts apply various special requirements to negligent infliction cases, and it is always wise to check the rules and cases of the particular jurisdiction in which your case lies.

emotional distress | Mental anguish. Nonphysical harm that may be compensated for by damages in some types of lawsuits. *Mental anguish* may be as limited as the immediate mental feelings during an injury or as broad as prolonged grief, shame, humiliation, despair, etc.

negligent infliction of emotional distress | Outrageous conduct by the tortfeasor that the tortfeasor reasonably should have anticipated would produce significant and reasonably foreseeable emotional injury to the victim.

Impact Rule

A minority of courts insist that some physical impact accompany the emotional injury. Thus, the tortfeasor must negligently do something that physically touches the victim if the victim is to recover damages for negligent infliction of emotional distress. This is often called the **impact rule,** and it has been severely criticized in the legal literature and judicial decisions.

The purpose of the impact requirement is to protect against false claims of emotional distress. Because mental anguish is largely invisible, courts at the turn of the century felt that the defendant had to make contact with the plaintiff to justify compensating something as easy to fake as mental harm. Modern courts utilizing the impact rule have seen impact in almost any physical touching. Something as casual as putting one's hand on a classmate's shoulder would be considered sufficient contact to satisfy the impact rule. Hence, it would seem that, as a safeguard against faked claims of emotional distress, the physical impact requirement does little or nothing to ensure honesty and sincerity for allegations of mental hurt.

Physical Manifestations Rule

The majority of courts have abandoned the impact rule in favor of the **physical manifestations rule.** This requires that, in addition to mental suffering, the plaintiff must experience physical symptoms as a result of the emotional distress. This rule is also thought to protect against bogus claims of emotional injury. After all, if a victim experiences some physical malady associated with an emotional harm, such as an ulcer, hives, sleeplessness, weight loss, or bowel dysfunction, then the probability is that the emotional harm is genuine.

Zone of Danger Rule

What happens when the negligent action occurs to someone else, and the plaintiff is a bystander who witnesses a negligent injury to another person? Could the tortfeasor be liable to the bystander for negligent infliction of emotional distress? Consider an example. Suppose parents witnessed their child being struck by a negligent driver. Would the parents have a cause of action against the driver for negligent infliction of emotional distress?

No impact occurred to the parents, although they may suffer physical manifestations as a result of witnessing their child's injury. The proper question, however, may be phrased in ordinary negligence terms: Did the driver owe (and breach) a duty of reasonable care to the parents by injuring their child? Did the driver's actions cause the parents' emotional suffering? Does proximate cause exist? Were the parents injured?

Certainly, the driver could not reasonably anticipate that any bystander would suffer emotional distress as a result of the driver's negligent act of hitting

---

impact rule | The rule (used today in very few states) that damages for emotional distress cannot be had in a negligence lawsuit unless there is some physical contact or impact.

physical manifestations rule | Doctrine applied in negligent infliction of emotional distress cases. The plaintiff may recover damages if physical symptoms accompanied his or her mental anguish.

a pedestrian. There must be some way to limit the scope of duty (and, hence, the range of foreseeable plaintiffs). Courts have attempted to establish such limits by creating the **zone of danger rule.** Under this rule, only bystanders who fall within the zone of danger can recover for negligent infliction of emotional distress. In other words, these individuals must have been threatened by the original negligent action (e.g., negligent driving of a vehicle) and have reasonably feared for their own safety, or have certain family relationships, as discussed next.

zone of danger rule | The rule in some states that a plaintiff must be in danger of physical harm, and frightened by the danger, to collect damages for the negligent infliction of emotional distress that results from seeing another person injured by the plaintiff.

THE CASE OF THE DISTRESSED BRIDE

In this case, one of a bride's worst nightmares occurs. Her carefully selected dream wedding venue and specified date are given to another bride months before the wedding. Could this have been avoided? The bride approached the situation with great seriousness and made sure that a contract was signed and a deposit given. Slowly this situation unraveled. What is the lesson here for future brides?

Maureen MURPHY
v.
LORD THOMPSON MANOR, INC.
No. 28106.
Appellate Court of Connecticut
Decided Jan. 29, 2008

We are born, some marry and we die. In this list of life events, it is only in marriage that we make choices. This appeal arises out of an action by the plaintiff, Maureen Murphy, to recover damages from the defendant, Lord Thompson Manor, Inc. (manor), for its failure to perform a contract for wedding related services and accommodations. Following a trial to the court, the court found the manor liable under theories of breach of contract and negligent infliction of emotional distress and awarded the plaintiff $17,000 in economic and noneconomic damages, plus costs.

The plaintiff considered the manor her ideal wedding site, as it could accommodate a "weekend celebration" consisting of a Friday night rehearsal dinner, a Saturday evening wedding reception and after party, and a Sunday brunch.

On February 21, 2003, the plaintiff and her mother, Sandra Powers, visited the manor and met with its owner and agent, Andrew Silverston. Silverston gave the plaintiff the manor's standard letter of agreement. Plaintiff signed the letter, and Powers submitted $2000 in deposit money on behalf of the plaintiff, thus fulfilling each condition the letter requested for finality. The letter further identified the date of the wedding as September 10, 2005.

In the two years following the signing of the contract, a Shakespearean drama of confusion and lost opportunities ensued that would result in the manor contracting with another wedding party for the September 10, 2005 date and the plaintiff holding her wedding at another location. This outcome was brought about by a series of miscommunications leading to Silverston's mistaken belief that the plaintiff was abandoning her wedding plans.

In February, 2005, Silverston became uncertain about whether the plaintiff's wedding was going forward. His insecurities were caused by his continued mistaken belief that there was no signed agreement or paid deposit. At the same time, Silverston had an inquiry from another couple who wanted to be married on September 10, 2005. He advised them that he might have a cancellation. On February 8, 2005, Silverston sent the plaintiff an express mail letter,

(continues)

asking her to contact him. The letter, however, contained no notice that the manor was uncertain of her wedding plans.

Silverston believed that his suspicions that the plaintiff's wedding was cancelled were confirmed by the lack of an immediate response from the plaintiff, as it was his experience that brides were anxious by nature and responded promptly to inquiries from their wedding coordinator.

On February 23, 2005, Silverston sent a letter to the plaintiff in which he inaccurately portrayed the February 21, 2003 letter agreement as tentative. Silverston's depiction of the parties' agreement as tentative was in direct contradiction of the agreement's language. He assumed that they were no longer interested in reserving the date of September 10, 2005.

The receipt of Silverston's letter stunned the heretofore unaware plaintiff.

During this period, the plaintiff's anxiety about her wedding plans increased, and feelings of extreme distrust for the manor developed. Because of her uncertainty that the manor would honor its contractual obligations, the plaintiff feverishly attempted to locate a venue that would accommodate her September 10, 2005 wedding date. After calling numerous sites, the plaintiff was able to find one venue. The wedding was a far cry from the weekend celebration the plaintiff originally had planned. The plaintiff testified that these events were the most stressful in her life.

A successful claim of negligent infliction of emotional distress "essentially requires that the fear or distress experienced by the plaintiffs be reasonable in light of the conduct of the defendants."

Here, we agree with the trial court that the actions of the manor's agent, Silverston, "created an unreasonable risk of causing [the plaintiff] emotional distress." The court noted in particular that "the manor gave [the plaintiff] no notice that it had questions about her wedding plans. The first direct notice she received of the manor's concerns was the manor's cancellation letter of February 23, 2005. [Although] the Manor's breach occurred approximately seven months before [the plaintiff's] wedding was to take place, it left her with limited options for alternative venues and the significant task of coordinating the details in light of a different venue and a different wedding day schedule, as well as informing 100 guests of the changes.... In addition, the Manor informed [the plaintiff] that it had given her date to another couple on February 16, 2005, when in fact it did not have a contract with the second party until March 6, 2005." The cumulative effect of the conduct described by the court undoubtedly would risk causing any bride emotional distress.

CASE QUESTIONS

1. Claimant was awarded $15,000 for her emotional distress. Do you think this was a fair amount?
2. Explain your answer to the above question.

Family Relationships Rule

family relationships rule | Doctrine used in negligent infliction of emotional distress cases. A bystander may recover damages if he or she witnesses the tortfeasor injuring one or more of the bystander's relatives.

Other courts have restricted recovery in negligent infliction cases to bystander plaintiffs who are related to the victim whom they witnessed being injured. This may be called the **family relationships rule.**

Sensory Perception Rule

Still other courts have insisted that the bystander perceive the traumatic, negligent event directly through the senses (e.g., seeing the collision; hearing the child's screams; feeling the heat of the car exploding; smelling the burning clothing). This may be labeled the **sensory perception rule.**

California Approach

The California courts were first to produce a further evolutionary development in negligent infliction law. In *Dillon v. Legg,* 68 Cal. 2d 728, 441 P.2d 912, 69 Cal. Rptr. 72 (1968), the California Supreme Court dispensed with the zone of danger rule and focused upon pure foreseeability. The straightforward question was, simply: Was the emotional injury reasonably foreseeable, given the tortfeasor's actions? This analysis neatly handled bystanders as well as immediate victims of negligent conduct. The court produced the following guidelines to decide the foreseeability issue:

1. The bystander's closeness to the emotionally disturbing incident *(physical proximity)*
2. The bystander's relationship to the injured party *(family relationships rule)*
3. The bystander's personal perception of the emotionally distressing occurrence *(sensory perception rule)*
4. Physical manifestations arising from the emotional distress.

The *Dillon* approach has been both praised and debunked by other courts and legal scholars. It presents another twist in negligent infliction cases, in a continuing attempt to clarify the circumstances in which a plaintiff may hold a defendant liable for this type of negligent tort.

The diversity of negligent infliction of emotional distress formulas used in different jurisdictions makes analysis dependent upon a specific state's version. The following hypothetical considers the varieties discussed in this section.

sensory perception rule |
Doctrine used in negligent infliction of emotional distress cases. A bystander may recover damages if he or she witnesses a tortfeasor injuring another person, so long as the bystander perceives the event directly through his or her own senses.

---

hypothetical

Lamar owns an apartment building. Duane and Tyrel are brothers who share an apartment. One day, while barbecuing on their apartment balcony, Duane stepped upon rotten floorboards, which collapsed. Lamar had known about this dangerous condition for months but had not corrected it. Duane fell through the balcony floor and hung upside down by one leg 30 feet above the ground. Meanwhile, Tyrel, who was waxing his car in the parking lot below, became very upset upon seeing this situation develop. As he ran upstairs to assist his brother, Duane fell and suffered debilitating injuries. Subsequently, Tyrel began having horrible nightmares involving endless falling. He would awaken nightly in cold sweats. He lost weight, had little appetite, and developed a phobia about

(continues)

heights. This phobia made it extremely difficult for Tyrel to continue his occupation as a roofing installer. Lamar's liability to Duane is an issue of land owner liability, which we discussed at the beginning of this chapter. Would Lamar be liable to Tyrel for negligent infliction of emotional distress?

Clearly, Tyrel suffered no physical impact as a result of Lamar's negligence. Tyrel did not come into contact with the rotten balcony when it gave way. In states following the impact rule, Tyrel could not recover damages against Lamar for negligent infliction.

In states following the zone of danger rule, Tyrel was not sufficiently close to the dangerous balcony to be threatened by its condition. He was not even below the point at which Duane fell, which would have placed him at risk. Under the zone of danger test, Tyrel could not recover.

In jurisdictions following California's approach, it was reasonably foreseeable that Tyrel would be emotionally harmed by witnessing Duane's life-threatening situation, which Duane became involved in because of Lamar's negligent maintenance of the balcony. Tyrel is Duane's brother, so the family relationship test is met. Tyrel saw Duane dangling from the balcony and knew that he could fall and be killed. This satisfies the sensory perception rule. Tyrel was standing close to the accident site, and thus met the physical proximity standard. He also displayed physical symptoms resulting from his mental anguish. All of the *Dillon* criteria have been satisfied. Accordingly, Lamar would be liable to Tyrel for negligent infliction of emotional distress, under the California theory.

Table 3-6 illustrates the various analytical approaches to negligent infliction of emotional distress.

TABLE 3-6
Elements of negligent infliction of emotional distress

Common Elements (applying standard negligence theory to emotionally distressing conduct)	(1) Outrageous conduct by tortfeasor, when (2) tortfeasor reasonably should have anticipated that behavior would produce (3) significant and reasonably foreseeable injury in plaintiff, (4) tortfeasor breached duty of reasonable care, and (5) victim was foreseeable plaintiff.
Impact Rule	Plaintiff must experience physical impact from defendant's actions to recover for negligent infliction of emotional distress.
Physical Manifestations Rule	No physical impact is required, but plaintiff must experience physical symptoms associated with mental anguish that defendant caused.
Zone of Danger Rule	Bystander witnessing negligent injury to third party must have been immediately threatened by the negligent activity.

Family Relationships Rule	Bystander must be a family relative of the person injured by the tortfeasor's negligent act.
Sensory Perception Rule	Bystander must perceive with his or her senses (sight, hearing, smell, touch, taste) the injury to another person as a result of the tortfeasor's negligent act.

TABLE 3-6 *(continued)*

▌ NEGLIGENCE PER SE

Negligence per se is negligence that is beyond debate because the law, usually a statute or ordinance, has established a duty or standard of care that the defendant has violated, thus causing injury to the plaintiff. When a statute defines certain conduct as negligent, and a tortfeasor violates the statute by engaging in that activity, then the tortfeasor is presumed to have been negligent by violating the statute. To meet the burden of proof, a plaintiff need only show that the defendant's actions violated the negligence statute. The defendant is then presumed negligent. This shifts the proof burden to the defendant, who must then present effective negligence defenses to avoid liability. A per se negligent defendant might also avoid liability by showing that he or she was not the proximate cause of the plaintiff's injuries. In other words, the defendant would have to prove that his or her violation of the statute did not proximately cause the plaintiff's harm.

negligence per se | Negligence that cannot be debated due to a law that establishes a duty of care that the defendant has violated, thus causing injury to another.

Defenses to Negligence Per Se

The negligence defenses of contributory negligence, comparative negligence, and assumption of risk also apply to negligence per se cases.

THE CASE OF THE UNYIELDING DRIVER

Sometimes liability of drivers in automobile accidents will be clear-cut. Here, one driver has the right of way and the other driver is faced with a stop sign, and a violation of state law requiring that vehicles stop at stop signs.

GERGIS
v.
MICCIO

N.Y. A.D. 2d Dept., 2007
Supreme Court, Appellate Division, Second Department, New York
Isis GERGIS, et al., respondents,
v.
Salvatore MICCIO, appellant
April 3, 2007

A driver who fails to yield the right-of-way after stopping at a stop sign controlling traffic is in violation of Vehicle and Traffic Law § 1142(a) and is negligent as a matter of law. A driver is required to "see that which through proper use of [his or her] senses [he or she] should have seen," and a driver who has the right-of-way is entitled to anticipate that the other motorist will obey the traffic law requiring him or her to yield.

(continues)

The defendant established, prima facie, his entitlement to judgment as a matter of law by demonstrating that the plaintiff driver, who was faced with a stop sign at the intersection of a parking lot exit and Route 25, negligently entered the intersection without yielding the right-of-way, and that this was the sole proximate cause of the accident. In opposition, the plaintiffs failed to submit evidence sufficient to raise a triable issue of fact.

CASE QUESTIONS
1. What statute was violated by the injured plaintiff?
2. If no statute were involved that was applicable to these same facts, would the duty owed by the plaintiff have been any different?

Plaintiff within Class of Persons Protected by Statute

Not every statutory violation constitutes negligence per se. To recover under negligence per se theory, the plaintiff must be within the class of persons protected by the statute or ordinance and the statute must be designed to protect the class of persons from the type of harm that occurred. For example, suppose a restaurant serves maggot-infested meat to its customers. This violates several state and local health statutes. Suppose Kent ate at the restaurant and became ill. He would fall within the class of persons protected by the health statutes that require restaurants to serve wholesome food to patrons. The restaurant's violation of the statutes would be considered negligence per se, and Kent would have an excellent cause of action against the establishment.

Absolute Liability Mislabeled as Negligence Per Se

Courts occasionally equate negligence per se with strict, or absolute, liability. However, the two tort theories are distinct. Negligence per se simply presumes negligence because of the tortfeasor's violation of a statute. Negligence is based upon the tortfeasor's failure to exercise reasonable care. Absolute liability holds the tortfeasor accountable, regardless of fault, for doing an abnormally dangerous activity. No degree of care is sufficient to avoid strict liability.

This confusion between absolute liability and negligence per se occurs because of the outcomes in each type of case. If the defendant violates a negligence statute, he or she automatically is presumed negligent. Liability is almost as certain as in strict liability cases. Thus, the two concepts are often equated, although they are substantially different.

Toxic Torts as Negligence Per Se

Statutes sometimes declare that violations of regulations regarding the transportation, disposal, or management of hazardous or toxic substances create a presumption of negligence as a matter of law. These statutory provisions boost plaintiffs' causes of action against tortfeasors who carelessly control abnormally dangerous materials.

Not every statutory violation is negligence per se. All elements must be satisfied for the doctrine to apply. The following hypotheticals further demonstrate this principle.

hypotheticals

Wes was driving his automobile at night along the Old River Road. Although it was pitch black, he did not have his headlights on. This violated a local county ordinance and state statute requiring headlight use at all times beginning an hour before sundown and ending an hour after sunrise. Wes collided with Mai Ling, a pedestrian walking along the side of the road. Mai Ling sues Wes for negligence per se. Was he negligent per se?

By driving without headlights, Wes violated an ordinance and statute that required motor vehicles to use lights at night. This was intended to protect other drivers and pedestrians from "invisible" vehicles hitting them in the dark. Mai Ling falls within the classification of persons protected by the statute and ordinance. Therefore, she could successfully sue Wes for negligence per se.

* * *

Consider another hypothetical. Barfly Beer Company sells "Brewster's Choice," a "light" beer low in calories. One of its distributors, the Brothers Emporium, sells the product in town. A state health statute requires any manufacturer or seller of items for human consumption to distribute them in containers free from foreign substances. Brothers collected empty bottles to send back to Barfly to be cleaned and reused. Sometimes, drinkers would put cigarette butts into the bottles. Neither Brothers nor Barfly checked the bottles for foreign substances; they were simply sent back to the Barfly plant, refilled, and redistributed. Ann drank one of the beers from a bottle with a cigarette butt floating in the bottom. As one might imagine, Ann became physically ill as a result. Aside from the clear products liability issue, has Barfly or Brothers been negligent per se?

The health statute was intended to protect consumers like Ann from injuries caused by foreign objects floating inside beverage bottles. Barfly and Brothers each violated the statute. Their negligence may be presumed.

Table 3-7 summarizes negligence per se.

TABLE 3-7 Elements of negligence per se	Defendant's actions are automatically considered negligent because they violated a negligence statute or ordinance
	Plaintiff must fall within class of persons protected by statute
	Defendant's actions must fall within the area for which the statute was created
	Defendant's statutory violation must proximately cause plaintiff's injuries
	Negligence defenses apply to negligence per se

▌ SUMMARY

Vicarious liability is the liability of one person (principal) for the negligent actions of another (agent). Many vicarious liability situations involve employer/employee relationships. Under the doctrine of respondeat superior, the employer must answer to the injured party for the employee's negligence when the employee has acted within the scope of his or her employment. This normally involves assigned tasks during normal working hours. Special rules apply for employees coming to and going from work, and for employees who frolic and detour from assigned tasks to pursue personal pleasures. A person hiring independent contractors is not vicariously liable for their negligence. Many states have motor vehicle consent statutes holding a vehicle owner liable for another driver's negligence.

In premises liability, owners and occupiers of land owe special duties of reasonable care to individuals who are injured while visiting the premises. Traditionally, courts have defined these duties differently, depending upon the injured party's status on the realty. There are three such distinctions: trespasser, licensee, and invitee. Land owners owe no duty of reasonable care to trespassers; they must simply refrain from intentionally injuring trespassers. Special rules, called attractive nuisance theory, apply to trespassing children. Licensees are persons that the owners permit to come onto their real estate. To licensees, land owners owe a duty to correct known dangers on the premises. Land owners owe a duty to discover and correct unknown risks on the premises for invitees, who have come onto the premises at the owners' expressed or implied invitation. The owner may limit the places on the land to which such invitation extends. Many courts have abandoned this three-tier analysis in favor of regular negligence theory.

Negligent infliction of emotional distress occurs when the tortfeasor engages in conduct that produces a reasonably foreseeable mental injury in a reasonably foreseeable victim. Many states have different rules to decide negligent infliction cases. A few courts require that the tortfeasor cause some physical impact to the emotionally distressed victim. Many courts hold that mental anguish is recoverable when accompanied by physical manifestations or symptoms. Others allow bystanders to recover when they witness negligent injuries to other people when the bystanders fall within the zone of danger. Courts that follow California's reasoning base liability upon foreseeability, using physical manifestations, physical proximity, family connection, and whether the bystander witnessed the injury to determine the outcome of negligent infliction litigation.

Negligence per se is any activity that violates a negligence statute. It is considered automatic negligence simply because the defendant's conduct violated the statutory provisions. To recover damages, the plaintiff must fall within the class of persons that the statute was intended to protect. The same defenses apply to negligence per se that apply to ordinary negligence cases. Furthermore, the defendant's statutory violation must have proximately caused the plaintiff's injuries.

▊ KEY TERMS

attractive nuisance	independent contractor	physical manifestations rule
attractive nuisance doctrine	invitee	respondeat superior
coming and going rule	licensee	scope of employment
emotional distress	negligence per se	sensory perception rule
family relationships rule	negligent infliction of emotional	vicarious liability
frolic and detour rule	distress	zone of danger rule
impact rule	occupier	

▊ PROBLEMS

In the following hypotheticals, determine which type of special negligence action applies, if any. For the sake of convenience, use the three-tier analysis for land owner/occupier liability.

1. Clint rents an apartment from Whisperwood Property Management, Inc. His next-door neighbor, Leslie, frequently visits to watch basketball on Clint's big-screen television. Clint had a can of aerosol cleaner in his utility closet. He set the can too close to the gas furnace, and the can slowly became overheated. One evening while watching the game, Leslie dropped and broke a glass. She opened the utility closet to fetch a broom to clean up the mess. Unfortunately, the cleaner can exploded just as she opened the closet door, injuring her severely.

2. Emily owns a pasture outside of town upon which she has her cattle and horses graze. Ted sometimes crosses the pasture as a shortcut to work. All around the property are posted signs stating in clear, red-and-black letters, "NO TRESPASSING! YES, *YOU!*" One day Emily saw Ted cutting across her land and warned him not to continue doing so in the future. Ted ignored the warning. Weeks later, Ted fell into a mud bog (which he could not see, because it was covered by fallen leaves). He sank to his chest and could not escape. He remained there for three days until a passing postal carrier stumbled upon his predicament. Ted suffered from severe malnutrition and exposure from the incident. As a result, he contracted pneumonia and was hospitalized for two weeks.

3. Davis operates a beauty shop. Kate comes in regularly for perms and haircuts. One of Davis's employees, Flower, absentmindedly left her electric shears on the seat of one of the hair dryers. Davis did not notice the shears when he had Kate sit in that chair to dry her newly permed hair. Unknown to everybody, the shears had an electrical short. When Davis turned on the hair dryer, the shears shorted out and electrocuted Kate, who was unknowingly sitting against the shears.

4. Susan hired Grass Goddess, a lawn care company, to fertilize and water her yard. One of the company's employees, Gupta, incorrectly mixed the fertilizer so that it contained 12 times the necessary amount of potassium. Gupta applied this mixture to Susan's grass. Honey, Susan's neighbor, came to Susan's party that

night and played volleyball in the backyard. She frequently fell and rolled on the grass while diving to return the ball over the net. The next day, Honey developed a painful rash all over her body. She usually noticed these symptoms, although less severely, when she ate bananas, which are high in potassium.

5. Jon is a sales executive for a local automobile dealership. He often drives to the manufacturing facility 150 miles from the dealership to check on new orders. Jon's employer reimburses him for gasoline, food, and lodging, and provides Jon with a dealer car to drive. While driving to the manufacturing plant, Jon decided to stop by his cousin's house for dinner. His boss accompanied him on the visit "to get a decent meal for a change." While on the way there, Jon collided with and injured a motorcyclist.

6. Matthew has a five-year-old son with whom he often plays catch in the front yard. Sometimes the wind catches their ball and blows it into the street. Matthew has warned his son never to chase the ball into the road, but one day, when the ball blew into the street, Matthew's son ran after it. A truck driver swerved and struck the boy with the edge of the vehicle's bumper. The child suffered only a few bruises and scrapes. Matthew, however, developed a nervous twitch, ulcers, and an extreme sensitivity to sudden movements. He lost weight and experienced terrible nightmares about the incident.

▌ REVIEW QUESTIONS

1. Define the three classes of plaintiffs to whom land owners and occupiers owe duties of reasonable care.

2. Describe the land owner/occupier's duty of reasonable care to trespassers. Does the rule apply to all trespassers?

3. What is attractive nuisance? To which type of plaintiffs would the doctrine apply? Why is the land owner/occupier's duty of reasonable care different for these plaintiffs?

4. Using common-law principles, discuss the land owner/occupier's duty of reasonable care to licensees. How do licensees differ from trespassers? From invitees?

5. Using common-law principles, what duty of reasonable care does the land owner/occupier owe to invitees? Why and how are invitees distinguishable from licensees and trespassers?

6. Explain how you might use traditional negligence theory to determine land owners'/occupiers' liability to persons injured on the real estate. Do you find this approach easier than the three-tier analysis discussed in problem 1? Why or why not?

7. Define vicarious liability. What types of relationships involve this theory? What is respondeat superior? Explain scope of employment, the coming and going rule, and the frolic and detour rule. Why are these important to your analysis? How does vicarious liability relate to independent contractors? To motor vehicle owners or passengers?

8. Explain negligent infliction of emotional distress. What are its elements? In what types of factual situations would the tort apply? Describe the different analytical approaches to this tort. Define the impact rule, the physical manifestations rule, the zone of danger rule, the family relationships rule, and the sensory perception rule. How have the California courts combined these concepts in negligent infliction cases?

9. What is negligence per se? How does negligence per se differ from negligence?

▌HELPFUL WEBSITES

This chapter focuses on special negligence actions. To learn more about special negligence actions, the following sites can be accessed:

General Information

http://www.findlaw.com

http://www.law.emory.edu

http://www.lawguru.com

http://www.prairielaw.com

http://www.courttv.com

STUDENT CD-ROM™

For additional materials, please go to the CD in this book.

ONLINE COMPANION™

For additional resources, please go to
http://www.paralegal.delmar.cengage.com

chapter 4

Defenses to Negligence

THE BIGGEST MISTAKES PARALEGALS MAKE & HOW TO AVOID THEM

Change Is Good?

One of the most embarrassing moments I ever experienced was the first time I submitted a brief to the senior attorney of my firm. I knew she was a stickler for detail and accuracy, especially with regard to good law. So I always validated that my caselaw citation references were strong, accurate, and onpoint. I found out that works if you are careful or not away from the office.

Changes do happen and validation information is electronically updated 24 to 48 hours from issuance of a judicial opinion. The day I left on vacation I failed to order automatic case citation updates for all the cases in my brief. If I had done so, my attorney would have had changes to reports of all the cases I used. Unfortunately, while I was gone, there was a sudden split of authority in my leading case

(continues)

that effectively rendered my brief useless. Upon realizing the situation, my attorney had to call upon another paralegal to do my work at the last minute. There was a stony silence when I returned to the office.

LESSON LEARNED: Always Shepardize your cases! Shepard's can even monitor the cases you choose, as well as alert you to changes. *Shepard's Citation Service,* the case validation citation service, is available exclusively from LexisNexis.

INTRODUCTION

Tort defenses are an important protection for defendants. They provide legal justification for the defendants' actions.

Defendants' defenses excuse negligent behavior. In effect, defenses provide defendants with a blame-shifting tool. Negligence defenses examine any plaintiff misconduct that was involved in causing the plaintiff's injuries. Even though the tortfeasor was negligent toward the victim, the tortfeasor's mischief may be forgiven (totally or partially) because of the victim's participation in producing his or her injuries.

This chapter discusses:

- How negligence defenses are used
- Contributory negligence
- Last clear chance
- Comparative negligence
- Assumption of risk
- Statutes of limitations.

Also see Chapter 12 where immunity from torts is discussed.

HOW NEGLIGENCE DEFENSES ARE USED

Once the plaintiff has alleged a cause of action for negligence in the complaint, it is assumed that the defendant has no defense unless he or she specifically pleads one (or more) in his or her answer. Always remember these basic analytical rules:

1. *Negligence defenses are used only by the defendant against the plaintiff.* Put more generally, these defenses are responses to negligence allegations. The party alleged to have been negligent can use defenses against the party alleging negligence.

2. *Negligence defenses are applied only in response to the plaintiff's allegations that the defendant acted negligently or with willful and wanton negligence, not to claims of intentional action.*

Once a plaintiff alleges the defendant's negligence, both parties' failure to be careful may be at issue.

3. *Ask who is alleging negligence and who is alleged to have been negligent.* The alleged tortfeasor, usually the defendant, is the person who may utilize defenses.

▌ CONTRIBUTORY NEGLIGENCE AND LAST CLEAR CHANCE

With this fundamental approach in mind, it is time to examine contributory negligence, used by a minority of jurisdictions. The majority use comparative negligence as a primary defense, which is described later in this chapter.

Contributory Negligence Defined

contributory negligence |
The plaintiff's own negligence that contributed to his or her injuries. In some jurisdictions this bars any recovery by a plaintiff.

Contributory negligence is the plaintiff's own negligence that contributed to his or her injuries. The elements of contributory negligence include duty, breach, causation, and injury. In some jurisdictions this doctrine totally bars an injured plaintiff from recovering anything. This is very harsh.

Duty of Care to Oneself. Suppose that Zelda is driving to school. Suppose that another driver runs a stop sign and the vehicles collide with one another. By failing to stop at the sign, the other driver breached the duty of reasonable care to other vehicle users such as Zelda. The other driver's negligence proximately caused injuries to Zelda and her vehicle. However, because Zelda was looking at herself in the mirror for a second, instead of looking at the road, she contributed to her own injuries.

Common Law Rule. At common law, contributory negligence barred the plaintiff from recovering any damages from the defendant. Even if the defendant were negligent in causing 99 percent of the plaintiff's harm, and the plaintiff were only 1 percent contributorily negligent, the courts ruled that the plaintiff could collect nothing against the defendant. Very few states still use contributory negligence as a defense. Because of the harshness of the rule, courts have sought ways to avoid it.

Last Clear Chance

last clear chance doctrine |
Even though the plaintiff was at fault in causing his or her own injuries, the defendant had the last opportunity to avert harm and failed to do so; therefore, the plaintiff can still recover.

When a defendant uses the contributory negligence defense against a plaintiff, the plaintiff has a responsive weapon to defeat this defense. This is called **last clear chance** and is a rebuttal to a contributory negligence defense. Last clear chance theory states that, although the plaintiff was contributorily negligent in causing his or her own injuries, the defendant had the last opportunity to avert harm and failed to do so; therefore, the plaintiff can still recover. This rule is not followed in all states and has many variations and names.

In other words, the defendant cannot escape liability for his or her negligence (by invoking the contributory negligence defense) if the defendant had the last clear chance to avoid the injury.

An example of last clear chance would be where a defendant enters a highway and goes in the wrong direction. The plaintiff sees the defendant's car coming at plaintiff in plaintiff's lane of traffic, and instead of trying to switch lanes or honk his horn to avoid the impending collision, the plaintiff does nothing and continues to drive in his lane of traffic. In the above example, it was the plaintiff who had the "last clear chance" to avoid the incident. The fact that the defendant was the one that was originally negligent does not affect plaintiff's obligation to try and avoid the collision.

Table 4-1 summarizes the different elements of contributory negligence and last clear chance.

CONTRIBUTORY NEGLIGENCE	LAST CLEAR CHANCE
Plaintiff's duty of reasonable care to himself or herself	Although plaintiff was contributorily negligent, defendant had the last reasonable opportunity to avoid harming plaintiff (as a consequence of defendant's negligence)
Plaintiff breaches duty	Nullifies contributory negligence defense
Plaintiff acts, or fails to act, which contributes to his or her injuries (causation and proximate cause)	Plaintiff uses last clear chance to respond to defendant's use of contributory negligence defense
Plaintiff is injured	

TABLE 4-1
Contributory negligence and last clear chance

▌COMPARATIVE NEGLIGENCE

The comparative negligence defense has replaced contributory negligence in most states' common law or statutes. Since the 1960s, courts and legislatures increasingly have adopted the defense as an alternative to the rigid, unfair results that contributory negligence often produced when a plaintiff could recover nothing if found even slightly at fault. The defense of comparative negligence enables the defendant's liability to be adjusted according to the extent of the plaintiff's contribution to his or her own injuries. **Comparative negligence** may be defined as a measurement and comparison of the plaintiff's and the defendant's negligence in causing the plaintiff's injuries.

comparative negligence | A legal rule, used in many states, by which the amount of "fault" on each side of an accident is measured and the side with less fault is given damages according to the difference between the magnitude of each side's fault.

Elements

The comparative negligence defense has three elements:

1. The plaintiff was negligent in contributing to his or her own injuries.
2. Calculation of the percentage of the plaintiff's negligence that contributed to his or her injuries.
3. Calculation of the percentage of the defendant's negligence that produced the plaintiff's injuries.

In some jurisdictions, a fourth element is included: the defendant must have been more negligent than the plaintiff.

Table 4-2 shows states' contributory and comparative negligence policies.

TABLE 4-2
States' contributory and comparative negligence policies

STATE	CONTRIBUTORY AND COMPARATIVE NEGLIGENCE POLICIES
California	Pure form of comparative negligence
Florida	Has comparative negligence. Any contributory fault by plaintiff lessens the proportionate amount of damages.
New Jersey	Contributory negligence can't be greater than negligence of defendants. Damages diminished by the percentage of damages attributable to plaintiff.
New York	Has comparative negligence. Contributory negligence does not bar recovery. Damages reduced in proportion to culpable conduct.
Pennsylvania	Contributory negligence doesn't bar recovery provided plaintiff's negligence is not greater than defendant's. Amount of damages is reduced in proportion to plaintiff's fault.
Texas	Contributory negligence limits a plaintiff's recovery. Plaintiff's negligence cannot be greater than defendant's. Award reduced in proportion to negligence.

The Balancing Act

Comparative negligence balances the degrees of each party's negligence that produced the plaintiff's harm. In effect, the plaintiff's and defendant's negligence are compared to see which was more responsible for causing injury. This comparative negligence balancing is typically measured in percentages of negligence. This is sometimes called **culpability factoring (liability apportionment).**

For instance, consider the stop sign example discussed earlier in this chapter. The defendant ran a stop sign. This is more negligent than a driver momentarily not paying full attention to the road, as the plaintiff's acts would not have produced the accident. It took the greater negligence of the defendant (i.e., failing to stop at the sign) to cause the damage. The defendant was more negligent than the plaintiff

culpability factoring (liability apportionment) | A defense to negligence. When the plaintiff's negligence contributed to his or her injuries, comparative negligence calculates the percentage of the defendant's and the plaintiff's negligence and adjusts the plaintiff's damages according to the numbers.

in that example. But what percentages of negligence would be assigned to the plaintiff (for contributing to the injuries) and the defendant (for negligently causing the harm)? Well, the defendant was more than half responsible, so the defendant's percentage must be higher than 50 percent. What percentages would be used? Defendant 75 percent, plaintiff 25 percent? 60/40? 90/10?

Readers may find this approach frustrating. What are the correct percentages? There is no exact formula. It depends upon the facts of each case. Whatever percentages are selected, readers and triers-of-fact probably rely on intuition and gut feeling as much as anything.

Who Decides the Percentages. The trier-of-fact decides the percentages in comparative negligence. Thus, the jury (or judge, in a bench trial) must closely examine the facts and assign negligence percentages to the plaintiff and the defendant.

Why Calculate Percentages. Comparative negligence is used to calculate the amount of the defendant's liability to the plaintiff. Assume that the following percentages were selected for the stop sign problem: defendant 75 percent negligent, plaintiff 25 percent negligent. What would be the outcome of the case? The defendant would be liable to the plaintiff for 75 percent of the amount the plaintiff received in damages. If the plaintiff recovered judgment against the defendant, receiving a $100,000 damages award, under this percentage the defendant would be liable for $75,000, with $25,000 having been subtracted out for the plaintiff's comparative negligence.

The advantages of comparative negligence are immediately apparent. Instead of completely barring the plaintiff's recovery (as common-law contributory negligence would have done), culpability factoring enables the plaintiff to recover damages for the defendant's share of responsibility in causing the injuries. Liability apportionment also protects the defendant from paying for the plaintiff's share in harming himself or herself. The result is a just and equitable outcome to the litigation. It allows a plaintiff to bring an action even though he or she is somewhat at fault.

Criticism of Comparative Negligence

Comparative negligence has been criticized for its arbitrary and capricious approach to assigning percentages of negligence. Critics complain that liability apportionment is imprecise and based entirely upon the emotional attitudes of the jury or judge. Think back to the stop sign illustration. If one disapproved of running stop signs more than driver inattention, would one not be more likely to raise the defendant's percentage of liability? Of course, juries are composed of several people, a fact that is intended to balance out such personal biases. Still, disapproval of comparative negligence continues in legal literature and court opinions.

Table 4-3 lists the elements of comparative negligence.

TABLE 4-3
Comparative negligence

ELEMENTS OF COMPARATIVE NEGLIGENCE
Plaintiff was negligent in contributing to his or her own injuries (defendant was also negligent in causing plaintiff's injuries)
Liability apportionment: Calculate each party's percentage of negligence (How much did plaintiff contribute to his or her own injuries?) (How much was defendant responsible for plaintiff's harm?)
In some jurisdications, defendant's percentage of negligence must be greater than plaintiff's percentage of negligence (modified comparative negligence)
In some jurisdictions, there is no minimum percent for defendants (pure comparative negligence)

THE CASE OF THE UN-EASY RIDER

Negligence is contagious. Those around a careless person sometimes find themselves infected by carefree, irresponsible attitudes. As a result, it is occasionally difficult to determine the degree to which each party is at fault.

The old contributory negligence defense made no effort to apportion fault. It simply and arbitrarily torpedoed the plaintiff's action if he or she were the least bit at fault for his or her injuries. Comparative negligence attempts to resolve this unfairness. The following case discusses last clear chance and contributory and comparative negligence.

PENN HARRIS MADISON SCHOOL CORPORATION, Appellant (Defendant below),
v.
Linda HOWARD, Individually and as Next Best Friend of David Howard, A Minor, Appellees (Plaintiffs below).

Supreme Court of Indiana
March 1, 2007

Two decades ago, the Legislature abolished the harsh doctrine of "contributory negligence" by which a man or a woman, injured through the fault of another, was denied any recovery if he or she was even slightly at fault. However, the defense of contributory negligence remains available to government entities like public schools.

David Howard attended Penn High School in the Penn Harris Madison School Corporation ("PHM"). Throughout high school, Howard helped his friend, Jon West, produce theatrical plays and build sets for those plays. West was a music teacher in a PHM elementary school.

During his senior year, Howard, age 17, helped West produce "Peter Pan" at the elementary school. Howard, who had experience rock climbing and rappelling, devised and constructed a pulley mechanism designed to allow the Peter Pan character to "fly" above the audience. Howard himself tested the apparatus several times.

On the night of dress rehearsal, Howard climbed a ladder that West was holding and connected himself to the webbing through a loop on the back of the harness. Howard jumped from the ladder. The apparatus failed and Howard fell to the gym floor, suffering serious injuries to his face, spleen, hands, and wrists.

Howard's mother, individually and as his next friend, sued PHM, alleging its negligence caused Howard's injuries. During the trial on their claims, the plaintiffs requested [that] the trial court give the jury certain instructions. The jury returned a verdict for the plaintiffs and awarded them $200,000 in damages.

At the plaintiffs' request, the trial court instructed the jury that in deciding whether Howard was guilty of contributory negligence, it must determine whether he had exercised the "reasonable care [that] a person of like age, intelligence, and experience would ordinarily exercise under like or similar circumstances."

The Court of Appeals properly determined that the instruction given by the trial court was not a correct statement of Indiana law. Children over the age of 14, absent special circumstances, are chargeable with exercising the standard of care of an adult.

The standard of care we impose on individuals over the age of 14 is a neutral principle of law, operating irrespective of whether the child is plaintiff (as here), defendant (e.g., a 14-year-old or 16-year-old driver), or even a non-party.

Even when a jury is given an incorrect instruction on the law, we will not reverse the judgment unless the party seeking a new trial shows "a reasonable probability that substantial rights of the complaining party have been adversely affected."

We are unable to find that PHM has made such a showing here. The offending instruction asked the jury to determine whether Howard exercised the "reasonable care [that] a person of like age, intelligence, and experience would ordinarily exercise under like or similar circumstances." We find the error in giving the instruction here to have been harmless.

At the plaintiffs' request, the trial court instructed the jury that it could find in favor of Howard, notwithstanding contributory negligence on his part,

if the plaintiffs established entitlement to recovery under the "last clear chance" doctrine.

The doctrine of last clear chance, as a general proposition, provides that the contributory negligence of a plaintiff does not prevent recovery by that plaintiff for the negligence and injuries caused by the defendant if the defendant by exercising reasonable care might have avoided injuring the plaintiff.

The Court of Appeals faithfully applied the last clear chance doctrine in this case. It properly noted that Howard had the burden of proving, among other elements, that the defendant "had the last opportunity through the exercise of reasonable care to avoid the injury." It quoted controlling authority that "the defendant... must have the last clear chance to avoid the injury to the plaintiff."

We agree with the Court of Appeals that there was no evidence that PHM had the last opportunity to "avert" or prevent Howard's fall.

[T]he undisputed evidence shows that Howard climbed the ladder of his own accord and attempted to hook himself to the pulley before he fell. While West was holding the ladder steady for Howard, there is no evidence that West or any other [PHM] employee assisted Howard in getting himself attached to the pulley. While no one knows for certain what mechanism failed and caused Howard's fall, the evidence clearly shows that Howard had the latest opportunity to avoid it. He had a choice whether to descend from the ladder or to attempt the stunt.

The instruction on last clear chance given by the trial court in this case was an accurate statement of law.

We affirm the judgment of the trial court.

CASE QUESTIONS

1. Which do you consider the more just doctrines: (a) contributory negligence and last clear chance, or (b) comparative negligence? Do you agree with this court's opinion? Explain.
2. Has your state adopted a statute similar to the Pennsylvania statute discussed here?

hypothetical

Ikeda Osaka manages and owns a hotel. Frances Borgioni is a guest. The smoke detector in Frances's room has a dead battery and does not function. None of Ikeda's employees has checked the detector recently, despite a management protocol instructing maintenance to check batteries every month. The customer staying in the room next to Frances's smoked in bed and started a fire. Smoke poured under the door adjoining the two rooms, but the malfunctioning detector did not awaken Frances before the room became filled with smoke. Frances awoke, coughing, and stumbled to the hallway door. He could not get the door open, however, because he had placed his own safety lock on the door, and that lock jammed as he was trying to escape. Frances passed out from smoke inhalation and suffered severe burns. Fortunately, the fire department rescued him.

Frances sued Ikeda for negligently failing to maintain an operative smoke detector in the room. Ikeda responded that Frances had contributed to his own injuries by placing his own lock on the door, so that he could not escape. May Ikeda invoke the defense of comparative negligence?

Was Ikeda negligent in failing to maintain a functioning smoke detector in Frances's room? Analyze the facts and apply the elements of negligence. If one decides that Ikeda was negligent (which is arguably the correct answer), then the comparative negligence defense should next be considered. Apply its elements. Was Frances negligent in contributing to his own injuries? Frances breached his duty of reasonable care to himself by placing a defective lock on the door, which prevented his escape during the fire. But for this act, Frances could have escaped before passing out from the smoke. Frances was negligent in harming himself. Next, decide if Ikeda's negligence exceeded Frances's. Would Frances have been endangered by the smoke at all if the smoke detector had activated? This would have given Frances more time to escape the room before the smoke thickened and knocked him unconscious. Ikeda's negligence exceeded Frances's. Now use liability apportionment. What percentages would be assigned? Ikeda's must be at least 51 percent. 60/40? 70/30? 80/20? There is no single correct answer here. A juror must use his or her best judgment based upon the facts.

▌ ASSUMPTION OF RISK

assumption of risk |
Knowingly and willingly exposing yourself (or your property) to the possibility of harm.

Assumption of risk is another defense to negligence. **Assumption of risk** means that the plaintiff assumed the risk of doing (or not doing) something that resulted in his or her injuries. Assumption of risk involves (1) the plaintiff's voluntary assumption of a known risk (2) with a full appreciation of the dangers involved in facing that risk. It is important to note that not all risks are assumed; just those that are reasonable.

Voluntary Assumption of Known Risk

For the assumption-of-risk defense to insulate the defendant from negligence liability, the plaintiff must have voluntarily decided to engage in an activity that the plaintiff knew (or reasonably should have known) was dangerous. In other words, the plaintiff must willfully face a known risk.

For instance, suppose Gilda's employer orders her to carry stacked boxes down a long flight of stairs. Her employer specifically instructs her to carry all the boxes in a single trip. To do this, however, Gilda must hold the boxes in front of her, blocking her forward vision. She knows that it is dangerous to descend stairs when she cannot see where she is going. Gilda slips and falls because her right foot misses a step. She sues her employer for negligence. The employer alleges that Gilda assumed the risk. Did she? No. Gilda did not voluntarily assume the dangerous activity. In fact, she was coerced into carrying all the boxes in one trip. She would not have done so but for her employer's command. Thus, Gilda did not voluntarily assume the risk of falling down the stairway.

Suppose that Brian slipped on some liquid somebody had spilled on the stairway. Brian thought the stairs were clean and dry, because he had walked up them just a few minutes earlier. He was unaware of the new danger that had appeared to threaten his safety. Brian did not assume a known risk.

Suppose that Gilda was carrying the boxes into a storeroom instead of down a stairway. The room was pitch black, and she knew that the ceiling lightbulb was burned out. Nevertheless, she carried the boxes into the room in which she could not clearly see. Gilda stumbled over a mop and broom on the floor, and the boxes fell upon and injured her. Again, she sues her employer for negligence in failing to replace the burned-out bulb. Her employer replies that Gilda voluntarily assumed a known risk—she knew the bulb was burned out. Further, she knew that the room was so dark that it would take her eyes several minutes to adjust. Still, she entered the room despite the obvious danger that she could fall over invisible objects. Gilda assumed the risk in this version of the facts.

What if Jonathan decides to go bungee jumping off the local bridge that spans a river? Lots of people go there for bungee jumping because the bridge is the perfect height and the river is so scenic. Jonathan uses a harness and follows all precautions from the company providing the equipment and instructions for the rides. Instead of jumping forward toward the river, Jonathan gets nervous and jumps swinging toward the bridge, hitting his head and sustaining a concussion. Has Jonathan assumed the risk, or can he bring an action against the company providing the bungee rides? Jonathan knew or should have known that bungee jumping is extremely dangerous. He assumed the risk of injury in this instance.

Full Appreciation of Danger

The plaintiff must fully understand the dangerous nature of the activity that he or she voluntarily undertakes. Suppose that Brett visits a friend's woods. He comes across a cavern and decides to explore it. He has no way of knowing that higher above him, on a nearby hill, a highway construction crew is preparing to detonate dynamite. They explode a powerful charge, which sends a shock wave through the ground and causes part of the cavern walls to collapse, trapping Brett inside the cave. He sues the highway company for negligence in detonating excessively powerful explosives. Run through the negligence formula to determine if the company was negligent toward Brett, closely examining foreseeability of the injury and foreseeable plaintiffs theory. Presuming that the company acted negligently, it responds with the defense of assumption of risk.

Did Brett voluntarily assume a known risk with a full appreciation of the dangers involved? He willfully entered the cave. He knew (or reasonably should have known) that cavern walls sometimes fall in. That risk was known, but he had no way to anticipate the additional danger created by a forceful explosion. He did not fully appreciate this aspect of the risk in entering the cave. Arguably, the dynamite was also an unknown risk to him. Thus, the company's defense would fail.

Proof of Assumption of Risk

There are two categories of assumption of risk. In *express assumption-of-risk* cases, a plaintiff voluntarily assumes a known risk by an express agreement. An example of this would be a plaintiff being given an agreement with a release clause to sign, thus acknowledging a particular danger associated with an activity and agreeing not to hold the other party liable; for example, a boxing match. This express assumption is valid so long as it does not violate **public policy,** such as a situation in which there is unequal bargaining power between the parties, and one of the parties is forced to waive his or her rights.

public policy | The law should be applied in a way that promotes the good and welfare of the people.

In *implied assumption of risk*, a plaintiff accepts a risk knowingly and voluntarily by reason of the plaintiff's knowledge. In implied assumption, while there is no express agreement, the assumption is implied based upon a party's conduct; for example, a plaintiff entering a barricaded structure despite seeing a large no-entry sign at the entrance. Just as with express assumption cases, the implied assumption cannot violate public policy, such as where a contractor fails to take adequate measures to protect the public and installs a defective barricade.

The Complete Defense

Assumption of risk is a complete defense to negligence in some jurisdictions. Like common-law contributory negligence, it totally bars the plaintiff's recovery. If the plaintiff assumed the risk, the defendant cannot be liable for negligence.

Assumption of the risk is commonly raised in spectator sport situations. There is a known risk that if you attend a baseball game, you might get hit by a ball hit into the stands. Likewise, observers of speed car races or demolition derbies might get hit by a car or piece of equipment hurled into the air. A spectator assumes these risks with full appreciation of the dangers and thus is barred from bringing suit as a result of any injuries sustained. Conversely, consider a situation in which bleachers collapse at a football stadium. Seats caving in is not a known or foreseeable risk, nor could the dangers be appreciated; thus, in this case assumption of the risk would not apply and suit would be allowed.

Assumption of risk is somewhat more difficult to establish than contributory or comparative negligence. The following example demonstrates how the elements must be carefully considered.

THE CASE OF THE FITNESS RELEASE

A woman joins a fitness club and signs a release at the same time as signing her membership agreement, releasing the club from liability for injuries. The woman tries to bring an action against the club, arguing as to the scope of the release.

Miriam PARDO et al., Plaintiffs and Appellants,
v.
L.A. FITNESS et al., Defendants and Respondents.

No. B182968.
Court of Appeal, Second District,
Division 7, California
(Los Angeles County Super.
Ct. No. LC068062)
May 9, 2007

Miriam Pardo signed a membership agreement with L.A. Fitness in February 2001 in which she expressly assumed all risks associated with use of L.A. Fitness's facilities and released L.A. Fitness from liability for injuries she might sustain while using any facility "for any purpose." Pardo regularly used the L.A. Fitness facility in Woodland Hills until she was injured in an automobile accident in May 2002. After her injury Pardo began receiving chiropractic treatment from Dr. Brian L. Campbell at Trillium, which had subleased from L.A. Fitness approximately 1,900 square feet on the second floor of the Woodland Hills facility.

The sublease provided that Trillium's patients could use L.A. Fitness's facilities "upon presentation to the front desk of a club-approved admission pass signed by Tenant" for a fee of $10 per patient.

According to Pardo, following her automobile accident she had stopped using L.A. Fitness's equipment except to "warm up" prior to her chiropractic treatments as directed by Dr. Campbell. On October 23, 2002, Pardo's last scheduled day of treatment, she tripped on a power strip lying between two exercise bicycles adjacent to the bicycle she had intended to use.

Pardo and her husband filed a complaint for premises liability and loss of consortium against L.A. Fitness on March 22, 2004. On August 10, 2004 the Pardos amended their complaint to name the Trillium defendants.

On March 14, 2005 the trial court granted L.A. Fitness's motion for summary judgment.

The liability of property owners for injuries sustained by individuals on their premises is generally governed by ordinary negligence principles, as set forth in Civil Code section 1714, subdivision (a). The

(continues)

controlling question is whether the property owner has acted as a reasonable person in the management of his or her property in view of the probability of injury to others. Recovery may be barred, however, if the plaintiff has signed an express contractual assumption of risk or release of liability before becoming injured. "[S]uch an agreement operates to relieve the defendant of a legal duty to the plaintiff with respect to the risks encompassed by the agreement and, where applicable, to bar completely the plaintiff's cause of action."

"It is obvious that patrons of health clubs sign release and assumption of risk provisions in contemplation of injuries that occur in the course of using the facilities for the primary purpose of exercising and using exercise equipment."

Pardo does not contest the general validity or broad scope of the release as it pertains to her as a member of L.A. Fitness. Rather, she argues the release applies only to her use of the equipment as a member of L.A. Fitness, not as a patient of Trillium, and contends there are triable issues of material fact relating to that issue.

The dispositive issue before this court is whether the release applies. . . .

"To be effective, a written release purporting to exculpate a tortfeasor from future negligence or misconduct must be clear, unambiguous, and explicit in expressing the intent of the subscribing parties."

The release Pardo signed is clear and unambiguous on its face. In consideration for the right "to enter any facility of L.A. Fitness . . . for any purpose including, but not limited to, observation, use of facilities, services or equipment, or participation in any way," Pardo released L.A. Fitness from liability for damages due to injuries arising from Pardo's use of the exercise equipment, which was precisely the cause of the injuries she sustained.

Pardo's contention [that] the release is ambiguous because it failed to indicate whether non-member patients of Trillium would also be required to release L.A. Fitness from any liability for injuries when using the facility lacks any merit.

Pardo asserts it was her understanding [that] the release would only be effective when she entered L.A. Fitness as a member, not as a Trillium patient. Pardos subjective intent and understanding, however, is not competent extrinsic evidence relevant to determining the meaning of the membership agreement.

Pardo contends there are triable issues of material fact concerning Trillium's exercise of control over the L.A. Fitness premises. "[T]he concept of control as developed in case law has been somewhat elastic. . . ."

There is no precise formula prescribing whether the presence of one factor or a combination of factors is determinative on the issue of control. For example, merely maintaining a portion of land belonging to a neighbor may not be sufficient to constitute an exercise of control.

Pardo does not present any competent evidence disputing that L.A. Fitness maintained its own premises; Trillium, its sublessee, did not have the right to manage or maintain the premises; Trillium was not responsible for placing the equipment at L.A. Fitness, including the power strip Pardo tripped over; and Trillium did not maintain any of the exercise equipment.

Indeed, Pardo did not submit any evidence of affirmative conduct by Trillium that is consistent with ownership of premises. Simply directing its patients to use the equipment at L.A. Fitness and its patients' ability to bypass L.A. Fitness's front desk is not, as Pardo suggests, the kind of affirmative action required to show that Trillium was treating the property as its own.

Given the lack of evidence of affirmative action by Trillium or evidence Trillium had knowledge of any dangerous condition at L.A. Fitness, Pardo has failed to demonstrate there is a triable issue of material fact Trillium exercised control over L.A. Fitness; thus, the trial court properly granted summary judgment in favor of Trillium.

CASE QUESTIONS

1. Why is the injured plaintiff arguing that the release she signed shouldn't apply to Trillium?
2. What effect does signing a release have on assumption of the risk?

hypothetical

Julie owns East of Tansmania, a tanning salon. Elizabeth is one of Julie's customers. She has been visiting the salon twice a week for ten years. She always uses the same tanning bed. Because of faulty equipment, Elizabeth was exposed during each session to five times more ultraviolet radiation than is normally emitted by tanning equipment. Elizabeth was diagnosed with skin cancer. She sues Julie for subjecting her to excessively intense ultraviolet light, which is a powerful carcinogen. Julie was negligent in exposing Elizabeth to such extremely high doses of ultraviolet radiation. Can she offer assumption of risk as a defense?

Did Elizabeth voluntarily assume a known risk with a full appreciation of the dangerous consequences? Clearly, she willfully visited the salon twice weekly for ten years. She chose to use the same bed each time. She knew (or reasonably should have known) that ultraviolet radiation is carcinogenic. But did she fully understand the danger? Did she realize that the equipment emitted five times more radiation than normal? Could she have known about this aspect of the threat? Not likely. Accordingly, she did not assume the risk, and the defense would not protect Julie from liability.

Suppose a warning were posted above the tanning bed that Elizabeth used, declaring, "DANGER! EMITS EXCESSIVE ULTRAVIOLET LIGHT. USE AT YOUR OWN RISK." Now Elizabeth would have been alerted to the threatening condition. She would have a full appreciation of the dangers involved in using the equipment. Under this version of the facts, Elizabeth would have assumed the risk, and Julie would not be liable for negligence.

Table 4-4 outlines the elements of assumption of risk.

ELEMENTS OF ASSUMPTION OF RISK
Plaintiff voluntarily assumes a known risk
Plaintiff fully appreciates the dangers involved in facing the risk

TABLE 4-4
Assumption of risk

▌ STATUTES OF LIMITATIONS

Statutes of limitations are statutes restricting the time within which a plaintiff may file a lawsuit for particular causes of action against a defendant. (In some jurisdictions, these statutes are called *limitations of actions*.) There are also such statutes for negligence actions. Many of these statutes specify that various negligence lawsuits must be filed within two years of the negligent acts giving rise to the plaintiff's claims.

States' statutes of limitations vary in numbers of years and among the different types of negligence. The period for medical malpractice claims, for instance, may be two years in one state and three years in another. Similarly,

statutes of limitations | Laws that set a maximum amount of time after something happens for it to be taken to court, such as a "three-year statute" for lawsuits based on a contract, or a "six-year statute" for a criminal prosecution.

lawsuits involving premises liability may have one-year statutes of limitations in one state and three-year statutes in another. One should become familiar with the specific statutes of limitations in one's own state for the various types of negligence causes of action.

Note that the statute of limitations is one of the few areas in the practice of law for which there is no remedy if one misses the deadline. Generally, there are provisions throughout the various civil practice acts that allow attorneys to amend, change, and supplement pleadings, and to remedy oversights in their handling of a case. Should a statute of limitations run out, though—no matter what the reason—judges are powerless to help you. Consequently, this is one of the areas in the practice of law in which malpractice claims most frequently arise.

practical **application**

To obtain malpractice insurance, attorneys must assure the malpractice insurance carrier that they have a reliable calendaring system. In fact, backup systems for recording important dates and deadlines are often required as well. Frequently, a paralegal is called upon to maintain a diary system and keep members of the firm alerted to approaching deadlines and dates. In addition, some firms automatically have all files pulled for review every three months, six months, and yearly to ensure that the cases are not being neglected.

THE CASE OF CONTINUOUS REPRESENTATION

The outcome of this lawsuit rests on the calculation of the applicable statute of limitations. In this case, the running of the statute of limitations for malpractice was found to be tolled or stopped, giving the plaintiff additional time in which to bring his action. Notice the ten-year lapse between the time the plaintiff initially sought legal counsel for his injuries and the time of this appeal.

POLLICINO
v.
ROEMER AND FEATHERSTONHAUGH P.C.
Supreme Court, Appellate Division, Third Department, New York
260 A.D.2d 52, 699 N.Y.S.2d 238
December 2, 1999

This appeal requires us to decide a question of first impression, namely, whether in a legal malpractice action a law firm's continuous representation of a client should be imputed to a former associate for purposes of tolling the Statute of Limitations against the associate. On the particular facts presented herein, we hold that it should be and reverse the contrary determination of Supreme Court.

On April 11, 1989, plaintiff retained the law firm of defendant Roemer and Featherstonhaugh P.C. (hereinafter the law firm) to represent him in connection with a July 1, 1988 accident wherein he lost sight in his right eye. His injury is alleged to have occurred when a New York City Transit

Authority bus ran over a glass bottle, the bottle exploded and a shard of glass struck plaintiff in the eye. In September 1989, the law firm moved for leave to serve a late notice of claim against the Transit Authority. Attached to its moving papers was a proposed notice of claim reflecting the accident date of July 1, 1988. After the motion was granted, however, a notice of claim incorrectly listing the accident date as June 30, 1988 was served. . . .

It was not until December 1, 1992 that the law firm moved on behalf of plaintiff for leave to serve an amended notice of claim to set forth the correct date of plaintiff's accident. . . .

While a cause of action for legal malpractice accrues on the date on which the claimed malpractice occurred, under the rule of continuous representation the Statute of Limitations is tolled while representation on the same matter in which the malpractice is alleged is ongoing. A twofold rationale underlies this rule, which is derived from the "continuous treatment" doctrine earlier crafted in medical malpractice actions. First, having sought professional assistance, the client 'has a right to repose confidence in the professional's ability and good faith, and realistically cannot be expected to question and assess the techniques employed or the manner in which the services are rendered' . . .

* * *

Here, it is uncontroverted that without application of the continuous representation rule, plaintiff's suit against defendant is time barred. The gravamen of plaintiff's malpractice claim is the erroneous accident date listed on the notice of claim, which led to dismissal of plaintiff's suit against the Transit Authority in 1994. His cause of action thus accrued when defendant allegedly committed the original error in November 1989 (or when he failed to correct it when a similar error in the summons and complaint was discovered and corrected in December 1989). Supreme Court held that since defendant's professional relationship with plaintiff ended when he left the law firm in September 1990, the rule of continuous representation did not apply. . . . Supreme Court's decision, however, failed to squarely address

the question presented: whether the law firm's continuous representation of plaintiff should be imputed to defendant so as to toll the Statute of Limitations against him.

We conclude that under the circumstances of this case, the principles underpinning the continuous representation rule militate in favor of its application to defendant. As a starting point, we observe that without application of this rule, the Statute of Limitations against defendant would have expired *before* plaintiff's action against the Transit Authority was dismissed based on the faulty notice of claim. We also note that beginning in December 1992 and continuing through May 1997, the law firm undertook efforts to rectify the 1989 error which, if successful, would have rendered plaintiff's malpractice claim moot.

Critical to our resolution of the question, however, is the fact that in retaining the law firm to represent him, plaintiff forged his professional relationship with the firm, not with any individual attorney. Defendant, as well as several other associates, worked on plaintiff's case as employees or agents of the law firm, whose representation of plaintiff was continuous and uninterrupted until May 1997. . . . Given the law firm's legal responsibility for the actions of defendant, its employee, commencing an action against defendant would have required plaintiff to sever his relationship with the law firm. Prevention of such a disruption in the professional relationship, together with any ongoing efforts, is a paramount value underlying the doctrine of continuous representation.

* * *

. . . "The Statute of Limitations was enacted to afford protection to defendants against defending stale claims after a reasonable period of time had elapsed during which a person of ordinary diligence would bring an action." Largely based on the same principles informing the continuous representation rule and rendering its application appropriate here, we do not believe it can be fairly said that plaintiff lacked diligence or failed to bring his action within a reasonable period of time.

(continues)

CASE QUESTIONS

1. Explain why the statute of limitations was tolled and what effect this had on the case.
2. How can you explain the ten-year passage of time between when legal counsel was originally retained and this appeal?
3. What lesson concerning the drafting of pleadings can a paralegal learn from this case?

Table 4-5 shows two typical statutes of limitations for negligence actions. Table 4-6 shows sample statutes of limitations for negligence by state.

TABLE 4-5
Sample negligence statutes of limitations

TWO-YEAR STATUTE OF LIMITATIONS	THREE-YEAR STATUTE OF LIMITATIONS
16.003. Texas Two-Year Limitations Period: (a) Except as provided by Sections 16.010 and 16.0045, a person must bring suit for trespass for injury to the estate or to the property of another, conversion of personal property, taking or detaining the personal property of another, personal injury, forcible entry and detainer, and forcible detainer not later than two years after the day the cause of action accrues. (b) A person must bring suit not later than two years after the day the cause of action accrues in an action for injury resulting in death. The cause of action accrues on the death of the injured person.	New York Civil Practice Law & Rules § 214 (McKinney): The following actions must be commenced within three years: * * * 5. an action to recover damages for a personal injury except as provided in sections 214-b, 214-c and 215; . . . [providing special rules concerning specific torts and time injury was detected].

TABLE 4-6
Sample statutes of limitations for negligence actions by state

STATE	NEGLIGENCE	MEDICAL MALPRACTICE
Alabama	2 years	2 years
California	2 years	3 years
Florida	4 years	2 years
Massachusetts	3 years	3 years
New York	3 years	2½ years
Texas	2 years	2 years
Washington	3 years	3 years
Wyoming	4 years	2 years

▌ SUMMARY

Negligence defenses are used only by the defendant against the plaintiff. The defenses are applied only in response to the plaintiff's allegations that the defendant acted negligently. To determine which party uses negligence defenses, one should ask who is alleging negligence and who is alleged to have been negligent.

Contributory negligence is the plaintiff's negligence that contributed to his or her own injuries. The plaintiff was negligent toward himself or herself and caused (in whole or in part) the harm. This defense exonerates the defendant whose negligence harmed the plaintiff. At common law, any amount of contributory negligence by the plaintiff, however small, would bar the plaintiff's recovery against the negligent defendant. Critics have argued that this defense is unreasonably harsh. Last clear chance is the plaintiff's response to the contributory negligence defense. Last clear chance means that, although the plaintiff was contributorily negligent, the defendant still had the last opportunity to avoid harming the plaintiff. Last clear chance nullifies the contributory negligence defense.

Comparative negligence is an alternative defense that has largely replaced contributory negligence in both the common law and statute. Comparative negligence measures and compares the negligence of both the plaintiff and the defendant. This allows the trier-of-fact to adjust the plaintiff's recovery to reflect more accurately each party's degree of negligence in causing the harm. The calculation is often in percentages of negligence. This is sometimes called culpability factoring or liability apportionment. These percentages are based entirely upon the trier-of-fact's subjective opinion regarding the specific facts of each case. Critics have criticized the defense for this uncertainty.

Assumption of risk is another negligence defense. It states that the plaintiff voluntarily assumed a known risk with full appreciation of the dangers involved. Like contributory negligence, assumption of risk is a complete defense to negligence. In other words, it totally excuses the defendant's negligence and erases the defendant's liability to the plaintiff.

Most state statutes of limitations restrict the time period within which a plaintiff may file a negligence cause of action against a defendant. In most states, these are two-year statutes, meaning that a plaintiff has two years from the date that the negligent act was committed within which to file a lawsuit against the tortfeasor. It is vital to research the specific statutes of limitations for each particular tort.

▌ KEY TERMS

assumption of risk
comparative negligence
contributory negligence

culpability factoring (liability apportionment)
last clear chance doctrine

public policy
statutes of limitations

▌ PROBLEMS

In the following hypotheticals, determine which negligence defense applies, if any.

1. The Tàpàjós Inn, owned by Guillermo Estaben, has a swimming pool with no lifeguards on duty. The pool is surrounded by a high-wire fence, and access to the pool is restricted to guests, who must use their room keys to reach the facility. Signs posted in several places on the fencing read, in bold, black lettering: "NO LIFEGUARD ON DUTY. SWIM AT YOUR OWN RISK! NO DIVING, RUNNING, OR

HORSE PLAY. ADULTS MUST SUPERVISE CHILDREN. BE CAREFUL!" Tony Harmon, a 16-year-old, and his family are staying at the Inn. Tony and his 17-year-old girlfriend, Tanya, went swimming in the pool after midnight. There were no signs indicating times when the pool was opened or closed. At 1:45 a.m., hotel maintenance activated the automatic pumps to drain the pool for cleaning. None of the Inn staff checked to see if the pool was being used. While swimming underwater, Tanya got her left foot caught in a pool drain as a result of the powerful suction of the pumps. She would have drowned had Tony not rescued her. She suffered torn tendons in her foot and ankle, and she developed an extreme phobia of water. She experienced nightmares and acute nervousness after the incident. There were no signs indicating that the pool could be drained remotely nor that the drains were dangerous when the pumps were running.

2. Farabee St. Claire owns an ice-skating rink. Charles and Kelly visited the rink on their tenth wedding anniversary. Charles had not skated since high school (fifteen years earlier), but Kelly often went skating at the rink. Because of a broken thermostat, one corner of the ice thawed and a small puddle formed. As Charles skated through the water, he slipped and fell to the ice, breaking his right arm. Kelly, who was skating close behind, collided with Charles and also fell to the ice, suffering a concussion. Kelly was a talented skater and could have avoided Charles by leaping over his body, but she did not think to do so in her surprise and confusion.

3. The Happy Hollow Mental Hospital houses many emotionally disturbed individuals. One patient, Jasmine, a convicted arsonist, escaped from her maximum-security room. No guards were on duty in that part of the hospital, and an attendant had left Jasmine's door unlocked. As Jasmine wandered out of a wooded area onto a highway, she hitchhiked a ride from Kate, who was driving back to the university at which she worked. Kate noticed that Jasmine was dressed in a hospital gown and blue jeans, but Jasmine explained that she was a medical student at the university and often wore these gowns because they were comfortable. Kate dropped Jasmine off at a bus stop located only a few hundred yards from Kate's home. Jasmine saw Kate stop at the house and then drive away again. Later that day, Kate's house burned down. Police arrested Jasmine for having set the fire.

4. Beth is an accountant. Ruben is one of her clients. Beth completed Ruben's federal and state tax returns for 2009. Beth made a critical addition error, however, and as a result, Ruben underpaid his taxes. Both the Internal Revenue Service and the State Department of Revenue assessed hefty penalties against Ruben for the underpayment. Ruben had signed the returns without reading them, although the instructions on each return clearly advised the taxpayer to read carefully through the returns to verify their accuracy, even if a professional tax preparer had been used.

5. Beau owns a sporting-goods store. Matt came in to buy a new shotgun. One of Beau's employees, Saul, handed Matt a shotgun that, unbeknownst to Saul or Matt, was loaded. Neither Saul nor Matt checked the gun to see if it was loaded. The trigger, however, had a keyed lock that prevented it from being pulled. Matt asked that the lock be removed so that he could feel the trigger's sensitivity. Saul opened the lock and Matt tested the trigger. The gun discharged, shooting another customer, Clay, in the stomach. Clay saw Matt aim the gun in his general direction. Instead of stepping aside, Clay jokingly shouted, "Hey, don't shoot me, I'm on your side!"

▌REVIEW QUESTIONS

1. How are negligence defenses used? Which party uses them? Against whom are the defenses used? What is the purpose of negligence defenses?

2. Define *contributory negligence*. What are its elements? What is the common-law rule? Why was contributory negligence a particularly effective defense? How would it arise today?

3. Explain last clear chance. How is it used? Who uses it against whom? What is its importance to contributory negligence?

4. Why is the contributory negligence defense unfair? What changes have courts and legislatures made to create a more equitable defense? What is this defense called?

5. Define *comparative negligence*. What are its elements? What is culpability factoring? Liability apportionment? Why are percentages used? Who decides these percentages? Is this defense more fair than contributory negligence? Why or why not?

6. What is assumption of risk? List its elements. Who uses the defense against whom? Must the risk be voluntarily assumed? What is "full appreciation of danger" and why is it significant? How effective is this defense in avoiding the defendant's liability? What level of risk does a person assume?

7. What are statutes of limitations? What time period is most commonly allowed for negligence causes of action? How can limitations statutes be used as a defense to negligence?

▌HELPFUL WEBSITES

This chapter focuses on defenses to negligence actions. To learn more about defenses to negligence actions, the following sites can be accessed:

General Information

http://www.uscourts.gov

http://www.courts.net

http://www.firstgov.gov

http://www.findlaw.com

STUDENT CD-ROM™
For additional materials, please go to the CD in this book.

ONLINE COMPANION™
For additional resources, please go to
http://www.paralegal.delmar.cengage.com

chapter 5

Intentional Torts:

Injuries to Persons

THE BIGGEST MISTAKES PARALEGALS MAKE *&* HOW TO AVOID THEM

How Do I Handle This Bozo?

As a paralegal at a big personal injury firm, I especially enjoyed the easygoing atmosphere that afforded good working conditions between attorneys and the staff. I was well-liked and I liked everyone in return. The only problem I had involved another firm that gave us referrals because they did not handle accident cases. The managing attorney of that firm, who was friendly with several partners at my firm, was always asking for favors like free tickets to plays and sporting events. It seemed that I was

designated the "go-to" girl for all his requests, and they became very frequent. One day he e-mailed me with an urgent request to get 4 tickets to a rock concert for his teenagers that night! As I tried to forward the request to my boss (with my added message "How do I handle this Bozo?"), I hit the "reply to all" prompt on the e-mail. The reaction from the managing attorney was fast and furious. He even demanded that I be fired. My firm went

(continues)

into damage control and I could sense my worth shrinking. Although I didn't lose my job, I could have no further contact with the other firm in any capacity—which made my job much harder because they handled cases for us as well.

LESSON LEARNED: There is never any excuse for name-calling of another professional, especially in writing! No matter how popular you are, that will not save you from a negative performance review (or worse) by jeopardizing the firm's integrity and revenue stream.

▌ INTRODUCTION

Generally, a person has a right to be free of threats and actual contact that injures or offends him or her. Therefore, one has a duty not to intentionally injure, offensively touch, or threaten other people. A person also has a right to be free of conduct that harms his or her property. Likewise, one has a duty not to intentionally harm the property of others. Intentional torts can be against both persons and property.

This chapter discusses:

- ▶ Intentional torts in general
- ▶ Assault and battery
- ▶ Patient dumping
- ▶ False imprisonment
- ▶ Sexual harassment
- ▶ Spoliation of evidence

▌ INTENTIONAL TORTS IN GENERAL

Intentional torts consist of conduct that is fashioned to harm another person or his or her property. The mischief is directed with the purpose of inflicting injury. All intentional torts include three elements: act, intent, and injurious behavior. **Intent** can be broadly defined as the desire to achieve a particular result. Specifically, the tortfeasor must intend to accomplish the harmful consequences of his or her actions. This does not require malice or ill will; the tortfeasor simply must intend to cause the consequences that give rise to the tort or the tortfeasor must know with substantial certainty that certain consequences would result from that act. Commonly, though, those consequences include some type of harm. These acts also must actually conclude in the injury that was intended.

For certain peculiar intentional torts, intent, strictly speaking, is not required. For example, for reckless infliction of emotional distress, intent is not essential. The tortfeasor need only know (or reasonably should know) that his or

intentional tort | An injury *designed* to injure a person or that person's property, as opposed to an injury caused by negligence or resulting from an accident.

intent | The resolve or purpose to use a particular means to reach a particular result. *Intent* usually explains *how* a person wants to do something and *what* that person wants to get done.

her outlandish or outrageous actions will produce emotional injury. This knowledge element acts as a substitute for intent.

Intentional torts involve intentional acts, and as such carry a high degree of risk of injury, and usually a low degree of social benefit. The risk generally greatly outweighs the benefit received. Therefore, the duty not to intentionally injure someone or something is great.

Intent and Action Together

Intent reflects the tortfeasor's state of mind and must occur simultaneously with the misconduct. For example, assume that David and Steven are carpenters. Steven tosses a piece of wood across a room into a pile, but before it lands the wood strikes David in the throat. Steven would not be liable for battery because, although the board struck David, Steven did not intend this to happen. Suppose David thought about throwing the board back at Steven, but did nothing and walked away. David would not be liable for assault because no action accompanied his desire.

Intentional torts present a relatively black-and-white image of the law, in which it is fairly easy to distinguish the "good" person from the "bad." The victim seems truly exploited, and the tortfeasor is clearly responsible and to blame (from a moral or ethical point of view) for having purposefully injured the victim. Our sense of fair play is rewarded when intentional tortfeasors are held accountable for their mischief.

Crimes versus Torts

It is important to note that a single act can be the basis for both a tort and a criminal action. Both crimes and torts involve wrongs. A *crime* is considered a wrong against the state or society as a whole, in addition to the actual victim. Therefore, the state brings actions against alleged criminals. With tort actions, one person brings suit against another individual; the action is brought by a private attorney on behalf of the injured party. Thus, a tort is considered a civil action.

Suppose that a person is walking down the street at night. Another person comes up, aims a gun, and then shoots the pedestrian. In this situation both an assault and a battery have occurred. The pedestrian was first put in fear of harm and then actually harmed. As a result of the same act, the attacker may face both criminal and civil prosecution. The state may seek criminal damages against the attacker. In addition, the injured party may proceed with a civil action to be reimbursed for injuries caused as a result of the attack. Table 5-1 compares torts versus crimes. Note that the civil and criminal definitions of acts constituting intentional torts are not necessarily the same.

	Tort	Crime
Goal	Compensation	Punishment and deterrence
Burden of Proof	Preponderance of evidence	Beyond reasonable doubt
Victim Harmed	Individual	Society
Rules of Evidence	Civil rules	Criminal rules

TABLE 5-1
Comparison of torts versus crimes

▌ ASSAULT AND BATTERY

The preceding example of the careless carpenters depicts two of the most common intentional torts: assault and battery. Of all torts, these are perhaps the most straightforward.

Assault Defined

Assault is the intentional threat, show of force, or movement that reasonably makes a person feel in danger of physical attack or harmful physical contact. There are three basic elements to this tort:

1. The tortfeasor attempts to make unconsented harmful or offensive contact
2. The victim is apprehensive for his or her physical safety
3. The threat of contact is imminent.

Actual physical contact is not necessary; in fact, contact converts an assault into a battery. Assault is distinguishable from battery in that no touching is required.

assault | An intentional threat, show of force, or movement that could reasonably make a person feel in danger of physical attack or harmful physical contact.

Imminent Threat of Contact. Assault involves the imminent or immediate threat that unconsented contact is about to occur. The fear arises from the likelihood that someone or something unwanted is about to strike. For instance, Michelle's threat to hit George while talking to him on the telephone does not present an immediate risk, as the task cannot be completed at the time the threat is made. Therefore, no assault has taken place.

Freedom from Apprehension. The rights being protected by recognition of this tort involve each person's right to control what touches his or her person. The tort of assault is also intended to protect individuals from the fear or apprehension that unconsented contact will take place. **Apprehension** means that a person reasonably fears for his or her physical safety in anticipation of being struck by the unconsented harmful or distasteful contact. This apprehension must be *reasonable,* meaning that the anxiety must be rational given the

apprehension | Fear or anxiety.

perceived threat of contact. For example, if a four-year-old warns that she is going to punch her father's head off, her father probably would not be overly concerned, as it would be unreasonable for an adult to fear a child's threatened battery under such circumstances. Threats at a distance do not present sufficient reason for alarm because it is physically impossible for the threatening party to fulfill the threat. This states the next legal requirement for assault: immediate threat of contact.

Examples should illustrate these elements. Although assault is a fairly straightforward tort, its elements can best be explored hypothetically.

THE CASE OF THE UNFRIENDLY NEIGHBORS

A husband and wife find themselves in the unenviable position of having to cross a neighbor's property in order to enter upon a portion of their own land. The testimony of the wife versus that of the alleged offending neighbor, which led up to this claim of assault and battery, is detailed below. Put yourself in the place of a juror. Try and determine whose version of the facts you would believe and whether an "assault and battery" actually occurred.

Jan WRONCY, Plaintiff-Appellant,
v.
Raymond Daniel KLEMP,
Defendant-Respondent.
219 Or. App. 578, 184 P.3d 1133
Court of Appeals of Oregon
Decided May 7, 2008

Plaintiff appeals a judgment for defendant on her claims for assault, battery, and intentional infliction of emotional distress.

Plaintiff and defendant are neighbors in rural Lane County. Horton Lane is a roadway in the country that crosses defendant's property and provides the only access to a portion of plaintiff's husband's property. Plaintiff and defendant have had disputes over plaintiff's right to use the roadway on defendant's property. On the morning of the incident that gave rise to plaintiff's claims against defendant, plaintiff walked up Horton Lane and encountered defendant and several other people who were in or standing near a pickup that was stopped in the roadway on defendant's property.

Defendant testified at trial that plaintiff initiated a confrontation with him by screaming obscenities at him. Plaintiff testified that defendant began the confrontation. According to plaintiff's testimony, she was speaking calmly with defendant's son, Jason, when defendant came around the pickup, got very close to her, and began screaming at her to leave his property. She further testified that, when she did not immediately depart, defendant grabbed the back of her hair, yanking her head backward while pushing her body forward. Plaintiff then sought to testify about an incident in which she had watched defendant run over a neighbor with his pickup truck during an argument over the use of the roadway.

Plaintiff's account of her confrontation with defendant, if believed, could support findings in her favor on her claims against defendant for assault, battery, and intentional infliction of emotional distress. Conversely, defendant's account, if believed, would foreclose findings in plaintiff's favor on her claims. Because the excluded evidence that plaintiff saw defendant run over a neighbor during a property dispute could make it more likely for a jury to believe plaintiff's account of the confrontation, the evidence was relevant. Hence, the court erred in excluding it.

The jury's decision likely turned on whose account of the confrontation between plaintiff and defendant the jury believed. Because the excluded evidence could well have affected the jury's resolution of that issue, we must reverse the judgment for defendant and remand the case for a new trial.

CASE QUESTIONS
1. Who is most credible? Explain.
2. Does the addition of the excluded evidence change your opinion as to credibility? Explain.

hypotheticals

Hong and Davis begin arguing in a bar. Hong balls up his fists and pulls his arm backward as if to swing at Davis. Davis ducks in anticipation of a punch. Has Hong committed assault?

Applying the legal elements of assault, as previously discussed (which are (1) the tortfeasor's attempt to make unconsented harmful or offensive contact, which (2) makes the victim apprehensive for his or her physical safety, and (3) the threat of contact is imminent), it is clear that Hong has assaulted Davis. Hong attempted to touch Davis in a harmful or offensive manner when he drew his arm back to swing. Davis did not consent to this action and feared for his safety, as is obvious because he ducked, expecting to be pelted with Hong's fist. The danger of contact was immediate, as Hong could complete his swing and punch within a matter of seconds.

* * *

Consider another example. Nabeel and Brandon are playing basketball in a gymnasium. Brandon yells that Nabeel stepped out of bounds as he dribbled the ball upcourt. Nabeel smiles and fakes a forceful pass to Brandon's head, causing Brandon to flinch in anticipation that the ball will hit him in the face. Has Nabeel committed assault?

Consent is the key to this hypothetical. Nabeel and Brandon had agreed to play basketball together. It is well known that sports activities such as this involve a certain degree of incidental contact to which participants consent. This could involve being struck by the ball as it is deliberately passed from one player to another. Because Brandon implicitly agreed in advance to such types of contact while playing the game, Nabeel did not assault him.

(continues)

All elements must exist for assault to occur. If any one feature is absent, then there is no assault. For instance, suppose in the first illustration that Davis had not reacted at all to Hong's arm gesture. Perhaps Hong and Davis often indulged in horseplay, such as by pantomiming fistfights, and so Davis assumed that it was just another joking episode. That would remove the apprehension element and thus there would be no assault. Suppose in the second example that Nabeel simply threw the ball down and shouted at Brandon, "Next time you call me a liar, I'll plant this right upside your head!" In that case, the threatened contact would not be imminent, as Nabeel warned only of behavior at some unspecified future time, which might in fact never take place. Accordingly, no assault would have happened.

Battery Defined

battery | An intentional, unconsented-to, physical contact by one person (or an object controlled by that person) with another person.

Strictly defined, a **battery** is the intentional, unconsented touching of another person in an offensive or injurious manner. There are three basic elements to this tort:

1. Nonconsensual physical contact
2. Offensive or harmful contact
3. The tortfeasor's intent to touch another person in an offensive or injurious manner.

Physical Contact Required. Actual touching is necessary for a battery to occur. However, contact need not be made with a person's body. It is sufficient for the tortfeasor to touch the victim's clothing, or an object that the victim is carrying, such as a purse, or an object in which the victim is sitting, such as a chair or automobile. These items are said to become *extensions* of the person which, if touched, translates into touching the person himself or herself.

Lack of Consent. Battery occurs only if the victim did not consent to the physical contact. Consent can be *expressed* or *implied*. Expressed consent is relatively easy to identify. For example, participants in sporting events readily consent to physical contact routinely associated with the activity. Implied consent arises out of particular situations in which individuals, by being involved, implicitly agree to some types of minor contact. For instance, people walking in crowds impliedly consent to incidental contact as they accidentally bump into passersby. It is reasonable and normal to expect that this will occur in crowded places, and those involved are (or should be) willing to tolerate some minor jostles. Consent is a defense to a battery claim.

Harmful or Offensive Contact.

Battery requires touching that is harmful or offensive. Although harmful contact should be relatively simple to perceive, offensive touching may present some surprises. Often, offensive contact may be intended as positive or complimentary, such as a pat on the back or kiss on the cheek from a co-worker. The recipient, however, may find these actions distasteful. This addresses the consent issue. People do not usually consent to touching that repulses them.

Whether or not the physical contact is offensive is judged by a **reasonable person standard.** Would a reasonable person have been insulted by the contact, given the same or similar circumstances? Reasonableness is often based upon the victim's actions in conjunction with the tortfeasor's. For example, if two friends are accustomed to "goofing around" by jokingly touching one another (pats on the back, fake punches, tickling, etc.), then such behavior would not reasonably be offensive. In effect, the participants consented to the activity. In contrast, a male supervisor touching a female employee in a sexually explicit fashion could reasonably be perceived as degrading and offensive.

reasonable person standard | What a reasonable person would have done in the same or similar circumstances.

Intent.

Like all intentional torts, battery includes an element of intent. The tortfeasor must have intended to make contact with another individual in a harmful or offensive manner. Thus, accidentally bumping into someone in an elevator as it jerked into motion would not be a battery, because the contact was unintentional. But pinching that person while leaving the elevator would be battery, as the act was purposefully designed to make offensive contact.

Transferred Intent.

Sometimes the tortfeasor tries to strike someone but ends up hitting someone else or intends one wrongful act and another occurs. For instance, if Robert threw a stone at Chad but struck Mark instead, then Robert has committed battery against Mark. Although Robert intended to strike Chad, his intent is said to be carried along by the object he set into motion— the stone—and his intent is thus transferred with the stone onto whomever it reaches—in this case, Mark. Note, too, that Robert has assaulted Chad by throwing the stone and missing, provided that Chad was placed in reasonable apprehension, and so on.

Transferred intent is an effective tool for protecting persons from misdirected physical contacts. It holds the tortfeasor accountable for the consequences of his or her actions even though, strictly speaking, he or she did not desire to hit the third person involved.

transferred intent | In tort law, the principle that if a person intended to hit another but hits a third person instead, he or she legally *intended* to hit the third person. This "legal fiction" sometimes allows the third person to sue the hitter for an intentional tort.

THE CASE OF THE TEACHER'S ASSAULT PAY

Teachers may joke that in some public schools there is so much violence that the teachers should receive "hazard pay" for their service. In this case, based upon a statutory plan, transferred intent becomes the key factor as to whether an injured teacher's pay will end after one year, or continue indefinitely throughout a disability.

John P. STOSHAK
v.
EAST BATON ROUGE PARISH SCHOOL BOARD.

959 So. 2d 996, 2006-0852
(La. App. 1st Cir. 2/21/07)
Court of Appeal of Louisiana, First Circuit
February 21, 2007

On August 20, 2004, John Stoshak, a teacher at Istrouma High School in Baton Rouge, was injured when he attempted to break up a fight between two of his students. During the course of the students' fistfight, one of the punches struck Mr. Stoshak in the back of the head, causing him to fall to the ground and lose consciousness.

Louisiana Revised Statute 17:1201(C) provides two different sick leave pay provisions for public school teachers who sustain injuries on the job, depending on the cause of the injury. Louisiana Revised Statutes 17:1201(C)(1)(a), commonly referred to as the "assault pay" provision, states, in pertinent part:

> Any member of the teaching staff of the public schools who is injured or disabled while acting in his official capacity as a result of assault or battery by any student or person shall receive sick leave without reduction in pay and without reduction in accrued sick leave days while disabled as a result of such assault or battery.

Louisiana Revised Statutes 17:1201(C)(1)(b)(i), commonly referred to as the "physical contact" provision, states, in pertinent part:

> Any member of the teaching staff of the public schools who while acting in his official capacity is injured or disabled as a result of physical contact with a student while providing physical assistance to a student to prevent danger or risk of injury to the student shall receive sick leave for a period up to one calendar year without reduction in pay....

The evidence reveals that on the morning of August 20, 2004, Mr. Stoshak was teaching a group of pre-GED students when a fight erupted in his classroom between 17-year-old Jordan and 18-year-old Orange. Jordan was seated at a computer when Orange entered the classroom and punched him from behind. Jordan chased Orange into the hallway and the two began fighting. Mr. Stoshak attempted to break up the fight. During the course of the fight, a punch thrown by one of the boys hit Mr. Stoshak in the back of his head. Neither boy admitted to hitting Mr. Stoshak. Mr. Stoshak stated that he did not believe either of the boys had punched him deliberately; rather, he got in the way of the fighting boys who, in his words, were "tear[ing] each other up."

Mr. Stoshak contends the student who hit him committed an assault or battery as those terms are defined under Louisiana's criminal and civil law, entitling him to benefits under the "assault pay" provision.

The Board contends that the "physical contact" provision applies in this case because it is undisputed that the student intended to cause harmful physical contact to the other student, but not to Mr. Stoshak.

Under the tort law, a battery has been defined as a "harmful or offensive contact with a person, resulting from an act intended to cause the plaintiff to suffer such a contact."

In defining what type of conduct constitutes a battery, our courts have employed the doctrine of transferred intent. Under this theory, if a person intended to inflict serious bodily injury while trying to hit another person, but missed and accidentally hit someone else instead, such intent is transferred to the actual victim.

The legislature authorized the highest level of benefits to a teacher injured as a result of "assault or battery by any student or person." There is no language in this provision requiring that the teacher be the intended victim of an assault or battery.

Accordingly, we construe the benefits provided for in the "assault pay" provision to apply whenever the teacher is the victim of a battery at the hands of a student. The benefits provided for under the "physical contact" provision apply to injuries a teacher sustains when coming to the aid of a student that result from physical contacts that do not rise to the level of an assault or battery.

Under the doctrine of transferred intent, the student who hit Mr. Stoshak while attempting to hit the other student is deemed to have had the requisite intent to commit a battery on Mr. Stoshak. Therefore, because Mr. Stoshak's injuries resulted from a battery by a student, the Board was obligated to provide him with leave without reduction in pay for the duration of his disability.

CASE QUESTIONS

1. How would the fact pattern of this case have to be changed so that the "physical contact" statute for leave and not the "assault pay" statute would have been applicable to Mr. Stoshak?
2. How was the "transferred intent" provision applicable to the injured plaintiff Stoshak?

Battery lends itself to a variety of boisterous hypotheticals. Consider the examples on the next page.

Table 5-2 summarizes the elements of assault and battery.

Assault	Battery
Attempt to make harmful or offensive contact with another person without consent	Unconsented physical contact
Placing the victim in reasonable apprehension for physical safety	Offensive or harmful contact
Threat of imminent contact	Intent to touch another person in offensive or injurious manner

TABLE 5-2
Elements of assault and battery

Other intentional torts are less straightforward than assault and battery. False imprisonment poses particular wrinkles and is discussed later in the chapter.

▌ PATIENT DUMPING

A new state cause of action has been created by Massachusetts to address **patient dumping** and protect patients who don't have medical insurance. The law provides

patient dumping | Denial of treatment to emergency patients or women in labor, or transferring them to another hospital while in an unstable condition.

hypotheticals

Erin is a production analyst for a local investment firm. She is one of only three women in the operation. Another analyst, Calvin, regularly flirts with her. Erin responds politely but coolly to these episodes. One day Calvin, while standing behind Erin, takes hold of her upper arms and leans over her shoulder as if to inspect the file she has before her on her desk. Calvin wisecracks about the "nice view," to which Erin responds by grimacing. Has Calvin committed battery against Erin?

The three basic elements of battery have been satisfied. Erin did not consent to Calvin's touching. Her previous encounters with Calvin did not establish a playful relationship in which she might have encouraged such actions; in fact, she expressly discouraged Calvin's flirting. A reasonable person would have found Calvin's behavior offensive. Erin was insulted by the contact, as evidenced by her expression. Calvin intended to touch Erin in a way she found distasteful. Accordingly, Calvin is liable to Erin for battery. If Calvin's behavior continues to be a problem, it might also be actionable as sexual harassment, which is discussed later in this chapter.

* * *

Consider another illustration. Shelley is a clerk at a hotdog stand in a football stadium. Ben, a customer, purchased lunch from another clerk. Shelley thought Ben was unusually rude, so, as Ben turned to walk away, Shelley threw Ben a plastic catsup bottle, shouting that he had forgotten his condiments. The bottle brushed Ben's jacket sleeve and caused him to spill his beverage onto his pants. The bottle then struck Iris in the head, covering her with catsup. Has Shelley committed battery against Ben and Iris?

Again, the elements unfold clearly. Ben did not consent to being touched. Shelley's intent to make contact transferred to the catsup bottle that struck Ben's clothing, which was an extension of his person. Shelley's contact was harmful because it caused Ben to spill his drink onto himself. Shelley purposefully touched Ben in a fashion that injured him. Furthermore, Shelley's intent to strike Ben was transferred with the bottle, so that in hitting Iris, transferred intent applied. Shelley is liable to both Ben and Iris for battery.

What if Shelley had been merely another spectator at the football game and, instead of throwing anything, had simply jostled Ben, causing the spillage onto both Ben and Iris, as they all were walking down the stairway to their seats? This would be considered incidental contact to which Shelley, Iris, and Ben impliedly consented. Thus, no battery would have happened.

that no patient who presents at a hospital with an emergency medical condition and who is unable to pay may be treated differently than patients who are covered by health insurance. It is important to note that this is not a cause of action for incorrect treatment, only for nonuniform treatment.

If a patient goes to a hospital that is a Medicare provider and has an emergency room or department, and the patient requests examination or treatment, and the patient has an emergency medical condition, and the patient is not provided with an appropriate medical screening exam, and as a result, the patient suffers direct harm, the patient will have a claim against the medical provider or institution.

The state law has been enacted to address the shortcomings of the federal Emergency Medical Treatment and Active Labor Act (EMTALA), which governs when and how a patient may be refused treatment or transferred from one hospital to another when he or she is in an unstable medical condition. EMTALA was passed as part of the Consolidated Omnibus Budget Reconciliation Act of 1986 (COBRA). The act applies to all patients, not just those on Medicare.

▌ FALSE IMPRISONMENT

False imprisonment occurs when the tortfeasor intentionally confines someone without that person's consent. This tort is meant to protect each individual's right to control his or her own freedom of movement. Essentially, there are four elements to false imprisonment:

false imprisonment | An unlawful restraint or deprivation of a person's liberty, usually by a public official.

1. Confinement without captive's consent
2. Tortfeasor's intent to confine victim
3. Confinement for an appreciable length of time
4. No reasonable means of escape.

Note that in some jurisdictions, knowledge or awareness of the confinement is required.

Confinement

All methods of confinement include (1) a restriction of the victim's freedom of movement, (2) the captive's awareness or fear of the restriction, and (3) the victim's nonconsent to the restriction. The second element prevents the victim from escaping, either because no routes of escape are available, or because the victim is afraid to attempt escape for fear of the tortfeasor's reprisals.

There are several ways in which the tortfeasor may confine his or her captive. These include physical barriers and express or implied threats of force. Table 5-3 illustrates the elements of false imprisonment.

Confinement without captive's consent
Intent to confine
Confinement for appreciable length of time
No reasonable means of escape

TABLE 5-3
Elements of false imprisonment

THE CASE OF THE MINOR IMPRISONMENT

A bus driver claims to have been so lost trying to find a school that it took four hours to take his only passenger to school. The outraged parents of the four-year-old special-needs student bring an action claiming false imprisonment among other things. Was this an extreme case of the bus driver having no sense of direction, or did something more occur?

The SCHOOL BOARD OF MIAMI-DADE COUNTY, FLORIDA, Appellant,

v.

Francisco and Lourdes TRUJILLO, individually as the natural parents of Christopher Trujillo, a minor, Appellees.

Nos. 3D04-77, 3D04-300.

906 So. 2d 1109 (Fla. Dist. Ct. App., 3d Dist.)
May 4, 2005

The pertinent facts are as follows: On the first day of school, a Miami-Dade County school bus picked up the Trujillo's four-year-old son, Christopher ("Christopher"), a special needs child. The bus arrived at 8:40 a.m., almost an hour later than his scheduled pick-up time. The bus driver then drove around the area and unsuccessfully attempted to pick up the other students and find Blue Lakes Elementary School.

Eventually, the driver obtained directions and arrived at the elementary school at 12:50 p.m. By this time, Christopher had urinated on himself at least once and appeared to be thirsty and dehydrated. Although Mr. Trujillo immediately took Christopher to a pediatrician, the pediatrician found no signs of abuse or physical injury. After the incident, however,

Christopher began having nightmares, started wetting his bed and appeared to develop a fear of school buses. The Trujillos decided that Christopher would no longer ride the school bus.

The Trujillos sued the School Board alleging negligence, false imprisonment and a violation of Christopher's civil rights. The Trujillos sought damages for Christopher's pain and suffering and for the additional child care and transportation costs they incurred because Christopher no longer rode the school bus.

Here, neither the pediatrician nor the psychologist who examined Christopher found any physical or emotional injuries.

Because Christopher did not suffer a physical injury or impact and his emotional injuries are intangible, the impact rule applies and therefore precludes recovery of damages.

There is no evidence that the School Board or its employees intended to confine Christopher, had knowledge that confinement would result, or that Christopher was prevented from leaving the bus or held against his will. Rather, the evidence shows that the bus driver picked Christopher up and thereafter got lost. This hardly amounts to false imprisonment.

CASE QUESTIONS
1. If the impact rule didn't apply, would the court's decision be different?
2. What facts would be needed to show false imprisonment?

Physical Barriers Restricting Movement. Physical barriers are the most common method of falsely imprisoning someone. Placing the captive in a locked room or a moving automobile (while refusing to stop) are common examples. However, the physical barriers need not be so small as a single room or vehicle.

A captive may be restricted to the grounds of a series of adjacent buildings. It is even possible for the victim to be penned in by such unexpected blockades as an automobile blocking the victim's access from a driveway to a street. The physical barrier need only restrict the captive's freedom of movement. This essentially traps the victim, either by some actual physical obstruction, such as a locked door, fence, or wall, or by an object which the tortfeasor is using to restrain the captive, such as the automobile blocking the driveway or even the tortfeasor's own body obstructing a doorway. In some jurisdictions, the victim must be aware of the confinement.

Express or Implied Threats of Force. Sometimes no locked door or wall is necessary to confine a person. Threats of physical or emotional violence can be quite effective, as are threats against the victim's family or property. In this way, confinement is achieved by expressed intimidation. The victim is afraid to escape for fear of physical or emotional injury. For example, when the tortfeasor warns, "If you leave this room, I will break your legs," the captive is likely to remain as instructed. Similarly, the tortfeasor could threaten, "If you leave this house, I will tell Joe that you wrecked his new car." In this situation, the victim is restrained by the threat of emotional injury, if certain information is revealed that would incriminate the captive.

These types of threats need not be explicit, however. Implied threats also work effectively. For instance, if a store manager tells a shoplifting suspect to wait in a room for questioning "so that nobody has to telephone the police," the threat of arrest and criminal prosecution is clearly implied, and the suspect will probably comply out of fear.

Captive's Consent to Confinement. The intentional tort of false imprisonment cannot occur if the victim consents to the captivity. **Consent** includes awareness and acceptance of the confinement. Thus, if a shoplifting suspect agrees to remain in a room pending questioning by store security, this would constitute consent, because the patron knows and accepts the restriction to the room. However, there could be instances where the suspect stays, and has not voluntarily consented.

consent | Voluntary and active agreement.

Intent to Confine. The tortfeasor must intend to confine the victim for false imprisonment to happen. Consider the example of an accidental lock-in at a department store, where a customer is inadvertently locked inside the store after closing hours. There would be no false imprisonment, because the store management had no desire to confine the patron.

Intent may be expressed or implied by conduct. The tortfeasor who states his or her intention to confine another person is easiest to identify. Often, however, intent is indicated by conduct. Again, the shoplifting illustration presents a good example. A shoplifting suspect is stopped by store security and is asked to accompany the guard. Without any word of explanation, the guard takes the suspect to a back room, has the suspect enter, closes the door, and departs. There have been no explicit indications of confinement—the door was not locked—but implicitly it is understood, based on the behavior of the guard, that the suspect is to remain in the room. Accordingly, the intent to restrain may be implied.

Confinement for Appreciable Time Period.

Although no definite time period is required, false imprisonment occurs only if the confinement has existed for an appreciable length of time. This depends upon the specific facts of each case. Usually, *appreciable confinement* is defined as unreasonable under the circumstances. That could be a matter of seconds, if someone is restrained in an extremely hazardous situation, such as in a burning building; or it could be a question of an hour or two, such as during a shoplifting investigation.

No Reasonable Means of Escape.

False imprisonment cannot happen if the captive has a reasonable avenue of escape. In other words, the confinement must be complete. If the victim could simply walk away from the situation, then no false imprisonment transpired. Reasonable means of escape depends upon the facts of each case, but usually includes any route that a reasonable person would use to flee given the circumstances. For example, if Wes makes improper advances upon Sarah in his automobile, and Sarah has only to open the door to leave, then she has a reasonable avenue of escape, and no false imprisonment has happened. However, if Wes made the same advances on Sarah in a fourth-floor apartment, in which the only exits were one door (which Wes blocked) and the windows, then false imprisonment would have occurred. Sarah could hardly be expected to escape by leaping from a fourth-story window.

Many false imprisonment cases involve shoplifting or alleged shoplifting. The difficulty in these cases stems from the conflicting interests involved: the patron's freedom to move about freely versus the business's right to protect its property from theft. Notice that there are competing tort interests here. The customer seeks protection from false imprisonment, while the store owner wishes to prevent conversion and trespass to chattel.

shopkeeper's privilege | A shopkeeper is allowed to detain a suspected shoplifter on store property for a reasonable period of time, so long as he or she has cause to believe that the person detained in fact committed, or attempted to commit, theft of store property.

Shopkeeper's Privilege.

In many states, there is a common-law right called the **shopkeeper's privilege** to stop and detain a suspected shoplifter at the store for a reasonable period of time, so long as the shopkeeper has reason to believe the person detained has actually stolen or attempted to steal property. This gives the shopkeeper the right to stop and question suspected shoplifters before they leave the store. It is important that the shopkeeper's acts be seen as reasonable. Questioning a suspect for a few minutes is acceptable. Hours of interrogation would not qualify for this privilege. A shopkeeper must have a reason to suspect the theft; mere hunch or assumption would not be acceptable.

THE CASE OF THE OVERZEALOUS STORE SECURITY OFFICER

Many false imprisonment cases involve shoplifting. All too often, store employees, anxious to curb theft of merchandise, become overzealous in their efforts. Suspected shoplifters, on the flimsiest circumstantial evidence, are occasionally subjected to unreasonable searches, confinements, interrogations, and the accompanying stresses and embarrassment. When the evidence against such suspects is extremely speculative, as in the case reprinted here, the result is often tort litigation. The suspect becomes the plaintiff. The store, as the defendant, suddenly finds itself attempting to justify its employees' conduct. In the following case, false imprisonment was successfully claimed.

ROGERS
v.
T.J.X. COS.
Supreme Court of North Carolina
329 N.C. 226, 404 S.E.2d 664 (1991)
June 12, 1991
Martin, Justice

The action arose out of events occurring on 17 July 1988 at the T.J. Maxx department store in Cary, North Carolina, owned by defendant T.J.X. Companies, Inc. Taken in the light most favorable to the plaintiff, as we must for summary judgment purposes, the evidence tends to show the following. Plaintiff entered T.J. Maxx, hereinafter "the store," about 4:30 P.M. shopping for linens. She wore bermuda shorts and a T-shirt and carried a pocketbook, approximately twelve inches by twelve inches. The purse contained two cosmetic bags, a wallet, two pens, a glasses' case, and a ziploc bag containing material and wallpaper samples. Plaintiff went first to the cosmetics area and then to the linens department. After leaving the linens department, she walked around a counter containing dishes and crystal and then left the store without making a purchase. Plaintiff never entered the lingerie department and never examined any items of lingerie.

As plaintiff exited the store, Michael Nourse stopped her, identified himself as a store security officer, and asked her to return to the store because he wished to talk with her about some merchandise. Nourse carried a badge of his own design and an identification card issued by the company; he showed these items to plaintiff. Plaintiff told him that he was making a mistake, but complied with his request and accompanied Nourse to his office at the back of the store. Plaintiff testified that she did not feel that she had a choice about accompanying Nourse because "he was the law of the store" and she had to obey him. On the way to the office, Nourse asked another store employee, Sheri Steffens, to join them and act as a witness.

Once inside the small office, plaintiff immediately dumped the contents of her purse onto the desk. Nourse told plaintiff to take a seat, but she refused, saying that this would not take long because she was a good customer and had not stolen anything. Nourse responded, "Good customers will steal," and again directed her to have a seat. Telling her he would soon return, he then left the office for five to fifteen minutes. Plaintiff testified that she believed that he might have gone to call the police, and she stepped out of the office to look for them. Seeing no

(continues)

one, she gathered up her belongings, but did not feel free to leave because Nourse had told her he would return. Steffens paged Nourse, who returned momentarily. He said to plaintiff, "Ma'am, all we want is our merchandise. What did you do with it? You were in our lingerie department." Plaintiff denied wrongdoing, again dumped her purse on the desk, and told him that he must have seen her putting the packet of material samples into her purse. As she reached to gather her belongings, Nourse instructed her not to touch anything.

Nourse pulled down a clipboard hanging on the wall and showed her a card which said that the store employees had the right to detain her if they had reason to believe she had been shoplifting. Nourse repeatedly questioned plaintiff about the location of the missing merchandise as she tried to read the card. Plaintiff told him to "shut up" so that she could concentrate. Nourse remarked to Steffens, "Usually the dog that barks the loudest is guilty." Nourse then told plaintiff that he could call the police if she wanted them to settle it; that he could handcuff her to a chair; and that he would call the police and have them put her in jail. Plaintiff continued to deny the allegations and asked if he wanted her to take her clothes off to prove that she had not done anything, even though she was a very modest person. Steffens testified that plaintiff was very upset throughout the incident and that Nourse's attitude and demeanor toward plaintiff was sarcastic.

Nourse instructed plaintiff to sign two forms, one of which was a waiver of Miranda rights. The other form released T.J. Maxx from liability for any claims arising out of the incident. Neither of the papers had been filled out when plaintiff signed. Plaintiff testified that she signed the release form only because she believed that she would not be allowed to leave the store and go home if she did not sign it. Nourse refused to give plaintiff copies of the forms, because it was not company policy. After signing the papers, plaintiff left the store and drove home. She had been in the security office approximately 35 minutes. About one-half hour after plaintiff left the store, Nourse announced to Steffens that he had found the missing merchandise, a beige brassiere.

False imprisonment is the illegal restraint of the person of any one against his or her will. The tort may be committed by words or acts; therefore, actual force is not required. Restraint of the person is essential, whether by threats, express or implied, or by conduct. The Court of Appeals held that plaintiff had established facts sufficient to support her claim for false imprisonment....

Taken in the light most favorable to the plaintiff, the evidence tends to show that (1) defendant Nourse impersonated a police officer by using a badge of his own design; (2) plaintiff was restrained against her will in the store security office for approximately one-half hour; (3) plaintiff was badgered, insulted and pressured to confess by defendant Nourse despite her efforts to prove her innocence; (4) plaintiff was frightened and upset and asked if she could leave; (5) defendant unlawfully detained plaintiff after [a] determination that no offense had been committed; (6) plaintiff was made to give up personal information including her driver's license number, telephone number, and social security number; and (7) plaintiff was forced to sign a release of liability as a condition to her release from Nourse's custody....

We hold that there was sufficient evidence of conduct constituting the false imprisonment, to survive defendants' motion for summary judgment.

CASE QUESTIONS

1. Given the facts in *Rogers,* did the plaintiff establish the elements (as discussed in this chapter) for assault and battery?
2. You might want to read and compare North Carolina's common law regarding false imprisonment with the law of your state.

hypotheticals

Consider Sophie's predicament. A cashier thought he spotted Sophie taking some merchandise and placing it in her purse without paying for it. As Sophie walked out the exit, store security grabbed her. She violently protested, but the guards, without explanation, bodily forced her into a small, unlit room in the rear of the store. They then locked the door, and Sophie sat for three hours until the store manager, who had been on a delivery errand, returned to question her. She was, in fact, innocent of any wrongdoing. Was there false imprisonment?

The confinement was without Sophie's consent, as evidenced by Sophie's protests of the guards' physical handling of her. The restraint was obvious because the door was locked. The store security guards intended to confine Sophie by locking her in the room. She was restrained there for three hours, which would probably be considered unreasonable, particularly because the room was small and unlit. She had no reasonable means of escape, again because the only door to the room was locked. Therefore, the store would be liable to Sophie for false imprisonment.

* * *

Consider also the case of Murphy. Murphy drove his automobile into a restricted area of a manufacturing plant. Plant security instructed him to remain parked in his vehicle pending the arrival of the supervisor. Murphy said he had no reason to hang around, as he had done nothing wrong. The security officers then left. There were no barriers preventing Murphy from simply driving off the premises, through an open gate, to the highway. Was there false imprisonment?

The critical element in this hypothetical is the reasonable route of escape. Murphy could easily have slipped away, and the guards made no implied or expressed threats (such as arrest and criminal prosecution if he attempted to leave). Accordingly, no false imprisonment took place.

█ SEXUAL HARASSMENT

Title VII of the Civil Rights Act of 1964 makes it unlawful for an employer to discriminate against an individual because of that individual's race, color, religion, sex, or national origin. 42 U.S.C. § 2000-2(a)(1). In addition to tort actions, **sexual harassment** claims can be brought under the provisions of Title VII. A claimant must show that the workplace is permeated with discriminatory intimidation, ridicule, and insult that alters the conditions of the victim's employment, thereby creating an abusive and hostile work environment. Tangible psychiatric injuries need not be proven.

It should not be very difficult to imagine other emotional damage infliction scenarios like those previously mentioned. However, there are many instances in which the behavior is more subtle.

sexual harassment | Unwelcome sexual advances, requests for sexual favors, and other verbal or physical conduct of a sexual nature, when this conduct affects an individual's employment, unreasonably interferes with an individual's work performance, or creates an intimidating, hostile, or offensive work environment.

THE CASE OF INCREDIBLE SEXUAL HARASSMENT

Two females detail graphic sexual harassment they allege occurred over the course of their employment. They both speak of vulgar and hurtful remarks made to them on a daily basis. The jury must weigh their testimony against that of the alleged harassers.

STATE OF OHIO
COUNTY OF LORAIN
KRISTINA CONTI, et al.
Appellants
v.
SPITZER AUTO WORLD
AMHERST, INC., et al.
Appellees

Ohio Court of Appeals,
Ninth Judicial District
2008 Ohio-1320
March 24, 2008

Conti, Dutton, and Smith (collectively "Employees") each worked for a period of time for a car dealership owned and operated by Appellee Spitzer Auto World Amherst, Inc. Employee benefits were provided to this dealership through Appellee Spitzer Management, Inc. At the time Employees worked at the dealership, the general manager was Joe Garrett, and the sales managers were Todd Meek and Tim Dalzell. Further, both Spitzer entities were owned and/or controlled by Alan Spitzer.

Employees alleged that during their employment they were subjected to sexual harassment on a near daily basis. Conti asserted that Meek and Dalzell routinely viewed pornography on work computers and forced her to view the pornography on numerous occasions. Conti also asserted that Meek rubbed up against her from behind and forced her to touch his buttocks on several occasions.

In order to demonstrate a prima facie case of sexual harassment, each plaintiff must produce evidence of the following:

"(1) she was a member of a protected class;
"(2) she was subjected to unwelcome sexual harassment in the form of sexual advances, requests for sexual favors or other verbal or physical conduct of a sexual nature;
"(3) the harassment complained of was based upon sex;
"(4) the charged sexual harassment had the effect of unreasonably interfering with the plaintiff's work performance and creating an intimidating, hostile or offensive working environment that affected the psychological well-being of the plaintiff and
"(5) the existence of respondeat superior liability."

In order to determine whether an environment is sufficiently hostile to warrant a finding of sexual harassment this Court examines the totality of the circumstances including:

"the frequency of the discriminatory conduct; its severity; whether it is physically threatening or humiliating, or a mere offensive utterance; and whether it unreasonably interferes with an employee's work performance. The effect on the employee's psychological well-being is, of course, relevant to determining whether the plaintiff actually found the environment abusive. But while psychological harm, like any other relevant factor, may be taken into account, no single factor is required." *Harris v. Forklift Sys. Inc.* (1993), 510 U.S. 17.

We also note that the standards for judging hostility are demanding such that "the ordinary tribulations of the work place, such as, sporadic use of abusive language, gender-related jokes, and occasional teasing" will not constitute a hostile work environment. *Faragher v. Boca Raton* (1998), 524 U.S. 775.

Moreover, the Sixth Circuit has established the standards by which employees might prove their constructive discharge claims based on sexual harassment. "A finding of constructive discharge in this circuit requires an inquiry into both the objective feelings of the employee and the intent of the employer. . . .

This court has . . . held that 'proof of discrimination alone is not a sufficient predicate for a finding of constructive discharge, there must be other aggravating factors.' We have also required some inquiry into the employer's intent and the reasonably foreseeable impact of its conduct on the employee...."

Accordingly, to prevail on their claim of constructive discharge premised on a hostile working environment, Smith and Dutton were required to demonstrate a hostile working environment and "show that a reasonable employer would have foreseen that [they] would resign, given the sexual harassment [they] faced."

Smith testified as follows. She was subjected to harassment by Meek on nearly a daily basis. Meek routinely asked if she was wearing underwear, and what color her underwear were. Once, Smith called in to tell Meek that she would be late for work that day. Meek responded by asking Smith to "scrub it" before coming to work. Smith understood this comment to be sexual in nature. On the final day of her employment, Smith was discussing the fact that her infant child had thrush. According to Smith, Meek then stated that the infant "shouldn't be sucking on my vagina." Smith went immediately to Ruth Sadowsky to report Meek's comment. Sadowsky, a financial manager for Spitzer, had Smith write a report detailing the harassment she described. Smith detailed the "scrub it" incident that had occurred six weeks earlier and Meek's comment that day. Smith did not report any other alleged harassment during her employment.

Dutton testified as follows. During the first week of her employment, when she was seventeen years old, Meek asked to see her breasts. Meek also asked whether Dutton and her boyfriend engaged in anal sex and whether Dutton had performed oral sex.

On another occasion, Meek walked past a van in Spitzer's showroom and asked Dutton if she would "get in there with him and give him a lap dance." On still another occasion, Dalzell asked her to spread her legs so that he could see up her skirt.

The jury was presented with two very different views of the workplace at Spitzer. Employees and their witnesses presented an atmosphere rife with crude comments and sexual innuendo. In contrast, Spitzer and its witnesses presented testimony that no inappropriate behavior took place at the dealership. There is little question that the jury was best situated to determine the credibility of these witnesses and determine which atmosphere existed at Spitzer. We find no error in the jury's apparent reliance on the testimony of Spitzer's witnesses. One relevant fact was undisputed. Smith and Dutton testified that the harassment occurred on a daily basis. Both, however, conceded that they had never mentioned this daily harassment to anyone in their lives prior to filing suit against Spitzer. From this admission, the jury was free to find that Smith and Dutton lacked credibility with respect to describing the frequency and severity of the alleged harassment.

Upon our review, the jury had before it competent, credible evidence to find in favor of the defendants on the claims brought by Dutton and Smith. The jury's verdict, therefore, was not against the manifest weight of the evidence.

CASE QUESTIONS

1. What part of the women's testimony was the key to the jury's decision? Explain.
2. Whose testimony did you find more convincing, that of the men or the women? Explain.

CONSENT DECREE

In another case, the U.S. Equal Employment Opportunity Commission (EEOC) announced on June 2, 2008, that a settlement of a retaliation and harassment lawsuit had been reached against the landmark New York restaurant Tavern on the Green, located in Central Park. The settlement was for $2.2 million. This case involved graphic comments, demands for various sex acts, and the groping of women's buttocks and breasts. There were also allegations of race and national origin discrimination against Black and Hispanic employees. The case was brought on September 24, 2007, in the United States District Court for the Southern District of New York. After the agency conducted an investigation, they tried to reach a voluntary settlement out of court. In addition to the above monetary settlement, the restaurant must now establish a telephone hotline for employees to use for harassment complaints; the restaurant must revise and distribute its policy on harassment, and provide training to all employees against discrimination and retaliation. Tavern on the Green is considered the highest grossing independently owned restaurant in the country, with annual revenues exceeding $34 million.

▌ SPOLIATION OF EVIDENCE

spoliation of evidence |
Withholding, hiding, or destruction of evidence relevant to a legal proceeding. This is a new tort.

Spoliation of evidence is deliberately withholding, hiding, or destroying evidence relevant to a legal proceeding. This is a criminal act. In some states, this is now a tort as well and a civil action can be brought. An example of this would be in a products liability case where the injured plaintiff who was in possession of the car that allegedly caused his serious injuries is unable to produce it at the time of trial. In these cases, the court can draw an adverse inference, preclude evidence or testimony, or dismiss a claim at the time of trial. Different states vary as to how they define the tort or whether they choose to acknowledge this tort.

THE CASE OF THE SPOILED EVIDENCE

A child born out of wedlock is deprived of his birthright and 5 million dollars. The court refuses to recognize the new tort of spoliation of evidence and provides its reasoning.

ROACH
v.
LEE, et al.
No. ED CV 03-286-RT.
369 F. Supp. 2d 1194 (C.D. Cal.)
May 9, 2005

Won Man Lee was the head of the Lee family, one of the wealthiest families in South Korea. Plaintiff is a United States citizen living in California. The Lee defendants were or are directors, officers, and/or controlling shareholders of defendant Kolon Industries and/or officers and directors of defendant Oh-Woon. Both Kolon Industries and Oh-Woon are incorporated in and have their principal place of business in South Korea.

Plaintiff was born in Seoul, South Korea on January 18, 1978. He was born out of wedlock to

Won Man Lee and an unnamed younger woman, who named him Dong Koo Lee. The Lee defendants forced his mother to give up legal custody of him when he was five years old. The Lee defendants also forced him to live in a small closet in their mansion, and to eat and sleep with the servants, under the supervision of an older relative.

In 1983, Won Man Lee passed control of Kolon Industries to his son, defendant Dong Chan Lee. Shortly thereafter, Won Man Lee had a stroke. Together with the other Lee defendants, Dong Chan Lee set out to erase any records of his father's out-of-wedlock children. The Lee defendants falsified Plaintiff's birth records, denied that Plaintiff had any relation to them, and placed him in a Korean orphanage. In 1985, Deanna and Martin Roach ("the Roaches"), an American family, adopted Plaintiff, took him to the United States, and changed his name to Peter Roach. The Lee defendants made this adoption possible through their influence over the orphanage and defendant Holt Children's Services, Inc. ("Holt"), an international adoption agency in South Korea.

After Won Man Lee's death in 1994, employees of Kolon Industries sought out the Roaches. On May 12, 1994, the Roaches had a meeting with these employees, whom the Lee defendants had instructed to give $100,000 to Plaintiff. The Roaches asked whether Won Man Lee was Plaintiff's father and whether Plaintiff had any brothers or sisters, to which the Kolon employees responded in the negative. In exchange for the $100,000, the Roaches signed a written agreement relinquishing the birthright of Plaintiff, who was a minor at the time. Kolon International, Inc. ("Kolon International"), acting on behalf of its parent company, Kolon Industries, wrote a letter thanking Holt International for locating Plaintiff and confirming a $10,000 payment for that service.

In May 2000, Plaintiff contacted a branch office of Kolon Industries in California ("Kolon California"). Plaintiff met twice with the branch's president, H.J. Park ("Park"). At the first meeting, Park agreed to contact defendant Woong Yeul Lee and ask whether Won Man Lee was Plaintiff's father. At the second meeting, Park told Plaintiff that the Lee family records did not indicate that he was a member of their family. Park then tricked Plaintiff into writing a letter to Woong Yeul Lee disclaiming any relationship to the Lee defendants.

Plaintiff later wrote an e-mail and a letter to Woong Yeul Lee inquiring whether any relationship existed between Plaintiff and Won Man Lee. Plaintiff sent a letter to the Lee family defendants through Holt International in Oregon, but received no response. In December 2002, Dae Ryung Song, Woong Yeul Lee's representative and Vice Chairman of Kolon Industries, denied that Plaintiff had an inheritance claim to the Estate of Won Man Lee. Dae Ryung Song stated that he would use the documents signed by Plaintiff and the Roaches to dispute any such claim.

Plaintiff would have received one-sixth of Won Man Lee's estate, estimated at $30 million. The Lee defendants used his inheritance to establish Oh-Woon as an alter-ego in 1994 to avoid paying any money they owed to him.

Plaintiff brings an intentional spoliation of evidence claim against Moving Defendants. They contend that a tort of intentional spoliation of evidence does not exist where the spoliation victim did not know nor should have known of the spoliation until after a decision on the merits of the underlying action.

The California Supreme Court held that there is no tort for "the intentional spoliation of evidence by a party to the cause of action to which the spoliated evidence is relevant [i.e., first-party spoliation], in cases in which . . . the spoliation victim knows or should have known of the alleged spoliation before the trial or other decision on the merits of the underlying action." The Court later held that there was no cause of action for intentional spoliation of evidence by a third party.

The California Court of Appeal extended these decisions to preclude causes of action for negligent spoliation by first or third parties.

In the instant case, Plaintiff alleges that Moving Defendants intentionally spoliated evidence related to the probate proceedings of Won Man Lee and that

(continues)

Plaintiff did not know nor should he have known about the spoliation until after the decision on the merits of the probate proceedings. California courts have not addressed the issue whether a tort for intentional spoliation of evidence exists "in cases of first party spoliation in which the spoliation victim neither knows nor should have known of the spoliation until after a decision on the merits of the underlying action."

This court must consider whether a tort for intentional first-party spoliation of evidence where the victim did not know and should not have known of the alleged spoliation prior to the termination of the underlying action ("purported tort") "would ultimately create social benefits exceeding those created by existing remedies for such conduct, and outweighing any costs and burdens it would impose." The relevant factors are (1) whether the purported tort contravenes the policy to limit torts arising out of litigation-related misconduct, (2) the existence of non-tort remedies, (3) the uncertainty of the fact of harm in spoliation cases, and (4) the costs imposed by the purported tort.

The first factor is whether the purported tort contravenes the policy of limiting torts arising out of litigation-related misconduct. The two main concerns here are whether this purported tort could spawn an endless cycle of litigation and whether it offends the need for the finality of adjudications.

In *Cedars-Sinai Medical Center*, the California Supreme Court warned that endless litigation was one of the dangers of creating a tort such as this one. Since the spoliation victim would not know and should not have known that evidence was spoliated in the underlying action, the only recourse for the victim would be another lawsuit. In the second lawsuit, spoliation could occur again without the victim's knowledge, spurring yet another lawsuit. Although spoliation victims in this situation would not be able to seek sanctions in the underlying action because they were unaware of any spoliation, the California Supreme Court has "recognized that even when sanctions within the lawsuit are not available, a tort

remedy may be rejected on the ground that such a remedy would produce endless derivative litigation."

The California Supreme Court was also concerned about the threat to the finality of adjudications. A spoliation victim who did not know and should not have known of the spoliation in the underlying action will always have to bring a new lawsuit to rectify the wrong, resulting to some extent in a retrial of the completed underlying action.

The second factor is the existence of non-tort remedies.

Two of the non-tort remedies cited by the California Supreme Court in *Cedars-Sinai Med. Ctr.*, would not apply in this case. Since the spoliation victim would not know and should not have known about the spoliation before a decision on the merits of the underlying action, the victim would not be able to seek discovery sanctions under California Code of Civil Procedure. The spoliation victim would also not be able to make use of the inference in California Evidence Code that "evidence which one party has destroyed or rendered unavailable was unfavorable to that party."

Yet, California Penal Code already criminalizes the spoliation of evidence, which creates an effective deterrent against this wrongful conduct. In addition, the State Bar of California would still be able to impose sanctions, including suspension and disbarment, on attorneys who spoliated evidence.

The California Supreme Court has clearly expressed a preference for non-tort remedies. Considering the rarity of cases involving the intentional spoliation of evidence, disciplinary sanctions and criminal penalties for the intentional spoliation of evidence will likely be sufficient for deterring this wrongful conduct.

The third factor is the uncertainty of harm in spoliation cases. In spoliation cases, "the fact of harm will be irreducibly uncertain" because "even if the jury infers from the act of spoliation that the spoliated evidence was somehow unfavorable to the spoliator, there will typically be no way of telling what precisely the evidence would have shown and how much it would have weighed in the spoliation victim's favor."

The fourth factor is the costs imposed by recognition of the purported tort. Many of the costs imposed by an intentional spoliation of evidence tort where the victim knew or should have known of the spoliation before a final decision on the underlying action also apply when the victim did not and should not have had that knowledge. First, the uncertainty of harm "would create the risk of erroneous determinations of spoliation liability (that is, findings of liability in cases in which availability of the spoliated evidence would have not changed the outcome of the underlying litigation)." Second, this risk of erroneous determinations "could also impose indirect costs by causing persons or entities to take extraordinary measures to preserve for an indefinite period documents and things of no apparent value solely to avoid the possibility of spoliation liability if years later those items turn out to have some potential relevance to future litigation."

"[T]he motive and opportunity to discover instances of spoliation are at their greatest during discovery in the underlying action," so "[t]here is no reason to conclude that instances of spoliation that remain hidden during discovery in the underlying action would come to light afterward solely by reason of the existence of a tort remedy."

In sum, it is this court's conclusion that the California Supreme Court would not recognize an intentional spoliation of evidence tort where the spoliation victim did not know nor should have known of the spoliation until after a decision on the merits of the underlying action.

CASE QUESTIONS

1. What facts did plaintiff need to allege to change this outcome?
2. Do you agree with the court's reasoning? Explain.

▌ SUMMARY

Intentional torts include actions designed to injure another person or his or her property. All intentional torts embrace an act, intent, and injurious conduct. These elements must occur together. Intentional torts harming the individual include assault, battery, false imprisonment, patient dumping, and spoliation of evidence.

Assault is the tortfeasor's attempt to inflict harmful or offensive contact upon another person without consent. Assault places the victim in fear of his or her physical safety, even if the anticipated contact would produce only a distasteful reaction. The threat of contact must be imminent. Battery is a completed assault. It is the intentional, unconsented touching of another person in a harmful or offensive manner. Physical contact is required, although it may occur only with the victim's clothing or objects held. Transferred intent means that the contact directed at one person carries over to another individual who was inadvertently struck; battery would thus have occurred to the unintended victim.

Patient dumping is the denial of treatment to emergency patients or women in labor, or transferring them to another hospital while they are in an unstable condition. This is a new tort to protect uninsured and poor patients from unequal medical treatment.

False imprisonment is the confinement of someone without his or her consent. Confinement must exist for an appreciable length of time. The victim must have no reasonable means of escape. The tortfeasor must intend to confine the victim and act to accomplish confinement. Confinement may be achieved either by physical barriers or by threat of force that intimidates the victim into remaining in the restricted area.

The shopkeeper's privilege allows a shopkeeper to detain a suspected shoplifter on store property for a reasonable period of time, so long as he or she has cause to believe that the person detained in fact committed, or attempted to commit, theft of store property. The key is reasonable time.

Sexual harassment constitutes unwelcome sexual advances, requests for sexual favors, and other verbal or physical conduct of a sexual nature, when this conduct affects an individual's employment, unreasonably interferes with an individual's work performance, or creates an intimidating, hostile, or offensive work environment. The EEOC is the federal agency that handles these kinds of claims. There are also state agencies that handle discrimination claims.

Spoliation of evidence, another new intentional tort, involves withholding, hiding, or destroying evidence relevant to a legal proceeding. Some jurisdictions do not feel that this tort is necessary, as there are other similar actions that cover this kind of situation.

▌ KEY TERMS

apprehension	intent	shopkeeper's privilege
assault	intentional tort	spoliation of evidence
battery	patient dumping	transferred intent
consent	reasonable person standard	
false imprisonment	sexual harassment	

▌ PROBLEMS

In the following hypotheticals, identify the intentional tort(s) committed, if any, and support your answer.

1. Alicia was waiting in line outside The Elegant Shop just before the store opened on the day of the shop's annual savings sale. Dozens of customers milled around the entrance in anticipation. Many patrons began to grow impatient. Suddenly, the doors were opened, and Alicia was knocked to the ground by Marie Harrington, another customer. Alicia covered her face with her arms in anticipation of being trampled. In her haste to enter, Marie stepped on Alicia's hand and broke Alicia's ring finger.

2. Malcolm is the manager of The Soft Touch, a ladies clothing store. Paris, a customer, was looking at accessory jewelry next to the full-length mirrors. Malcolm glanced at the mirrors and thought he saw Paris place something in her purse. He thought it might be jewelry, but he did not actually see the object. As Paris began to exit the store, Malcolm asked her politely to stop. She did so, whereupon Malcolm identified himself and requested that she accompany him to the back room for questioning. She refused. Malcolm insisted, threatening to telephone the police if she attempted to leave the store. She then agreed and the two went to a small room at the rear of the store. Inside, Malcolm asked Paris to empty her pockets and purse, which she did. No jewelry was found. He asked her a few questions about the jewelry and what he had seen. She explained that she had put a handkerchief into her purse, and there was in fact a kerchief inside it. Malcolm apologized for any inconvenience and Paris then left. The interview in the room lasted five minutes.

3. Patty Patient arrives via ambulance at Mercy General Hospital emergency room. Her first words to the triage nurse are, "I don't have insurance, did they bring me to the right place?" Then Patty starts moaning and passes out. The triage nurse Henry is glad he heard Patty's last words and whispers to the Emergency Medical Technician Pete, who has just wheeled Patty in, "Take her out of here." Off goes Patty to the County Medical Center. En route to that hospital, she dies.

4. Gina Lee loves her new job as office assistant. She can't believe her good luck: there are so many good-looking guys working in her department. Gina is determined to start dating someone new by the end of the month. When Gina sees her co-worker Brad each morning, she tries to think of something different and provocative to say. Brad seems kind of quiet and it's hard to get a reaction out of him. Gina isn't sure if he is just trying to play it cool or what. Gina tells Brad in detail about her exciting nights with her last boyfriend. Brad does not seem to care, but Gina still thinks he is playing it cool. The next morning, Gina decides she needs to be more forward. Gina asks Brad about his sex life and whether he thinks John or Scott in the next cubicle would make good lovers. Again no response from Brad. Gina brushes against Brad's crotch with her hip and walks away.

5. Sean, Leroy, the driver of one vehicle, has sued another driver, Ethan Rogers, concerning a motor vehicle accident that seriously injured both drivers. Rogers was unemployed at the time of the crash and desperately needed to sell his vehicle and some other possessions for cash. Rogers takes the first offer to buy his car, despite the fact that his attorney had just advised that Rogers needs to make the car available for inspection by Leroy's expert mechanic.

▌ REVIEW QUESTIONS

1. Define *assault* and *battery*. How are they similar? Distinguishable? Is intent required?

2. Define *patient dumping*. Is this a cause of action for incorrect treatment or nonuniform treatment? Explain.

3. Define *sexual harassment*. How can sexual harassment be distinguished from innocent flirting?

4. Define *spoliation of evidence*. What are some other similar legal actions that could be brought instead of using this new tort?

5. What is the shopkeeper's privilege? Do you think this is used appropriately in most instances, or does it create more problems than it solves? Explain.

▌ HELPFUL WEBSITES

This chapter deals with intentional torts and injuries to persons. To learn more about personal injury law, the following sites can be accessed:

General Information

http://www.lawguru.com
http://www.jurist.law.pitt.edu
http://www.emory.edu
http://www.hg.org
http://www.ilrg.com

Publications

http://www.law.com
http://www.lawresearch.com

Medical Information

http://www.webmd.com
http://www.healthfinder.gov
http://www.mayohealth.org
http://www.health.nih.gov

Expert Witnesses

http://www.expertpages.com

STUDENT CD-ROM™
For additional materials, please go to the CD in this book.

ONLINE COMPANION™
For additional resources, please go to
http://www.paralegal.delmar.cengage.com

chapter 6

Intentional Torts:

More Injuries to Persons

THE BIGGEST MISTAKES PARALEGALS MAKE & HOW TO AVOID THEM

The $64,000 Question

Because all of the trial attorneys were out of the office one afternoon, I was asked by the managing attorney to conduct the initial intake examination of a man who had been injured in a car accident and was recently released from the hospital. Following the intake exam, the client asked me what his chances were of clearing $100,000 on his accident claim. I had no idea and told him so. He insisted and said, "Just a ballpark guess? I just want some idea if I should bother." I do

know that every accident claim is not compensable, depending on a host of reasons. "I am not a lawyer," I said. The client smiled and said, "I know, but my wife wants me to find out a range where accidents like this one might settle." I knew another claim like his had settled for $64,000 and gave him that figure as "safe," if it didn't go to trial and was the perfect case.

The client's new appointment was with one of our attorneys one week later. When he failed to

(continues)

arrive, I was asked to call the man. When I called, his wife answered. She said he had retained another firm for his claim. When I asked why, she said another attorney said his claim was worth more than the $64,000 I quoted! Even though I told the man I was not a lawyer, he assumed I was making a promise in behalf of the firm.

As a paralegal I am not empowered to speak for the firm or give legal advice. What sounds like the perfect case initially can easily fall apart once the facts are presented by all sides.

LESSON LEARNED: The client (or his wife) will always remember any promises not kept, and they may even be the basis for a malpractice action against the firm.

INTRODUCTION

In the preceding chapter, several intentional torts designed to injure a person were discussed: assault, battery, patient dumping, false imprisonment, and spoliation of evidence. All required an act, intent, and injurious behavior. The tortfeasor needed to intend to accomplish the harmful consequences of his own action. In this chapter, more intentional injuries to persons are detailed:

- Infliction of emotional distress
- Fraud and misrepresentation
- Malicious prosecution and abuse of process
- Invasion of privacy
- Defamation: libel and slander.

Some of these torts are the kind you see in the newspapers and on-line with celebrities headlining the stories.

INFLICTION OF EMOTIONAL DISTRESS

We have all encountered episodes in our lives in which other persons have intentionally caused us emotional upset. Anyone with a sibling can relate to misconduct designed to annoy and distress. In the law of intentional torts, infliction of emotional distress has developed as a separate cause of action to protect injured parties from other people's efforts to cause shock, fright, or other psychological trauma. One owes a duty to others not to intentionally inflict emotional distress. The breach of that duty is called intentional infliction of emotional distress.

emotional distress | Mental anguish. Nonphysical harm that may be compensated for by damages in some types of lawsuits. *Mental anguish* may be as limited as the immediate mental feelings during an injury or as broad as prolonged grief, shame, humiliation, despair, etc.

Emotional distress can be broadly defined as mental anguish caused by a tortfeasor. Synonyms such as fright, anxiety, shock, grief, mental suffering, or emotional disturbance are commonly used by the courts to describe this tort. The condition can include shame or embarrassment as well.

The critical aspect of infliction of emotional distress is that the victim suffers from mental anguish rather than from some physical injury caused by the tortfeasor. It is the psychological harm that this tort intends to remedy.

Not just any insult or offensive behavior will result in this tort, however. The misdeed must be so outrageous that a reasonable person would suffer severe emotional injury as a consequence. This is the key element in all infliction of emotional distress cases. Minor annoyances or indignities are part of everyday life, and these are not included in this tort. If it were otherwise, the courts would overflow with lawsuits, based upon the irritations we all encounter from other people almost daily. Obviously, the law cannot reshape the world into the loving, peaceful utopia we might prefer, but it can discourage flagrant actions tailored to cause mental suffering.

In the field of intentional torts, there are two varieties of infliction of emotional distress: intentional and reckless. A third version, negligent infliction, is discussed in Chapter 3.

Intentional Infliction

Intentional infliction of emotional distress consists of three elements:

1. Outrageous conduct by the tortfeasor
2. Conduct intended to cause severe mental anguish in the victim
3. The victim's suffering of severe mental anguish as a consequence of the tortfeasor's behavior.

intentional infliction of emotional distress | An intentional tort that occurs when the tortfeasor's outrageous conduct, which is intended to cause severe emotional anguish in the victim, actually causes the victim such emotional suffering as a result of the tortfeasor's actions.

Outrageous Conduct. As noted earlier, the tortfeasor's behavior must be sufficiently outrageous. The common test for outrageous conduct is one of reasonableness. Would a reasonable person suffer substantial emotional distress as a result of the tortfeasor's actions? Were these activities so outlandish as to *shock the conscience* of a reasonable person? Or, put another way, would a person of *ordinary sensibilities* suffer mental pain as a consequence? This generally excludes all but the most extreme types of egregious conduct.

Examples of outrageous conduct abound in legal literature. Tasteless practical jokes often provide fodder for emotional distress litigation. Consider the person who places a dead mouse inside a soda-pop bottle from which someone is drinking and then tells the drinker about the mouse. Or the heartless prankster who tells a parent that his or her child has just been struck and killed by an automobile when, in fact, this never occurred, as the joker knew perfectly well. Or the person who places revealing photographs of a nude sunbather all around the sunbather's place of employment for fellow workers to see. Or the individual who repeatedly telephones another at all hours of the day and night over several weeks. These are clear instances of outrageous conduct that most people would agree are highly offensive and would cause intense emotional dismay to the victims.

Intentional Acts. Obviously, intentional infliction cases must include the element of intent. The tortfeasor must purposefully behave so as to create mental anguish in the victim; the tortfeasor desires to cause anguish. This separates intentional infliction from reckless infliction, which does not require that the tortfeasor tailor his or her acts to cause mental suffering, as is discussed later in this section.

Actual Emotional Distress. Naturally, the victim must actually suffer emotionally as a result of the tortfeasor's antics. Again, the test for anguish revolves around the way a reasonable person of ordinary sensibilities would react to the tortfeasor's actions. Courts have often complained that determining genuine emotional suffering from faked distress is extremely difficult, because anyone can pretend to be upset by something. However, physical symptoms usually accompany mental distress, such as loss of sleep, weight, appetite, or vigor; illnesses brought on after the mental shock; or other signs of effect, such as tremors, twitches, or sensitivity to loud or sudden noises. It is important to note, though, that modern courts do *not* require physical manifestations in intentional infliction cases. Mental suffering alone, unaccompanied by physical effects, is sufficient, provided that the trier-of-fact is convinced of the authenticity of the distress.

THE CASE OF THE BASHFUL BAD BOY

In this case, a couple's intimate moments are shared with the reader because the defendant failed to disclose his sexual history to his girlfriend. The defendant is accused of negligent infliction of a sexually transmitted disease. The court found that the defendant breached his duty by failing either to warn of his condition or to abstain from relations.

DEUSCHLE
v.
JOBE
Missouri Court of Appeals, Western District
30 S.W.3d 215
October 31, 2000

Ms. Deuschle contends that Missouri recognizes a cause of action for reckless infection of a sexually transmitted disease. She alleges that her sexual partner, Mr. Jobe, infected her with herpes and genital warts. Ms. Deuschle claims Mr. Jobe knew he was infected with the diseases at the time he had sexual relations with her, and he failed to disclose his condition.

There is no statutory basis for this cause of action. But since 1986, Missouri common law has recognized a cause of action for negligently transmitting herpes.

* * *

In our case, the parties are unmarried. However, we find no justification for excluding an unmarried individual from bringing suit against her sexual partner for transmitting herpes under general tort law. . . .

Here, Ms. Deuschle alleged both intentional and negligent transmission of the disease. In Missouri, it has long been established that the elements of a negligence action are "(1) [a] legal duty on the part of the defendant to conform to a certain standard of conduct to protect others against unreasonable risks; (2) a breach of that duty; (3) a proximate cause between the conduct and the resulting injury; and (4) actual damages to the claimant's person or property."

. . . Missouri courts have long recognized the importance of preserving public health and welfare by creating legal duties, which help prevent the spread of dangerous, communicable diseases.

In furtherance of this objective, we hold that one has a legal duty to exercise reasonable care by disclosing a contagious venereal disease before entering into sexual relations with another. Several other jurisdictions that recognize this cause of action support this proposition. In an action for negligent transmission of a venereal disease, a person is liable if he knew or should have known that he was infected with a disease and failed to disclose or warn his sexual partner about this unreasonable risk of harm before engaging in a sexual relationship.

In order to establish whether or not this duty has been breached, we must determine if the foreseeability of actual harm exists. . . . The standard for foreseeability is measured by "whether or not a reasonably prudent person would have anticipated danger and provided against it."

When a disease such as herpes is almost exclusively spread through sexual contact, it is foreseeable that one's sexual partner is susceptible to the contagion if the infected partner is aware he has the disease or suffers from symptoms of the disease. . . .

Ms. Deuschle also alleges in the petition that Mr. Jobe's actions were the direct and proximate cause of her medical conditions. . . . As with any incurable sexually transmitted disease, once infected we infer that actual harm exists. Hence, a negligence action has been sufficiently pled by Ms. Deuschle in the petition.

As noted previously, the petition in some respects sounds like an intentional tort claim in alleging that Mr. Jobe knowingly failed to tell her of his disease, and knowing she was likely to become infected, that he intended injury, and that his conduct was outrageous. It is unclear exactly what intentional tort she is attempting to plead. . . . We direct the trial court to allow her to amend the petition to allege a specific intentional tort.

CASE QUESTIONS

1. What is the difference between negligent infliction of a disease and intentional infliction of a disease?
2. Is there an intentional tort in Missouri that would have been applicable to Ms. Deuschle's claim?

THE CASE OF THE HUMILIATED NEWSPAPER LADY

In this case, the court debated what it was "worth" to ninety-six-year-old Nellie Mitchell to suffer the humiliation, embarrassment, damage to reputation, and mental suffering of having her picture inserted in a supermarket tabloid. This case focused on the tort of intentional infliction of emotional distress.

MITCHELL

v.

GLOBE INTERNATIONAL PUBLISHING, INC.

United States District Court, W.D. Arkansas, Harrison Division

817 F. Supp. 72 (W.D. Ark. 1993)

March 15, 1993

Waters, Chief Judge

In the October 2, 1990, edition of *The Sun*, a supermarket tabloid published by defendant, Globe International Publishing, Inc., a photograph of Nellie Mitchell, a 96-year-old resident of Mountain Home, Arkansas, was used to illustrate a story about "Paper Gal, Audrey Wiles" in Sterling, Australia, who had become pregnant by one of her customers, a "reclusive millionaire" she met on her newspaper route. In fact,

(continues)

Mrs. Mitchell made her living running a newspaper stand and delivering newspapers in Mountain Home.

She sued Globe for defamation, invasion of privacy, and intentional infliction of emotional distress, and the case was tried to a jury in Harrison, Arkansas, beginning on December 2, 1991. The jury found that the defendant's conduct had invaded Mrs. Mitchell's privacy by placing her in a false light and had amounted to an intentional infliction of emotional distress. She was awarded compensatory damages in the amount of $650,000 and punitive damages of $850,000.

* * *

[I]t is the court's duty, as directed by the Court of Appeals, to reduce the compensatory damage award by some unspecified amount with the only guideline received from the Court of Appeals being that it should be "substantial."

The Court of Appeals said:

Though we are convinced that sufficient evidence exists to sustain a compensatory award for damage to Mitchell's reputation and her mental suffering, we also conclude the amount of the award is shocking and exaggerated.

Thus, it appears that it is this court's duty to determine, in whatever manner, what it is "worth" to Mrs. Mitchell to suffer the humiliation, embarrassment, mental suffering, and damage to her reputation caused by the egregious conduct by defendant in placing her picture and her very existence in the middle of an odious supermarket tabloid which, among other things, had a "road kill cannibal" describing his preference for human flesh from adults over that of children. . . . This court still believes that the Harrison, Arkansas, jury, chosen from all walks of life, was better situated to make that decision than this court is, but, as indicated, that is beside the point, because this court has been directed to do it.

This is an especially difficult task where the damages to be awarded are based upon intangibles such as damage to reputation and mental suffering. . . .

Of course, because of the nature of the damages in this case, there are no identifiable amounts that can be deducted, so any remittitur will, by its very nature, have to be somewhat arbitrary and speculative. . . .

In short, this court has been directed to order a "substantial remittitur" so it must do so. For reasons stated in the earlier opinion, this court is convinced that Mrs. Mitchell suffered substantial damages to her reputation and was caused mental suffering by being a part, against her will, of a detestable publication issued and sold across the country by the defendant.

Vada Sheid, a friend of Mrs. Mitchell described the humiliation that she suffered beginning at page 156 of Vol. I of the trial transcript as follows:

And I called Nellie and told her that I had the paper, and she came to the store to see this paper, and she said, where did you get this and how did this get into your store? . . . And she says, well, that's me, but you know that I'm not pregnant. And I said, of course not. . . . [S]he became so disturbed and so humiliated, and she said, but what will my kids think about this? Do you think they'll believe this, and how will I ever explain it to the people in town? And then she said, I'm going to buy up all the papers there is in this town so people in Mountain Home won't know about this.

* * *

[S]he went home, and she did not stir out for a few days. . . . [S]he was very depressed and humiliated, and she just didn't deliver her papers even for the following week.

* * *

Nellie was hurt. She said, I don't know why they're doing this to me; why it was done to me. She said, I've tried not to hurt anyone . . . why did they do it? . . . But she was hurt, and after that, she said that people would come in and, they'd—She said they look down at my belly, and they'll say, well, Nellie, haven't you had that baby yet? Nellie, when are you going to have that baby? Nellie, you should have had that baby by now.

And she said that it bothered her.

What is all that "worth"? A Harrison, Arkansas, jury believed that it was worth $650,000, but this court has been directed to reduce that award by ordering a "substantial remittitur." . . .

This court recognizes, and recognized from the very first, that Mrs. Mitchell did not show at the trial a great deal of outward evidence of the humiliation, anger, and disgust that many would express under the same circumstances, but the court attributed a great deal of that to her advanced age. . . . Admittedly, the court cannot take the evidence and point to any "specials" as lawyers call them, or any other identifiable dollar figures which can, with any certainty, justify an award of damages satisfactory to those who believe that these matters should be determined by some kind of formula. However, under all of the circumstances, the court is convinced that it is "worth" a minimum of $150,000 for Mrs. Mitchell to have been forced to endure what defendant heaped upon her, and the court,

therefore, determines that a "substantial remittitur" in this case, as directed by the Court of Appeals, is $500,000. A reduction of a half million dollars is certainly "substantial", and the court believes that an award of at least $150,000 in compensatory damages is justified by the evidence.

This court will deny the motion for a new trial filed herein in behalf of the defendant on the express condition that plaintiff has, within 14 days of the date of this opinion, accepted a remittitur in the amount of $500,000. If, within such period, plaintiff has not notified the court of acceptance of a remittitur in such amount, the motion for a new trial will be granted, and a new trial ordered.

CASE QUESTIONS

1. Why was the United States District Court so reluctant to reduce or change the award originally made by the jury?
2. Do you feel the original jury verdict was excessive? Explain.

Reckless Infliction

In general, recklessness is often a substitute for intent in tort law. Many **reckless infliction of emotional distress** cases include the mishandling of the remains of deceased persons. Consider a common fact pattern: A funeral home cremates the deceased instead of following the family's clear and explicit instructions regarding burial. Even though the funeral home did not intend this error, the conduct could be construed as so reckless as to fall within this tort.

Another type of fact situation involves the unanticipated effect of a practical joke. Consider the pranksters who vandalized someone's automobile by smearing it with manure, knowing that the vehicle owner took enormous pride in the car's appearance. The jokers knew that the owner had a weak heart, but were only expecting to shake up the owner. When the owner saw his prize automobile, he collapsed from a heart attack. This illustrates wanton misconduct. Although the pranksters did not intend the victim to suffer heart failure as a consequence of their deed, the tortfeasors' behavior revealed utter disregard for the health and well-being of the victim, and accordingly they would be liable for reckless infliction of emotional distress.

Claims of reckless infliction of emotional distress are sometimes made regarding unwanted, insulting, and demeaning sexual advances from a supervisor or co-worker at a place of employment. These claims are also known as sexual harassment suits.

reckless infliction of emotional distress | An intentional tort that occurs when the tortfeasor's outrageous conduct causes the victim to suffer severe mental anguish. Intent to produce the emotional suffering is not necessary. Instead, it is sufficient that the tortfeasor knew, or reasonably should have known, that his or her misbehavior would produce emotional distress. The tortfeasor's conduct is wanton, with no apparent regard for the victim's suffering.

hypotheticals

Fantasia could offer an example. She owed money on a charge account at a local appliance store. Unfortunately, she missed several payments because of financial difficulties. Susan, the store sales manager, began repeatedly telephoning Fantasia at work and late in the evenings at home, demanding that Fantasia pay the balance due. The calls continued over several weeks. Fantasia's supervisor became angry that Fantasia was wasting company time taking these phone calls. The calls at night woke Fantasia several times and agitated her enough to keep her awake. As a result, Fantasia's job performance slumped. Fantasia lost weight and became irritable because of lack of sleep. Has Susan intentionally inflicted emotional distress upon Fantasia?

Susan's actions were designed to upset Fantasia greatly to coerce Fantasia to pay the overdue debt. Susan acted in an outrageous manner—reasonable persons would find repeated telephone calls late at night and on the job to be highly offensive. Fantasia suffered substantial mental anguish (with physical manifestations) as a result of Susan's conduct. Accordingly, Susan would be liable to Fantasia for intentional infliction of emotional distress.

***

Consider another illustration. Gupta and Colin are accountants with the same firm. Gupta planted a fake letter of termination on Colin's desk, in which the office manager accused Colin of misappropriation of client funds. Upon reading the letter, Colin became distraught, shaking and sweating violently and feeling nauseous. Colin burst into the manager's office to deny the allegations, at which time Gupta disclosed his gag. Has Gupta inflicted emotional distress upon Colin?

All the elements are present in this hypothetical, including intent to cause mental anguish. Gupta should tally his own personal accounts, because he will be liable to Colin for intentional infliction of emotional distress.

Table 6-1 summarizes the elements of infliction of emotional distress.

TABLE 6-1
Elements of infliction of emotional distress

INTENTIONAL INFLICTION	RECKLESS INFLICTION
Outrageous conduct	Outrageous conduct
Conduct intended to cause severe mental anguish	Conduct known (or reasonably should be known) to cause severe mental anguish Recklessness is a substitute for intent
Victim suffers severe mental anguish as result	Victim suffers severe mental anguish as result
Example: Deliberately playing a joke on someone; telling them a family member died.	**Example:** Carelessly burying the wrong corpse in a cemetery plot.

▌ FRAUD AND MISREPRESENTATION

Fraud, or **deceit** as some states call it, occurs when a tortfeasor makes false statements to entice the victim to give up something of value to the tortfeasor. Fraudulent **misrepresentation** exists when the tortfeasor knowingly makes false statements or purposefully behaves in such a way as to deceive the victim. The two torts are quite similar. Both involve false statements or actions. Both include deception as the tortfeasor's objective. Yet fraud features the element of underhanded economic gain: the victim surrenders something valuable to the tortfeasor as a result of the false comments. As a practical matter, however, a tortfeasor who commits fraud also commits misrepresentation, although they technically are not the same tort. Still, many courts view them as synonymous. Note, when a salesperson uses puffery (exaggerates), this is not considered a misrepresentation.

fraud (deceit) | Any kind of trickery used to cheat another of money or property.

misrepresentation |
1. *Innocent misrepresentation* is a false statement that is not known to be false.
2. *Negligent misrepresentation* is a false statement made when the one making the statement should have known better.
3. *Fraudulent misrepresentation* is a false statement known to be false and meant to be misleading.

Definitions and Distinctions

Fraud. For fraud, the following must exist:

1. The defrauder must intend to deceive by making a false representation of material fact
2. The defrauder must know that the statements made are false
3. The purpose of the false statements must be to entice the victim into giving the tortfeasor something of value
4. The innocent party must justifiably rely on the misrepresentation
5. The innocent party must be injured.

Misrepresentation. For misrepresentation, the first two elements of fraud must occur. Some courts, however, also add the other elements to misrepresentation, making it identical to fraud. In such jurisdictions, the two concepts are thus redundant. Table 6-2 outlines the elements of fraud and misrepresentation.

Fraud	Misrepresentation
False statements intended to deceive	False statements intended to deceive
Knowledge of falsity of statements	Knowledge of falsity of statements
Plaintiff relies on the statement	Plaintiff relies on the statement
Statements designed to entice victim into surrendering something of value	
Innocent party is injured	Innocent party is injured

TABLE 6-2
Elements of fraud and misrepresentation

material | Significant or important.

False Statements Intended to Deceive

A tortfeasor commits fraud or misrepresentation by making **material** false statements designed to delude the victim. For example, if Aaron tells Stephanie that he can repair her broken dishwasher for $100, when Aaron knows that he lacks the requisite skill and knowledge to do so, then Aaron has made false statements intended to mislead Stephanie into paying him the money for work he cannot perform.

Knowledge of Falsity of Information

The tortfeasor must have known or should have known that the information given to the victim is false for fraud or misrepresentation to happen. For instance, if Henry sells Michelle a new computer with a defective floppy disk drive of which Henry is totally unaware, then Henry has not engaged in either fraud or misrepresentation, because he did not know about the product defect when he made the sale.

Tortfeasor's Profit from Deception

For fraud, the defrauder must make false statements tailored to encourage the victim to surrender something of value to the tortfeasor. In the preceding example, Aaron duped Stephanie in order to receive her money. This constitutes fraud.

Justifiable Reliance

The injured party must justifiably rely on the false statement. This means the party must know about the statement. The false statement must be a substantial factor in the plaintiff's decision, or reason for an action taken based upon the statement. However, the false statement need not be the sole factor in the decision or action.

Innocent Party's Injury

Like all torts, the innocent party must prove actual injury as a consequence of the false statements or misrepresentation.

THE CASE OF CONTINUING ABUSE

This case represents just one of the thousands of cases of abuse brought against clergy and the archdiocese in recent times. As evidenced by the specific pleadings and facts of this case, each case is different. Here, even though it appears most likely that abuse did occur, the plaintiff's case was dismissed. The plaintiff waited until he was in his late twenties to bring this action.

John DELANEY, Appellant

v.

ARCHDIOCESE OF PHILADELPHIA, Cardinal Justin Rigali and Cardinal Anthony Bevilacqua, Appellees.

2007 WL 1334479 (Pa. Super.)

No. 1759 EDA 2006

Superior Court of Pennsylvania

Filed May 8, 2007

This is an appeal from an order granting judgment in favor of Appellees Archdiocese of Philadelphia, Cardinal Justin Rigali, and Cardinal Anthony Bevilacqua on the basis that the claims of Appellant John Delaney were barred by the statute of limitations. We affirm.

The record discloses that in 1982, at the age of eleven, Appellant became acquainted with Father Brzyski while a parishioner at St. Cecilia in Philadelphia, Pennsylvania. Appellant was also being educated in the parish school, worked in the parish rectory, and served as an altar boy for the parish. Father Brzyski routinely sexually abused Appellant at the child's residence and at the parish rectory. These abuses lasted for approximately four years and even continued after Father Brzyski transferred from St. Cecilia in 1983 or 1984—Father Brzyski maintained the relationship with Appellant's family in order to perpetuate the sexual abuse of the minor child, which was all done with the alleged knowledge and concealment of Father Brzyski's pedophilia by Appellees Archdiocese of Philadelphia, Cardinal Justin Rigali, and Cardinal Anthony Bevilacqua.

The reasons Appellant's parents did not know of the abuse were twofold: 1) Father Brzyski ordered Appellant to refrain from telling anyone; and 2) Appellant, his parents, and other parishioners were told by Appellees that Father Brzyski's removal from St. Cecilia was ascribed to "sick leave." This lulled Appellant's parents into allowing Father Brzyski to have continuing access to the minor child. In fact, Appellees' failure to inform Appellant and his family of Father Brzyski's history of sexual abuse of children before and after his removal from St. Cecilia and

placement on "sick leave" prompted Appellant and his parents to relax their vigilance and refrain from investigating any potential claims against Appellees until August 6, 2005.

> [Appellant] first learned of the [. . .] reports [from a former principal of St. Cecilia or another person affiliated with St. Cecilia] regarding Father Brzyski['s abuse of Appellant and/or others at St. Cecilia and it being reported to the Archdiocese and/or its representatives] on or about Sunday, August 6, 2005 when he read about the same in that day's edition of the *Philadelphia Inquirer*.

Once Appellant discovered Appellees' role in concealing knowledge of sexual abuse by Father Brzyski and other predator priests in the Archdiocese, Appellant filed suit in September of 2005 against Appellees. Appellees asserted that Appellant's claims were barred by the applicable statute of limitations.

Appellant alleges that the running of the statute of limitations was tolled based upon Appellees' fraudulent concealment of Father Brzyski's abuse of children. First, the concealment referred to by Appellant is in the nature of a "general, systematic fraudulent conduct on the part of Archdiocesan [Appellees,]" *i.e.*, systematically concealing the danger that predator priests present by misrepresenting them as priests in good standing; creating a misperception in the mind of Appellant and his parents that priests in general and Father Brzyski in particular engaged in isolated incidents of spurious conduct.

The incidents of fraud recited above are the predicate for Appellant's argument that the statute of limitations should be tolled until he learned in August of 2005, from reading the *Philadelphia Inquirer,* of Appellees' concealment and misrepresentation to the public regarding the systematic "cover-up" of its knowledge of the pervasiveness of predator priests within the Archdiocese.

[. . .] The child abuse is the injury in this matter, not the alleged cover-up by the Archdiocese (otherwise, any member of the Catholic Church could conceivably bring suit against the Archdiocese, absent any abuse, alleging injury from the Archdiocese's general conduct).

(continues)

The Archdiocese [. . .] claim[s] that even if this no-specific conduct is considered concealment, [Appellants] cannot be considered to have relied on any representations or omissions of the Archdiocese because [Appellants] did not make any effort to investigate their claims and the Archdiocese did not prevent them from investigating their claims.

We agree with the Archdiocese that the doctrine of fraudulent concealment does not toll the statute of limitations here.

Appellant has not put forth any evidence to indicate that he made any inquiries of Appellees prior to August of 2005 regarding his potential causes of action. Appellant does not allege that Appellees' reassignment of Father Brzyski and listing him on "sick leave" misled Appellant or his parents into believing that the alleged sexual abuse did not occur, that it had not been committed by Father Brzyski, or that the alleged sexual abuse had not resulted in injury to Appellant. Appellees never concealed from Appellant or his parents the fact of the injury itself. Nor does Appellant allege that he or his parents were lied to by Appellees with regard to the identity of his abuser or his abuser's place within the Archdiocese, which if relied upon would have caused him and/or his parents to suspend pursuit of their claims.

The essence of Appellant's fraudulent concealment argument is that Appellees' general conduct and/or listing Father Brzyski on "sick leave" concealed from him and his parents an additional theory of liability for the alleged sexual abuse from the offending priest to his employers/supervisors/principals/Appellees. "This argument misses the mark [. . .] for a cause of action to accrue, the entire theory of the case need not be immediately apparent [. . .] as soon as [the plaintiffs] became aware of the alleged abuse, they should also have been aware that the [defendants], as the priests' employers, were potentially liable for that abuse."

With the systematic conduct alleged by Appellant failing to constitute an affirmative act for purposes of the fraudulent concealment exception, and Appellant's failure to show that he relied upon any affirmative act of concealment by Appellees which caused him to forego pursuit of his causes of action, we shall affirm the judgment in favor of Appellees.

CASE QUESTIONS

1. Do you think this decision was harsh? Explain.
2. Why do you think the plaintiff waited so long to bring suit?

Classic illustrations of fraud or misrepresentation seem to utilize used car sales situations, which have become the brunt of many jokes. Still, the examples profile the elements quite well.

hypotheticals

Ask Mayfield, for instance, who purchased an automobile from Honest Eddy's Used Car Palace. Honest Eddy himself assured Mayfield that the chosen vehicle had been driven only 5,000 miles by a driving instructor from Ontario, that the brakes had just been replaced, and that the engine had been re-tuned. Honest Eddy knew that none of this was true and merely wanted to make the sale at all costs. Mayfield bought the car and drove away. Much to Mayfield's horror and embarrassment, within a week the automobile began to emit huge plumes of blue smoke from its exhaust. It also shook violently upon acceleration and made grinding noises. Has Honest Eddy committed fraud and misrepresentation against Mayfield?

The elements piece together. Honest Eddy knew that the automobile was defective, but lied about its condition to induce Mayfield to buy it. Mayfield surrendered to Honest Eddy something of value (namely, money—the car's purchase price). Because there was deception, misrepresentation exists. Honest Eddy is liable to Mayfield for fraud and misrepresentation.

* * *

Richard supplies another good illustration. He purchased a home from Quality Construction Company (QCC). QCC's sales director assured Richard that the house had been treated for termites when, in fact, it had not. QCC had paid an exterminator to inspect the house, and the exterminator's report advised of the need for termite treatment. After living in the house for a few months, Richard discovered a serious termite infestation. Did QCC engage in fraud or misrepresentation?

The critical elements here are intent and knowledge. Did QCC's sales director know that no termite treatment had been done? QCC had received the exterminator's report recommending treatment. Thus, the sales director should have known that treatment was necessary and should have known that QCC had not performed this task. Thus, knowledge may be *imputed* under the circumstances. Intent, however, is more difficult to ascertain. Did the sales director purposefully mislead Richard? Since the director should have known that no treatment had been applied, his contrary statement to Richard demonstrated his desire to delude Richard. This equals intentional deception. Thus, misrepresentation can be proven. Also, because QCC's objective was to entice Richard to buy the house, the third element of fraud exists.

MALICIOUS PROSECUTION AND ABUSE OF PROCESS

Usually the common law distinguishes malicious prosecution from abuse of process in this way: Malicious prosecution occurs in criminal prosecutions, whereas abuse of process happens in civil litigation. They are similar intentional torts.

Malicious Prosecution

Malicious prosecution arises when a private citizen files with the prosecutor a groundless criminal complaint against another person (who is named as the defendant in the subsequent criminal proceeding). This tort is comprised of the following elements:

1. Groundless criminal prosecution against the accused without probable cause
2. The complainant's malice in filing the spurious charges

malicious prosecution | A tort committed by bringing charges against someone in order to harm that person and with no legal justification for doing it.

3. The accused's acquittal from, or dismissal of, the criminal charges

4. Injury to the accused as a result of the prosecution.

Groundless Criminal Prosecution.

The individual registering a criminal complaint with the police or prosecutor is sometimes called the **complainant.** The complainant's actions are considered bogus if he or she preferred criminal charges without probable cause that the accused was guilty of the crime. **Probable cause** is routinely defined as the reasonable belief that the accused is guilty of the alleged crime. This belief need exist only at the time the criminal charges are initiated for probable cause to exist. However, if it later becomes obvious through investigation that the accused did not commit the alleged crime, then the complainant's insistence on the government's continuing prosecution would be malicious prosecution.

complainant | 1. A person who makes an official complaint. 2. A person who starts a lawsuit.

probable cause | A reasonable belief that the accused is guilty of the alleged crime.

Malice.

Malice in filing spurious criminal charges may be inferred from the circumstances surrounding the case. If the complainant knew (or reasonably should have known) that the accused did not commit the alleged crime, then malice is implied. Also, if the complainant is using the criminal prosecution to obtain some improper objective, such as intimidating the accused into settling a disputed civil claim or to extort money from the accused, then this likewise implies malice.

malice | 1. Ill will. 2. Intentionally harming someone. 3. In defamation law, with knowledge of falsity or with reckless disregard for whether or not something is false.

Accused's Acquittal from, or Dismissal of, the Criminal Charges.

To recover successfully for malicious prosecution, the accused must have been acquitted of the groundless criminal charges initiated by the complainant, or the prosecution must have been otherwise disposed of in the accused's favor (dismissal of charges, for instance).

Injury to the Accused.

Like all torts, the accused must prove actual injury as a consequence of the wrongful prosecution. This is most often accomplished by showing damage to the accused's reputation in the community or financial standing, mental anguish, or legal expenses associated with defending the criminal charges.

Abuse of Process

abuse of process | Using the legal system unfairly; for example, prosecuting a person for writing a "bad check" simply to pressure him or her to pay.

Abuse of process is the civil equivalent of malicious prosecution. It occurs when the tortfeasor misuses a legal proceeding against another person to achieve an unlawful objective. The elements of abuse of process are

1. Misuse of a legal proceeding, or threat of such misuse

2. Misuse to achieve unlawful objectives

3. Injury to the victim as a result of the misuse.

Misuse of Legal Proceedings to Achieve Unlawful Goals.

The tortfeasor must intentionally misuse (or threaten to misuse) a legal proceeding against another person to accomplish an objective to which the process abuser is not legally entitled. The tortfeasor normally threatens frivolous civil litigation in an attempt to frighten the victim into paying a disputed claim. For example, the process abuser might file a groundless lawsuit against an innocent defendant in an attempt to "scare up some quick money." This occasionally occurs in personal injury litigation when fault is difficult to assign and prove; the personal injury plaintiff abuses process by suing a convenient (but innocent) defendant (who usually has assets or insurance but seems unlikely to defend a frivolous lawsuit).

Litigation is not the only legal process that may be misapplied, however. Creditors filing improper mechanic's liens against debtors to collect on disputed debts, or a wife accusing her spouse of sexually abusing their children to gain an advantage in a custody hearing, when there are no grounds for the claim and she knows the claim is false, would also be guilty of abuse of process.

The pivotal aspect of abuse of process is the tortfeasor's misuse of a legal proceeding to gain some indirect benefit to which he or she is not legally entitled. The tortfeasor has an ulterior motive for manipulating the legal proceeding. The following hypotheticals illustrate how legal process may be exploited in this way.

When tortfeasors engage in malicious prosecution and abuse of process, their victims are often left with an unpleasant taste as a result of the experience. The victims develop a cynical bitterness toward the apparent ease with which the legal system was manipulated against them. But tort law strives to restore the balance (and the victims' faith in the system) by affording remedies against these intentional torts.

Table 6-3 specifies the elements of malicious prosecution and abuse of process.

MALICIOUS PROSECUTION	ABUSE OF PROCESS
Groundless criminal prosecution	Misuse of legal proceeding (or threat of misuse)
Complainant's malice	Misuse to achieve unlawful objectives
Accused's acquittal or dismissal of charges	
Accused's injury	Injury to victim

TABLE 6-3
Elements of malicious prosecution and abuse of process

The following examples demonstrate how the legal system reacts when misused in this manner.

hypotheticals

Andrew was offended when a bookstore that sold provocative literature opened in his neighborhood. He registered with the prosecutor a criminal complaint for pornography against the bookstore in the hope that it would shut down or move away. Nothing that the bookstore sold violated the city's pornography ordinance, as the prosecutor informed Andrew. Nonetheless, Andrew exerted pressure on the prosecutor (through a contact in the mayor's office) to proceed, and subsequently the court dismissed the charges upon the bookstore's attorney's motion. The bookstore lost substantial business as a result of adverse publicity in the newspapers surrounding the case. Has Andrew maliciously prosecuted?

Andrew's criminal complaint against the bookstore was frivolous, because its merchandise did not violate any criminal ordinance. The prosecutor had told Andrew that the bookstore was not acting illegally, so Andrew lacked probable cause to believe in the bookstore's guilt. Andrew's malice could be inferred, because he knew of the bookstore's innocence but insisted on pressing the criminal prosecution to coerce the bookstore into closing or moving. The bookstore successfully had the criminal charges dismissed. It also suffered financial injury as a result of Andrew's actions. Accordingly, Andrew is liable to the bookstore for malicious prosecution.

* * *

Jennifer's Shipping Company delivered a shipment of desks to Northern Office Supply Corporation. One of Northern's employees, Tony, damaged several desks while moving them into storage with a fork loader truck. The desks were undamaged previously. Northern's president, Carrie, filed suit against Jennifer's, claiming that the desks had been damaged in shipment by Jennifer's employees. Has Northern abused process against Jennifer's?

Carrie knew that Jennifer's was not responsible for the marred desks, as she had observed Tony carelessly operate the fork loader and damage the desks. Thus, Northern's lawsuit against Jennifer's was groundless. Filing frivolous litigation constitutes misuse of legal process. It may be deduced that Carrie's purpose in filing Northern's lawsuit was to intimidate Jennifer's into settling the case out of court through its insurance carrier. Jennifer's injury exists in that it must defend against this baseless legal action, incurring attorneys' fees, litigation expenses, and lost time for employees required to testify. The lawsuit could also damage Jennifer's reputation if the business community became aware of the action, which could easily occur, as lawsuits are a matter of public record. Northern will therefore be liable to Jennifer's for abuse of process.

THE CASE OF THE DUKE LACROSSE PLAYERS

In this headline-making case, the victims, three Duke University lacrosse players, were ultimately declared innocent by the North Carolina Attorney General Roy Cooper, after falsely being accused of rape by a stripper. Not only were the criminal charges dropped after 395 days of public accusations, but the prosecutor, attorney Mike Nifong, was ultimately disbarred for his actions. Nifong was accused of multiple ethics violations, including of the prohibition against making comments that have a substantial likelihood of heightening public condemnation of the accused.

More than three dozen current and former Duke lacrosse players and their family members filed a lawsuit for the emotional distress they suffered during this public media circus that arose regarding the prosecutor's targeted investigation and overzealous rush to judgment. None of the parties filed a suit against the woman who alleged she was raped, who had been referred to as a deeply disturbed, drug-dependent woman who attended North Carolina Central University. This case inflamed racial tensions and evoked discussion of class because the players were white and from an elite private school, and the accused was a black woman from a public university.

Dave Evans, Collin Finnerty, Reade Seligmann, et al., plaintiffs.
v.
Duke University, President Richard Brodhead, Duke Medical Center, City of Durham, et al., defendants.
United States District Court
Middle District of North Carolina

The players in this lawsuit filed on February 21, 2008, accuse the City of Durham Officials of fraud, abuse and breach of duty for supporting the prosecution of this case. The lawsuit against the private university was for allegedly implying the team was guilty when the accusations surfaced, and for ignoring and suppressing evidence while the team members suffered abuse and harassment on campus. The City of Durham is charged with responsibility for Nifong's investigation and actions.

While Nifong won indictments against the three lacrosse players after the woman accused them of rape in the Spring 2006, the case quickly fell apart as the woman's story changed and there was a lack of evidence. The twenty-eight-year-old woman was hired to perform as a dancer at a lacrosse team party. When she alleged she was gang raped this started the unending media headline coverage.

This case caused a huge uproar on campus. Duke cancelled the rest of the team's 2006 season games. The lacrosse coach resigned after faculty took sides, some supporting the athletes, and others who accused the athletes of "frat boy" behavior.

In December, nine months after the charges broke, the prosecutor became the accused. The bar cited 41 different quotes and 8 paraphrased statements that Nifong made to the media, many of them focused on his characterization of the character and credibility of the players, or their unwillingness to cooperate with Nifong. When questioned by reporters, Nifong referred to the three lacrosse players as "a bunch of hooligans," and stated that he was sure there was a rape. Nifong even stated that he wondered why they needed an attorney if they claim they hadn't done anything wrong and were not charged. Nifong also said he was disappointed that none of the lacrosse players was "enough of a man to come forward."

According to the bar, when DNA testing failed to find any evidence that a lacrosse player raped the accused, Nifong told the reporter that the players might have used a condom. Yet, Nifong was in possession of a report from an emergency room nurse who was advised by the female in question that her attackers

(continues)

did not use a condom. Only after the female wavered in her story and advised that she no longer was certain that she was penetrated vaginally with a penis, did Nifong drop the rape charges. Yet, Nifong still pursued the kidnapping and sexual offense charges even though the legal experts warned Nifong that the case appeared to be weak.

In addition to the weak DNA evidence and the alleged victim's changing story, one player claimed to have an alibi supported by time dated receipts, and the defense claimed that the police photo lineup used to identify the accused violated police procedures and was skewed against the men.

Attorney General Roy Cooper, assigned to the case after Nifong was charged with ethics violations, stated the case shows the "enormous consequences of overreaching by a prosecutor." The attorney general stated that, after investigating, they were led to conclude that no attack occurred.

There has been no decision in this case yet.

CASE QUESTIONS
1. How can this "rush to justice" be avoided in the future?
2. Who would you hold responsible in this matter: Nifong, or others? Explain.

▌ INVASION OF PRIVACY

Invasion of privacy is largely a twentieth-century concept. In 1888, Judge Cooley of the Michigan Supreme Court, in his famous torts treatise, analyzed a series of nineteenth-century court decisions on defamation, trespass upon a personal property right (such as lectures or publications), and breach of confidence under implied contract law. Cooley surmised that a broader right was being protected and defined the legal interest in the famous phrase *the right to be let alone* (Cooley, *Torts* 29 [2d ed. 1888]). In 1890, a famous *Harvard Law Review* article co-authored by (later United States Supreme Court Justice) Louis Brandeis substantially expanded Cooley's theory, coining the phrase *right to privacy* (Warren & Brandeis, "The Right to Privacy," 4 *Harv. L. Rev.* 193 [1890]). American courts and legislatures throughout the twentieth century have incorporated this tort into their common law and statutes. It may be fairly said that this cause of action arose primarily because of this law-review article.

invasion of privacy | A violation of the right to be left alone.

Simply put, **invasion of privacy** exists when someone publicly exploits another person's private affairs in an unreasonably intrusive manner. In tort law, there are four separate types of invasion of privacy:

1. Appropriation
2. Unreasonable intrusion
3. Public disclosure of private facts
4. False light in the public eye.

Appropriation

Appropriation occurs when the tortfeasor uses a person's name or likeness without permission to gain some benefit. For example, if an advertising company used a person's photograph to sell a product without that person's consent, then the firm would be liable to the person for invasion of privacy by appropriation. Most cases involving this variety of invasion of privacy consist of the unauthorized use of photographs, artist's sketches, or quotations associated with names to sell someone else's goods or services.

appropriation | Taking something wrongfully.

THE CASE OF THE FALSE STILL

In this case, computer technology is used to alter famous still photography. Despite this false depiction, the actor is left powerless.

HOFFMAN
v.
CAPITAL CITIES/ABC, INCORPORATED
United States Court of Appeals, Ninth Circuit
255 F.3d 1180 (9th Cir. (Cal.))
Argued and Submitted Oct. 10, 2000
Filed July 6, 2001

In 1982, actor Dustin Hoffman starred in the movie "Tootsie," playing a male actor who dresses as a woman to get a part on a television soap opera. One memorable still photograph from the movie showed Hoffman in character in a red long-sleeved sequined evening dress and high heels, posing in front of an American flag. The still carried the text, "What do you get when you cross a hopelessly straight, starving actor with a dynamite red sequined dress? You get America's hottest new actress."

In March 1997, Los Angeles Magazine ("LAM") published the "Fabulous Hollywood Issue!" An article from this issue entitled "Grand Illusions" used computer technology to alter famous film stills to make it appear that the actors were wearing Spring 1997 fashions. The sixteen familiar scenes included movies and actors such as "North by Northwest" (Cary Grant), "Saturday Night Fever" (John Travolta), . . .

"Gone with the Wind" (Vivian Leigh and Hattie McDaniel). . . . The final shot was the "Tootsie" still. The American flag and Hoffman's head remained as they appeared in the original, but Hoffman's body and his long-sleeved red sequined dress were replaced by the body of a male model in the same pose, wearing a spaghetti-strapped, cream-colored, silk evening dress and high-heeled sandals. LAM omitted the original caption. The text on the page identified the still as from the movie "Tootsie," and read, "Dustin Hoffman isn't a drag in a butter-colored silk gown by Richard Tyler and Ralph Lauren heels."

LAM did not ask Hoffman for permission to publish the altered photograph. Nor did LAM secure permission from Columbia Pictures, the copyright holder. . . .

California recognizes, in its common law and its statutes, "the right of a person whose identity has commercial value—most often a celebrity—to control the commercial use of that identity." Hoffman claims that LAM violated his state right of publicity by appropriating his name and likeness. He also claims that LAM violated his rights under the federal Lanham Act.

LAM replies that its challenged use of the "Tootsie" photo is protected under the First Amendment. We evaluate this defense aware of "the careful balance

(continues)

that courts have gradually constructed between the right of publicity and the First Amendment and federal intellectual property laws."

LAM argues that the "Grand Illusions" article and the altered "Tootsie" photograph contained therein are an expression of editorial opinion, entitled to protection under the First Amendment. Hoffman, a public figure, must therefore show that LAM, a media defendant, acted with "actual malice," that is, with knowledge that the photograph was false, or with reckless disregard for its falsity. Because Hoffman did not produce clear and convincing evidence that LAM acted with actual malice, LAM contends that all Hoffman's claims are barred by the First Amendment.

* * *

"Commercial speech" has special meaning in the First Amendment context. . . . Such speech is entitled to a measure of First Amendment protection. . . . Commercial messages, however, do not receive the same level of constitutional protection as other types of protected expression. . . . [C]ommercial speech receives limited amount of protection compared to speech at core of First Amendment and may freely be regulated if it is misleading. When speech is properly classified as commercial, a public figure plaintiff does not have to show that the speaker acted with actual malice.

In many right of publicity cases, the question of actual malice does not arise, because the challenged use of the celebrity's identity occurs in an advertisement that "does no more than propose a commercial transaction" and is clearly commercial speech. . . . In all these cases, the defendant used an aspect of the celebrity's identity entirely and directly for the purpose of selling a product. Such uses do not implicate the First Amendment's protection of expressions of editorial opinion.

Hoffman points out that the body double in the "Tootsie" photograph was identified as wearing Ralph Lauren shoes and that there was a Ralph Lauren advertisement (which did not feature shoes) elsewhere in the magazine. (Insofar as the record

shows, Richard Tyler, the designer of the gown, had never advertised in LAM.) Hoffman also points to the "Shopper's Guide" in the back of the magazine, which provided stores and prices for the shoes and gown.

These facts are not enough to make the "Tootsie" photograph pure commercial speech. . . . LAM did not use Hoffman's image in a traditional advertisement printed merely for the purpose of selling a particular product. . . . "Grand Illusions" appears as a feature article on the cover of the magazine and in the table of contents. It is a complement to and a part of the issue's focus on Hollywood past and present. Viewed in context, the article as a whole is a combination of fashion photography, humor, and visual and verbal editorial comment on classic films and famous actors.

* * *

We conclude that LAM's publication of the altered "Tootsie" photograph was not commercial speech.

* * *

We have concluded that LAM is entitled to the full First Amendment protection accorded noncommercial speech. Because a public figure such as Hoffman can recover damages for noncommercial speech from a media organization such as LAM only by proving "actual malice," we now must determine whether the district court was correct in concluding that LAM acted with "reckless disregard for the truth" or a "high degree of awareness of probable falsity." . . .

To show actual malice, Hoffman must demonstrate by clear and convincing evidence that LAM intended to create the false impression in the minds of its readers that when they saw the altered "Tootsie" photograph they were seeing Hoffman's body. It is not enough to show that LAM unknowingly misled readers into thinking Hoffman had actually posed for the altered photograph. Mere negligence is not enough to demonstrate actual malice. . . . The evidence must clearly and convincingly demonstrate that LAM knew (or purposefully avoided knowing) that the photograph would mislead its readers into thinking that the body in the altered photograph was Hoffman's.

We do not believe that the totality of LAM's presentation of the article and the "Tootsie" photograph provides clear and convincing evidence that the editors intended to suggest falsely to the ordinary reader that he or she was seeing Hoffman's body in the altered "Tootsie" photograph. All but one of the references to the article in the magazine make it clear

that digital techniques were used to substitute current fashions for the clothes worn in the original stills.

* * *

Because there is no clear and convincing evidence of actual malice, we must reverse the district court's judgment in Hoffman's favor and the court's award of attorney fees.

CASE QUESTIONS

1. Explain why the altered "Tootsie" photograph was not considered commercial speech.
2. Explain why the court concluded that there was no actual malice.

Unreasonable Intrusion

Unreasonable intrusion involves an excessive and highly offensive assault upon one's seclusion or solitude. Several illustrations should clarify. If store security personnel demand that a suspected shoplifter disrobe, or if they rifle through the suspect's personal belongings in an illegal search, this would be considered unreasonable intrusion. Intentional eavesdropping upon a private conversation is another example. Recall the Fantasia/Susan hypothetical discussed in connection with infliction of emotional distress. Susan's incessant telephone calls would also constitute unreasonable intrusion. Searching another's mail to discover private information or obtaining unauthorized access to someone's bank account or tax records are yet other instances. Courts have also found that illegal, compulsory blood tests equal unreasonable intrusion. Simple trespassing onto an individual's land to snoop would also violate this version of privacy.

unreasonable intrusion | One type of the intentional tort of invasion of privacy. Occurs when the tortfeasor engages in an excessive and highly offensive invasion upon another person's seclusion or solitude.

Public Disclosure of Private Facts

When a tortfeasor communicates purely private information about a person to the public without permission, and a reasonable person would find this disclosure extremely objectionable, then invasion of privacy by **public disclosure of private facts** has taken place. Truth is *not* a defense against this tort, because it is the unauthorized and offensive public revelation of private facts that is being protected against.

The most common example of such disclosure involves communications by the mass media. For example, if a newspaper article mentions an ordinary citizen by name and discusses in detail his or her drug dependency problems, and the person did not consent, then public disclosure of private facts has occurred. Public figures, however, generally do not succeed in lawsuits against the media when such disclosures are made without malice.

public disclosure of private facts | One type of the intentional tort of invasion of privacy. Occurs when the tortfeasor communicates purely private information about a person to the public without permission, and a reasonable person would find this disclosure extremely objectionable.

THE CASE OF THE VIEWING ROOM COVERED BY THE UMBRELLA

In some cases, the statement "truth is stranger than fiction" really rings true. As a paralegal you will be privy to numerous stories—some of which, if you heard them outside the law office, would cause you to burst out laughing in disbelief. As a professional, you must learn to maintain your composure no matter what the client reveals to you. In this example, you get to see a case from an insurance company's perspective.

LINEBERRY
v.
STATE FARM FIRE & CASUALTY CO.

885 F. Supp. 1095 (M.D. Tenn. 1995)
United States District Court
Middle District of Tennessee
April 4, 1995
Echols, District Judge

Plaintiffs, Dewey Lineberry and Bill Robinson, seek a declaratory judgment requiring State Farm Fire & Casualty Co. ["State Farm"] to defend and indemnify them against actions in state court pursuant to personal liability policies of insurance ....

Plaintiffs are currently defending four separate actions brought in the Circuit Court of Wilson County, Tennessee by four women. The allegations of all four suits are essentially the same. Lineberry apparently had sexual relationships with the four women over the period of time stated in the lawsuits. In the course of building himself a new office building, Lineberry enlisted the help of Robinson to construct a "secret" viewing room adjoining the recreation room and the restroom of Lineberry's personal office. Two-way mirrors were constructed into the walls of the recreation room and restroom so that anyone in the viewing room could look through the mirrors and observe occupants of the recreation room and bathroom without the occupant's knowledge. The occupants of the recreation room and restroom could see only their own reflections in the mirrors. Lineberry and Robinson set up a video camera in the viewing room so that the persons and activities in the recreation room and restroom could secretly be filmed through the two-way mirrors.

On occasions Lineberry brought the unsuspecting females to his office where Robinson, who was hiding in the viewing room, secretly videotaped their sexual activities. Lineberry contends this scheme was approved or suggested by his attorney as a way to preserve proof of his sexual activities in the event one of his unsuspecting female guests falsely accused him of some impropriety. He maintains that this extraordinary precaution was taken only for his own protection, and that he had no intention of disclosing the video tapes of his sexual escapades to any other person. At some later time, Lineberry and his attorney had a dispute. Subsequently, Lineberry's attorney notified the Wilson County District Attorney of Lineberry's clandestine videotaping activities. After a search warrant was obtained, Lineberry's office was searched, and the tapes were seized by local law enforcement officials. The women depicted in the videotapes were then asked to come to the Sheriff's Department, identify themselves on the videotapes, and explain their actions. All four women deny they were aware they had been filmed.

Each of the four women filed a separate lawsuit in the Circuit Court of Wilson County. The suits charge Lineberry and Robinson with outrageous conduct, intentional infliction of emotional distress, fraud or constructive fraud, misrepresentation, appropriation, and invasion of their rights to privacy. Each of the women seek recovery for humiliation, mental distress, and emotional pain and suffering which resulted from the actions of Lineberry and Robinson.

Both Lineberry and Robinson possess personal liability umbrella insurance policies with State Farm. They contend that pursuant to the provisions of those policies, State Farm must defend and indemnify them against the claims for invasion of privacy in the four lawsuits filed in Wilson County, Tennessee.

* * *

The policies also contain a provision which excludes coverage for intentional acts or acts which are expected. . . .

Plaintiffs contend that State Farm, having specifically insured them against losses caused by the invasion of the right to privacy, must both defend them against the claims presented in the four lawsuits and indemnify them for any damages awarded to the four women. State Farm contends it is not required to defend or indemnify against these claims because the losses were not the result of an "accident" and the claims fall within the policy's exclusion for intentional or expected acts.

Plaintiffs counter Defendant's arguments by pointing to the language in the policy which defines "personal injury" by specifically listing a number of intentional torts, including invasion of the right of privacy. In other words, the losses insured against are those resulting in personal injury, which under the policy's definition includes certain types of intentional torts. An intentional tort is a civil wrong or injury which occurs as a result of the intentional act of another person. For example, one cannot commit an act of assault and battery accidentally. . . .

Defendant alleges that the insurance policy provisions are not contradictory and the coverage is not illusory, because an invasion of the right to privacy is not necessarily an intentional tort. If that were correct, the policy would not necessarily be ambiguous, as the policy would cover injuries resulting from unintentional invasions of the right of privacy and would exclude those which are intentional.

* * *

In the instant case, the umbrella policy expressly covered injuries resulting from invasion of the right of privacy, an inherently intentional tort, but excluded injuries which were intended or expected. Therefore, the Court finds the coverage is illusory, and the policy is ambiguous and must be interpreted against the insurer and in favor of the insured. Accordingly, State Farm must idemnify Plaintiffs for injuries (humiliation, mental distress, emotional pain and suffering) arising from Plaintiffs' alleged invasion of rights to privacy.

The Court will now turn to State Farm's duty to defend. . . . The obligation to defend arises whenever the complaint against the insured alleges a claim upon any ground for which there might be a recovery within the terms of a policy. . . . The purpose of such duty . . . is for the insured to obtain protection against the expense of defending suits, whether meritorious or groundless, *within the area and scope of liability covered by the policy.*

Because this Court has found that the claims for injuries resulting from the alleged invasion of the right to privacy fall within the coverage of the policies, State Farm has a duty to defend against that portion of the complaints against Lineberry and Robinson.

For the foregoing reasons, Lineberry's Motion for Summary Judgment is GRANTED, Plaintiff Robinson's Motion for Summary Judgment is GRANTED, and Defendant State Farm's Motion for Summary Judgment is DENIED.

CASE QUESTIONS

1. Why did the court find that the defendant insurance company had an obligation to defend the plaintiffs?
2. Do you think that insurance was designed to cover deliberate and intentional acts of insureds? Explain.

False Light in the Public Eye

Invasion of privacy by placing a person in a **false light in the public eye** happens if the tortfeasor publicly attributes to that individual false opinions, statements, or actions. For instance, if a magazine uses someone's photograph and name

false light in the public eye | One type of the intentional tort of invasion of privacy. Occurs when the tortfeasor publicly attributes to another individual false opinions, statements, or actions.

without permission and in an embarrassing fashion, this would place the victim in a false light publicly. One fact pattern repeated in many court cases concerns a plaintiff's photograph and name appearing in a newspaper adjacent to a negative story appearing on the same page, when the story and photograph appear in such a way as to suggest a connection between the two. Another example would be the advertisement mentioned previously regarding appropriation.

THE CASE OF THE NOT SO BAD LIGHT

This case raises many interesting points. Madonna's bodyguard, James Albright, claims among other things that he has been defamed, that his privacy has been invaded, and that he has been shown in a false light because a photograph of an "outspoken homosexual" was incorrectly labeled as being him. Albright asks the court to recognize a new tort that other states recognize that is not recognized in Massachusetts, the tort of false light. However, Albright must overcome a major hurdle: he must first prove defamation (that a false statement about him was made and published), and then additionally he must show that it would have been highly offensive to the reasonable person. Unlike defamation, the statement need not harm his reputation, but show him in a false light. Sometimes these two standards can be quite similar. This is why some courts refuse to recognize the tort of false light. They feel that defamation covers most situations. Defamation is covered in the next section.

**AMRAK PRODUCTIONS, INC.;
JAMES ALBRIGHT,
Plaintiffs, Appellants,
v.
ANDREW MORTON; MICHAEL O'MARA;
MICHAEL O'MARA BOOKS LIMITED et al.,
Defendants, Appellees,
NEWS GROUP NEWSPAPERS, LTD.,
Defendants.
APPEAL FROM THE UNITED STATES
DISTRICT COURT FOR THE DISTRICT
OF MASSACHUSETTS**

No. 04-1449
United States Court of Appeals for the First Circuit.
June 3, 2005

Amrak employed Albright—who has been involved in the personal and professional security business for over ten years—as a professional bodyguard. From January to July 1992, Albright served as Madonna's bodyguard, during which time he became

romantically involved with the artist and remained so until 1994.

In December 2000, Albright entered into a contract with O'Mara Books to sell information about Madonna for an upcoming biography. The book, entitled *Madonna*, was written by author Andrew Morton and published by O'Mara Books in the United Kingdom and by St. Martin's Press in the United States in 2001. Chapter 11 of the book details Albright's relationship with Madonna.

The book also contains forty-eight pages of photographs, including one in which Madonna is accompanied by two men. The man to the left is wearing black pants, a black and white shirt, a black leather jacket, tinted sunglasses, a string necklace, and an earring. The caption states:

Madonna attends ex-lover Prince's concert with her secret lover and one-time bodyguard Jimmy Albright (left). Albright, who bears an uncanny resemblance to Carlos León, the father of Madonna's daughter, enjoyed a stormy three-year relationship with the star. They planned to marry, and had even chosen names for their children.

This photograph allegedly defamed Albright because the man pictured was, in fact, José Guitierez, an "outspoken homosexual" who "often dressed as a woman," and engaged in what appellants describe as "homosexual, sexually graphic, lewd, lascivious, offensive, and possibly illegal" conduct. Guitierez was employed as one of Madonna's dancers.

On November 12, 2001, *People* magazine, a publication of Time Inc., published the same photograph along with the erroneous caption. News of the World, a publication of News Group Newspapers, Ltd., published the same on March 17, 2002.

Appellants subsequently sued for defamation, invasion of privacy, negligence, negligent and intentional infliction of emotional distress, along with violations of state statutory prohibitions on unfair trade practices, and unauthorized commercial use of a name or likeness.

The district court granted appellees' motion to dismiss on all counts. First, the court held that no reasonable view of the photograph and text would suggest that Albright is homosexual, and thus the publication cannot be construed as defamatory. Alternatively, the court held that imputing homosexuality cannot be considered defamatory per se in Massachusetts, particularly given the rationales in the U.S. Supreme Court's decision in Lawrence v. Texas (invalidating state statute criminalizing same-sex sexual conduct), as well as the decision in Goodridge v. Dep't of Pub. Health (invalidating limitations to civil marriage for same-sex couples under state equal protection principles). Given appellants' failure to state a defamation claim, the court dismissed the derivative claims of commercial use, false light invasion of privacy, emotional distress, negligence, and unfair trade practices.

To prevail in a defamation claim, plaintiffs must establish that "defendant[s] w[ere] at fault for the publication of a false statement regarding the plaintiff, capable of damaging the plaintiff's reputation in the community, which either caused economic loss or is actionable without proof of economic loss." This threshold question, "whether a communication is reasonably susceptible of a defamatory meaning, is a question of law for the court."

A communication is susceptible to defamatory meaning if it "would tend to hold the plaintiff up to scorn, hatred, ridicule or contempt, in the minds of any considerable and respectable segment in the community." The communication "must be interpreted reasonably," leading a "reasonable reader" to conclude that it conveyed a defamatory meaning. Context matters in assessing such claims: The Massachusetts Supreme Judicial Court, for example, has required that allegedly defamatory photographs or headlines be interpreted in light of the entire context of the publication.

The miscaptioned photograph in the instant case is not reasonably susceptible of a defamatory meaning. Nothing in Guitierez's appearance, particularly given the accompanying caption stressing Albright's heterosexuality (e.g., Madonna's "secret lover"), gives any indication that Albright is homosexual. To draw such an inference, the reader—who would have to view homosexuals with "scorn, hatred, ridicule or contempt"—must follow Madonna and her cohort closely enough to recognize Guitierez as a gay man, but not closely enough to know Guitierez's name or what Albright looks like. Few, if any, readers would fall into this "considerable and respectable segment in the community."

The context of the text accompanying the photograph further deflates any argument that the photo conveys a defamatory meaning. When we "consider all the words used" in the accompanying text, including phrases such as Albright's "long-time girlfriend," his "hot and heavy" affair with Madonna, their sexual encounters, and Albright's "fling" with a "girl at a club"—we find that no reasonable reader could conclude that Albright is homosexual. This conclusion is supported by the caption, which states that Albright was Madonna's "secret lover," that they

(continues)

"enjoyed a stormy three-year relationship," and that they planned to marry. Similarly, the caption for the People Weekly photograph states that Albright felt "overwhelming love" for Madonna.

Given appellants' failure to satisfy the threshold question of defamatory meaning, we affirm the court's dismissal of the defamation claim.

We have considered appellants' derivative claims—commercial use, negligent and intentional infliction of emotional distress—and find them all without merit. We likewise reject appellants' urging that the false light invasion of privacy claim should be recognized in Massachusetts, particularly given the state court's repeated refusal to do so.

CASE QUESTIONS

1. Do you think Albright has been harmed? Explain.
2. What would harm Albright more, the photo in the book, or the publicity surrounding this suit? Explain.

Perhaps no other intentional tort excites the public indignation more than invasion of privacy. Almost everyone desires a sanctuary from the daily intrusions that dominate our urbanized, highly technological, and mobile society. However, the popular conception of the right to privacy does not always afford legal remedies. The following hypotheticals illustrate how the tort elements must first be satisfied.

hypotheticals

T.J. rents a house from Eric. After T.J. had lived there for six months, Eric notified T.J. to move out of the house within ten days, because Eric needed the house for his bedridden mother. T.J. refused, pointing out that the lease ran for a full year and that it could not be terminated by either party without thirty days' advance notice. After ten days, Eric moved into the house with his mother and her two grandchildren. T.J. refused to leave the house, and everyone lived in a state of considerable tension for two weeks before T.J. could not stand it any longer and left. Did Eric invade T.J.'s privacy by unreasonable intrusion?

Eric's actions interfered with T.J.'s solitude in an excessive and highly offensive manner. T.J. had complied with the lease agreement and had a legal right to occupy the premises. Eric's invasion with his invalid mother and two grandchildren substantially disrupted T.J.'s domestic tranquility. The stress among the house occupants became so extreme that T.J. was at last compelled to abandon his residence. Accordingly, Eric would be liable to T.J. for invasion of privacy by unreasonable intrusion.

* * *

Aaron was aghast when he opened the day's newspaper to see an advertisement with his picture, in which he was holding a can of Bartell's Beenie-Weenies. Under the photograph was the caption, "Bartell's Makes the Best Beenie-Weenies!" Aaron could not recall ever buying this brand and made no such endorsement to anyone associated with the product. He did not give his permission to use the photograph. Has Bartell's invaded Aaron's privacy by appropriation?

Bartell's used Aaron's likeness in its photograph without his consent. Bartell's hoped to profit from increased sales as a result of this "customer's" endorsement. Bartell's would thus be liable to Aaron for invasion of privacy by appropriation.

Furthermore, Bartell's publicly attributed a spurious opinion to Aaron in its photograph caption. This would place Aaron in a false light in the public eye. Thus, Bartell's would also be liable to Aaron for this type of invasion of privacy.

Table 6-4 summarizes the elements of the four types of invasion of privacy.

APPROPRIATION	UNREASONABLE INTRUSION	PUBLIC DISCLOSURE OF PRIVATE FACTS	FALSE LIGHT IN THE PUBLIC EYE
Unconsented use of person's name or likeness for profit	Excessive and highly offensive invasion of one's seclusion or solitude	Public communication of private information about person without permission	Publicly attributing false opinions, statements, or actions to a person
		Reasonable person finds disclosure extremely objectionable	

TABLE 6-4
Elements of invasion of privacy

DEFAMATION: LIBEL AND SLANDER

Defamation consists of two varieties: libel and slander. **Libel** is a written false and disparaging statement about an individual that the tortfeasor communicates to a third party. **Slander** is an oral false and disparaging statement about a person that the tortfeasor communicates to a third party. Courts often refer to this communication element as **publication.** Publication of the defamatory information must injure the victim's reputation in the community. The elements can be outlined as follows:

1. Written (libel) or oral (slander) statement
2. False and defamatory statement about a person

defamation | Transmission to others of false statements that harm the reputation, business, or property rights of a person. Spoken defamation is *slander* and written defamation is *libel.*

libel | Written defamation. Publicly communicated, false written statements that injure a person's reputation, business, or property rights.

slander | Oral defamation. The speaking of false words that injure another person's reputation, business, or property rights.

publication | Making public; communicating defamatory information to a person other than the person defamed.

3. Tortfeasor's communication of the statement to a third party

4. Harm to the victim's reputation in the community.

Although the first element is obvious, the others require some elaboration.

Nature of the Statement

For libel, the statement must generally be written in some fashion. This does not necessarily mean writing, such as handwriting, or printed words, such as those appearing on this page. There are many forms of written expression, including such unusual methods as billboards, skywriting with smoke or banners pulled by an airplane, or placing objects such as stones into the shapes of letters. The critical element of writing is whether the information is communicated visually through means of an alphabet. Libel can also appear in the form of films, records, DVDs, and computer downloads.

For slander, the statement must be orally delivered. But it does not have to be words. Gestures, particularly obscene ones, also qualify, provided that the meaning of the gestures is sufficiently clear to onlookers to be defamatory.

✴   THE CASE OF THE FAMILY FEUD VIA INTERNET   ✴

This case brings to light a whole new avenue for defamation: defamation via Internet. Five years after a contentious divorce, the partners are fighting again in a whole new domain. A sheriff's former wife has set up websites and posted a good deal of information from the divorce file on the Net for all to read. Allegations against her husband include alleged physical abuse and harassment against the wife. The sheriff, on learning of this public display of private matters, sought an injunction to stop the "slanderous" conduct against him, which he claimed is an invasion of privacy.

THOMAS C. EVANS, Plaintiff and Respondent,
v.
LINDA A. EVANS, Defendant and Appellant.
No. GIC 881162, Superior Court
of San Diego County on appeal
No. D051144 (Cal. App. Ct., 4th Dist., Div. One)
May 12, 2008

Thomas is a law enforcement officer with the San Diego County Sheriff's Department. He and Linda were married in 1985, and separated in 1998. In 2002, the court entered a judgment dissolving the marriage. During the next five years, the parties had substantial ongoing conflict over custody, child support and other issues.

In March 2007, Thomas filed a complaint against Linda, alleging harassment, slander and defamation, various common law torts, breach of privacy claims, and breach of contract. The gist of the allegations was that Linda has engaged in a series of acts intended to harass Thomas and cause him severe emotional stress and injury to his reputation and career.

Shortly after, Thomas moved for a temporary restraining order and preliminary injunction.

Thomas said that in April 2005, Linda filed a complaint with the Sheriff's Department, alleging "a number of departmental and state law violations," including "child abuse, lying, falsifying departmental reports, [and] abuse of position...." After a criminal and internal investigation, these allegations were found to be unsubstantiated and/or unfounded. Twenty months later, in December 2006, Thomas "was informed by [his] superiors... that the District Attorney and Sheriff had both received letters about [Thomas] that were very defaming in nature." Thomas did not say who wrote these letters, but in a supplemental declaration, Thomas said information about these letters would be "fleshed out through discovery" in the action. Thomas also stated that in March 2007, Linda filed another "harassing request" to the Sheriff's Department.

Thomas said he "believe[d]" these prior communications with the Sheriff's Department were "a major factor" in his "inability to [be] promote[d] within the Department." Thomas also asserted that the "embarrassment" resulting from Linda's conduct caused him to decide to "seek a less prominent job within the Department."

With respect to the Internet postings, Thomas stated that: "In December 2006, I was informed that there were internet websites posted by [Linda and Preddy] with numerous defaming comments and statements about me as a sworn law enforcement officer, and the lawyers, judges, and counselors involved in our family court case." Thomas also said he "discovered in December 2006 and January 2007 that [Preddy] had apparently inappropriately gained access to both my family court medical records and financial records, and had published information from them on the internet."

Thomas also submitted copies of Web site pages in which it appeared that Linda posted statements accusing Thomas of physical abuse against her and her son, and statements suggesting that several San Diego Superior Court judges were biased and/or "incompetent." Thomas also stated "[a]s recently as February 19, 2007, a Google search of my name on thepetitionsite.com generated a blurb posted by [Linda] stating the following: 'Our eldest son was returned to my "Primary Care" after his father,

San Diego County Sheriff's Sergeant, Thomas C. Evans, struck him with a belt repeatedly....' This statement is entirely false.

Five days later, on April 18, the court issued the preliminary injunction challenged in this appeal. The preliminary injunction stated: "1. [Linda and Preddy] are enjoined from publishing false and defamatory statements and/or confidential personal information about [Thomas] on the internet; and [¶] 2. [Linda and Preddy] are enjoined from contacting [Thomas's] employer via e-mail or otherwise regarding [Thomas]. Since [Thomas] is employed by the San Diego Sheriff's Department, this injunction should not be construed to prohibit defendants from calling 911 to report criminal conduct."

An order prohibiting a party from making or publishing false statements is a classic type of an unconstitutional prior restraint. "While [a party] may be held responsible for abusing his right to speak freely in a subsequent tort action, he has the initial right to speak freely without censorship."

The California Supreme Court recently recognized this fundamental principle, but held the rule does not apply to an order issued after a trial prohibiting the defendant from *repeating specific statements found at trial to be defamatory*.

The California Supreme Court held that although other aspects of the injunction were overbroad, the defendant's "right to free speech would not be infringed by a properly limited injunction prohibiting defendant from repeating statements about plaintiff that were determined at trial to be defamatory."

To establish a valid prior restraint under the federal Constitution, a proponent has a heavy burden to show the countervailing interest is compelling, the prior restraint is necessary and would be effective in promoting this interest, and less extreme measures are unavailable.

Even if an injunction does not impermissibly constitute a prior restraint, the injunction must be sufficiently precise to provide "a person of ordinary intelligence fair notice that his contemplated conduct is forbidden." An injunction is unconstitutionally

(continues)

vague if it does not clearly define the persons protected and the conduct prohibited.

The court's preliminary injunction prohibiting Linda from publishing any "false and defamatory" statements on the Internet is constitutionally invalid. Because there has been no trial and no determination on the merits that any statement made by Linda was defamatory, the court cannot prohibit her from making statements characterized only as "false and defamatory."

This portion of the order is also invalid as unconstitutionally vague and overbroad. The injunction broadly prohibited Linda from publishing any defamatory comments about Thomas. This sweeping prohibition fails to adequately delineate which of Linda's future comments might violate the injunction and lead to contempt of court.

In addition to enjoining "false and defamatory statements," the court also enjoined Linda from "publishing . . . confidential personal information about [Thomas] on the internet."

A prohibition against disclosing confidential information constitutes a prior restraint. However, because it also potentially concerns the countervailing right of privacy protected under the California Constitution, a prohibition may be proper under certain compelling or "extraordinary" circumstances.

In determining whether such circumstances exist, courts generally apply a balancing test, weighing the competing privacy and free speech constitutional rights. Relevant factors include whether the person is a public or private figure, the scope of the prior restraint, the nature of the private information, whether the information is of legitimate public concern, the extent of the potential harm if the information is disclosed, and the strength of the private and governmental interest in preventing publication of the information.

We cannot determine whether the court properly applied the balancing test in this case because the order is ambiguous as to the meaning of "confidential personal information." The order does not contain a definition of "confidential personal information" and it is not reasonably possible to determine the scope of this prohibition from any other source. Without a definition, the injunction is not sufficiently clear to determine whether Thomas's privacy rights to the information substantially outweigh Linda's free speech rights.

In his appellate briefs, Thomas seeks to justify this portion of the order by suggesting that Linda will place (or has placed) his telephone number, address, and Social Security number on the Internet. He argues the disclosure of the information will put his safety and well-being in jeopardy, particularly because of his job as a deputy sheriff. We agree.

However, in the proceedings below, Thomas did not specifically request an order preventing his identifying information from being placed on the Internet. Instead, Thomas focused primarily on his concern that Linda and/or her mother had placed, or planned to place, information about the divorce proceedings on the Internet, including information that had been contained in the family court file. However, the mere fact that information is contained in court files or concerns divorce proceedings does not necessarily mean it is confidential and cannot be disclosed.

An order enjoining the disclosure must be narrowly tailored to protect only these specific interests and should not unnecessarily interfere with a person's free speech rights.

Accordingly, we conclude the order preventing Linda from placing any "confidential personal information" about Thomas on the Internet is vague, overbroad, and not narrowly tailored. On remand, the court should reevaluate Thomas's request. After determining the information that Thomas seeks to be kept private, the court should engage in a balancing test to determine whether there is a compelling reason that such information be kept private.

The record did not support the conclusion that Thomas would prevail on his causes of action challenging Linda's complaints to the Sheriff's Department. A citizen's report to law enforcement personnel seeking investigation of alleged wrongful activities is absolutely privileged. "'An absolute privilege exists to protect citizens from the threat of litigation for communications to government agencies whose function it is to investigate and remedy wrongdoing.'"

Additionally, there are less intrusive means to limit Linda's filing false complaints with the Sheriff's Department. Government agencies can establish reasonable requirements before an individual may be permitted to file a complaint. If the Sheriff's Department believes the complaints are unwarranted, it has the authority to take administrative action.

Based on the record before us, the court's order enjoining Linda from contacting the Sheriff's Department about Thomas absent an emergency was overbroad and was not justified by the evidentiary record.

The preliminary injunction order is reversed. The matter is remanded for the court to reconsider the order with the views expressed in this opinion.

CASE QUESTIONS
1. What did Thomas need to do to succeed with his injunction request?
2. When the court advises Thomas to wait for actual defamation to occur before seeking relief on this ground, does this meet your expectations? Explain.

Publication

The tortfeasor must communicate the false and derogatory statement to a third party. That means that statements made by the tortfeasor directly to the victim are defamatory only if seen or heard by another or others.

Publication takes place through any means by which the false information is disseminated. This includes anything spoken, either in person or over amplification (megaphone or loudspeaker at a ballpark, for instance), radio, television, or telephone; or anything written, including letters, telegrams, scribbled messages, billboards, or printed and published works (such as a letter to the editor in the local newspaper, for instance).

Harm to Reputation in the Community

A statement is considered *defamatory* if it causes the fourth element—namely, injury to the victim's reputation in the community. For purposes of libel and slander, **community** is narrowly defined as a significant number of persons acquainted or familiar with the victim. Although some courts have held that "a community of one" is sufficient under certain circumstances, most courts maintain that larger numbers are required. Nevertheless, certain expressions, such as "a handful," "a closely associated group," and "associates in the neighborhood or workplace," suggest small numbers in most instances.

Many courts define the victim's injury in more emotional terms. For example, it has commonly been held that statements are libelous or slanderous if they ridicule, humiliate, or subject the victim to contempt or hatred from among his or her peers.

community | 1. Neighborhood, locality, etc. A vague term that can include very large or very small areas.
2. A group with common interests.
3. Shared.

Public Figures

Public figures, such as movie and television celebrities or public officers and employees who exercise substantial governmental power, are treated differently than private individuals. These people are used to being under the public eye and have greater access to the media to refute untrue charges than the ordinary person. Accordingly, not as much protection is afforded to public figures. To be successful in claiming defamation, a public figure must show that a statement was made with actual malice. Because this is very hard to prove, few public figures bring lawsuits to challenge statements about them even when they know the assertions to be totally false.

Slander Per Se

Per se is a term indicating that something is automatic or presumed. Some words in and of themselves are defamatory; therefore, injury and damage need not be proven when slander per se is shown. For example, words that imply criminal conduct, or words that are harmful to one's business, or words implying that one has a loathsome and communicable disease are all presumed to damage one's reputation, so the victim need not prove damages to be successful in a slander per se claim.

Truth and Privilege as Absolute Defenses

Truth is considered an absolute defense in defamation cases. If the information the tortfeasor communicates is true, then no libel or slander occurred. To successfully use this defense, the tortfeasor must prove the veracity of the statement.

What is true is often a matter of opinion. It always depends upon the nature of the derogatory comments. For example, to call a person born out of wedlock a "bastard" is technically accurate, but in today's society the term is rarely used as defined in the dictionary. Similarly, to refer to a sexually promiscuous individual as a "whore" or a "John" could be deemed factual by reasonable persons, particularly those who are morally opposed to the conduct described. Courts have struggled with the elasticity of truth, and a variety of formulas for pinpointing truth have been posited in court opinions. The most common court opinion states that literal truth in every detail is unnecessary. If the statement is substantially true, so that a reasonable person would decide that the accusations were justified given the facts, then truth will operate as a defense to defamation actions.

Privilege is also considered an absolute defense in defamation cases. Statements made by attorneys and judges during trials are privileged and cannot be the grounds for a defamation charge. Likewise, legislators are immune from liability for false statements made during debate, even if the lawmakers deliberately make the untrue statements. Members of Congress have an absolute privilege while speaking on the floor of Congress. Privilege allows all these persons to do their best jobs without fear of repercussions should a statement they make later prove to be untrue.

Defamation is another intentional tort, like assault and battery, that virtually everyone has experienced, either as victim or tortfeasor (or both). One need only recall a recent imprudent remark to mentally invoke accusations of slander or libel. Nevertheless, the elements determine whether defamation has occurred, as the following illustrations show.

Table 6-5 lists the elements of libel and slander.

Libel	Slander
Written statement	Oral statement
False and defamatory statement	False and defamatory statement
Publication to third party	Publication to third party
Injury to victim's reputation in the community	Injury to victim's reputation in the community

TABLE 6-5
Elements of libel and slander

THE CASE OF THE LIVING DEAD

Imagine one's horror at opening the daily newspaper and, while glancing quickly at the obituaries, spotting oneself listed as recently deceased! Although this may be a shocking revelation, it is the type of mistake that newspapers easily and promptly correct. As the following case illustrates, an erroneous obituary does not always constitute defamation.

DECKER
v.
PRINCETON PACKET, INC.
116 N.J. 418, 561 A.2d 1122 (1989)
Supreme Court of New Jersey
August 8, 1989
Handler, J.

This case involves a tort action brought against a newspaper seeking damages for defamation and emotional distress attributable to the publication of a false obituary. The Court is called on to address whether an obituary that reports a death, this being the only false statement, can possibly have a defamatory interpretation. . . . The trial court and Appellate Division held that defamation and emotional-harm claims were without merit as a matter of law.

Plaintiffs appeal these rulings arguing that defendant's publication of a false obituary without verifying its accuracy caused damage to reputation and emotional harm that should be compensated under our tort law.

On February 15, 1985, the defendant, a newspaper, The Princeton Packet, Inc. ("The Packet"), which publishes on Tuesday and Friday of each week, reported the following obituary for Marcy Goldberg Decker, the plaintiff:

Marcy Goldberg Decker of Princeton died suddenly Feb. 11. She was 31.
Ms. Goldberg was the fiance of Robert J. Feldman of Princeton.
She was a lifelong resident of Princeton and is survived by a son, Jackson T.; her mother, Charlotte

(continues)

Goldberg of Trenton; and a brother, Ronald Goldberg of California.

Funeral arrangements were incomplete at press time.

This obituary is incorrect because Marcy Decker was not dead.

All other information in the obituary—her age, residence, and family relationships—was accurate. . . . Plaintiff notified defendant by a telephone call two days after the publication that she was in fact alive. The Packet printed the following retraction on February 19, 1985:

> The Packet erroneously reported in Friday's edition that Marcy Decker of Princeton died Feb. 11. The obituary was false. The Packet regrets the error and any inconvenience this may have caused Ms. Decker or her family.

* * *

Plaintiffs deposed three employees of defendant to establish their claims that The Packet was unaware of who had submitted the obituary, [and] that it took no steps to determine the validity of the notice. . . .

* * *

A defamatory statement is one that is false and is "'injurious to the reputation of another' or exposes another person to 'hatred, contempt or ridicule' or subjects another person to 'a loss of the good will and confidence' in which he or she is held by others." Thus, if the statement of Marcy Decker's death in the false obituary could be interpreted by a reasonable person to expose the plaintiff to "hatred, contempt, ridicule or disgrace or subject . . . [her] to loss of the good will and confidence of the community," then her action for defamation could proceed to trial.

The principle generally endorsed by most authority throughout the country is that an obituary in which the only false statement concerns the death of the individual, published without malicious intent, is not defamatory *per se*. These cases suggest that publication of a notice of death is usually not defamatory because it does not injure one's reputation. As one court explained, "one is [not] demeaned or belittled by the report of his or her death."

The general rule, however, does have an exception where the false obituary contains additional false information that may be defamatory. . . .

This Court finds that the general rule and its limited exception should govern this case and other similar cases. Here, the only false aspect of the obituary was the death of plaintiff Marcy Decker. Therefore, under the general rule, the obituary is not defamatory *per se* because the reported death of an individual when viewed from the perspective of a reasonable person of ordinary intelligence and experience does not impugn reputation. As the trial court observed, the publication of the death notice did not impute to the plaintiff any wrong and did not hold her up to ridicule. Death is a natural state and demeans no one.

. . . Moreover, the chance of an obituary being incorrect appears slight, and the newspaper can promptly publish a correction, which occurred in this case. Thus, the plaintiffs did have an adequate remedy to correct any false statement and the published correction should have prevented the false obituary from causing any continuing effects.

. . . Therefore, we hold that where a newspaper mistakenly prints an obituary for a person who is still alive and then retracts its mistake, there is no defamation *per se*, since announcing the death of someone is not by itself injurious to one's reputation.

* * *

Accordingly, the judgment below is affirmed.

CASE QUESTIONS

1. Do you believe the facts in *Decker* satisfy an action for intentional or reckless infliction of emotional distress? For invasion of privacy? Explain.
2. If the plaintiff could discover who planted the false obituary at the newspaper's offices, could she recover for any intentional torts discussed in this chapter against this unknown person? Why or why not?

hypotheticals

Randy owns an automobile painting service. One of his customers, Jewel, was dissatisfied with Randy's paint job on her automobile; several spots that had not been polished stood out against the rest of the finish. Rather than complain directly to Randy, Jewel called in to a live local radio station and said that Randy was a "con artist" and that he had swindled many other people with sloppy work. Has Jewel slandered Randy?

Jewel communicated information about Randy to third persons, and so publication occurred. The information was false, as Jewel's dissatisfaction with a single paint job hardly documented Randy's dishonesty. The critical issue is whether Jewel's statements were defamatory. It is likely that Jewel's accusations about Randy's honesty and integrity will substantially injure Randy's business reputation in the community. This is particularly true because the allegations suggest criminal conduct by an innocent person. Thus, Jewel has slandered Randy and is liable to him for damages.

* * *

Consider the hypothetical of Britney. She enjoyed writing letters to the editor and her missives regularly appeared in the newspaper. One day Britney turned to the editorial page and read the following response to one of her letters:

> Dear Editor:
>
> In response to Britney Gold's letter in last week's edition, I must say that this woman is mentally ill and needs psychiatric treatment. She suffers from delusions and cannot be trusted. How can she make those ridiculous statements about the city's snow removal policy? I happen to work for the city street department, and I know that we regularly clear side streets after handling the main streets. It usually only takes a few extra days to get to the side streets, not weeks as she said. Why doesn't she take her medicine and get a grip?
>
> Jackson Winderson

Has Jackson libeled Britney? Jackson's written communication was published—literally—by appearing in the newspaper. Many people would have been exposed to the letter. Britney's reputation in the community undoubtedly will suffer from Jackson's accusations that she is "mentally ill." Although it may be true that Britney was uninformed about the city's snow removal policy, truth as to these matters is irrelevant—the defamatory remarks pertained to Britney's mental capacity. Jackson would be liable to Britney for libel.

THE CASE OF THE "WOODCHIPPER MURDERER"

In this case, a man's wife—a stewardess—disappeared. A news broadcaster suggested that the pilot-husband had murdered his wife like another pilot had in a similar case. Is mere inference enough, or must defamation be proved by explicit words?

BROWN
v.
HEARST CORP.

54 F.3d 21 (1st Cir. 1995)
United States Court of Appeals, First Circuit
May 11, 1995
Boudin, Circuit Judge

In March 1987, Regina Brown, the then-wife of appellant Willis Brown and mother of three children, disappeared. At the time Regina was employed as a flight attendant, and Willis as a pilot, for American Airlines; the couple had lived together in Newtown, Connecticut, but had been separated for four months and were living apart. The police investigated the disappearance and found Regina's car abandoned in New York but no trace of her. The investigation remains open. It is not known whether Regina is alive or dead.

Later in the same year the Browns were divorced in a Connecticut state court, the contested proceedings being completed in Regina's absence. The state court trial was prolonged and a detailed opinion was written by the trial judge pertaining to custody and support. . . .

The trial was widely reported in the press, and publicity continued even after the decree. This was due partly to further litigation and the continuing police investigation, but also to a freakish coincidence. About six months before Regina's disappearance, another woman who lived in Newtown, a Pan Am flight attendant married to an Eastern pilot, had disappeared. Fragments of her bone were found in a nearby river, and her pilot husband was convicted in the so-called woodchipper murder.

In November 1990, appellee Hearst Corporation d/b/a WCVB-TV Channel 5 in Boston ("Channel 5") broadcasted from Massachusetts a segment entitled "The Other Pilot's Wife" as a part of the station's regular "newsmagazine" program. It was prepared by Mary Richardson, a journalist with the station, who conducted a substantial amount of research and a number of interviews in preparing the broadcast.

The broadcast opens with the leitmotif—"Tonight the bizarre story of a small New England town where one stewardess is dead, another is missing"—and then offers a brief reprise of the 1986 murder of the Pan Am flight attendant. Next, turning to the Browns, the broadcast describes and depicts an apparent storybook marriage going sour, the divorce petition, and Regina's disappearance. "In the days following Regina's disappearance," says Richardson, "Willis showed no interest in what had happened to her."

* * *

There is other incriminating information about Willis recounted in the program, and the police are described as having suspected Willis and as believing still that "Mr. Brown knows more about the disappearance of his wife than he is letting on." No evidence even remotely exculpatory of Willis is described. On the other hand, Mary Richardson, the "voice over" throughout the program, never asserts that Willis is guilty or even says that she thinks he is guilty. Formally, the program describes the disappearance as a mystery or, at worst, a possible murder still unsolved.

In February 1993, Willis brought the present action against Channel 5 in state court in Texas. The case was removed to federal court and thereafter transferred to the federal district court in Massachusetts. As subsequently amended, Willis' complaint charged defamation, invasion of privacy under Mass. Gen.L. ch. 214 § 1B, "false light" invasion of privacy, and intentional infliction of emotional distress.

After discovery, Channel 5 moved for summary judgment. In a detailed opinion dated July 21, 1994, the district court granted the motion. As to the defamation claim, the court relied in different respects on lack of falsity, the limited protection available for statements of opinion, the "fair report" privilege, and lack of fault. The privacy and intentional infliction claims were dismissed on grounds described below. Willis has now appealed, asserting that all of his claims should have been submitted to a jury.

On appeal from a grant of summary judgment, we review the decision de novo, drawing inferences in favor of the party opposing the motion. . . .

Channel 5 does not appear to dispute that the broadcast charges Willis with murder or at least that a jury would be entitled to find this to be the import of the program. The broadcast never flatly expresses that accusation. Indeed, it says that the murder is unsolved and makes clear that the police have nothing much in the way of direct evidence against Willis. But defamation can occur by innuendo as well as by explicit assertion, and the suggestion here is a fairly strong one.

* * *

The broadcast makes clear that the police suspect Willis, and Regina's parents are filmed making even stronger statements of suspicion. Material from the divorce trial is used to establish or buttress doubts about Willis' character and history. The suggestion of murder runs through the program like a gold thread. The broadcast opens with the dramatic footage relating to the woodchipper murder and closes with Richardson's rhetorical question, could "someone" get away with murder?

A common defense to a charge of defamation is "truth." The Supreme Court tells us that in a suit like this one against the media the burden is upon the defamed plaintiff to show that the statements are not true. Neither side addresses this issue. Perhaps each assumes that to carry his burden of proof, Willis could testify at trial that he did not murder his wife and a jury might believe him. In all events, we take the case as one in which a jury might find that murder had been charged and that the charge was false.

Channel 5's primary response is that "[m]uch of the [b]roadcast, and the entirety of its allegedly defamatory sting, is in essence a 'fair report' of the Brown's divorce trial in Connecticut" and thus falls under the Massachusetts privilege allowed for media coverage of an official proceeding. Such a privilege certainly exists in Massachusetts, and there is little doubt that much of the material in the broadcast is drawn from, and attributed to, the divorce proceeding.

For present purposes, we will assume that the privilege extends to non-contemporaneous reports and that the program—so far as it related to the divorce proceeding and the information developed there—conveyed a fair and accurate report of the proceeding. But only a portion of the broadcast purported to be drawn from the proceeding. And, while that portion may be privileged, we are skeptical of Channel 5's claim that the the entire "sting" of the broadcast is privileged material.

* * *

Where the evidence is thus enlarged and the charge cast in a more lurid light, it is not clear to us that the fair report privilege automatically shields the larger whole.

The problem for Willis, we think, is that the Supreme Court has instructed that a state libel-suit plaintiff must demonstrate fault on the part of the media; and this requirement applies even where the plaintiff is not a public official or public figure. In such cases Massachusetts has imposed a requirement that the newspaper or broadcaster be shown to be negligent or worse. Thus, even if a false charge of murder has been made, it remains to see whether Willis provided evidence of negligence to justify submitting the case to a jury. . . .

So far as the murder goes, Willis points to nothing to suggest that Channel 5 was negligent in its mustering of the available evidence. Some might think the broadcast gaudy journalism; certainly the interpolation of the woodchipper murder is largely gratuitous. . . .

Willis' brief says tersely that the police admitted that they had no evidence against him; and he reasons that it was thus "negligent disregard for the

(continues)

truth" for Channel 5 to "insinuate" that "[he] murdered his wife and disposed of her body in the same fashion as did [the woodchipper murderer]." . . .

A different problem is presented by Willis' suggestion that the broadcast charged him with disposing of his wife's body "in the same fashion" as the woodchipper murder. Patently, the broadcast did not so charge; no reasonable juror could draw such an inference. Willis offers no argument to support such an inference, and it is not surprising that elsewhere in his brief he retreats to a more cautious assertion: that the juxtaposition "conveys the message that Brown also murdered his wife and disposed of her body *in some insidious fashion*" (emphasis added).

* * *

Even if all of these doubts are resolved in Willis' favor, we think this narrow remaining claim is too thin to survive summary judgment. About the most one can get from the woodchipper episode is the suggestion that, if Willis killed his wife, he also took steps to assure that her body would not be found.

* * *

A writing or program is normally viewed as a whole; and that requirement has special force here because the woodchipper episode was assertedly about someone else, and its connection to Willis depended upon the rest of the program. We conclude as a matter of law that the broadcast, taken as a whole, cannot reasonably be taken to charge that Willis brutally disposed of his wife's body.

Willis' non-libel claims do not require much discussion. On appeal, Willis has narrowed his privacy claim to the contention that the program places him in a false light by leaving the viewer with "a false impression," *i.e.*, that Brown killed Regina and disposed of her body in the same fashion as did the woodchipper murderer. The district court thought it sufficient that Massachusetts has never adopted the false light theory of privacy invasion.

* * *

Lastly, Willis charged Channel 5 with intentional infliction of emotional distress. This is a recognized tort under Massachusetts law requiring intended or foreseeable infliction of such distress, "extreme and outrageous conduct," and causation of distress so severe that no reasonable person could be expected to endure it. The district court said that Channel 5's conduct was not negligent and therefore could hardly be "extreme and outrageous."

In all events, many of the legitimate news stories that appear in the media involve foreseeable distress for the subject of the story, probably severe distress in some cases. Regina's disappearance and the divorce trial were news stories, and so was her continued absence and the failure of the police to solve the case. Willis provides no basis to think that generally accurate coverage in such a case is even remotely close to conduct "beyond all possible bounds of decency" and "utterly intolerable in a civilized community."

Affirmed.

CASE QUESTIONS
1. Which of the parties is described as having a privilege?
2. What was the effect of the privilege?

▍SUMMARY

Intentional torts include actions designed to injure another person or his or her property. All intentional torts embrace an act, intent, and injurious conduct. These elements must occur together. Intentional torts harming the individual include infliction of emotional distress, fraud, misrepresentation, malicious prosecution, abuse of process, invasion of privacy, and defamation.

Intentional infliction of emotional distress involves outrageous conduct designed to cause severe mental anguish in the victim. The victim must actually suffer emotional turmoil as a result of the tortfeasor's actions. Reckless infliction of emotional distress includes outrageous conduct that the tortfeasor knew, or reasonably should have known, would produce significant emotional injury to the victim. The conduct is considered outrageous if it shocks the conscience of a reasonable person with normal emotional sensibilities. Therefore, intent is not necessary.

Fraud consists of false statements made to entice the victim to surrender something of value to the defrauder. Misrepresentation includes false statements or behavior designed to deceive the victim. In many jurisdictions, the two intentional torts are considered virtually identical and interchangeable. The tortfeasor must know that the statements made are false and intend to deceive the victim.

Malicious prosecution happens when a private citizen files a groundless criminal complaint with the prosecutor against an innocent person who is named as the defendant in a criminal prosecution action. To sue the complainant, the innocent defendant must be either acquitted or otherwise victorious in the criminal lawsuit. The complainant must have filed the frivolous criminal charges out of malice for the innocent defendant, and malice may be implied from the circumstances surrounding the case. The innocent defendant must be injured as a consequence of the baseless prosecution. Abuse of process is the misuse (or threat of misuse) of a legal proceeding against another to obtain an unlawful objective. The victim must be harmed by the frivolous legal action. It is the civil equivalent of malicious prosecution.

Invasion of privacy consists of four independent varieties: appropriation, unreasonable intrusion, public disclosure of private facts, and false light in the public eye. Appropriation is the use of a person's name or likeness, without consent, for profit in some way. Unreasonable intrusion involves excessive and highly offensive interference with an individual's seclusion or solitude. Public disclosure of private facts happens when a tortfeasor publicly communicates purely private information about another person and such a disclosure would offend a reasonable person. False light in the public eye occurs when a tortfeasor publicly attributes to another false statements, opinions, or actions.

Defamation includes libel and slander. Libel is written communication of false and disparaging statements about an individual to third parties. Slander involves oral communication that does the same thing. Communication to third persons is called publication. The misinformation disseminated must injure the victim by harming his or her reputation in the community. Community can be narrowly defined as a small number of persons who know the victim. Even one third party is sufficient in some cases for publication to exist. Truth is an absolute defense in defamation actions. Public figures must prove actual malice to succeed in a defamation claim.

▌ KEY TERMS

abuse of process
appropriation
community
complainant
defamation
emotional distress
false light in the public eye
fraud (deceit)

intentional infliction
  of emotional distress
invasion of privacy
libel
malice
malicious prosecution
material
misrepresentation

probable cause
publication
public disclosure of private facts
reckless infliction of emotional
  distress
slander
unreasonable intrusion

▌ PROBLEMS

In the following hypotheticals, identify the intentional tort(s) committed, if any, and support your answer.

1. Eugene Bagley III was an aspiring literature student at the state university. He had submitted several short stories and poems to *Rhapsody*, a college literary magazine. Steve lived in Eugene's dormitory and had a reputation for playing pranks on fellow dorm residents. Steve wrote a fake letter of rejection on *Rhapsody* letterhead, which a friend had taken from the magazine's office supplies. The letter was a scathing indictment of Eugene's work as plagiarism and amateurish. The letter threatened to notify the English department and academic dean about the alleged plagiarism. Steve signed the editor of the magazine's name. When Eugene received the letter, he became physically ill and had to visit the university hospital for medication to sleep and concentrate.

2. Mike was a salesperson at a local hardware store. Samuel was a customer looking to buy exterior paint for his storage shed. When Samuel told Mike he needed paint that could be used on metal siding, Mike indicated a wood paint. Samuel inquired about this, but Mike said that it was not just for wood but for any surface. In fact, the paint would not adhere to any surface other than wood. Mike had worked in the store for only a few days and knew nothing about any of the paint supplies. Samuel bought the paint and applied it. Within two weeks, the paint peeled off.

3. Maria is an honor student at a small college. She is worried that another student, Alex, will take her place as number one in the class and apply for the same scholarship she desperately needs to continue her schooling. Maria calls Alex and pretends that she is a nurse calling from the emergency room of Alex's hometown local hospital. Maria tells Alex that his mother was in an accident and was gravely injured, and that he needs to come there right away. Alex is distraught and returns home immediately. He is so upset he totally forgets about the scholarship deadline and fails to apply.

4. Celeste and David are involved in a bitter custody dispute over their children. After losing the marital home, Celeste decides she is not going to let her husband get one more thing from her. Celeste calls the police after carefully coaching her children and complains that her children have been repeatedly sexually abused by David. David is immediately arrested at work. Celeste is granted temporary custody over the children. David is later cleared of the false charges of sexual abuse.

5. Newspaper sales have been declining for weeks for the *Gazette Herald*. The owner of the paper knows that people are curious and would like to know more about the personal lives of the residents in town. A reporter is sent to attend meetings of Alcoholics Anonymous and plastic surgeon Dr. John Glassgow's seminars on facial rejuvenation. A new feature is included in the paper, "What You Don't Know About Your Neighbors." A list of those attending Alcoholics Anonymous and those attending the doctor's seminars who are considering plastic surgery is published. As expected, sales of the newspaper increase immediately.

▌ REVIEW QUESTIONS

1. Define *fraud* and *misrepresentation*. How are they similar? Distinguishable? Is intent required? What objectives must the tortfeasor have in giving false information?

2. Describe malicious prosecution and abuse of process. Can you determine why they are separate intentional torts? What makes criminal prosecution groundless? What is malice? Must the victim win in criminal litigation? What injury is required? For abuse of process, how can legal proceedings be misused? To what purpose?

3. What are the four varieties of invasion of privacy in tort law? How is each defined? Do you see any similarities between invasion of privacy and any other intentional torts?

4. What are the two aspects of defamation? How are they comparable? What is publication? What makes a statement false and defamatory? What is the role of truth in defamation?

5. In the field of intentional torts, what is the intentional infliction of emotional distress? What is mental anguish? Outrageous conduct? When is intent necessary?

▌HELPFUL WEBSITES

This chapter deals with intentional torts and injuries to persons. To learn more about personal injury law, the following sites can be accessed:

General Information

http://www.personalinjurylaw.com

http://www.lawnewsnetwork.com

Publications

http://www.lawtechnews.com

http://www.nylj.com

Medical Information

http://www.nlm.nih.gov

http://www.webmd.com

Expert Witnesses and Consultants

http://www.nocall.org

http://www.findlaw.com

STUDENT CD-ROM™
For additional materials, please go to the CD in this book.

ONLINE COMPANION™
For additional resources, please go to
http://www.paralegal.delmar.cengage.com

chapter 7

Intentional Torts:

Injuries to Property

THE BIGGEST MISTAKES PARALEGALS MAKE & HOW TO AVOID THEM

An Elephant Never Forgets and a Paralegal Better Not Either

The firm assigned me to a toxic torts class action with a potential fee of $100 million for my attorneys. I kept track of all the clients and the thousands of calls and e-mails regarding their information and requests. My job for months was 70 percent consumed by this case because there were more than 100 claimants.

Another aspect of my job was to track the myriad of deadlines associated with all the various

courts and jurisdictions while we attempted to move it to federal court. Unfortunately, the case was not certified by the federal court because I failed to make one key filing deadline, in spite of all the other work that was done on this case. I lost my job and unemployment benefits because I was fired for cause. I still feel guilty for letting my firm down and especially all the deserving clients who trusted me.

(continues)

LESSON LEARNED: Most offices employ a double or triple diary system (at least one electronic plus one hard copy) to track all deadlines. A client's case may be dismissed permanently because you did not file in time or you forgot to file. Either way, it is an unforgivable act because the clients' cases could be permanently dismissed because of your dereliction of duty.

INTRODUCTION

The previous two chapters (Chapters 5 and 6) examined intentional torts involving injuries to persons (an owner's duty to others). This chapter deals with injury to the rights of a property owner or possessor.

This chapter includes:

- Intentional torts dealing with injuries to property rights
- Trespass to land
- Toxic torts
- Trespass to chattel
- Conversion
- Slander of title
- Commercial disparagement
- Defamation by computer.

TRESPASS TO LAND

Trespass is an ancient concept in tort law. In medieval English law, torts originated from trespass and trespass on the case. Under modern American law, trespass is recognized in two varieties: trespass to land and trespass to chattel.

Elements of Trespass to Land

Trespass to land occurs when a tortfeasor enters upon a land owner's real estate without consent. The tortfeasor trespasses when he or she intentionally acts in such a way as to violate the land owner's exclusive right to use the land. The elements of trespass to land are threefold:

1. Unauthorized entry upon another person's real estate
2. Tortfeasor's intent to enter without consent
3. Tortfeasor's actions interfering with the land owner's exclusive right to use the land (possession).

trespass | A wrongful entry onto another person's property.

Entry Defined

entry | The act of entering [as
upon real property].

The tortfeasor must enter upon a land owner's real estate without permission.
Entry occurs when the tortfeasor acts so as to interfere with the land owner's
exclusive right to use the property. For example, walking across someone's front
lawn constitutes entry, because the tortfeasor entered the land. Also, entry happens if a person throws trash in a neighbor's backyard, because the trash de-
positor placed an unwanted substance (trash) on the land. Both these examples
include the interference element. The front-lawn owner cannot utilize his or her
property exclusively if someone is walking across it. The neighbor's use of his or
her backyard is severely hampered by the accumulation of another's trash. The
tortfeasor's conduct in either case has disrupted the land owner's exclusive use of
the real estate. This is the foundation of trespass to land.

No Actual Harm Required

It is important to note that, under trespass law, the unauthorized entry need
not cause any damage to the real estate. It is sufficient that the transgression
occurred. Trespass law presumes that injury has happened simply because the
tortfeasor has interfered with the land owner's use of the realty. Thus, simply
walking across someone's front lawn without permission is trespass to land,
although no actual harm arises from the conduct. These types of trespasses to
land are often called *technical trespasses.* Courts generally award only nominal
damages. In technical trespass cases, courts usually award a paltry sum, such as
one dollar in nominal damages, because no actual injury resulted from the trespass. The judgment award is ceremonial or symbolic of the technical invasion of
the land owner's property rights.

As a practical matter, few lawsuits involve technical trespasses. It is simply
too expensive to litigate a trespass action when no injury has resulted. Litigants
frequently speak of suing "as a matter of principle," but plaintiffs are rarely sufficiently affluent to afford it.

Unauthorized Entry

The entry must be without consent. This essentially translates as a permission
element. For instance, if a farmer allows a person to cross his fields to reach a lake
in which to fish, then that person has not committed trespass—the entry was
authorized. Similarly, homeowners may invite visitors onto their premises by
extending an implied welcome, such as clearing sidewalks of snow up to a house
door or placing doorbells outside the doors. This suggests that people may come
upon the property to speak with the land owner. Consequently, door-to-door
salespersons would not necessarily be trespassing if they had reason to believe
that the homeowner welcomed their presence. However, if the yard were fenced

in, with a "no soliciting" sign displayed, then the salespersons would know that they did not have permission to enter the property.

Sometimes persons have a lawful right to enter upon another's land. For example, if the land owner gives an easement to a utility company to install utility lines across his or her property, then the utility company has the legal right to enter the premises to install and maintain the lines. Accordingly, no trespass to land could happen. Also, a process server, such as the county sheriff, generally has the legal right to enter the defendant's land to deliver a plaintiff's complaint and summons. No trespass to land would occur in such an instance.

One's lawful right to be upon another's premises may be withdrawn, however. Consider the example of the patron of a store. Customers are invited to come upon the premises to spend money. Suppose one such individual becomes disruptive, annoying other shoppers and employees. The store manager could demand that the agitator leave immediately. At this point, the customer becomes a trespasser, because remaining means that he or she is present upon another's land without consent. Although the customer was originally invited into the store as a patron, once he or she is ordered to leave, trespass occurs.

Intentional Interference

The tortfeasor must have intended to enter the land owner's real estate without consent. Thus, if Twila is forced to cross a neighbor's front yard to escape a pursuing wild animal, she has not committed trespass to land. Twila did not intend to cross her neighbor's property without permission; rather, she was essentially forced across by the chasing animal. However, if she deliberately strolls across her neighbor's yard, the entry was intentional.

Possession: Land Owner's Exclusive Right to Use

To constitute trespass to land, the tortfeasor's unauthorized entry must interfere with the land owner's **exclusive right** to use his or her realty. This is sometimes called the **exclusive right of possession,** which entitles the land owner to use the property without anyone else's meddling. Recall the illustrations from the discussion of entry: the neighbor could not use his or her land exclusively if someone else's trash was being dumped on it. Nor could someone use his or her front lawn exclusively if another person walked across it.

This exclusivity requirement may at first appear overly harsh. One might well ask what wrong has been done just by crossing someone's land. Trespass intends to protect one's real estate in much the same way as assault and battery are intended to protect one's person. The objective is protection from undesired interferences. In this respect, trespass seeks merely to protect one's realty from other people encroaching upon it, just as assault and battery are meant to deter unwanted physical contact.

exclusive right | A right granted to no one else.

exclusive right of possession | A land owner's right to use his or her property without interference from other persons.

Trespass Above and Below Land: Is the Sky the Limit?

Trespass to land may occur not only upon the surface of the realty, but also above and below it. In property law, a Latin phrase summarizes the extent of one's ownership of land: *cujus est solum ejus est usque ad coelum* ("he who has the soil owns upward unto heaven and downward to perdition"). Thus, it is possible for trespass to occur in the air above one's land. For instance, if a utility company erects wires across one's land without consent, this would constitute trespass to land, because the land owner owns the air above the soil. This could present insurmountable difficulties for aircraft. Fortunately, modern common law implies an exception for aircraft to fly over private property.

Similarly, one owns the resources under the earth. Although this enters into the complex area of oil, gas, and mineral law (within which special legal theories have evolved), it may be said generally that one owns the mineral resources beneath one's real estate. Accordingly, if someone mines under a person's land without permission, trespass to land has occurred. Cave exploration cases provide an interesting aspect of this theory. In a famous Indiana court case, *Marengo Cave Co. v. Ross,* 212 Ind. 624, 10 N.E.2d 917 (1937), the Supreme Court of Indiana stated that it was a trespass for the cave company to charge admission for tourists to explore caves below the surface of a land owner's property.

The sanctity of land is an ancient aspect of the human psyche. For millennia, people have used physical force and, as civilization progressed, force of law to protect against invasions. Today, trespass to land remains an active intentional tort, as these hypotheticals demonstrate.

hypotheticals

Burrough Excavating Company was digging a basement for a new home. Burrough's backhoe operator dumped the dirt on a vacant lot next to the construction site. This lot was owned by Liza, who never gave Burrough permission to use her lot. Has Burrough trespassed to land against Liza?

The elements line up nicely. Liza did not consent to Burrough's dirt dumping, and so Burrough engaged in unauthorized entry upon another's realty. Burrough obviously intended this entry, as the backhoe operator dumped the dirt on Liza's lot. This dumping interfered with Liza's exclusive use of her property, because she will now have to contend with the dirt pile if she wishes to use her lot. Therefore, Burrough has committed trespass to land against Liza.

* * *

Consider another hypothetical. Bryan owns a house next to Elizabeth. Elizabeth planted several oak trees on her property with branches that hang over a fence separating her property from Bryan's. Bryan thought the trees were unsightly and trimmed the limbs that hung over onto his yard. He did not ask Elizabeth for permission to remove the limbs. Has a trespass occurred?

Who has trespassed? By allowing her tree branches to cross over onto Bryan's property, Elizabeth committed unauthorized entry onto another's land without consent. Her trees interfered with Bryan's exclusive right of possession, because the branches obstructed Bryan's use of this part of his property. Recall, too, that Bryan owns to the top of the sky under the *ad coelum* doctrine discussed earlier. Anything encroaching upon his airspace constitutes entry. Intent may be implied, as Elizabeth knew the trees crossed the fence but did nothing to remove the overhanging limbs. Thus, Elizabeth has trespassed upon Bryan's land.

Somewhat more problematic is the inverse inquiry: namely, did Bryan trespass against Elizabeth by pruning the trees? Because the trees grew on Elizabeth's property, Bryan's trimming (without permission) encroached upon Elizabeth's use of her trees. But does this constitute unauthorized entry onto another's land? The branches hung over onto Bryan's property, so he did not actually enter upon Elizabeth's land to cut the limbs. He was simply "defending" his property from the encroaching branches. Accordingly, Bryan did not commit trespass to land against Elizabeth.

Recent trespass actions have involved one of the most complex and dynamic developing areas of tort law—namely, toxic tort litigation. The next section discusses this type of trespass.

▌ TOXIC TORT ACTIONS

A significant percentage of modern tort litigation is devoted to actions involving toxic chemicals, pollution, hazardous waste disposal and transportation, and other environmentally sensitive issues. These are sometimes referred to as **toxic tort actions.** These lawsuits cover causes of action involving the following: trespass to land, negligence, absolute liability for ultrahazardous substances, products liability, and nuisance. This chapter focuses on the trespass to land aspects of toxic tort litigation.

toxic tort actions | Actions involving toxic chemicals, pollution, hazardous waste disposal and transportation, and other environmentally sensitive issues. Many tort theories, including trespass to land, negligence, absolute liability for ultrahazardous substances, products liability, and nuisance apply.

Nature of the Problem

For much of this century, toxic waste disposal was considered simple. Manufacturers or chemical processors applied a centuries-old approach: "out of sight, out of mind." Hazardous waste was simply buried, dumped into waterways, or burned. Much toxic waste found its way into public and private landfills, rivers, and smoke-belching incinerators. This did not eliminate the noxious nature of the waste products; it simply shifted the problem to another location. As the years passed, barrels buried at the underground sites rusted and leaked, sending lethal seepage through the soil, contaminating underground water supplies, and injuring people who drank contaminated well water. Toxic burial leakage also percolated from underground through springs, exposing innocent bystanders to carcinogenic or otherwise lethal substances in surface waters. Rivers and streams simply carried the sludge to haunt downstream land owners, who came into contact with the poisons through irrigation or otherwise working with the polluted waters. Residents near the incineration plants suffered a variety of lung ailments from poisonous air pollutants.

Traditionally, all these intrusions fell neatly within the intentional tort of trespass to land. Nuisance provided neighboring land owners another cause of action with which to litigate against the industrial toxic polluters. Absolute liability also applied under the ultrahazardous substances theory. Negligence lent further legal aid to plaintiffs seeking relief against injuries from the unwanted and toxic invaders.

THE CASE OF THE POLLUTING PLUME

This is a case of buyer beware. The owners of real property find themselves in the middle of a huge lawsuit with the California Department of Toxic Substances Control. Dry cleaning chemicals from the prior businesses located on the property leached into the groundwater and contaminated it. Who should bear the cost of cleanup?

CALIFORNIA DEPARTMENT OF TOXIC SUBSTANCES CONTROL, Plaintiff,
v.
PAYLESS CLEANERS; College Cleaners; Heidinger Cleaners; Norge Village Cleaners; Defendants, et al.
368 F. Supp. 2d 1069
United States District Court, E.D. California
March 4, 2005

This action arises out of a two-mile wide perchloroethylene ("PCE") "plume" located south of the central business district of Chico, California. On October 31, 2002, the California Department of Toxic Substances Control ("DTSC") filed a cost recovery action against various individuals and companies alleging rights under the Comprehensive Environmental Response, Compensation, and Liability Act (CERCLA), 42 U.S.C.

§§ 9601 et seq. and state law based claims. The DTSC named several dry cleaning businesses as well as the property owners of the sites where those businesses operated upon its belief that the PCE emanated from those businesses. Among the defendants are the Peters. The DTSC seeks to recover its costs in investigating and remediating the contaminated groundwater.

The Peters are the owners of property in the City of Chico from which hazardous substances, including PCE, were allegedly released when a dry cleaner business operated on the property. The Peters bring suit against Maytag as Norge Corporation's ("Norge") successor-in-interest, which, according to the Peters, manufactured and provided the dry cleaning equipment and PCE used on their property.

The Peters allege that, prior to their ownership, third party defendant CAVA, Inc. ("CAVA") constructed, owned, and operated Norge Village

Cleaner ("Dry Cleaner") on the property at issue. Pursuant to a franchise agreement, CAVA purchased and used dry cleaning machines and solvents for their dry cleaning operation from Norge, who designed and manufactured the machines and solvents. The dry cleaning machines were designed to use, process and discharge solvents containing PCE. Norge also decided and controlled the layout of the Dry Cleaner, including where the machines were installed and the location of floor drains for disposal of waste water.

According to the Peters, Norge installed the machines to use, process, and dispose of wastewater laden with PCE through a floor piping connected with the City of Chico's sewer system.

Maytag contends that the Peters fail to allege sufficient facts to support a claim for liability under CERCLA.

CERCLA allocates the rights and responsibilities of those involved in hazardous waste remediation. In creating CERCLA Congress provided a right of recovery for potentially responsible parties ("PRPs") who have incurred hazardous waste cleanup costs by expressly allowing a contribution action against other PRPs. Thus, a PRP who is found to be jointly and severally liable for response costs can sue to recover those expenses paid in excess of its own liability by spreading the costs to other PRPs. The Peters bring suit against Maytag for contribution in their capacity as a PRP to the DTSC.

To establish a prima facie case against Maytag, the Peters must show that: (1) PCE is a hazardous substance; (2) there has been a release of PCE at the Peters' facility; (3) the release or threatened release caused the Plaintiffs to incur response costs; and (4) defendants are within one of four classes of persons subject to CERCLA's liability provisions. Maytag challenges only the last of these elements, asserting

that it does not fall within any of the four classes as required to be held liable.

The Peters allege that Maytag "designed, manufactured, and actually installed the dry cleaning machines that produced PCE at the Dry Cleaner and/or CAVA."

Maytag's transaction can be described only as the sale of a useful good which, through its normal use, created a waste byproduct.

Although the machines were designed to discharge waste water through a hose, the Peters could have connected that hose to and collected the waste in a tank or disposed of the waste through other means. In sum, these facts do not by themselves establish Maytag's actual authority and control over the disposal of the PCE, rather, that control remained with the Peters.

The Peters allege that Maytag physically installed the dry cleaning machines, including "physically connecting the [machines'] discharge piping" to the building drain, which was itself connected to the sewer system. This fact, along with the facts concerning Maytag's role as the franchisor, establishes that it had the authority to and did actually control the disposal of the waste water laden with PCE.

If Maytag chose the locations of the floor drains and then inspected to ensure that the waste water was disposed into the sewer system, then the Peters did not exercise independent decisionmaking regarding the disposal, but rather, at the very least, shared this control with Maytag. Although these facts alone seem sufficient to subject Maytag to liability, the Peters present even more compelling allegations that establish Maytag's control over the PCE disposal.

Accordingly, the Peters can seek contribution from Maytag.

CASE QUESTIONS

1. What is the purpose of CERCLA?
2. Has the purpose of CERCLA been met by this case?

Toxic Trespass

Trespass to land occurs when toxic substances enter upon another's property. The trespass elements remain the same:

1. Unauthorized entry upon another person's real estate
2. Tortfeasor's intent to enter without consent
3. Tortfeasor's actions interfering with the land owner's exclusive right to use the land (possession).

In the case of toxic substances, the unauthorized entry is seepage or accumulation of the hazardous material on the victim's land. Few owners consent to having toxins placed over, upon, or under their realty. Most people want such materials to be taken as far away from them as possible.

The tortfeasor's intent to enter without permission may be implied from the disposal method used. For instance, toxic waste buried in metal barrels will, over time, rust through and seep into the underground soil, unless the material is contained in an isolated fashion, such as an underground concrete crypt. If the tortfeasor failed to take sufficient precautions to prevent subterranean seepage, then the intent to trespass may be implied. Another example of implied intent is dumping toxic fluids into waterways. The tortfeasor desired the river or stream to carry the dangerous substances downstream, which would plainly deposit the toxins on the shores of other people's property.

The tortfeasor's interference with the plaintiff's exclusive possession of his or her land is equally clear. The toxic residues are a highly offensive and potent invasion, making some real estate uninhabitable. A more significant illustration of trespass would be difficult to imagine.

When land owners' underground water supplies are contaminated with buried toxic waste seepage, trespass to land occurs. A quick review of the elements shows that they are readily satisfied. Many cases in the court reports tell sad tales of families irreparably harmed through long-term consumption of chemically contaminated well water, poisoned as a result of improper underground waste disposal.

THE CASE OF THE NUISANCE LAKE

The owner of property near an artificial lake brought this action for nuisance and trespass against both the owner of the lake and the operator of a textile mill. The plaintiff claims that the mill discharged wastewater, which polluted the lake. The plaintiff further alleges that the owners of the lake allowed this to occur, thereby harming the plaintiff's neighboring property. Even though the plaintiff's expert testified concerning the contaminants in the lake, the court was not willing to make the inference that the plaintiff's land was actually contaminated.

RUSSELL CORPORATION
v.
SULLIVAN et al. AVONDALE MILLS, INC.

2001 WL 29264
Supreme Court of Alabama
January 12, 2001

Russell and Avondale Mills operate textile plants in Alexander City. As part of their operations, they discharge directly into the Sugar Creek Plant large volumes of wastewater containing dyes used in processing textiles. After the wastewater is treated at the Sugar Creek Plant, it is discharged into Sugar Creek at a rate of five to six million gallons a day. This output flows through Sugar Creek, runs into Elkahatchee Creek, and, eventually, into Lake Martin. The plaintiffs are all residents of the Raintree subdivision located on Lake Martin. [APCo owns Lake Martin, a manmade lake APCo uses to generate power.]

The wastewater from Russell and Avondale constitutes 70–80% of the water treated daily at the Sugar Creek Plant. This wastewater contains dyes, salts, acid surfactants, and heavy metals, making the water difficult to treat. At least one type of dye treated at the Sugar Creek Plant, azo dye, has been shown to have carcinogenic properties. The plaintiffs presented evidence indicating that the dyes, which are resistant to fading, are also difficult to remove from the wastewater during treatment. As a result of problems in removing color from the treated water, the City of Alexander City installed a chlorination/dechlorination facility at the Sugar Creek Plant.

The Sugar Creek Plant uses an activated-sludge process to treat the wastewater. In that process, the waste is combined with oxygen and bacteria; it then forms a sludge that is removed from the water. The remaining water is decontaminated and is then discharged into Sugar Creek. . . .

Testimony at trial indicated that the plaintiffs noticed the [floating sediment] flocs floating in the lake water near their property. At times, they claim, the water was so stained by the dyes that it would color

T-shirts. . . . No evidence was presented to indicate that the dyes or any of the components released by Russell and Avondale in their wastewater were actually found on any of the plaintiffs' properties. The plaintiffs relied on the testimony that waves and high waters could wash the materials ashore. The plaintiffs testified that because the water in Lake Martin is contaminated, their property is not as valuable as it could have been.

. . . The plaintiffs' action against APCo rests on the theory that APCo has a duty to keep Lake Martin clean, and that it breached that duty by allowing Russell and Avondale to discharge contaminants into Lake Martin.

Trespass requires an intentional act by the defendant. . . . [T]hat in order for one to be liable to another for trespass, the person must intentionally enter upon land in the possession of another or the person must intentionally cause some 'substance' or 'thing' to enter upon another's land.

The plaintiffs argue that APCo committed trespass by allowing Russell and Avondale to discharge contaminants into Lake Martin and then by allowing those contaminants to remain on the bottom of the lake. . . . In this case, there is no agency relationship between APCo, on the one hand, and Russell and Avondale, on the other. No evidence was presented to indicate that APCo directed Russell and Avondale to discharge their waste in any manner or to indicate that APCo aided or participated in the discharge. Therefore, there was no intentional act by APCo to support a claim of trespass.

* * *

APCo operates Lake Martin pursuant to a license issued by the Federal Energy Regulatory Commission ("FERC"). During the trial, the plaintiffs, over APCo's objection, placed that license in evidence.

> "In the construction, maintenance, or operation of the project, *the Licensee shall be responsible for, and shall take reasonable measures to prevent,* soil erosion on lands adjacent to streams or other waters, stream sedimentation, and *any form of water or air pollution.* . . ."

* * *

(continues)

Where a plant discharges effluent into a stream that ultimately runs into a reservoir created by a dam, the owner of the reservoir cannot be liable for maintaining a nuisance, absent evidence indicating that it authorized or participated in the deposit of pollutants or that it had control over the deposits. The only prong of this test that arguably might apply to APCo is the "control-over-the-deposits" prong. However, as previously noted, that control cannot be grounded upon the FERC license charging APCo with a duty to take reasonable measures to prevent water pollution. The record is devoid of any other basis for concluding that APCo had any control over the activities of Russell and Avondale.

We therefore reverse the trial court's judgment as to APCo and render judgment for APCo on both the trespass claim and the nuisance claim.

* * *

In this case, whether water actually splashed onto the plaintiffs' property is sharply contested. . . .

In summary, several conclusions urged by the plaintiffs are unsupported by evidence: . . . The ultimate conclusion that any chemicals were deposited onto the plaintiffs' properties is, at best, speculative. . . .

The lack of scientific evidence indicating the presence of any chemicals causing "actual substantial damage" to the plaintiffs' properties or to support any of Dr. Gould's opinions is fatal to the plaintiffs' trespass claims. . . .

"A 'nuisance' is anything that works hurt, inconvenience or damage to another. The fact that the act done may otherwise be lawful does not keep it from being a nuisance. The inconvenience complained of must not be fanciful or such as would affect only one of fastidious taste, but it should be such as would affect an ordinary reasonable man." Therefore, although Russell and Avondale argue that their actions were in accordance with state and federal regulations and that they were permissible under various permits, the plaintiffs may still maintain an action against Russell and Avondale if they can prove the elements of nuisance.

In Alabama, a nuisance can be either private or public. "A public nuisance is one which damages all persons who come within the sphere of its operation, though it may vary in its effects on individuals. A private nuisance is one limited in its injurious effects to one or a few individuals."

The distinction between a private and a public nuisance is an important one. "A private nuisance gives a right of action to the person injured" while "a public nuisance gives no right of action to any individual, but must be abated by a process instituted in the name of the state." . . . In order to support an individual's cause of action for a public nuisance, the nuisance must cause a "special damage" that is different in "kind and degree from [the damage] suffered by the public in general." Therefore, if the nuisance allegedly created by the discharge of wastewater into Sugar Creek, and ultimately into Lake Martin, is a public one, the plaintiffs in this case must show that the discharge has caused them special damage, i.e., damage that is different than that suffered by others. . . .

The plaintiffs in the present case, however, have presented no evidence indicating such special damage. The plaintiffs alleged that Russell's and Avondale's actions resulted in the loss of the use and enjoyment of Lake Martin.

The plaintiffs claim that the nuisance they suffered was a private nuisance. . . .

Russell and Avondale correctly argue that the nuisance, if any, is a public nuisance, because, they say, the alleged nuisance is in the water of Lake Martin, a public waterway whose bed is owned solely by APCo. The discharge of contaminants into a public body of water constitutes a public nuisance. Russell and Avondale argue that the plaintiffs never proved that the alleged nuisance prevented them from using or enjoying their "own" property. While the plaintiffs offered evidence that they were unable to use and enjoy the lake, the use and enjoyment of a public area is a public right. . . . Any nuisance caused by the discharge of contaminated wastewater into Lake Martin is a public, not a private, nuisance.

Because the plaintiffs expressly waived any claim to recovery under a public-nuisance theory, thereby avoiding the necessity of proving that they suffered special damage not suffered by members of the general public, it is unnecessary to address whether the record contains substantial evidence of such damage.

The trial court erred in denying Russell, Avondale, and APCo's motion for a judgment as a matter of law. Therefore, its judgment is reversed and a judgment is rendered in favor of Russell, Avondale, and APCo.

CASE QUESTIONS
1. Explain the difference between a public and a private nuisance.
2. Why was no trespass found?

Importance of Environmental Statutes

Aside from trespass, nuisance, absolute liability, and negligence, there are a variety of federal, state, and local statutes regulating environmental toxins. One important federal statute is the Toxic Substances Control Act. This act regulates the manufacture, distribution, processing, use, and disposal of hazardous materials. Detailed recordkeeping regarding the hazardous materials must be maintained, 15 U.S.C. § 2601 *et seq.* (1992). The Hazardous Materials Transportation Act establishes strict requirements for transporters of hazardous waste. Detailed recordkeeping is required to ensure compliance with the act, 49 U.S.C. §§ 1801–1812 (1992). Another federal statute, the Comprehensive Environmental Response, Compensation and Liability Act (CERCLA), addresses any "imminently hazardous chemical substance or mixture" and allows the federal Environmental Protection Agency (EPA) to file civil lawsuits when the use of such a material will pose imminent risk to health or the environment and the EPA has not issued a final rule to protect against such risk.

Trespass to land is merely one type of trespass action. Trespass to chattel is the other.

▌ TRESPASS TO CHATTEL

A tortfeasor commits **trespass to chattel** when he or she possesses someone's personal property without consent. A **chattel** is personal property, as opposed to real property, which is land. An automobile, a textbook, a pet dog or cat, and a desk are examples of chattels. Trespass to chattel has elements similar to those of trespass to land:

1. Unauthorized possession of, or interference with the use of, another individual's personal property
2. Intent to deprive (or interfere with) the owner's possession or exclusive use of his or her chattel.

trespass to chattel | Occurs when the tortfeasor intentionally deprives or interferes with the chattel owner's possession or exclusive use of personal property. The tortfeasor's possession or interference must be unauthorized, which means that the owner cannot have consented.

chattel | Item of personal property. Any property other than land.

Unauthorized Possession of Another's Chattel

Suppose Nadene takes a neighbor's textbook during class. Unless Nadene obtained the neighbor's consent before seizing the text, Nadene has engaged in unauthorized possession of another's personal property. The book's owner did not give Nadene permission to possess the chattel. When a tortfeasor takes possession of another's personal property without consent, this is sometimes described as the act of **dispossession.**

dispossession | Wrongfully taking away a person's property by force, trick, or misuse of the law.

Consent may be implied under certain circumstances. For instance, if Alfred gives his car keys to a friend, the implication is that the friend may use Alfred's motor vehicle. Similarly, hotel guests may presume that the management intended them to use the electricity, water, soap, and tissues supplied to the rooms. However, if a patron takes the hotel's pillows, sheets, and towels, this would be unauthorized possession, as staying in a hotel does not implicitly entitle guests to keep such items.

Unauthorized Interference with Use

It is possible to trespass to chattel without actually wrenching possession of the personal property from its rightful owner. Interference with the chattel owner's use of the property is sufficient. For instance, if a tortfeasor purposely fed Reggie's prize hogs a contaminated food, so that the hogs became ill and lost weight, then the tortfeasor engaged in unconsented interference with Reggie's use of the animals. If Cherrie's landlord shuts off the electricity to her apartment without permission, then this would also constitute unauthorized interference with the use of her personal property (provided, of course, that Cherrie had paid her electric bill).

THE CASE OF THE PERSONAL-PROPERTY PET

Frequently, legal decisions must define exactly how property is characterized under the law. In this case, man's best friend is defined as personal property, nothing more. A dog's owner has sued the treating veterinarian, and seeks emotional damages as a result of alleged malpractice.

KOESTER
v.
VCA ANIMAL HOSPITAL
244 Mich. App. 173, 624 N.W.2d 209
Court of Appeals of Michigan
December 26, 2000

Plaintiff left his dog at defendant VCA's kennel for a weekend. Plaintiff left explicit instructions not to use a collar on the dog because of a salivary gland problem for which VCA had previously treated the pet. Upon returning for the dog, plaintiff noticed that the dog's neck area was swollen. Within a few days, when the dog continued to exhibit swelling in the neck area, plaintiff returned to defendant VCA. Defendant Field, a veterinarian, treated the dog by draining its enlarged gland and bandaging its neck and head. When plaintiff returned to pick up his dog after the procedure, he noticed that the dog appeared to have trouble breathing and asked defendant Field whether the bandages were too tight. Field responded that the dog would be fine once it calmed down. Later that same day, plaintiff left the dog alone for ten to fifteen minutes to run an errand. When plaintiff returned home, he discovered the dog laying motionless on the floor, having apparently choked to death. An autopsy determined that the dog suffocated to death because the bandages were wrapped too tightly.

Plaintiff brought the instant negligence action pleading damages that included plaintiff's pain and suffering, extreme fright, shock, mortification, and the loss of the society and companionship of his dog. Defendants moved for summary disposition pursuant to MCR 2.116(C)(8), for failure to state a claim upon which relief could be granted, arguing that plaintiff was not entitled to the damages pleaded as a matter of law. The trial court agreed, holding that emotional damages for the loss of a dog did not exist.

* * *

On appeal, plaintiff alleges that the trial court erred in summarily disposing of his negligence claim. Plaintiff primarily argues that companion animals should not be considered merely personal property. In support of his argument, plaintiff offers the alleged practice of other jurisdictions which have acknowledged the value of companion animals by awarding damages for emotional distress associated with the loss of a pet. Although we recognize that domesticated pets have value and sentimentality associated with them which may not compare with that of other personal property, we cannot agree with plaintiff.

. . . In this matter, plaintiff pleaded damages of emotional distress and loss of society and companionship of his dog. Pets have long been considered personal property in Michigan jurisprudence (see *Ten Hopen v. Walker,* 96 Mich 236, 239; 55 NW 657 (1893)). Consequently, the issue before this Court is whether plaintiff can properly plead and recover for emotional injuries he allegedly suffered as a consequence of his property being damaged by defendants' negligence. There is no Michigan precedent which permits the recovery of damages for emotional injuries allegedly suffered as a consequence of property damage. Plaintiff requests that we allow such recovery when a pet is the property that is damaged, arguing that pets have evolved in our modern society to a status which is not consistent with their characterization as a "chattel." . . . Although this Court is very sympathetic to plaintiff's position, we defer to the Legislature to create such a remedy.

There are several factors that must be considered before expanding or creating tort liability including, but not limited to, legislative and judicial policies. In this case, there is no statutory, judicial, or other persuasive authority that compels or permits this Court to take the drastic action proposed by plaintiff. Case law on this issue from sister states is not consistent, persuasive, or sufficient precedent. We refuse to create a remedy where there is no legal structure in which to give it support. . . .

We decline to allow the recovery of emotional distress damages arising from negligence committed against plaintiff's pet; therefore, plaintiff's complaint failed to plead legally cognizable damages and was properly dismissed by the trial court.

Affirmed.

CASE QUESTIONS
1. Why couldn't the dog owner recover for emotional distress?
2. Do you think tort liability should be expanded to cover emotional injuries for damages to property?

Intent to Deprive or Interfere

To commit trespass to chattel, the tortfeasor must intend to interfere with or deprive the chattel owner of possession or the exclusive use of his or her personal property. Intent may be expressed, as it was when Nadene took her neighbor's book. It may also be implied under the circumstances. For example, assume that Cherrie's landlord changed the locks on her apartment door in order to lock her out, although she had paid her rent and had done nothing to violate her rental agreement. This would imply the landlord's intent to deprive Cherrie of possession of her personal property inside the apartment. Her use of the chattels would definitely be hindered.

Similarly, lack of intent may be implied. For example, assume Bud found his neighbor's cow grazing along a public highway and took the animal to his barn for safekeeping until he could telephone the neighbor. Although Bud took possession of the cow without his neighbor's consent, Bud did not intend to interfere with the neighbor's use of the cow. Nor did he wish to deprive his neighbor of possession. Bud simply wished to protect the animal from harm. This is emphasized by his efforts to contact his neighbor to come claim the cow. Thus, Bud lacked intent to trespass to chattel.

Table 7-1 summarizes the elements of trespass to land and trespass to chattel.

TABLE 7-1
Elements of trespass to land and trespass to chattel

TRESPASS TO LAND	TRESPASS TO CHATTEL
Unauthorized entry upon another person's real estate	Unauthorized possession of another individual's personal property *or* unauthorized interference with another's use of his or her chattel
Intent to enter without consent (no harm to land required)	Intent to dispossess or interfere with owner's use of his or her personal property
Interference with land owner's exclusive right to use land (possession)	Similar to conversion, which also requires tortfeasor to put dispossessed chattel to his or her own use

A CASE OF NOT-SO-GUT-WRENCHING CONFLICT

Not every invasion of one's personal property constitutes trespass to chattel. Actual dispossession must occur. A trifling interference, fleeting and momentary, will be tolerated under the law. As the following case demonstrates, the invasion of this plaintiff's chattel was insufficient to give rise to this cause of action.

KOEPNICK

v.

SEARS, ROEBUCK & CO.

Court of Appeals of Arizona
158 Ariz. 322, 762 P.2d 609 (1988)
June 16, 1988
Froeb, Presiding Judge

. . . The issues presented on appeal are: . . . whether the trial court erred in granting Sears' motion for judgment notwithstanding the verdict (judgment n.o.v.) on Koepnick's trespass to chattel claim. . . .

FACTS

Koepnick was stopped in the Fiesta Mall parking lot by Sears security guards Lessard and Pollack on December 6, 1982, at approximately 6:15 P.M. Lessard and Pollack suspected Koepnick of shoplifting a wrench and therefore detained him for approximately 15 minutes until the Mesa police arrived. Upon arrival of the police, Koepnick and a police officer became involved in an altercation in which Koepnick was injured. The police officer handcuffed Koepnick, placed a call for a backup, and began investigating the shop-lifting allegations. Upon investigation it was discovered that Koepnick had receipts for the wrench and for all the Sears merchandise he had been carrying. Additionally, the store clerk who sold the wrench to Koepnick was located. He verified the sale and informed Lessard that he had put the wrench in a small bag, stapled it shut, and then placed that bag into a large bag containing Koepnick's other purchases. The small bag was not among the items in Koepnick's possession in the security room. To determine whether a second wrench was involved, the police and Lessard searched Koepnick's truck which was in the mall parking lot. No stolen items were found. Having completed their investigation, the police cited Koepnick for disorderly conduct and released him. The entire detention lasted approximately 45 minutes.

Koepnick sued Sears for false arrest, assault, trespass to chattel, invasion of privacy and malicious

prosecution. The trial court directed a verdict in favor of Sears on all charges except false arrest and trespass to chattel. After a trial on these claims, a jury awarded Koepnick . . . $100 compensatory damages and $25,000 punitive damages for trespass to chattel. Sears timely moved for judgment n.o.v. and alternatively for a new trial. The trial court . . . granted Sears' motion for judgment n.o.v. on the trespass to chattel charge. . . .

Koepnick appeals, challenging the trial court's order granting Sears . . . judgment n.o.v. on his trespass to chattel claim. . . .

We find no reversible error and therefore affirm the trial court's order granting . . . judgment n.o.v. on the trespass to chattel claim.

* * *

TRESPASS TO CHATTEL

Arizona courts follow the Restatement (Second) of Torts absent authority to the contrary. The Restatement provides that the tort of trespass to a chattel may be committed by intentionally dispossessing another of the chattel or using or intermeddling with a chattel in the possession of another. Restatement (Second) of Torts § 217 (1965).

The Restatement (Second) of Torts § 221 (1965) defines dispossession as follows:

A dispossession may be committed by intentionally
   (a) taking a chattel from the possession of another without the other's consent, or

   . . .

   (c) barring the possessor's access to a chattel . . . .

Comment b to § 221 provides that dispossession may occur when someone intentionally assumes physical control over the chattel and deals with the chattel in a way which will be destructive of the possessory interest of the other person. Comment b further provides that "on the other hand, an intermeddling with the chattel is not a dispossession unless the actor intends to exercise a dominion and control over it inconsistent with a possession in any other person other than himself."

(continues)

The Restatement (Second) of Torts § 218 (1965) provides:

> One who commits a trespass to a chattel is subject to liability to the possessor of the chattel if, but only if,
>   (a) he dispossesses the other of the chattel, or
>   (b) the chattel is impaired as to its condition, quality, or value, or
>   (c) the possessor is deprived of the use of the chattel for a substantial time, or
>   (d) bodily harm is caused to the possessor, or harm is caused to some person or thing in which the possessor has a legally protected interest.

Koepnick argued at trial that Lessard's participation in searching his truck constituted an actionable trespass to the truck. He was awarded $100 damages by the jury which he characterizes as damages for a dispossession pursuant to subsection (a) or deprivation of use pursuant to subsection (c) of § 218.

* * *

Sears' actions with respect to the trespass consisted of Steve Lessard accompanying a Mesa police officer out to the parking lot and looking in the truck. There is no evidence in the record of an intent on the part of Sears' employee to claim a possessory interest in the truck contrary to Koepnick's interest. No lien or ownership interest claim of any kind was made. Further, there is no evidence that Sears intentionally denied Koepnick access to his truck.

Koepnick was in the City of Mesa's custody at the time of the search and Sears had no control over how the police department conducted its investigation. . . .

. . . In order that an actor who interferes with another's chattel may be liable, his conduct must affect some other and more important interest of the possessor [than for harmless intermeddlings]. Therefore, one who intentionally intermeddles with another's chattel is subject to liability only if his intermeddling is harmful to the possessor's materially valuable interest in the physical condition, quality, or value of the chattel, or if the possessor is deprived of the use of the chattel for a substantial time. . . . Sufficient legal protection of the possessor's interest in the mere inviolability of his chattel is afforded by his privilege to use reasonable force to protect his possession against even harmless interference.

Side bar: The *Koepnick* court stated that an owner could protect his or her chattel from harmless interference through the defense of property defense, discussed in Chapter 8. The court felt this was sufficient legal protection of the chattel owner's interests. But how could Koepnick protect his truck from intrusion by the police officer and Sears' security guard, as the defense would lawfully premit, when he was hand-cuffed and held elsewhere?

The search in question took approximately two minutes. Neither the truck nor its contents were damaged in any manner by the police or Sears' employee. As a matter of law, Sears' action did not constitute an actionable trespass under § 218(c).

. . . For a deprivation of use caused by a trespass to chattel to be actionable, the time must be so substantial that it is possible to estimate the loss that is caused. The record in the present case lacks any evidence to permit a jury to estimate any loss caused to Koepnick [as a result of the police officer and Lessard's search of his truck].

* * *

We conclude that there was no dispossession of the vehicle as contemplated under § 218 of the Restatement nor was Koepnick deprived of its use for a substantial period of time. . . .

The judgment of the trial court is affirmed. . . .

CASE QUESTIONS

1. Why do you suppose the jury awarded Koepnick such a large damages award, which prompted the trial court to grant judgment notwithstanding the verdict (judgment n.o.v.)? Do you think the jurors would agree that Koepnick suffered no harm as a result of the defendants' actions? Do you?
2. Do you believe that Koepnick satisfied the elements for assault, invasion of privacy, and malicious prosecution?

CONVERSION

In the early history of tort law, trespass to chattel was frequently subject to litigation, often in cases involving domestic livestock. Court opinions from the nineteenth century abound. More recent cases, however, have tended to focus upon conversion, which is a similar but separate tort.

History

Conversion occurs when a tortfeasor, without consent, deprives an owner of possession of the owner's chattel and puts or *converts* the property to the tortfeasor's own use. It is essentially a broader version of trespass to chattel, but both torts developed separately.

conversion | Any act that deprives an owner of property without that owner's permission and without just cause.

   Conversion evolved from the common law action of *trover,* which appeared in England during the fifteenth century as a specific type of trespass on the case action. In trover lawsuits, the court determined that the plaintiff, the chattel owner, had a legal right to possess the personal property (namely, because of ownership), and that the defendant, the tortfeasor, had taken possession of the chattel for his or her own use. Gradually, this element (taking for one's own use) was described in the English court opinions as "converting the property for one's own use." Thus, the term *conversion* began to replace *trover,* and the modern tort of conversion emerged.

Elements of Conversion

Under modern tort law, conversion consists of three elements:

1. Depriving the owner of possession of a chattel
2. Intent to deprive possession and convert the property to one's own use
3. The owner's nonconsent to the tortfeasor's possession and use of the chattel.

Depriving of Possession

Under conversion, the tortfeasor must actually deprive the owner of possession of personal property. The common law usually employs the phrase *exercising dominion and control over the chattel which is inconsistent with the owner's right to exclusive use.* This means that the tortfeasor controls another's personal property so as to prevent the owner from using it. For example, suppose Nadene took her neighbor's textbook and refused to return it. Nadene's "dominion and control" over the book prevents the neighbor from using his or her chattel.

Extent of Deprivation.
Normally, conversion is differentiated from trespass to chattel based upon the scope of the deprivation. With trespass to chattel, many courts have held that the deprivation need only be minor or temporary.

With conversion, several courts have ruled that the deprivation must be so extensive as to suggest a desire to deprive the owner of possession permanently. There is considerable disagreement among different jurisdictions as to this issue, however. The majority of courts maintain that conversion has occurred simply because the tortfeasor deprived the owner of dominion and control over the chattel, regardless of length of time or permanent intent.

Methods of Depriving. Deprivation of possession may occur in a variety of ways. *Physical possession* of the chattel is most common, although deprivation may happen through *damage or destruction* of the personal property. For instance, if someone plows under Kathy's garden to plant grass seed, this amounts to deprivation of possession, because Kathy can no longer use her vegetables. Similarly, if someone opens a window during a thunderstorm, and rain floods Sig's stereo, the injury has deprived Sig of the use of his chattel.

Deprivation may also take place simply through use. Some forms of personal property cannot be picked up and carried away. For instance, electricity, free-flowing liquids, and other intangible items are commonly defined as chattels under state commercial codes. One possesses such things by using them. If Morgan, Colleen's neighbor, plugs his garage heater into her electric outlet without permission, and Colleen's electric bill suddenly soars, Morgan has deprived her of dominion and control over her electricity. This translates as deprivation of possession.

Intent to Deprive and Convert to Own Use

First of all, conversion requires that the tortfeasor intend to deprive the owner of possession of his or her chattel. This is comparable to trespass to chattel. However, unlike trespass to chattel, conversion also requires that the tortfeasor convert the personal property to his or her own use. For example, assume Joey and Lisa are acquaintances at school. Then suppose that Joey found Lisa's earrings on a bench at the mall. Joey might keep the earrings until he saw Lisa at school later in the week. Because Joey did not intend to use the earrings himself, he is not guilty of conversion. However, if Joey wore the earrings to the school dance, he would have converted them to his own use.

It is important to note that the tortfeasor does not have to injure the chattel to convert it. Conversion occurs simply because the owner has been deprived of the use of the personal property without having given permission. Injury occurs to the owner's right to exclusively use the chattel.

Lack of Consent

Naturally, the owner cannot have granted permission to someone to use or possess the chattel. If Victoria allows a classmate to borrow her text overnight to study, then the classmate has not converted the book. Consent may be expressed, as in the book-borrowing situation, or it may be implied. For example, suppose that when Bob leaves his automobile at a mechanic's for an oil replacement the mechanic also repairs a broken valve and pipe. The mechanic did not convert Bob's property, because Bob impliedly gave the mechanic permission to possess the vehicle for repair purposes. Of course, Bob did not authorize the additional work, but that is a breach-of-contract question. However, if the mechanic went joy-riding in Bob's car after changing the oil, this would be conversion, because Bob did not implicitly consent to that use of his car.

Even though the chattel owner may have consented to a tortfeasor's possession, this permission may be revoked. This could result in a conversion. For example, Bob complains that he did not authorize the additional work done on his automobile, but he is willing to pay for the oil change, which he did request. The mechanic insists that Bob also pay for the unauthorized repairs and refuses to return Bob's car until he pays the extra amount. Because Bob did not agree to these additional charges, he insists that his vehicle be returned immediately. Thus, Bob has revoked the permission he originally gave the mechanic to possess the chattel. If the mechanic does not comply with Bob's demand, the mechanic will be liable for conversion.

THE CASE OF THE CONVERTED QUARTERS

A grandparent sues his own daughter and her former spouse because of the acts of a grandchild. The court must decide who can be held responsible for the deliberate torts of the child.

ALFRED T. READING, Plaintiff-Appellant,
v.
MATTHEW MAHON and DONNA MAHON,
Defendants-Respondents.
Docket No. A-0404-06T3
Superior Court of New Jersey, Appellate Division
Argued April 24, 2007—Decided

Plaintiff commenced this litigation to hold defendants Donna and Matthew Mahon accountable for their eldest son's conversion of his property.

The child is plaintiff's grandson. His parents are divorced. Although the parents share custody of their sons, the boys live with their mother in their

grandparents' home "most of the time." Their father lives nearby and in the same neighborhood.

Plaintiff and his wife have been saving rolls of quarters since 1999. They were stored on shelves in the basement of their home. On April 26, 2006, plaintiff discovered that $3800 worth of coins had been removed. At plaintiff's request, defendant Donna Mahon questioned her sons about the money. The eldest boy admitted that he took the quarters and spent the money.

As a consequence of the boy's admission, plaintiff prepared an agreement for the signature of the boy and his parents evidencing a promise to repay him $3800. The boy and defendant Donna Mahon

(continues)

agreed and signed. The boy's father refused to agree or sign.

Plaintiff sought a judgment declaring both parents responsible for repayment of the $3800 taken by their son. Judge McManimon concluded that plaintiff failed to establish grounds for holding defendant Matthew Mahon accountable for his son's theft. We agree that the evidence is inadequate.

"The mere existence of the relationship of parent and child does not render a parent liable for his child's torts." Absent statutory authority, agency, direction, consent or approval, parents are generally not liable for the intentional torts of their child. Our courts have recognized an exception based on a parent's duty to exercise reasonable care to control their children so as to avoid their intentionally harming others. That exception, however, is limited and applies only if the parent "has the ability to control [the] child" at the relevant time and "knows or should know of the necessity and opportunity for exercising such control."

While there was evidence that defendants had joint custody of the child, there was no evidence from which the court could have found that defendant Matthew Mahon knew or should have known about the quarters or his son's intention to acquire them. Nor was there evidence that would support a finding that the father had the ability to control the child while he was in plaintiff's home. Accordingly, there were no facts that would warrant a finding of liability on defendant Matthew Mahon's part based on his failure to provide supervision or "control in connection with the incident in question."

Affirmed.

CASE QUESTIONS

1. Do you agree with the court's decision? Explain.
2. Who was most likely in the best position to repay the grandfather?

Conversion as a Crime

Many state statutes define conversion as a criminal offense. Some statutes use the term *theft* instead of *conversion*. Simultaneously, conversion is considered an intentional tort under the common law. This means that the chattel owner may sue in a civil action under the tort theory of conversion and may also contact the county prosecutor (or other local law enforcement authority) to file a criminal complaint for conversion. These separate legal actions are commonly pursued simultaneously in most jurisdictions.

Conversion, like trespass to chattel, is a mobile tort, as it is easy in most instances to grab and carry away someone else's personal property. If the personal property can be carried away, it may be converted. Hence, there are an infinite variety of fact situations involving conversion. Both torts fire the victim's blood. While reading the following examples, imagine that your own chattels have been converted; your emotional response may make clear why so many such cases are brought.

Table 7-2 outlines the elements of conversion.

TABLE 7-2
Elements of conversion

Depriving owner of possession of his or her personal property (dispossession)

Intent to dispossess and convert chattel to tortfeasor's own use

Chattel owner did not consent to tortfeasor's possession and use of personal property

hypotheticals

Nichole is painting her wooden fence in her backyard. Her neighbor, Jason, needs some paint for his garage door. He notices that Nichole has more than enough paint to finish the fence, and so Jason "borrows" two gallons to paint his door. Has Jason converted Nichole's paint?

Jason deprived Nichole of possession of the paint. Jason clearly intended to deprive her of possession and convert the paint to his own use, as he applied the paint to his garage door. Nichole did not consent to Jason's use of the paint. Jason has committed conversion.

* * *

Consider Sherry, who works at an advertising agency. One of her duties is to telephone clients to discuss accounts. Frequently, however, Sherry telephones long-distance to relatives to discuss family matters. The company has strict regulations prohibiting use of company phones for personal calls. Has Sherry engaged in conversion?

Deprivation of possession becomes a perplexing query in this hypothetical. Did Sherry deprive her employer of possession of the telephone? The actual property right being taken here is the use (and cost) of the telephone for placing long-distance calls. Most courts would agree that this satisfies the deprivation requirement. Sherry intended to use the company's phones for personal use. The company expressly forbade such activities, and so consent was lacking. Accordingly, Sherry has converted her employer's rights in the telephone system.

SLANDER OF TITLE, COMMERCIAL DISPARAGEMENT, AND DEFAMATION BY COMPUTER

The intentional torts of slander of title, commercial disparagement, and defamation by computer involve defamed property interests. The trio has a common ancestry. All arose from the intentional tort of defamation, which concerns personal challenges as to the truth of statements.

Slander of Title

Slander of title results when a tortfeasor makes false statements about an individual's ownership of property. The false statements are not designed to defame

slander of title | Occurs when a tortfeasor makes false statements about an individual's ownership of property.

the owner personally; rather, the purpose of the negative criticism is to injure the owner's ability to use the property. Slander of title contains three basic elements:

1. False statements regarding a person's ownership of property
2. Intent to hinder or damage the owner's use of the property
3. Communication (publication) of the falsehoods to third parties.

False Statements Regarding Ownership. A tortfeasor commits slander of title by making false statements about a person's ownership of property. This usually occurs when the tortfeasor falsely impugns the title to another's property. Normally, cases involving this tort include real estate and the filing of spurious liens. Often, businesses that provide services to customers who do not pay will file liens against the customers' real estate. The lien attaches to the title of the land so that the property cannot be leased or sold without the lien. Suppose a business threatens to file a lien against a customer who does not owe the business any money. If the lienholder wrongfully files a lien, then the lien has defamed the integrity of the land owner's title. The improper lien falsely suggests to the world that the land owner has not properly paid his or her debts to the lienholder. Anyone thinking of buying or leasing the property will think twice, because lien property may be sold under certain circumstances to satisfy the debt. Few buyers or tenants would want to become entangled with property that is encumbered by a lien. Thus, a spurious lien could injure the land owner's ability to use the property, even though in actuality the lienholder has no legal right to file the lien against the land owner. This improper lien filing constitutes making false statements about someone's ownership of property.

Intent to Hinder or Damage Owner's Use of Property. By making the false statements about ownership, the tortfeasor must intend to hamper or injure the owner's use of his or her property. This is visibly demonstrated in the preceding lien example. The lienholder filed the lien to prevent the land owner from selling or using his or her realty without first paying the debt supposedly owed to the lienholder. But, in fact, no money was due, so the lien was falsely filed.

Communication (Publication) to Third Parties. The false statements about another's property ownership must be transmitted to third parties in slander of title actions. The slander in the preceding lien example is communicated to the public when the lien is recorded at the county recorder's office. It then becomes a matter of public record for the world to take notice.

Commercial Disparagement

Another type of slander focuses directly upon the chattel itself: commercial disparagement. **Commercial disparagement** may be defined as false statements

commercial disparagement | An intentional tort that occurs when a tortfeasor communicates false statements to third parties about a person's goods, services, or business enterprise. The tortfeasor must intend to harm the victim's ability to use goods, furnish services, or conduct business.

communicated (published) to third parties about a person's goods, services, or business enterprise. The intentional tort of commercial disparagement includes three varieties: disparagement of goods, disparagement of services, and disparagement of business. Like slander of title, *disparagement of goods* impedes the chattel owner's ability to use his or her personal property. *Disparagement of services* interferes with a service provider's ability to engage in provision of services. *Disparagement of business* occurs when the tortfeasor impugns the integrity of another's business venture. Commercial disparagement can be divided into three elements:

1. False statements about an individual's goods, services, or business
2. Intent to injure the victim's ability to use goods, furnish services, or conduct business
3. Communication (publication) to third parties.

False Statements about Goods, Services, or Business. The tortfeasor must express false statements about another's personal property, services, or business reputation (sometimes called *goodwill*). For example, if someone carries a sign in front of a grocery store declaring, "This store sells spoiled fruit!," when in fact the store carries fresh and wholesome fruit, then the sign carrier has made disparaging remarks about the quality of the grocery's foodstuffs. This impugns the integrity of both the goods themselves and the store's reputation. Similarly, if someone tells his or her friends that a particular dentist uses inferior materials to fill cavities when, in reality, the dentist uses professionally acceptable materials, then the dentist's services and reputation have been wrongfully impaired.

THE CASE OF THE ERRANT LOT LINE

Slander of title is usually limited to cases involving improperly filed liens. However, the intentional tort surfaces in other lawsuits, such as the one excerpted here. In *Hossler* the dispute involved an uncertain property line. In addition to slander of title, the case demonstrates why it is vital to obtain correct surveys before purchasing or selling real estate.

HOSSLER
v.
HAMMEL
Court of Appeals of Indiana
587 N.E.2d 133 (Ind. Ct. App. 1992)
February 24, 1992
Hoffman, Judge

This appeal arises from a property dispute between Roger and Sandra Hossler (plaintiffs) and Michael Hammel (defendant), owners of adjoining lots in Austin's Addition to the original plat of the town of Etna, Indiana.

The facts relevant to the appeal disclose that the Kecks and the Wheelers, the original owners of the

(continues)

lots, had surveys made in 1953, after which they agreed upon a common boundary line. When plaintiffs purchased their lot in 1970, they agreed to the established boundary line without a survey, and when defendant purchased his lot in 1977, he, too, agreed to the established boundary line without a survey. Plaintiffs rented their lot for several years and had a survey made in 1988 in order to sell the lot. The survey indicated the Addition was 9 feet longer east to west than shown in the original plat, and the surveyor allocated the extra footage equally among 6 lots. When defendant became aware of the survey, he insisted that the entire 9 feet be allocated to his lot due to his previous purchase of property in the original plat. After numerous threats from defendant to demolish 8 feet of their garage, plaintiffs filed an action to quiet title in the disputed strip of land. Following a bench trial, the court entered findings of fact and conclusions of law establishing the property line as that which the parties had originally agreed upon but denying damages to plaintiffs for slander of title.

The sole issue for our review is whether plaintiffs failed to meet their burden of proving the elements necessary to prevail on their slander of title claim.

To prevail in a slander of title action, the plaintiff must prove that the defendant made false statements regarding the plaintiff's ownership of the land in question, that the defendant made the statements with malice, and that the statements caused the plaintiff pecuniary loss. As plaintiffs note [in] their brief, "[t]he bone of contention in this case is whether the Defendant uttered statements with malice." Malicious statements are those made with knowledge of their falsity or with reckless disregard for whether or not they were false.

In *Freiburger v. Fry*, this Court found malice where, despite the description in his deed, the Defendant had actual knowledge of an existing fence separating the property and that the owner of the other side refused to move it. The instant case is similar to *Freiburger* in that, while defendant may have been relying on the results of plaintiffs' survey in making his statements, he had actual knowledge of the boundary line from the realtor who sold him the lot as well as from the survey. Moreover, the evidence was undisputed that the boundary line had been agreed upon for over 30 years, and once a person possesses property for 10 years in a continuous, adverse, notorious and exclusive manner, title vests in that person by operation of law.

As the party with the burden of proof on the slander of title issue, plaintiffs are appealing from a negative judgment. Therefore, to be successful they must establish that the judgment is contrary to law. As both parties note, defendant did not testify at trial, and neither of his two witnesses testified as to any statements he made regarding the boundary line. Plaintiffs, on the other hand, presented evidence that defendant threatened to bulldoze their garage, cut holes in their garage with a chainsaw, and keep livestock in their garage. Because this evidence and the evidence of defendant's actual knowledge of the agreed-upon boundary line was without conflict and led to a conclusion opposite that reached by the trial court, the judgment of the trial court is contrary to law and reversed.

Reversed and remanded for determination of damages.

CASE QUESTIONS

1. Would the defendant's actions, rather than statements, have been sufficient to constitute slander of title? Assume that the defendant did not communicate with the plaintiffs. What if the defendant had parked a bulldozer next to the plaintiffs' garage? What if the defendant had placed livestock on his property adjoining the plaintiffs'? Would these actions satisfy the Indiana common-law elements? Would they satisfy the elements discussed in this chapter?
2. Assuming the hypothetical facts from question one, what additional tort(s) would the defendant have committed through his actions?

Intent to Harm Victim's Ability to Use Goods, Supply Services, or Conduct Business. Disparagement of goods requires that the tortfeasor intend to injure the victim's capability to use chattels, provide services, or engage in business. Normally, cases involving goods relate to sales. In the preceding illustrations, the sign carrier obviously desired to discourage other shoppers from buying fruit at that particular grocery. The person criticizing the dentist wished to dissuade friends from seeking the dentist's services. The clear underlying objective in both examples is to hamper the ability of these enterprises to conduct business.

Communication (Publication) to Third Parties. Like slander of title, commercial disparagement requires that the false statements be communicated to third parties. In the examples, the sign carrier transmitted the false complaints to anyone reading the sign. The friends of the disgruntled patient heard the falsehoods about the dentist. Like the intentional torts of slander and libel (defamation) discussed in Chapter 6, publication may occur through oral or written means. The preceding examples illustrate both media.

Defamation by Computer

Defamation by computer is a relatively recent intentional tort. Because of the proliferation of computerized databases that can store virtually any information about anyone, the likelihood of mistakes has increased. Further, as access to computerized material expands, the dissemination of inaccurate information can become enormously damaging to the victim.

Computerized Credit Reporting. Customers who are the subjects of credit reports are protected by the stringent guidelines of the Fair Credit Reporting Act (FCRA), 15 U.S.C. § 1681 *et seq.* Defamation by computer most frequently involves cases concerning erroneous credit information entered into a readily accessible computer database. A credit company reports to a national credit reporting agency that a particular individual has become delinquent in account payments. This bad credit rating can have alarmingly negative effects upon the person being reported. If the information reported is false, the injury is especially annoying, as future credit may hang in the balance of good credit reports.

Defamation by computer can be defined as the inclusion of false information about a consumer's credit rating in a computer recordkeeping system that harms the consumer's ability to secure credit. The tort includes four elements:

1. False information about a person's credit rating
2. Entering such erroneous data into a computerized recordkeeping system

defamation by computer | An intentional tort that occurs when the tortfeasor includes false information about a person's credit or credit rating in a computer database. This false information must be communicated to third parties, and must injure the victim's ability to obtain credit.

3. Communication (publication) of the incorrect information to third parties
4. Injuring the victim's ability to obtain credit as a result of the false computerized data.

THE CASE OF THE REJECTED CHECK

Imagine your frustration if, when shopping, you got all the way up to the cashier and realized you had forgotten to bring your checkbook. In this case, a man was shopping with his secretary. Upon discovering that he did not have his checkbook, the man returned to his office with his secretary and then sent the secretary back with a check to pay for the merchandise. Can the store request a consumer report before accepting a check for a transaction, or is this an invasion of privacy?

ESTIVERNE
v.
SAK'S FIFTH AVENUE

9 F.3d 1171 (5th Cir. 1993)
United States Court of Appeals Fifth Circuit
December 28, 1993
Davis, Jones, and Duhé, Circuit Judges

Appellant, Nicolas Estiverne, appeals from the district court's grant of summary judgment for the Defendants, Sak's Fifth Avenue and JBS, Inc., and the imposition of Rule 11 sanctions. Estiverne sued Defendants for discrimination under 42 U.S.C. § 2000a and invasion of privacy when Sak's declined to honor a check written by Estiverne. . . .

On November 26, 1991, Nicolas Estiverne and his secretary went to Sak's Fifth Avenue in New Orleans to purchase a watch. After selecting a watch, Estiverne realized that he had left his checkbook at his office. After returning to his office, Estiverne gave his secretary a signed check, together with a credit card and his driver's license, to return to the store to pay for the watch. After receiving the check, the Sak's salesclerk, in accordance with standard policy, submitted it to JBS for approval. Sak's declined to honor the check after JBS refused to approve it. Estiverne sued both JBS and Sak's alleging that his check was not accepted because he is black. He also alleged that Sak's and JBS's inquiry into his credit information was an invasion of privacy.

The district court granted summary judgment for Defendants and imposed Rule 11 sanctions against Estiverne totaling more than $15,000. Estiverne appeals. . . .

There is no genuine issue of material fact in dispute in this case. The only issue as to summary judgment Estiverne raises on appeal is whether the district court correctly applied the Fair Credit Reporting Act ("FCRA"), 15 U.S.C. §§ 1681 1681t, specifically §§ 1681a(d) and 1681b(3)(E). The district court held that JBS's reports were consumer reports under § 1681a(d) and that Sak's had a "legitimate business need" under 15 U.S.C. § 1681b(3)(E) for the reports for the purpose of deciding whether to accept or reject Estiverne's check. Estiverne argues that paying by check is not a business transaction that authorizes Sak's to obtain a credit history report under the FCRA because he made no application for credit.

This is an issue of first impression for this Court. Section 161a(d) provides that a consumer report is:

any written, oral, or other communication of any information by a consumer reporting agency bearing on a consumer's credit worthiness, credit standing, credit capacity, character, general reputation, personal characteristics, or mode of living which is used or expected to be used or collected in whole or in part for the purpose of serving as a factor in establishing the consumer's eligibility for . . . (3) other purposes authorized under § 1681b of this title.

Section 1681b(3)(E) states that one of the authorized purposes for disclosure of consumer information is "a legitimate business need for the information in connection with a business transaction involving the consumer."

* * *

The FTC has interpreted the definition of consumer report to include lists devised to inform merchants about consumers who have had checks previously dishonored. The FTC stated in its commentary:

> *Bad check lists.* A report indicating that an individual has issued bad checks, provided by printed list or otherwise, to a business for use in determining whether to accept consumers' checks tendered in transactions primarily for personal, family or household purposes, is a consumer report. The information furnished bears on consumers' character, general reputation and personal characteristics, and it is used or expected to be used in connection with business transactions involving consumers. . . .

We defer to the FTC's interpretation of the statute and hold that JBS's reports fall squarely within the definition of a consumer report and that Sak's obtaining of this report for the purpose of deciding whether to accept or reject a check in payment is a "legitimate business need." This holding is also in accord with results reached by other courts that have addressed this issue. Accordingly, the district court did not err in granting summary judgment for JBS and Sak's.

Estiverne does not contest the imposition of Rule 11 sanctions; rather, he contends that sanctions totaling more than $15,000 are unreasonable. We review a district court's calculation of sanctions for an abuse of discretion.

The district court has broad discretion in imposing sanctions reasonably tailored to further the objectives of Rule 11. . . .

The district court adopted the amounts found by the magistrate judge as the proper sanctions in line with the objectives of Rule 11. It represented less than the attorneys fees and expenses incurred by Defendants. Estiverne failed to produce any evidence to support his allegations that his check was refused because of his race. The facts alleged in his complaint were misleading and factually incorrect. . . . [W]e find no abuse of discretion in the amount of sanctions imposed against Estiverne.

Invoking Federal Rule of Appellate Procedure 38, Sak's seeks sanctions against Estiverne for filing a frivolous appeal. . . . Because the issue regarding the FCRA was novel to this Court, we decline to impose sanctions on appeal.

For the foregoing reasons, the district court's grant of summary judgment for Defendants and imposition of Rule 11 sanctions against Estiverne is AFFIRMED.

CASE QUESTIONS

1. Why do you think Sak's Fifth Avenue's employee requested a consumer report before accepting Mr. Estiverne's check?
2. Is it an invasion of privacy for a store to request a consumer credit report before deciding whether to accept a customer's check?
3. What kind of facts would Mr. Estiverne have needed to include in his complaint for the court to have considered his claims of racial discrimination?

Creation of a New Tort. Legal commentators occasionally spur the development of tort law through their law review articles and treatises. Perhaps the best example is law professor William L. Prosser's writings, which have had significant and immeasurable influence over courts for decades. Prosser's tort handbook is the bible for legal students and remains the best available dissertation on the subject.

Other commentators have entered onto the tort scene with exciting new ideas that spurred courts and legislatures to change the course of the law. The article excerpted here, first published in 1977, blazed the trail for establishment of the intentional tort of defamation by computer. From G. Stevens & H. Hoffman, "Tort Liability for Defamation by Computer," 6 *Rutgers Journal of Computers & the Law* 91 (1977) (footnotes omitted):

> Protection of the individual from the misuse of computerized personal information has received considerable scholarly attention, but little has been written on the tort liability of the information processor. Eventually, courts will be faced with questions concerning the processor's legal responsibilities for defamation and invasion of privacy. Actions to recover damages for such injuries are possible not only against recipients of computerized reports who make the information public, but also against information processors and suppliers. . . .

Defamation

> Under common law, a prima facie case for defamation is established if the plaintiff successfully pleads that he was identified in a defamatory matter through a "publication" of the charge by the defendant. The message need only be communicated to one person other than the defamed to be actionable, and any means through which a third party receives it can be considered a publication. While an oral statement may be classified as slander and a written statement as libel, a defamatory message designed for visual perception will be considered libelous. . . . Liability could be extended to a key punch operator or a programmer under the theory that without their neglect of duty a defamatory statement might not have appeared.
>
> * * *
>
> The States should enact uniform guidelines for those in the computer information processing chain. . . .

hypotheticals

Heather moved from her apartment in the city of Shelbydale to a house in the town of Wellington. Heather had a charge account with The Prime Account, a national credit card company. Heather wrote all of her credit card companies to report her address change. The Prime Account failed to change Heather's address in its computer billing system and continued to send its monthly invoices to Heather's Shelbydale address. After 90 days, The Prime Account reported Heather's account as delinquent to a national credit rating service. The service indicated Heather's delinquency in its computerized records, which were included in various credit reports to banks. When Heather applied at the Wellington State Bank for a mortgage loan, the bank refused her request, based upon the bad credit information. Is The Prime Account liable to Heather for defamation by computer?

The Prime Account reported that Heather's account was delinquent, and this was accurate. However, the delinquency was due to Heather's failure to receive her monthly statements. The mailing mistake was The Prime Account's fault. However, this error does not negate the truth of Heather's delinquency. The information reported in the computerized credit systems was correct, and thus defamation by computer has not occurred.

* * *

Sylvia owns a bowling alley. Zach is a professional bowler who frequents one of Sylvia's competitors but occasionally bowls at Sylvia's establishment. Zach's scores were repeatedly lower at Sylvia's than at any other bowling alley in town. One day, after a particularly frustrating series, Zach lay down to "sight" the levelness of the alleys. To his eyes, the lanes looked uneven. Zach telephoned the American Bowling Federation (ABF) to report that Sylvia's alleys did not comply with their standards. If such a criticism were true, the ABF could revoke its certification of Sylvia's facility. This could result in lost business if bowling leagues relocated to other alleys. In fact, the alleys complied with ABF standards. Has Zach disparaged Sylvia's business enterprise?

Zach's comments about Sylvia's alleys were false. The defamed article was the quality of Sylvia's bowling alleys, which would include the integrity of the business itself. Zach communicated these falsehoods to a third party by telephoning the ABF. Zach's intent may be implied by his conduct. What purpose could he have furthered by telephoning the ABF? The reasonable response would be that he hoped that the ABF would remove its certification from Sylvia's and thus discourage patronage. This translates as intent to injure another's ability to conduct business. The damage to Sylvia's goodwill would be substantial if the ABF revoked its certification. Therefore, Zach has committed commercial disparagement.

Table 7-3 illustrates the requirements for slander of title, commercial disparagement, and defamation by computer.

SLANDER OF TITLE	COMMERCIAL DISPARAGEMENT	DEFAMATION BY COMPUTER
False statements regarding person's property ownership	False statements about person's goods, services, or business	False information about a person's credit rating
Intent to impede or injure owner's use of property	Intent to harm victim's ability to use goods, furnish services, or conduct business	Inputting false information into computerized database

TABLE 7-3
Elements of slander of title, commercial disparagement, and defamation by computer

(continues)

TABLE 7-3 *(continued)*

SLANDER OF TITLE	COMMERCIAL DISPARAGEMENT	DEFAMATION BY COMPUTER
Communication (publication) of falsehoods to third parties	Communication (publication) of falsehoods to third parties	Communication (publication) of falsehoods to third parties
Usually involves filing of spurious liens against real estate	Includes disparagement of goods, disparagement of services, and disparagement of business	Injury to victim's ability to secure credit, as a result of erroneous credit data

THE CASE OF THE INTENTIONAL CYBER SQUATTER

In the ever-expanding law of computer torts, this court explores the rights associated with the owner of a domain name. A cyber squatter with a confusingly similar domain name intends to profit from the goodwill associated with the owner of the domain name joecartoon.com.

SHIELDS

v.

ZUCCARINI

2001 WL 671607 (3d Cir. (Pa.))
United States Court of Appeals, Third Circuit
June 15, 2001

John Zuccarini appeals from the district court's grant of summary judgment and award of statutory damages and attorneys' fees in favor of Joseph Shields under the new Anticybersquatting Consumer Protection Act ("ACPA" or "Act"). In this case of first impression in this court interpreting the ACPA, we must decide whether the district court erred in determining that registering domain names that are intentional misspellings of distinctive or famous names constitutes unlawful conduct under the Act. . . .

Shields, a graphic artist from Alto, Michigan, creates, exhibits and markets cartoons under the names "Joe Cartoon" and "The Joe Cartoon Co." His creations include the popular "Frog Blender," "Micro-Gerbil" and "Live and Let Dive" animations. Shields licenses his cartoons to others for display on T-shirts, coffee mugs and other items, many of which are sold at gift stores across the country. He has marketed his cartoons under the "Joe Cartoon" label for the past fifteen years.

On June 12, 1997, Shields registered the domain name joecartoon.com, and he has operated it as a web site ever since. Visitors to the site can download his animations and purchase Joe Cartoon merchandise. Since April 1998, when it won "shock site of the day" from Macromedia, Joe Cartoon's web traffic has increased exponentially, now averaging over 700,000 visits per month.

In November 1999, Zuccarini, an Andalusia, Pennsylvania "wholesaler" of Internet domain names, registered five world wide web variations on Shields's site: joescartoon.com, joecarton.com, joescartons.com, joescartoons.com and cartoonjoe.com. Zuccarini's sites featured advertisements for other sites and for credit card companies. Visitors were trapped or "mousetrapped" in the sites, which, in the jargon of the computer world, means that they were unable to exit without clicking on a succession of advertisements. . . .

In December 1999, Shields sent "cease and desist" letters to Zuccarini regarding the infringing domain names. Zuccarini did not respond to the letters. Immediately after Shields filed this suit, Zuccarini changed the five sites to "political protest" pages and posted the following message on them:

> This is a page of POLITICAL PROTEST
> —Against the web site joecartoon.com—
> joecartoon.com is a web site that depicts the mutilation and killing of animals in a shockwave based cartoon format—many children are inticed [sic] to the web site, not knowing what is really there and then encouraged to join in the mutilation and killing through the use of the shockwave cartoon presented to them.

* * *

On November 29, 1999, the ACPA became law, making it illegal for a person to register or to use with the "bad faith" intent to profit from an Internet domain name that is "identical or confusingly similar" to the distinctive or famous trademark or Internet domain name of another person or company (see 15 U.S.C. § 1125(d) (Supp. 2000)). The Act was intended to prevent "cybersquatting," an expression that has come to mean the bad faith, abusive registration and use of the distinctive trademarks of others as Internet domain names, with the intent to profit from the goodwill associated with those trademarks.

* * *

To succeed on his ACPA claim, Shields was required to prove that (1) "Joe Cartoon" is a distinctive or famous mark entitled to protection; (2) Zuccarini's domain names are "identical or confusingly similar to" Shields's mark; and (3) Zuccarini registered the domain names with the bad faith intent to profit from them.

Under § 1125(d)(1)(A)(ii)(I) and (II), the district court first had to determine if "Joe Cartoon" is a "distinctive" or "famous" mark and, therefore, is entitled to protection under the Act. . . .

Shields runs the only "Joe Cartoon" operation in the nation and has done so for the past fifteen years. This suggests both the inherent and acquired distinctiveness of the "Joe Cartoon" name. In addition to using the "Joe Cartoon" name for

fifteen years, Shields has used the domain name joecartoon.com as a web site since June 1997 to display his animations and sell products featuring his drawings. . . .

Joe Cartoon T-shirts have been sold across the country since at least the early 1990s, and its products appear on the web site of at least one nationally known retail chain, Spencer Gifts. . . . Shields's cartoons and merchandise are marketed on the Internet, in gift shops and at tourist venues. The Joe Cartoon mark has won a huge following because of the work of Shields. In light of the above, we conclude that "Joe Cartoon" is distinctive, and, with 700,000 hits a month, the web site "joecartoon.com" qualifies as being famous. Therefore, the trademark and domain name are protected under the ACPA.

Under the Act, the next inquiry is whether Zuccarini's domain names are "identical or confusingly similar" to Shields's mark. The domain names—joescartoon.com, joecarton.com, joescartons.com, joescartoons.com and cartoonjoe.com—closely resemble "joecartoon.com," with a few additional or deleted letters, or, in the last domain name, by rearranging the order of the words. To divert Internet traffic to his sites, Zuccarini admits that he registers domain names, including the five at issue here, because they are likely misspellings of famous marks or personal names. The strong similarity between these domain names and joecartoon.com persuades us that they are "confusingly similar." . . .

The statute covers the registration of domain names that are "identical" to distinctive or famous marks, but it also covers domain names that are "confusingly similar" to distinctive or famous marks. . . .

> [C]ybersquatters often register well-known marks to prey on consumer confusion by misusing the domain name to divert customers from the mark owner's site to the cybersquatter's own site, many of which are pornography sites that derive advertising revenue based on the number of visits, or "hits," the site receives. . . .

(continues)

We conclude that Zuccarini's conduct here is a classic example of a specific practice the ACPA was designed to prohibit. The district court properly found that the domain names he registered were "confusingly similar."

* * *

CASE QUESTIONS
1. What is the definition of cybersquatting?
2. For what purpose did Zuccarini deliberately use a confusingly similar domain name to "joecartoon.com"?

▌SUMMARY

Trespass to land occurs when a tortfeasor enters upon another's real estate without permission. The tortfeasor must intend to invade the premises without consent. Also, the tortfeasor's entry must interfere with the land owner's exclusive right to use the land, which is called possession.

Toxic tort actions involve toxic chemicals, pollution, hazardous waste disposal and transportation, and other environmentally sensitive issues. This litigation applies many tort theories, including trespass to land, negligence, absolute liability for ultrahazardous substances, products liability, and nuisance. The same formula for trespass to land applies in cases involving toxic substances that invade an innocent land owner's property through underwater seepage or surface or air contamination.

Trespass to chattel occurs when the tortfeasor possesses or interferes with the use of another's personal property without permission. The tortfeasor must intend to dispossess the owner of his or her chattel, or to interfere with the owner's exclusive use of the chattel.

Conversion deprives a chattel owner of possession of personal property, which the tortfeasor converts to his or her own use. The tortfeasor must intend to dispossess the owner of the chattel and then use it without consent. Conversion occurs whenever the tortfeasor deprives the owner of dominion and control over the personal property. In many jurisdictions, statutes define conversion as a crime, in addition to the common-law intentional tort.

Slander of title occurs when false statements are made about an individual's ownership of property. The tortfeasor's intentions are to handicap or harm the owner's use of the property. Commercial disparagement includes disparagement of goods, of services, and of business. Commercial disparagement involves false statements about a person's goods, services, or business intended to injure the victim's ability to use the property, supply the services, or conduct business. Defamation by computer concerns false information about a person's credit rating that is entered into a computer database. Communication, or publication, of the false information to third parties is required of all three of these intentional torts.

▌KEY TERMS

chattel	dispossession	slander of title
commercial disparagement	entry	toxic tort actions
conversion	exclusive right	trespass
defamation by computer	exclusive right of possession	trespass to chattel

▌ PROBLEMS

In the following hypotheticals, identify the intentional tort(s) committed, if any, and support your answers.

1. Pestro Chemical Corporation manufactures *Dredroxiphine,* a poison used in insect sprays. A railway line delivers tanker cars full of the chemical to be unloaded into the plant. On breezy days, the fumes from the unloading stations drift across the highway onto Elmer Parsley's farm. The odors are pungent and are especially irritating to the sinuses. When Elmer and his family work outside on windy days, they are constantly besieged by the poison's smells. Their eyes water excessively, their noses run, and they are gripped by sneezing fits. Other farmers in the area have complained of similar symptoms. Visits to the family physician have revealed that Elmer has absorbed minute amounts of the chemical in his lungs and through his skin. Medical studies link exposure to the chemical with several forms of cancer. Elmer has farmed on his property since 1999. Pestro constructed its plant in 2001.

2. Ben left the Pick-Em-Up saloon after an evening of heavy drinking. Intoxicated, he stumbled across the street to the Tao, an oriental restaurant, and ordered a hamburger. The waitress, an exchange student at the local high school, did not understand English well, and because Ben's speech was slurred, she misunderstood him. When she returned with an oriental dish, Ben jumped from his chair and shouted loudly, "I didn't order this stinking slop! Get it outta my face!" Several customers stared at Ben as he yelled at the waitress, "I'll get the health department to shut this dump down, before somebody else gets poisoned!" The manager ran out from the kitchen and demanded that Ben leave the premises immediately. Ben refused to leave.

3. Alexa operates a day-care center for children. Jay, a nine-year-old, attended the center after school while his parents worked. Alexa discovered Jay's parents were delinquent in paying their fees by three months. One day Jay brought in his father's portable computer for show-and-tell. Alexa asked Jay if he would like her to keep the computer locked up for safekeeping. Jay agreed. At the end of the day, Jay asked Alexa to return the computer, but she refused, stating that she would keep the computer until Jay's parents paid their bill.

4. Theresa rented an apartment from Whisperwood Apartments. Under the lease, she was responsible for paying for electricity and gas heat. When she moved into the apartment, she noticed that the electricity and gas were already on; the apartment owners paid for the utilities while apartments were vacant. She did not contact the utility companies to have the accounts transferred into her name, and she did not notify the apartment manager about the situation. Theresa lived in the apartment for three months before the error was discovered. She never paid any money for utilities, although utility bills for the apartment totaled $250 for this time period.

5. Steve is a mason. He installed a concrete patio at the home of Jose and Elena Garcia. Elena stopped by Steve's house one day and paid his wife (in cash) for the work. Elena did not get a receipt. Steve's wife, however, never told Steve about the money. Steve sent several invoices to the Garcias', but they ignored them. Thinking the bill remained unpaid, Steve filed a mechanic's lien against the Garcias' real estate. Once the Garcias discovered the lien, they angrily telephoned Steve and explained about the cash payment. Steve's wife admitted to receiving the money, so Steve considered the matter settled. However, Steve did not release the lien at the county recorder's office.

6. Ryan owed his dentist for oral surgery. Ryan faithfully made monthly payments to the dentist. The dentist's accountant reported to a local credit rating service that Ryan had defaulted on the bill. The service included this information in its computerized credit files. Ryan applied for a credit card at a local department store, but was denied as a result of the bad credit rating. The department store was a client of the credit-rating service and received monthly credit-rating summaries.

▌ REVIEW QUESTIONS

1. What are the intentional torts that involve injuries to property rights? How are these distinguishable from intentional torts in which the harm is focused on persons?

2. Define *trespass to land* and *trespass to chattel.* How do the two intentional torts differ? How are they similar? What is entry? What is exclusive use? What is possession? Can trespass occur above or below land? What role does consent play in trespass? Is harm to the property required? Must the trespass be intentional? Why or why not? Must trespass to chattel involve dispossession?

3. What are toxic torts? What causes of action are available for injured persons? What federal statutes exist to regulate hazardous or toxic substances? What are the provisions of these statutes?

4. What is conversion? How is it different from trespass to chattel? How is it similar? To what extent must the chattel owner be deprived of possession? How might such deprivation occur? Must the tortfeasor do more than simply dispossess the chattel owner? What are dominion and control, and why are they important? What are the roles of intent and consent in conversion? Can conversion also be a crime? Why?

5. Explain slander of title. How might false statements be made about one's ownership of property? Provide an example of this intentional tort. What intent is involved? What is publication and why is it necessary?

6. List the different types of commercial disparagement. What are the elements of this category of intentional tort? What intent is involved? Why is communication important?

7. What is defamation by computer? Under what circumstances is this intentional tort most likely to arise? Why is communication significant?

▌ HELPFUL WEBSITES

This chapter deals with intentional torts to property. To learn more about intentional torts to property, the following sites can be accessed:

Governmental Agencies

http://www.statelocal.gov
http://www.findlaw.com

Legal Discussion Groups

http://www.lib.uchicago.edu
http://www.paralegalgateway.com

Attorneys

http://www.martindale.com
http://www.lawoffice.com

State Law and Codes

http://www.washlaw.edu
http://www.law.cornell.edu

STUDENT CD-ROM™

For additional materials, please go to the CD in this book.

ONLINE COMPANION™

For additional resources, please go to
http://www.paralegal.delmar.cengage.com

chapter 8

Defenses to Intentional Torts

THE BIGGEST MISTAKES PARALEGALS MAKE & HOW TO AVOID THEM

What Happens When You Assume Something?

Our client slipped and fell outside her favorite nail salon. During the intake interview, the client said she fell at Hanoi Nails. Actually she was unaware that the salon had been sold to new owners and they had yet to change the sign to the new name, Miss Saigon. Additionally, the sidewalk in front of the salon was city property. Also, unbeknownst to her, a contractor working at a shop next door spilled oil on his way to the truck parked in front of the salon. While I proceeded to work on a suit against Hanoi Nails, my firm should have named Miss Saigon instead with two other defendants: the city and the contractor.

(continues)

LESSON LEARNED: A proper initial investigation by me would have revealed all these facts. Fortunately, my state allows attorneys to freely amend pleadings and we were able to correct the defects, but some jurisdictions are not so forgiving. Assume nothing!

INTRODUCTION

Sometimes intentional torts are legally justified; thus, the person engaging in the intentional tort is not liable to the victim. These are collectively called **defenses** to intentional torts. For instance, conduct that normally would constitute an intentional tort, such as battery, could be excused under the theory of self-defense. Defenses are commonly used by the defendant in a civil lawsuit to exonerate the defendant from liability to the plaintiff.

A legal defense arises only when one party responds to another party's allegations in a lawsuit. Usually, the defendant answers the plaintiff's complaint with defenses. However, if the defendant counter-claimed against the plaintiff, it would be the plaintiff who replied with defenses. If third parties were involved in the litigation through cross-complaints, these third parties would answer with defenses. This presumes, of course, that defenses are available with which to respond.

This chapter focuses on *justification of intentional tortious conduct through defenses.* The following questions may be helpful:

1. May the tortfeasor use a defense to excuse his or her misconduct?

2. Which defenses apply to which intentional torts?

Intentional torts involve intentional acts. Thus, they carry a high degree of risk of injury to others, and usually there is a low degree of social benefit from the act involved. The risk of injury outweighs the benefits received from the act. Therefore, the duty not to intentionally injure someone or something is great.

There are several types of legal defenses to intentional torts. This chapter describes:

- Consent (defense to all intentional torts)
- Self-defense (defense against assault, battery, or false imprisonment)
- Defense of persons or property (defense against assault, battery, or false imprisonment)
- Rightful repossession (defense against trespass to land, trespass to chattel, conversion, assault, and battery)
- Mistake (defense to most intentional torts)
- Privilege (broad category of defense against intentional torts)

defense | 1. The sum of the facts, law, and arguments presented by the side against whom legal action is brought.
2. Any counter-argument or counter-force. A defense can relieve a defendant of the liability of a tort.

> ▶ Necessity (defense to various intentional torts)
> ▶ Public officer's immunity for legal process enforcement, and law enforcement and private citizen's defense for warrantless arrest
> ▶ Statutes of limitations (defense to all intentional torts)
> ▶ Workers' compensation.

Because intentional torts are rarely covered by insurance, intentional torts and their defenses are far less common in legal practice than negligence actions.

▌ CONSENT

consent | Voluntary and active agreement.

Consent is a broad defense applicable to every intentional tort. **Consent** occurs when the victim of an intentional tort voluntarily agrees to the tortfeasor's actions, provided that the victim understands (or reasonably should understand) the consequences of the tortfeasor's deeds. This knowledge factor is sometimes called **informed consent.**

informed consent | A person's agreement to allow something to happen (such as surgery) that is based on a full disclosure or full knowledge of the facts needed to make the decision intelligently.

The consent defense contains the following elements: (1) Voluntary acceptance of an intentionally tortious act (2) with full knowledge or understanding of the consequences. Actually, consent is not a legal defense at all. As shown in the previous two chapters, it is a deliberately missing element of intentional torts. If consent existed, then the intentional tort could not have occurred. The ancient common law applied the Latin maxim, *volenti non fit injuria,* which translates as, "No wrong may occur to one who is willing." As a practical matter, courts over the centuries have treated consent as a defense to intentional torts.

Informed Consent: Voluntary Acceptance

Consent will be a successful defense to an intentional tort action only if the victim willingly and knowingly agreed to the tortfeasor's conduct. Accordingly, a victim who is coerced into tolerating an intentional tort cannot consent to it, because the victim was compelled to undergo the tort. Further, the victim must comprehend the implications of the tortfeasor's actions to consent to them.

For instance, suppose Randy agrees to wrestle Ralph. Assume that both Randy and Ralph understand the repercussions of wrestling, including possible inadvertent injury. Randy and Ralph will have mutually consented to battery, and so neither could sue the other for this intentional tort if harm did happen.

Part of the voluntary, or *volition*, factor of consent is the victim's mental capacity to agree. Some persons simply lack sufficient mental abilities to understand the consequences of a tortfeasor's actions. Severely retarded or mentally incapacitated individuals, for example, might not grasp the implications of a tortfeasor's misbehavior. Intoxicated individuals may also have insufficient mental faculties to comprehend the results of an intentional tort. Children, particularly when very young, may lack cognitive development adequate to grasp the ramifications of intentional torts. For such persons, consent could become virtually impossible.

Implied Consent

Consent may be expressed, either orally or in writing, or it may be implied by conduct or circumstances. For instance, public officials or famous persons are assumed to consent to adverse publicity merely by placing themselves in the public limelight. Consent to publicity is therefore implied, and public officials or celebrities cannot recover for libel or slander, unless malice is proven.

The most common example of implied consent involves emergency medical treatment. If a patient is unconscious and is taken to a hospital emergency room, the medical personnel may presume that the patient consents to treatment, at least to the extent of the emergency condition. Thus, if someone is found unconscious on the pavement, suffering from gastrointestinal bleeding, and an ambulance takes her to the hospital, the patient is presumed to agree to treatment of the emergency condition, in this case a "G.I. bleed," which is often life-threatening. Later, if the patient regains consciousness and protests against the treatment (perhaps upon religious grounds), the patient cannot sue for battery for the unauthorized emergency care. However, once conscious and clear-minded, the patient could insist that further treatment be forgone. Failure to stop treatment would then constitute battery. Suppose, instead, that the medical personnel treated beyond the emergency condition, such as removing a portion of diseased skin while treating the intestinal bleeding. Implied consent does not apply to nonemergency treatment, and thus battery would have occurred.

Consent is sometimes characterized as the "you asked for it" defense. However, as the following hypothetical demonstrates, there can be doubt as to what the "it" was to which the victim consented.

THE CASE OF THE MORE-THAN-TOUCH FOOTBALL GAME

Almost everyone has played contact games. Children delight in games such as "tag," "keep-away," and "hide-and-seek," which usually involve some physical contact. Older children and adults engage in rougher sports in which implied consent accepts incidental contact. Sometimes, however, a player forgets that there are limits to the reasonable force to which participants consent. In the following case, it becomes clear that the plaintiff felt that the defendant went well beyond these acceptable lines. The California Court of Appeal, however, was unimpressed. Perhaps none of the judges had ever played a rough game of touch football.

(continues)

KNIGHT
v.
JEWETT

232 Cal. App. 3d 1142,
275 Cal. Rptr. 292 (1990)
November 27, 1990
Review granted, 278 Cal. Rptr. 203,
804 P.2d 1300 (Cal. 1991)
Todd, Acting Presiding Justice

Kendra Knight appeals a summary judgment granted in favor of Michael Jewett in her lawsuit against Jewett for negligence and assault and battery stemming from a touch football game in which she was injured. Knight contends . . . it was error to apply the doctrine of assumption of risk to defeat the assault and battery cause of action and . . . there were triable issues of fact that should have precluded the granting of summary judgment.

FACTS

On January 25, 1987, Knight and several other individuals, including Jewett, gathered at the Vista home of Ed McDaniels to observe the Super Bowl football game. Knight and Jewett were among those who decided to play a game of co-ed touch football during half-time using a "pee-wee" football often used by children. Apparently, no explicit rules were written down or discussed before the game, other than the requirement that to stop advancement of the player with the ball it was necessary to touch that player above the waist with two hands. Knight and Jewett were on different teams.

Previously, Knight had played touch football and frequently watched football on television. Knight voluntarily participated in the Super Bowl half-time game. It was her understanding that this game would not involve forceful pushing, hard hitting or hard shoving during the game. She had never observed anyone being injured in a touch football game before this incident.

About five to ten minutes after the game started, Jewett ran into Knight during a play and afterward Knight asked Jewett not to play so rough. Otherwise, she told him, she would stop playing.

On the next play, Knight suffered her injuries, when she was knocked down by Jewett and he stepped on the little finger of her right hand. Kendra had three surgeries on the finger, but they proved unsuccessful. The finger was amputated during a fourth surgery.

According to Jewett, he had jumped up to intercept a pass and as he came down he knocked Knight over. When he landed, he stepped back and onto Knight's hand.

According to Knight's version, her teammate Andrea Starr had caught the ball and was proceeding up the field. Knight was headed in the same direction, when Jewett, in pursuit of Starr, came from behind Knight and knocked her down. Knight put her arms out to break the fall and Jewett ran over her, stepping on her hand. Jewett continued to pursue Starr for another 10 to 15 feet before catching up with her and tagging her. Starr said the tag was rough enough to cause her to lose her balance and fall and twist her ankle.

Jewett did not intend to step on Knight's hand and did not intend to hurt her.

* * *

Knight contends her cause of action for assault and battery is viable and she should be allowed to proceed to trial on it.

. . . Jewett argued it must fail because Knight consented to the physical contact.

Consent is a viable defense to the tort of assault and battery. "A person may, by participating in a game, or by other conduct, consent to an act which might otherwise constitute a battery." Here, however, we need not dwell on whether Jewett can successfully interpose a defense of consent to Knight's assault and battery cause of action.

Inasmuch as this case reaches us on appeal from a summary judgment in favor of Jewett, it is only necessary for us to determine whether there is any possibility Knight may be able to establish her case.

A requisite element of assault and battery is intent. Here, however, there is no evidence that Jewett intended to injure Knight or commit a battery on her. Moreover, the record affirmatively shows Knight does not believe Jewett had the intent to step on her hand or injure her. Without the requisite intent, Knight cannot state a cause of action for assault and battery.

A motion for summary judgment is addressed to the sound discretion of the trial court and, absent a clear showing of abuse, the judgment will not be disturbed on appeal. On this record, we discern no abuse of discretion; the granting of summary judgment was proper. . . . Affirmed.

CASE QUESTIONS

1. *Knight* demonstrates how the defense of consent cannot be reached unless the elements of intentional torts (in this case, assault and battery) are satisfied. Although the evidence suggested that the defendant lacked the necessary intent to cause injury, could you imply such intent from Jewett's rough conduct during the game?
2. Presume that Knight had proven Jewett's intent to harm her, thus making a prima facie case for assault and battery (the other elements being satisfied under the facts of the case as given in the opinion). Would Jewett's consent defense prevail? Did Knight consent to the harsh play that Jewett was engaging in? If so, did Knight withdraw her consent when she told Jewett to stop playing so roughly?
3. Are there any other intentional tort defenses that were not discussed in *Knight* but that would apply? What are they? Why do you think they would succeed or fail?

hypothetical

Colleen attended a company banquet in her honor as "sales director of the year." The dinner was a "roast" at which co-workers made humorous remarks about the guest of honor. Several of these comments were loaded with sarcasm and a few were in questionable taste. However, none of the comments was taken seriously by the audience, which understood that it was all in good fun. Under other circumstances, however, some members of the audience might have been offended. Colleen, however, took offense at the more colorful character references. Could she sue her co-employees for slander?

Colleen voluntarily agreed to attend the banquet with a complete understanding that co-workers would use the forum to tease and joke about her. She should have known that some of her fellow employees would push the limits of propriety with a few harsh remarks. Because the audience was not offended (given the "roast" atmosphere), and because Colleen knowingly accepted the potentially slanderous conduct, consent would be a defense to Colleen's slander claim.

The components of consent are listed in Table 8-1.

Consent is clearly the most pervasive defense to intentional torts.

Voluntary acceptance of an intentionally tortious act
Full knowledge or understanding of the consequences

TABLE 8-1
Elements of consent

SELF-DEFENSE

Of the legal defenses, self-defense is probably the most familiar to the average person. It is most commonly applied to the intentional torts of assault and battery, but it may also be used in cases involving false imprisonment. **Self-defense** is the exercise of reasonable force to repel an attack upon one's person or to avoid confinement. The nature of the action is simple: the victim of an assault or battery may use that degree of force necessary to prevent bodily injury (or offensive contact) from the attacker. Similarly, the victim of false imprisonment may use the force needed to prevent or escape confinement.

self-defense | Physical force used against a person who is threatening physical force or using physical force. This is a right if your own family, property, or body is in danger, but sometimes only if the danger was not provoked. Also, deadly force may (usually) only be used against deadly force.

Consider this likely scenario. Jake is angry at Zach and throws a punch at Zach's face. Zach responds by blocking Jake's fist, grabbing his wrist, and twisting his arm behind his back until he agrees to calm down. This illustrates assault and self-defense: by throwing the punch, Jake placed Zach in reasonable apprehension of an unconsented contact that endangered his physical safety. Under self-defense, Zach was entitled to use whatever force was necessary to repel the attack.

The issue of self-defense would arise only if Jake (as plaintiff) sued Zach (as defendant) for battery. Jake would allege that Zach committed battery by grabbing his wrist and twisting his arm. Zach would reply with the legal defense of self-defense, which justified his actions. Remember that the defendant uses legal defenses to avoid liability to the plaintiff. In our hypothetical, Zach's self-defense argument would defeat Jake's complaint for battery. Bear in mind that Zach would have his own cause of action against Jake for assault, and Jake would not be able to use self-defense as a defense because he initiated the attack upon Zach.

The elements of self-defense are (1) use of reasonable force (2) to counter an attacking or offensive force that is (3) necessary to prevent bodily injury, offensive contact, or confinement.

Reasonable Force

reasonable force | Force that is reasonable, limited to that which is necessary to dispel the attacking force for self-defense.

The neutralizing force a person uses in self-defense is limited. The force cannot be greater than what is reasonably necessary to dispel the attacking force. This is called **reasonable force.** In the preceding example, Zach applied only as much force as needed to prevent Jake from striking Zach. Had Zach broken Jake's arm in retaliation, this would clearly have been excessive force, because breaking Jake's arm was unnecessary to stop the assault. Thus, Zach could not use self-defense as a legal justification. Instead, Zach would have become the aggressor and have engaged in battery against Jake. Common law maintains that the victim of an assault or battery may not turn aggressive once the assailant is incapacitated. Thus, if Jake collapsed after Zach twisted his arm, Zach could not kick Jake into unconsciousness and then claim self-defense.

What constitutes reasonable force varies depending upon the circumstances of each case. If Jake attacked Zach with an axe, then deadly force would be involved. Zach would therefore be warranted in responding with deadly force to repulse the onslaught. If Jake threw rocks at Zach, his force would threaten severe bodily harm. Thus, Zach could react with similarly powerful force, such as knocking Jake down with a pole.

Deadly Self-Defense. The reasonableness issue is difficult to reduce to clearly defined, black-and-white terms. Much depends upon the options available to the victim. Many courts hold that, in the face of deadly force, if a victim might reasonably escape from the attack, then this choice must first be selected before deadly force may be used in self-defense. Several courts apply the same rule to situations involving threats of serious bodily injury. However, the majority of jurisdictions maintain that a person is not required to flee his or her home if threatened by an intruder. This is sometimes called the **castle doctrine,** in which a dweller is considered "king" or "queen" and may use any amount of force, including deadly force, to resist an intruder, such as a burglar. This varies greatly by state law.

castle doctrine | The principle that you can use any force necessary to protect your own home or its inhabitants from attack. Also called *dwelling defense doctrine*.

Countering an Attacking or Offensive Force

The party exercising self-defense must be opposing an attacking or offensive force. Jake's fist is obviously an attacking force. But suppose Jake spit at Zach. This would be an example of an offensive force, as it is contact by which Zach would probably be offended.

Force Necessary to Prevent Injury, Offensive Contact, or Confinement

The force used in self-defense must be necessary to prevent bodily injury or offensive contact, or to avoid confinement. **Necessary force** is that which is reasonably perceived as required to rebuff an attack or confinement. When Zach grabbed Jake's wrist and twisted his arm, Zach felt this action was required to prevent Jake from continuing his assault. The question again becomes one of reasonableness: Did Zach respond with reasonable force necessary to allay Jake's attack? Or was Zach's force unnecessary (and thus excessive) given Jake's actions? Suppose Jake had only tapped Zach on the shoulder with his finger. Zach's wrist-and-arm twist in response would then be considered unreasonable, unneeded, and extreme. Thus, Zach could not avail himself of a self-defense argument against Jake's battery claim.

necessary force | That degree of force reasonably perceived as required to repel an attack or resist confinement. It is an aspect of self-defense.

Say that Jake was attempting to lock Zach in a room against Zach's will. In self-defense, Zach could reply with as much force as required to avoid being confined. This means that Zach could use that degree of force necessary to escape Jake.

Self-defense is perhaps the easiest legal justification to illustrate. Almost any child who has engaged in a playground shoving match can explain the fundamental concept. However, the legal elements require a more discerning eye, as shown in the following example.

hypothetical

Jake Nesmith sat alone at a table in a local tavern. He was waiting to meet a friend from work when two men standing nearby got into a shoving match. One of the men, John, pushed the other man, Bruce, into Jake. Jake shoved Bruce back into John, knocking them both to the floor.

John committed battery against Bruce by pushing him. Under the doctrine of transferred intent, when Bruce bumped into Jake, John transferred his battery onto Jake. By pushing Bruce away, Jake used reasonable force to repel an attacking force to prevent injury to himself. Accordingly, Jake could claim self-defense against John.

There remains a puzzling question, however. Could Jake claim self-defense against Bruce, or did Jake commit battery against Bruce? Bruce was essentially the instrumentality that John put into motion to strike Jake, albeit accidentally. Bruce did not intend to contact Jake. Therefore, Bruce did not commit battery or assault against Jake.

Jake could still claim self-defense against Bruce, however. Jake responded to protect himself against injury from both participants in the shoving match. Thus, self-defense would apply. Further, because Bruce was a voluntary participant in the struggle with John, Bruce consented to physical contact associated with a shoving match. This would include inadvertently bumping into an innocent bystander like Jake. Accordingly, Jake did not commit battery against Bruce, because Bruce impliedly consented to the incidental contact involved, which would include Jake's return shove.

The elements of self-defense are summarized in Table 8-2.

Assault and battery may be justifiable in the defense of others or of property, as discussed in Chapter 5.

TABLE 8-2
Elements of self-defense

Use of reasonable force
Countering an attacking or offensive force
Actions necessary to prevent bodily injury, offensive contact, or confinement

DEFENSE OF PERSONS OR PROPERTY

As a legal justification for assault or battery, defense of other persons or defense of injury to property is similar to self-defense. A person who would otherwise have committed assault or battery may be excused if the action was taken to protect another individual or property from harm. This would include freeing someone subject to false imprisonment.

Defense of Persons: Elements

Defense of persons as a legal justification for assault or battery has the following elements: (1) use of reasonable force (2) to defend or protect a third party from injury (3) when the third party is threatened by an attacking force. For example, if Marie were about to throw a vase at Marjorie, Simon could use reasonable force to subdue Marie before she could complete the throw. Simon would not have committed battery, because he grabbed Marie to prevent her from harming Marjorie. Simon would be entitled to the legal defense of defense of another person to avoid liability for battery.

The same principles used in self-defense to define reasonable force also apply to defense of persons. Thus, Simon could not use excessive force to repel Marie's attack against Marjorie. For instance, if Simon struck Marie sharply in the head with a two-by-four, this would be unnecessarily brutal force to subdue the vase attack.

Also, like self-defense, the repelling force must be used to counter an attacking force. If Marjorie telephoned Simon to complain that Marie had just thrown a vase at her, Simon could not run over and strike Marie and then claim defense of another as an excuse. The defender steps into the shoes of the third person, and only gets the defense if the third person was in the right. Hence, Simon would have the same rights as Marjorie.

Defense of Property: Elements

Conduct that otherwise might be assault or battery may be vindicated if the action is taken to defend property from damage or dispossession. A property owner has the right to possess and safeguard his or her property from others. The elements of **defense of property** are (1) use of reasonable force (2) to protect property from damage or dispossession (3) when another person, the *invader*, attempts to injure or wrongfully take possession of the property.

The reasonable force contemplated here is essentially identical to that discussed in regard to self-defense. Many courts, however, restrict the defensive force to the least amount necessary to protect the property from harm or dispossession. This is a narrower definition of *reasonableness,* suggesting that human well-being is more important than the safety of property. Under this theory,

defense of persons | A defense to the intentional torts of assault, battery, and false imprisonment. Its elements include the use of reasonable force to defend or protect a third party from injury when the third party is threatened by an attacking force.

defense of property | A defense to the intentional torts of assault and battery. Its elements include the use of reasonable force to protect property from damage or dispossession when another person, called the *invader*, attempts to injure or wrongfully take possession of the property.

most courts would not allow deadly force or extreme force likely to cause serious bodily injury to be used to defend property under any circumstances.

The property owner or possessor uses reasonable force to repulse an attacking force that is attempting to harm or possess the property. For example, if Frederick is in the process of committing conversion or trespass to chattel, then Helen, who owns the personal property in danger, may use reasonable force to dispel Frederick's efforts at dispossession.

ejectment | The name for an old type of lawsuit to get back land taken away wrongfully.

The use of reasonable force to expel a trespasser to land is called **ejectment.** Defense of real property cases frequently involve land owners who have placed dangerous traps for trespassers. The trespassers are often seeking to steal personal property and usually violate various criminal statutes involving theft or burglary. Nevertheless, land owners may not set up deadly traps to inflict serious bodily injuries upon such criminals. Spring-loaded guns have been the most common snares litigated. A land owner places a shotgun inside a barn or outbuilding that is triggered by a trip-wire placed across a window or doorway. The thief steps upon the wire while trying to enter and is shot. Courts universally condemn this use of deadly force to defend property.

It should be relatively easy to imagine situations in which reasonable force is used to defend another person from attack. Defense of property, however, may be more difficult to conjure.

THE CASE OF THE DEFIANT TRUCKER

In 1966 the Bobby Fuller Four recorded a popular rock song in which the refrain declared, "I fought the law, and the law won." As this case demonstrates, this is usually the result. However, note the dissent's approach to defense of property against an arguably unlawful seizure by law enforcement officers. Although this case involved criminal law, the court's discussion of defense of property is relevant to tort law.

JURCO
v.
STATE
825 P.2d 909 (Alaska Ct. App. 1992)
Court of Appeals of Alaska
February 14, 1992
Mannheimer, Judge

David Jurco was convicted, following a jury trial in district court, of disorderly conduct and resisting arrest. These offenses resulted from a confrontation between Jurco and members of the State Troopers who had come to Jurco's residence to serve a court order directing them to take possession of Jurco's truck; the Kenai District Court had ordered forfeiture of the vehicle because Jurco had used it in furtherance of a violation of the fish and game laws.

Unbeknown to the troopers, Jurco had recently filed for bankruptcy. The federal bankruptcy court had directed Jurco not to sell or transfer any of his property or allow creditors to take any of his property without court order. Jurco believed that the bankruptcy court's directive obliged him to resist the troopers' attempt to seize his truck. At first, Jurco argued with the troopers. Finding he could not dissuade them, Jurco got into the truck and started it. With Trooper Eugene Kallus trying to hang on to the side of the truck, Jurco drove the truck away to a different location on his property. Jurco then got out of the truck, removed the battery from the vehicle, and began to let the air out of the truck's tires.

At this point, Trooper Kallus informed Jurco that he was placing him under arrest for disorderly conduct....

But even if we assume for purposes of argument that Jurco's interpretation of bankruptcy law is correct, the question remains whether Jurco was entitled to forcibly resist the troopers when they came to execute the Kenai District Court's warrant. We conclude that Jurco was not entitled to forcibly resist the troopers even if he reasonably believed that the seizure of his truck was illegal.

* * *

[At common law] a property owner was entitled to use force to resist an unlawful taking of his property. "One whose lawful possession of property is threatened by the unlawful conduct of another, and who has no time to resort to the law for its protection, may take reasonable steps, including the use of force, to prevent or terminate such interference with the property." This ... common-law rule has also been codified in Alaska; AS [Alaska Statutes] 11.81.350-(a) provides:

> Justification: Use of force in defense of property and premises.
>
> (a) A person may use nondeadly force upon another when and to the extent the person reasonably believes it is necessary to terminate what the person reasonably believes to be the commission or attempted commission by the other of an unlawful taking or damaging of property or services.

For purposes of deciding this appeal, we assume that Jurco reasonably believed that the Kenai District Court's order to seize his truck ran afoul of the federal bankruptcy court's order to keep his property together. [Another Alaska statute, Alaska Stat. § 11.81.420, authorized law enforcement officers to use reasonable force, including deadly force, to enforce a court order to seize property, even if the court decree is later determined to have been unlawful.] In such a situation, the joint operation of Alaska Stat. §§ 11.81.420 and 11.81.350(a) would seemingly allow Jurco to use force against the troopers to resist the taking of his truck while at the same time authorizing the troopers to respond with force of their own against Jurco— creating an escalating confrontation that would end only when the troopers resorted to deadly force against Jurco. . . .

This could not have been the legislature's intention. With emotions running high on both sides, a property owner who sees that non-deadly force is not enough to make law enforcement officials back down might well begin (unlawfully) to use deadly force on the officers. Or, in the heat of the moment, the officers might mistakenly conclude that the property owner has begun to use deadly force upon them and respond in kind. Both possibilities could easily lead to the infliction of serious injury or death.

Thus, the question presented by Jurco's case is: which of these two statutes did the legislature intend to take precedence when law enforcement officers attempt to execute a court order calling for a seizure of property?

We conclude that a person is not entitled to use force to resist the taking of property by law enforcement officers pursuant to a court order.

* * *

It follows that Jurco was not entitled to forcibly resist the State Troopers' efforts to seize his truck under the order issued by the Kenai District Court.

* * *

The judgment of the district court is AFFIRMED.

BRYNER, Chief Judge, dissenting.

(continues)

I disagree with the court's decision.... In my view, Jurco was entitled to [a jury instruction] on his theory of defense ... that he was seeking to protect his property from what he reasonably believed to be an unlawful taking.

* * *

The majority of this court effectively amends the defense of property statute by engrafting to it an exception that the legislature evidently chose not to include. The court does so in reliance on its own notions of desirable social policy.

CASE QUESTIONS

1. Do you agree with the majority that the legislature intended the law officer enforcement-of-court-orders statute to override the defense-of-property statute? Explain.
2. Do you agree with the dissent that the majority rewrites the two statutes to suit its own vision of preferred social policy?

hypothetical

Consider the case of Isaac, who discovered two teenage hoodlums throwing bricks and stones at his house windows. Isaac crept up behind the duo and leapt from behind some bushes. The delinquents were taken by surprise, and Isaac knocked one to the ground and kicked him in the stomach and tackled the other. Although both hoodlums suffered minor abrasions and bruises, neither was injured severely. The two hoodlums claim that Isaac has committed battery against them. Does Isaac have a defense?

Isaac used force against the rowdies to prevent damage to his property. The hoodlums were attempting to injure Isaac's house. The primary question is whether Isaac used reasonable force to prevent the property damage. Because neither of the two teenagers suffered severe harm as a result of Isaac's actions, the force should be deemed reasonable to neutralize the teenagers. Accordingly, Isaac could successfully apply defense of property against the allegation of battery.

The elements of defense of persons or property are listed in Table 8-3.

TABLE 8-3
Elements of defense of persons or property

DEFENSE OF PERSONS	DEFENSE OF PROPERTY
Use of reasonable force	Use of reasonable force
To defend or protect a third party from harm	To protect property from damage or dispossession
Third person is threatened by attacking force	Someone attempts to harm or wrongfully possess property

Defense of property is often used in situations in which sellers repossess property from defaulting buyers.

▌ RIGHTFUL REPOSSESSION

An owner of personal property generally has the right to repossess, by force if necessary, a chattel that has been wrongfully taken or withheld. This is the defense of **rightful repossession.** The defense is generally applied to allegations of trespass to land, assault, battery, and sometimes conversion and trespass to chattel. However, the amount of force that may be used is extremely limited. Generally, the elements of rightful repossession include the following: (1) use of reasonable force (2) in prompt repossession (3) to retake possession of personal property (4) of which the owner has been wrongfully dispossessed (or to which the owner is denied possession). For this defense, reasonable force is defined along the same lines as defense of property.

rightful repossession | A defense to trespass to land, trespass to chattel, conversion, assault, and battery. It includes the use of reasonable force to retake possession of personal property of which the owner has been wrongfully disposed, or denied possession.

Retaking Possession of Personal Property

Reasonable Force. The chattel owner seeks to repossess personal property to which he or she is entitled. This is the crux of the defense. If someone has wrongfully dispossessed an owner of his or her chattel, then the owner is entitled to enter upon the dispossessor's land to recover the chattel. This provides a defense to trespass to land. Reasonable force may be applied to recover possession of the personal property.

To illustrate, suppose Raymond took Carl's motorcycle without asking permission and drove the cycle back to his own garage. Carl would be entitled to enter Raymond's garage to recover the cycle. If Raymond attempted to prevent Carl from entering, Carl could use reasonable force to vanquish Raymond and recover the cycle. Carl would not be liable for either trespass to land or battery, because he would have the defense of rightful repossession.

Prompt Repossession Efforts

Older common law cases held that a chattel owner's efforts to repossess personal property must occur soon after the chattel had been wrongfully taken away. However, just how promptly this had to occur was not clearly defined. Many nineteenth-century opinions ruled that hot pursuit was necessary. Hot pursuit is usually defined for purposes of criminal law, but its meaning is the same for this tort defense. **Hot (fresh) pursuit,** in this context, may be described as a rapid chase as soon as possible after the owner has discovered that his or her chattel is missing. This presumes, of course, that the personal property owner knows who took the chattel.

hot (fresh) pursuit | The right of a person who has had property taken to use reasonable force to get it back after a chase that takes place immediately after it was taken.

Wrongful Denial of Possession

The chattel owner need not be dispossessed of the personal property for this defense to apply. Consider the example of someone who originally took possession of the chattel with the owner's consent, but later wrongfully refuses to return it. If the owner then attempted to retake possession and was accused of trespass to land, assault, or battery, the owner could apply rightful repossession as a defense.

Most cases involving denial of possession deal with bailments, in which the owner has delivered possession of the chattel to someone else for a specific purpose, with the explicit understanding that the chattel is to be returned at a certain time or upon demand. When an automobile is taken to a mechanic for repair, for instance, there is a bailment. The mechanic would have lawful possession of the vehicle, because the owner left it for repairs. Suppose, however, that the mechanic made unauthorized repairs and sought to charge the owner. If the owner demanded return of the car and the mechanic refused, then this refusal would constitute wrongful denial of possession. The owner could use reasonable force to enter the mechanic's premises to retake the chattel. The owner would not be liable to the mechanic for trespass to land because of the rightful repossession defense.

Note that this result would be different if there had been a dispute over authorized repairs. Most state statutes provide mechanics with possessory liens, which empower repair persons to keep possession of vehicles until repair charges have been paid. However, some statutes provide that the amounts due must be undisputed.

Wrongful Dispossession

For the defense of rightful repossession to apply, the owner's chattel must have been unlawfully dispossessed, or its return have been unlawfully denied. This means that the dispossessor or retainer must not have a legal right to possess (or deny return of) the chattel.

In the preceding bailment example, the mechanic did not possess the automobile unlawfully because the owner had left it for repairs. However, when the mechanic performed unauthorized work and sought payment, and the owner demanded the car's return, then the mechanic wrongfully possessed the vehicle—specifically, the repair person committed trespass to chattel and possibly conversion. Thus, the owner would be entitled to repossess with reasonable force and could use that defense against the mechanic's lawsuit for trespass to land, assault, or battery.

Rightful repossession seems a noble defense, albeit more difficult to conceptualize than self-defense or defense of others and property. One might express the emotional essence of the doctrine as, "It's mine and I'm taking it back now!" The defense appeals to a sense of entitlement. As you read the following hypothetical, with whom do your sympathies lie?

THE CASE OF THE FREE-ROAMING FELINE

The following case illustrates an unusual application of rightful repossession. Any pet owner, however, will immediately sympathize with the Blanchards. The court discusses self-defense and defense of property, but the case is a classic rightful repossession scenario.

SHEHYN
v.
UNITED STATES

256 A.2d 404 (D.C. 1969)
District of Columbia Court of Appeals
August 7, 1969
Fickling, J.

Appellant was convicted by a jury of assault, D.C. Code § 22-504. After the court charged the jury on assault and self-defense, the instruction [on defense of property] ... was given and objected to on the ground that it did not correctly state the law on the defense of one's property. The objection was well taken. However, we hold it was harmless error in the context of the case as a whole.

Mr. Blanchard, the complainant, and his wife, who were next door neighbors of appellant, went upon appellant's parking lot to retrieve their pet cat which had escaped from their house and had hidden in appellant's air shaft. Appellant ordered the Blanchards off his property. After they refused, he went inside his house and got a wooden camera tripod about four feet in length and again ordered them to leave. When they refused to leave until they recovered their cat, appellant pushed Mrs. Blanchard aside and struck Mr. Blanchard with the tripod causing injury to his hand, requiring five stitches, and lacerations to his chest. The testimony is conflicting as to why appellant struck Mr. Blanchard. Appellant testified he went into the house to get the tripod because Mr. Blanchard picked up a brick. Blanchard testified he picked up a brick after appellant came out of his house with the tripod, and then he dropped the brick as appellant was advancing upon him because he did not want to strike appellant, who is an elderly man.

It is well settled that a person may use as much force as is reasonably necessary to eject a trespasser from his property, and that if he used more force than is necessary, he is guilty of assault. This is true regardless of any actual or threatened injury to the property by the trespasser, although this would be a factor in determining the reasonableness of the force used. However, in the instant case, Blanchard was not a trespasser. He had a privilege to go peaceably upon appellant's property to retrieve his cat. In *Carter v. Thurston*, 59 N.H. 104 (1877), where logs went upon a riparian owner's property because of a flood, the court stated:

> This right of pursuit and reclamation [of logs] rests upon the same natural right as that which permits the owner of cattle to pursue into an adjoining field and recover his beasts straying from the highway; but in the pursuit and recovery of his cattle or his logs, the owner must do no unnecessary damage, and is responsible for any excess or abuse of his right.

In an assault case where the complainant was injured while recovering his carpenter's plane, the court stated in *Stuyvesant v. Wilcox*, 92 Mich. 233, 52 N.W. 465, 467 (1892):

> But it is a rule well settled that one has such a right in personal property that he may recapture it and take it into his own possession whenever and wherever he may peaceably do so.

This principle was also followed in *Pierce v. Finerty*, 76 N.H. 38, 76 A. 194, 196 (1910), which involved reclamation of trees upon the land of another:

> There is a right of recaption or reclamation of personal property upon another's land without fault of the owner. In such cases, under certain circumstances, the owner of personal property has a right

(continues)

to enter to retake his property, and is not a trespasser if he does so.... But the right does not extend to cases where the situation is created by the fault or wrong of such owner.

The applicable rule, which we adopt, is stated in *Restatement (Second) of Torts* § 198 (1965):

(1) One is privileged to enter land in the possession of another, at a reasonable time and in a reasonable manner, for the purpose of removing a chattel to the immediate possession of which the actor is entitled, and which has come upon the land otherwise than with the actor's consent or by his tortious conduct or contributory negligence.

(2) The actor is subject to liability for any harm done in the exercise of the privilege stated in Subsection (1) to any legally protected interest of the possessor in the land or connected with it, except where the chattel is on the land through the tortious conduct or contributory negligence of the possessor.

In this case there is no evidence in the record which would indicate that the Blanchards acted in an unreasonable manner or at an unreasonable time when they went upon the parking lot to get their cat. The [jury] instruction, even though erroneous, was actually beneficial to appellant since he had no right to eject the Blanchards while they were exercising a privilege given to them by law, and appellant was not entitled to any defense of property instruction.

Affirmed.

CASE QUESTIONS

1. Although Shehyn, the appellant, was prosecuted under a criminal statute for assault, the defenses used in the case would be identical to those pleaded in a civil lawsuit involving the tort of assault or battery. Did you notice that the Blanchards were alleged to have committed trespass to land? What were their defenses as discussed in *Shehyn*? What portions of the court's opinion alerted you to these defenses?

2. Although the court in *Shehyn* quoted several persuasive precedents from other jurisdictions, it chose to adopt the rule stated in the *Restatement (Second) of Torts* § 198. Why did the *Shehyn* court quote these other state court opinions? Why do you think it adopted the *Restatement* rule, which is considered secondary legal authority, as opposed to the quoted court cases, which are primary authority?

3. Are there any other intentional tort defenses that were not discussed in *Shehyn* but that would apply? What are these? Why do you think they would succeed or fail?

4. Would the decision in *Shehyn* have been different if the Blanchards' cat had entered the appellant's land as a result of the Blanchards' actions? Suppose Mr. Blanchard threw a cat toy too high into the air, causing it to land on top of the appellant's roof, thereby enticing the cat to climb up onto the roof and become trapped there. Would the Blanchards have been legally justified in entering the appellant's real estate under these circumstances?

hypothetical

Ann was buying an automobile from Bryce. Ann wrote a check to Bryce for the final payment and this check bounced (i.e., the bank did not pay it because there were insufficient funds in Ann's account). Bryce angrily went over to Ann's house and drove away in the car. As soon as Ann discovered the check problem, she telephoned Bryce's apartment and left a message on his answering machine that she would be over directly to pay cash.

The first issue is whether Bryce had the right to repossess the automobile once Ann's check bounced. This would depend upon the terms of their agreement or, if the agreement did not address the problem, then upon creditors' rights statutes. For the sake of example, assume that no statutes address the question and that the parties' contract was silent as well. Although it is true that Ann breached her contract by bouncing her payment check to Bryce, she also swiftly corrected the error. Most courts would hold that Bryce could not use self-help remedies such as repossession without first contacting Ann to see if she could make good on the check. By repossessing the car without first talking with Ann, and because Ann has paid nearly the entire purchase price (and thus has a substantial equity, meaning property interest, in the vehicle), Bryce has committed trespass to chattel. Thus, Ann has been wrongfully dispossessed of her chattel. She could then enter Bryce's real estate to recover her automobile without being liable to Bryce for trespass to land. Ann would be entitled to the defense of rightful repossession.

It should also be noted that Bryce would not be able to claim rightful repossession as a defense to trespass to chattel. Because Bryce did not first communicate with Ann regarding the bad check and alternative means of payment, most courts would say that Bryce could not defend his retaking of the car on the grounds of rightful repossession. However, if Bryce had telephoned Ann about the check, and she had replied that she could or would not make the final payment, then Bryce would be legally entitled to repossess the vehicle. Under this set of circumstances, Bryce could use rightful repossession as a defense to trespass to chattel.

A synopsis of rightful repossession appears in Table 8-4.

Use of reasonable force
Prompt repossession
To repossess personal property
Owner has been wrongfully dispossessed of the chattel or has been improperly denied possession

TABLE 8-4
Elements of rightful repossession

▌ MISTAKE

Sometimes people act based upon inaccurate information or incorrect interpretations of events. The actor intended the result of his or her conduct but behaved under false beliefs. Often, had a person known the true state of affairs,

mistake | An unintentional
error or act.

he or she would have behaved differently. Tort law recognizes this tendency toward error, in which everyone has engaged at one time or another. The defense of mistake provides individuals with an escape route from intentional tort liability. As a legal defense, **mistake** is the good-faith belief, based upon incorrect information, that one is justified in committing an intentional tort under the circumstances. The elements may be detailed as follows: (1) Good-faith conviction that one's actions are justified (2) with the belief based upon faulty information; and (3) the conduct would otherwise be considered tortious but for the erroneous belief.

The *Restatement (Second) of Torts*

In the *Restatement (Second)*'s chapter 45, justification and excuse to tort liability are discussed. The following is an excerpt applicable to the mistake defense.

> ### *Restatement (Second) of Torts* § 890
> ### Comments a & f
> ### American Law Institute (1979)
>
> In some cases the law creates a privilege.... [A] privilege is given although it adversely affects the legally protected interests of another. This is ordinarily true when the actor is protected although mistaken (see Comment *f*), as when one acts in self-defense against another whom he reasonably but erroneously believes to be an aggressor....
>
>   *f. Mistake.* ...
>
>   When the privilege is conditional, a person is sometimes protected by his reasonable belief in the existence of facts that would give rise to a privilege, even though the facts do not exist. Thus one is not liable for using reasonable force in the protection of himself or another against what he reasonably believes to be an aggression of another ... ; a policeman is not liable for mistakenly arresting one whom he believes to have committed a felony ... and a private person is similarly protected if a felony has been committed ... ; a parent or teacher is not liable for mistakenly but reasonably disciplining a student.

Copyright © 1979 by The American Law Institute. Reprinted with the permission of the American Law Institute.

Mistake is summarized in Table 8-5.

TABLE 8-5
Elements of mistake

Good-faith conviction that actor's conduct is justified
Belief based upon erroneous information
Behavior would be tortious except for incorrect belief

hypothetical

Diedra was shopping at a local convenience store. The manager thought she saw Diedra put a pack of chewing gum into her purse. When Diedra left the store without stopping at the cashier, the manager asked her to step back inside the store to see the contents of her purse. The manager explained that she thought she had seen Diedra take merchandise without paying. Diedra emptied her purse, but no store items were included. If Diedra claimed that the manager had committed false imprisonment, defamation, or infliction of emotional distress, could the manager use mistake as a defense?

Assume that the manager's acts arguably constituted any one of these intentional torts. Nevertheless, courts would readily rule that, under these circumstances, the manager was justified in detaining Diedra for questioning. So long as the interrogation was conducted reasonably (such as in private for a short time period), then the courts would consider the manager's behavior to be acceptable. The manager had a good-faith belief that Diedra had shoplifted (although, in fact, she had not). The manager acted based upon this erroneous conviction, expecting that her conduct would be legally excused under the circumstances.

▍PRIVILEGE

As an intentional torts defense, **privilege** is a legal justification to engage in otherwise tortious conduct in order to accomplish a compelling social goal. This defense is based upon the right of a person to do what most people are not permitted to do. It is a right conferred on a person by society. For example, as a land owner, one may eject a person from one's own property, but other people may not do this. Only the land owner is thus privileged.

privilege | As a defense against an intentional tort, *privilege* is a legal justification to engage in otherwise tortious conduct in order to accomplish a compelling social goal.

Privilege is most commonly a defense to trespass to land, trespass to chattel, conversion, assault, battery, and false imprisonment, although it may be applied against other intentional torts as well. Privilege includes the following considerations:

1. Do the actor's motives for engaging in an intentional tort outweigh the injury to the victim or his or her property?
2. Was the actor justified in committing the intentional tort to accomplish his or her socially desirable purposes, or could a less damaging action have been taken instead?

This formula shows how courts balance values between the socially acceptable motives of the tortfeasor (actor) and the tort victim's compensation for injury.

Privilege presumes that the intentional tort is legally justified because of the higher purposes to be achieved.

Motives and Socially Desirable Goals

Motive describes the goal that a participant wishes to accomplish by taking a particular action. Motive may be discovered by probing the mental state of the actor. This mind-reading occurs in many areas of law. For example, in criminal law, *mens rea* loosely translates from the Latin as "evil thoughts" and suggests a psychological component to criminal conduct. In tort law, motive is synonymous with **intent,** which is broadly defined as the desire to attain a certain result. For purposes of the privilege defense, motive must be socially advantageous to a point that excuses intentional harm to another person or his or her property. The example of trespassing to save a drowning child's life sharply illustrates the clearly superior social objective that would give rise to the defense against the land owner's trespass-to-land lawsuit.

motive | The reason why a person does something.

intent | The resolve or purpose to use a particular means to reach a particular result. *Intent* usually explains *how* a person wants to do something and *what* that person wants to get done, while *motive* usually explains *why*.

Less Injurious Alternatives

With privilege defenses, courts frequently ask whether the tortfeasor's objectives could have been reached through behavior that would have been less harmful to the victim. Suppose Sinbad discovers an automobile on fire next to a natural gas storage facility. Given the likelihood that the burning car will ignite the gas tanks, which would explode along with a sizeable portion of the surrounding neighborhood, Sinbad sprays the flaming vehicle with water, irreparably damaging the engine. The car owner would complain against Sinbad's conversion or trespass to chattel. Sinbad would defend by arguing privilege. The court would query: Could Sinbad have saved the storage facility (and surrounding area) through a less damaging act?

The answer to this question depends upon the extent of the fire. If only a small portion of the automobile were burning, such as something in the trunk, Sinbad could have isolated the danger by concentrating water only into the trunk compartment. If the interior were also ablaze, Sinbad would be forced to expose more car to the water to put out the fire. Still, he might have spared the engine compartment. However, if the inferno had engulfed the entire vehicle, he would have no choice other than to inundate it with water.

Similarity between Privilege and Other Defenses

Several distinct intentional tort defenses, such as rightful repossession, self-defense, or defense of others or property, are simply particular types of privilege. Each has a social benefits component that justifies otherwise tortious misconduct. Necessity is another form of privilege that has also become a separate defense in its own right. The same is true of public officers' immunity for legal process enforcement, warrantless arrest, and reasonable discipline. These defenses to intentional torts are discussed in the remaining sections of this chapter.

The *Restatement (Second)* Position

Restatement (Second) of Torts § 890 focuses on privileges, noting that the term is broadly defined to include many of the specific defenses discussed throughout this chapter. The illustrations in the Comments are particularly helpful in understanding the scope of privilege.

Restatement (Second) of Torts § 890 & Comments
American Law Institute (1979)

§ 890. Privileges
One who otherwise would be liable for a tort is not liable if he acts in pursuance of and within the limits of a privilege of his own or of a privilege of another that was properly delegated to him.

Comment

a. As stated in § 10, the word "privilege" is used throughout this Restatement to denote the fact that conduct that under ordinary circumstances would subject the actor to liability, under particular circumstances does not subject him to the liability.

* * *

In some cases the law creates a privilege … as when the owner of land is given a privilege to eject a trespasser upon his land or to enter the land of another to abate a private nuisance, or when a citizen is given the privilege of arresting a felon. . . .

c. Purpose of privilege—Conditional privileges created by rule of law. Most of the privileges that are not based on consent are conditioned upon their being performed for the purpose of protecting the interest for which the privilege was given. This is illustrated in cases in which force is used against another; in self-defense or in defense of a third person … ; in the defense of the possession of land … ; in the recapture of land or chattels … ; in an arrest by a private person or a peace officer … ; in the prevention of crime … ; in the disciplining of children. . . .

d. Purpose of privilege—Absolute privileges. In certain cases in which the interests of the public are overwhelming, the purpose of the actor is immaterial. Thus for some or all statements, complete immunity from civil liability exists as to defamatory statements made during the course of judicial proceedings . . . , as well as to statements by legislators and certain administrative officers while acting in the performance of their functions.

Anastasia owns a grocery in town. One of her customers notified her that several cans of Buddy Boy's Baked Beans were bulging, which is a symptom of contamination. Anastasia opened these cans and discovered that the food had spoiled. She placed an advertisement in the local newspaper warning her customers to return any can of Buddy Boy's, whether bulging or not, because of spoilage. In fact, only four cans of the product were defective. Buddy Boy's manufacturer, E. I. Wilcott & Company, sued Anastasia for disparagement of goods. Anastasia claimed privilege, arguing that her motive was to protect the public from food poisoning. Would the defense carry the day?

Truth is an absolute defense in any type of defamation action, including commercial disparagement. In our hypothetical, however, the truth was exaggerated. Only a few cans were tainted. Nonetheless, there was no way of determining this without recalling as many cans as possible from Anastasia's customers. A court would rule that Anastasia was justified in advertising the warning to her customers, and so Anastasia would not be liable to E. I. Wilcott & Company for disparagement of goods.

The elements of privilege are abstracted in Table 8-6.

TABLE 8-6
Elements of privilege

Actor's motives in committing intentional tort outweigh injury to victim or property
Actor was justified in engaging in intentional tort to accomplish socially desirable goals
No less-damaging alternative action could have been taken
Exception: Absolute privilege of judges, legislators, etc. These actors' motives are immaterial.

An example of privilege is where force can be used for self-defense.

NECESSITY

Necessity is another variety of privilege that excuses otherwise tortious misconduct. Under this defense, the tortfeasor is justified in engaging in an intentional tort to prevent more serious injury from an external force. **Necessity** contains four elements: (1) Committing an intentional tort (2) to avert more serious injury (3) caused by a force other than the tortfeasor (4) and the tortfeasor's actions were reasonably necessary to avert the greater harm. This defense is based on the

necessity | Often refers to a situation that requires an action that would otherwise be illegal or expose a person to tort liability.

theory that the benefit—prevention of a greater harm—outweighs the risk of the intentional injury (competing harms).

Thwarting a More Substantial Harm

In a necessity situation, the tortfeasor is usually faced with having to choose between the lesser of two evils. On the one hand, the tortfeasor must inflict injury upon a victim or the victim's property. On the other hand, the tortfeasor could do nothing and watch a greater havoc occur. For example, suppose Antonio is aboard a ship that suddenly begins to sink. There are several passengers aboard, including Antonio, as well as valuable cargo. If the cargo were thrown overboard, the boat could stay afloat long enough for help to arrive. So Antonio elects to jettison the cargo and save the passengers' lives. The cargo owner could sue Antonio for trespass to chattel, but the defense of necessity would insulate Antonio from liability. Although Antonio committed an intentional tort, he sought only to prevent greater harm caused by a force beyond his control (namely, the ship's sinking).

External Forces

For necessity to operate as a defense to an intentional tort, the more significant danger being averted must originate from a source other than the tortfeasor. For instance, in the previous illustration, the boat began to sink through no fault of Antonio's. However, suppose he had caused an explosion in the engine room by improper fuel mixing, and thus blew a hole in the hull of the craft. Because Antonio created the greater hazard, he could not claim necessity in throwing the cargo overboard. Had it not been for his misconduct in the engine room, the extreme peril would never have happened. The necessity defense cannot protect a tortfeasor who creates the catastrophic condition and then must engage in an intentional tort to resolve the crisis.

Reasonably Necessary Action

As is generally true with privilege, necessity requires that the tortfeasor's conduct be reasonably necessary to prevent the more substantial danger. Thus, the tortfeasor must use only that degree of force required to avert the greater risk. Using the sinking ship example, suppose that the leak in the ship's hull occurred not because of Antonio's misbehavior but because of faulty sealing techniques. If Antonio could plug the leak rather than abandon ship, it would not be necessary for him to jettison the cargo to save the passengers.

Fires further illustrate this aspect of reasonably required action; many necessity cases involve burning buildings. Several nineteenth-century court opinions discussed "row" structures, which were many discrete buildings attached in long rows down a street. If one were to catch fire, it was likely that the entire block would burn to the ground. To avoid this calamity, the flaming building was often destroyed. There simply was no less-damaging alternative when the building was fully ablaze. If the building owner sued for trespass to land, the courts routinely applied the necessity defense to protect the tortfeasor from liability to the building owner.

The *Restatement (Second)* Position

The *Restatement (Second)* addresses necessity as a defense in emergency situations in which the tortfeasor is compelled to immediate action by a crisis. In such cases, the defense operates to protect the defendant from liability. Note how the *Restatement's* elements are distinguishable from those previously discussed in the text.

Restatement (Second) of Torts §§ 890, 892D & Comments
American Law Institute (1979)

[§ 890, Comment a.] [The emergency defense exists] when the protection of the public is of overriding importance, as when one is privileged to destroy buildings to avert a public disaster. . . .

§ 892D. Emergency Action Without Consent

Conduct that injures another does not make the actor liable to the other, even though the other has not consented to it[,] if

(a) an emergency makes it necessary or apparently necessary, in order to prevent harm to the other, to act before there is opportunity to obtain consent from the other or one empowered to consent for him, and

(b) the actor has no reason to believe that the other, if he had the opportunity to consent, would decline.

Comment

a. The rule stated in this Section covers a group of exceptional situations in which the actor is privileged to proceed without the consent of another and without any manifested or apparent consent, on the assumption that if the other had the opportunity to decide he would certainly consent. This privilege must necessarily be a limited one and can arise only in situations of emergency, when there is no time to consult the other or one empowered to consent for him, or [if] for reasons such as the unconsciousness of the other his consent cannot be obtained. The mere possibility that the other might consent if he were able to do so is not enough; and the conduct must be so clearly and manifestly to the other's advantage that there is no reason to believe that the consent would not be given. If the actor knows or has reason to know, because of past refusals or other circumstances, that the consent would not be given, he is not privileged to act. . . .

Necessity can be a puzzling defense. Its elements compel courts to balance competing interests, employing somewhat more value judgment than usual. This hypothetical illustrates.

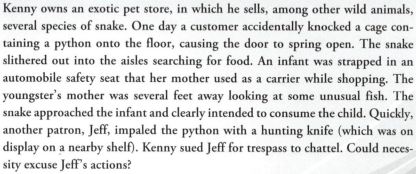

hypothetical

Kenny owns an exotic pet store, in which he sells, among other wild animals, several species of snake. One day a customer accidentally knocked a cage containing a python onto the floor, causing the door to spring open. The snake slithered out into the aisles searching for food. An infant was strapped in an automobile safety seat that her mother used as a carrier while shopping. The youngster's mother was several feet away looking at some unusual fish. The snake approached the infant and clearly intended to consume the child. Quickly, another patron, Jeff, impaled the python with a hunting knife (which was on display on a nearby shelf). Kenny sued Jeff for trespass to chattel. Could necessity excuse Jeff's actions?

Reasonably necessary action is the critical element in this hypothetical. Jeff's actions were reasonably necessary. He would not be liable for trespass to chattel.

A short review of the elements of necessity is provided in Table 8-7.

Committing intentional tort
Purpose to avert more harmful injury
Harm threatened by force other than tortfeasor
Tortfeasor's actions were reasonably necessary to prevent danger of greater harm

TABLE 8-7
Elements of necessity

▌ PUBLIC OFFICER'S IMMUNITY FOR LEGAL PROCESS ENFORCEMENT

Public officials often engage in activity that normally would be considered intentionally tortious. However, because such persons are authorized by law to engage in such conduct, they are protected from liability. Several types of governmental action fall within this protected class. The most common include: (1) process serving; (2) execution sales; (3) attachment or replevin; (4) arrest by warrant; (5) prosecutors acting in official capacity; and (6) judges acting in official capacity.

Service of Process

Process, process serving, or **service of process** are the methods by which a defendant in a lawsuit is notified that a plaintiff has filed suit against the defendant. The cases of actual physical delivery give rise to litigation. The defendant might sue the sheriff for trespass to land when the sheriff arrived on the defendant's real estate to deliver the summons. However, the sheriff has the power to enter another person's land to serve process. The land owner's lawsuit against the sheriff would fail.

Execution Sales

When a plaintiff wins judgment against the defendant in a civil action, the defendant usually has a certain period of time to pay the judgment. If the defendant fails to pay, the plaintiff may return to court requesting the court to order the defendant's property sold to satisfy the judgment. These forced sales are often referred to as **execution sales** or **sheriff's sales,** because the sheriff is frequently the public official responsible for seizing and selling the defendant's property. The defendant might sue the sheriff for trespass to land, trespass to chattel, and conversion after the sheriff comes and gets the defendant's property. However, the sheriff is legally protected.

Attachment or Replevin

Attachment is a court-ordered remedy in a lawsuit. When a plaintiff is entitled to a remedy against the defendant in a lawsuit, and the defendant is likely to dispose of his or her property to avoid losing it in a subsequent action, the plaintiff may ask the court to attach the property. The court then orders a law enforcement officer, such as the sheriff, to seize the defendant's property. The defendant might sue the sheriff for conversion or trespass to chattel. The sheriff is authorized by statute or common law to take the defendant's property.

Replevin is another court-ordered remedy. A plaintiff sues a defendant who wrongfully possesses the plaintiff's chattel and refuses to return it. The plaintiff asks the court for replevin, which means that the court would order the defendant to return the personal property to the plaintiff. If the defendant refuses, the court could instruct the sheriff to seize the chattel.

Arrest by Warrant

Police officers often arrest suspected criminals under a warrant for arrest. Suppose the suspect was innocent of any crimes. Could the suspect sue the police department for false imprisonment and infliction of emotional distress for having been arrested? If the law enforcement personnel were acting pursuant to an arrest warrant properly ordered by a judge, and if they acted in good faith, then they would not be liable for any intentional torts.

process | A court's ordering a defendant to show up in court or risk losing a lawsuit; a summons.

process serving | The method by which a defendant in a lawsuit is notified that the plaintiff has filed suit against the defendant. Also called *service of process*.

service of process | The delivery (or its legal equivalent, such as publication in a newspaper in some cases) of a legal paper by an authorized person.

execution sale | A forced public sale held by a sheriff or other public official of property seized to pay a judgment.

sheriff's sale | A sale (of property) held by a sheriff to pay a court judgment against the owner of the property.

attachment | Formally seizing property (or a person) in order to bring it under control of the court. This is usually done by getting a court order to have a law enforcement officer take control of the property.

replevin | A legal action to get back property wrongfully held by another person.

Prosecutors and Judges

Prosecutors and **judges** acting in the scope of their positions are privileged and immune from liability for their actions. If this were not so, no one would accept such a position. It is inherent in these positions to occasionally intentionally injure someone mentally, emotionally, and by reputation. Liability for their mistakes would have a chilling effect on their performance; that is, they would be too afraid of making a mistake and thus err against social benefit. Therefore, public policy has always been to allow these persons immunity from liability in the honest performance of their positions.

There are exceptions to the privilege and immunity doctrines. 42 U.S.C. § 1983 permits liability of public officers (usually other than prosecutors and judges) if the performance of their duties involves activities that deprive persons of their civil rights. Such an action is called a civil rights action or a "1983" action (*1983* is the section number of the law permitting this action, not the year it was passed). If a police officer arrests someone without a warrant and without probable cause, it is a violation of civil rights and the officer may be liable.

prosecutor | A public official who represents the government's case against a person accused of a crime.

judge | The person who runs a courtroom, decides all legal questions, and sometimes decides entire cases by also deciding factual questions.

 THE CASE OF THE DEFIANT TRUCKER (PART II)

In *Jurco v. State,* partially reprinted earlier, the Alaska Court of Appeals addressed conflicting defenses: namely, defense of property versus law enforcement officers' immunity for legal process enforcement. Reread the case as it applies to this latter defense and as a refresher for the facts. The court also discussed warrantless arrests, which are discussed in a further analysis of this case in the next section.

JURCO
v.
STATE
825 P.2d 909 (Alaska Ct. App. 1992)
Court of Appeals of Alaska
February 14, 1992
Mannheimer, Judge

At common law, a public officer was authorized to use reasonable force against other persons when executing a court order requiring or authorizing the officer to seize another person's property. This common-law rule has been codified in Alaska; [Alaska Statutes §] 11.81.420 provides:

Justification: Performance of public duty.
(a) Unless inconsistent with AS 11.81.320—
11.81-410, conduct which would otherwise

constitute an offense is justified when it is required or authorized by law or by a judicial decree, judgment, or order.
(b) The justification afforded by this section also applies when . . . the person reasonably believes the conduct to be required or authorized by a decree, judgment, or order of a court of competent jurisdiction or in the lawful execution of legal process, notwithstanding lack of jurisdiction of the court or defect in the legal process[.]

Under this statute, law enforcement officers are empowered to use force to execute court decrees, even if it is later shown that the court had no authority to issue the decree. Thus, in Jurco's case, the State Troopers were authorized to use all reasonable force to execute the Alaska District

(continues)

Court's order to seize Jurco's vehicle, even if Jurco was correct in claiming that the pendency of his bankruptcy petition deprived the state district court of the judicial authority to issue orders affecting his property.

---

hypothetical

Emily sued Rupa. The sheriff delivered a copy of the summons and Emily's complaint to Rupa's house. Rupa did not appear at trial, and Emily won a default judgment against Rupa. After thirty days, Rupa had failed to pay the judgment. Emily filed a writ of execution with the court, which ordered the sheriff to seize Rupa's property. The sheriff again returned to Rupa's house to garner the chattels that could be sold at an execution sale. The proceeds from the sale went to satisfy Emily's judgment. Rupa sued the sheriff for trespass to land, trespass to chattel, and conversion. The sheriff applied the defense of legal process enforcement.

This hypothetical is probably the easiest to answer of any in the text. The sheriff was acting under court order to enforce legal processes, and so the defense would succeed. Rupa's lawsuit would be promptly dismissed.

The elements of the legal process enforcement defense are listed in Table 8-8.

TABLE 8-8
Types of legal process enforcement defenses and elements of warrantless arrest defenses

Legal Process Enforcement	Warrantless Arrest
Process serving	Law enforcement officers' power to arrest if a felony is committed or if reasonably believe a felony occurred (witness a felony or breach of peace)
Execution sales	Citizen's arrest (felonies or breaches of peace)
Attachment or replevin	
Arrest by warrant	

▍WARRANTLESS ARREST BY LAW ENFORCEMENT OFFICIALS OR CITIZENS

Police officers, and sometimes even ordinary citizens, engage in *warrantless arrests*. Could they be liable for false imprisonment, battery, assault, trespass to land, and infliction of emotional distress?

Statutes and common law authorize law enforcement personnel to arrest criminal suspects, even without court-issued warrants, under certain circumstances. For example, when a police officer witnesses a felony, he or she may arrest the suspect immediately. This proper enforcement of a legal process would be a defense against the suspect's intentional torts lawsuit.

Private citizens, too, may take suspected criminals into custody under the theory of *citizen's arrest.* Under the common law, a private citizen may take a suspect into custody if the citizen has witnessed the suspect commit a felony or breach of the peace. This would include situations in which the citizen reasonably thinks that the suspect has committed a felony. Historically, this defense was often used to protect store owners who detained suspected shoplifters from liability for false imprisonment actions.

Normally, modern warrantless arrest does not involve private citizen participation to the extent the pre-twentieth-century cases did. However, private police, such as company security, are often involved in today's cases.

The warrantless arrest defense, together with the defense of legal process enforcement, are both summarized in Table 8-8.

hypothetical

Carter is a night watchman at a local factory. He noticed someone suspicious lurking in the shadows near a restricted-access building containing company records and other valuables. He turned his flashlight on the suspect, whom he did not recognize. He demanded identification and the reason the stranger was present on factory grounds. The stranger said nothing and attempted to flee. Carter tackled the individual, forcibly returned him to the security office, and telephoned the police. The stranger turned out to be an employee of a competitor to Carter's employer. The stranger sued Carter for battery, false imprisonment, and infliction of emotional distress. Would Carter be entitled to a defense under citizen's arrest theory?

Carter witnessed a simple trespass to land, which is not a felony under either statutory or common law. The stranger had merely trespassed onto the factory's property. Further, the stranger had not breached the peace. However, Carter reasonably believed that the suspect was about to engage in a felony (namely, burglary or theft). In his experience as a security guard, Carter had seen many felons behave just as the stranger had acted. Thus, Carter's reasonable belief that the suspect was about to commit a felony was sufficient to justify his behavior. Carter would not be liable to the stranger for any of the intentional torts.

THE CASE OF THE DEFIANT TRUCKER (PART III)

Jurco v. State, discussed earlier, also involved warrantless arrest. As it had done with Jurco's previous issues on appeal, the Alaska Court of Appeals, with "arresting" analysis, ruled against the appellant. Although the court's discussion did not involve tort liability as a result of a warrantless arrest, it is clear that there could be no such liability, because the arrest was lawful.

JURCO
v.
STATE
825 P.2d 909 (Alaska Ct. App. 1992)
Court of Appeals of Alaska
February 14, 1992
Mannheimer, Judge

Jurco also argues that his arrest was illegal because the troopers did not have an arrest warrant. Jurco acknowledges that [Alaska Stat. §] 12.25.030 authorizes police officers to arrest without a

warrant when a misdemeanor is committed in their presence. . . .

Finally, even if some additional justification were needed for the troopers' decision to make an arrest instead of issue a citation, that justification was present. It was clear that Jurco was intent on thwarting the troopers' performance of their duty under the court order directing seizure of Jurco's truck; the troopers could reasonably conclude that Jurco would continue to impede their efforts unless he were physically taken into custody.

▌ STATUTES OF LIMITATIONS

Statutes of limitations are statutes restricting the time within which a plaintiff may file his or her lawsuit for particular causes of action against a defendant. All states have statutes of limitations for almost all tort actions, including intentional torts. (Sometimes they are called *limitation of actions.*) The most common tort statutes of limitations are two years. This means that the plaintiff has two years from the date that an intentional tort occurred to file his or her lawsuit against the defendant. If the plaintiff fails to file within this statutory time period, then his or her cause of action against the defendant is barred forever.

Although two years is a common statute of limitations period for many torts, the exact time period varies among states and different types of torts. One should always research the specific statute of limitations for each cause of action, whether in tort or in other areas of law. This is a vital piece of information for both the plaintiff and the defendant. If the statute of limitations has expired, the defendant may respond with this defense and have the plaintiff's case dismissed or otherwise disposed of (usually by summary judgment). The plaintiff's attorney must be aware of the statute of limitations and file the lawsuit in a timely manner, or risk a malpractice suit.

▌ WORKERS' COMPENSATION

Another defense to an intentional tort action might be that the action is prevented by a state's workers' compensation statute. These statutes cover workers who are injured or killed or become ill as a result of incidents occurring during the course and scope of their employment. Workers' compensation statutes bar tort actions against the employer and are considered a worker's sole remedy for on-the-job injuries and death, regardless of fault, in most states. Workers' compensation is also addressed in Chapter 12 in relation to tort immunities.

Workers' compensation is insurance that provides cash benefits and/or medical care for workers who are injured on the job or who become ill as a result of their job. Employers pay for this insurance. This is a form of strict liability, a no-fault system by state. In workers' compensation cases, no one party is found to be at fault. However, an employee's injury must "arise out of" and occur in the "course of employment." This means that an injury that occurs at work and is related to work will be covered. In contrast, if an employee is on the way to or from work and injuries are sustained, they will generally not be covered.

The amount a worker collects is not based upon, nor is it affected by, whether an employer is at fault. Unlike a traditional negligence claim, the employee does not have to worry that his or her claim will be defeated by the employer's assertion of defenses such as the employee's contributory negligence, assumption of the risk, or that the injury was actually caused by a fellow employee rather than the employer.

It is important to note that while workers' compensation statutes all but eliminate suits between injured employees and employers, an employee still retains the right to bring an action against a third party who may have also caused or contributed to the injuries. Workers' compensation only bars suits against the employer, not outside third parties. Accordingly, an employee might bring a workers' compensation claim and still sue a private entity such as a janitorial service that left a floor dangerously slippery with wax, or a manufacturer that produced a defective product that was used at work.

However, if an employee intentionally tries to injure himself or herself, or is injured as a result of drug or alcohol intoxication, then the employee cannot collect benefits. Workers' compensation statutes specify which type of employers and which employees are covered by the acts. Not all employees or all forms of employment are covered by workers' compensation.

Employees must report workplace injuries to their employer and fill out a claim form in order to apply for benefits. Generally, there is a waiting period before the employee can collect benefits. An employer cannot fire an employee solely because the employee has filed for benefits.

The injured employee's medical provider determines the extent of disability, if any. Cash benefits are based upon and determined according to disability classifications ranging from temporary partial disability to permanent total disability. In the event of the death of an employee as a result of a workplace injury, the surviving spouse and family may be entitled to a cash benefit. In the event an employee can no longer return to his or her previous type of work, vocational rehabilitation is offered to train the employee for a new career.

THE CASE OF COMPENSATION

As a paralegal, you will run into a lot of different fact patterns when dealing with workers' compensation claims. While this case regarding a mounted police officer getting shoes for his horse appears to address a seemingly uncommon fact pattern, the important thing to remember is that all compensation cases must still go through the same legal analysis. Were the injuries sustained "arising out of and in the course of employment"?

Michael RASH, Petitioner,
v.
WORKERS' COMPENSATION APPEALS BOARD,
Stanislaus County Sheriff's Department et al.,
Respondents.

No. F051520
(WCAB No. STK 197752)
Court of Appeal, Fifth District, California
May 25, 2007

A sheriff's deputy asks whether the injuries he sustained while returning from a college horseshoeing course to prepare his privately owned horse for mounted duty arose out of and in the course of his employment.

Michael Rash worked as a deputy with the County Sheriff's Department (Department). As a member of the Department's horse-mounted unit, Rash was required to privately own, care for, train, and transport a horse certified for mounted duty to be available for service 24 hours a day, seven days a week.

Lieutenant James Silva is a commander in the Department. He adopted a constant shoeing requirement so that horses approved for mounted duty would be ready at a moment's notice. To replace horseshoes, farriers either travel to the horse or ask the owner to bring the horse to the farrier.

Lieutenant Silva and his wife signed up for a horseshoeing class at Merced College. Due to insufficient enrollment, Lieutenant Silva asked Rash to join the class and advanced his $150 to $160 tuition, which Rash later reimbursed. On about half of the course days, Lieutenant Silva and Rash carpooled.

Department Sergeant Giles New called Rash on Monday, and they agreed Rash would cover a shift of another mounted deputy at the Rodeo the following Saturday and Sunday. Later that afternoon, Rash examined his horse, Indian, and discovered its right rear shoe was missing. Rash decided to shoe Indian at the horseshoeing class.

Rash loaded the horses in his privately owned truck and trailer at the end of Wednesday's class and on the way home went to lunch in Merced approximately one mile from the college. Following lunch, Rash was driving along Route J-59 when another vehicle struck him head-on. As a result of the accident, Rash filed a claim for workers' compensation benefits alleging injury to "multiple body parts," including both legs.

The Department concluded that Rash's injuries were not employment-related and denied his claim for workers' compensation benefits. Following hearings in March and May 2006, a workers' compensation administrative law judge (WCJ) agreed with the Department.

An employer is liable for workers' compensation benefits only where an employee sustains an injury "arising out of and in the course of the employment. . . . "

This two-pronged requirement is the cornerstone of the workers' compensation system.

An injury arises out of employment when there is a causal link between the injury and the job. In other words, the injury must have been sustained while performing a particular act reasonably contemplated by the employment; accordingly, the nature of the act, the nature of the employment, the custom and usage of a particular employment, the terms of the contract of employment.

In determining whether an injury arises out of and in the course of employment, the judicially created "going and coming" rule generally precludes workers' compensation recovery for injuries sustained during a local commute en route to a fixed place of business at fixed hours. The rule is based on the notion that an employee usually does not render services for the benefit of the employer while traveling to and from work. Exceptions to the going-and-coming rule exist, however, " 'where the trip involves an incidental benefit to the employer, not common to commute trips by ordinary members of the work force.'" As a result, "[w]hen an employee engages in a special activity that is within the course of employment, an injury suffered during the activity or while traveling to and from the place of such activity also arises out of the employment." This type of activity is also known as a "'special mission,'" where "'"[s]pecial" means extraordinary in relation to routine duties, not outside the scope of the employment.'"

An employee performs services arising out of and in the course of employment "when he engages in conduct reasonably directed toward the fulfillment of his employer's requirements, performed for the benefit and advantage of the employer." The burden of proving that an injury arose out of and in the course of employment falls on the employee and generally presents a question of fact.

Agreeing with the WCAB's determination that his injury *arose out of* his employment, Rash asks this court also to consider whether his injury also occurred *in the course of* his employment. The WCJ found that the injury did not occur in the course of employment because Rash created his own "special mission that his employer did not request." It appears, however, that the WCAB failed to consider whether Rash's activity—taking Indian to Merced College to be shod for an impending work-related event—was necessary or impliedly permitted under the terms of his employment as a mounted deputy. There is no indication that taking Indian to be shod at Merced College several days before an assignment exceeded the scope of duties contemplated by Rash's employment as a mounted officer.

Rash's conduct on April 6, 2006, of taking Indian to be shod at the class in the most convenient and inexpensive manner in preparation for duty was both a subjectively and objectively reasonable expectancy of his employment as a mounted deputy and was therefore compensable.

CASE QUESTIONS

1. Did Rash's injuries from the automobile accident arise out of and in the course of his employment? Explain.
2. Did the "special mission" doctrine apply here? Explain.

▮ SUMMARY

Consent may be a defense to all intentional torts. Consent occurs when a victim of an intentional tort voluntarily agrees to endure the tortious actions. Voluntary agreement involves the victim understanding the consequences of the tortfeasor's conduct. This is called informed consent. Consent may be expressed or implied based upon the behavior of the parties.

Self-defense is the exercise of reasonable force to repel an attack upon one's person or to avoid confinement. Self-defense counters an offensive force that threatens bodily injury, repugnant contact, or sequestration. The amount of force a person may use in self-defense is limited to that amount necessary to repel the attacking force. Any greater resistance is excessive and the defense would be ineffective. The defense is used against allegations of assault, battery, or false imprisonment.

Defense of persons or property is another legal justification for assault or battery. Defense of persons involves the use of reasonable force to defend or protect a third party from injury when the third person is threatened by an attacking force. Here, reasonable force is defined identically as for self-defense. Defense of property allows reasonable force to protect property from damage or dispossession when an invader attempts to injure or wrongfully take custody of the property. Reasonable force to protect property is usually defined as less force than would ordinarily be allowed to protect persons. Courts generally do not permit deadly force to be used to protect property, although one may apply deadly force in defense of one's home against intruders, under the castle rule.

Rightful repossession empowers a chattel owner to enter upon another's real estate to legally repossess personal property that has been wrongfully taken or withheld. The chattel owner would not be liable for trespass to land, trespass to chattel, or conversion, because he or she was justified in retaking control of the property. The defense also may protect against claims of assault or battery. Reasonable force may be used to repossess the chattel. Reasonable force is defined along the same lines as for defense of property. The efforts to regain possession must occur promptly after the property is first taken from the owner, or from the time the possessor wrongfully refuses to return the property to the owner. For the defense to succeed, the chattel owner must have been wrongfully dispossessed, or return of the property must have been improperly refused.

As a defense to intentional torts, mistake is a good-faith belief, based upon incorrect information, that a person is justified in committing an intentional tort under the circumstances. This belief must be reasonable, and reasonableness is determined on a case-by-case basis. This belief must be based on erroneous details which, if they had been true, would have excused the intentional torts committed.

Privilege is sometimes considered a broad category embracing all the other defenses discussed in this chapter. To use the defense, one must ask if the actor's motives for engaging in the intentional tort outweigh the injury to the victim or property. Further, one must ask if the actor was justified in committing the intentional tort to achieve socially desirable goals (which outweigh the injury factor). Could these goals have been accomplished without inflicting the harm to the victim?

The necessity defense allows a tortfeasor to commit an intentional tort to prevent more serious injury from an external force. The tortfeasor's actions must be reasonably necessary to avert the more substantial danger. Necessity is basically a choice between the lesser of two evils. The tortfeasor cannot cause the greater threat of harm if the necessity defense is to insulate him or her from liability.

Public officials are immune from intentional tort liability for the proper enforcement of legal processes, such as service of process, execution sales, attachment, replevin, or arrest by warrant. Both statutes and common law protect governmental employees involved in these activities, as legal process enforcement is necessary to implement the judicial system. Normally, law enforcement officers, such as sheriffs, participate in these processes.

Law enforcement officials are authorized by statutes and common law to make warrantless arrests, usually when a felony is committed or suspected in their presence. Under the defense of citizen's arrest, private persons may restrain suspected felons without liability for assault, battery, false imprisonment, infliction of emotional distress, trespass to land, or other intentional torts.

Most state statutes of limitations restrict the time period within which a plaintiff may file his or her intentional tort causes of action against a defendant. In most states, these are two-year statutes, meaning that a plaintiff has two years from the date that the intentional tort was committed within which to file his or her lawsuit against the tortfeasor. It is vital to research specific statutes of limitations for each particular tort.

State workers' compensation statutes bar tort actions against workers' employers regardless of fault.

▍ KEY TERMS

attachment	informed consent	process serving
castle doctrine	intent	prosecutor
consent	judge	reasonable force
defense	mistake	replevin
defense of persons	motive	rightful repossession
defense of property	necessary force	self-defense
ejectment	necessity	service of process
execution sale	privilege	sheriff's sale
hot (fresh) pursuit	process	

▍ PROBLEMS

In the following hypotheticals, identify the intentional torts and available defenses involved, if any, and support your answers.

1. Kim drives a delivery truck for The Dough Boy, a local bakery. One day, while making a delivery, Kim saw an automobile parked along the side of the street begin to move. There was no one inside the car, and it appeared to have slipped out of gear. The car rolled with increasing speed down a hill toward a crowded sidewalk along which several businesses were having outdoor sales. None of the shoppers saw the runaway vehicle approaching. Kim rammed her truck into the rear right side of the car, causing it to spin sideways. This stopped it from rolling into the pedestrians. The auto owner sued Kim for damaging the car, and the owner of The Dough Boy also sued Kim for injuring the delivery truck.

2. Todd, a student at the city college, visited the school bookstore to purchase some notebooks. Outside the bookstore were a series of locking boxes within which students placed their backpacks, briefcases, or other belongings that the bookstore forbade customers to bring into the store. Todd placed his backpack into one of the lockers and entered the bookstore. However, he forgot to take the key from the box. Luke, another student, opened the box and thought the backpack was his, as he owned a pack almost identical to Todd's. Luke had placed his own pack in one of the boxes but had also forgotten to take the key. Later, Todd discovered the pack missing, and a bookstore cashier described Luke as the culprit. Luke had not examined the pack closely but had thrown it into his car trunk and forgotten about it. Todd sued Luke.

3. Leroy frequented a pub called Bottom's Up! Late one Saturday night, an intoxicated man began shouting obscenities at a woman sitting at the table next to Leroy's. The woman ignored the man and continued to drink her beer. The man approached the lady, looking ominous. Leroy stood and asked the fellow over to the bar for a drink. The man grumbled that Leroy should mind his own business. The man reached out and

grabbed the woman's wrist, and Leroy neatly twisted the man's other arm behind his back while restraining him with a neck hold. The man protested vehemently, but Leroy did not let go. Leroy placed the man firmly into a chair and told him not to move or else Leroy would have to punch him. The woman told Leroy that the man was her husband and asked him to leave them both alone. Leroy left the bar. The man sued Leroy.

4. Peter Delaney works as an assistant manager at a local clothing store. One evening, while emptying trash outside the back of the store, Peter saw someone toying with a lock on the back door of another store. He could not see who the person was. Peter telephoned the police from inside his store and returned to the alley. He yelled out to the mysterious person not to move, because he was armed, and the police were coming. In fact, Peter did not possess any weapons, but bluffed to scare the culprit. The suspicious character turned out to be a new employee at the neighboring store who was trying to determine which key opened the rear door lock. Peter did not know this individual. The person sued Peter.

5. Alyssa was purchasing some merchandise on layaway at a local department store. She had made her final payment and had requested that the items be delivered to her house. After a few days, she telephoned the store manager to complain that the goods had not been delivered. The manager explained that she would first have to pay the entire purchase price before delivery would be possible. Alyssa protested that she had, in fact, paid in full. She went to the store and showed the layaway clerk her payment receipts. The clerk refused to produce the merchandise. Alyssa walked behind the counter, went up the stairs to the layaway storage area, and retrieved her items. The clerk notified store security, who took Alyssa into custody and locked her in an empty storeroom next to the restrooms. The room was unlit and not heated. The police arrived after an hour to question Alyssa, and after a few minutes she was released. Alyssa sued the store and the store counter-claimed against Alyssa.

▌REVIEW QUESTIONS

1. What are defenses? How are they applied against intentional torts? In what type of situation would a defense most likely be raised?

2. Describe consent. Is the defense widely applicable to intentional torts? What is informed consent? Implied consent?

3. Explain self-defense. Against which intentional torts might this defense be used? What is reasonable force? How is it defined? How is it similar to necessary force?

4. Discuss defense of persons or property. How is it similar to self-defense? Different? How is defense of persons different from defense of property? Similar? How is reasonable force defined for this defense?

5. What is rightful repossession? What type of property is involved? Against which intentional torts might this defense be applied? How is reasonable force defined? What is the role of wrongful dispossession or denial of possession? Must the property owner's efforts to repossess be taken within a certain time frame? What is this called?

6. Explain mistake. What is the role of the good-faith conviction? Why must the information believed be inaccurate? How broad is the defense?

7. Does privilege include all defenses to intentional torts? Why? Against which intentional torts would the defense be utilized? What are its characteristics? What is the role of motive? Of socially acceptable goals? Of less injurious alternatives?

8. What are the elements of necessity? How is it used as an intentional tort defense? What is the significance of external forces? Why must the action be reasonably necessary?

9. Discuss the various types of public official immunity for legal process enforcement. What intentional torts might apply to these cases? How does the defense operate in each such instance?

10. What is warrantless arrest? Citizen's arrest? How are these protected from intentional tort liability?

11. What are statutes of limitations? What is the time period most commonly used for tort causes of action? How can statutes of limitations be used as a defense to intentional torts?

12. What kinds of activities that result in injury at work would not be covered under workers' compensation?

▌HELPFUL WEBSITES

This chapter focuses on defenses to intentional torts. To learn more about defenses to intentional torts, the following sites can be accessed:

General Information

http://www.uscourts.gov

http://vls.law.vill.edu

http://www.atra.org

http://www.law.indiana.edu

http://www.dri.org

STUDENT CD-ROM™

For additional materials, please go to the CD in this book.

ONLINE COMPANION™

For additional resources, please go to
http://www.paralegal.delmar.cengage.com

Strict, or Absolute, Liability

THE BIGGEST MISTAKES PARALEGALS MAKE & HOW TO AVOID THEM

Loose Lips Sink Paralegal Ships

While I was at the courthouse law library researching several issues for a major client, I stopped by the county clerk's office to file some judgments for the attorneys at the firm. While waiting in line, I met a lawyer about my age named Glenn Edwards who struck up a conversation with me. By the time I reached the front of the line, it was already noon and Glenn had asked me to lunch in the courthouse cafeteria. We were laughing and joking during lunch and he decided to walk back to the library with me. Trying to impress, I said I had to spend the rest of the afternoon working on issues where our client Viacom was expecting to sue Google.

When I returned to the office I asked a lawyer if she knew Attorney Edwards. "Well, yes . . . he's the guy you will serve with a summons because he is the designated agent for Google." I thought I was going to be sick, not so much that I was interested

(continues)

in Glenn, but that I had compromised our client's cases by informing our adversary prematurely.

LESSON LEARNED: Never discuss clients, facts of the case, or any proprietary information (confidential issues learned on the job) in public places—such as elevators, restaurants, libraries, because you never know who may be parties to an action or who is listening to your conversation.

INTRODUCTION

Intentional torts and negligence account for the bulk of torts. However, there remain several important torts to study. The remainder primarily consists of strict, or absolute, liability. Products liability is one form of strict liability. The terms *strict liability* and *absolute liability* are interchangeable. Strict liability differs from intentional torts and negligence in that fault is unnecessary to establish liability. From the defendant's standpoint, absolute liability can be serious trouble.

This chapter discusses the following:

- An overview of strict liability
- Animal owners' liability
- Abnormally dangerous activities
- Proximate cause
- Mass torts and class actions.

AN OVERVIEW OF STRICT LIABILITY

Under intentional torts and negligence, tortfeasors are held accountable for their wrongful actions. Fault is an essential part of the reasoning. What was the defendant's misconduct that hurt the plaintiff? Was it intentional, willful, and wanton, or was it negligent action? Placing the blame is second nature in negligence or intentional torts analysis.

Fault Is Irrelevant

Absolute (strict) liability holds the tortfeasor responsible for his or her behavior regardless of fault. In other words, the tortfeasor could have used every possible degree of care to protect against injuring the victim, but this would not prevent liability. Fault is irrelevant to absolute liability. The tortfeasor would be strictly liable just because he or she did something specific that hurt the plaintiff.

absolute (strict) liability | The legal responsibility for damage or injury, even if you are not at fault or negligent.

Limitations to Absolute Liability

One's sense of fair play may rebel against strict liability. One might think that it is unfair to hold a defendant accountable even if he or she did not intentionally or negligently misbehave. This fault concept extends throughout every area of law. This is why absolute liability is restricted to certain types of activities, such as abnormally dangerous tasks and defectively manufactured products, where the risk involved substantially outweighs the benefit.

Public Policy Objectives behind Strict Liability

Under strict liability, society (through its courts and legislatures) has decided that the person engaged in certain ventures should bear the risk of liability to individuals innocently injured as a consequence of the dangerous or defective item or action. It is society's decision that persons owning wild animals, using fire or explosives, or manufacturing defective products are in the best economic position to pay for plaintiffs' injuries arising from these activities.

Insurance Analogy

Absolute liability resembles insurance. Defendants are insuring, or guaranteeing, the safety of plaintiffs who come into contact with what tort law calls **abnormally dangerous (ultrahazardous) instrumentalities.** These activities or objects are dangerous by their very nature. Even if all precautions are taken, an injury might still occur.

Historical Development

Ancient English common law held the owners of animals, slaves, or objects absolutely liable for causing the death of another person. For instance, suppose a boat broke its mooring and floated downstream, colliding with and drowning a swimmer. In medieval England, the boat would be considered a *deodand,* because it killed someone. The term originated from the Latin *Deo dandum,* which translates as "a thing to be given to God." The ecclesiastical courts insisted that the offending, sinful property be seized and placed into God's service. Deodands had to be forfeited to the church or the crown, or sometimes to the injured party's surviving family, to be used in pious pursuits. It was seen as a charitable redemption: the owner would pay for his or her sinful chattel by giving it up. It did not matter that the chattel killed accidentally. This was probably one of the earliest forms of strict liability. As times change, so can "ultrahazardous" instrumentalities. For example, when first invented, airplanes were ultrahazardous, but are now considered a very safe form of transportation.

▌ANIMAL OWNERS' LIABILITY

Modern absolute liability first arose in the common law involving private ownership of wild animals and the use of fire or explosives. This section discusses owners' liability for injuries inflicted by their wild animals.

abnormally dangerous (ultrahazardous) instrumentalities | Activities or objects that are, by their very nature, extremely hazardous to persons or property. These are relevant to strict (absolute) liability cases.

Wild Animals Defined

The ancient common-law cases use the Latin term ***ferae naturae,*** meaning "wild nature," to refer to wild animals. These are animals that have naturally wild dispositions, as opposed to tame animals, which are called ***domitae naturae,*** meaning "domesticated nature." Examples of *ferae naturae* include deer, bison, elk, bear, snakes, bees, stream or ocean fish, coyotes, foxes, wild birds, lions, tigers, gophers, raccoons, opossums, or prairie dogs.

ferae naturae | (Latin) "Of wild nature." Naturally wild animals.

domitae naturae | (Latin) "Domesticated nature." Tame, domestic animals.

Ownership of Wildlife

Under ancient English common law, the king owned all wildlife in the realm. This is why poachers were often hanged or beheaded for taking the crown's property during medieval times. As English law evolved, an average person could claim ownership of a wild animal—the trick was to catch the beast. Once someone had control over a wild animal, it was considered to be his or her property until it escaped to its natural, free state. The common-law cases call this ownership the exercise of **dominion** and **control** over the wild animal. American common law holds that the state (or the federal government), under its police power, owns wildlife in trust for the benefit of all citizens. This is why one must obtain state or federal hunting or fishing licenses to take wildlife.

dominion | Legal ownership plus full actual control over something.

control | The power or authority to direct or oversee.

For example, suppose Kathleen has an apiary—in other words, she is a beekeeper. The bees are wildlife, *ferae naturae*. However, if Kathleen catches and places them in her apiary hives, they may stay and produce honey for her. Now Kathleen owns the bees. As long as she exercises dominion and control over the insects, they are hers. But once the bees fly away, they are *ferae naturae* again, and Kathleen does not own them (that is, unless she catches them again).

Importance of Wildlife Ownership

Wildlife ownership is important for purposes of absolute liability. If a wild animal injures someone, the victim cannot sue the beast (or, at the very least, cannot easily collect judgment). Instead, the plaintiff looks to the animal's owner for compensation. Owners are strictly liable for the injuries their wildlife inflicts. It does not matter that the owner exercised every precaution to safeguard others from being hurt by the wild animals. If the beast attacks and hurts someone, the owner must compensate the victim for the injuries. Because the common law presumes that wild animals are dangerous by nature, strict liability applies to any injuries they cause.

Suppose Ken's pet bear mauls a visitor to Ken's home. The victim will sue Ken under strict liability. One might argue that premises liability, using negligence theory, should apply instead, because Ken owns the land and the chattels that harmed the plaintiff, but this argument would lose. Because bears are wildlife, Ken is absolutely liable for his pet's mischief.

Comparison with Domesticated Animals

Domitae naturae are animals that the law presumes to be harmless. Examples of domestic animals include dogs, cats, pet birds, or livestock such as pigs, horses, cows, or sheep. When domesticated animals hurt someone, the common law states that the owner is liable if he or she was negligent in handling the animals. Liability would also arise if an owner intentionally used domestic animals to hurt someone. For example, suppose an attack dog's owner ordered the animal to attack a victim. This is a form of battery, as the animal would be considered an extension of the tortfeasor's body.

---

practical **application**

Check to find out if your local jurisdiction has an applicable leash law. Many municipalities have local laws requiring pet owners to keep their pets fenced in or on a leash. Should a victim be injured by a stray dog, you should inquire about local leash laws.

Vicious Propensity Rule

Owners may be held absolutely liable for injuries caused by their domestic animals if the animals exhibit vicious tendencies. When a dog growls or snarls, when a bull paws the ground and snorts, or when a cat arches its back and hisses, these are all demonstrations of vicious propensities. When a domestic animal routinely displays these characteristics to the point that it gets a reputation for viciousness, it is said to have *vicious propensities*. An owner of such an animal will be held strictly liable for any injuries the beast inflicts, under the so-called **vicious propensity rule.** All states except Indiana have adopted this common-law principle. Indiana has a hybrid vicious propensity rule, peculiar to its common-law heritage, under which an owner's negligence in handling the animal must be proven, whether or not the animal displays a vicious propensity.

vicious propensity rule | Doctrine in absolute liability cases involving domestic animals. Normally owners are not strictly liable for injuries caused by their domestic animals. However, if the animals display vicious propensities and hurt someone or their property, then the owner is absolutely liable.

Defenses in Animal Absolute Liability Cases

Normally, negligence or intentional tort defenses are ineffective against strict liability. However, certain exceptions have arisen in the common law for particular types of absolute liability, such as cases involving animals. The following defenses can protect an animal owner from strict liability:

1. Assumption of risk
2. Contributory and comparative negligence
3. Consent
4. Self-defense and defense of others

Assumption of Risk. If the individual injured by a wild (or vicious-propensity domestic) animal voluntarily assumed a known risk, with full appreciation of the dangers involved, then the owner is not strictly liable for the inflicted injuries. Courts justify this defense on equitable grounds. It would be unfair to hold owners absolutely liable for harm their animals caused if the victims chose to subject themselves to the danger.

Contributory and Comparative Negligence. Courts often rule that the plaintiff's contributory or comparative negligence in an animal attack will prevent the owner's absolute liability. Some courts state that a plaintiff's contributory negligence bars strict liability altogether. This means that the plaintiff would have to prove that the defendant (owner) was negligent in keeping the animal that attacked and hurt the plaintiff. Other courts simply ignore absolute liability theory and reshape the case in a negligence mold, in which the plaintiff's and defendant's respective degrees of negligence are compared.

Consent. An injured plaintiff might have consented to exposure to a dangerous animal. Consent is usually based upon a person's employment responsibilities while working around animals. For example, suppose Gordon works for a police-dog training facility, where he serves as an attack victim. He knows from observation and experience that the dogs are dangerous. Even if Gordon was not wearing his protective padding, and he was bitten by one of the dogs, he has implicitly consented to this danger as part of his job. Basically, this is assumption of risk couched in consent terms. The same reasoning would apply for keepers, trainers, or feeders of wild animals for zoos or circuses.

Self-Defense and Defense of Others. When a wild or vicious domestic animal attacks a victim, but the owner used the animal as a means of self-defense or defense of other persons, then the owner would not be strictly liable for the inflicted injuries. For instance, suppose someone attacks Arthur while he is out walking his dog, which has a vicious reputation around the neighborhood. To repel the danger, Arthur commands his dog to attack. His assailant is knocked to the ground, chewed up a bit, and scared away. Arthur would not be absolutely liable for the injuries caused by his dog. The same scenario would arise if Arthur saw someone attacking a member of his family or a friend and he used the dog to protect that person. However, remember the limitations to these defenses; one may not become the aggressor and still use them to escape liability. Hence, if Arthur's dog had chased the fleeing attacker down the street, Arthur could not use these defenses to avoid liability.

Dog-Bite Statutes

Most jurisdictions have statutes that have changed the common-law owner liability (and the available defenses) in dog-bite cases. These statutes can substantially affect a dog owner's liability and defenses. A few states even impose strict liability for dogs with no known vicious propensities.

Dog-bite hypotheticals present interesting applications of absolute liability. In the following example, consider the vicious propensity rule and its effects on the canine owner's liability.

 THE CASE OF THE KNOWLEDGEABLE LANDLORD

Thousands of dog-bite cases are reported each year, with the more sensational injury-causing cases making headlines. Here, the landlord as well as the owners of a dog are being sued for injuries sustained by a couple and their dog. The outcome of the case focuses on notice.

Johanna A. GORDON et al.
v.
Joey WINSTON et al.

No. CV0650040955
Superior Court of Connecticut,
Judicial District of Hartford
November 28, 2006

This case arises from an incident which allegedly occurred on March 19, 2006. The plaintiffs allege that they were both injured when a dog owned by defendants Winston and Williams attacked their leashed dog while they were on their own property.

Defendant Peter Sztaba owns the apartment building where the co-defendants lived with their dog. This building is located in close proximity to the plaintiffs' residence. Plaintiffs have sued defendant Sztaba in four counts. The Third and Fourth Counts allege that Mr. Sztaba is liable to them under *Conn. Gen.Stat.* § 22-357. In the Fifth and Sixth Counts, plaintiffs allege that the attack was caused by Mr. Sztaba's negligence, because he had prior notice "of the vicious propensities of [the dog], and said dog being allowed to roam at large by via (sic) numerous complaints from neighbors as well as a previous event in which said dog killed

a dog belonging to a neighbor." Plaintiffs allege that Mr. Sztaba was negligent in that he allowed the defendant tenants to keep the dog despite a lease provision prohibiting dogs and by failing to warn neighbors of the dog's propensities.

Defendant Sztaba has moved to strike all four counts against him.

The motion to strike is granted as to the Third and Fourth Counts. A landlord is not a "keeper" of a dog "merely because a tenant owns a dog and keeps the dog on the premises." The Third and Fourth Counts contain no allegations that Mr. Sztaba exercised sufficient control over the dog to make him a "keeper" within the meaning of § 22-357.

In *Stokes v. Lyddy,* our Appellate Court affirmed summary judgment in favor of a landlord who was sued by a nontenant bitten by a tenant's dog, with the incident occurring away from the leased premises.

Here, plaintiffs have alleged that [p]rior to said incident, the defendant, Peter S. Sztaba, was made aware of the vicious propensities of said pit bull terrier dog, and [sic] said dog being allowed to roam at large by via [sic] numerous complaints by neighbors as well as a previous event in which said dog killed a dog belonging to a neighbor.

If plaintiffs can establish, through the discovery process, that Mr. Sztaba had actual or constructive notice of the dog's prior misconduct, then it is entirely conceivable that this case would survive a summary judgment motion. The motion to strike the Fifth and Sixth Counts is therefore denied.

CASE QUESTIONS

1. Why do you suppose the plaintiffs are trying to bring an action against the landlord in addition to the owner of the dog?
2. Why would the landlord's notice of the dog's propensities change the outcome of a court decision?

hypothetical

Toby Jones owns a towing service. He uses Doberman pinscher dogs to guard the parking lot in which he keeps towed vehicles. The area is surrounded by large, barbed-wire fences with "no trespassing" signs attached every few feet. The guard dogs would bark, snarl, bite, and lunge at anyone who came near the fencing. Early one morning, Chet Paisley stopped by to claim an automobile that had been towed for illegal parking. After paying the storage fees, Chet walked back to the holding area. Toby had forgotten to chain the dogs from the night before, and they were running loose in the parking lot. When they saw Chet, they attacked and severely injured him.

The common law presumes that dogs are harmless, domestic creatures. However, there is considerable evidence that Toby's Dobermans displayed vicious propensities. Accordingly, the harmlessness presumption falls aside, and the dogs are viewed as potentially dangerous, like wild animals. Under absolute liability, Toby would be responsible for Chet's injuries. Toby's negligence or intent are irrelevant here. It only matters that the dogs were abnormally dangerous instrumentalities, because of their vicious propensities. Once strict liability applies, the result is easy: the animal owner must compensate the victim for his or her injuries.

Would the result have been different if Toby had posted signs stating, "WARNING! DANGEROUS ATTACK DOGS! DO NOT ENTER WITHOUT AUTHORIZED PERSONNEL TO ACCOMPANY YOU"? If Chet had seen such signs but entered regardless, he would have assumed the risk. Chet would have voluntarily assumed a known risk (the dangerous dogs) with full appreciation of the threat involved (being bitten or mauled). Chet would also have been contributorily negligent in entering the enclosed parking lot without Toby or another employee accompanying him.

Table 9-1 summarizes animal owner strict liability and the available defenses.

TABLE 9-1
Animal owners' absolute
liability and defenses

WILDLIFE (FERAE NATURAE)	DOMESTIC ANIMALS (DOMITAE NATURAE)	DEFENSES
Owner strictly liable for injuries caused by wild animals	Owner absolutely liable for injuries caused by domestic animals *only* if such animals display vicious propensities, or liability is imposed by statute or local ordinance	1. Assumption of risk 2. Contributory and comparative negligence 3. Consent 4. Self-defense and defense of others

▌ ABNORMALLY DANGEROUS ACTIVITIES

Abnormally dangerous activities are inherently perilous because of the actions and the devices involved. Common examples include the use of explosives, flammable substances, noxious gases, poisons, hazardous wastes (the so-called **toxic tort actions**), or (in some jurisdictions) electricity, natural gas, and water supplied through unprotected utility lines. Many early twentieth-century cases refer to *ultrahazardous activities*. This is the term used by the original *Restatement of Torts* § 520 (the *First Restatement*). Although some courts split hairs distinguishing ultrahazardous from abnormally dangerous, the expressions are essentially interchangeable.

toxic tort actions | Actions involving toxic chemicals, pollution, hazardous waste disposal and transportation, and other environmentally sensitive issues. Many tort theories, including trespass to land, negligence, absolute liability for ultrahazardous substances, products liability, and nuisance apply.

Restatement (Second) Rule

Restatement (Second) of Torts § 520 declares that persons engaged in abnormally dangerous activities shall be strictly liable for injuries caused by their actions. The *Restatement* lists several criteria for absolute liability:

1. The abnormally dangerous activity created a high risk of substantial injury to an individual or his or her property.
2. This risk could not be removed through the use of reasonable care.
3. The activity is not commonly undertaken (the common usage principle).
4. The activity was inappropriately undertaken in the place in which the victim was harmed.
5. The hazards that the activity creates outweigh the benefits that the activity brings to the community.

High Risk of Substantial Injury. To be abnormally dangerous, the defendant's activity must create a great threat of seriously injuring the plaintiff or the plaintiff's property. For instance, consider a highway construction company that uses dynamite to excavate rock and earth. Dynamite is dangerous stuff. It presents an enormous risk of injuring others nearby if it is not used properly. The threat of harm is significant, as people could be killed or their property destroyed if the dynamite is not used correctly.

Reasonable Care. If the tortfeasor could have eliminated the risk of harm through the use of reasonable care, then the activity is not abnormally dangerous, and absolute liability does not apply. For example, a utility company could exercise reasonable care and protect citizens from the great threat posed by electricity or natural gas simply by using insulated wires or double-sealed underground pipelines. Reasonable care could easily eliminate the risks of electrocution or explosion. If the utility company actually used these (or other) reasonable precautions, then the activity (supplying electricity or natural gas) would not be ultrahazardous, even if a victim nonetheless was injured.

Note the hidden implication in this element, though. Failure to use reasonable care to safeguard others from the risks involved in the activity could make it abnormally dangerous. For instance, suppose a utility company ran electricity through uninsulated wires. Many courts have held that this would make the activity ultrahazardous, so the utility company would be strictly liable for injuries. However, not all courts interpret the *Second Restatement*'s reasonable care standard in this way.

Common Usage Principle. Abnormally dangerous activities and substances are those not commonly undertaken or used in everyday life. This is sometimes called the **common usage (use) principle.** For instance, consider explosives, toxic chemicals, or poisonous gases. How often does the average person use them? Does anyone in the reader's neighborhood? What about the manufacturing plant across town? In other words, it could be said that the vast majority of the public does not use such substances. These, then, would be examples of abnormally dangerous substances, because they are not commonly used.

> **common usage (use) principle** | Doctrine in strict liability cases that defines abnormally dangerous activities and substances as those not commonly undertaken or used in everyday life.

What about flammable substances? Many courts have included these as ultrahazardous items. But virtually everyone uses gasoline every day. Would gasoline not fall within common usage? Whether gasoline is abnormally dangerous depends upon how it is being used. Suppose SludgeCo Oil Company operates a gasoline refinery, with several massive fuel tanks storing hundreds of thousands of gallons. Few people in a community have such facilities in their backyards. Gasoline may be commonly used, but not in the way this storage facility uses it. The gas one keeps in his or her garage for the lawn mower would not be ultrahazardous; however, the huge storage tanks would be abnormally dangerous.

Inappropriate Use in Certain Place. To be ultrahazardous, the activity or substance must have been inappropriately performed or used in the place in which the victim was harmed. For example, suppose a chemical manufacturer opened a plant adjacent to a housing subdivision that uses well water. Suppose that the plant dumped toxic chemicals into holding ponds on its premises. Harmful chemicals could seep into the ground and contaminate the water supplies of nearby residents. Perhaps several of these homeowners became ill as a consequence. The activity (using toxic chemical retention ponds) is abnormally dangerous because it created a serious risk of substantial harm, was not of common usage, and was inappropriately undertaken at the location in which the plaintiffs were harmed (adjacent to residences).

Hazards Outweigh Benefits: Balancing Test. Courts often apply a balancing test to decide if an activity is abnormally dangerous. Such an analysis compares the dangers created by the activity with the benefits that the community derives from the activity. This is similar to the benefits analysis used in many nuisance cases.

For example, suppose a local builder is building a new road to improve access between hospitals and an isolated rural town. The construction crew uses dynamite to clear the area for the road. A nearby homeowner suffers structural damage to her house as a result of the blasting and sues the builder under strict liability theory. Courts following the *Second Restatement* would balance the benefits derived against the risks involved. The road would improve the community's access to hospital facilities. The dangers created by dynamite use, which in this case involved structural damage, are probably outweighed by these benefits.

Many courts have applied the *Second Restatement*'s approach throughout this century. Several jurisdictions, however, have rejected the rule, either in whole or in part. Still, the *Second Restatement* provides a comprehensive, general formula for analyzing abnormally dangerous activities and absolute liability.

Defenses

Many state legislatures have enacted statutes protecting certain abnormally dangerous activities from strict liability. These statutes usually shield public utilities distributing electricity and natural gas, private contractors performing construction (particularly highway) work for the government, and municipal zoos or parks that maintain wild animals. Under these statutes, the protected entities cannot be held absolutely liable for injuries caused by wild animals or ultrahazardous activities. Instead, plaintiffs must prove that the protected defendants were negligent or committed intentional torts, unless the defendants have purchased liability insurance to cover injuries under these circumstances.

THE CASE OF THE ULTRAHAZARDOUS ACTIVITY

Land owners are becoming increasingly concerned with the safety of their groundwater. In this case, the plaintiffs claimed that the use of certain industrial solvents, which were used as degreasers in preparation for painting, was an ultrahazardous activity, and that defendants should be strictly liable.

CEREGHINO
v.
BOEING CO.

826 F. Supp. 1243 (D. Or. 1993)
United States District Court for the District of Oregon
May 10, 1993
Jelderks, United States Magistrate Judge

Plaintiffs Joseph A. Cereghino, on his own behalf and as personal representative of the estate of Angelo Cereghino, and Mario Cereghino (collectively Cereghinos) bring this action, based on the release of certain chemicals, against the Boeing Company (Boeing), International Controls Corporation (ICC), Datron Systems, Inc. (Datron), and Elecspec Corporation (Elecspec). . . .

The Cereghinos own farmland in Multnomah County, Oregon, located on the north side of Northeast Sandy Boulevard near the intersection of Northeast 185th Avenue and Sandy Boulevard. Industrial activities giving rise to this action began in 1964 on the south side of Sandy Boulevard, opposite the Cereghinos' land. At that time, Electronic Specialty Company (ESC), which is not a party to this action, began to operate a manufacturing facility on the site.

* * *

In early 1986, Boeing discovered that groundwater on the industrial site contained hazardous industrial solvents. It reported this finding to the United States Environmental Protection Agency, and to the Oregon Department of Environmental Quality. In July 1986, Boeing entered into a Consent Order and Compliance Agreement with those agencies. . . .

In August 1986, the Cereghinos were notified that the groundwater in their land was contaminated with trichloroethylene (TCE). They subsequently learned

that TCE and trichloroethane (TCA) had migrated into their groundwater from neighboring property. TCE and TCA are industrial solvents used as degreasers and in preparation for painting. These compounds are listed as hazardous wastes under the Federal Resource, Conservation and Recovery Act. 40 C.F.R. § 261.31. Boeing stopped using TCE in 1980. The levels of TCA detected in the groundwater on the Cereghinos' property do not exceed federal drinking water standards. TCE levels do exceed those standards.

Plaintiffs filed this action in January 1992. Their amended complaint, filed in January 1993, asserts that Boeing has owned the industrial site and has operated industrial facilities on that site "from about 1963 to the present, and at all material times there- to. . . ." They also allege that, from 1968 to 1985, ICC, Datron, and Elecspec operated manufacturing facilities on the land owned by Boeing, and that these defendants "used, handled, stored and disposed of hazardous substances, including but not limited to [TCE] and [TCA], in the course of the operation of the manufacturing and/or industrial facilities located on Boeing's land."

* * *

[The court's discussion of issues other than the ultrahazardous activity claim have been omitted.]

Plaintiffs' ultrahazardous activity claim asserts that defendants' "use, handling, storage and disposal of hazardous substances" constituted an ultrahazardous activity. This claim adds that defendants knew, or in the exercise of reasonable care should have known, that releases resulting from these activities would substantially harm landholders such as themselves.

Strict liability may be imposed on those who engage in "ultrahazardous" activities. An activity is

(continues)

considered ultrahazardous if it is "extraordinary, exceptional, or unusual, considering the locality in which it is carried on; when there is a risk of grave harm from such abnormality; and when the risk cannot be eliminated by the exercise of reasonable care. . . ." No Oregon court has decided whether the use of solvents such as TCE and TCA constitutes an ultrahazardous activity.

Boeing has submitted the uncontroverted affidavit of an expert who states that TCE and TCA are commonly-used degreasing agents, and opines that "it is entirely feasible to use both TCA and TCE

in ways that would prevent any contamination of soil or groundwater." Boeing has also submitted uncontroverted evidence that use of degreasing solvents is common in the area around its property, and that plaintiffs themselves use solvents in maintenance of their farming equipment.

Boeing has shown the absence of material issues of fact as to whether use of the solvents in question here constituted an ultrahazardous activity. Use of solvents cannot be classified as ultrahazardous in this case and the motion for summary judgment on this claim should be granted.

CASE QUESTIONS

1. Do you agree with the United States District Court's decision?
2. What could a home purchaser do to prevent being surprised about potentially toxic chemicals being found on land years after the purchase?

THE CASE OF ASBESTOS IN THE AIR

John Maiorana, a 40-year-old man, died of cancer. Thirteen years prior to his death, Maiorana was exposed to asbestos on the job. How can his estate show a definite connection between the cancer and the asbestos? In toxic tort actions, plaintiff's counsel has the difficult task of proving causation, when the onset of disease may occur many years after exposure to a potentially harmful substance.

IN RE JOINT EASTERN & SOUTHERN DISTRICTS ASBESTOS LITIGATION

United States District Court of Appeals,
Second Circuit
52 F.3d 1124 (2d Cir. 1995)
April 6, 1995
Cabranes, Circuit Judge

This case marks the convergence of epidemiological evidence, probabilistic causation in carcinogenic torts, and the important issue of the extent to which a trial court may assess the sufficiency of

scientific evidence, in light of the Supreme Court's recent holding in *Daubert v. Merrell Dow Pharmaceuticals, Inc.*, ____ U.S.___, 113 S.Ct. 2786, 125 L.Ed.2d 469 (1993). That decision enlarged district courts' "gatekeeping" roles in appraising the admissibility of scientific evidence. The central question before us is the standard governing federal judges' evaluation of the *sufficiency*—as opposed to admissibility—of scientific evidence already admitted.

In 1983, John Maiorana ("Maiorana") died of colon cancer. His widow, plaintiff/appellant Arlene M.

Maiorana ("plaintiff"), claimed that her husband's illness was caused by exposure to Cafco D., an asbestos spray manufactured by defendant-appellee United States Mineral Products Co. ("USMP"). This spray was used for insulation on two construction sites—the World Trade Center in New York City and Meadowbrook Hospital in Nassau County, New York—where Maiorana was employed as a sheet metal worker.

The scientific community is divided on whether asbestos exposure significantly increases the risk of contracting colon cancer. At trial in the United States District Court for the Southern District of New York . . . , both plaintiff and USMP brought expert witnesses and numerous epidemiological studies to bear on their likely causal factors. After considering this evidence, the jury on February 10, 1993, returned a verdict in favor of the plaintiff.

In an opinion dated July 23, 1993, the district court granted USMP's motion for judgment as a matter of law, setting aside the jury verdict. We believe that the district court . . . inappropriately usurped the role of the jury. . . .

Cafco D is a fireproof asbestos spray formerly used for insulating construction sites. In the fall of 1969 and spring of 1970, two major construction projects where Cafco D was used were the World Trade Center ("WTC") in Manhattan and the Meadowbrook Hospital ("Meadowbrook") in Nassau County, New York.

Maiorana was employed as a sheet metal worker for a small company which performed sheet metal work on both the WTC and Meadowbrook projects. Plaintiff contends that Maiorana and the other sheet metal workers—who worked in close proximity to the asbestos sprayers—were exposed to asbestos through contact with Cafco D.

In January 1983, Maiorana was diagnosed with colon cancer. Six months later, on June 16, 1983, Maiorana died from the disease. He was 40.

Plaintiff filed her original complaint on July 28, 1987, in connection with a case brought by sixteen plaintiffs on behalf of themselves and their deceased spouses against a number of manufacturers of

asbestos-containing products. These manufacturers included USMP, the producer of Cafco D. By way of several third-party complaints and impleaders, a number of third-party defendants were added to the litigation. . . .

In a series of rulings in 1991, the district court awarded summary judgment in favor of defendants, including USMP, on the grounds that the epidemiological and clinical evidence of causation were insufficient to meet the preponderance standard.

On appeal, we reversed the grant of summary judgment and remanded for further proceedings, concluding that the evidence was sufficient to survive summary judgment. We found that plaintiff had presented not only epidemiological studies in support of a causal connection between asbestos exposure and colon cancer, but also clinical evidence—in the form of Maiorana's own medical records and personal history, which plaintiff's experts used to exclude other possible causal factors. We found that the statements of the plaintiff's experts, viewed in the light most favorable to plaintiff, were the "equivalent of stating that asbestos exposure more probably than not caused the colon cancer."

From January 20 to February 10, 1993, the case was tried before a jury. By the time the jury was ready to deliver its verdict, all the original direct defendants but USMP had settled. The jury found in favor of plaintiff in the amount of $4,510,000. After allocating percentages of fault among USMP and third-party defendants, the jury found USMP 50% responsible for plaintiff's damages and found three of the third-party defendants approximately equally negligent (both Tishman and Castagna were assessed to be 14% responsible; subcontractor Mario & DiBono was assessed to be 15% responsible). In addition, the jury absolved the Port Authority of any liability.

On March 10, 1993, USMP moved for judgment as a matter of law. . . .

In an extensive and thoughtful opinion dated July 23, 1993, the district court granted USMP's motion for judgment as a matter of law. The district court based its decision on its findings that (1) plaintiff's epidemiological evidence was insufficient to support

(continues)

a causal connection between asbestos exposure and colon cancer, and (2) plaintiff had failed to present affirmative clinical evidence to overcome the paucity of statistically significant epidemiological proof.

Epidemiology is the study of disease patterns in human populations. It "attempts to define a relationship between a disease and a factor suspected of causing it." As the district court observed, epidemiological evidence is indispensable in toxic and carcinogenic tort actions where direct proof of causation is lacking.

Epidemiologists speak in the statistical language of risks and probabilities. . . .

In order for plaintiff to present a jury question on the issue of causation, the district court noted that she bore the burden of demonstrating that asbestos exposure was "more likely than not" the cause of Maiorana's colon cancer.

* * *

Plaintiff's expert witnesses—Dr. Steven Markowitz and Dr. Carl Shy—testified at trial that there was a causal relationship between asbestos exposure and colon cancer. The district court, however, conducted an independent and detailed analysis of many of the epidemiological studies and concluded that there was no basis for plaintiff's experts' conclusions. . . . The district court criticized the methodologies employed in these studies, however, and found that when considered in the context of all the studies, plaintiff's evidence "establishe[d] only the conclusions that the association between exposure to asbestos and developing colon cancer is, at best, weak, and that the consistency of this purported association across the studies is, at best, poor."

* * *

Given plaintiff's failure to show that any asbestos fibers were found in Maiorana's cancerous tissues, the district court found that the sum total of plaintiff's evidence did not justify the jury's finding of causation, and that "the jury's finding could only have been the result of sheer surmise and conjecture."

* * *

In the present case, the sufficiency inquiry bears on the factual issue of causation—whether the body of plaintiff's evidence was sufficient to persuade a rational jury that Maiorana's exposure to asbestos more likely than not caused his colon cancer. Causation in toxic torts normally comprises two separate inquiries: whether the epidemiological or other scientific evidence establishes a causal link between c (asbestos exposure) and d (colon cancer), and whether plaintiff is within the class of persons to which inferences from the general causation evidence should be applied.

For the reasons stated below, we hold that the district court overstepped the boundaries set forth in *Daubert*. It impermissibly crossed the line from assessing evidentiary reliability to usurping the role of the jury. Accordingly, we reverse the district court's entry of judgment as a matter of law with respect to the jury verdict in favor of plaintiff.

* * *

The issue before the district court in this case, then, was whether the epidemiological and clinical data already in evidence was sufficient to justify the jury's verdict finding causation.

* * *

In rejecting plaintiff's experts' differential diagnosis, the district court gave little weight to Maiorana's relatively young age of death. While conceding it was "uncommon for a 40-year-old man to develop colon cancer," the court emphasized the absence of asbestos fibers in Maiorana's colon cancer tissues and the typical latency period of more than 20 years for colon cancer, compared to only 13 years for Maiorana. The district court's conclusions regarding latency periods, however, ignored Markowitz's testimony on the study by Seidman which indicated an increased incidence of gastrointestinal cancer among individuals exposed to asbestos 10 years previously. That a latency period of 13 years was too short appeared to constitute an independent medical conclusion by the district court.

For the above reasons, we hold that the district court erred in ruling that plaintiff presented insufficient epidemiological and clinical evidence to support the jury's verdict finding causation. In our view, the district court impermissibly made a number of independent scientific conclusions—without granting plaintiff the requisite favorable inferences—in a manner not authorized by *Daubert*.

* * *

By way of summary:

On the issue of causation, we reverse the district court's entry of judgment as a matter of law, and we reinstate the jury verdict in favor of plaintiff. The district court erred in failing to draw all reasonable inferences in favor of plaintiff. . . .

In view of the conditional order for a remittitur, we remand to the district court to provide plaintiff with the requisite opportunity to decide whether to accept the reduced verdict or submit to a new trial.

CASE QUESTIONS

1. Normally, the statute of limitations for tort actions is just a few years. Is it fair to hold a defendant liable for an incident that may have occurred ten, twenty, or more years ago? Explain.
2. What are some of the potential problems a defendant would face in defending a matter based on an occurrence that transpired many years ago?

Public Policy Objectives behind Statutory Immunity

Legislatures often justify immunity statutes on the grounds that government (and the private companies that often work under governmental contracts) must be protected from the harshness of strict liability if certain essential activities are to be performed. How, the argument goes, can governments build roads, operate zoos or parks, supply utilities, or enable private industry to satisfy energy demands, if these activities carry the burden of strict liability whenever someone inadvertently gets hurt? This reasoning is similar to the benefits balancing act that courts often apply under the *Second Restatement* approach. Because legislatures enact statutes, and the public can change the legislature (through voting) and thus change the statutes, citizens who disagree with the immunity laws can elect new legislators to modify these provisions.

Cases involving toxic substances often revolve around absolute liability theory, applying the abnormally dangerous activity analysis. Of all the causes of action usually associated with toxic torts (including trespass to land, negligence, nuisance, and strict liability), absolute liability offers the best common-law avenue for plaintiffs to recover.

THE CASE OF THE SATURDAY NIGHT SPECIAL

Many Americans recall the 1981 assassination attempt on President Ronald Reagan. Several bystanders were seriously injured when John Hinckley fired his fateful shots. Searching for a deeper pocket than Hinckley's, one injured person sued the manufacturer of Hinckley's gun, commonly called a "Saturday Night Special," under ultrahazardous activity and products liability theories. The D.C. Court of Appeals shot down the appellants' attempt to hold the manufacturer absolutely liable.

(continues)

DELAHANTY

v.

HINCKLEY

District of Columbia Court of Appeals
564 A.2d 758 (D.C. 1989)
October 11, 1989
Ferren, Associate Judge

Thomas and Jean Delahanty, appellants, filed suit in the United States District Court for the District of Columbia against John Hinckley for injuries Thomas suffered when Hinckley attempted to assassinate President Ronald Reagan. The Delahantys also sued the manufacturer of the gun, R.G. Industries, Inc., its foreign parent company, Roehm, and individual officers of Roehm.

Appellants advanced three legal theories for holding the gun manufacturers liable in these circumstances: negligence, strict products liability . . . , and a "social utility" claim apparently based on strict liability for abnormally dangerous activities under *Restatement (Second) of Torts* §§ 519, 520 (1977). . . .

The District Court dismissed appellants' complaint against the gun manufacturers and their officers for failure to state a claim upon which relief could be granted. On appeal, the United States Court of Appeals for the District of Columbia Circuit *sua sponte* asked this court . . . to decide whether, in the District of Columbia, "manufacturers and distributors of Saturday Night Specials may be strictly liable for injuries arising from these guns' criminal use." On consideration of this question, we conclude that traditional tort theories—negligence and strict liability under the *Restatement (Second) of Torts*—provide no basis for holding the gun manufacturer liable. . . .

We reject each of the theories appellants have advanced in the federal courts and in this court. . . .

Appellants also present what they call a "social utility claim," arguing that the manufacturer should be held strictly liable because the type of gun in this case is "inherently and abnormally dangerous with no social value." Appellants appear to base this claim . . . on liability for abnormally dangerous activities, *Restatement (Second) of Torts* §§ 519, 520, a doctrine not yet explicitly adopted in the District of Columbia. . . .

Like other courts that have considered the issue . . . we reject application of the "abnormally dangerous activity" doctrine to gun manufacture and sale.

Appellants argue that the marketing of the guns is the abnormally dangerous activity for which the manufacturers should be held liable. We cannot agree. The cause of action under *Restatement* § 519 applies only to activities that are dangerous in themselves and to injuries that result directly from the dangerous activity. "The marketing of a handgun is not dangerous in and of itself, and when injury occurs, it is not the direct result of the sale itself, but rather the result of actions taken by a third party." Furthermore, handgun marketing cannot be classified as abnormally dangerous by applying the factors of *Restatement* § 520. . . . For example, any high degree of risk of harm, or any likelihood that such harm will be great, would result from the use, not the marketing as such, of handguns. . . .

In sum, given appellants' proffered theories, we perceive no basis under the facts alleged for holding the gun manufacturers and their officers liable under the law of the District of Columbia for Hinckley's criminal use of the gun.

CASE QUESTIONS

1. Apart from negligence or strict liability, is there another avenue by which manufacturers and sellers of "Saturday Night Specials" could be held absolutely liable for resulting injuries when the weapons are used in crimes? What governmental agency would have to be involved in this process?
2. What does *sua sponte* mean, as used in the court's opinion?

hypothetical

Suppose local businesses operated a Fourth of July fireworks celebration, which involved shooting the fireworks into the air high above town. Suppose excessive explosives were used in the fireworks. When they were detonated, flaming debris fell onto nearby houses, causing many fires. Could the homeowners succeed in a strict liability lawsuit against the companies responsible for the fireworks display?

Were the fireworks abnormally dangerous activities? Apply the *Second Restatement*'s criteria for absolute liability. Fireworks exploding in mid-air create a tremendous risk that flaming debris could fall onto buildings' roofs, setting fires. The threat and the harm are substantial. Could reasonable care have avoided the risk? Fireworks that explode in the air are going to fall somewhere, perhaps in flaming pieces. No degree of reasonable care could prevent the danger of resulting fires. Aerial fireworks of the types described in this example are not commonly used by the public. The fireworks were inappropriately used in the area in which the fires occurred, because the power used was excessive and the fireworks detonated above the houses, subjecting them to the severe fire risk. The threat of harm outweighs the benefits to the community, as fireworks displays are conducted only once or twice per year and the benefits are purely aesthetic and momentary. The fireworks promoters will be strictly liable to the homeowners. (This conclusion assumes, of course, that there are no state statutes or local ordinances granting the fireworks promoters immunity from absolute liability.)

Table 9-2 summarizes absolute liability for abnormally dangerous activities. All absolute liability cases, as discussed in this chapter, must satisfy the requirements of proximate cause.

Definitions and Examples	Defenses
Abnormally dangerous = Ultrahazardous	Statutory immunities for certain types of ultrahazardous activities
These activities are, by their very nature, perilous	Most often include governmental activities involving uses of explosives, chemicals, or energy service
Examples: use of explosives, flammable substances, noxious gases, or poisons	Immunities reflect public policy objectives to balance necessary public services against individual right to compensation for injury
Some courts include unprotected use of utilities (electricity, natural gas, water)	

TABLE 9-2
Absolute liability for abnormally dangerous activities and defenses

▍ SCOPE OF LIABILITY: PROXIMATE CAUSE

Proximate cause in absolute liability cases is defined similarly to proximate cause in negligence cases. Animals or abnormally dangerous activities must proximately cause the victim's injuries if the tortfeasor is to be held strictly liable. For absolute liability purposes, **proximate cause** has the following elements:

1. The plaintiff's injuries must have been a reasonably foreseeable consequence of the defendant's actions.
2. The victim must have been a foreseeable plaintiff (meaning that it must have been reasonably foreseeable that the plaintiff would be injured as a result of the defendant's activities).

These elements are defined the same as in negligence theory.

proximate cause | The "legal cause" of an accident or other injury (which may have several actual causes). The *proximate cause* of an injury is not necessarily the closest thing in time or space to the injury.

No Duty of Reasonable Care

Negligence is irrelevant to strict liability; therefore, the duty of reasonable care, as used in negligence, is also irrelevant.

In the hypotheticals discussed throughout this chapter, apply the proximate cause standard to each example. Did the tortfeasor's actions proximately cause the victim's injuries? A variety of answers are possible. As with negligence, proximate cause in absolute liability cases can be a puzzle. Exhibit 9-1 shows a notice for a proposed class action settlement.

▍ MASS TORTS AND CLASS ACTIONS

A **mass tort** occurs when a large group of people are injured as a result of a single tortious act. As the world becomes more densely populated, the chances for mass injury to people resulting from a single incident, product, or exposure greatly increases.

mass tort | When large groups of people are injured as a result of a single tortious act. A mass tort typically involves thousands of claimants, years of litigation, and millions of dollars in attorneys' fees and costs. Generally, a smaller number of defendants are involved.

A mass tort combines many legal cases into a single trial. Each plaintiff of a mass tort is treated like an individual with his or her own individual lawsuit, rather than as a member of a group. In mass torts, many cases that are similar are argued together, saving time and money. Some examples of mass torts that have recently been brought involve the following issues: Accutane, Asbestos, Bextra/Celebrex, Ciba Geigy, Depo-Provera, HRT, Mahwah Toxic Dump Site, Ortho Evra, Risperdal/Seroquel/Zyprexa, Vioxx, and Zometa/Aredia. These cases generally involve a large number of claims regarding a single product, and common facts and legal issues.

The tragic events of September 11, 2001, when planes crashed into the World Trade towers in New York, are examples of a mass tort. More than a hundred thousand people in New York were affected by this attack through loss of life, injury, property, or lost jobs. Countless others have been displaced from their apartments and offices.

If You Are a Licensed Driver
Or Own a Motor Vehicle

A Proposed Class Action Settlement May Affect Your Rights

Para Una Notificacion en Espanol, Llamar o Visitar Nuestro Website

There is a Proposed Settlement in a class action lawsuit, *Fresco, et al. v. Automotive Directions, Inc., et al.,* Case No. 03-61063-CIV-MARTINEZ, in the U.S. District Court for the Southern District of Florida.

The Proposed Settlement affects a "Class", or group, of people that may include you. This notice is just a summary of your rights. To get complete information you should visit www.DPPAsettlement.com or call 1-888-279-4224.

What Is the Case About?

The people who filed this lawsuit, the plaintiffs, claim that the Settling Defendants knowingly obtained, used or disclosed personal information from motor vehicle records in violation of a federal law, the Driver's Privacy Protection Act ("DPPA").

The companies that were sued, the Settling Defendants, don't think they did anything wrong. They agreed to the Proposed Settlement to avoid the further expense, inconvenience, and burden of this litigation.

Who Is Involved?

The Class includes all persons whose Personal Information or Highly Restricted Personal Information (as those terms are defined by the DPPA) was obtained, used or disclosed by any of the Settling Defendants from April 1, 1998 through the date that the Court approves the Final Judgement.

Settling Defendants are: Automotive Directions, Inc.; ChoicePoint Inc.; ChoicePoint Precision Marketing Inc.; ChoicePoint Public Records Inc.; ChoicePoint Services Inc.; eFunds Corporation; Experian Information Solutions, Inc.; KnowX LLC; Reed Elsevier Inc.; and Seisint, Inc. Two other Defendants in the lawsuit, Acxiom Corporation and R.L. Polk & Co., have not agreed to this Proposed Settlement. The lawsuit will continue against these Defendants.

What Does the Proposed Settlement Provide?

The relief provided is injunctive. This means that the Settling Defendants have agreed to design, implement and maintain specific and substantial procedures to enhance compliance with the DPPA when they obtain, use or disclose information regulated by the DPPA. There will be no monetary recovery for Class Members. However, if you have actual money damages, you can file a lawsuit on your own.

Who Represents Me?

The Court has appointed attorneys to represent the Class. Class Counsel will request that the Court award attorneys' fees and expenses in an amount not to exceed

EXHIBIT 9-1
Legal notice for a proposed class action settlement

(continues)

EXHIBIT 9-1 *(continued)*

$25 million. You may hire your own attorney, if you wish. However, you will be responsible for your attorney's fees and expenses.

What Are My Legal Rights?

If the Court approves the Proposed Settlement, you will be bound by the Court's decisions. You will not be able to sue the Settling Defendants for the claims that were made in this lawsuit, including claims for statutory liquidated damages. But you will be able to sue for actual money damages in an individual lawsuit. For full information about the rights you are giving up, please read the *Notice of Proposed Class Action Settlement.*

You can tell the Court if you do not like the Proposed Settlement. To object or comment, you must send a letter that is mailed and postmarked no later than September 25, 2007, as outlined in the *Notice of Proposed Class Action Settlement.*

Will the Court Approve the Proposed Settlement?

The Court will hold a Final Approval Hearing on October 24, 2007 at 10:00 A.M. to consider whether the Proposed Settlement is fair, reasonable, and adequate and the motion for attorneys' fees and expenses. If comments or objections have been received, the Court will consider them at this time.

For complete information on the Proposed Settlement, and to get a copy of the *Notice of Proposed Class Action Settlement,*

Call: 1-888-279-4224, Visit: www.DPPAsettlement.com, Or Write: DPPA Settlement Administrator, P.O. Box 296, Minneapolis, MN 55440-0296.

Recent cases brought against the tobacco companies, manufacturers of silicone breast implants, and securities companies are just a few other examples of large numbers of people injured as a result of the same incident, accident, product, exposure, or misrepresentation. Very few law firms could handle the enormous time and money constraints posed by mass tort claims. Accordingly, some firms have joined together to act in representing those injured by mass torts.

Class Action

A mass tort is distinguishable from a **class action.** A class action encompasses a smaller group of plaintiffs that are harmed. In a class action a lawsuit is brought by an individual for himself or herself and other persons in the same situation. To bring a class action, you must convince the court that there are too many

class action | A lawsuit brought for yourself and other persons in the same situation. To bring a *class action*, you must convince the court that there are too many persons in the class (group) to make them all individually a part of a lawsuit and that your interests are the same as theirs, so that you can adequately represent their needs.

persons in the class (group) to make them all individually a part of the lawsuit and that your interests are the same as theirs so that you can adequately represent their needs (i.e., wage and hour claim against employer). There have been several recent class actions against fast-food restaurants claiming they are the cause of obesity and conditions such as diabetes, high blood pressure, and heart disease. One such case was brought in the District of Columbia by a physician.

THE CASE OF THE MASS TOXIC TORT

This case involves a mass toxic tort litigation concerning a colorless, liquid chemical, benzene. It was used at multiple manufacturing plants and work sites by multiple defendants without issue for many years. Benzene is obtained from coal tar and used as a solvent for resins and fats and used in the manufacture of dyes. It is very difficult to allege at what point in time which chemical made with benzene caused a plaintiff's particular illness. Here, two different plaintiffs involved in this case have repeatedly attempted to amend their pleadings to give better notice to the defendants. The court weighs the competing interests of the plaintiffs who are trying to bring their claims for injuries, versus the defendants who seek to properly defend themselves.

IN RE BENZENE LITIGATION.
Roy Hamill and Joyce Hamill, his wife.
Kay Heddinger, Individually and as Surviving Spouse of Harold Heddinger, Deceased.
C.A. Nos. 05C-09-020-JRS (BEN),
06C-05-295-JRS (BEN)
Superior Court of Delaware, New Castle County
Submitted: October 26, 2006
Decided: February 26, 2007

Several defendants in this mass tort litigation have filed motions to dismiss complaints on the grounds that plaintiffs have failed to plead sufficient facts relating to their long term occupational exposure to benzene to meet Delaware's pleading req.uirements and to state a cause of action. The motions ask the Court to measure the adequacy of the complaints.

Mr. and Mrs. Hamill filed their original complaint on September 1, 2005, alleging injuries resulting from Mr. Hamill's occupational exposure to products containing benzene. The defendants were divided into two categories: product defendants and premises

defendants. The product defendants included those who allegedly manufactured or distributed the benzene-containing products to which Mr. Hamill was exposed. The premises defendants included those who owned or operated the properties where Mr. Hamill alleged his exposure occurred.

Between November 3, 2005 and December 30, 2005, multiple defendants moved to dismiss the first Hamill complaint for failure to state a claim upon which relief may be granted and for failure to plead fraud and negligence with particularity.

After announcing the standard it would apply to the motions, the Court dismissed the first amended Hamill complaint because it did not adequately identify the benzene-containing products to which Mr. Hamill allegedly was exposed or the locations where the exposure allegedly occurred. The dismissal was entered without prejudice and with leave to amend.

In reaching its decision on the first motions to dismiss, the Court attempted to balance the defendants' need for sufficient notice of the facts supporting the

(continues)

plaintiffs' claims against the potential prejudice the plaintiffs might suffer if required to plead too many details.

On August 31, 2006, Mr. and Mrs. Hamill filed their Fifth Complaint.

The Fifth Hamill Complaint is 47 pages long, 34 of which are devoted to pleading facts. The facts appear to be divided into three parts: the first addresses Mr. Hamill's employment experience and generally describes his alleged exposure to benzene at six identified work sites. In the second section, Mr. Hamill describes in more detail the premises where he alleges he was exposed to benzene. The third section identifies the products to which Mr. Hamill alleges he was exposed during his work history.

Six of the twenty-three named defendants moved to dismiss the Fifth Hamill Complaint. All six are premises defendants.

On May 26, 2006, more than a month after the Court ruled on the first motions to dismiss and set the standard governing the degree of particularity required in her complaint, Kay Heddinger filed her original complaint.

On September 13, 2006, apparently in response to several motions to dismiss her initial complaint, Mrs. Heddinger filed her First Amended Complaint ("the Second Heddinger Complaint") in which she dropped the misrepresentation claims against all defendants.

The Second Heddinger Complaint is 28 pages long with 11 pages devoted to pleading facts.

Four product defendants and the lone premises defendant have moved to dismiss the Second Heddinger Complaint (hereinafter collectively "the Heddinger defendants").

Among the unique difficulties presented in toxic tort litigation is the well-recognized phenomenon whereby plaintiffs who were unwittingly exposed to the hazardous substance years before any injury is manifested are unable, years later, to identify the product(s) and/or the manufacturer(s) of the product(s) to which they were exposed.

There are several compelling reasons to require a plaintiff meaningfully to identify the product or premises at issue and the time and place of exposure. First, in toxic tort cases, plaintiffs typically name multiple defendants. These defendants are entitled at the pleading stage to isolate the wrong they are alleged to have committed. Second, product defendants must be able to ascertain whether other entities—e.g., component part manufacturers, designers, distributors—should be brought into the litigation as third-party defendants. This can only occur after the defendants are advised of the specific product(s) at issue, and the time frame of the alleged exposure. Finally, defendants must be able to evaluate the condition and composition of the products and/or premises at issue at the time of alleged exposure and compare these conditions to those that have existed at other relevant time frames in order to determine if others may be liable for subsequent alterations.

The Court attempted to strike a balance between the competing interests when it issued its oral ruling on April 3, 2006. Toxic tort plaintiffs usually cannot identify the products by brand name or the premises by address, nor should they be expected to do so. But, by virtue of the fact that they cannot provide the kind of product or premises identification typically provided in a products or premises liability action, plaintiffs must attempt to draw a picture for these defendants by pleading factual circumstances that may not otherwise be required.

By necessity, this effort will require the plaintiffs to plead more facts to make the point that they could make more succinctly if they possessed a specific product name or a specific property location.

With respect to claims against product defendants, when a plaintiff is unable specifically to identify the product at issue, it is reasonable to expect the plaintiff to identify a class of products within which the allegedly defective product fits. In the benzene litigation, the allegedly defective products all seem to take a liquid form of one sort or another. Vague descriptions such as "liquid," "fluid," "solvent," "fuel," without more, do not provide fair notice of the product at issue. These descriptions, however, when coupled with a meaningful explanation of the location and manner in which the product was used, will begin to draw a picture from which the defendants can ascertain which of their products are involved in the litigation. Plaintiffs' pre-filing due diligence must narrow the time frame to no more than a span of years, not decades. Defendants should not bear the burden of pouring through their inventory of products over many years, with little guidance from the plaintiffs, in order to track down potentially relevant products, particularly given that the benzene litigation is in its relative infancy with little institutional history to narrow the products potentially at issue.

To summarize, a plaintiff may identify the premises at issue by: (1) describing its location with the degree of precision dictated by the circumstances of the claim; (2) the type of facility located on the premises and a description of the toxic substances used there; and (3) the activity on the premises that gave rise to the exposure.

When read in a light most favorable to the plaintiffs, the pleading alleges that Mr. Hamill was injured by exposure to benzene while working on the moving defendants' oil fields in Southwestern Kansas, the Panhandle of Oklahoma, and Eastern Colorado. Mr. Hamill has described the nature of his work on these oil fields and the types of benzene-containing products to which he was exposed. He has also identified each of his employers and has stated the time frames in which these employers provided services on the defendants' premises. A search of company records for references to Mr. Hamill's various employers and the locations where these firms provided services to the defendants will likely further narrow the scope of potential sites.

The Court has determined that the Fifth Hamill Complaint complies with Superior Court Civil Rules in that it sufficiently identifies the premises at issue and further identifies factual bases upon which claims of premises liability can rest. The motions to dismiss the Fifth Hamill Complaint are DENIED.

The Second Heddinger Complaint adequately pleads claims against some defendants, but not against others.

CASE QUESTIONS

1. In toxic tort cases, usually the plaintiff can't name the offending product by brand name. Why does this occur?
2. Why is the time frame of a toxic tort considered so significant? Explain.

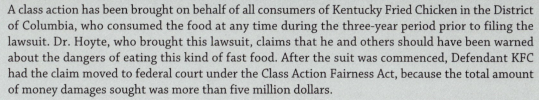

THE CASE OF THE FATTY CHICKEN

A class action has been brought on behalf of all consumers of Kentucky Fried Chicken in the District of Columbia, who consumed the food at any time during the three-year period prior to filing the lawsuit. Dr. Hoyte, who brought this lawsuit, claims that he and others should have been warned about the dangers of eating this kind of fast food. After the suit was commenced, Defendant KFC had the claim moved to federal court under the Class Action Fairness Act, because the total amount of money damages sought was more than five million dollars.

(continues)

Arthur HOYTE, M.D.
v.
YUM! BRANDS, INC. d/b/a/ KFC.

06-1127
Superior Court, District of Columbia
June 12, 2006

Dr. Hoyte seeks money for himself and any District of Columbia consumer in the amount up to $74,000 per person for injuries sustained as a result of KFC's use of dangerous trans fats to prepare food for consumers. The suit is for all people who purchased food at KFC in D.C. which was prepared containing trans fats. The class is so numerous that joinder of the parties in impracticable; thousands of people are involved. Dr. Hoyte's claims are typical of the class. He and others have been injured by the wrongful conduct. All KFC's in D.C. used partially hydrogenated oil, which is very high in trans fats. Trans fats have been classified as more harmful to the public than saturated fats.

A pot pie at KFC contained 14 grams of trans fat. The large popcorn chicken contained 7 grams of trans fats. Dr. Hoyte claims he should have been warned that even KFC's "best food," the Tender Roast and Honey BBQ chicken, contained trans fats. Dr. Hoyte alleged that the food was not fit for consumption, that this violated the implied warranty of merchantability, and that KFC was negligent in its misrepresentation. Since the suit, KFC switched its cooking style in 5,500 of its restaurants. KFC announced plans to discontinue the use of all trans fats in its other restaurants by April of 2007.

KFC maintains that it had no duty to warn. KFC alleged that the case was similar to the class actions against McDonalds regarding obesity which were dismissed on the basis that it is well known that fast foods contain high levels of cholesterol, fat, salt and sugar. As of this writing the decision is still pending.

CASE QUESTIONS

1. Who do you think will prevail? Explain.
2. Los Angeles County, California, is trying to ban the opening of any new fast-food chains in certain areas where there is a high percentage of obese residents, and no alternative food sources. Do you think this legislation will pass? Explain.

▍SUMMARY

Fault is irrelevant to strict liability. If the tortfeasor is found to be absolutely liable, his or her negligence or intent does not affect the liability. This may seem harsh and unfair, because a tortfeasor might exercise every degree of care to avoid injuring others and still be held responsible under absolute liability. Strict liability is limited to cases involving abnormally dangerous instrumentalities, such as wild animals, vicious domestic animals, ultrahazardous activities, and products liability. Through its courts and legislatures, the public has established absolute liability as an insurance measure to protect innocent victims from harm caused by particularly perilous pursuits.

The common law calls wild animals *ferae naturae* ("wild nature") and domestic animals *domitae naturae* ("domesticated nature"). At common law wild animals are presumed to be naturally dangerous, whereas domestic animals are assumed to be harmless and docile creatures. Wild animals may be owned by individuals who capture and restrain the beasts. This is called exercising dominion and control. Owners are absolutely liable for injuries their wild animals inflict. However, owners are strictly liable only for injuries caused by their domestic animals if these animals exhibited vicious propensities. The defenses of assumption of risk, contributory and comparative negligence, consent, and self-defense or defense of others apply to animal liability cases.

Abnormally dangerous, or ultrahazardous, activities are inherently perilous. Use of explosives, flammable substances, noxious gases, poisons, hazardous wastes, and sometimes electricity, natural gas, or water utilities are examples. *Restatement (Second) of Torts* § 520 states that persons engaged in abnormally dangerous activities are strictly liable for injuries caused by these activities. The activity must create a high risk of substantial harm, which risk could not have been eliminated through the exercise of reasonable care; the activity or substance must not be commonly undertaken or used; the activity must have been inappropriately used in the place in which the injury happened; and the activity's hazards must outweigh the activity's benefits to the community. As a defense to strict liability, many legislatures have enacted statutes protecting certain activities from absolute liability. Some toxic torts have injured so many people that mass tort actions or class actions were needed for legal recourse.

Absolute liability in animal and abnormally dangerous activity cases is limited by proximate cause. For strict liability to apply, the defendant's actions must have proximately caused the plaintiff's injuries. This means that the plaintiff's injuries must have been reasonably foreseeable as a consequence of the defendant's conduct, and it must have been foreseeable that the plaintiff could be injured as a result of the defendant's actions. This is called the foreseeable plaintiffs theory. There is no duty of reasonable care in strict liability cases, because the duty involves negligence theory, which is irrelevant to absolute liability.

▌ KEY TERMS

abnormally dangerous (ultrahazardous) instrumentalities	common usage (use) principle	mass tort
	control	proximate cause
absolute (strict) liability	dominion	toxic tort actions
class action	*domitae naturae*	vicious propensity rule
	ferae naturae	

▌ PROBLEMS

In the following hypotheticals, determine if absolute liability applies and if the tortfeasor will be strictly liable to the injured party. Are any defenses relevant? If so, how would they be applied?

1. Heather works at the municipal zoo. She cleans the cages of and feeds the various species of monkey on exhibition. One day, Heather received a telephone call from "Spider," exhibits supervisor, who instructed her to report to the exotic bird building to substitute for another employee who was ill. Heather had never worked with these birds before and was unfamiliar with their habits, although she received feeding and watering instructions from Spider. As she was cleaning one of the walk-in cages, a toucan landed on the back of her neck, scratching and biting at her ears. The scratches required stitches. There were no municipal ordinances discussing the zoo or its operation, apart from the enabling act that established the zoo and its supervision by the city's department of parks and recreation.

2. Willie owns a bulldog, which he kept chained in his backyard. The dog often barked and growled at anyone passing by the house on the sidewalk. One morning, Lisa, an employee of the electric company, visited Willie's house to read the meter, which was located in the backyard. Lisa had read Willie's meter before and knew about the dog. She peeked around the house but could not see the dog. She assumed it was inside the house, because the chain was lying on the ground. As she walked over to the meter, the dog leaped from the bushes, knocked Lisa down, and chewed on her arms and hands. Lisa was hospitalized as a result of these injuries.

3. Olaf owns a gas station. While a tanker truck was filling his underground fuel tanks, Olaf was using a welding torch inside his garage area to repair a customer's car. He inadvertently knocked over the torch, still lit, which fell into a puddle of gasoline from the tanker. The puddle ignited and burned across the ground to the tanker pipe connected to the underground tanks. Both the tanker truck and the fuel in the underground tanks then ignited and exploded. Several patrons were severely injured and their vehicles damaged.

4. The Belladonna Pharmaceutical Company manufactures medicines. It uses certain chemical solutions that turn bad and must be destroyed. These solutions are kept in steel barrels in the firm's back lot, awaiting pickup from a local waste disposal company. Brad works for the trash company. He had never collected trash from Belladonna before, as he normally rode the residential trash routes. Brad's supervisor failed to instruct him to take a special sealed tank truck to get Belladonna's chemicals. Instead, Brad drove an open-top trash truck used to haul dry garbage. Brad tossed the barrels into the truck, and several of them ruptured and leaked. As Brad drove down the highway to the dump, chemical sludge spilled out the back of the truck onto an automobile driven by Madison. Madison stopped and touched the sludge caked across the front of his car. It made his hands burn. Frightened, Madison drove to a local hospital emergency room. His skin had absorbed much of the chemical waste, and he became severely ill and had to be hospitalized for several weeks.

❚ REVIEW QUESTIONS

1. How is strict, or absolute, liability different from negligence and intentional torts? What role does fault play in absolute liability? What are the limitations to strict liability? What are the public policy objectives behind absolute liability? How is strict liability like insurance?

2. How does the common law define wild animals? Domestic animals? What does the common law presume about each type of animal? How can wildlife be owned? Why is this important to the question of liability? When does strict liability apply to injuries inflicted by wild animals? By domestic animals? What is the vicious propensity rule? What defenses apply to animal-owner absolute liability cases?

3. What are abnormally dangerous activities? Ultrahazardous activities? How does the *Restatement (Second) of Torts* define the term? What elements are required for absolute liability to apply? What is the function of reasonable care? What is the common usage principle? What balancing test do courts apply in abnormally dangerous activity cases?

4. How is proximate cause defined in strict liability cases? Why is it important?

5. What is a mass tort?

6. How is a class action different from a mass tort?

▌HELPFUL WEBSITES

This chapter focuses on strict and absolute liability. To learn more about strict or absolute liability, the following sites can be accessed:

General Information

http://www.productslaw.com

http://www.rand.org

http://www.toxlaw.com

http://www.osha.gov

http://www.thefederation.org

http://www.access.gpo.gov

Mass Torts

http://www.njcourtsonline.com

STUDENT CD-ROM™
For additional materials, please go to the CD in this book.

ONLINE COMPANION™
For additional resources, please go to
http://www.paralegal.delmar.cengage.com

chapter 10

Products Liability

THE BIGGEST MISTAKES PARALEGALS MAKE & HOW TO AVOID THEM

How Do You Spell Your Names?

The firm where I work has voluminous files of forms developed from precedents created in the past. The extensive search capability developed by our librarians and IT staff allows one to find anything that can be adapted to a similar fact pattern. This process saves hours of work by "cutting and pasting" new information into these templates. However, proofreading is the key when working off templates of previous matters. Once, I did not fully proofread a retainer agreement

and the consequences were not good. Since I thought I had carefully read through the entire agreement, when the phone rang, I put the agreement in my "completed" pile. Imagine the surprise of everyone when it was time to sign the agreement and the names were not those of the new clients. I had left the names of the clients from a previous matter on the signature page! We salvaged the appointment by quickly printing the correct signature page with the new clients' names.

(continues)

LESSON LEARNED: While they said very little about the error, the clients seemed uneasy about beginning a new relationship with a firm that produced such a sloppy document. No matter how much work went into producing a good product, misspelling or otherwise messing up the names of clients is not acceptable.

▌ INTRODUCTION

Products liability is any form of liability arising out of the use of a defective product. A plaintiff can bring three different causes of action depending on the facts: strict tort liability, negligence, or breach of warranty. This chapter focuses on the cause of action for strict liability in tort. Generally, under products liability, the manufacturer or seller of a product is absolutely liable for any injuries caused by a defect in the product. Products liability occupies a prominent position in torts study, as it is involved in a sizeable portion of tort litigation. It is probably the most significant development in tort law since the courts accepted negligence theory as a separate tort.

This chapter includes:

- The parties in products liability cases
- The elements of products liability
- *Restatement (Second) of Torts* § 402A
- The defenses to products liability
- Comparison of products liability with contract law warranties.

product(s) liability | The responsibility of manufacturers (and sometimes sellers) of goods to pay for harm to purchasers (and sometimes other users and even bystanders) caused by a defective product.

▌ PRODUCTS LIABILITY THEORY AND HISTORY

Products liability was established as a distinct tort theory in the landmark case of *Greenman v. Yuba Power Products, Inc.,* 59 Cal. 2d 57, 377 P.2d 897, 27 Cal. Rptr. 697 (1962). In this case, the California Supreme Court completed more than 100 years of legal evolution that culminated in strict products liability.

Public Policy Objectives behind Products Liability

Products liability is society's decision, through its courts and legislatures, that businesses manufacturing and selling defective products are in the best economic position to bear the expenses incurred when a faulty product injures an innocent user. The theory may be simply put: Why should the hapless victim shoulder the burdens (medical costs, permanent injuries, etc.) produced by a defectively made product? Instead, should not the manufacturer or seller of that product be liable for the resulting harms? Does that not seem reasonable and ethical? If one has ever been hurt by a defective product, one might answer affirmatively. A manufacturer or seller, however, might feel differently.

Historical Development of Products Liability

In the early nineteenth century, English and American common law held that persons injured by defective products had to sue under contract law rather than tort law. These courts felt that the appropriate cause of action was breach of contract or, more precisely, breach of warranty. A **warranty** is a guarantee that a product or service meets certain quality standards. If a product fails to meet such standards, as is the case when a product is defective, then the warranty has been breached.

Under early nineteenth-century English and American common law, only persons who had made contracts with the manufacturer or seller of a defective product could recover damages for breach of warranty or breach of contract. This contractual relationship is called **privity of contract.** Privity exists when parties are directly engaged in an agreement between them. If Joseph enters into a contract with Harris, in which Joseph agrees to sell Harris a product for a certain price, then there is privity of contract between them. The landmark case that announced the privity rule was *Winterbottom v. Wright*, 10 Meeson & Welsby 109, 152 Eng. Rep. 402 (1842). In this case, the plaintiff drove a horse-drawn coach for the postmaster general. This coach was manufactured especially for the postmaster general by the defendant. The plaintiff was maimed when the vehicle's axle broke and threw him from the carriage seat. The plaintiff sued the defendant for failing to properly maintain the coach under a service contract. The court held that the plaintiff was not a party to either the service agreement or the manufacturing agreement. Thus, the plaintiff lacked privity of contract and therefore could not recover for the injuries caused by the defectively assembled coach. The only party that could sue under such circumstances would be the postmaster general, with whom the defendant contracted to make the carriage. But in this case the postmaster general was not harmed. The injured plaintiff was left without compensation.

Almost immediately, American courts began to carve out exceptions to the privity-of-contract rule. In *Thomas v. Winchester,* 6 N.Y. 397 (1852), the New York Court of Appeals ruled that a mislabeled medicine (which actually contained poison) was inherently dangerous, and accordingly the injured party did not have to have privity of contract with the manufacturer or seller to recover damages. In this case, the plaintiff's husband had purchased a bottle, labeled "dandelion extract," that in actuality contained belladonna, a deadly poison. The defendant manufacturer who mislabeled the product sold it to a druggist, who resold it to a physician, who prescribed it to the plaintiff. There was no privity of contract

warranty | Any promise (or a presumed promise, called an *implied warranty*) that certain facts are true. . . . In consumer law, . . . any obligations imposed by law on a seller that benefit a buyer; for example, the warranty that goods are merchantable and the warranty that goods sold as fit for a particular purpose are fit for that purpose.

privity of contract | A legal relationship that exists between parties to a contract. In some cases privity must exist in order for an individual to make a claim against another.

between the plaintiff and the defendant. Nonetheless, the court permitted the plaintiff to recover damages for injuries caused when she took the poison from the mislabeled bottle. The court reasoned that poisons are imminently dangerous by their very nature. Accordingly, remote users of a mislabeled drug could be seriously injured. Thus, privity of contract is unnecessary if the defective product (such as a mislabeled poison) is imminently dangerous. Later courts characterized this as the **imminent danger exception** to the privity-of-contract rule.

Throughout the nineteenth century, the New York Court of Appeals, and many courts following its lead, expanded the imminent danger rule to include spoiled food, explosives, improperly assembled scaffolding, an exploding coffee urn, and defectively made automobile wheels. Many courts found liability in contract warranty law, but this still required privity of contract. The landmark case in this century, which is often said to have sparked modern products liability law, is *MacPherson v. Buick Motor Co.*, 217 N.Y. 382, 111 N.E. 1050 (1916). Writing for the majority, Justice Cardozo declared that privity of contract was obsolete. If a product, because of its defective manufacture, became unreasonably dangerous, then the manufacturer or seller would be liable for injuries caused by the defective product. Cardozo applied negligence theory to determine whether the defective product was unreasonably dangerous. The manufacturer had to be negligent in making the faulty product.

MacPherson ushered in a cascade of court opinions following and expanding its precedent. In *Escola v. Coca Cola Bottling Co.*, 24 Cal. 2d 453, 150 P.2d 436 (1944), Justice Traynor of the California Supreme Court, in his concurring opinion, opined that negligence was no longer necessary for defective product manufacturers to be liable. Instead, he proposed strict liability. It took eighteen years before the California Supreme Court adopted this view in *Greenman v. Yuba Power Products.* Many other state courts quickly joined the new common-law theory.

The American Law Institute followed *Greenman* with its famous *Restatement (Second) of Torts* § 402A, which virtually every American jurisdiction has adopted (in some form or another) as the definitive rule for strict products liability. The *Restatement*'s position is discussed in greater detail later in the chapter.

imminent danger exception | A nineteenth- and early twentieth-century exception to the privity of contract requirement in defective product cases.

Types of Warranties

Three different kinds of possible warranties are involved under strict products liability. To recover under these warranties, a plaintiff need not show that a defendant was negligent or acted intentionally to cause harm. The plaintiff must show a breach of the following warranties:

1. Express warranty, or
2. Implied warranty of merchantability, or
3. Implied warranty of fitness for a particular purpose.

Express Warranty. Express warranties are very common. They are a statement that a particular promise or set of facts is true. When a seller or manufacturer makes such a promise to the buyer, the buyer is relieved of responsibility to verify such information. If the facts are not as represented, the purchaser will have a claim for any loss as a result. Examples of express warranties vary from statements such as "this car is guaranteed for three years or 30,000 miles" to a label on a shirt that states, "never needs ironing." Express warranties address the quality, fitness, and character of goods. A seller's opinion, such as "you'll love this car," or sales puffery, such as "this is the finest camera you'll see," are not considered express warranties. There is no expectation that the buyer will purchase a product based on these statements.

Implied Warranty of Merchantability. Unlike an express warranty in which a specific statement is made, an implied warranty arises by virtue of the law. When a product is sold, the law imposes an implied warranty that the goods sold will be "merchantable," meaning they are fit for their ordinary purpose. If you purchase a vegetable peeler, there is an implied promise that you will be able to peel most vegetables with the peeler without too much effort. If you purchase a chair, there is an implied promise that the furniture will support you when you sit down. When you buy food, there is an implied warranty that it is fit for consumption. If you come down with food poisoning after eating canned tuna, then the implied warranty that food is fit for human consumption has been broken. Likewise, if there is glass in food, or other foreign objects, the implied warranty of merchantability has been breached. Additionally, products must be properly contained, packaged, and labeled. A product labeled suntan lotion that doesn't protect you from the sun's harmful rays would be considered in breach of the implied warranty of merchantability.

Implied Warranty of Fitness for a Particular Purpose. Least common is the implied warranty of fitness for a particular purpose. This warranty generally involves an interaction between the buyer and seller. A purchaser goes into a hardware store and says, "I'm looking for a product that will cover up water stains on my ceiling tiles." The seller's employee or representative then recommends a water-sealing paint product for the buyer's particular needs. The law imposes an implied warranty of fitness for a particular purpose. If the product does not work as needed, then the buyer can return the product. In these cases the buyer relied on the expertise of the seller and bought a product based upon his or her recommendation.

▌ PARTIES

Three classes of parties are involved in products liability cases: the product manufacturer, the seller, and the ultimate user.

THE CASE OF THE HOT CAR

Two cousins go out drinking. The cousin who is driving hears some noise from his van on the way home. Then the car stalls, and he tries to restart the van several times. The driver is severely injured when a rear seat explodes into fire. The court reviews consumer expectations.

Krzysztof SOBCZAK, Plaintiff-Appellant,
v.
GENERAL MOTORS CORPORATION,
Defendant-Appellee.

No. 1-05-2154
Appellate Court of Illinois, First District,
Third Division
May 23, 2007

At about 9 P.M., on August 28, 1999, Sobczak drove his father's Chevrolet Astro van (YF7 configured, M/L model) to pick up his cousin Arthur. Sobczak and Arthur went to two nightclubs over the course of several hours. Sobczak consumed at least five beers.

After dropping off Arthur, Sobczak noticed that the van was sluggish and was making noises. The car stalled and Sobczak tried to start the car by putting the transmission into neutral and turning the key. The car started but the motor sounded like it was "jumping up and down." Sobczak put his foot on the brake pedal and put the van in gear, but the motor died. This occurred about 10 times in 10 minutes. Sobczak started the van once more but smelled something coming from the back. He climbed over the seat and went to the back bench seat. He started to check around when the seat exploded into flames. His shirt and hair caught on fire. The next thing Sobczak could recall was waking up in the hospital one month after the accident.

John Orisini, the head of the fire and arson investigative unit for the Cook County sheriff's police, testified the fire started near the rear tire on the passenger side. He drew this conclusion based on the fact that the metal in that area was exposed and whitening occurred. There was also evidence of heavy burning in the area of the kickup and the rear wheel. The carpet padding in front of the two rear seats was completely burned away. Orisini concluded that the fire started underneath the van either in or near the muffler and the heat had conducted up through the flooring and traveled inside the van.

At trial, Sobczak pursued his claims for negligence and strict products liability based on design defect that GM had defectively designed the van's heat shields, muffler and fuel management system; and negligently designed the van's heat shields.

A plaintiff may establish a strict liability claim based on a design defect in one of two ways: the consumer-expectation test or the risk-utility test. The consumer-expectation test provides that a product is "unreasonably dangerous" when it is "dangerous to an extent beyond that which would be contemplated by the ordinary consumer who purchases it, with the ordinary knowledge common to the community as to its characteristics." *Restatement (Second) of Torts* § 402A, Comment *i*, at 352 (1965).

Under the risk-utility test, a plaintiff must demonstrate that a design defect exists by presenting evidence that the risk of danger inherent in the design of the product outweighs the benefits of the design. In other words, "[t]he utility of the design must therefore be weighed against the risk of harm created" and "[i]f the likelihood and gravity of the harm outweigh the benefits and utilities of the product, the product is unreasonably dangerous."

As previously stated, a plaintiff may prevail under the consumer-expectation test if he or she can demonstrate that the product failed to perform as an ordinary consumer would expect when used in an intended or reasonably foreseeable manner.

The purpose of the heat shielding system is to disburse and deflect any heat created from the operation of the vehicle away from the vehicle.

(continues)

Clearly, an ordinary consumer purchasing an M/L van would give little or no thought to the heat shielding system selected by GM, but would expect that little or no heat would be transferred from underneath their YF7 configured M/L van into the vehicle compartment.

It is reasonably foreseeable that if the M/L van stalled, an ordinary consumer would make numerous attempts to restart the van without much thought as to whether the heat shielding system would withstand the high temperatures that may be created by revving the engine. Specifically, an ordinary consumer would expect his M/L van either to start or not to start, but would not expect the interior of the van to ignite.

Verdict for Sobczak.

CASE QUESTIONS

1. Did this van meet consumer expectations? Explain.
2. Do you think General Motors Corporation was aware of this defect? Explain.

Manufacturers and Sellers

product manufacturer | The maker of a product that, if defective, gives rise to product liability.

seller | One who sells property, either its own or through contract with the actual owner.

wholesaler | One who sells goods wholesale, rather than retail.

retailer | One who makes retail sales of goods.

purchaser | One who acquires property through the purchase of said property.

The **product manufacturer** makes the defective product that gives rise to the entire products liability lawsuit. **Seller** includes anyone who is in the business of selling goods such as the one that is faulty. This includes the manufacturer as well as wholesalers and retailers. **Wholesalers** are businesses that buy and sell goods to **retailers,** which in turn sell the products to customers, usually individual persons.

The Ultimate User

When we buy a product, we are **purchasers.** In products liability law, however, the party injured by flawed merchandise need not be the original buyer. Instead, a member of the purchaser's family, or a friend of the buyer, could recover damages if hurt by a defective product. The key is whether it is reasonably foreseeable that the user would have utilized the product. This individual is called the **ultimate user,** because that person eventually used the product that caused an injury.

ultimate user | In products liability law, a person who is injured by a defective product. It must have been reasonably foreseeable that the injured party would use the defective product.

deep pocket | The one person (or organization), among many possible defendants, best able to pay a judgment; the one a plaintiff is most likely to sue.

In products liability litigation, the ultimate user becomes the plaintiff who sues various defendants: the retailer, the wholesaler(s), and the manufacturer. The plaintiff uses a shotgun approach to products liability—namely, sue all the sellers. This may seem excessive, but the plaintiff has a logical explanation. The plaintiff sues all the sellers along the product distribution chain to ensure that one of them (probably the manufacturer) will have sufficient monies to pay a judgment. In tort law, this is called "going for the **deep pocket.**" In other words, the plaintiff tries to sue defendants that have money and could satisfy a damages award. Exhibit 10-1 shows the product distribution chain between manufacturers,

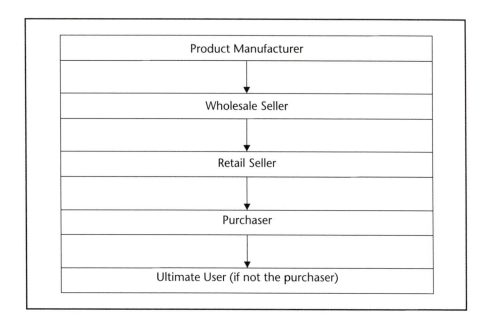

Exhibit 10-1
Product distribution chain

sellers, purchasers, and ultimate users. The deficient product passes through many hands before reaching its unfortunate victim.

Now that we have met the parties to products liability actions, it is time to investigate the elements of products liability.

▌ ELEMENTS

Products liability is defined as strict, or absolute, liability for the seller or manufacturer of a defectively made product that injures a user of the item.

No Privity of Contract Requirement

Privity of contract is not required in products liability. The ultimate user need not have purchased the merchandise directly from the seller or manufacturer, although some states require that a sale of the product have occurred somewhere between the manufacturer and the ultimate user. However, it need not be a direct transaction between the two.

Negligence Is Irrelevant

Remember that the seller or manufacturer's negligence is irrelevant to strict liability. It does not matter how much care the seller or manufacturer used in making or maintaining the product. Every possible precaution could have been utilized, but that simply makes no difference. If the product was defective, and a user was harmed as a result, absolute liability applies—period.

A Typical Products Liability Formula

There are five elements of products liability, as defined by most state courts or statutes:

1. The defect must render the product unreasonably dangerous to use.
2. The seller or manufacturer must be in the business of selling products such as the flawed one(s).
3. The product cannot have been substantially changed between the time it left the seller or manufacturer's hands and the time it reached the ultimate user.
4. The defect must have proximately caused the ultimate user's injuries.
5. The ultimate user must have used the product properly, that is, in the way that the product was designed to be used.

In some jurisdictions, several additional elements are required:

6. The ultimate user must have been foreseeable (foreseeable plaintiffs theory).
7. The seller or manufacturer must have been responsible for the condition in which the product was maintained.
8. In a few states, a sale of the product must have occurred. This could be a sale between the manufacturer and a wholesaler, or a wholesaler to a retailer, or a retailer to a customer. Basically, someone at some point had to buy the defective item.

Restatement (Second) Rule

Section 402A of the *Restatement (Second) of Torts* contains fewer elements than those just discussed. It states:

(1) One who sells any product in a defective condition unreasonably dangerous to the user or consumer or to his property is subject to liability for physical harm thereby caused to the ultimate user or consumer, or to his property, if

    (a) the seller is engaged in the business of selling such a product, and

    (b) it is expected to and does reach the user or consumer without substantial change in the condition in which it is sold.

(2) The rule stated in Subsection (1) applies though

    (a) the seller has exercised all possible care in the preparation and sale of this product, and

    (b) the user or consumer has not bought the product from or entered into any contractual relation with the seller.

THE CASE OF THE PREMATURE VIEWING

A casket breaks apart and a body flies out in full view of the family. Who are the injured parties and what kind of claim can they bring? Is this a strict products claim, or does the claim really pertain to the wrongful mishandling of a corpse?

S. Randall SWEENEY; George Allen Sweeney; Suzanne Sweeney, Individually; and Suzanne Sweeney, as Guardian for Lorin Neal Sweeney, Appellants

v.

AURORA CASKET COMPANY, INC. and Victoriaville Caskets Limited, Appellees.

No. 2005-CA-001569-MR
Court of Appeals of Kentucky
February 9, 2007

OPINION

HENRY, Senior Judge.

This appeal is taken from the Hancock Circuit Court's entry of a directed verdict and judgment as to a number of claims brought by the appellants in connection with an unfortunate incident relating to the burial of their father. Upon review, we affirm.

The facts of the case are as follows: Sherroll Sweeney died in August 2001. Soon after his death, his son, Randall Sweeney, made funeral arrangements with Taylor-Raymond-Spear Funeral Home for Spear to conduct Sherroll's funeral, which was to be held on August 31, 2001. Part of this process included selling Randall a casket for his father's burial. The casket Randall chose was one that Spear had purchased from Aurora Casket Company. Aurora, in turn, had purchased the casket from its manufacturer, Victoriaville Caskets Limited.

Following Sherroll's funeral service, he was to be interred at Lewisport Cemetery after a planned gravesite service. After the funeral procession arrived at the gravesite, J. David Spear, owner of the funeral home, assembled the pallbearers, and they began to remove Sherroll's casket from the funeral coach. When the casket was approximately three-fourths of

the way out of the coach, Spear heard a loud pop and a heavy weight—the edge of the casket bottom—hit his foot. Apparently the bottom of the casket where Sherroll's head had been resting had become detached from the rest of the casket, resulting in his head and half of his body spilling forth in clear view of the Sweeney family. Sherroll's body was subsequently returned to the funeral home, where it was placed in another casket before being returned to the gravesite for continuation of the service and burial.

On August 22, 2002, Sherroll's widow, Joan Sweeney, filed a complaint in the Hancock Circuit Court against the appellees and Spear. A week after Joan filed her original complaint, Sherroll's adult children-Randall Sweeney, George Allen Sweeney, Suzanne Sweeney, and Lorin Neal Sweeney (through a guardian)—filed their own complaint in the Hancock Circuit Court against the same parties.

Joan's claims were eventually settled, and she is not a party to this appeal. Spear is also not a party, as the trial court granted the funeral home's unopposed summary judgment motion in an order entered on April 2, 2004. The remaining claims of the Sweeney children against Aurora and Victoriaville proceeded to trial on March 23 and 24, 2005. At the conclusion of the Sweeneys' proof at trial, the trial court directed verdicts in favor of Aurora and Victoriaville as to the negligence, strict liability, and implied warranty claims. The court allowed the remaining outrageous conduct claim to go the jury; however, the jury found in favor of Aurora and Victoriaville. This appeal followed.

On appeal, the Sweeneys challenge the trial court's directed verdict in favor of Aurora and Victoriaville as to their negligence, strict liability, and implied warranty claims. The jury verdict as to the outrageous conduct claim is not part of this appeal.

(continues)

We first address the Sweeneys' contention that they were entitled to recover damages against Aurora and Victoriaville for mental and emotional anguish under both negligence and strict liability theories due to a manufacturing defect in their father's casket.

As both Aurora and Victoriaville point out, Kentucky courts have consistently held that "damages may not be recovered for shock or mental anguish unaccompanied by physical contact or injury." It is undisputed that the Sweeneys had no physical contact relating to the incident in question and accordingly suffered no resulting physical injuries. Instead, they were simply bystanders to the event. Consequently, a general claim of damages for mental anguish is unavailable to them.

In possible recognition of this fact, the Sweeneys correctly point out that a plaintiff may recover damages for mental anguish arising out of the wrongful mishandling of a corpse, and suggest that this cause of action should have been available to them here to allow for such recovery. In reviewing the record, however, we question whether this cause of action was ever properly presented against Aurora or Victoriaville in the Sweeneys' original and amended complaints or at any other point throughout this litigation. Aurora and Victoriaville argue that a wrongful mishandling of a corpse claim was never made against them, and the Sweeneys provide nothing in their brief to refute this position. In any event, such a claim is also unavailable to them here, as a suit for the mishandling of a corpse is only available to the deceased's "next of kin"—in this case, Sherroll's surviving spouse, Joan. Accordingly, the trial court's entry of a directed verdict against the Sweeneys as to their negligence and strict liability claims against Aurora and Victoriaville was appropriate, and the appellees' remaining arguments in this respect need not be considered.

The Sweeneys also contend that their breach of warranty claim against Aurora should have gone to the jury because the Taylor-Raymond-Spear Funeral Home "was not the true seller of the casket" and only facilitated Aurora's sale of the casket. Consequently, the Sweeneys contend that there was privity of contract between Aurora and themselves, and the claim should have been allowed to proceed to the jury. The Sweeneys provide absolutely no authority in support of this position, so we therefore reject it.

It is undisputed that Randall Sweeney was the only purchaser of the casket in question. None of his siblings had a contract with any of the defendants involved in this case, and they therefore have no viable breach-of-warranty claim against Aurora. As for any such claim that Randall might have, the Sweeneys have provided us with nothing of substance to suggest that such buyer-seller privity exists here between Randall and Aurora. Instead, the record reflects that Spear sold the casket and Randall purchased it. We therefore conclude that the Sweeneys' implied warranty claim against Aurora was rightfully dismissed via directed verdict, and the appellees' remaining contentions in this respect need not be considered.

The judgment of the Hancock Circuit Court is affirmed.

CASE QUESTIONS
1. What was the court's decision?
2. Did any of the plaintiffs' claims survive? Explain.

Subsection (2)(a) of § 402A indicates that the seller is liable regardless of the degree of care used to safeguard the public from injury by the defective product. Subsection (2)(b) states that privity of contract is unnecessary for strict liability to apply. Table 10-1 illustrates tort recovery, and Table 10-2 lists the elements required.

Negligence	Express Warranty	Implied Warranty	Strict Liability
Personal injuries	Personal injuries	Personal injuries	Personal injuries
Property damage	Property damage	Property damage	Property damage
Economic loss	Pure economic loss	Pure economic loss	Economic loss if there is also personal injury or property damage

TABLE 10-1
Tort recovery

Negligence	Express Warranty	Implied Warranty	Strict Liability
Duty	Statement of fact that is false	Sale of goods by merchant	Seller
Breach	Made with the intent or expectation that the statement will reach plaintiff	The goods are not merchantable	Defective product that is unreasonably dangerous to people or property
Causation	The plaintiff relies on the statement	Causation	Causation
Damages	Damages	Damages	Damages

TABLE 10-2
Elements required for tort recovery

Unreasonably Dangerous Products

The product must be unreasonably dangerous as a result of its defect. Courts look to see if the product has become unreasonably threatening because of its defect. There are four types of unreasonably dangerous defects: (1) fault in product design; (2) error in product manufacture or assembly; (3) improper product maintenance; and (4) manufacturer/seller's failure to warn.

Faulty Product Design. Products can be unreasonably dangerous if they have a defective design. Courts look to see whether the product is inherently dangerous because of a poor design but for which (that is, if such a defect did not exist) the product would have been safe to use. For instance, suppose a manufacturer assembles a toy with small, removable parts that can be swallowed by an infant, and thereby cause serious injury or death. The toy would be inherently dangerous, because the removable-parts design would expose small children to the dangers of choking. This design defect makes the product unreasonably dangerous.

Courts decide faulty design (which make products unreasonably danger-ous) in terms of three tests: the consumer contemplation test, the danger/utility test, and the state-of-the-art discoverability test.

Consumer Contemplation Test. In its Comments, *Restatement* § 402A states that a product is unreasonably dangerous if the consumer ordinarily would not appreciate the threat inherent in its design. The defect becomes unreasonably hazardous because the reasonable person would not be expected to anticipate the danger created by the faulty design. Legal commentators and courts have labeled this the **consumer contemplation test.**

For example, suppose that Nicholas bought a top-loading washing ma-chine. He had to lean across the control panel to load his clothing inside. In doing so, he might accidentally press the start button with his body. This might start the machine while his hands were inside the washing drum, injuring him.

Under the consumer contemplation test, a reasonable person would have anticipated this situation. Nicholas should have seen where the start button was located. He knew that the machine could begin operating once this button was pushed. He should have contemplated the risk inherent in the product's poor design. The product was not unreasonably dangerous.

Danger/Utility Test. Many courts have formulated another test to determine if a product is unreasonably dangerous by its design: the **danger/utility test.** A product is unreasonably hazardous if the danger created by its design outweighs the benefits derived from its use. Consider the previous washing-machine ex-ample. Normally, Nicholas derives tremendous benefits from the device—he gets clean clothes. If he is cautious about where he stands, he should be able to avoid the accidental start risk. Using the danger/utility test, the washer is not unreasonably dangerous.

State-of-the-Art Discoverability Test. If manufacturers could have discovered hazards created by defective product designs, using current, state-of-the-art tech-nologies, then failure to do so makes a design-flawed product unreasonably dan-gerous. For example, suppose an automobile manufacturer installed ordinary glass in the small vent windows in a vehicle's doors. State-of-the-art crash testing would quickly indicate that this glass shatters into sharp fragments during a collision. If the car maker did not discover this defect through modern testing procedures, then it would be strictly liable for any injuries caused by the fragile windows.

Error in Product Manufacture or Assembly. Safely designed prod-ucts may become unreasonably dangerous as a result of improper assembly or manufacture. For instance, if a lawn-mower manufacturer failed to tighten

consumer contemplation test | If a reasonable person would not have anticipated the danger created by the fault in the product, then the product is unreasonably dangerous.

danger/utility test | A theory in products liability design that makes a product unreasonably dangerous. Under this test, a product is unreasonably danger-ous if the danger created by its design outweighs the benefits derived from its use.

the bolt holding the blade with sufficient torque, the blade could fly off during use. Suppose this happened to a purchaser, who was severely cut by the blade. The lawn mower, although designed properly, became unreasonably dangerous because it was not suitably assembled. This is sometimes called an **assembly defect.**

Improper Product Maintenance. Sellers occasionally fail to maintain merchandise properly. When a buyer purchases the product, it might not function correctly because of a **maintenance defect.** For example, suppose a lawn and garden shop sells chain saws. The chain on such a saw must be oiled frequently to operate appropriately. Suppose the seller forgot to keep oil in its chain saws. While displaying one model to a customer, the saw froze up and the chain snapped, sailing into the face of the surprised customer. The product was unreasonably dangerous because the seller did not properly maintain it.

The seller was negligent in forgetting to keep oil in the saw. The seller would also be liable under negligence theory, as well as products liability.

Seller or Manufacturer's Failure to Warn. Sometimes products are unreasonably dangerous by their very nature. Lawn mowers, chain saws, poisons, and chemicals can be lethal if not cautiously used. However, purchasers may not always spot the obvious dangers. Accordingly, manufacturers and sellers have an obligation to warn the ultimate user about inherent product dangers. Failure to warn could result in strict liability. If one uses rat poison or insect sprays, the containers warn not to ingest the contents or get them in one's eyes. These are examples of warnings used to avoid absolute liability. If the user is warned, then the user knows the risks. To apply, the warning must be in an obvious and noticeable place.

Business Requirement

Section 402A of the *Restatement (Second) of Torts,* and most common law and statutory versions of products liability, insist that the manufacturer or seller be engaged in the business of selling products such as the defective item(s) that injured the ultimate user. Its purpose is to exclude products liability for people who are not in the business of selling such goods. For example, suppose Laurie sold Micron a vacuum cleaner, which she had bought from a department store. Because of a design defect, it exploded and injured Micron. Products liability is not intended to hold Laurie liable for this mishap, because she neither manufactured nor was in the business of selling such merchandise. Under products liability, Micron would need to sue the department store and manufacturer.

assembly defect | A theory in products liability concerning whether a defective product is unreasonably dangerous. Errors in production, manufacture, or assembly may render a product unreasonably hazardous despite safe design.

maintenance defect | A theory in products liability concerning whether a defective product is unreasonably dangerous. If a seller fails to maintain a product properly, and the product later causes injury to the ultimate user, then the product was unreasonably dangerous.

Substantially Unchanged Condition Requirement

For products liability to apply, the product must reach the ultimate user without any substantial changes in its condition from the time it left the manufacturer or seller. This is a crucial requirement. If something happened along the product distribution chain to alter the product (perhaps creating the unreasonably dangerous condition), then it would be unfair to hold manufacturers or sellers accountable for something they did not cause.

For instance, suppose Rachel purchased milk at a nearby grocery. The milk was fresh when she bought it. However, during the drive home, Rachel gets caught in traffic and it takes her more than an hour to arrive home. During this period, the milk spoiled. A visiting relative later drank the milk and suffered food poisoning. The relative wishes to sue the grocery. However, products liability would not apply, because the milk did not reach the ultimate user (Rachel's relative) in a substantially unchanged condition.

In some states, for strict liability to exist, the manufacturer or seller must be responsible for how the defective product was maintained. If the seller were not in any way responsible for how the product was assembled or stored (until it was sold or used), then that seller would have no control over the products it distributes. Products liability attempts to place the blame on the party responsible for the defect, to protect innocent sellers from absolute liability for product defects caused by someone else.

Proximate Cause

Recall the discussion of proximate cause in strict liability cases. That analysis also applies in products liability cases: the defective product must have been the proximate cause of the plaintiff's injury if liability is to attach.

Proper Use Requirement

The ultimate user must use the defective product properly in order for products liability to apply. In other words, the user must use the product for some function for which it was designed or intended to be used. For example, if Cliff wanted to climb onto his roof, he would probably use a ladder. If one of the ladder's rungs broke (because of the manufacturer's failure to use proper glues), and Cliff fell and broke bones, he would be entitled to sue the manufacturer and seller under products liability. However, if he had used stacked vegetable crates to climb upon, and these collapsed, Cliff could not sue under products liability. Vegetable crates are neither designed nor intended for people to climb on. See the next section on defenses where "foreseeable misuse" of a product is covered. If misuse can be anticipated, in most cases it will be considered proper use.

THE CASE OF THE NOT-SO-BRIGHT LIGHT

This case demonstrates the risk versus utility analysis used in evaluating allegedly dangerous products. The court must decide whether, as a matter of social policy, the risk of loss should be placed on the manufacturer or supplier of a butane lighter that was not childproof.

SMITH
v.
SCRIPTO-TOKAI CORP.

170 F. Supp. 2d 533 (W.D. Pa. 2001)
United States District Court, W.D. Pennsylvania
November 2, 2001

This is a case for damages arising out of a residential fire started by plaintiffs' three-year-old child using a butane utility lighter manufactured by defendants. On June 15, 2000, we granted defendants' motion to dismiss all claims except negligence. As to the negligence claim, we explained that we were bound to follow the Court of Appeals' decision in *Griggs v. BIC Corp.*, 981 F.2d 1429 (3d Cir. 1992), and chastised defendant's counsel for his lack of candor to the tribunal in failing to acknowledge that case.

* * *

As set forth in *Griggs*, 981 F.2d at 1434, plaintiff must establish the following elements of a negligence action: (1) defendants had a duty; (2) defendants failed to conform to the standard required; (3) there was a causal connection between defendants' conduct and the resulting injury; and (4) damages. The "duty" element has two components: foreseeability and unreasonableness. Although foreseeability is not part of a strict liability claim, forseeability "is an integral part of a determination that a duty does exist in Pennsylvania negligence law." . . .

In this case, the Aim 'n Flame lighter is a consumer product and there is "abundant empirical data demonstrating that Tokai could have foreseen the risk of an unsupervised child causing injury by using a lighter." Further, the risk is unreasonable because the high social value placed on the safety of people and property threatened by childplay fires, the high gravity and considerable probability of the risk, and the likelihood of a reasonably available alternative (childproofing) outweigh defendants' interest in producing its lighters without childproofing features. Thus, as the Court of Appeals held in *Griggs*, "if a manufacturer of cigarette lighters may reasonably foresee that they will fall into the hands of children, who, albeit unintended users, can ignite them with a probability of serious injury to themselves and others, and if childproofing the lighters is economically feasible, the manufacturer would have a duty to guard against the unreasonable risk of harm by designing the lighter to be childproof." Accordingly, plaintiffs have established the "duty" element of their negligence claim. Plaintiffs have also established that defendants breached that duty. Indeed, defendants do not seriously contend that the Aim 'n Flame lighter at issue here had appropriate safety features.

There are material disputes of fact that prevent causation from being established as a matter of law. Plaintiffs point out that an Aim 'n Flame lighter was recovered from the wreckage of the home, underneath the point of origin of the fire. Defendants, not so subtly, seek to imply that this evidence was planted. If defendants wish to risk alienating the jury by pursuing this line of reasoning, they shall have that opportunity.

Finally, the existence of damages is undisputed. However, a jury will have to determine the amount of such damages.

. . . Plaintiffs have established, as a matter of law, that defendants had a duty to manufacture a childproof lighter and breached that duty. The case will proceed to trial on the issues of causation and damages.

A defendant may be liable for negligence if he (1) knows that the chattel is in a dangerous condition;

(continues)

(2) has no reason to believe that those for whose use the chattel is supplied will realize the dangerous condition; and (3) fails to warn those for whose use the chattel is supplied of the dangerous condition. A warning is sufficient if it adequately notifies the intended user of the unobvious dangers inherent in the product.

* * *

Pennsylvania adopted the Restatement (Second) of Torts Section 402A as the law of strict products liability. [T]he Pennsylvania Supreme Court announced a threshold question of law for the court to decide: whether, as a matter of social policy, the product's condition justifies placing the risk of loss on the manufacturer or supplier. A risk-utility analysis, using the Dean John Wade factors, is appropriate in performing this threshold social policy inquiry. If the claim survives this threshold determination, "the jury must determine whether, under the facts, the product, at the time it left the defendant's control, lacked any element necessary to make it safe for its intended use or contained any condition that made it unsafe for use."

* * *

We conclude that reinstatement of the products liability claim is appropriate. Developments of the law in the Pennsylvania intermediate courts and in the Court of Appeals have clearly indicated that the threshold products liability question should be based on the risk-utility analysis. The Superior Court has applied this analysis in a closely analogous case and we have no reason to believe that the Supreme Court would apply risk-utility factors any differently. . . .

CASE QUESTIONS

1. How would you apply a risk-utility analysis in this case?
2. Why would Scripto have produced a lighter that was not childproof?

Table 10-3 lists different kinds of defective products.

TABLE 10-3
Different kinds of defective products

Type	Example
1. Design defect	Product designed improperly. Parts scrape against each other when in motion
2. Manufacturing defect	Product manufactured with insufficient screws or bolts
3. Improper product maintenance	Product not kept at proper temperature
4. Failure to warn by manufacturer or seller	No warning label on box or product insert

Foreseeable Plaintiffs Theory

In some jurisdictions, it must have been reasonably foreseeable that the ultimate user would use the defective product. This is called the zone of danger (or foreseeable plaintiffs) theory in negligence. Some ultimate users are not reasonably foreseeable and no duty is owed to them. For example, it is highly improbable that a one-year-old infant would come into contact with industrial cleaners used in manufacturing processes. Such a person could not be a reasonably foreseeable ultimate user of such a product. However, members of a product purchaser's family, or the buyer's neighbors, could be foreseeable users of defective goods. How many times in one's family has more than one individual used an appliance or tool? Have you ever borrowed products from your neighbors?

Consider Diana, who borrowed a pen from a classmate with which to take notes during the lecture. The pen had a manufacturing defect that made the plastic casing unusually brittle. While she is writing, the pen shatters in Diana's hand, and she is cut by the many tiny fragments. Was Diana a reasonably foreseeable ultimate user? Yes. Classmates often share pens, pencils, notebooks, and many other products during classes. It was reasonably foreseeable that someone might borrow a pen to take notes in class. Diana could sue the pen manufacturer under products liability as a foreseeable plaintiff.

Having analyzed the various elements of products liability, we may now proceed to apply the theory to hypotheticals.

hypotheticals

Burgess Primer Corporation manufactures paint. Didi bought Burgess's "Supreme Ease" paint at Painter Place, a local retailer that carried Burgess products. Didi selected various colors, which store employees mixed together. While applying the paint indoors, Didi noticed that the paint stung her skin as it splattered from her roller. Apparently, Didi was allergic to certain oils that had been mixed into the paint. When she showered later that day, she noticed that the paint had left her arms and face mottled with burn marks. Many of these became infected. Medical tests indicated that a significant percentage of the population suffered this allergic reaction to the paint mix.

Are Burgess Primer Corporation (as manufacturer) and Painter Place (as seller) strictly liable for an unreasonably dangerous product? Applying the generic formula, first ask if the defect made the product unreasonably dangerous. The fault here is product assembly (i.e., how the paint was mixed). Using the consumer contemplation test, would a reasonable person anticipate that he or she might be allergic to paint oils? This is not an obvious hazard that an ordinary person would detect from a can of paint. Thus, the product's dangerous condition rendered it unreasonably dangerous to the ultimate user, Didi. Under the danger/utility test, the hazard in using the product outweighed the benefits, as many people were allergic to the particular mix.

Both Burgess and Painter Place were engaged in the business of selling paint. The product reached the ultimate user, Didi, in the same condition as it left the retailer. Also, Didi used the paint properly, in a way in which paint is intended to be used.

(continues)

It was reasonably foreseeable that Didi would use the paint she bought at a retail store, so she is a foreseeable plaintiff. Both Burgess and the retailer were responsible for how the paint was maintained. Further, a sale occurred (for those jurisdictions requiring it). So far, even with the extra elements, it seems as though strict liability will favor Didi.

But who was the proximate cause of Didi's injuries? Burgess manufactured the paint base and the various colors. However, the paint did not become unreasonably dangerous until Painter Place's employees mixed it. Therefore, Burgess, as manufacturer, did not proximately cause Didi's injuries. Painter Place was clearly the proximate cause of the harm. Proximate cause is a crucial determination, because it absolves Burgess from strict products liability. Painter Place is absolutely liable for Didi's injuries under products liability theory.

* * *

Consider another hypothetical. Fairfield Seed Company sold sweet corn seeds to retail variety stores. Fairfield had erroneously treated the seeds with a toxic insecticide used for field corn seeds. As the corn grew, this chemical was absorbed into the ears of sweet corn. When the gardeners (who had bought the seed from the retailers) ate the corn, they became ill.

Would the retail variety stores and Fairfield be strictly liable for the gardeners' injuries from an unreasonably dangerous product? Apply either the consumer contemplation test or the danger/utility test. The reasonable gardener would not expect sweet corn seeds to be treated with a poison harmful to humans. The risks far outweigh the benefits. Both Fairfield and the retailers were in the business of selling garden seeds. Fairfield improperly prepared the seeds, which would be a manufacturing defect. The dangerous seeds reached the ultimate users in the same condition as when they left the manufacturer. Fairfield was responsible for the condition of the product. Fairfield's insecticide coating proximately caused the gardeners' injuries, because the ultimate users ate the contaminated ears of corn grown from the poisoned seed. The gardeners used the product as it was designed (i.e., to grow corn to eat) and were foreseeable plaintiffs. All the elements of products liability have been met; thus, Fairfield is strictly liable for the gardeners' injuries caused by the poison corn.

What about the retailers' liability, however? There are two critical queries here. First, did the retailers proximately cause the ultimate users' injuries? Second, were the retailers responsible for the condition in which the defective product was maintained?

The retailers did not contaminate the seeds. The seeds came in sealed packages, which the retailers simply stocked on shelves for customers to pick up and purchase. Thus, the retailers did nothing to proximately cause the gardeners' injuries. Furthermore, the retailers had no control over the manufacturing processes that contaminated the seeds. They were not responsible for how the seeds were prepared. The retailers maintained the condition of the seeds just as they were supposed to, namely, by stocking their shelves with sealed packages. Under this analysis, the retailers would not be strictly liable for the harm to the gardeners.

THE CASE OF THE SATURDAY NIGHT SPECIAL (THE SEQUEL)

In the last discussion of this case, the D.C. Court of Appeals ruled that the sale of a "Saturday Night Special" handgun was not an ultrahazardous activity for purposes of absolute liability. The appellants also argued products liability theory, but as in the first round, the court once again guns down this proposition, exempting the manufacturer from strict liability. Reread the earlier excerpt in Chapter 9 for the facts and procedural history.

DELAHANTY
v.
HINCKLEY

564 A.2d 758 (D.C. 1989)
District of Columbia Court of Appeals
October 11, 1989
Ferren, Associate Judge

Appellants advanced three legal theories for holding the gun manufacturers liable in these circumstances: negligence, strict products liability under the *Restatement (Second) of Torts* § 402A (1965), and a "social utility" claim apparently based on strict liability for abnormally dangerous activities. . . . Appellants alleged in their complaint that: Hinckley needed an easily concealable weapon for his assassination attempt; the gun manufactured by [the defendant] is an easily concealable, inexpensive handgun; the gun is poorly constructed, unreliable, and therefore not useful for legitimate purposes such as military use, target practice, or self-defense; as a result of the gun's low price,

it is used for criminal purposes; and the manufacturers knew of the gun's criminal uses.

* * *

Appellants first claim the manufacturers of the gun used by Hinckley are strictly liable for sale of a defective product. They rely on *Restatement (Second) of Torts* § 402A, which imposes liability for the sale of "any product in a defective condition unreasonably dangerous to the user or consumer . . .". We join the other courts which have rejected the application of this theory in circumstances such as these. Appellants point to no malfunction of the gun caused by improper design or manufacture that led to Thomas Delahanty's injuries. Instead, appellants argue that the manufacturers had a duty to warn of the dangers of criminal misuse of the gun. There is no duty to warn, however, "when the danger, or potentiality of danger, is generally known and recognized." *Restatement (Second) of Torts*, § 402A comment j. Because hazards of firearms are obvious, the manufacturer had no duty to warn.

CASE QUESTIONS

1. Suppose that, when Hinckley fired at the president, the handgun had exploded because of a defective firing pin. Suppose also that Delahanty had been injured by the flying shrapnel. Would Delahanty's products liability claim against the manufacturer have succeeded under these facts? Would Delahanty have been the ultimate user under these facts? Explain.

2. What if the bullets that struck Delahanty had been defectively manufactured, so that they exploded upon impact. Would Delahanty then have had a products liability claim against the bullet manufacturer? Would Delahanty have been the ultimate user under these facts? Explain.

Table 10-4 summarizes the elements of products liability under the generic, common-law formula.

TABLE 10-4
Elements of products liability

TYPICAL COMMON-LAW OR STATUTORY FORMULA	ADDITIONAL ELEMENTS NEEDED (IN SOME STATES)
1. Defect makes product unreasonably dangerous	Ultimate user must be reasonably foreseeable (foreseeable plaintiffs theory)
2. Manufacturer or seller must be in business of selling products such as the defective one(s)	Manufacturer or seller must be responsible for condition in which defective product was maintained
3. Defective product cannot have been substantially changed from time it left manufacturer or seller until it was used by ultimate user	A sale of the defective product must have occurred
4. Defect must have proximately caused the ultimate user's injuries	
5. Ultimate user must have used the product properly (in the way in which it was designed or intended to be used)	
6.	Some states, by statute or common law, require a sale

▊ DEFENSES

There are several defenses to absolute liability. Some of those defenses also apply to products liability.

Contributory or Comparative Negligence Not a Defense

Courts have generally held that contributory negligence is not a defense in products liability cases. This seems logical, because contributory negligence is a defense to negligence and negligence has no place in strict liability cases.

Ultimate User's Misuse of Product

Saying that contributory or comparative negligence is not a defense is not to say, however, that the plaintiff (the ultimate user) can use a defective product irresponsibly or wantonly. The ultimate user is expected to use the product properly, as it was intended to be used. This is an element of products liability, although some courts consider product misuse to be a defense. If the ultimate user misuses a defective product and is injured as a consequence, his or her products liability claim against the manufacturer or seller will be denied. This defense is effective even though the misused product was defective.

Foreseeable Misuse. Some product uses may be unusual, but are not actually considered misuses. For example, chairs are designed to be sat on. Yet how often have you used a chair as a stepping stool to reach something stored on a high shelf? Using a chair as a ladder is not a misuse of the product, because it is reasonably foreseeable that one might use a chair for such a purpose. In other words, reasonably foreseeable uses, even though the product may not originally have been intended or designed for such functions, are acceptable uses. A products liability claim would not be barred if the ultimate user used the product in a reasonably foreseeable fashion.

Removal of Safety Devices. Adult smokers commonly remove the "child-proof" safety devices on butane lighters, increasing the risk of injury.

Employees who are under great pressure to produce a lot while working on an assembly line or in a factory may deliberately dismantle the very safety device that is there to protect them. If the safety device is removed, a machine might run faster than was intended, or it may become easier to get to the interior of the machine when it jams or needs cleaning. For these injured parties, a products liability cause of action will not be available, because the product was misused and altered.

---

practical **application**

> Unfortunately, you will frequently see misuse of products by injured parties who will tell you that they removed the guard or safety device from a machine at work.

Assumption of Risk

Assumption of risk, however, is usually accepted as a defense. The ultimate user assumes the risk of being injured by a hazardous product in three ways: (1) by discovering the defect but disregarding it and using the product anyway; (2) by failing to properly maintain the product; and (3) by failing to follow instructions or heed warnings for safe product use.

Ignoring a Discovered Defect. Recall the basic definition of assumption of risk. **Assumption of risk** is the plaintiff's voluntary assumption of a known risk with a full appreciation of the dangers involved in facing that risk. In products liability cases, the plaintiff is the ultimate user. The ultimate user assumes the risk by discovering a product defect and then ignoring the risks involved and using the product anyway. For example, suppose Steve discovers that his circular saw blade is bent. The warp would cause the blade to rub

assumption of risk | Knowingly and willingly exposing yourself (or your property) to the possibility of harm. In most states, a person who assumes a risk of harm cannot win a negligence lawsuit against the person responsible for the harm.

against the saw's protective sheathing when it rotated. This would create sparks, which could burn him. Steve decides that the risk is worth taking and he uses the saw. Sparks fly into his eyes (because he does not wear protective eyewear). Steve assumed a known risk with a full comprehension of the possible hazardous consequences.

Failure to Properly Maintain Product. Ultimate users cannot recover in products liability if they failed to properly maintain the product for safe uses. Courts often characterize this as an assumption-of-risk defense. The circular saw example illustrates this type of assumption of risk. Steve did not maintain the saw so that it could be safely used. The blade was bent. Before using it, he should have replaced the damaged blade with a new blade.

Consider another illustration. Suppose Gil failed to put motor oil in his automobile. If he proceeded to drive for hundreds of miles, his motor would undoubtedly burn out. Gil could not recover under products liability from the manufacturer or seller. He assumed the risk of ruining his car by not properly maintaining it.

Failure to Follow Instructions or Heed Warnings. How often have you used a product without first reading the instructions? Surely everyone has done this. Most of the time the products we use are sufficiently simple that we can use them properly after a quick glance. With a complex product, however, following instructions could prevent injuries. Products liability plaintiffs often argue that defectively designed products are unreasonably dangerous. However, sometimes these plaintiffs did not follow the manufacturer's instructions or disregarded manufacturer's warnings that specifically point out the dangers inherent in the product design. Both of these actions are types of assumption of risk. Likewise, if a consumer ignores a safety recall notice sent by the dealer or manufacturer of a product, and fails to cooperate and bring the product to be fixed, the consumer assumes the risk of injury as a result.

Assume, in the saw example, that the manufacturer printed on the side of the saw, "WARNING! DO NOT USE IF BLADE IS BENT!" If Steve disregarded this warning and were hurt from the bent saw, he could not recover damages for a defectively designed product. Steve assumed the risk by ignoring the warning.

Suppose, instead of a bent blade, that the blade was merely loose. The instructions included directions for blade tightening. If Steve did not read or follow these directions, and he was hurt because the blade flew off while he was using the saw, he could not recover damages under products liability. Steve assumed the risk by failing to follow instructions to properly maintain the product.

THE CASE OF THE TOXIC FIRE PAINT

Product misuse does not always require an unusual use of an item. Sometimes the product may be applied to achieve the results for which it was intended, but the actual operation of the item is inappropriate and causes the user's injuries. As the following case illustrates, the paint was used as paint is ordinarily intended. However, the way in which the paint was applied was the misuse. Nor were the firefighters reasonably foreseeable plaintiffs. Although one cannot help but sympathize with the plaintiffs, the Fourth Circuit's analysis of products liability theory reaches the correct result.

HIGGINS
v.
E.I. DUPONT DE NEMOURS & CO.
863 F.2d 1162 (4th Cir. 1988)
U.S. Court of Appeals, Fourth Circuit
December 23, 1988
Murnaghan, Circuit Judge

Plaintiffs Higgins and Jones appeal from the district court's order granting summary judgment in favor of defendant, E.I. DuPont de Nemours & Co., Inc. ("DuPont"), regarding their survival actions. Plaintiffs also appeal the dismissal of their wrongful death actions. . . .

Plaintiffs brought the actions to recover for the deaths of their children and fetuses who allegedly died from the teratogenic effect of chemicals contained in Imron paint. Each of the husbands had worked for the Baltimore City Fire Department in the same fire house, where they used Imron paint to "touch up" the fire engines. Plaintiffs claimed that the deaths were caused by glycol ether acetates and lead supplied by Dow and contained in Imron paint which was developed, manufactured and distributed by DuPont. DuPont advertised Imron paint for sale through distributors for use by industrial professionals, such as fleet truck and transit systems, body shops, marinas, car dealers and manufacturers of aircraft, fire engines, heavy duty construction equipment, and utility vans. Imron was sold and delivered by DuPont to C & R Paint Supply, Inc. ("C & R"), which in turn, sold and delivered the product to the Key Highway repair yard of the Baltimore City Fire Department, where fire apparatus was regularly painted and repainted. C & R never sold or delivered Imron paint

directly to the City firehouses nor did it directly solicit business from the Fire Department through sales representatives. Furthermore, it is undisputed that C & R understood that the City's fire vehicles were repaired and painted only at the Key Highway repair shop. Nothing suggests that C & R even suspected that Imron paint was sent out to the individual fire houses until 1985 when it received an unusual request from the City Fire Department for some empty quart containers.

However, from 1979 to 1985, the City Fire Department's Key Highway facility redistributed quantities of Imron in both marked (i.e., with DuPont's labels affixed) and unmarked one-gallon paint cans, coffee cans, or glass jars to the plaintiffs for their use in touching up fire apparatus in the firehouse. The city did not provide the plaintiffs with separate instructions or warnings as to the use of Imron, or with protective clothes to wear while applying the Imron paint.

Each of the labels affixed to the Imron paint products which C & R sold to the City Fire Department stated in clear lettering on the front of the cans:

FOR INDUSTRIAL USE ONLY by professional, trained personnel. Not for sale to or use by the general public.

This warning was accompanied by instruction on the back of the label which required the use of a supplied-air respirator, eye protection, gloves, protective clothing and adequate ventilation. Furthermore, C & R supplied Material Safety Data Sheets ("MSDS") to the City Fire Department which repeated the safety precautions. . . . However, none of the information constituting a warning specifically warned of the possible teratogenic effects of the product.

* * *

(continues)

The district court found that the firefighters were not "professional, trained personnel" for the obvious use of Imron products, i.e., painting. That they were professional firefighters and not professional painters was evidence from the manner in which they mixed and applied the paint. The evidence shows that the firefighters painted in their fire department work uniforms, mixed the paint in cups and sometimes with their fingers and did not heed any of the label precautions which a professional painter would have taken seriously. We agree with the district court that the labels were adequate enough to warn plaintiffs that they were not sufficiently well-trained to use Imron paint. Therefore, DuPont did not distribute a product which was unreasonably dangerous when used for a purpose and in a manner that is reasonably foreseeable, i.e., for industrial use by trained painters. Imron paint was not defective.

Because plaintiffs did not fall into the class of foreseeable users of Imron paint which DuPont had specifically circumscribed to limit its potential liability, the district court held that had the City heeded the warning and not redistributed Imron paint in unlabeled cans to the firehouse, plaintiffs would not have been injured. Likewise, plaintiffs could not complain when they failed to observe the warnings on the Imron paint cans which the City redistributed to them in the original, labeled cans. The district court held that such a misuse of the product barred recovery as a matter of law. Although our sympathy rests with the plaintiffs who have suffered unspeakable losses, we must agree with the district court that plaintiffs' real complaint lies with the City Fire Department and not DuPont.

* * *

Misuse of a product may bar recovery against the manufacturer where the misuse is the sole proximate cause of damage, or where it is the intervening or superseding cause. Product misuse is defined as use of a product in a manner that could not reasonably be foreseen by the defendant. Reasonably foreseeable uses include " 'the incidental and attendant consequences that accompany normal use.' " The district court found that the normal use of Imron paint was restricted to industrial purposes for which professional painters, who appreciated the attendant risks, were required. The district court held that DuPont could not reasonably foresee that either the City would redistribute Imron paint in either labeled or unlabeled containers or that plaintiffs, who were amateur painters, would use Imron paint after reading the various conspicuous warnings contained on the labeled cannisters [sic] which did reach them. . . . [W]e still agree with the basic reasoning of the district court, . . . that the firefighters were not professional, trained personnel. Plaintiffs failed to provide any contradictory evidence. DuPont had a right to rely on its warning to cut off the chain of causation and to insulate it from becoming a virtual insurer against all injuries arising from its product.

Affirmed.

CASE QUESTIONS

1. Was it not reasonably foreseeable that Imron paint might be shifted into unmarked containers for easier use? Why or why not? What is the significance of DuPont's labeling for this issue?
2. Two of the multiple defendants in this case were the mayor and city council of Baltimore, Maryland. Do you believe the plaintiffs would succeed against them, under respondeat superior, for the torts of the Baltimore City Fire Department? Explain the tort theories that the plaintiffs could successfully apply.

Defenses are a defective product manufacturer's best friend. Even if every products liability element is satisfied, defenses can spare the seller from the wrath of strict liability, as the following hypotheticals illustrate.

hypotheticals

Mike owns a tire repair shop. He sells new tires from all the national brands and repairs old tires. Hailey came into the shop one day with a punctured tire. Mike agreed that it could be patched and repaired, but he instructed Hailey to use the tire only as a spare for emergencies. He recommended that she purchase a reconditioned tire for regular use. Hailey insisted that Mike put her patched tire back onto her car. Mike warned that the patch might not hold up over long-term, constant use. Nevertheless, he had the repaired tire re-mounted on her car. Later the following month, while Hailey was driving to work, the patch failed and the tire blew out. Hailey's car ran off the road, collided with a telephone pole, and injured her.

Hailey's products liability claim against Mike would fail. Hailey assumed the risk of using the patched tire contrary to Mike's specific instructions and warnings. She voluntarily assumed a known risk with a full appreciation of the hazards involved. The defense of assumption of risk would protect Mike from strict products liability.

* * *

The Oasis Sprinkler Company manufactures underground lawn sprinkler systems. Oasis offers a do-it-yourself kit for handy customers. Sarah purchased one of these kits. The detailed assembly instructions directed her to attach the sprinkler heads to the underground pipe using a special copper clamp. "Be certain to crimp the clamp with pliers to ensure a snug connection," read the instructions. Sarah did not crimp the clamps, although she did put them in place. Later, while the sprinkler system was in use, one of the sprinkler heads flew into the air under the force of the water pressure. It struck Sarah's daughter, Janice, in the forehead, causing a wound that required several stitches.

Could Janice and Sarah win a products liability lawsuit against Oasis? Not if the assumption-of-risk defense can be successfully applied. Sarah disregarded the manufacturer's specific instructions for assembling the product. However, Oasis failed to warn about the possible dangers that could occur if the clamps were not crimped. So we have a manufacturer's failure-to-warn situation versus a user's failure-to-follow-instructions defense. Which wins? Is the manufacturer's failure to warn sufficient to hold Oasis liable for an unreasonably dangerous product? Or is Sarah's failure to obey instructions a complete defense under assumption of risk?

The key to this problem is whether a reasonable ultimate user (i.e., a reasonable person) would have anticipated that the sprinkler heads might fly off under high water pressure if the clamps were not crimped. Most people know that water carried through pipes is under great pressure, which makes the water a powerful, focused force. A loose connection could easily give way and send a

(continues)

sprinkler head flying in any direction. Reasonable persons know this from everyday experience with garden hoses or plumbing. Sarah should have anticipated this risk; therefore, it is considered a known risk that she voluntarily assumed, despite a full appreciation of the dangers involved. Assumption of risk will overpower the manufacturer's failure to warn of this particular hazard. Accordingly, the defense of assumption of risk will protect Oasis from strict products liability.

* * *

The Comfort King Corporation manufactures recliner chairs. When Nathan visited a friend who owned such a recliner, Nathan noticed that a lightbulb was burned out in his friend's hallway. He used the recliner as a ladder to reach the light fixture. As he stood on the chair, it reclined, sending him sprawling across the hall where he smashed his head into a closet doorknob. Nathan thought the chair was unreasonably dangerous, so he sued Comfort King under products liability.

Comfort King, however, shrugged off the lawsuit. The product misuse defense was there to protect the company from strict liability. Recliner chairs are not designed or intended to be used as ladders or stoops. After all, recliners *recline.* They cannot be safely stood upon for that reason. Nathan should have reasonably anticipated the danger created by misusing the chair in this fashion. Nathan's misuse of the product is a solid products liability defense for Comfort King.

Table 10-5 lists the defenses to products liability.

TABLE 10-5
Defenses to products liability

CONTRIBUTORY NEGLIGENCE	ASSUMPTION OF RISK	PRODUCT MISUSE BY ULTIMATE USER
Not considered a defense in products liability cases	Ultimate user's voluntary assumption of known risk with full appreciation of dangers involved	If ultimate user misuses the product, then he or she cannot recover under products liability
	Occurs when ultimate user ignores a discovered defect and uses the product while knowing of its dangerous condition	Reasonably foreseeable uses are *not* misuses of products
	Occurs when ultimate user fails to properly maintain product	
	Occurs when ultimate user fails to follow instructions or heed warnings for safe product use	

◼ COMPARISON TO CONTRACT LAW WARRANTIES

Express Warranties

Products liability has roots in contract law warranties. A *warranty* is a guarantee that a product seller gives a buyer. The guarantee states that the product will perform to certain standards or will not break down over a period of time. This warranty is part of the contract between the buyer and the seller.

If the product fails to comply with the guarantee, the warranty is *breached.* This **breach of warranty** is also a violation of the parties' agreement that the product shall remain in a particular condition while used.

breach of warranty | The violation of either an express or implied warranty.

Implied Warranties

The Uniform Commercial Code (UCC) is a model (suggested) statute concerning the sale of goods that has been adopted by all states. One of its provisions, § 2-314, concerns implied warranties that all sellers of goods provide with their goods as to the goods being "merchantable," which means that all goods must be of fair average quality and fit for their ordinary purpose. This warranty protects the buyer against defective goods.

Another provision of the UCC, § 2-315, provides that if the seller knows of a particular purpose for which the buyer is buying, then the goods must be fit for that purpose.

These two provisions have allowed liability for injuries sustained as a result of defects in products. Because the UCC has been adopted by all states, decisions on these points tend to be similar nationwide.

◼ BAD FAITH

A tort is society's method of addressing the injuries that occur to people and property. As evidenced by all the new tort actions in this chapter, the tort field has greatly developed in response to modern problems; legal theories that allow an injured party to prevail can be flexible to fit the times. An example of this is the tort of **bad faith,** which has developed from California legal cases.

When an insurance company unreasonably denies a claim or fails to pay it in a timely fashion within the policy limits, this is called the *tort of bad faith,* or *bad faith liability.* Obviously, where liability is not clear-cut or certain, this tort will not apply. Insurance companies are expected to negotiate in good faith on behalf of an insured person and promptly settle claims for which liability is reasonably clear.

bad faith | Dishonesty or other failure to deal fairly with another person.

An example of bad faith would be when a plaintiff is willing to settle a lawsuit within the defendant's insurance policy limits, the defendant is clearly responsible for the plaintiff's injuries, and the defendant's insurance company refuses to settle the claim or even make a settlement offer. The plaintiff might then proceed to trial, and the jury may end up awarding a verdict greatly in excess of the amount of the defendant's insurance coverage. In this instance, the defendant ends up owing money to the claimant out of pocket, when this did not need to occur. If an insurance company refuses to bargain in good faith when there was available coverage for an incident, this defeats the purpose of insurance and subjects an insured to unnecessary liability.

The tort of bad faith demonstrates how tort law and contract law can intersect. When an insurance company fails to settle a tort case, the company may be liable to its insured on the basis of contract law as set forth in the terms of the insurance policy.

Table 10-6 lists states' statutes of limitations for products liability cases.

TABLE 10-6
State statutes of limitations for products liability cases

STATE	STATUTE OF LIMITATIONS FOR PRODUCTS LIABILITY CASES
California	Action must be brought within two years from time when injury is or should have been discovered
Florida	Action must be brought within two years from time when injury is or should have been discovered
Massachusetts	Action must be brought within three years of date on which injury occurred
New Jersey	Action must be brought within two years of date on which injury occurred
New York	Action must be brought within three years of date on which injury occurred
Ohio	Action must be brought within two years of date on which injury occurred
Pennsylvania	Action must be brought within two years of date on which injury occurred
Texas	Action must be brought within two years of date on which injury occurred

▌ SUMMARY

Products liability became a distinct tort theory in the early 1960s. For more than 100 years, American and English courts combined contract law and negligence to hold manufacturers and sellers liable for injuries caused by defective products. Finally, in 1962, strict liability was applied to such cases. As a matter of public policy, products liability places the risk of harm created by unreasonably dangerous products upon those who make and sell them. The law presumes that the innocent user should not be forced to bear the costs associated with harmful products.

The parties in products liability cases include the manufacturer, other sellers (such as retailers or wholesalers), and the consumers, or ultimate users, of the product. Often the ultimate user is a member of the product buyer's family or a neighbor or friend. By looking at a product's distribution chain, it becomes clear how the product leaves the manufacturer and reaches the ultimate user.

Products liability is strict, or absolute, liability. No privity of contract is required between the manufacturer or seller and the ultimate user. The manufacturer or seller's negligence is irrelevant. The product must contain a defect rendering it unreasonably dangerous to use. This fault may arise in a design defect, by improper product maintenance, or by the manufacturer or seller's failure to warn the buyer of hazards inherent in using the product. The manufacturer or seller must be engaged in the business of selling products like the defective one. The product cannot be substantially changed from the time it left the manufacturer or seller and reached the ultimate user. The defect must proximately cause the ultimate user's injuries. The ultimate user must use the product in the way in which it was designed or intended, or foreseeable.

Contributory negligence is not a defense to products liability. Product misuse is a defense, although it is often included as an element in the products liability formula. If the ultimate user misuses the product, even though the product is defective, the manufacturer and seller will not be strictly liable for the harm. Assumption of risk is another defense to products liability. If the ultimate user ignores a discovered defect and, by using the product, is hurt, the user has assumed the risk, and the manufacturer or seller would not be strictly liable. The same is true if the ultimate user fails to properly maintain a product, follow instructions, or heed warnings for safe use.

Products liability is similar to contract law warranties. First, both involve absolute liability. Second, both involve defective or unreasonably dangerous products. Third, under many warranty statutes and common law, the ultimate user is protected even if he or she was not the original product purchaser.

The tort of bad faith occurs when an insurance company fails to reasonably or timely settle a case that could have been settled within the policy limits.

▌ KEY TERMS

assembly defect	deep pocket	purchaser
assumption of risk	imminent danger exception	retailer
bad faith	maintenance defect	seller
breach of warranty	privity of contract	ultimate user
consumer contemplation test	product manufacturer	warranty
danger/utility test	products liability	wholesaler

▌ PROBLEMS

1. WedgeCorp manufactures golf clubs. The clubs have rubberized grips that golfers hold onto to swing them. Chase bought his wife a set of clubs for her birthday. Cindy is an avid golfer and uses the clubs three times a week at the local country club. When WedgeCorp manufactured the clubs, they used an improperly mixed glue that did not tightly bond the grips to the end of the clubs. While Cindy was swinging a five iron, the grip came loose and the club sailed through the air, striking Cindy's golfing partner, Betty, in the forehead.

2. Better Bovine, Inc. (BB) sells dairy cattle to farmers. These livestock are raised on one of the BB's pasturing farms outside of town. To control weeds, BB's employees sprayed pasture land with herbicides. The cattle ate this grass and absorbed the chemicals into their systems. These chemicals reduced the cows' milk production. Several farmers who purchased BB cows suffered substantial economic losses when the animals' milk productivity plummeted.

3. Whopper Toys Corporation manufactures "Mr. Killjoy," a combat doll. Mr. Killjoy comes equipped with sharp plastic swords that you can fit into his hands for mock battles. Whopper indicated on its packaging that this toy was not suitable for children under the age of six years. This was the only warning printed on the package. Franco bought a Mr. Killjoy figure for his four-year-old son, Francisco. While playing with Charlotte, a three-year-old neighbor girl, Francisco had the doll "attack" her. Its sword stabbed Charlotte through her nose, leaving a permanent scar.

4. Omar is an accountant who lives in an apartment next to Joyce. Omar sold his electric stove to Joyce for $200. Omar had never kept the electric heating elements on top of the stove particularly clean. In fact, they were caked with grease and dirt. The first time Joyce turned on the stove, the heating elements caught fire and set Joyce's long hair ablaze.

5. The Steak Out restaurant has a reputation for excellent steaks. One day it received a meat shipment from the Midwestern Meat Packing Company, a national meat distributor. When the shipment left Midwestern, it was shipped in a refrigerated truck. However, en route to The Steak Out, the truck's refrigeration system broke down, but the driver never noticed. The meat spoiled. When the Steak Out's employees unloaded the truck, they did not notice that the meat smelled bad. In fact, the meat did not smell much, if at all. Nevertheless, customers served from this shipment of beef became seriously ill from food poisoning.

6. Vlad bought a large screwdriver, made by the Hand Tool Manufacturing Company, from his local hardware store. Unknown to anyone, the screwdriver had a microscopic crack in its shaft. If excessive pressure were exerted on the screwdriver, it would snap. Vlad used the screwdriver to pry open sealed crates that he received at work. One day, while he was prying open a crate, the screwdriver broke, severely cutting the tendons in Vlad's left hand.

7. Chase works for the United States Department of Defense. One day he noticed that his paper-shredding machine made a loud grinding noise during operation. He opened the maintenance door, but could see nothing wrong with the parts inside. Chase continued using the machine, despite the horrible noise. Several co-workers complained to him about it. The grinding occurred because the machine was out of lubricating oil, which, according to the machine's instruction manual, should have been checked at least monthly. No one had checked the oil level since the machine was purchased more than a year ago. While Chase was using the machine, its gears froze up and broke loose the paper-shredding blades. These lodged in Chase's thighs, cutting him deeply.

▌▌ REVIEW QUESTIONS

1. What are the public policy objectives behind products liability? How are they similar to the public policy objectives mentioned in Chapter 9 for "regular" strict liability?

2. How did modern products liability evolve? What were some of the landmark cases during the nineteenth and early twentieth centuries that led to these developments? What was the imminent danger exception? It was an exception to what rule?

3. How is negligence relevant to products liability? Is privity of contract required? Who are the parties in products liability cases? Who is the ultimate user?

4. Discuss the elements of a typical products liability formula. How are these different from the elements in *Restatement (Second) of Torts* § 402A? How are they similar?

5. How would you define an unreasonably dangerous product? What is faulty product design? Explain the consumer contemplation test, the danger/utility test, and the state-of-the-art discoverability test. Why are these tests important?

6. Explain how errors in product manufacture or assembly make a product unreasonably dangerous for products liability purposes.

7. In products liability, what role does improper product maintenance play? Manufacturer or seller's failure to warn of product hazards?

8. Define (a) the business requirement, (b) the substantially unchanged condition requirement, and (c) the proper use requirement. Why are they relevant to products liability? Does proximate cause play any role?

9. Is contributory negligence a defense to products liability? Why or why not? What about product misuse?

10. Explain how assumption of risk operates as a defense to products liability. Identify the three ways in which the ultimate user assumes the risk of using a defective product.

11. How does the tort of bad faith intersect with contract law?

▌ HELPFUL WEBSITES

This chapter focuses on products liability. To learn more about products liability, the following sites can be accessed:

General Information

http://www.personalinjurylaw.com

http://www.hg.org

OSHA

http://www.osha.gov

Products Liability

http://www.productslaw.com

Toxic Torts

http://www.toxlaw.com

United States Product Safety Commission

http://www.cpsc.gov

Directory of Experts

http://www.expertpages.com

Internet Drug Index

http://www.rxlist.com

Mayo Clinic

http://www.mayoclinic.com

STUDENT CD-ROM™
For additional materials, please go to the CD in this book.

ONLINE COMPANION™
For additional resources, please go to
http://www.paralegal.delmar.cengage.com

chapter 11

Special Tort Actions

THE BIGGEST MISTAKES PARALEGALS MAKE & HOW TO AVOID THEM

Paralegal Gone Wild!

My state's paralegal association was hosting an annual meeting in the state capital one weekend. I decided to go, especially since none of the other women from my firm could attend. My boss even allowed me to expense my hotel and mileage if I agreed to share what I learned with my colleagues!

When I arrived at the convention hotel, there was a singles' mixer following registration, where I met a great group who were attending from all over the state. Someone suggested we go to the "Mardi Gras" night at the hotel bar where they featured karaoke. Everyone was having a good time, and we took turns singing and buying rounds of drinks. When it was my turn to go up to the bar to buy a round, the bartender smiled and said, "Since it is 'Mardi Gras' the drinks are free for women who 'flash' me." I was a little surprised and a little drunk so I unbuttoned a couple of buttons and revealed some

(continues)

cleavage. "The whole round was free!" I said when I returned to the table. When I explained my discount, the others quickly finished their drinks and excused themselves. I was so embarrassed and somewhat ashamed. The next morning I packed up and returned home without attending the meeting. I didn't put in for the expenses and when my boss asked why not, I said I was sick and didn't attend.

Later I found out people told him they had seen me at the registration.

LESSON LEARNED: Becoming too familiar or careless at a professional meeting, even when not officially representing your firm, has consequences that may affect your career. One must always maintain professional behavior in public and know when not to cross that line.

▌ INTRODUCTION

You have now reached an area of torts that is often overlooked in paralegal education. These forgotten torts are just as important as the major torts of negligence and strict liability.

Special tort actions include nuisance, which involves issues of both tort and property law, and negligence per se, which is often a statutory tort. Tort litigation also often includes wrongful death actions, which are usually associated with negligence claims. Within the past thirty years a new, related tort, *wrongful life*, has emerged in the appellate courts.

This chapter investigates these special tort actions. Much of our discussion will incorporate negligence and absolute liability theories. Specifically, the following torts and issues are discussed:

- ▶ Private nuisances
- ▶ "Coming to the nuisance" defense
- ▶ Public nuisances
- ▶ Nuisances per se
- ▶ Nuisance remedies: abatement, injunctions, and damages
- ▶ Wrongful death and survival statutes
- ▶ Wrongful birth actions
- ▶ Wrongful life actions.

▌ PRIVATE NUISANCES

nuisance | 1. Anything that annoys or disturbs unreasonably, hurts a person's use of his or her property, or violates the public health, safety, or decency.
2. Use of land that does anything in definition 1.

A **nuisance** is an unreasonable or unlawful use of one's real property that injures another person or interferes with another person's use of his or her real property. Nuisances are defined by common law and by statute. There are two types of nuisances: private and public. Occasionally, the same activity constitutes both a private and a public nuisance. These are sometimes called *mixed nuisances*.

Private Nuisance Defined

A **private nuisance** occurs when someone (1) uses his or her land in such a way as to (2) unreasonably and substantially interfere with (3) another person's use and enjoyment of his or her land. (4) The defendant's activity proximately causes the plaintiff's injuries. The tortfeasor (defendant) is the land user whose activities offend his or her neighbors. The neighboring land user (plaintiff) sues the tortfeasor for engaging in a private nuisance. The second element in commission of a private nuisance, unreasonable and substantial interference, is the most susceptible of interpretation.

private nuisance | A tort that requires a showing of special harm to you or your property and allows the recovery of damages for the harm as well as an injunction.

Unreasonable and Substantial Defined. Whether the tortfeasor's use of real estate is unreasonable and substantially interferes with another's land use is usually defined in terms of offensiveness. The critical question is: How offensive is the tortfeasor's land use? Offensiveness is determined by applying the reasonable person standard. Would a reasonable person with ordinary sensitivities find the tortfeasor's land use unreasonably offensive? If so, then the tortfeasor has unreasonably and substantially interfered with the plaintiff's use and enjoyment of his or her land. Therefore, the tortfeasor has committed a private nuisance.

Community Standard. The reasonable person standard is normally a community standard. In other words, it asks how people living in the community in which the alleged nuisance is taking place would react to the activity. This *reasonable community* reaction supposedly evaluates whether the tortfeasor's land use is unreasonable and a substantial interference with neighboring land uses. The finder of fact, usually a jury, makes this determination.

Use and Enjoyment. *Use and enjoyment* is a term of art in nuisance law. The two are always used together. The term *use* would be sufficient, but *enjoyment* imparts an emotional aspect to nuisance law. The alleged nuisance activity ruins the pleasure neighbors gain through the ways in which they use their real estate. This seems to make the tortfeasor's activities more blameworthy.

Classic Examples

There are many common examples of private nuisances to which to apply the elements just explained. These situations can be classified in broad categories: (1) physical effects on land; (2) health hazards or offending sensibilities; and (3) unwanted associations with neighboring uses.

Physical Effects on Land. Neighboring land users often complain if a tortfeasor's use of realty creates constant vibrations, pollution of water or soil, destruction of crops, flooding, excessive clutter, or unwanted excavations.

Ground Vibrations. For example, suppose a manufacturing plant next door to Jenny's house operates twenty-four hours a day. This plant uses heavy machinery that produces powerful vibrations. These vibrations can be felt for hundreds of feet in all directions. The ground actually shakes slightly from the effect. Over several years, this phenomenon has caused Jenny's house foundation to crack. She would argue that these constant vibrations were an unreasonable and substantial interference with her use and enjoyment of her home. In short, the manufacturing plant would be creating a private nuisance.

Pollution of Water or Soil. Consider another example. Suppose a chemical processing plant dumped its waste waters onto vacant land behind its buildings. These wastes seeped into the soil and polluted underground water supplies. The chemicals also spread across the soil surface onto neighboring lands, making them sterile. These are unreasonable and substantial interferences with the neighboring land owners' use and enjoyment of their realty. The chemical plant has produced a private nuisance.

Crop Destruction. Take another hypothetical. The Blackout Power Company burns coal to produce electricity. Thick, black smoke belches from its tall smokestacks. As the wind disperses the smoke, coal dust settles on the neighbors' land, upon which grow corn and soybeans. The neighbors' crops grow poorly because of the coal dust on their leaves. Blackout's activity is an unreasonable and substantial interference with the neighboring farmers' use and enjoyment of their land. A private nuisance exists.

Flooding. Flooding can also be a private nuisance. Suppose Deatra lives along a small creek. Several miles downstream, another land owner erects a dam to create a small lake for fishermen. However, the lake extends beyond the downstream user's land and floods Deatra's property, including her home. Although this case could involve issues of *riparian* (water) law, in terms of nuisance law, the downstream land owner has unreasonably and substantially interfered with Deatra's use and enjoyment of her real estate by flooding her out.

Excessive Clutter. Few individuals would ever want to live adjacent to a junkyard or trash dump. Most people find such land uses to be offensive to many senses, one of which is sight. Having to look at junk or trash piled high next door can be aesthetically depressing. Many courts have found such uses to be private nuisances for this reason, although neighbors are more commonly also offended by refuse odors.

Unwanted Excavations. Excavation companies sometimes purchase soil from vacant lot owners to haul away and use in construction projects. These excavations leave deep and, for some people, unsightly holes in the vacant lots. Suppose Andy's house is next to several vacant lots that have been excavated in this fashion. A quick search of the caselaw reveals that several courts would find this to be a private nuisance.

Health Hazards or Offending Sensibilities. People's **sensibilities** are ways in which their physical senses (sight, hearing, smell, taste, and touch) and their emotional senses (what they find disgusting, repulsive, threatening, and so forth) are affected. Private nuisances offend a person's sensibilities. They can also create health hazards.

sensibilities | In nuisance law, ways in which people's physical and emotional senses are affected.

Noxious Odors. Land uses that produce harmful, obnoxious odors are frequent candidates as private nuisances, as in the previous trash-dump example. Suppose Nicki lives next to a livestock farm, a chemical processing plant, or a paper mill. These may not create any bad smells at all, but sometimes they emit a powerful and dreadful stench. Much nuisance litigation has involved offensive odors produced by activities such as these.

Smoke and Dust. Smoke and dust emissions can produce serious health hazards for neighbors. Consider the Blackout Power Company example. Neighbors who breathe the coal-dust-laden air could suffer severe respiratory injury. If this happened, the courts would probably rule that Blackout was involved in creating a private nuisance.

Excessive Noise and Temperatures. Land uses that produce excessive noise can harm neighbors' health. In nuisance litigation, many plaintiffs have complained of sleep loss, nervousness, and associated physical and emotional symptoms because of a neighbor's excessive noise. Imagine how Eric might be affected if he lived next to a motor-vehicle racetrack that ran late-night races on weeknights.

Factories producing extreme heat might also pose health problems for neighbors. Persons living adjacent to steel mills have sued for nuisance because of the high temperatures produced by the blast furnaces. The heat from these operations can raise air temperatures to uncomfortable levels. When the heat becomes unreasonable, the courts may find private nuisances.

Toxic Tort Nuisances. The disposal and transportation of hazardous wastes or toxic chemicals are frequently grounds for private nuisance actions. Underground or surface water supplies that are contaminated by leaking toxic-chemical dumps, or air that is filled with poisonous dusts (such as uranium dust vented from a nuclear power plant) are excellent examples of private nuisances. Much of the toxic tort litigation brought today involves nuisance actions.

Incessant Telephone Calls. Creditors occasionally use intimidation tactics to coerce customers to pay delinquent accounts. A favorite technique is the late-night telephone call. The creditor might telephone a delinquent customer several times late at night, every day for weeks or even months, to try to persuade the patron to pay the overdue amounts. Customers subjected to such harassment often suffer emotional distress and related physical manifestations.

Courts routinely determine that such activity constitutes a private nuisance. It is an unreasonable interference with the customer's use and enjoyment of the privacy of his or her home life. In fact, plaintiffs besieged with incessant phone calls often sue the culprit under several causes of action—namely, the intentional torts of invasion of privacy or intentional infliction of emotional distress—along with nuisance.

Unwanted Associations with Neighboring Uses.

For decades, land owners have rushed to the courthouse to file private nuisance actions against the owners of houses of ill repute, X-rated movie theaters, adult bookstores, and liquor or gambling establishments. These cases illustrate clearly the personal nature of offensiveness. Some persons simply cannot abide living in the vicinity of these types of activities. They do not wish to be associated with these land uses. These persons typically become plaintiffs in nuisance lawsuits in an attempt to drive out activities that they find repugnant.

In cases such as these, courts often struggle with community standards to decide if the activities are private nuisances. Are the plaintiffs overreacting, or are their objections reasonable? Would reasonable persons agree that having to live adjacent to establishments engaged in these pursuits is an unreasonable and substantial interference with the use and enjoyment of the realty? This is not an easy question to answer, as can be seen by reading some of the hundreds of appellate court opinions discussing the subject.

"Coming to the Nuisance" Defense

Often, a person will move into a neighborhood in which one of the activities previously described is already situated. In many cases, the manufacturer, trash dump, junkyard, or adult bookstore has been doing business in the same location for years. The plaintiff came to the area after the alleged nuisance was already there. When this happens, and the plaintiff then sues for private nuisance, the defendant may plead the "coming to the nuisance" defense. The **coming to the nuisance defense** involves the plaintiff who owns or uses land at a location in which the alleged nuisance activity was already occurring. If the plaintiff came to the nuisance, then he or she cannot recover against the defendant. The defense is similar to the defense of assumption of risk, in that the plaintiff knew (or reasonably should have known) that the preexisting activity would offend

coming to the nuisance defense | A defense to private nuisance lawsuits that may be used successfully when a plaintiff owns or uses land at a location in which the alleged nuisance activity was previously occurring. The plaintiff is said to have "come to the nuisance" and thus cannot recover against the defendant.

THE CASE OF THE COUNTRY CLUB NUISANCE

The success of a pro se litigant's action against a country club hinges on the applicable statute of limitations. Though living on lands adjoining a country club is often considered desirable, these litigants would beg to differ.

SILVESTER
v.
SPRING VALLEY COUNTRY CLUB

344 S.C. 280, 543 S.E.2d 563
Court of Appeals of South Carolina
February 12, 2001

In 1983, the Silvesters purchased a residence in Spring Valley subdivision. The rear of their lot adjoins a portion of the Club's golf course. Water from the Club's land channels onto the Silvesters' lot, allegedly causing erosion, the deposit of trash, and a potentially hazardous condition due to standing water. . . . The problem manifested itself shortly after the Silvesters occupied the house in 1984.

The Silvesters brought this action in April 1996. They alleged for a first cause of action a trespass occurring in 1992 when the Club constructed a french drainage system to collect and concentrate surface water, thereby exacerbating the Silvesters' drainage problem. . . . For their second cause of action, the Silvesters allege [that] the Club's actions constitute a continuing nuisance affecting the enjoyment of their land.

The action was called to trial on June 17, 1998, with the Silvesters proceeding *pro se.* Prior to selecting a jury, the court heard the Club's motion to dismiss. During argument on the motion, Mr. Silvester admitted they realized the severity of the water problem by 1991. . . .

Mrs. Silvester argued the action should not be dismissed based on the statute of limitations because it was an ongoing nuisance. . . .

The trial court granted the motion to dismiss based on the statute of limitations. The Silvesters appeal.

* * *

The Silvesters pled trespass as the first cause of action in their complaint. However, at the hearing before the trial court, the continuing nuisance claim was the only issue clearly addressed. . . . We therefore find the grant of summary judgment to the Club on the trespass cause of action is not presented to this court as an issue appropriate for appellate review. . . .

The Silvesters contend [that] the trial court erred in granting the Club summary judgment on their continuing nuisance cause of action. We agree.

South Carolina follows the common enemy rule which allows a landowner to treat surface water as a common enemy and dispose of it as he sees fit. However, an exception to this rule prohibits a landowner from using his land in such a manner as to create a nuisance.

The traditional concept of a nuisance requires a landowner to demonstrate that the defendant unreasonably interfered with his ownership or possession of the land. The distinction between trespass and nuisance is that trespass is any intentional invasion of the plaintiff's interest in the exclusive possession of his property, whereas nuisance is a substantial and unreasonable interference with the plaintiff's use and enjoyment of his property.

A nuisance may be classified as permanent or continuing in nature. A continuing nuisance is defined as a nuisance that is intermittent or periodical and is described as one which occurs so often that it is said to be continuing although it is not necessarily constant or unceasing. A permanent nuisance may be expected to continue but is presumed to continue permanently, with no possibility of abatement. As to a permanent nuisance, such as a building or a railroad encroaching on a party's land, the injury is fixed and goes to the whole value of the land.

(continues)

When the statute of limitations begins to run hinges on whether a nuisance is classified as permanent or continuing. When the nuisance is permanent in nature and only one cause of action may be brought for damages, the applicable statute of limitations bars the action if not brought within the statutory period after the first actionable injury. When the nuisance is continuing and the injury is abatable, the statute of limitations does not run merely from the original intrusion on the property and cannot be a complete bar. Rather, a new statute of limitations begins to run after each separate invasion of the property.

In discussing the limitations period applicable in a continuing nuisance action, our supreme court has stated:

> Since every continuance of a nuisance is a new nuisance, authorizing a fresh action, an action may be brought, for the recovery of all damages, resulting from the continuance of a nuisance, within the statutory period of the statute of limitations, for which no previous recovery has been had, even though the original cause of action is barred, unless the nuisance has been so long continued, as to raise the presumption of a grant, or in case of injury to real property, unless the plaintiff's right of entry is barred. . . .

Furthermore, although the statute of limitations may bar a nuisance action for damages, it "is not a defense in an action based upon nuisance for injunctive relief since such statutes do not bar the equitable relief of injunction."

The Silvesters argue [that] water channels from a man-made ditch dug by the Club onto their property. The Club maintains [that] water channeling through a naturally occurring stream passes over a portion of the Silvesters' lot and only "occasionally" overflows their yard. However, Mr. Silvester testified at the hearing "there was an enormous amount of water coming through the property," and Mrs. Silvester stated "our property daily is being damaged." After reviewing the record, we find there exist genuine issues of material fact making summary judgment inappropriate in this case.

The Silvesters alleged a continuing nuisance and requested damages and injunctive relief. The trial court summarily applied the three year statute of limitations to the continuing nuisance cause of action without considering the possibility of abatement, the Club's alleged negligence, or the Silvesters' request for injunctive relief. Viewing the evidence in the light most favorable to the Silvesters, we agree the trial court erred in applying the statute of limitations to their continuing nuisance claim and accordingly reverse the grant of summary judgment on this issue.

. . . We find no evidence in the record [that] the trial judge's ruling was based on or influenced by any bias against either the Silvesters or *pro se* litigants as a class.

Based on the foregoing, the order on appeal is affirmed as to the dismissal of the trespass cause of action and reversed and remanded as to the nuisance cause of action.

CASE QUESTIONS

1. Do you think this case would have had a different outcome if the Silvesters had not appeared *pro se*? Explain.
2. What effect does classifying a nuisance as permanent or continuing have on the statute of limitations?

him or her. Consequently, a reasonable person would not have chosen to buy or use land adjacent to a known, present, and distasteful land use. In essence, the plaintiff assumes the risk of obnoxiousness from the nuisance activity by coming to the place while knowing that the nuisance is already there, waiting to offend the plaintiff. Note, as is discussed later in this chapter, the defense of coming to the nuisance cannot be used against public nuisances.

Private nuisance hypotheticals provide the reader with some of the earthiest factual situations in tort law. Students can easily relate to intrusions upon their senses or values. However, one must guard against identifying too strongly with the offended individual over the business allegedly creating the nuisance. As the following examples illustrate, each party in the nuisance story has its side to tell.

THE CASE OF INTRUSION ON HOG HEAVEN

Incompatible land uses often make unhappy neighbors. Unfortunately, it is not always apparent that such incompatibilities will exist until after the activities have cohabited for some time. Then one of the land owners usually is harmed by the other, and a nuisance action enters the picture. As the case here illustrates, a business can create a nuisance through its own actions or those of its customers.

SHERK
v.
INDIANA WASTE SYSTEMS, INC.
495 N.E.2d 815 (Ind. Ct. App. 1986)
Court of Appeals of Indiana
July 31, 1986
Conover, Judge

Plaintiff-Appellant Dale J. Sherk (Sherk) appeals a negative judgment in his nuisance action against Defendants-Appellees Indiana Waste Systems, Inc. (IWS) and Prairie View Farms, Inc.

We reverse.

ISSUES

Sherk presents three issues for review. Because we reverse we consider only two issues. Restated, they are

1. whether the trial court erred in finding IWS and Prairie View were not responsible for noise generated by others, and
2. whether the trial court erred in finding IWS's use of the land was reasonable and thus a good defense to this action.

FACTS

Sherk raises hogs. IWS operates a landfill on land adjacent to Sherk's former hog breeding facility. IWS leases its land from Prairie View. Sherk's hogs suffered a 50% reduction in conception rates from the time IWS started its operation there. Eventually, Sherk had to close down his hog breeding facility at that location because of such losses.

Sherk, attributing that reduction to noise from the landfill operation, sued IWS and Prairie View Farms, Inc. (hereinafter collectively IWS). Sherk alleged IWS operated its landfill in such a noisy manner it constituted a nuisance and damaged him.

The case was tried by the court. . . .

The trial court found *inter alia* (1) noise generated by IWS's operation of its landfill did not cause Sherk's problem, (2) truck traffic increased as a result of the opening of the landfill, (3) noise emanating from the increased truck traffic caused the reduction in conception rates, and (4) IWS's operation of the landfill was reasonable. The trial court entered judgment against Sherk. He appeals.

* * *

(continues)

Sherk contends the trial court erred when it concluded IWS was not responsible for the noise and vibration generated by the trash hauling trucks entering and leaving its landfill. Sherk also contends the trial court erred when it decided reasonableness of use is a defense to an action for a nuisance and IWS's use of its land is reasonable. . . .

When deciding whether one's use of his property is a nuisance to his neighbors it is necessary to balance the competing interests of the landowners. In so doing we use a common sense approach. Mere annoyance or inconvenience will not support an action for a nuisance because the damages resulting therefrom are deemed *damnum absque injuria* in recognition of the fact life is not perfect. Thus, "reasonable use" of one's property may be a defense to a nuisance action where the use merely causes *incidental* injury to another. Where, however, one uses his property for his profit so as to practically confiscate or destroy his neighbor's property he should be compelled to respond in damages, for it can hardly be said such use is reasonable. Whether one's use of property is reasonable is determined by the effect such use has on neighboring property. Liability is imposed in those cases where the harm or risk thereto is greater than the owner of such property should be required to bear under the circumstances.

Sherk argues but for the landfill operation there would have been no noise obstructing the free use of his property as a hog breeding facility. Thus, he opines, IWS should be liable for the noise generated by the trash hauling trucks. IWS in turn argues because the trial court found its use of its property was reasonable IWS is absolved of any responsibility for its customers' noisy trucks.

. . . [A] business may be liable for the acts of its customers or others if acts by them upon the business property or in going to or leaving it obstruct a neighbor's use of his property.

The facts found by the trial court here show (1) the conception rate of Sherk's pigs ranged between 70% and 90% before the landfill began its operations; (2) the rate was reduced to 30% following the opening of the landfill; (3) the reduction in rate of conception was due to the noise generated by the trash hauling trucks traveling to and from the landfill.

It is apparent but for the landfill there substantially would have been no noisy truck traffic in the vicinity of Sherk's pigs, and they would have continued breeding successfully in the peace and tranquility which they apparently require. The interference here is more than a mere annoyance or incidental harm. The use of IWS's property has destroyed the usefulness of Sherk's property as a hog breeding facility. The evidence and all reasonable inferences from it leads inescapably to the conclusion IWS's use of its property was unreasonable in relation to Sherk's use of his property as a hog breeding facility.

Because the trial court found no liability, it made no findings as to damages. While a proper remedy for nuisance may consist of damages or injunction or some combination of the two . . . , Sherk seeks no injunction, only damages.

Reversed, and remanded for hearing and determination as to Sherk's damages only.

CASE QUESTIONS
1. Do you agree with the court that IWS's use of its property was unreasonable? Why or why not?
2. Suppose that IWS had begun operating its landfill before Sherk established his hog breeding facility. Would the outcome of the case be different? Explain.

There are literally thousands of different factual patterns involving private nuisance to be found in the court reporters. This tort can be quite interesting to study, given the variety and peculiarity of the fact scenarios that allegedly produce nuisances. One might wish to consult the index to the *American Law Reports* series, published

hypotheticals

Sajjad bought a house in a residential subdivision in 2000. His real estate is adjacent to seventy acres of pasture land. In 2007, the pasture was sold to the Waste Away Company, which erected a trash processing plant and landfill in 2008. This plant began compacting trash for landfill use as well as incinerating trash. Early in 2009 Sajjad began smelling unpleasant odors and smoke from the trash piles and smokestacks. In warm weather, the smell was extremely nasty. Fumes seemed to hover all around the neighborhood. Does Sajjad have a cause of action for private nuisance?

When Sajjad bought his home in 2000, he assumed that he would be living next door to pasture land, which is free from odors and has a clear, natural view. He probably anticipated that wildlife or livestock would graze the realty next door. This rustic expectation was shattered in 2007 when Waste Away transformed the land into a trash processing facility and landfill.

Using the private nuisance formula, first ask whether Waste Away's use of its real estate unreasonably and substantially interfered with Sajjad's use and enjoyment of his property. Every day, odors and smoke floated across Sajjad's land from the trash facility. The neighborhood became inundated with the foul smell of piled or burning trash. Reasonable persons with ordinary sensibilities (or, as it is sometimes called, sensitivities) would find such odors and smoke to be offensive. Most subdivision residents in Sajjad's community could reasonably be expected to react adversely to the invading stench. Waste Away has created a private nuisance.

* * *

The Sanctified Brethren Church purchased a building site for a new cathedral in July 2008. Across the street, one block away, were several taverns, an X-rated movie theatre, and an adult bookstore. Once construction began, members of the church filed suit against the owners of these businesses, claiming private nuisance. Would the church's lawsuit be successful?

No. Assuming that the church could first prove that these businesses constituted a private nuisance, the businesses could avail themselves of the coming to the nuisance defense. The church knew that these businesses were already located in the neighborhood when it purchased its building site. The church voluntarily decided to situate its cathedral within close proximity to activities that church members found offensive. Therefore, the church would fail in its lawsuit.

by The Lawyers' Cooperative Publishing Company. (These are abbreviated as ALR, ALR2d, ALR3d, ALR4th, ALR5th, ALR6th, and ALR Fed.) Each series contains many annotations involving different examples of nuisances. These are often entertaining as well as enlightening—one reason that nuisance is frequently regarded as a "fun" tort subject in law study. Table 11-1 lists the elements to private nuisance.

TABLE 11-1

Elements of private
nuisance

ELEMENTS	EXAMPLES	DEFENSE
Defendant uses his or her land	Physical effects on land (vibrations, pollution, crop destruction, flooding, junk clutter, or excavations)	Coming to the nuisance
In an activity that unreasonably and substantially interferes	Health hazards and offending sensibilities (noxious odors, smoke, dust, extreme noise or temperature, incessant telephone calling)	
With use and enjoyment of another's land		
Defendant's activity must proximately cause plaintiff's injuries	Unwanted associations with neighboring uses (prostitution houses, distributors of explicit sexual material, gambling institutions)	

▌ PUBLIC NUISANCES

public nuisance | Activity by the tortfeasor that unreasonably and substantially interferes with the public's use and enjoyment of legal rights common to the public.

In addition to private nuisances, there are also public nuisances. A **public nuisance** is a land use that injures the public at large rather than just a single individual. A public nuisance unreasonably interferes with the public's enjoyment of legal rights common to the public. The elements of public nuisance may be broken down as: (1) The tortfeasor's activity that (2) unreasonably and substantially interferes with (3) the public's use and enjoyment of legal rights common to the public.

Unlike private nuisances, which can adversely affect a single person, a public nuisance must harm the general public. More than one person *must* be affected (or, at least, potentially affected) by the alleged nuisance activity. This does not require a multitude of angry citizens. Residents of a single neighborhood would suffice.

The standard of unreasonable and substantial interference is identical to that used in private nuisances, except that the interference must be to the public rather than a sole plaintiff.

Use and Enjoyment of Common Legal Rights

The use and enjoyment element in public nuisance is significantly different from the one discussed in private nuisances. With public nuisances, the tortfeasor's obnoxious land use interferes with the public's common legal rights, such as the right to peaceably assemble in public places, the right to use public streets and sidewalks without being subjected to offensive activities, or the right to safe and healthy conditions in one's neighborhood.

Governments as Plaintiffs

Although citizens often file public nuisance complaints with their local governmental agencies, it is the government, through its municipal governing bodies (e.g., city council, county commissioners) or its prosecuting attorneys, that sues defendants alleged to be committing public nuisances. This is because the government represents the public at large and must enforce its citizens' legal rights against tortfeasors. At common law, or by statute or, in some states, by state constitutional provision, state and local governments have the authority to protect their citizens from public nuisances. The source of this power is the states' **police powers,** which give governments authority to file lawsuits or enact legislation to protect the public's health, welfare, safety, or morals. These are usually very broad powers that give governments considerable flexibility to forbid certain offensive activities.

police power | The government's right and power to set up and enforce laws to provide for the safety, health, and general welfare of the people.

Types of Public Nuisances

Almost all public nuisances are defined by statute or ordinance. Many such laws focus on land uses *that legislators believe* a majority of the population would find offensive, unhealthy, or immoral. The reader may know from personal experience that this belief may be unfounded or exaggerated. That, of course, depends upon whether one agrees or disagrees with what the government has labeled a public nuisance. Common targets of public nuisance laws include institutions devoted to (1) gambling, (2) prostitution, (3) distribution of sexually explicit materials, (4) sale of alcohol, or (5) toxic waste management. Other typical public nuisances include (1) allowing certain weeds or poisonous plants to grow on one's land; (2) failing to comply with health code provisions by keeping one's residence clean and vermin-free; and (3) keeping unrestrained wild or vicious animals on one's property. However, public nuisances may also include many of the same activities discussed in the private nuisances section.

Mixed Nuisances

Often, the same activity can constitute both a private and a public nuisance. These are sometimes called **mixed nuisances.** Apply this rule of thumb in such cases: The greater the number of persons adversely affected by an allegedly offensive land use, the more likely it will be considered a public, as well as a private, nuisance.

mixed nuisance | A nuisance that is both public and private.

Nuisances Per Se

Courts often consider activities violating public nuisance statutes to be **nuisances per se.** *Per se* is Latin meaning "by itself." In tort law, it usually means that some behavior has violated a statute, and therefore the defendant is automatically liable. Sometimes courts, in the common law, decree that certain conduct is per se tortious. Negligence per se is an example. Per se nuisances have also been established by common-law court decisions.

A public nuisance per se is an activity that violates the statute and is automatically considered a public nuisance. The tortfeasor thus loses from the start of litigation, simply by violating the statute. Statutes (and, rarely, common law) may also declare certain private nuisances to be per se nuisances.

"Coming to the Nuisance" Not a Defense

Generally, courts do not recognize the coming to the nuisance defense in public nuisance cases. This defense focuses on the individual plaintiff who purchases or uses land next to a preexisting, private nuisance activity. Public nuisances, by definition, affect the public at large, and the very existence or continuation of the public nuisance activity is considered harmful, whether it was preexisting or not.

As *Jacobs* demonstrates, what constitutes a public nuisance or a nuisance per se is generally a question of common-law interpretation and statutory construction. But underlying questions of substance and form are the value judgments implicit in all nuisance per se or public nuisance cases. The following examples present such choices. Despite the temptation to become caught up in "good" versus "bad," one must concentrate on the legal elements and their application to the facts. However, the remedy of ordering an injunction may involve a balancing of interests.

THE CASE OF THE DOOR-TO-DOOR SOLICITATION

Many people commonly think of door-to-door salespersons as nuisances, but the law does not automatically define them as such. As the following case suggests, not all forms of solicitation are included in public nuisance ordinances.

JACOBS

v.

CITY OF JACKSONVILLE

762 F. Supp. 327 (M.D. Fla. 1991)
U.S. District Court, Middle District of Florida
April 8, 1991
Moore, II, District Judge

This cause was tried before the Court on March 11, 1990. . . . [T]he Court now issues the following findings of fact and conclusions of law.

* * *

Plaintiff, Jerry L. Jacobs, does business under the fictitious name of Youth Opportunities Unlimited (hereinafter "Y.O.U."), and is a person who, personally and through his employees, sells or offers for sale merchandise by traveling from door-to-door, while carrying such merchandise. Y.O.U. is a for-profit organization which derives income through the sale of cookies, candy, and other items. These sales are conducted primarily by teenagers who are Y.O.U. members. Plaintiff holds a city permit to operate as a peddler of merchandise.

* * *

Plaintiff and the Y.O.U. salespersons conduct the door-to-door activities in various neighborhoods in Jacksonville on a rotating basis; as a result, sales in any particular neighborhood are made no more than a few times per year. Each individual Y.O.U. product item is sold to the consumer for $4.00. . . . No evidence was introduced to show that a large number of the residences solicited found Y.O.U.'s sales activities to be annoying or injurious, although the evidence did show that Y.O.U. salespersons are occasionally unwelcome at a few residences.

* * *

The City of Jacksonville, through Officer J.P. Baptist of the Jacksonville Sheriff's Office, has threatened Plaintiff with arrest under [Jacksonville ordinance] § 250.303, for engaging in residential door-to-door peddling activities without invitation. . . .

In most instances, Plaintiff has not been expressly "requested or invited" by the owner or occupant of the private residence before engaging in door-to-door sales activity. Plaintiff does not solicit at any private residence where a "No Solicitation" sign is visible.

. . . The Court finds that Plaintiff is a "peddler" as defined in the Code, . . . subject to the prohibition on door-to-door peddling set forth in J.O.C. § 250.303.

* * *

Under Florida law, unless a homeowner manifests externally in some manner his or her wish to remain unmolested by the visits of solicitors or peddlers, a solicitor or peddler may take . . . an implied invitation to call upon residences . . . . (*Prior v. White*, 132 Fla. 1, 180 So. 347, 355 (1938)). In *Prior*, the Florida Supreme Court invalidated an anti-peddling ordinance of New Smyrna Beach, Florida, as applied to

the door-to-door sales activities of a Fuller Brush Company salesman. The New Smyrna ordinance was virtually identical to the Jacksonville ordinance now at issue. The court held that peddling and soliciting in New Smyrna was not a public nuisance because custom and usage established an implied invitation to solicit sales at private residences, and therefore could not be punished as a crime or misdemeanor. The court further held that a municipality cannot, through an attempted exercise of its police powers, declare by ordinance or otherwise that an activity is a public nuisance, when in fact such activity is not proved to be a public nuisance.

Prior v. White is still good law in Florida, never having been overruled by the Florida Supreme Court. Recent cases also have held that a municipality may not declare an activity to be a public nuisance unless that activity does in fact constitute a public nuisance. In addition, Florida courts continue to recognize the implied invitation theory. Since the principles set forth in *Prior* remain part of the law of Florida, *Prior* is binding upon this Court in its interpretation of Florida law. . . . Thus, the facts of each case must be examined carefully to determine whether the type of door-to-door peddling engaged in by the parties in that case constitutes a public nuisance.

A public nuisance is defined as an activity that "violates public rights, subverts public order, decency or morals, or causes inconvenience or damage to the public generally." It is not completely clear under *Prior* which party bears the burden of proving that peddling is or is not a public nuisance. . . .

In this case, door-to-door peddling in Jacksonville, Florida has not been proved to be a public nuisance. The Defendants have introduced virtually no evidence that proves peddling in Jacksonville by Y.O.U. or by others is a public nuisance, and have made little attempt to make such a showing. . . .

Even assuming the Plaintiff bears the burden of proving that door-to-door peddling . . . is not a public nuisance, the Court finds that Plaintiff has met this burden. The evidence introduced at trial showed that

(continues)

Y.O.U. sold 90,000 items in Jacksonville in 1990, an average of roughly one item per residence solicited. The evidence showed that a sizeable number, approximately one-half, of the residences solicited made a purchase from Y.O.U. Thus, thousands of customers in Jacksonville evidently did not find Plaintiff's organization materially annoying to them personally, which demonstrates that Y.O.U.'s activities do not materially inconvenience the public at large or subvert public order. . . . Thus, Plaintiff has affirmatively proved, in the absence of any effective rebuttal evidence by the Defendants, that Y.O.U.'s activities do not inconvenience the public in a manner that amounts to a public nuisance. Accordingly, under the authority of *Prior v. White,* the ordinance is unreasonable and an invalid exercise of the police power as applied to the Plaintiff and the Y.O.U. organization.

* * *

ORDERED AND ADJUDGED:

. . . Defendants are permanently enjoined from arresting or prosecuting Plaintiff or any members of Youth Opportunities Unlimited under color of Jacksonville Ordinance Code § 250.303.

CASE QUESTIONS

1. How does the court's definition of a public nuisance differ from that discussed in this chapter?
2. Do you agree with the court that the plaintiff's activities did not violate the ordinance? Explain.

hypotheticals

Carter has an apiary in his backyard. He lives in a suburban neighborhood. Several hundred honeybees congregate in Carter's hives. The bees produce honey that Carter sells at local groceries. Frequently, children in the area have been stung by honeybees. Parents complained to Carter, but he simply shrugged off each incident, stating that there was no proof that his bees were responsible. However, there were no other honeybee colonies in the neighborhood. A town ordinance prohibits the keeping of wildlife within the city limits. Has Carter committed a public nuisance, a private nuisance, or a nuisance per se?

Carter's use of his land (maintaining an apiary) substantially and unreasonably interfered with his neighbors' use and enjoyment of the public streets and sidewalks in the area, as well as their own realty. Children were often stung by honeybees, and the only large honeybee colony in the neighborhood was Carter's. A trier-of-fact could reasonably infer that Carter's bees were responsible for the attacks. This would be a private nuisance. A local governmental agency could sue Carter for public nuisance. Reasonable persons would find these bee encounters to be offensive and dangerous. The public at large was threatened by Carter's *ferae naturae.* The bees unreasonably and substantially interfered with citizens' use of public streets and sidewalks.

Under its police power, the local government would have authority to sue Carter for public nuisance.

Carter also violated the local ordinance prohibiting the keeping of wildlife within the city limits. This constitutes a nuisance per se, giving the town government another cause of action against Carter.

* * *

Dave operates a massage parlor across from the local public high school. Although there is no evidence of prostitution at the establishment, Dave offers nude massages, during which both customers and masseurs disrobe. From across the street, high-school students can see clearly through the windows of Dave's building. Is Dave engaged in a public nuisance?

Dave's use of his land could adversely affect the students. The erotic views could disrupt school activities as children (and adults) cluster around windows to catch the revealing sights next door. Arguably, this is an unreasonable and substantial interference with a public right—namely, the right to use the public school for educational pursuits. Under its police powers, the municipal government could sue Dave for public nuisance.

Admittedly, cases such as Dave's involve value judgments and presume a threat to the public morals. One may agree or disagree with the alleged public threat produced by a massage parlor next to a school. However, many cases have involved exactly these fact situations, and courts promptly conclude that public nuisances have occurred.

Table 11-2 lists the elements of public nuisances, mixed nuisances, and nuisances per se.

ELEMENTS	EXAMPLES	DEFENSE
Public Nuisance Activity that unreasonably and substantially interferes with public's use and enjoyment of legal rights common to public at large	Prostitution establishments Pornography distributors	Coming to the nuisance *not* a defense to public nuisances
Plaintiff is governmental agency responsible for protecting public interest harmed by public nuisance activity	Historically, gambling and alcohol establishments were often considered public nuisances, although not normally at the present time	

TABLE 11-2
Elements of public nuisances, mixed nuisances, and nuisances per se

(continues)

TABLE 11-2 *(continued)*

ELEMENTS	EXAMPLES	DEFENSE
State and local governments have authority to litigate public nuisances under general police powers to protect public health, safety, morals, and welfare	Allowing noxious weeds to grow on one's land. Failing to comply with public health statutes. Keeping unrestrained wild animals on one's land	
Mixed Nuisance Mixed nuisances include public and private nuisances		Coming to the nuisance defense effective against private nuisance portion of mixed nuisance actions
Nuisances Per Se Nuisances per se are nuisance activities that violate statutes or ordinances		Coming to the nuisance defense not usually effective against nuisance per se actions

▌ REMEDIES FOR NUISANCES

When one has identified a private or public nuisance, what does one do about it? In other words, what remedies are available to plaintiffs against defendants? **Remedies** are the relief that plaintiffs receive against defendants in lawsuits. The most common remedy in tort actions is *money* **damages,** in which the defendant must pay the plaintiff a sum of money to satisfy the judgment. The trier-of-fact sets the amount owed after a trial has been held.

Other, nonmonetary remedies are also available for torts such as nuisance. These are called equitable remedies. **Equitable remedies** do not involve money damages; instead, the court orders the defendant to do (or, more commonly, *not* to do) something. When the court orders a defendant to do or not to do something, it is called an **injunction.** When a court orders a governmental official to perform a nondiscretionary act, this is called a **mandamus** order.

For centuries, money damages were considered inappropriate in nuisance cases. Courts would apply only equitable remedies. In nuisance law, the most common equitable remedies include (1) abatement and (2) injunction, although now money damages are occasionally permitted in nuisance cases.

Abatement

In nuisance cases, abatement is the most common remedy plaintiffs seek. With **abatement,** the defendant is ordered to cease, or *abate*, the nuisance activity.

remedy | The means by which a right is enforced or satisfaction is gained for a harm done.

damages | Money that a court orders paid to a person who has suffered damage (a loss or harm) by the person who caused the injury.

equitable relief (remedy) | A remedy available in equity; generally non-monetary relief.

injunction | A judge's order to a person to do or to refrain from doing a particular thing.

mandamus | (Latin) "We command." A *writ of mandamus* is a court order that directs a public official or government department to do something.

abatement | Reduction or decrease . . . [or] complete elimination.

Abatement is often permanent. The defendant must desist from conducting the nuisance activity after a judgment for abatement is entered. This provides complete relief for the plaintiff, because the nuisance activity will be discontinued. Abatement can create harsh economic consequences for defendants, but the public policy behind abatement is clear: Nuisance tortfeasors have injured someone (or, if the public, many people). As long as the nuisance continues, the plaintiff(s) will continue to be hurt. The only certain solution is to stop the nuisance altogether.

Injunctions

Courts enforce abatement through injunctive relief. *Injunctions* are court orders to defendants to cease and desist from engaging in nuisance activities. There are two types of injunctions: (1) temporary injunctions, including temporary restraining orders (TROs); and (2) permanent injunctions.

Temporary Injunctions.
Temporary injunctions are often used from the time a plaintiff files suit until the first court hearing. The plaintiff, in his or her complaint, asks the court to issue a **temporary restraining order (TRO),** forbidding the defendant from conducting an alleged nuisance activity until a court hearing can be held to determine if the activity constitutes a nuisance. Under most rules of civil procedure, TROs may be issued for up to ten days, while the court convenes a hearing to decide if a nuisance has occurred. After the hearing, if the evidence convinces the judge that a nuisance is happening, the court may order further temporary injunctive relief, banning the defendant's nuisance activity until a trial on the merits may be held.

> **temporary restraining order (TRO)** | A judge's order to a person to not take a certain action during the period prior to a full hearing on the rightness of the action.

The purpose of temporary injunctions is to protect the plaintiff from further harm if a nuisance is in fact occurring. Plaintiffs often must post bonds to compensate the defendant if the court or jury later decides that the defendant did not engage in a nuisance. This is to protect the defendant from economic losses suffered while the injunctions were in effect and the defendant was not permitted to conduct the nuisance activity (which could mean lost profits or extra expenses). The court must balance the hardship to the defendant against the interference suffered by the plaintiff.

Permanent Injunctions.
Permanent injunctions are abatement orders instructing the defendant to permanently stop doing the nuisance activity. They are usually issued after a trial on the merits, once the trier-of-fact has concluded that a nuisance exists. If the defendant fails to obey a permanent injunction by continuing the nuisance, the court can punish the defendant by holding him or her in **contempt.** This punishment may involve monetary fines or even imprisonment.

> **permanent injunction** | Abatement orders instructing the defendant to permanently stop doing the nuisance activity. Usually issued after a full hearing.
>
> **contempt** | 1. An act that obstructs a court's work or lessens the dignity of the court. . . . 2. A willful disobeying of a judge's command or official court order.

Money Damages

When abatement could impose an unreasonably severe economic burden upon the nuisance tortfeasor, courts have broken with the ancient common-law tradition and awarded plaintiffs money damages instead of abatement. This way, the plaintiffs can be compensated for their injuries produced by the nuisance activities, and the defendant can survive (economically) by staying in business, even though the nuisance also continues. Courts using this alternative are usually attempting to balance interests between conflicting land uses.

THE CASE OF THE POLLUTING TOLL BOOTH

Federal and state statutes often provide private citizens and public agencies with authority to litigate against public agencies concerning public or private nuisances. Private citizens may enforce nuisance actions under the Clean Air Act, Clean Water Act, and a variety of other environmental-protection statutes. However, there are certain precise statutory requirements to follow in order to proceed with these actions. This case clearly demonstrates the difficulties a pro se litigant can encounter in handling complex legal matters.

UNITED STATES ENVIRONMENTAL PROTECTION AGENCY

v.

THE PORT AUTHORITY OF NEW YORK AND NEW JERSEY, et al.

162 F. Supp. 2d 173 (S.D.N.Y. 2001)
United States District Court, S.D. New York
March 30, 2001

Plaintiffs Kevin McKeown ("McKeown") and his organization No More Tolls (collectively "plaintiffs") commenced this *pro se* citizen's suit against defendants, state authorities and officials responsible for operating toll roads, bridges and tunnels in New York, New Jersey, Delaware and Maryland, alleging that they operate and maintain toll booth facilities in violation of the Clean Air Act, ("CAA"), the Clean Water Act ("CWA"), the Resource Conservation and Recovery Act ("RCRA"), Occupational Safety and Health Administration ("OSHA") regulations, Federal Highway Administration regulations, nuisance law, and civil rights law.

* * *

Plaintiff No More Tolls is a public interest organization in Washington D.C. It is "dedicated to the protection and enhancement of the environment of the United States. . . . [I]t supports effective enforcement of Federal and State CAA, CWA, RCRA, and other Federal and State laws." Plaintiff McKeown is the Executive Director of No More Tolls.

Defendants are state authorities and their directors who are responsible for the administration of public transportation including the operation of toll booths in New York (the "New York defendants"), New Jersey (the "New Jersey defendants"), Delaware (the "Delaware defendants") and Maryland (the "Maryland defendants").

On November 29, 1999, plaintiffs sent defendants a Notice of Intent to Sue. The Notice of Intent to Sue states that plaintiffs believe defendants are violating the CAA, CWA and RCRA by operating toll booths.

On February 3, 2000, plaintiffs filed this action by order to show cause, requesting a temporary restraining order and a preliminary injunction.

* * *

The CAA, CWA and RCRA all permit a citizen to bring a civil action to enforce those statutes on their own behalf. . . . Moreover, McKeown and No More Tolls have not offered any reason why the EPA and

Browner are necessary parties. ("The [CAA] citizen suit provision contemplates actions against the Administrator where he fails to perform a non-discretionary act. Alternatively, the citizen, after giving sixty days notice to the Administrator, can proceed directly against the violator. When the plaintiff elects this later course, the Administrator has the right to intervene in the suit, but he is not required to be a participant in such litigation and his absence does not render the action infirm.")

Accordingly, defendants' motions to strike the EPA and Browner from the amended complaint are granted. . . .

Defendants argue that the complaint should be dismissed for lack of standing because plaintiffs have not alleged an injury in-fact, or alternatively, that any alleged injury is not redressable by this action.

An organization such as No More Tolls may have standing to "seek judicial relief from injury to itself and to vindicate whatever rights and immunities the association itself may enjoy. . . ." No More Tolls, however, has not asserted injury to itself.

. . . The only known member of No More Tolls is McKeown. . . .

The only personalized injuries alleged in the amended complaint are that McKeown "has sustained damages as a result of the operation of toll booths" and that "[d]efendant[s'] operation of toll booths damage the business, property and health of the [p]laintiff" in violation of antitrust laws. Neither of those allegations is concrete or particularized, nor do they constitute a "distinct and palpable injury."

* * *

Further, even if plaintiffs could establish that they have standing to sue, they failed to comply with the mandatory notice requirement with respect to the Maryland and New Jersey defendants.

* * *

Accordingly, the New Jersey defendants' motion to dismiss plaintiffs' CAA, CWA and RCRA claims for failure to comply with the mandatory notice provisions pursuant to those statutes is granted.

Even if plaintiffs had complied with the notice requirements, venue is improper as to the Maryland, New Jersey and Delaware defendants. Moreover, plaintiffs have failed to state a claim upon which relief can be granted.

* * *

The CAA was implemented to prevent and control air pollution by providing "[f]ederal financial assistance and leadership . . . for the development of cooperative Federal, State, regional, and local programs to prevent and control air pollution."

* * *

Plaintiffs claim that defendants have violated the CAA by slowing "vehicular movement which unnecessarily increases toxic tailpipe emissions." However, the complaint does not identify any violations of specific emissions standards, or limitations under the CAA or legally enforceable strategies or commitments that the defendants made under a current SIP.

Plaintiffs also claim that toll booths are major sources of hazardous air pollutants under 42 U.S.C. The CAA defines a "major source" as a "stationary source that emits or has the potential to emit considering controls, in the aggregate 10 tons per year or more of any hazardous air pollutant or 25 tons per year or more of any combination of hazardous air pollutants . . ." (42 U.S.C. § 7412(a)(1)). A stationary source is defined as "any building, structure, facility, or installation which emits or may emit any air pollutant," (42 U.S.C. § 7411(a)(3)).

Plaintiffs do not allege that toll booths emit or have the potential to emit air pollutants. They claim that motor vehicles emit the air pollutants. Motor vehicles, however, are specifically excluded from the definition of stationary source.

* * *

Accordingly, defendants' motions to dismiss plaintiffs' CAA claims for failure to state a claim are granted.

(continues)

Citizen suits under the CWA are permitted only to enforce "an effluent standard or limitation" or "an order issued by the [EPA] Administrator or a State with respect to such a standard or limitation" (33 U.S.C. § 1365(a)). Effluent standards and limitations are administratively established regulations of particular types of dischargers on the amounts of pollutants that may be discharged.

Plaintiffs assert that "[t]oll booth operators violate 'an effluent standard or limitation' under . . . 33 U.S.C. [§] 1365(a)(1)(A) because of illegal and unpermitted discharges of leachate from toll booth locations," that "[d]efendants violate CWA Section 311 by continuing to cause the dimunition of water quality of the surface and subterranean waters by release of pollutants into the surface waters and ground waters under and adjacent to toll booth areas," . . .

Plaintiffs' sweeping allegations do not charge defendants with violating any effluent standards or limitations.

* * *

Moreover, the "leachate" that plaintiffs claim is released from toll booths, including carbon monoxide, nitrogen oxide and sulfur, are air emissions and not water pollutants, covered by CWA.

* * *

For all of the above stated reasons, defendants' motions to dismiss plaintiffs' CWA claims are granted.

CASE QUESTIONS

1. What were the fatal flaws in the plaintiffs' claim?
2. Do the precise requirements of the environmental statutes interfere with their intent?

Review of Hypotheticals

Review the hypotheticals from the previous sections of this chapter. Consider which remedies are suitable. In class or study groups, one may wish to discuss whether money damages is an appropriate alternative to abatement. Table 11-3 restates the remedies available in nuisance lawsuits.

TABLE 11-3
Remedies for nuisances

EQUITABLE REMEDIES	MONEY DAMAGES
Abatement (permanent prohibition against nuisance activity)	Money damages may be awarded if abatement would put unreasonable economic burdens on the defendant
Temporary injunctions (forbidding nuisance activity during litigation process)	
Permanent injunctions (used for abatement)	

SURVIVAL STATUTES AND WRONGFUL DEATH STATUTES

Under common law, when a plaintiff died his or her tort action also died, and the spouse and children would lose all right to recovery. To avoid this harsh result, all states have passed survival statutes. Also under common law, a defendant could injure a person and still be liable; but if the defendant died, then there would be no recovery at all.

Survival statutes allow recovery to families of persons killed by tortious actions. In this way the injured party's claim survives his or her death. If successful, damages are awarded to the decedent's estate. This is contrasted with **wrongful death statutes,** which give the surviving family members of a deceased tort victim a cause of action against the tortfeasor whose negligence or intentional torts resulted in the victim's death.

Typical Facts in Wrongful Death Cases

The factual pattern in wrongful death actions may be summarized as follows: (1) a tortfeasor commits a tort against the victim; (2) the victim dies as a result of the tortfeasor's actions; (3) the victim's spouse, children, estate, or person who relied on the deceased person for economic support, or all of them, sue the tortfeasor for wrongfully causing the victim's death.

Plaintiffs in Wrongful Death Actions

Under wrongful death statutes, the surviving family members, usually the victim's spouse or children, become the plaintiffs. However, some statutes allow the victim's parents or siblings to become plaintiffs. The victim's estate may also be permitted to sue the defendant for wrongful death damages under some statutes. Some states have a limit on damages for wrongful death.

Damages

Wrongful death statutes usually define the types of damages that plaintiffs may recover against defendants. These damages include lost lifetime earnings potential and loss of **consortium.**

survival statute | A state law that allows a lawsuit to be brought by a relative for a person who has just died. The lawsuit is based on the cause of action the dead person would have had.

wrongful death statute | [Statute that allows] a lawsuit [to be] brought by the dependents of a dead person against the person who caused the death. Damages will be given to compensate the dependents for their loss if the killing was negligent or willful.

consortium | The rights and duties resulting from marriage. They include companionship, love, affection, assistance, cooperation, and sexual relations.

---

practical **application**

Be sure to check the precise wording of the wrongful death statute in your jurisdiction. In some states, such as California, the statute of limitations for wrongful death runs from the date of death, not the date of the accident.

Lost Lifetime Earnings Potential.

A tort victim's surviving family members may recover damages for the lost income that the victim would likely have earned had he or she not been killed by the tortfeasor. Wrongful death statutes usually define these damages in terms of the decedent's lost earnings potential based upon income at the time of death. This income base is projected over time. The future time period used is normally the victim's life expectancy, which is calculated from insurance actuarial tables. The projected earnings potential is usually adjusted for the victim's projected living expenses, had he or she survived. An economist is usually hired as an expert witness to introduce this evidence at trial.

Loss of Consortium.

Wrongful death statutes often permit a tort victim's surviving family to recover damages for the lost love and companionship of the decedent. This is similar to pain and suffering damages. However, many statutes do not allow recovery of such damages. Wrongful death statutes (or courts interpreting them) often label this type of damages **loss of consortium.** Many statutes define *consortium* as both economic and intangible benefits lost to a victim's surviving family because of the victim's death. The intangible element could include lost love, companionship, and even the survivors' mental anguish upon losing a loved one.

loss of consortium | The loss of one or more of a spouse's services.

Defenses

In wrongful death actions, the tortfeasor may use any defense applicable to the specific tort that produced the victim's injury. For example, suppose the victim had been contributorily or comparatively negligent, or assumed the risk of the defendant's actions that killed the victim. Suppose the tortfeasor killed the victim while acting in self-defense or defense of others. The tortfeasor may escape liability for wrongfully causing the victim's death if any of the suitable tort defenses apply in the case. Defenses are available in a wrongful death action just as if the victim were still alive and, as plaintiff, were suing the defendant.

A CASE OF "DEATH-BEFORE-LITIGATION"

Some issues that come before appellate courts seem to have obvious answers. Some are so obvious, in fact, that one wonders why an appeal was necessary to answer them. The Montana Supreme Court may have been thinking this very question as it wrote the following straightfaced opinion, in response to a perfectly serious Ninth Circuit Court of Appeals query. Note Justice Gray's remarkable judicial restraint in the opinion. (Case questions are omitted following the case, as there is nothing left to ask.)

CARROLL
v.
W.R. GRACE & CO.
830 P.2d 1253 (Mont. 1992)
Supreme Court of Montana
January 14, 1992
Gray, Justice

This case is before us on certified questions from the Ninth Circuit Court of Appeals concerning the point at which a Montana wrongful death action accrues. . . .

Appellant (and defendant), W.R. Grace and Company, claims that the action accrues at the date of injury. Respondent (and plaintiff), Edith Carroll, claims that a wrongful death action accrues at the death of the injured person. We conclude that a wrongful death action does not accrue until the death of the injured person.

Charles Carroll (decedent) was employed by W.R. Grace and Company (Grace) at its vermiculite mine located in Libby, Montana, from 1958 until 1976; he underwent yearly chest x-rays provided by Grace from 1967 until 1976. Decedent retired in 1976, but continued to seek medical help regarding shortness of breath and a heart condition.

Mr. Carroll died in 1989, thirteen years after retirement. His autopsy report listed the cause of death as "severe interstitial fibrosis with pulmonary failure, apparently due to 'asbestosis.'" Decedent's medical records show that he had been diagnosed as suffering from asbestosis as early as 1972.

Edith Carroll, wife of decedent, filed a survival claim and a wrongful death claim against Grace, her husband's former employer, asserting that her husband's asbestosis was related to his employment at Grace's mine. She contends that she did not know his death was related to his employment until she read the autopsy report. She filed her suit as a diversity action in the United States District Court within two months of her husband's death.

Grace moved for summary judgment based on the running of the statutes of limitations for both survival and wrongful death claims. The U.S. District Court granted summary judgment, holding that the statute of limitations had run on both claims. Edith Carroll appealed to the United States Court of Appeals for the Ninth Circuit. The Ninth Circuit affirmed the District Court's holding that the survival claim was barred by the applicable three-year statute of limitations, but stated that Montana law was not definitive on the issue of when a wrongful death action accrues. . . .

Wrongful death claims are creatures of statute in Montana. As such, the question of when a wrongful death claim accrues requires an analysis of the general accrual statute and the wrongful death statute itself.

The general accrual statute for all actions in Montana provides:

> [A] claim or cause of action accrues when all elements of the claim or cause exist or have occurred, [and] the right to maintain an action on the claim or cause is complete. . . .

The wrongful death statute reads:

> Action for wrongful death. When injuries to and the death of one person are caused by the wrongful act or neglect of another, the personal representative of the decedent's estate may maintain an action for damages against the person causing the death. . . .

The language of Montana's general accrual statute is plain and straightforward: "all elements" of a claim must exist before the claim can accrue. The meaning is equally clear and not susceptible to differing interpretations: only when all elements exist is a claim complete. [The general accrual statute] applies, by its terms, to all claims and causes of action. Thus, a wrongful death claim, like any other cause of action, accrues only when all elements of the claim have occurred; the claim simply does not exist until that time. The question, then, is whether death is an element of a wrongful death claim.

The wrongful death statute references ". . . injuries to *and the death* of one person. . . ". (Emphasis
(continues)

added.) When these occurrences are caused by the "wrongful act or neglect of another," a wrongful death action may be maintained against the person who caused the death of the injured person. It is clear from the legislature's use of the conjunctive "and" that the death of the injured person is an element of a wrongful death claim.

The wrongful death statute contains additional language mandating the conclusion that death is an element of the claim. "[T]he personal representative of the decedent's estate . . ." files a wrongful death action. A "decedent" is indisputably a person who has died and a personal representative of an estate cannot be appointed until there is a decedent. Thus, the death itself is a critical element in a wrongful death action.

To summarize, no claim exists until all elements of a cause of action occur pursuant to [the general accrual statute], and death is an element of a wrongful death claim under . . . Montana's wrongful death statute. Therefore, we hold that a wrongful death action in Montana accrues at the time of decedent's death.

The following example illustrates how a wrongful death action might arise under a hypothetical statute.

hypothetical

Yee Wen owns a cement manufacturing plant. One of her employees, Sean, drives a cement truck. One of Yee Wen's customers is Sally, who was installing a swimming pool at her home. Sean came to pour cement for the pool. Sally's husband, Abraham, stood beneath the truck inside the excavated pool area. Without first checking to see if anyone was in the way, Sean dumped the entire truckload of cement on top of Abraham, who suffocated and died. Assume that this jurisdiction's wrongful death statute permits family survivors to sue tortfeasors for "negligently, wantonly, or intentionally" causing a victim's death. What is the likely result?

Sally could sue Sean (and, by respondeat superior, Sean's employer, Yee Wen) for causing the wrongful death of her husband, Abraham. Sean was negligent in pouring the cement without first seeing if anyone was inside the dangerous dumping area. Because Abraham died, Sally has a cause of action for wrongful death.

The family survivors' specific legal rights are entirely dependent upon the language of each wrongful death statute. It is important to become familiar with the wrongful death statutes in one's state, if one intends to work with plaintiffs for this special tort action. Table 11-4 summarizes the standard ingredients of wrongful death statutes.

Tortfeasor commits tort against victim, causing victim's death
Victim's surviving spouse and children (or victim's estate) may sue tortfeasor to recover damages under wrongful death statute
Most statutes or courts allow damages for victim's lost lifetime earnings potential and for loss of consortium
Same tort defenses apply in wrongful death actions, depending upon the specific tort tortfeasor committed against deceased victim

TABLE 11-4
Elements of wrongful death statutes

▌WRONGFUL BIRTH

Wrongful birth actions are lawsuits for the wrongful birth of a child. The plaintiffs are usually the surprised parents, and the defendant is normally the genetic counselor who missed or failed to reveal a genetic problem. Wrongful birth, then, can be considered another form of medical malpractice, which is negligence.

wrongful birth | The birth of a child having serious defects that results from a doctor's failure to provide proper information (to advise, diagnose, or test properly).

Typical Fact Pattern: Genetic Counseling Gone Awry

The typical situation involving unwanted pregnancy is as follows: A couple visit a physician and rely on the physician's expertise in making their decisions to conceive a child or continue with a pregnancy.

The plaintiffs (parents) then sue the physician for the unwanted birth of a child born with birth defects or other congenital problems. The parents would seek to be reimbursed for the added expenses of raising a severely disabled child. This may occur when a doctor assures a couple that an unborn child will not be harmed by a disease the mother contracted during pregnancy, but when born, the child does in fact have substantial birth defects caused by the mother's infection. Another such situation involves a child who is born with genetic defects that a doctor assured the parents were not present or inheritable.

Damages. The parents sue to recover for emotional distress, the cost of prenatal care and delivery, and expenses associated with the child's impairment.

Table 11-5 lists the elements of wrongful birth.

Usually a form of medical malpractice in which physician has negligently counseled parents concerning genetic issues
May include cases involving children born with birth defects
Damages include parents' medical expenses for unwanted birth and, in some jurisdictions, the costs of raising the child

TABLE 11-5
Elements of wrongful birth actions

Wrongful Life: The New Tort

Wrongful life actions are a recent tort invention, having arisen within the last twenty-five to thirty years. This is typically an action by or on behalf of an unwanted child who is impaired. The child is seeking damages. This new tort has received mixed reviews from appellate courts across the United States. Some jurisdictions reject the tort altogether; others permit it in circumstances involving birth deformities; and still others allow the action even for healthy but unwanted children when sterilization has failed. Wrongful life litigation demonstrates the ingenuity of attorneys and legal scholars searching for new sources of recovery for harmed plaintiffs.

Damages. The child seeks (and sometimes recovers) damages from the responsible physician(s) for the difference in value of an impaired life versus an unimpaired life. Clearly, this is very difficult to calculate and is only allowed in a minority of states.

Wrongful life and birth cases often carry powerful emotional implications, but the temptation to become lost in value judgments must be resisted. Once again, focusing upon the legal elements carries the reader to the appropriate conclusions, as the following example demonstrates.

THE CASE OF THE ABSENCE OF A PHYSICIAN/PATIENT DUTY

A cause of action for wrongful life is brought on behalf of an injured child against his mother's former obstetrician. The obstetrician argues that he owed no duty of care to a child not yet in existence, when he failed to properly document that in the mother's first delivery, her first child received trauma from birth. The court refuses to find a cause of action in Florida for wrongful life and decides the case on medical malpractice grounds. (The mother has a separate related action for wrongful birth that is not a part of this action.)

Maria TORRES, as parent and natural guardian of Luis Torres, a minor child, Appellant,
v.
SARASOTA COUNTY PUBLIC HOSPITAL BOARD, d/b/a Sarasota Memorial Hospital; Gary W. Easterling, M.D.; Gary W. Easterling, M.D., P.A.; and Sarasota County Health Department, Appellees.

No. 2D04-1634
District Court of Appeal of Florida,
Second District
April 13, 2007

During delivery, Luis sustained a brachial plexus injury. The complaint alleges that Dr. Sullivan was negligent because he failed to obtain a complete obstetrical history from Mrs. Torres.

Luis's complaint alleges that the Hospital is vicariously liable for Dr. Sullivan's negligence and the negligence of the nurse who assisted him in obtaining Mrs. Torres's history.

During her pregnancy with Luis and during an earlier pregnancy, Mrs. Torres received prenatal care from the Department of Health. The allegations of negligence against the Department pertain in one way or another to the medical records created and kept by the Department during those pregnancies.

A year before Luis was born, Dr. Easterling delivered Luis's sister, Isaura. The complaint alleges that the standard of care applicable to Dr. Easterling required him to document in Mrs. Torres's medical records Isaura's condition at birth and the complications Mrs. Torres experienced during labor and delivery. It also alleges that he was obligated to tell Mrs. Torres that Isaura had suffered an Erb's Palsy because of birth trauma and that Mrs. Torres should provide this information to future health care providers. The complaint alleges that Dr. Easterling failed to do any of these things and that had he done them, Dr. Sullivan or a reasonable obstetrician under the same circumstances would have performed a Caesarean section.

We write only to discuss the question of whether Dr. Easterling owed a duty to Luis.

Dr. Easterling argues that the summary judgment in his favor was proper because he did not owe a duty of care to Luis. Citing *Pate v. Threlkel*, Dr. Easterling contends that Luis was not his patient and "before a physician can be found to owe a legal duty of care to a third party not under the care of that physician, it must be shown that the physician is aware of the existence of the third party." Dr. Easterling contends that he could not have been aware of Luis's existence because Luis did not exist at the time of his alleged negligence. Dr. Easterling also argues that "the concept of legal duty is based upon whether the defendant's actions place the plaintiff within a zone of danger" and that the question of duty "presupposes the actual existence of the plaintiff as a member of society capable of being injured as the result of the defendant's actions."

In medical malpractice actions, as in other negligence actions, a plaintiff must establish a duty owed to the plaintiff by the defendant, a breach of that duty by allowing conduct to fall below the applicable standard of care, and an injury proximately caused by the defendant's breach of duty. We agree that no physician-patient relationship existed between Luis and Dr. Easterling.

The absence of a physician-patient relationship between Luis and Dr. Easterling is not necessarily fatal to his claim, however, because Florida has extended a physician's duty to third parties in limited circumstances. The question of whether a child has a medical malpractice cause of action for injuries allegedly caused by the negligence of a physician when that negligence occurs before the child is conceived appears to be one of first impression in Florida.

Courts have dubbed the type of claim Luis asserts against Dr. Easterling a "preconception tort." *See, e.g., Grover v. Eli Lilly & Co.* Preconception tort actions are generally defined as actions in which the plaintiff is seeking redress for injuries caused by negligent conduct that occurred before the plaintiff's conception. A claim for "wrongful life" is a preconception tort. A "wrongful life" claim is a malpractice action in which the plaintiff child alleges that if the defendant physician had not been negligent in providing medical advice or treatment to the plaintiff's parents, the plaintiff would not have been born. Most courts that have considered the issue have refused to recognize such an action because of the nature of the "right" invaded-the right not to be born—and the nature of the damages.

The normal measure of damages in tort actions is compensatory. Damages are measured by comparing the condition plaintiff would have been in, had the defendants not been negligent, with plaintiff's impaired condition as a result of the negligence. The infant plaintiff would have us measure the difference between his life with defects against the utter void of nonexistence, but it is impossible to make such a determination. This Court cannot weigh the value of life with impairments against the nonexistence of life itself. By asserting that he should not have been born, the infant plaintiff makes it logically impossible for a court to measure his alleged damages because of the impossibility of making the comparison required by compensatory remedies.

The claim Luis asserts is not a claim for "wrongful life," and the damages he seeks are those typically sought in a claim for medical malpractice. Instead of adopting a blanket no-duty rule based on the timing of

(continues)

the physician's alleged negligence. We believe it is appropriate to assess the viability of Luis's claim as we would any other medical malpractice claim brought against a physician by someone other than a patient.

In this case, the parties' experts on the standard of care agreed that it required Dr. Easterling to document Isaura's difficult delivery and the injury she sustained as a result. The information is "useful to those who subsequently care for and provide" obstetrical care for the patient. In this case, the standard of care is premised on the possibility that in the future the patient will have another child. Applying the rationale of *Pate* to this case, we conclude that Dr. Easterling's duty extended to Luis.

CASE QUESTIONS

1. If Dr. Easterling had taken a complete obstetrical history from Ms. Torres, would this have changed the outcome of Luis's birth?
2. Did the court consider this a wrongful life claim?

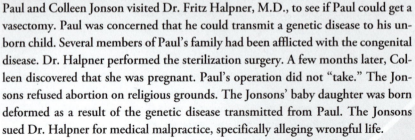

hypothetical

Paul and Colleen Jonson visited Dr. Fritz Halpner, M.D., to see if Paul could get a vasectomy. Paul was concerned that he could transmit a genetic disease to his unborn child. Several members of Paul's family had been afflicted with the congenital disease. Dr. Halpner performed the sterilization surgery. A few months later, Colleen discovered that she was pregnant. Paul's operation did not "take." The Jonsons refused abortion on religious grounds. The Jonsons' baby daughter was born deformed as a result of the genetic disease transmitted from Paul. The Jonsons sued Dr. Halpner for medical malpractice, specifically alleging wrongful life.

Dr. Halpner's vasectomy operation did not prevent Colleen from becoming pregnant. Worse yet, the Jonson child was afflicted with congenital deformities because of Paul's genetically defective sperm. This child would not have been born in this unfortunate condition but for the doctor's negligence in performing the faulty operation. The Jonsons would appear to have a valid claim against Dr. Halpner for the tort of wrongful life.

▋ SUMMARY

A private nuisance is an unreasonable and substantial interference with another person's use and enjoyment of his or her land. Whether a nuisance activity is unreasonable and substantial depends upon its degree of offensiveness. The reasonable person standard is applied to test offensiveness and is based upon the community standard for persons living in the vicinity of the nuisance activity. Private nuisances often involve physical effects on the land, such as vibrations, pollution, and flooding. Private nuisance may also produce health hazards, such as poison gases, hazardous wastes, smoke, or dust, or effects offending the plaintiffs' sensibilities, such as odors or even incessant telephone calling. Private nuisances also include unwanted associations with neighboring uses, such as prostitution houses or gambling emporiums. "Coming to the nuisance" is the primary defense in private nuisance actions.

Public nuisances are activities that harm the public at large rather than a single individual. These nuisances unreasonably and substantially interfere with the public's use and enjoyment of legal rights common to the public. Governmental agencies litigate against public nuisance tortfeasors to enforce the general public's legal rights. State and local governments have the authority to litigate public nuisances under the police powers of the states. Public nuisances often involve so-called immoral activities, such as gambling, prostitution, distribution of sexually explicit materials, or the sale of alcohol. Others include permitting noxious weeds to grow on one's property, carelessly disposing of toxic substances, or violating public health laws. Often, nuisances may be both private and public. These are called mixed nuisances. Nuisances per se are activities that violate statutes or ordinances. Public nuisances are often per se nuisances. "Coming to the nuisance" is usually not a defense in public nuisance cases.

Equitable remedies are usually awarded in nuisance litigation instead of money damages. Money damages are sometimes given when equitable remedies would be excessively harsh to the defendant. The relief most often granted involves injunctions. In injunctions, the court orders the defendant to act or to cease and desist the nuisance activity. Permanent injunctions forbid the activity forever. Temporary injunctions, such as temporary restraining orders (TROs), merely halt the defendant's nuisance activity until the court can conduct hearings or a trial on the merits. Defendants who disregard injunctions may find themselves in contempt of court, for which they can be fined or imprisoned.

Survival statutes allow an injured party's claim to survive his or her death. The victim's estate pursues this action. Wrongful death statutes provide surviving family members of a deceased tort victim with the right to sue the tortfeasor for wrongfully causing the victim's death. The tortfeasor's wrong may include negligence or intentional torts. Wrongful death damages usually consist of the victim's lost lifetime earnings potential and loss of consortium. Consortium includes the lost love and companionship between the dead victim and his or her family. The tortfeasor may use any defenses applicable for the alleged tort that caused the wrongful death. If the tortfeasor were accused of negligently causing the victim's death, then negligence defenses would apply. If the tortfeasor's intentional tort killed the victim, then intentional tort defenses would apply.

Wrongful birth actions are lawsuits for the wrongful birth of a child. Usually, parents sue a physician for malpractice for negligently counseling them about genetic issues and concerns. Wrongful life cases often involve actions brought by children born with birth defects. The tort has developed within the past quarter-century. Court reactions to the tort have been mixed. Some jurisdictions reject the tort altogether, while others embrace it in whole or in part.

▌ KEY TERMS

abatement	mandamus	remedy
coming to the nuisance defense	mixed nuisance	sensibilities
consortium	nuisance	survival statute
contempt	nuisance per se	temporary restraining order
damages	permanent injunction	(TRO)
equitable relief (remedy)	police power	wrongful birth
injunction	private nuisance	wrongful death statute
loss of consortium	public nuisance	

▌ PROBLEMS

In the following hypotheticals, identify the relevant cause(s) of action, suitable defense(s) (if any), and appropriate remedies.

1. Pestro Chemical Corporation manufactures *Dredroxiphine*, a poison used in insect sprays. A railway line delivers tanker cars full of the chemical to be unloaded into the plant. On breezy days, the fumes from the unloading stations drift across the highway onto Jorge's farm. The odors are pungent and are especially irritating to the sinuses. When Jorge and his family work outside on windy days, they are constantly besieged by the poison's smell. Their eyes water excessively, their noses run, and they are gripped by sneezing fits. Other farmers in the area have complained of similar symptoms. Visits to the family physician revealed that Jorge has absorbed minute amounts of the chemical in his lungs and through his skin. Medical studies link exposure to the chemical with several forms of cancer. Jorge has farmed on his property since 1947. Pestro constructed its plant in 1972.

2. Wowser's Video Palace rents X-rated videotaped movies. A local ordinance restricts rental of such materials to persons over the age of 18 years. Wowser's employees never check customer identifications, however, and often rent X-rated movies to underage individuals. Citizens Rallying Against Pornography, a local citizen's group, has asked the county prosecutor to take action against Wowser's. The prosecutor has asked you to summarize the appropriate cause(s) of action in a short paragraph.

3. Quintin and Ursella Xenopher were driving along Interstate 928 on the beltway around the city. Terri was driving while intoxicated. Her blood alcohol level was .214, and a state criminal statute provides that .10 is legally drunk. A related state civil statute provides injured parties with a tort cause of action against a tortfeasor who causes injuries while violating criminal statutes. Terri's automobile collided with the Xenopher's vehicle, killing Quintin. Ursella suffered permanent disability in her left leg.

4. Dr. Sarah Davis, M.D., performed a tubal ligation upon Jennifer Colfield to prevent impregnation. Jennifer was a single, 24-year-old woman who had a sexual relationship with her boyfriend, Scott. Six months after her operation, Jennifer discovered that she was pregnant. She could not afford the costs of raising a child, but she did not want to get an abortion. Scott refused to subsidize Jennifer's medical expenses or contribute to the child's upbringing. The local adoption agencies (managed by rigid-thinking administrators) refused to speak with Jennifer, because she had a history of narcotic abuse. She did not consult with out-of-town adoption agencies, which would have been happy to assist her in placing the child in a foster home.

▌ REVIEW QUESTIONS

1. Define private nuisance. Who are the parties to this litigation? What is unreasonable and substantial interference? How is it determined? What is the role of the community standard? What is use and enjoyment?

2. Name the common types of private nuisance. Can you provide hypotheticals to illustrate each? What is "coming to the nuisance"?

3. What is a public nuisance? How is it distinguishable from a private nuisance? Who is affected by a public nuisance? Who acts as plaintiff? What are some common examples of public nuisance? Does "coming to the nuisance" apply? What are common legal rights? What are mixed nuisances? What is a nuisance per se?

4. What remedies are used in nuisance cases? What about money damages? What is abatement? What are injunctions? Explain the difference between temporary and permanent injunctions. When is a TRO used? What is contempt?

5. What are wrongful death statutes? Who are the plaintiffs in wrongful death litigation? What types of torts can be involved? What damages are awarded? What defenses apply?

6. What is wrongful birth? What are the usual fact situations involving this special tort? What damages may be awarded? What is wrongful life?

▌HELPFUL WEBSITES

This chapter focuses on special tort actions. To learn more about special tort actions, the following sites can be accessed:

General Legal Sites

http://www.law.vill.edu

http://www.findlaw.com

http://www.law.cornell.edu

http://www.law.indiana.edu

Administrative Office of the United States Courts

http://www.uscourts.gov

Legal Dictionary

http://www.lectlaw.com

Law Libraries

http://www.washlaw.edu

STUDENT CD-ROM™
For additional materials, please go to the CD in this book.

ONLINE COMPANION™
For additional resources, please go to
http://www.paralegal.delmar.cengage.com

chapter 12

Tort Immunities

THE BIGGEST MISTAKES PARALEGALS MAKE & HOW TO AVOID THEM

The Devil Is in the Details, or How Many Beers Did You Have?

An elderly lady fell off a stool at a bar and hurt herself. She visited the firm where I worked as a paralegal and sought legal counsel. Before she met with the attorney, at the intake interview, I asked what she was drinking and she said, "Beer, just the usual." At the time of the examination before trial, the opposing attorney asked her if she had any nicknames. "Yes, they call me Twiggy," the skinny old woman answered. "So, Twiggy, in the space of an hour you spent at the bar, how many beers did

you have?" asked the lawyer. "Oh, the usual . . . 5–6 mugs," Twiggy deadpanned.

My attorney was dumbfounded because nothing from my intake interview prepared him for these answers. To say nothing that Twiggy lost her wig in the fall, which was also revealed!

LESSON LEARNED: Follow through on all the answers the client offers, no matter how trivial. The sweet grandmother at my office was made to look like a

(continues)

drunken fool at the examination before trial because I failed to ask the right questions. Prepare a thorough intake interview that fleshes out all the facts, no matter how insignificant. Do not presume that you know what a client means when he or she is vague. And try to listen carefully as well as observe nonverbal cues. Since memories fade with time, all the details should be recorded for future reference in preparation for trial years later.

▌INTRODUCTION

Up to now, something has been missing from the torts analysis. That something is **tort immunities**—absolute defenses against a plaintiff's tort claims. If the defendant successfully invokes an immunity defense, he or she cannot be held liable for any torts committed. It is the reverse of absolute liability. Tort immunities absolutely protect the defendant from tort liability. There are many types of tort immunity, but the most common include sovereign (governmental) immunity and legal infirmities such as infancy or insanity. Tort immunities are similar to **privileges** and the terms are often used interchangeably.

> **immunity** | An exemption from a legally imposed duty, freedom from a duty, or freedom from a penalty.

This chapter includes a discussion of

- ▶ Sovereign (governmental) immunity
- ▶ Public officials' immunity
- ▶ Young children's immunity
- ▶ Family immunity
- ▶ Workers' compensation.

> **privilege** | 1. An advantage; a right to preferential treatment. 2. An exemption from a duty others like you must perform. . . . 3. A special advantage, as opposed to a right; an advantage that can be taken away.

▌SOVEREIGN, OR GOVERNMENTAL, IMMUNITY

Sovereign (governmental) immunity has a long and storied history throughout the annals of tort law. To understand modern applications of this doctrine, one must trace its roots and development.

History

In the history of tort law, governments have held an enviable position. Until the twentieth century, governments were immune from liability for torts committed by their employees. This immunity was called **sovereign immunity** or, in modern times, **governmental immunity.** It stemmed from the ancient English (and Western European) legal tradition that a king could not be sued by his subjects unless he consented. Official tortfeasors thus enjoyed an enviable immunity from liability unless they agreed to be sued, which consent one would naturally not give if one had committed any torts.

> **sovereign (governmental) immunity** | The government's freedom from being sued. In many cases, the United States government has waived immunity by a statute such as the Federal Tort Claims Act.

Courts applied the legal maxim *The king can do no wrong.* This maxim traces its origins to pre-Roman times when the emperor was considered divine and, thus, incapable of errors that the law could remedy.

Modern Applications

For centuries, sovereign immunity protected the Crown and all its subordinates. Later, English and American common law spoke of governmental bodies (and their employees) as enjoying sovereign immunity. The term *king* was replaced with *government* in the American system, because our sovereigns are elected officials serving as presidents, governors, mayors, legislators, or (at the state and local level) judges.

Beginning in the early twentieth century, American courts began to whittle away at the governmental immunity doctrine. Many state courts have abolished sovereign immunity as an absolute defense to governmental liability. Legislatures have enacted statutes, such as the Federal Tort Claims Act, that specifically authorize lawsuits against torts committed by governmental employees (for which governmental agencies could be responsible under respondeat superior).

Early Twentieth-Century Cases.
Many courts found the absolute defense of sovereign immunity to be unreasonably harsh on the plaintiffs. To avoid the full force of the immunity, early in the twentieth century American courts began distinguishing the different types of governmental activities that were or were not exempt from tort liability. The result was two categories: governmental and proprietary. This is sometimes called the *governmental/proprietary distinction.*

Governmental Actions.
governmental function |
An action performed for the general public good by a governmental agency . . . or by a private organization closely tied to the government. . . . These functions are state actions.

When governmental bodies perform certain public protection activities, such as providing fire, police, or ambulance services, they are considered to be undertaking **governmental functions.** Persons performing governmental functions are immune from tort liability, under the early twentieth-century court decisions. Even if the fire, police, or ambulance departments committed torts against a citizen while performing their duties, the old caselaw would define these as governmental actions immune from liability.

Proprietary Actions.
proprietary actions | Certain business-like activities performed by governmental bodies that are usually associated with the private sector, and are not given immunity from tort liability.

Governmental bodies also perform certain business-like activities (usually associated with the private sector). These are defined as **proprietary actions** and do not carry immunity from tort liability. For example, a municipality may provide utility services to its residents, such as water, sewer, electric, or natural gas, but this activity more closely resembles a private business enterprise than a public, governmental function. If the governmental agency providing such services committed torts, the government would be liable, and the immunity defense would not prevent liability.

Difficulty with the Governmental/Proprietary Distinction

Courts have struggled with the governmental/proprietary distinction for decades. What about cities that provide garbage collection? What about public parks? Are these governmental or proprietary functions? Courts often decide based upon whether a fee is assessed to users of these services. If a fee is charged, then the activity is considered proprietary. If not, then it is governmental. This may be called the **fee standard.**

Similar to the fee standard is the *pecuniary benefit test.* When governments provide services for profit, then the activities are proprietary. If governments offer services for the common public good, without economic benefit to the governmental units themselves, then the activities are governmental.

fee standard | A test courts use in applying the governmental/proprietary distinction. If a governmental agency assesses a fee for an activity, the activity is considered proprietary; if not, it is considered governmental.

Modern Steps to Eliminate the Distinction

Within the past twenty years, many state courts have abolished the governmental/proprietary distinction and with it the defense of sovereign immunity. These courts now focus upon whether the governments committed any torts—just as courts would handle any other tort lawsuit. Many state legislatures and Congress have enacted statutes eliminating or restricting sovereign immunity to particular types of services, such as public parks or utilities.

Suits against States

Even though many courts have abolished sovereign immunity and allow tort suits, not all states permit all kinds of tort suits to be brought against them. The individual state can decide just what suits it will or will not allow. In fact, in some states there is a special court just for tort claims against the state. In New York, it is called the Court of Claims, and a notice of claim is required to bring the action.

Federal Tort Claims Act—Suits against the United States

The Federal Tort Claims Act (FTCA) of August 2, 1946, is a statute enacted by Congress allowing private parties to sue the United States in federal courts for most torts committed by persons acting on behalf of the United States. Suit is allowed for negligent or wrongful acts or omissions of employees of the United States government occurring during the scope of their employment. Liability is limited to those instances in which a private person would be liable to the claimant, according to the laws of the place where the act occurred. Actions must first be presented to the appropriate federal agency where the alleged harm occurred.

The act does not apply and does not permit suit regarding conduct that is uniquely governmental, that is, that cannot be performed by a private individual. The FTCA exempts and does not permit suits for three major kinds of cases, even where a private person could have been liable for such suits under state law (*Feres* doctrine): (1) failure to perform discretionary functions that involve a degree of judgment or choice; (2) suits by the military for injuries sustained while in the service; and (3) suits for many intentional torts such as liable, assault, battery, misrepresentation, false imprisonment, false arrest, and abuse of process. Suits for injuries caused by medical malpractice while in the military, and suits by victims of atomic testing are also prohibited against the United States government under the FTCA.

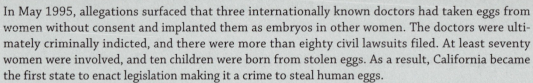

THE CASE OF THE MISSING EGGS

In May 1995, allegations surfaced that three internationally known doctors had taken eggs from women without consent and implanted them as embryos in other women. The doctors were ultimately criminally indicted, and there were more than eighty civil lawsuits filed. At least seventy women were involved, and ten children were born from stolen eggs. As a result, California became the first state to enact legislation making it a crime to steal human eggs.

This case addresses tort issues from almost every chapter in this text. There are allegations of lack of consent (medical malpractice), conversion, intentional and negligent infliction of emotional distress, spoliation of evidence, breach of duty to defend, fraud, issues regarding agency standard for review, California's State Torts Claim Act, scope of employment, and governmental versus private acts, to name a few. Here, the court narrowed the case down to a single issue: scope of employment. For this issue, clarification of the relationship of the defendants is needed. The Regents of the University of California is a state agency, which was in charge of the state university that maintained the health center where Dr. Stone worked and also saw private patients. As is discussed in the next chapter, the proper naming of parties and understanding of their legal status is essential in the investigation of a tort case.

SERGIO C. STONE, Plaintiff and Respondent,
v.
THE REGENTS OF THE UNIVERSITY
OF CALIFORNIA, Defendant and Appellant.
77 Cal. App. 4th 736, 92 Cal. Rptr. 2d 94 (1999)
Court of Appeal of California,
Fourth Appellate District
December 16, 1999, decided

Stone is a physician, board certified in obstetrics and gynecology. From 1990 to 1995, he was a partner in the Center for Reproductive Health (CRH), along with two other infertility specialists, Ricardo Asch and Jose Balmaceda. The CRH's offices were on the University of California at Irvine (UCI) campus. The university provided the doctors with space, management and administrative services, and support staff, and charged patients an administrative fee to cover

the cost of these services. The university also provided professional liability insurance for the faculty of the department of obstetrics and gynecology (which included Stone) "while working within the course and scope of their University employment," which it stated "includes the management of private patients in facilities which have been previously approved by the University. . . ."

In 1995, Susan and Wayne Clay sued Stone (along with Asch, Balmaceda, CRH, UCI and the Regents). Susan Clay was a former CRH patient. The Clays alleged their eggs, sperm and embryos were implanted in another woman without their knowledge or consent. The suit was brought after allegations of "egg stealing" and other improprieties at CRH surfaced, and after the Regents had completed two investigations into the charges and were in the midst of others.

In 1994, two UCI employees working at CRH had notified the university they believed improper activities were taking place in both medical and financial matters. The university appointed an outside clinical panel to investigate the medical allegations.

In March 1995, the clinical panel delivered its report. The report sustained two allegations implicating or involving Stone that are germane to this action. The more serious was the finding that egg stealing took place—human eggs were taken from one patient and implanted in another without the consent of the donor. However, among the three doctors, the panel was unable to say who did what. None of the physicians cooperated in the investigation. They refused to provide patient charts, records, or information about procedures for obtaining patient consents, and they declined to allow the panel to interview patients.

In May 1995, the Regents sued Stone, Asch and Balmaceda to obtain the sought-after documents. Alleging the doctors removed documents from UCI offices to hinder the investigations, and Asch attempted to alter or modify some records, the complaint set out causes of action for conversion (of university records), replevin (of university records), destruction of documents and spoliation of evidence, among other things. The record does not reveal the outcome of this litigation.

At about the same time, the Clays notified Stone they intended to sue for professional negligence. The Clays sued in September 1995, alleging negligence, fraud (based on the representation the eggs/sperm/embryos would only be implanted in Susan Clay), conversion (of the eggs/sperm/embryos), intentional and negligent infliction of emotional distress, battery (taking Susan Clay's eggs for implantation in another without her consent), spoliation of evidence (alteration and destruction of embryo logs, medical records and genetic material), and a conspiracy to take and use the Clays' genetic material in other women for the purpose of increasing CRH's success rate. The complaint did not specify who did what, with the exception that alleged the Regents' failure to adequately

supervise. Nor did it allege what Stone's role was in the Clays' treatment.

Stone wrote to the Regents on May 25, 1995 requesting a defense. The Regents replied they would defend Stone in the anticipated Clay suit but reserved the right to "withdraw that defense at any time."

The Regents refused to defend Stone. John F. Lundberg, deputy general counsel, took the position the conduct alleged was outside the scope of employment, and it was intentional and fraudulent. The trial judge ruled the Regents acted arbitrarily in refusing to defend Stone.

The Regents successfully moved for reconsideration.

The Regents' argument is that they did not abuse their discretion in refusing to defend Stone. We agree.

Stone petitioned for a writ of ordinary mandate under Code of Civil Procedure section 1085. Ordinary mandate is used to review an adjudicatory decision when an agency is not required to hold an evidentiary hearing. The scope of review is limited, out of deference to the agency's authority and presumed expertise: "The court may not reweigh the evidence or substitute its judgment for that of the agency." . . . 'A court will uphold the agency action unless the action is arbitrary, capricious, or lacking in evidentiary support.'

Under Government Code section 995.2(a), the Regents could refuse to provide Stone with a defense if they determined any one of the three excluding situations existed: conduct outside the scope of employment; conduct involving actual fraud, corruption or malice; or a conflict of interest. They had to reach a decision quickly, because section 995.2(b) required the Regents to respond to Stone's written request for a defense within 20 days, and give their reasons if he was turned down.

Section 995.2 is part of the California Tort Claims Act, which provides that in the usual civil case brought against a public employee, a public entity must provide a defense to the employee and pay any claim or judgment against him. Where the public entity refuses to defend, the employee can seek a writ of mandate, as Stone did.

(continues)

On the record before us, we conclude there was substantial evidence to support the Regents' decision the conduct alleged in the Clays' suit took place, Stone participated, and his actions were outside the scope of employment. By the time Stone asked for a defense, the Regents had before them the clinical panel report that concluded egg stealing took place at CRH. They did not know if Stone participated, but that was because he refused to cooperate in the investigation by not producing requested medical records or patient charts. We think a reasonable inference was that Stone was involved.

At some point in time, the Regents learned Stone had seen Susan Clay only once, to perform an ultrasound examination. Even if we assume the scenario most favorable to Stone, that the Regents knew this when they turned down his defense, the choice was still reasonable. This fact would eliminate the possibility Stone himself took Susan Clay's eggs without her consent, but not the possibility it was done pursuant to an agreement between Stone and his colleagues to engage in such conduct, as alleged in the conspiracy count in the Clays' action.

Stone's position appears to be that his private practice at CRH was within the scope of employment, so he was entitled to a defense against any suit arising out of it. Stone argues he acted within the scope of employment because he paid the university a portion of his fees from seeing private patients, he reported to the dean of the medical school, and he only performed an ultrasound on Susan Clay, which was "reasonably foreseeable for a physician member of the faculty . . . [and] incident to his responsibilities."

But the issue is not whether seeing private patients or performing one ultrasound was within Stone's employment—the question is whether the alleged conspiracy to misappropriate and misuse Clay's eggs was a part of his employment. Stone, understandably, offered no evidence it was.

Scope of employment is a question of fact, but all that can be required of the Regents when asked for a defense is that their decision be within the range of reason. It was. We cannot say as a matter of law it is typical of the risks of a medical school faculty practice that a physician, for 18 years a tenured professor, with a renowned and successful fertility clinic, would be part of a scheme to enrich himself by using a patient's eggs without her consent. Put in terms of the foreseeability test, this *is* such startling and unusual conduct that we cannot say, as a matter of law, it would be fair to impose these risks on a university. To the extent the conduct may be viewed as an abuse of job-created authority, it was again a reasonable conclusion the motivations were the purely personal ones of financial reward and professional acclaim.

Stone supplied ammunition for the Regents' argument when he refused to turn over CRH patient records because they were "private patient charts, and are not and have never have been the property of the [university]."

Having concluded the Regents did not abuse their discretion in turning down Stone's defense because the conduct alleged was outside the scope of his employment, we need not consider their other arguments.

The judgment is reversed. The Regents are entitled to costs on appeal.

CASE QUESTIONS

1. What was the Regents' reason for not defending Stone?
2. Do you agree with this decision? Explain.

An exception to the prohibition against intentional tort suits is if the act was committed by federal law enforcement or investigative officials. The government can be held liable for some of their intentional torts, including false arrest, false imprisonment, abuse of process, and malicious prosecution.

Tort claims must be presented to the appropriate federal agency within two years after the claim accrues, or unless action is begun within six months after the date of mailing of notice of final denial of the claim by the agency where presented. The attorney general is responsible for defending actions under the FTCA.

---

practical **application**

The paralegal must be careful when preparing a tort claim against a state to see if there are any special rules. Your jurisdiction might require special procedures for bringing tort claims against the state. The pleadings might be different and have different or shorter time limits than usual. Because suits against the state were not always allowed, there may not be a provision for jury trial when the state is sued. Be sure to sue the correct party. For example, name the state in the suit if you also name in the suit the agency such as State Police or State Department of Transportation.

▌PUBLIC OFFICERS

Somewhat different from sovereign immunity is the individual tort immunity granted to certain public employees engaged in their official capacities. Certain governmental officials are immune from personal liability for any torts committed while they were performing their public duties.

Exceptions

There are exceptions to the privilege and immunity doctrines. 42 U.S.C. § 1983 permits liability of public officers (usually other than prosecutors and judges) if the performance of their duties involves intentional or reckless activities that deprive persons of their civil rights. Such an action is called a civil rights action or a "1983" action; 1983 is the section number of the law permitting this action, not the year it was passed. If a police officer arrests someone without a warrant and without probable cause, the arrest is in violation of the detainee's civil rights and the officer may be liable. If excessive force is used in an arrest, it is a violation of civil rights and the officer may be liable (*Tennessee v. Garner*, 471 U.S. 1 (1985)). If any action under color or authority of the government—whether local, state, or federal—violates civil rights, the actor(s) may be liable regardless of immunity. Note that these exceptions do not address negligent acts.

Who Is Protected

Legislators and judges enjoy an absolute immunity from tort liability for acts in their official governmental capacities. In performing legislative or judicial functions, it is

354   chapter 12

possible that these public officials might commit torts against individual citizens. An example of a judge's absolute immunity is when, in the judge's official capacity, the judge renders an opinion in a case, and some of the statements in the decision offend one of the parties. However, judges are not immune from torts committed in their administrative capacity. For example, when hiring someone, a judge cannot violate the hiring laws and discriminate just because he or she is a judge. The common law protects judges and legislators from any liability whatsoever for having committed such torts. Executive branch officials, however, do not receive this blanket immunity, although administrative officers serving judicial or legislative functions do receive absolute immunity. For example, an agency adjudication officer, prosecutor, or county council legislator would be protected completely from tort liability.

Rationale for Immunity

Governmental official immunity is intended to ensure that legislators and judges may pursue their public duties without the chilling effect that fear of tort liability might create. Imagine how cautious legislators or judges would have to be in decision making if, with each sensitive topic, they had to worry about tort liability. These officials might become paralyzed by second-guessing, and the liability spectre could influence their public-policy decisions. This rationale for such immunity is often repeated in the common law. To encourage maximum public benefit from the services of the public's judges and legislators, the law must totally protect these officials from tort liability.

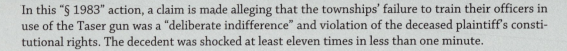

THE CASE OF THE DEADLY TASER

In this "§ 1983" action, a claim is made alleging that the townships' failure to train their officers in use of the Taser gun was a "deliberate indifference" and violation of the deceased plaintiff's constitutional rights. The decedent was shocked at least eleven times in less than one minute.

Richard LIEBERMAN, Sr. and Richard Lieberman, Jr., as Co-Administrators of the Estate of Kris Lieberman, Plaintiffs,

v.

David MARINO, et al., Defendants.

Civil Action No. 06-2745
United States District Court, E.D. Pennsylvania
March 13, 2007

At the time of his death, Decedent, Kris Lieberman, was 32 years old, and living at a residence on his

parent's property. On the evening of June 24, 2004, Decedent, after performing various helpful tasks at home, rode his motorcycle to his brother, Richard Lieberman, Jr.'s home. There, Decedent drove his motorcycle around his brother's pool until Richard Lieberman, Sr. joined the brothers. Decedent took a picture of his family with a disposable camera, and rode away on his motorcycle.

At about 8:46 P.M. that evening, the Northampton County 911 Emergency Center received two telephone calls about a man yelling and screaming. Upon his arrival at the scene, Officer Marino radioed the Emergency Center to request medical personnel for a possible mental health issue; Marino observed Decedent pulling up tufts of grass and throwing them in the air, and yelling obscenities. Thereafter, Defendent Sean Stuber arrived at the scene, and took control as the ranking officer.

Marino unholstered his Taser, and the two Bushkill Township police officers entered the field to approach Decedent. Decedent and Stuber recognized each other, and Decedent called to Stuber by his first name. Apparently misidentifying Marino as one of Decedent's old schoolmates, Decedent called out to "Homoki." Marino gave Decedent verbal commands to "calm down," and "relax." Decedent, apparently oblivious to the officers' commands, continued spinning on the ground and screaming.

He ignored further commands from the officers to stay on the ground, and instead charged at Marino. Marino activated his Taser, discharging a jolt of electricity into the upper body of Decedent. Decedent collapsed to the ground, face-first. As Stuber straddled Decedent in an attempt to immobilize and handcuff him, Marino administered a second jolt from his Taser. Stuber directed Marino to administer a third, continuous discharge from the Taser. One of the Taser wires had broken, however use of the Taser continued, and Stuber ordered Marino to insert a fresh cartridge into the Taser. Records downloaded from the Taser itself indicate the Decedent was shocked at least eleven times within less than one minute.

Plaintiffs assert that Decedent was kept lying prone on his stomach throughout this time with the weight of at least one defendant on his back, even after his hands had been cuffed behind. Defendant Stubar revised his earlier request to slow the arrival of emergency medical personnel, and requested that the EMTs expedite their arrival to the scene. Decedent was transported to Easton Hospital, where he was declared dead.

Count I alleges violations of 42 U.S.C. § 1983. Defendants move to dismiss the claims against the Townships, arguing they are not liable because the alleged constitutional deprivation did not result from an official policy or custom. Plaintiffs contend that such a policy or custom did exist.

Municipal custom or policy can be demonstrated either by reference to express, codified policy or by evidence that a particular practice, although not authorized by law, is so permanent and well-settled that it constitutes law. Further, Plaintiffs must demonstrate causation, as "a municipality can be liable under § 1983 only where its policies are the moving force behind the constitutional violation." Additionally, for liability to attach under a failure-to-train theory, Defendants' failure to train their employees must "reflect a 'deliberate' of 'conscious' choice by [a] municipality" such that one could call it a policy or custom. The focus must be on whether the program is adequate to the tasks the particular employees must perform. Moreover, such liability arises "only where a municipality's failure to train its employees in a relevant respect evidences a 'deliberate indifference' to the rights of its inhabitants."

Plaintiffs clearly accuse Bushkill and Upper Nazareth Townships of failing to train their officers in what Plaintiffs would characterize as the proper use of a Taser, and that this failure to train shows Defendants' deliberate indifference to Decedent's constitutional rights. Plaintiffs seek to hold Defendants liable for "deliberately failing to train all the Defendants in the recognition of, and proper response to, known dangers created by the use of the taser [sic] device." Plaintiffs clearly allege that deficient training and operating manuals caused the individual defendants to misuse the Taser and defibrillator in such a way as to deprive Decedent of his constitutional rights, and that the Townships should have known this was the case. Plaintiffs' Complaint goes well beyond the requirements of notice pleading, and is sufficient to require Defendants to defend the case. Accordingly, Defendants' motions as to Plaintiffs' § 1983 claims against Bushkill Township and Upper Nazareth Township will be denied.

(continues)

CASE QUESTIONS
1. Would Taser training have changed the result for the deceased plaintiff? Explain.
2. Would municipal immunity apply here? Explain.

CHILDREN OF TENDER YEARS

Definition

tender years | Minors; usually those under the age of seven.

minor | A person who is under the age of full legal rights and duties.

Children of **tender years** are usually defined as young children under the age of seven years. Under traditional common law, any person under the age of twenty-one (and in the past twenty-five or so years, eighteen) is classed as a **minor.** However, only very young children normally enjoy the tender-years immunity.

Absolute Immunity for Intentional Torts

Most states still follow the ancient common law rule that children of tender years are incapable of committing intentional torts; thus, they are immune from intentional tort liability. This immunity is based upon the concept that young children are mentally and emotionally incapable of having the proper intent to commit an intentional tort. Because they are so young, they lack the experience and development to appreciate fully the significance of their actions, which sometimes are tortious in nature.

Immunity from Negligence

Most courts do not grant absolute negligence immunity to young children. Instead, the child tortfeasor's age is merely one factor to be considered in determining the standard of reasonable care that the reasonable child of tender years would have used in a particular case.

SPOUSAL/FAMILY IMMUNITY

Spousal and family immunity defenses protect certain family members from lawsuits.

Spousal Immunity

Originally, common law dictated that spouses were immune from suit by each other. A husband and wife were considered to act as one unit. Additionally, there was a concern that if family members could sue each other, there was more apt to be fraud or collusion. This tort immunity for spouses has now been abolished to some degree by the majority of states. Some states have only abolished the immunity from suit for specific kinds of tort actions.

THE CASE OF PARENTAL CONTROL

As the two-wage-earner family becomes more and more common, a question frequently asked is "Who is minding the children?" When a minor kills another minor, can the killer's mother and grandparents be sued for negligent failure to control a minor? This case presents a threat to all grandparents who take on the role of babysitter to their grandchildren.

WELLS
v.
HICKMAN

657 N.E.2d 172 (Ind. Ct. App. 1995)
Court of Appeals of Indiana
November 8, 1995
Najam, Judge

Cheryl Wells ("Wells") filed a complaint for the wrongful death of her son, D.E., at the hands of L.H., the son of Gloria Hickman ("Hickman") and the grandson of Albert and Geneva Hickman (the "Grandparents"). L.H. beat D.E. to death while the two boys were in the woods behind the Grandparents' home. Wells alleged that Hickman and the Grandparents failed to control L.H. when they were aware or should have been aware that injury to D.E. was possible and that their negligence resulted in D.E.'s death.

* * *

Several issues are presented on appeal which we restate as follows:

1. Whether Indiana Code § 34-4-31-1 precludes the recovery of damages in a common law action for parental negligence by limiting parental liability for the wrongful acts of the parent's child.
2. Whether Hickman had a parental duty to exercise reasonable care to control L.H. for the safety of D.E.
3. Whether the Grandparents had a duty to protect D.E. from harm.

D.E. and his mother, Cheryl Wells, were neighbors to L.H. and his mother, Gloria Hickman. L.H. and Hickman lived in a trailer located on land owned by L.H.'s grandparents, Albert and Geneva Hickman.

The trailer was parked within 100 feet of the Grandparents' house and L.H. was often at their home. Hickman worked the night shift and usually left for work at 10:00 P.M. The Grandparents cared for L.H. while Hickman was at work, and L.H. often ate his meals and snacks at the Grandparents' home. Either Hickman or the Grandparents always knew L.H.'s whereabouts.

Between the Fall of 1990 and October 15, 1991, L.H. killed a pet dog by beating it to death, and he killed a pet hamster. L.H. had also expressed his desire to commit suicide. L.H. often exhibited anger and, on one occasion, he came home from school with a black eye, cuts and bruises. . . .

On October 15, 1991, D.E. was celebrating his twelfth birthday. After school, fifteen year old L.H. invited D.E. over to play video games. Wells, D.E.'s mother, agreed. The boys did not play video games and neither Hickman nor the Grandparents were aware that D.E. and L.H. were together. Around 6:30 P.M., L.H. returned home and appeared to be very nervous. Later, L.H. told his mother that he thought he had killed D.E. After a search, D.E.'s body was found lying beside a fallen tree on the Grandparents' property.

* * *

A negligence action is rarely an appropriate case for summary judgment. . . . To be liable the parent must know that her child "had a habit of engaging in the particular act or course of conduct which led to the plaintiff's injury." The duty to control one's child is described in the Restatement (Second) of Torts as follows:

A parent is under a duty to exercise reasonable care so to control his minor child as to prevent it from

(continues)

intentionally harming others or from so conducting itself as to create an unreasonable risk of bodily harm to them, if the parent

(a) knows or has reason to know that he has the ability to control his child, and

(b) knows or should know of the necessity and opportunity for exercising such control.

* * *

The critical issue in this case is foreseeability and we must determine whether Hickman knew or with due care should have known that L.H. would injure D.E. . . .

The record indicates Hickman knew that L.H. was a troubled child and she could anticipate the same type of conduct that he had exhibited in the past. Upon the advice of a school principal and from her personal observations, Hickman was aware that L.H. needed professional help. Nevertheless, we cannot conclude, based upon L.H.'s cruelty to animals and his comment about committing suicide, that it was reasonably foreseeable he would kill a neighborhood friend. . . . Neither the type of harm inflicted nor the victim in this case was foreseeable and, thus, cannot support the imposition of a duty upon Hickman.

Public policy supports the imposition of a duty to control on a parent under the proper circumstances, but it does not in this case. Parents are in a unique position in society because they have a special power to observe and control the conduct of their minor children. . . . Parents have a duty to exercise this power reasonably, especially when they have notice of a child's dangerous tendencies. . . .

We hold that a cause of action for parental negligence in the failure to control may be maintained in Indiana, but we decline to find a duty in this case. A duty may be imposed upon a parent for her failure to control her child when the parent knows or should know that the child has engaged in a particular act or course of conduct and it is reasonably foreseeable that this conduct would lead to the plaintiff's injuries. We conclude, as a matter of law, that Hickman had no duty to exercise control over L.H. because the harm and the victim were not reasonably foreseeable. . . .

Wells next contends that the failure to control exception may be extended to the Grandparents in this case because they assumed a parental role over L.H., their grandson. We cannot agree.

As we have already stated, imposition of a duty under this exception requires that the parent knew or should have known that injury to another was reasonably foreseeable. . . . [W]e concluded that Hickman could not have reasonably foreseen that L.H. would kill or even harm D.E. and, likewise, we conclude that the Grandparents could not have foreseen this occurrence. . . .

Wells also asserts that the Grandparents are liable based on a negligent entrustment theory and claims that because L.H. was entrusted to their care, they are responsible for the death of D.E. Again, we must disagree.

There is a well recognized duty in tort law that persons entrusted with children have a duty to supervise their charges. . . . The duty exists whether or not the supervising party has agreed to watch over the child for some form of compensation.

* * *

[T]he Grandparents were unaware of D.E.'s presence on their property. There was no relationship between the Grandparents and D.E. that would give rise to a duty under a negligent entrustment theory.

* * *

CASE QUESTIONS

1. Based on the facts presented, do you feel that the death of D.E. was foreseeable? Explain.
2. What kind of facts would have had to be present for the court to have sustained an action for negligent failure to control?

Family Immunity (Parent/Child)

At common law, suits between parents and children were also prevented, in the interest of maintaining family harmony and avoiding fraud. In some states this family immunity has now been abolished. This is particularly true where automobile accidents are concerned. Since most car accidents are typically covered by a policy of insurance, it is thought that there is less chance for causing family disharmony, as the suit would no longer be directly against a family member. It is important to note that the family immunity doctrine only covers parent and child, and not suits between brothers and sisters or other relatives.

▌ WORKERS' COMPENSATION

In most states, workers who are injured or killed as a result of incidents occurring during the course and scope of their employment are covered for their injuries by state workers' compensation statutes. An employee is covered regardless of the employer's fault. Recovery is limited to the amount set forth in statutory tables. This is generally much less than would be awarded for similar injuries in a common-law tort claim. As a result of these workers' compensation statutes, employers are immune from most employee suits. Workers' compensation is considered the employee's sole remedy. Note also that there are some federal workers' compensation statutes, which apply to certain employees of the United States government.

Types of Injuries

Some examples of injuries arising out of employment include a slip and fall where an employee injures his or her back, a chemical splash that burns a worker's skin, or a car accident when an employee is making deliveries, resulting in broken bones and a concussion. Some jurisdictions might also include a psychiatric injury caused by witnessing a theft or shooting at work, or other traumatic incident.

Whereas such injuries are caused by a single event, a claim might also arise out of repeated exposures at work, such as to chemical vapors, loud noise, or vibrations. An employee might claim damage to his or her lungs from toxic vapors, a hearing loss from loud noise, or carpal tunnel syndrome to the wrists from using a power drill repetitively.

Benefits

Depending on the state, benefits could include medical care paid for by the employer. If an employee is unable to work, he or she might receive lost wages called disability benefits. Usually there is a time limit up until which these are paid. Permanently injured workers also receive disability payments, and in some areas can elect to receive these in a lump sum instead of weekly payments over time. Vocational rehabilitation is offered to those who are unable to return to their old jobs and need retraining for a new career. If an employee dies as a result of injuries or illness, a death benefit is usually paid to the spouse or children who are dependent on the employee. A burial allowance is also paid.

Reporting and Filing Requirements

Workers' compensation is highly regulated in order to avoid false claims and fraud. Employees are required to immediately report on-the-job injuries to their employers. There are strict time limits for filing a claim to collect benefits. After an employee files a claim, the employer is required to fill out the employer's version of what occurred (the employer portion of the claim form) and submit it to the insurance company. The employer has strict time limits for authorizing medical treatment for the injured employee, or advising as to the reason for denial.

Workers' compensation is also discussed in Chapter 8 regarding defenses to intentional torts.

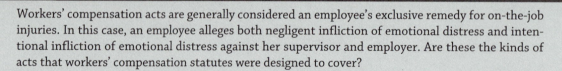

THE CASE OF THE EXCLUSIVE WORKERS' COMPENSATION

Workers' compensation acts are generally considered an employee's exclusive remedy for on-the-job injuries. In this case, an employee alleges both negligent infliction of emotional distress and intentional infliction of emotional distress against her supervisor and employer. Are these the kinds of acts that workers' compensation statutes were designed to cover?

VORVIS
v.
SOUTHERN NEW ENGLAND TELEPHONE CO.

821 F. Supp. 851 (D. Conn. 1993)
United States District Court
for the District of Connecticut
May 25, 1993
Edginton, Senior District Judge

Plaintiff, Joyce Vorvis, was employed by defendant, Southern New England Telephone Company ("SNET"), from July 13, 1981 to June 2, 1989, under the terms and conditions of an employment contract. Frank Kulaga was her direct supervisor beginning September 1, 1988. From this time until the end of her employment, plaintiff alleges that she was subjected to extreme and outrageous harassment by Kulaga. She claims he continually subjected her to verbal abuse and caused her to work extra hours without compensation. She alleges that Kulaga made at least one false verbal statement about her job performance, which, along with the harassment, damaged her reputation. She alleges that Kulaga unfairly disciplined her for certain incompleted work assignments. As a result, she claims she suffered physical and emotional harm and was forced to leave her job on June 2, 1989. Defendants benefited from her departure, she contends, because SNET was in the process of reducing its workforce.

* * *

In Counts I and II, plaintiff alleges intentional infliction of emotional distress against Kulaga and SNET. She claims that from September 1, 1988 through June 2, 1989, SNET intentionally directed

Kulaga to treat her in such a way as to cause severe emotional distress which would lead to her departure from SNET. This treatment began after she returned from foot surgery and while she was coping with the illness and death of her sister. The treatment allegedly took place almost every day for a period of over one year, and included chastising, criticism, humiliation in front of coworkers, threats to fire her, extra work assignments for the purpose of causing anxiety, uncompensated work on weekends and evenings, unwarranted vulgar remarks, and disciplinary actions for matters beyond her control. . . .

The exclusivity provision of the Connecticut Worker's Compensation Act provides that:

> An employer shall not be liable to any action for damages on account of personal injury sustained by a employee arising out of and in the course of his employment or on account of death resulting from personal injury so sustained, but an employer shall secure compensation for his employees as follows, except that compensation shall not be paid when the personal injury has been caused by the wilful and serious misconduct between employer and employees . . .

Conn.Gen.Stat. § 31-284(a). Under the Workers' Compensation Act, an employee surrenders his or her right to bring common-law action against employer. Intentional tort claims are not barred if the actor is acting with the knowing authorization of the employer. Thus, a claim will not be barred by the Workers' Compensation Act where the tort is intentional and where the defendant employer directed the supervisor to commit the tort.

Here, the exception for "personal injury . . . caused by the wilful and serious misconduct between employer and employees" applies as to plaintiff's claims of intentional infliction of emotional distress. Plaintiff alleges an intentional tort that was knowingly authorized by the actor's employer. Thus, the Worker's Compensation Act does not bar this cause of action.

The next step is to determine whether plaintiff has made a claim for intentional infliction of emotional distress. Viewing the allegations in the complaint in the light most favorable to the plaintiff, the court finds that she does. Plaintiff has alleged in the complaint that: (1) defendant intended or knew that emotional distress would likely result from defendant's conduct; (2) defendant's conduct was extreme or outrageous; (3) defendant's conduct caused plaintiff's distress; and (4) plaintiff's emotional distress was severe.

Accordingly, the motion to dismiss must be denied as to Counts I and II.

Plaintiff alleges negligent infliction of emotional distress against Kulaga in Count III, and against SNET in Counts IV and V.

* * *

Under Connecticut law, the issue of compensability under the Workers' Compensation Act is determined by whether or not the worker's injury is one "arising out of and in the course of employment." . . .

In the instant case, plaintiff's claim for negligent infliction of emotional distress is barred by the Connecticut Workers' Compensation Act because her alleged injuries arose out of and in the course of her employment, and because the exception for intentional torts does not apply.

Therefore, the motion to dismiss Counts III, IV, and V alleging negligent infliction of emotional distress must be granted.

CASE QUESTION

1. The plaintiff's claims of negligent infliction of emotional distress and intentional infliction of emotional distress were treated differently by the United States District Court. Explain which of the claims, if any, were covered under workers' compensation, and which were permitted as separate claims.

▌ SUMMARY

Tort immunities are absolute defenses against a plaintiff's tort claims. Sovereign, or governmental, immunity is an ancient common-law defense that protected governments from tort liability. The doctrine was based on the presumption that "the king could do no wrong," which, in America, translated that the government could not be sued without its consent. American courts drastically reduced or eliminated sovereign immunity during the twentieth century. In the early decades of the century, courts avoided the immunity by distinguishing between governmental and proprietary actions in which government agencies were engaged. Many states have abolished sovereign immunity altogether as an absolute defense.

Public officers, such as judges or legislators, are immune from personal liability for any torts committed while they are performing their official duties. This ensures that governmental officials may act independently and freely to perform their civil responsibilities, without fear of constant tort liability for their every public action that might tortiously affect individual citizens in some way.

"Children of tender years" are very young children, often under the age of seven years, although many courts have defined the term as including children to age twelve or even through the teenage years. Children of tender years are immune from intentional tort liability in most jurisdictions. Often, a specific age boundary is used. Many courts state that children under seven years are absolutely immune. Others do not rigidly follow any age barrier. For negligence, most courts apply a reasonable child-of-tender-years standard to decide whether negligence has occurred. A minority of states use definite age limits, such as the seven-year-old rule, for negligence cases.

At common law, various family members were immune from suit. Spouses could not sue spouses, and children and parents could not bring actions against each other. These immunities have been abolished in varying degrees depending on jurisdiction.

State workers' compensation statutes prevent suits by injured employees against employers.

▌ KEY TERMS

fee standard	minor	sovereign (governmental)
governmental function	privilege	immunity
immunity	proprietary actions	tender years

▌ PROBLEMS

1. Superior Court Judge Emily Doud McKinnley granted summary judgment to the defendant in a negligence lawsuit. The plaintiff had sued the defendant for negligently causing personal injuries. The plaintiff suffered extensive injuries and was unable to work for the remainder of his life. Upon appeal, the state court of appeals reversed Judge McKinnley's summary judgment order. The appellate court admonished the trial judge for refusing to accept certain key evidence that the plaintiff offered at hearing. The appellate court stated that there was no legal basis for granting summary judgment in the case. The trial transcript clearly indicated that the judge had become angry at the plaintiff's counsel's attempts to admit the evidence despite warnings to desist. After the appeal, the plaintiff wished to sue Judge McKinnley for judicial malpractice.

2. Shelby Sarville drives a garbage truck for the City of New Ventura. The city charges its customers a monthly trash-hauling fee, which is based upon the size of the trash container used. Citizens may use the city's service, although many people hire private trash companies instead. One day, while backing up to empty a trash dumpster, Shelby failed to look in his rearview mirrors. A five-year-old girl tried to squeeze between the truck and the dumpster on her bicycle. She mistimed the squeeze, and the truck crushed her against the dumpster, causing severe internal injuries. (Be sure to address the contributory negligence issue in this case.)

3. Daphne is an eight-year-old girl who often plays with her neighborhood friends. While hiking through the woods on Saturday afternoon, two of Daphne's neighbors, Paul (age seven) and Anne (age ten), decided to "ditch" Daphne, that is, the duo would abandon Daphne in the woods and flee the scene. The sun had just gone down, and it was becoming quite dark when Paul and Anne ditched Daphne. Once Daphne realized she was alone in the forest, she became frightened and ran toward home. She twisted her ankle and fell, striking her head against a tree root. She was knocked unconscious. Several hours later, a police search party located her. She suffered a concussion and dehydration.

▌ REVIEW QUESTIONS

1. What are tort immunities? What is their function in tort litigation? Who do they protect?

2. Define sovereign, or governmental, immunity. What is the historical rationale behind the defense? How have modern American courts applied the doctrine?

3. What is the governmental/proprietary distinction? How it is used? How are governmental actions defined? Proprietary actions? What is the significance of these distinctions?

4. How has the sovereign immunity defense changed during this century?

5. What are public officers' immunities? Who do they protect? Why are these governmental officials granted immunity?

6. Define *children of tender years*. Who is protected by this defense? How does the immunity differ for intentional torts and negligence?

7. What are the two family immunities?

8. What is the purpose of workers' compensation?

▌ HELPFUL WEBSITES

This chapter focuses on tort immunity. To learn more about tort immunity, the following sites can be accessed:

Workers' Compensation

  http://www.law.cornell.edu

  http://www.dol.gov

State Courts

  http://www.courts.net

State Resources

http://www.findlaw.com

http://www.statelocal.gov

United States Supreme Court

http://www.supremecourtus.gov

United States Government Agencies

http://www.lib.lsu.edu

United States Department of Labor

http://www.dol.gov

Employment Discrimination Laws

http://www.eeoc.gov

STUDENT CD-ROM™

For additional materials, please go to the CD in this book.

ONLINE COMPANION™

For additional resources, please go to
http://www.paralegal.delmar.cengage.com

chapter 13

Tort Investigation

THE BIGGEST MISTAKES PARALEGALS MAKE & HOW TO AVOID THEM

There Is No Investigation Like an Accident Scene Investigation

My firm's client was interviewed in the hospital following an accident that crushed her pelvis. As the paralegal assigned to the matter, I interviewed the client, who told me a neighbor's parked car rolled toward her, pinning her body against the outside of her garage door. Further, she stated there were no witnesses to the accident and she waited thirty minutes to be rescued by a passing police cruiser. I also noticed that the police report stated, "No witnesses." The attorney who was handling the case asked me to get a digital camera and photograph the scene ASAP. I forgot all about it because of my heavy workload.

That weekend I was in a convenience store when I heard the cashier telling his manager about a woman who was hit by a runaway car across the street. Suddenly realizing I was in our client's neighborhood,

(continues)

I asked the cashier if he had witnessed the accident. He said, "No, but if you want to see the video I have that!" The surveillance camera on the outside of the store recorded the parking lot and the area across the street. The cashier showed me the tape where our client was hit and pinned by the neighbor's car. I ordered a copy of the tape.

LESSON LEARNED: Jumping to the conclusion of no witnesses, even when the client's version is supported by a police report, was wrong—as was my forgetting to visit the scene as directed by my attorney. One never knows what visiting the actual accident scene will reveal.

▌ INTRODUCTION

Investigating the facts and circumstances surrounding tortious injury or death offers many challenges. Every tort case presents the following fundamental questions, which journalists use every day in a reporting context: *Who? What? Where? When? Why? How?* In tort cases, the paralegal queries: Who injured the victim (plaintiff)? What injuries happened? How did the victim (plaintiff) get hurt? Where and when did the injuries occur? Why did the victim (plaintiff) incur injuries (that is, did the defendant(s) cause the victim's/plaintiff's injuries)? How did the injuries occur? What were the actions of the defendant?

This chapter examines the procedures paralegals use to investigate tort cases.

This chapter includes:

▶ Tort investigation
▶ The importance of tort case investigation
▶ Witness interview techniques and questions
▶ Determining and locating defendants
▶ Documenting the scene
▶ Public and private sector resources
▶ Additional areas to investigate
▶ Investigating different types of tort cases

▌ TORT INVESTIGATION

Approximately 10 percent of the paralegals in the United States specialize in personal injury litigation. Many more paralegals work on personal injury cases from time to time, as it is one of the many areas of law routinely handled by general-practice firms.

Some of the many tasks a personal injury paralegal performs are:

- Interviewing clients to elicit the particular facts of their cases
- Obtaining witness statements
- Investigating the accident, condition, or occurrence
- Assisting in the preparation of legal documents, such as the summons, complaint, answer, or reply
- Preparing settlement summaries
- Ordering medical authorizations and records
- Preparing discovery requests, tracking and monitoring responses to discovery requests, and summarizing deposition transcripts
- Researching legal issues and assisting in preparing motions
- Scheduling witnesses and experts for trial
- Preparing exhibits for trial
- Organizing evidence for trial
- Preparing cases for arbitration
- Preparing subpoenas for trial and arranging for service of process
- Aiding in preparing clients for testifying at trial
- Being present at trial to assist the attorney
- Assisting in the preparation and research of appellate briefs
- Researching different legal theories
- Drafting documents to collect a money judgment.

▮▮ THE IMPORTANCE OF TORT CASE INVESTIGATION

Key facts must be ascertained if a law firm is to properly handle a personal injury or property damage lawsuit. This entails an **investigation.**

investigation | A systematic examination, especially an official inquiry.

Paralegals and Investigators

Each attorney or law firm has its own specialized methods for conducting investigations. Some have in-house investigators; others hire outside investigators or investigation services. Some attorneys hire specialists for specific aspects of a tort case. Some rely on law clerks, paralegals, or other staff members to perform certain aspects of investigations.

Even if the paralegal is not required to conduct investigations, it is essential that he or she know what is needed for each type of case in order to supervise or monitor the investigation. Paralegals need to know when a particular piece of information may lead to something else and therefore merits additional investigation. Conversely, paralegals should develop a sense of what items of information are not useful or relevant. One must be able to review the investigation, make sure it has been done properly and completely, and ascertain whether further research is needed.

Many paralegals handle particular aspects of investigation, either in the stages of case evaluation and development or in the course of case management. This is especially true when the trial team is determining potential defendants or defenses and ascertaining the basic facts of what happened and why. At times, a knowledgeable paralegal will spot legal issues early on that have a significant bearing on the case investigation. For example, the paralegal might learn of the existence of photographs taken by a rescue squad that show details about the condition of an accident scene.

Customizing the Investigation

The tort trial team will want to adapt the investigation to fit the case. Investigations can be quite simple or highly complex and technical. Factors such as the severity of the injury involved and resources available to the plaintiff or defendant often control the scope of the investigation. "Resources available" are such factors as the client's ability to pay, the attorney's ability to advance the costs of investigation, the financial condition of prospective parties, and the existence of insurance, all of which must be considered.

Details, Details, Details!

In litigation, details are very important. An overlooked detail could make a real difference in the outcome of the case. Investigations must be customized, with more than a little creativity. For example, suppose that you are investigating an automobile accident. You cannot understand why the driver of the vehicle did not stop for the pedestrian in the crosswalk. A witness tells you that she noticed the driver was wearing glasses, but this should *not* be enough proof for you to automatically conclude that the driver could see properly. It is possible that the driver was only wearing reading glasses when distance glasses were needed. It is also possible that the driver was wearing an old pair of glasses and never bothered to get a new prescription. Little details like these can make or break a case.

Goals of Tort Case Investigation

Factual investigation is designed to shed light on liability and damages. Information is gathered in terms of what happened to the injured party, who may or may not have been responsible for the injuries, and any act or omission by the injured party that contributed to the accident.

If all else fails, it may be necessary to turn over the investigation, or portions of it, to a professional investigator who has expertise with a particular subject and other special resources. However, this is not practical in a small case or in a case where the firm's client has limited financial resources.

█ WITNESS INTERVIEW TECHNIQUES AND QUESTIONS

Witnesses will explain their account of the circumstances before and after the accident, how the accident occurred, and the damages or injuries received by the people involved. Some firms prefer that such interviews be electronically recorded, or written and signed by the witness for future reference or use. Witnesses sometimes forget or change their testimony. It is important to interview witnesses as soon as possible; they will be easier to locate, and their recollections will be clearer. Exhibit 13-1 shows a sample witness statement.

Narrative Questions

There are different kinds of questioning styles you might develop, depending on the type of case and the personality of the witness. Sometimes a narrative of the event in question is most helpful. This allows the witness to tell a story without interruption. You can start out with an open-ended question as general as, "Can you tell me what happened on the day of the incident?" and see what the witness has to say. This allows the witness to speak from memory without any breaks in the story. You want to avoid breaking the stream of memory. This kind of open response seems to be more accurate than when the witness is prompted by individual questions from the interviewer. Allow the witness to pause, and do not make the witness feel uncomfortable when thinking or gathering thoughts.

Closed-Ended Questions

If needed, you can follow up with closed-ended questions for more details. You might need to ask, for instance, "So what was the color of the other car?" or "What time did you leave your house that day?" Sometimes when asked specific questions, the witness becomes more self-conscious and thinks you are looking for a certain answer or that there is a correct answer. The paralegal's goal is to encourage the witness to speak freely, even if the statements made seem trivial or insignificant.

Leading Questions

Occasionally, based upon some information in your file, you might need to ask leading questions, which tend to suggest to the witness the answer you are looking for. An example of this is asking, "Was the other car red?" Of course you want to caution the witness not to guess about any answers. It is better to have the witness tell you that he or she does not know, rather than to guess as to what occurred.

WITNESS STATEMENT

14 Fern Dr.	Albany	N.Y.	5/03/09
LOCATION	CITY	STATE	DATE

1. My name is Kris J. McGrail. I reside at 14 Fern Drive,
2. Albany, NY. I am employed by the Albany Police
3. Department. My date of birth is 10/10/80. On 4/28/09 I
4. witnessed an accident on Sand Creek Road east of Wolf
5. Road. I was sitting on my motorcycle at the Hess
6. Station on Sand Creek and Wolf Road. I was just
7. finished getting gas and was getting ready to leave when
8. I witnessed an accident. I was just about to leave the
9. gas station when I noticed a motorcycle heading across
10. Wolf Road going eastbound. This motorcycle had a green
11. light as it crossed Wolf Road on Sand Creek Road. I
12. noticed the motorcycle because the driver was wearing a
13. T-shirt and I thought he was brave because although it
14. was nice out it wasn't that warm. There was a gold-
15. toned vehicle behind me at the pumps at the Hess
16. Station facing north. This vehicle, which I later learned
17. was driven by Deborah Lawrence, pulled around me at
18. the pump and began to exit from the Hess Station. Ms.
19. Lawrence used the exit of the Hess Station going onto
20. Sand Creek Road. Ms. Lawrence came to a gliding stop
21. and exited the driveway going westbound. Ms. Lawrence
22. never brought her car to a full stop as she exited the
23. driveway. Ms. Lawrence did not have the directional
24.
25.
26.
27.   Wit: Cathy Okrent   Kris McGrail

▲━━━━━━━━ **DO NOT WRITE BELOW THIS LINE** ━━━━━━━━▲

EXHIBIT 13-1   Sample witness statement

WITNESS STATEMENT

	LOCATION	CITY	STATE	5/03/09
				DATE

1. light of her vehicle on as she made the turn. Ms.
2. Lawrence then broadsided the motorcycle on the
3. motorcyclist's right side. The front bumper of her vehicle
4. collided with the side of the motorcycle. The motorcycle
5. was knocked down and continued to slide east by the
6. force of the impact. Bob Green, the motorcyclist, went up
7. in the air and landed on the ground of the road. Mr.
8. Green then got up and was hopping on one leg. My
9. wife went over to Mr. Green to offer aid. I went over to
10. Ms. Lawrence and told her to pull into the parking lot
11. of Ace Transmissions which she did. At the time of the
12. accident, Mr. Green was not traveling fast on his
13. motorcycle. He was traveling at a rate of speed no more
14. than 25-30 miles per hour. I went over to Mr. Green
15. and he complained about his leg and ankle, which looked
16. quite injured to me. His leg was cut, swollen, and
17. purple and he complained of pain. Someone from a
18. nearby business called the police and ambulance. Ms.
19. Lawrence at the scene said she never saw the motorcycle.
20. Ms. Lawrence was alone in her vehicle. She did not have
21. anyone in the car as a passenger. Mr. Green was
22. wearing a helmet and the headlight of the motorcycle was
23. on. I do not know of any other witnesses to the
24.
25.
26.
27. Wit: Cathy Okrent   Kris McGrail

DO NOT WRITE BELOW THIS LINE

EXHIBIT 13-1   Sample witness statement *(continued)*

WITNESS STATEMENT

5/03/09

LOCATION	CITY	STATE	DATE

1. accident. I believe this accident was caused by Ms.
2. Lawrence's inattention and failure to yield the right of
3. way to Mr. Green, the motorcyclist.
4.
5. I have read the above statement and it is true to the
6. best of my knowledge.
7.
8.
9.   Kris McGrail
10.
11.
12.
13.
14.
15.
16.
17.
18.
19.
20.
21.
22.
23.   Cathy Okrent
24.   Notary Public State of New York
                             Qualified in Schenectady County
25.   Commission Expires July 31, 2010
26.
27.

DO NOT WRITE BELOW THIS LINE

EXHIBIT 13-1   Sample witness statement *(continued)*

Pictures and Diagrams

Having a witness draw a picture or diagram is often quite helpful. This is great with very old or young witnesses, or when the subject of the inquiry is complex or involves directions of vehicles, or location of people. Sometimes the witness's idea of direction does not match actual compass or map directions, and it is important that you both mean the same thing when you refer to left, right, or north and south, or even close and far. At the end of the interview, always be sure to ask, "Is there anything else you need to tell me or that we have not discussed?" Then be sure to caution the witness not to speak with others about the case before discussing this with the attorney assigned to the case. Finally, thank the witness, and encourage the witness to stay in touch with you, and to feel free to contact you if anything additional is remembered about the occurrence.

Client Interview Techniques

Personal injury paralegals are often involved in interviewing clients and witnesses. Some firms will have the client fill out an initial information questionnaire that is specifically geared to garner the information needed to handle a personal injury case. (See the client information questionnaire in Appendix A.) Other firms might desire a more informal initial contact with clients, and prefer that a paralegal or attorney greet the clients and interview them.

It is always important to put the client at ease. Be sure the client is comfortable with you and the law-office surroundings before getting down to details. Small talk of a general nature helps. When the client sees that you care about him or her as a person, rather than as the next slip-and-fall case, he or she will be more apt to confide in you and provide you with the information needed for the best possible representation.

It is important to remember that, for many clients, this injury claim represents the first time they have been to an attorney's office. For some clients, an appointment with an attorney is a very intimidating experience, particularly when the attorney hastily greets them and then must excuse himself or herself to go to court at the last minute. The clients are left feeling that the attorney was too busy to see them. The paralegal then becomes an invaluable bridge between the attorney and the client. Eventually, the client will see that the paralegal often has more time to speak with the client and is more readily accessible by telephone, e-mail, or for office conferences than the trial attorney. Some clients prefer to speak with the paralegal working on their case for this very reason. You might even notice that clients will tell you things that they are reluctant to tell the attorney. Some clients are hesitant to take up the attorney's time, or feel that the attorney will think less of them, or will not want to represent them if they tell the attorney all the details of the case.

This is one reason why the role of the paralegal is so important. A paralegal who encourages the client to talk and thoroughly interviews the client about the accident provides a wealth of information for the attorney and other members of the litigation team who might later work on the file.

Depending on your jurisdiction, it could take anywhere from months to four or five years for a personal injury case to reach the trial date. At the time of trial, your client's only recollection of the accident may be that which previously was told to you and recorded in the file. The same is true of witnesses. The importance of a thorough interview, and possible followup interviews, at the outset of a case cannot be emphasized enough. In time, each paralegal develops his or her own method of interviewing. Some think of an interview like a tree. You proceed up the main trunk, but at any time, your client might say something that causes you to branch off to focus on specific facts or issues. Then it is up to you to determine if you need to return to your main series of questions, or if perhaps the new information obtained should be pursued first.

▌ DETERMINING AND LOCATING DEFENDANTS

Besides the client, the most critical participants in any tort litigation are any potential defendants and witnesses. If a plaintiff's attorney cannot find someone to sue successfully, then the client's tort case comes to a halt. A paralegal may be asked to locate all prospective defendants and witnesses. In most tort cases, determining defendants to sue is done through in-house investigation, although occasionally it will be necessary for an investigator with more extensive resources to locate a defendant or research information (for example, regarding the principals of a defunct partnership or corporation).

It is sometimes difficult to identify and locate parties. This is particularly true if a business operating under a trade name has been dissolved or has otherwise "vanished" since the tort was committed. Even individuals can "disappear," as debt collectors and skip-tracers become acutely aware when searching for fleeing debtors. Some tortfeasors lie low to avoid service of process and liability. Some businesses create dummy corporations or partnerships to "front" for shareholders, who may be individuals, other corporations, or partnerships that hope to remain hidden from potential tort actions. In some instances, the client may simply be unaware of the defendant's correct corporate name.

Using Discovery to Locate Defendants

Discovery is the phase in a lawsuit when information is exchanged between the parties and the issues for trial are narrowed. Occasionally, discovery will

discovery | 1. The formal and informal exchange of information between sides in a lawsuit.... 2. Finding out something previously unknown.

be served upon known defendants to uncover information about unknown defendants or ones that cannot be located. The paralegal should check the rules of civil procedure and discovery in his or her jurisdiction to see if prelitigation discovery is allowed, and if a court order is needed. If not, discovery will have to be conducted after the lawsuit commences.

Examination before Trial (Deposition). There are various discovery methods, which vary slightly by name and rules from state to state and at the federal level as well. One of the main forms of discovery is the examination before trial (EBT), sometimes referred to as the deposition of the parties. Through questioning of the parties early in the proceedings, the attorneys can narrow the issues and be better aware of the value of their case. This form of discovery is not used for all cases, as it can be expensive and time consuming. Generally, a court stenographer is hired to take the testimony and produce a written transcript of the proceedings.

Written Interrogatories. Another method of discovery includes written interrogatories. Written questions are sent to the opposing party, and the party is required to respond under oath, in writing, in a timely fashion. This is very helpful in a contract or business matter where inquiry is made as to the availability of business documents and records. This might be used when there is no need to observe the character or demeanor of the witnesses in person, or if a matter does not involve substantial sums of money.

Notice to Admit. Sometimes, notices to admit (requests for admissions) are sent to the opposing party. The party must admit the truth or falsity of certain statements. When you are not certain as to the precise name of a defendant, or there are a few key issues that must be resolved, a notice to admit might help narrow the issues or provide some clarity.

Request for Documents. A paralegal might be asked to send requests for the production of documents. This might be done to find out the kind of evidence the opposing party possesses. For instance, you might demand a copy of a contract, receipts, accident reports, photographs, written statements, reports, inventory records, bills of lading, or computer records in the other party's possession. This request, like all the other discovery requests, is subject to various rules and limitations that the paralegal must be familiar with before sending out a request.

Physical or Mental Examination. In cases where a party's physical or mental condition is in issue, a physical or mental examination of the party might be requested. Again, keep in mind that a host of rules limit the scope and manner in which these can be conducted, not to mention the cost of paying an expert to perform an examination and write a written report, as well as HIPAA concerns. See the discussion on HIPAA later in the chapter.

Permission to Enter on Land. Depending on the type of case, you might want to request permission to enter another party's land or business for inspection. Once an incident has occurred at a private location, you are going to need specific permission to gain entry and observe the area where an incident occurred. Absent this permission, you risk a trespassing claim, not to mention certain ethical violations. Make sure you are familiar with all aspects of your jurisdiction's discovery rules and procedures to ensure that the greatest amount of information you discover will eventually be admissible at trial.

Study Documents Carefully

Every piece of paper a paralegal obtains regarding a client's tort case is a prospective source of information regarding potential defendants and witnesses. Police accident reports are an obvious example in personal injury cases, but there are many others. Letters, invoices, leases, articles in newspapers, ambulance reports, witnesses' statements, and other documents often contain vital leads for finding parties. Any document connected to the parties and the circumstances involved in the tort might contain information a paralegal could use to locate defendants. Frequently one finds a clue about the accident through which one may determine a person's name, address, or parent company name—perhaps from the fine print in the document.

Exhibit 13-2 is a sample copy of a traffic ticket.

Use Caution When Naming Parties

Paralegals must be certain to have the correct parties before a tort lawsuit is filed. If one files notice, sues the wrong person, or fails to name a proper party, serious problems may arise. For instance, the attorney or law firm may be subject to legal action and/or disciplinary proceedings for filing a frivolous lawsuit against the innocent party. Additionally, the statute of limitations or a notice requirement may run on a client's lawsuit without the correct person(s) having been notified or sued. Mistakes in this area may even result in a claim of malpractice by the client against the attorney.

The paralegal should check all available resources to ensure that the correct individual or business entity is being identified as the defendant. Investigatory novices might be satisfied by pulling a company or individual's name out of the telephone directory, but this practice can be disastrous if the purported defendant turns out to be an innocent "same-name" person or business.

New York State Department of Motor Vehicles
TRAFFIC TICKET

GG9900G3SP

To be completed by Police Officer and given to Motorist.

POLICE AGENCY
NEW YORK STATE POLICE
Local Police Code

Last Name	First Name	M. I

Number and Street	Apt. No.	Photo Lic Shown ⬭

City	State	Zip Code	Owner is Open ⬭	Lic Closed Type

Cites ID Number	Sex	Date of Birth

Lic State	License Expires	Veh. Type	Veh. Year	Veh. Make	Veh. Color

Plate Number	Reg. State	Registration Expires

OAB XXXXXXX

New York State Department of Motor Vechicles
TRAFFIC TICKET

POLICE AGENCY

LAST NAME FIRST NAME M. I LOCAL POLICE CODE

NUMBER & STREET ADDRESS APT. NO. PHOTO LIC SHOWN ⬭

CITY STATE ZIP CODE Owner is Open ⬭ LIC CLASSED TYPE

I.D NUMBER SEX DATE OF BIRTH (MMDDYY)

STATE LICENSE EXPIRES (MMDDYY) VEH. TYPE VEH. YR VEH. MAKE VEH. COLOR

Exhibit 13-2
Sample traffic ticket
Source: http://www.nysdmv.com/pleadandpay/pmtsamples.htm

Using the Telephone as a Research Tool

Telephone calls occasionally may be useful in uncovering details concerning defendants, particularly when the person called is cooperative and talkative. If a shopping center, apartment complex, or similar business or building is involved, someone at the office may tell a paralegal over the phone who the owners are or will reveal the name of the management company. Oral communication skills are at a premium here. A good investigative paralegal, like a good journalist, knows how to get information without giving away any secrets or motives. In general, information should flow *to* the paralegal from nonclient witnesses; the paralegal should be wary of giving out information.

Internet Resources

A large part of tort investigation can now be completed using the Internet. A wide array of telephone, professional, and other directories can now be accessed on the Web. You can research companies, get proper corporate names and addresses, and obtain other information needed for suit directly from a company's Web site. Most government offices, courts, and agencies have Web sites where you can obtain information and even forms and brochures detailing the proper method for bringing or defending a claim before the particular agency or jurisdiction. A variety of the procedures described in this chapter for investigating a tort claim can also be conducted via the Internet.

Obtaining Information about Corporations

Most jurisdictions require corporations to be registered with the state in which they were incorporated, created, or are doing business.

Secretaries of State Offices.
To locate a corporation, a paralegal should first contact the state agency that is responsible for keeping business organizational records. This is usually the secretary of state's corporate division for each state. A paralegal may determine the correct names, addresses, officers, directors, and contact persons for service of process upon a corporation operating in a particular state by contacting the secretary of state's office. One may also discover the name of a parent corporation by searching the secretary of state's records. Exhibit 13-3 shows a sample request to a secretary of state's office.

For a minimal fee, in most states the secretary of state's office will furnish other written documentation, such as a corporation's articles of incorporation, that has been filed with the governmental agency. Most of this information should be available on-line.

business directory | A listing of corporations and other business organizations by name, geographic location, product or service, brand name, advertising, and other subject headings.

Business Directories.
Business directories are another excellent source of information about business defendants. **Business directories** list corporations and other business organizations according to name, geographic location, product or service, brand name, advertising, and other subject headings. Most public or university libraries have these reference texts on reserve. Various private services, such as Dun & Bradstreet, Inc., also provide this information, in print or on-line; sometimes a fee is involved.

Public Business Records.
Other potential sources of information about business defendants include:

- Company annual reports
- The state attorney general's office
- The state or federal Departments of Commerce
- The Securities and Exchange Commission (SEC)
- On-line services.

VAN & LIAL, P.C.
10 Church Street, New York, N.Y. 10007
Telephone (212) 732-9000

August 12, 2009

Department of State
Corporation Division
Albany, New York

Re: Koche v. Patrick

Gentlemen:

Kindly advise whether you have any filing for the following corporation:
D. B. Associates, Inc., doing business out of Albany, New York.
Please indicate whether the above corporation is a New York corporation, and if so, when it was incorporated, where its principal office is, and whether the above designation is correct.
If it is not a New York corporation, kindly advise us in what state it was incorporated and if it is authorized to do business in the State of New York.
Thank you for a prompt reply to the undersigned.

Very truly yours,

VAN & LIAL, P.C.

By: _____
        Tyrah Williams, paralegal

TW/kn

EXHIBIT 13-3
Sample request to
a secretary of state's office

SEC reports are surprisingly fertile sources of corporate information. The reports that companies are required to file with the SEC typically contain much more detailed information than is found in annual reports to stockholders. Also, SEC reports have the advantage of being more accessible than shareholder reports, which companies often consider confidential.

Obtaining Information about Partnerships

Partnerships can be more elusive than corporations. Investors sometimes form partnerships for specific projects, such as shopping centers or housing developments, and then disband them after the project is complete. Some jurisdictions require that partnerships be registered, in which case they can be located through the partnership section of the secretary of state's offices. However, there are fewer requirements for partnership registration than for corporations in some states. Most jurisdictions allow service of process upon any partner as notice to the partnership. **Process service** is the delivery of the summons to the defendant as a means of notifying the defendant of a pending action and compelling the defendant to appear in court.

service of process (process service) | The delivery (or its legal equivalent, such as publication in a newspaper in some cases) of a legal paper by an authorized person.

Obtaining the Names of Sole Proprietors and Partners

Many jurisdictions require that partnerships and individuals doing business under a trade name or assumed, **fictitious name** file a *doing business as (d/b/a)* certificate or affidavit with an appropriate governmental agency. Many local governments require sole proprietors and partnerships doing business in the county or city to file d/b/a certificates and affidavits with the local recorder's office.

fictitious name | A trade or assumed name used by a corporation for the purpose of conducting business.

Ambulance Services and Fire Departments as Defendants

Even the people called upon for assistance can end up being defendants in a lawsuit. If the fire department or ambulance service is called, and there is an unusual delay in their arrival, or if they do not have standard and appropriate equipment, the department may be liable. If equipment is not working properly, personnel are not properly trained to use it, or personnel are not supervised adequately, they may be potential defendants.

Usually the agency for which the offending individuals, firefighters, or ambulance service persons are working is added to the lawsuit for failure to supervise, failure to adequately train, or failure to provide appropriate and functional equipment. Of course, the theories of liability would depend upon the circumstances.

A fire department or ambulance service is often owned or supervised by a governmental agency, such as the city, county, or town. However, there may be a volunteer organization in a small town or a rural or unincorporated area. If so, its contract with the cities or counties in the service area should be reviewed, if possible. **Freedom of information laws (FOIL)** in each state usually provide for the disclosure of such information from governmental entities. Exhibit 13-4 shows a typical request for information. Some local governments contract out ambulance services to private companies. Ambulances may also be owned and operated by hospitals and funeral homes.

Freedom of information law (FOIL) | A law requiring (or assisting) public access to government records.

Paralegals should carefully follow statutes or procedural rules for special notice requirements when suing governmental agencies. Some municipalities and governmental entities require prior notice of a condition or defect before a suit is permitted, if at all.

EXHIBIT 13-4
Sample request
for information
to government agency

EVANS AND MYERS, P.C.
12 State Street, Albany, New York
(518) 474-3691

January 25, 2009

Albany County Clerk
Office of the County Clerk
Albany, New York 12207

Re: FREEDOM OF INFORMATION REQUEST
of January 11, 2009
Airplane Crash of December 1, 2008
in the Town of Knox, County of Albany,
New York

Dear Sir or Madam:

   Thank you for your letter dated January 16, 2009 and the investigative report of the Albany County Sheriff's Department with respect to the above airplane crash.

   On Page 3 of said report, the third paragraph mentions that photographs were taken by I.D. Officer George Dinell. If possible, this office would like copies of the prints of said photographs pursuant to the Freedom of Information Act.

   Would you please be so kind as to inform the undersigned, in writing, of the necessary procedures to procure said photographs, and the fee for obtaining same.

   Again, I thank you for your assistance and your fine efforts, and I look forward to hearing from your office soon with respect to the above mentioned photographs.

Very truly yours,

By: _____
         Anna Lee Chin, Paralegal

AC/km

practical **application**

When handling reports about situations in which negligence may be a factor, a paralegal should study the documents not only to determine the *facts* of what happened, but also to identify *who* was responsible.

Investigating Licensed or Regulated Businesses

Most states have a central department or agency that oversees licensed and regulated businesses. For example, in Texas this agency is the Texas Department of Licensing and Regulation. To uncover additional information about a licensed or regulated business, a paralegal should consult the state governmental listings in the telephone directory in the state in which the business is located, or go on-line.

Agencies can also provide listings of all state licensing requirements. By checking with the state agency, one may discover whether a potential business defendant's license, certification, or insurance has lapsed or is not in good standing. Also, information might be available about the defendant's proper name, address, and telephone number.

Typically, one must complete a request form to gain access to the information on file for a particular business at the state licensing agency. These documents will range from the business's initial application for the license to a copy of its insurance certificate. Many agencies have this information available on the Internet.

practical **application**

If the defendant is local, the paralegal should check the display advertisements in the telephone directory, or the company's Web site. Many businesses include their business license number in the advertisement or post it for inspection at the place of business. Having this information available may speed up one's request for information.

Sample Defendant Search

Consider the following hypothetical defendant search. The accident report lists Axtco Construction as the owner of a truck that struck the client's vehicle. The accident report will also have Axtco's address.

If Axtco is listed in the local telephone directory, the paralegal could first call to obtain the name of the president, owner, or chief executive officer. If the address on the accident report is an out-of-town address, obtain the number from directory assistance for that area code.

The paralegal should be prepared to reach an uncooperative Axtco employee who will not divulge any of this information without first knowing the reason. One should be extremely cautious regarding how much information to disclose during such direct telephone contact with a potential business defendant. Also recall that ethical considerations are involved in such direct contact. The paralegal should consult with his or her supervising attorney to decide how much to tell the company personnel to obtain the names and addresses of the company chief executive officer, president, or other officer who can be sent a notice or demand letter and, subsequently, service of process. Usually, it is best to reveal as little as possible and to truthfully downplay any legal implications for which the information is being requested. Also, business directories (often found in reference sections of libraries) can be consulted for information about a business, as can on-line resources.

Assuming that the direct-contact approach yields little or no useful information regarding Axtco, the paralegal could next consult the secretary of state's corporate or partnership divisions to see if Axtco is a corporation or partnership authorized to conduct business in the state. If not, the paralegal could next contact the city or county governmental agency in which assumed or trade names are registered (e.g., the county recorder's office). The agency to consult will be located in the city or county in which Axtco's business offices are found. Then the paralegal could look up Axtco's trade or assumed name certificate or affidavit on file with the agency. Also, online resources might contain the needed information.

In case the accident report is unavailable or contains incomplete information about Axtco, the paralegal should look at any photographs of the vehicle from the accident scene. Do the company's name and address appear on the truck's doors or body? If not, the information may be available from the state's Department of Motor Vehicles.

Knowing who and where the defendants are is an important initial stage in every tort investigation. Another critical investigatory aspect involves the circumstances surrounding the victim/plaintiff's injuries. The next section considers how paralegals document tort accident scenes.

▌ DOCUMENTING THE SCENE

Although legal staff are almost never on the scene when a tort actually occurs, it is critical to document the scene of a tort injury as soon as possible.

Obtaining Visual Documentation, Measurements, and Other Details

Paralegals may take photographs or videotape recordings of accident scenes. Also, paralegals take measurements and describe physical conditions at the location itself. Documenting the scene should be done as soon as possible, because valuable evidence is often lost as conditions change over time. Accident scenes can alter naturally due to environmental changes; or, more frequently, people might deliberately modify conditions to prevent others from being harmed or to conceal possible liability.

Paralegals should be exceedingly thorough when documenting the scene of an accident or other tort. What seems insignificant at the time may be found to be important after more is known about the accident itself. For example, the distance between steps on a stairway, and whether the stairs were tiled or carpeted, could be vitally important in a slip-and-fall case. Also, it is meaningful when re-constructing an accident to have as much information as possible about the actual scene at the time of the accident.

practical **application**

The scene of an accident should be documented as soon as possible. The paralegal should keep in mind that places and situations change, some-times rapidly. Weather conditions can change streets and roads, construc-tion projects may start or end, streetlights may be installed, or lighting that was on at the time of an accident may go out. A place of business may put up warnings or fences. A pool may be covered or drained. One may safely presume that potential defendants, if they are aware of their pos-sible liabilities, will act quickly to have the cause of an accident repaired to prevent others from being injured.

Knowing the Evidentiary Rules for One's Jurisdiction

Every state has rules of evidence that regulate the admissibility of evidence. Not all evidence will automatically be admitted into evidence at the time of the trial. Sometimes the evidence must be in a specific form. You may have to obtain original records rather than photocopies. These rules can generally be obtained on-line.

As the tort investigation is conducted, the paralegal should put each item to be used at trial in admissible form. Rules of evidence from your jurisdiction should be consulted. Even evidence that will be used only for in-house purposes, or for settlement brochures or mediation packages, should be maintained in a form that could be admitted at trial if necessary. Documents that the trial team plans to use for evidence at trial *must* be suitable to present at trial. Otherwise, a paralegal may find himself or herself tracking down these documents at the last minute, having to put them into admissible form (such as certified copies, which also usually requires another fee), and generally wasting time that could have been better spent on other aspects of trial preparation. Sometimes opposing counsel will cooperate in stipulating to the admissibility of certain documents; sometimes not.

Using Proper Evidentiary Form

Looking ahead to trial, paralegals should consult the relevant state, local, or fed-eral procedural and evidentiary rules to determine the form in which evidence must be submitted into the trial record and what type of documentation is required. For instance:

▶ Does the court require supporting affidavits for admission of medical records and bills into evidence?

▶ Is there a certain form or language for business records? If not, how are they proved in court? Are original records necessary, or will copies suffice?

▶ Are there chain-of-custody rules that you need to comply with?

▶ Are you prepared to prove that a videotape or photo has not been altered?

▶ Can documents or pleadings—the formal statements of the parties, such as the complaint and the answer—from other cases be used as evidence in one's case? If so, must they be certified by a court clerk or someone else?

Hearsay Problems

Hearsay is an out-of-court statement offered as evidence to prove the fact contained in the statement. Statements may be verbal, written, or even gestural.

Some documents may not be admissible because they are considered hearsay. At times, only portions of documents may be admissible. For example, all or part of a police or ambulance report may be considered hearsay because the police officer and/or ambulance attendant who wrote the report did not actually see the accident. This person's report will contain information from someone else, such as the injured party or a witness. Hearsay is not admissible, but there are numerous exceptions to this rule.

The trial team will want to review the documents and the evidence rules. They may want to offer the reports into evidence simply as business records (an exception to the hearsay rule), or use them to refresh the memory of a testifying police officer or paramedic, without offering them as evidence.

hearsay | A statement about what someone else said (or wrote or otherwise communicated).

Video and Computer Technologies

Videotape and computer animation are routinely used in accident reconstruction, "day-in-the-life" documentaries, and settlement brochures. Even video news footage is being utilized in the courtroom. Paralegals should know how to document the authenticity of this type of evidence so that it can be used during trial.

▌ PUBLIC AND PRIVATE SECTOR RESOURCES

Governmental agencies and private entities are sources of a variety of information that may be germane to the paralegal's tort case investigation. On-line computer networks may be the information superhighway, but some information is still stored the old-fashioned way—on paper, microfilm, microfiche, or other archival media—and paralegals need to know where to look to uncover this material.

Local Governmental Agencies

Governmental agencies are literal stockpiles of information that the paralegal will find invaluable in tort case investigation. Freedom of information laws provide for governmental disclosure of most contracts. Archives contain vital statistics, marriage licenses, civil suit records, and probate and estate records. One can obtain information from automobile license tag records, such as the name and current address of the owner of a vehicle involved in an accident. Also, information can be obtained from driver's license records, deeds, and liens. The tax assessor's office can provide property-ownership information by name or address of the property. In some states, some of the information will be protected by privacy protection acts limiting the amount of information that can be obtained or distributed to others.

Newspapers

Newspapers and newspaper personnel can be good sources of information. For instance, an article about the tort incident might quote a witness about whom the paralegal did not know. There could also be helpful information about how the accident happened or who was involved. The paralegal should find out if a newspaper reporter took any photographs of the scene, even if none were printed in the newspaper.

There may be information about one's client or other parties in the archives of the newspaper. The paralegal should look beyond articles about the tort incident for photographs or profiles of people involved. There may be information to document a client's activities before an accident or to aid in service on an individual or business. Many newspapers are now on-line, allowing for easy access to prior publications.

Television and Radio News Reports

If the accident that is the basis of the tort lawsuit was reported on the news, one may want to get an audiotape, videotape, or transcript of what was reported to the public. It may be useful if a jury trial is anticipated, because prior publicity may affect jurors and even the venue of the case.

Additionally, if video news footage was taken, the paralegal should obtain a copy. It may have scene footage that is not obtainable from any other source. This footage may also have been taken closer in time to the actual incident than later documentary efforts by the law firm. The trial team may be glad to have this footage when preparing a video settlement brochure or video recreation of the accident for trial. If the television station will not cooperate, consult your rules of discovery; it may be possible to subpoena the footage.

Paralegals should also give some thought to any local conditions that might have contributed to the accident. If a fire or storm occurred at the time, and was significant, it is possible that it was reported on the local news. For example, a client's case might involve a storm-damaged building that was not repaired. The client was later injured at that business when a portion of the roof caved in. In this case, it would be a good idea to check local television stations for any news footage that might have been taken of the storm or wind shears on the day the building was believed to have been originally damaged. If found, this footage would dramatically help document not only when the building was damaged, but also that the owner or manager of the building knew, or reasonably should have known, that the building needed repair, well in advance of the injury occurring.

Official weather statistics are frequently obtained from the National Oceanic and Atmospheric Administration (NOAA), which is part of the United States Commerce Department. These statistics can be found at major airports. For local information, the department of meteorology at a local university or television station will have weather statistics. Such statistics are frequently used in arbitration and litigation.

Computerized Databases

There are many types of computerized databases and networks, each holding a wealth of information. Different jurisdictions have rules and requirements about how much information is accessible to the public or admissible at trial. Even with these restrictions, it is surprising what can be learned. Databases can be used to uncover:

- Driving records
- Driver's information
- Driver's licenses, which provide a history of residences
- Vehicle registration
- Credit reports
- Criminal history
- Public record filings, such as deeds and liens
- Business filings, such as assumed names, corporate filings, partnership filings, bankruptcy, and company officers and incorporators
- Civil lawsuits, including divorces
- Asset and other financial information.

Following are samples of documents obtained from the Internet that can be used in investigations depending on the type of case involved. Exhibit 13-5 shows a chemical database available through the U.S. Department of Labor to research chemicals.

OSHA/EPA Occupational Chemical Database

Welcome to the OSHA/EPA Occupational Chemical Database. OSHA and EPA jointly developed and maintain this database as a convenient reference for the occupational saftey and health community. This database compiles information from several government agencies and organizations. Available database reports include: "Physical Properties," "Exposure Guidelines," "NIOSH Pocket Guide," and "Emergency Response Information," including the DOT Emergency Response Guide. In additon, an all-in-one report, "Full Report," is available.

SEARCH OPTIONS

Chemical Name: [Benzene]   *Exact Match*
(or name fragment)

CAS Number: [   ]
(e.g., 7782-50-5, or CAS # fragment, e.g., 7782-5)

[Search]

View All Chemicals with:

- PELs
- Carcinogen Designations
- Skin Designations
- IDLH Values

[View]

CHEMICAL NAME / CAS NUMBER INDEX

Table of Contents by Chemical Name:

A B C D E F G H I J K L M N
O P Q R S T U V W X Y Z

[Note: Chemicals beginning with p⁻, m⁻, and o⁻ are listed alphabetically, e.g., m-xylene is found under "M" rather than "X."]

Table of Contents by [CAS Number]

Total number of records returned: 79

Chemical Name	CAS #	Formula	Synonyms	Reports Available				
1,2,4-TRICHLOROBENZENE	120-82-1	C6H3Cl3	unsym-Trichlorobenzene; 1,2,4-Trichlorobenzol	Full Report	Physical Properties	Exposure Guidelines	NIOSH Pocket Guide	Emergency Response Information
1,2-EPOXYETHYLBENZENE	96-09-3			Full Report	Physical Properties	Exposure Guidelines	NIOSH Pocket Guide	Emergency Response Information
2,4 DINITROTOLUENE	121-14-2	C7H6N2O4	Dinitrotoluol; DNT; Methyldinitrobenzene [Note: Various isomers of DNT exist]	Full Report	Physical Properties	Exposure Guidelines	NIOSH Pocket Guide	Emergency Response Information
2,4-DIAMINOANISOLE AND ITS SALTS	615-05-4		1,3-Diamino-4-methoxybenzene; 4-Methoxy-1,3-benzene-diamine; 4-Methoxy-m-phenylene-diamine Synonyms of salts vary depending upon the specific compound.	Full Report	Physical Properties	Exposure Guidelines	NIOSH Pocket Guide	Emergency Response Information
2,6 DINITROTOLUENE	606-20-2	C7H6N2O4	Dinitrotoluol; DNT; Methyldinitrobenzene	Full Report	Physical Properties	Exposure Guidelines	NIOSH Pocket Guide	Emergency Response Information
2-CHLOROANILINE	95-51-2	C6H6ClN	1-amino-2-Chlorobenzene; 2-chlorobenzenamine; 2-Chlorophenylamine; o-Chloroaniline	Full Report	Physical Properties	Exposure Guidelines	NIOSH Pocket Guide	Emergency Response Information
2-CHLORONITROBENZENE	88-73-3	C6H4ClNO2	o-Chloronitrobenzene; 1-Chloro-2-nitrobenzene; 2-Chloro-1-nitrobenzene o-Nitrochlorobenzene; Chloro-o-nitrobebzene; ONCB; 2-CNB; o-Nitrochlorobenzene	Full Report	Physical Properties	Exposure Guidelines	NIOSH Pocket Guide	Emergency Response Information
3,5-DINITROTOLUENE	618-85-9	CH3C6H3(NO2)2	Dinitrotoluol; DNT;Methyldinitrobenzene	Full Report	Physical Properties	Exposure Guidelines	NIOSH Pocket Guide	Emergency Response Information
4,4'-THIOBIS(6-TERT-BUTYL-M-CRESOL)	96-69-5	C22H30O2S	4,4'-Thiobis(3-methyl-6-tert-butylphenol); 1,1'=Thiobis(2-methyl-4-hydroxy-5-tert-butylbenzene)	Full Report	Physical Properties	Exposure Guidelines	NIOSH Pocket Guide	Emergency Response Information
4-CHLORO-2-METHYANILINE AND ITS HYDROCHLORIDE SALT	95-69-2	C7H8ClN	4-Chloro-o-Toluidine; 2-Amino-5-chlorotoluene; 5-Chloro-2-aminotoluene; 4-Chloro-2-methylbenzeneamine; 4-Chloro-2-toluidine; 4-Chloro-6-methylaniline; Fast Red TR; Fast Red TR 11; Fast Red TR Base; P-Chloro-o-toluidine	Full Report	Physical Properties	Exposure Guidelines	NIOSH Pocket Guide	Emergency Response Information
4-CHLOROANILINE	106-47-6	C6H6ClN	p-Aminochlorobenzene; 1-Amino-4-chlorobenzene; p-Chloroaniline; p-Chlorobenzenamine; 4-Chlorobenazmine	Full Report	Physical Properties	Exposure Guidelines	NIOSH Pocket Guide	Emergency Response Information
4-DIMETHYLAMINOAZOBENZENE	60-11-7	C14H15N3	Butter yellow; DAB; p-Dimethylaminoazobenzene; N,N-Dimethyl-4-aminoazobenzene; Methyl yellow	Full Report	Physical Properties	Exposure Guidelines	NIOSH Pocket Guide	Emergency Response Information
4-NITROBIPHENYL	92-93-3	C6H5C6H4NO2	p-Nitrobipheny; p-Nitrodiphenyl; 4-Nitrodiphenyl; p-Phenylnitrobenzene; 4-Phenylnitrobenzene; PNB	Full Report	Physical Properties	Exposure Guidelines	NIOSH Pocket Guide	Emergency Response Information
ANILINE	62-53-3	C6H7N	Aminobenzene; Aniline oil; Benzenamine; Phenylamine	Full Report	Physical Properties	Exposure Guidelines	NIOSH Pocket Guide	Emergency Response Information
BENZENE	71-43-2	C6H6	Benzol; Phenyl hydride	Full Report	Physical Properties	Exposure Guidelines	NIOSH Pocket Guide	Emergency Response Information
BENZYL CHLORIDE	100-44-7	C7H7Cl	Chloromethylbenzene; alpha-Chlorotoluene	Full Report	Physical Properties	Exposure Guidelines	NIOSH Pocket Guide	Emergency Response Information

EXHIBIT 13-5   OSHA/EPA occupational chemical database
Source: http://www.osha.gov/web/dep/chemicaldata/default.asp#target

Exhibit 13-6 is from the National Transportation Safety Board (NTSB) database detailing aviation crashes.

Exhibit 13-7 is a sample form that can be obtained on-line from the state motor vehicle department to obtain a copy of a motor vehicle report from an accident. Most states have similar motor vehicle forms.

Depending on the type of case being investigated, the paralegal might find several documents available on-line from federal or state agencies.

Information Regarding Criminal Acts

If the incident that is the basis of the tort lawsuit also involves a criminal act, such as a shooting or other type of assault or battery, there will be a criminal investigation, and additional information resources may be available to the trial team. The paralegal will want to review and possibly obtain copies of the following:

- Police report
- Criminal record of the perpetrator
- Trial transcript of any criminal trial, conviction, or judgment
- Exhibits used at criminal trial
- 911 or other emergency telephone call audiotapes and/or transcripts
- Floor plans or diagrams of the incident location
- Map of the area
- Crime statistics of the specific law enforcement jurisdiction.

Most tort cases involve damages, insurance coverage, and other elements that must be researched. The next section investigates these considerations.

▌ ADDITIONAL AREAS TO INVESTIGATE

Tort damages present a variety of details to investigate. These items include degree and permanence of the injury, employment and lost wages, injury expenses, insurance coverage, prior tort claims, preexisting injuries, past criminal records, and driving history, to name but a few.

Employment and Lost Wages

The plaintiff's damages may be based in part on the dollar amount of wages lost due to injuries. Another factor that is often considered is impairment of future earning capacity. The paralegal needs this earnings information for in-house evaluation, but the defendants will also be entitled to obtain certain information regarding wages. See Exhibit 13-8, a report of occupational injury or illness.

The plaintiff's income must be documented. It is not sufficient for a client to simply testify, "I could have made $175,000 this year if it weren't for this injury." Income and income potential must be substantiated by independent evidence.

Enter your word string below: (Searches both synopsis and full narrative; will slow the query performance)

[   ] NEW *(see Search Tips)*

NTSB Status

Accident Number   Report Status   Probable Cause Issued between

[   ]   [All   ]   [   ] and [   ]

                                     (mm/dd/yyyy)   *(mm/dd/yyyy)*

Sort by: [Date   ] in [Descending] order. Show [10] records per page.

[Submit Query] [Reset]

Current Synopsis	PDF Report(s)	Event Date	Probable Cause Released	Location	Make / Model	Regist. Number	Event Severity	Type of Air Carrier Operation and Carrier Name (Doing Business As)
Factual	Factual	7/22/2007		San Salvador, El Salvador	Robinson R22 Beta II	HR-ASO	Fatal(1)	Non-U.S., Non-Commercial
Preliminary	Preliminary	7/20/2007		Stratford, OK	Rotorway 162F	N888TD	Nonfatal	Part 91: General Aviation
Preliminary	Preliminary	7/20/2007		Destin, FL	Larry J. Cook Lancair 320	N52LC	Nonfatal	Part 91: General Aviation
Preliminary	Preliminary	7/20/2007		Slaton, TX	Air Tractor AT-502	N15400	Nonfatal	Part 91: General Aviation
Factual	Factual	7/17/2007		Sao Paulo, Brazil	Airbus Industrie A320-233	PT-MBK	Fatal(186)	SCHD Non-U.S. Commercial TAM Linhas Aéreas
Preliminary	Preliminary	7/16/2007		Laurel, IA	Air Tractor AT-402A	N203DM	Fatal(1)	Part 137: Agricultural
Preliminary	Preliminary	7/16/2007		Benchmark, MT	Bell UH-1H	N667HP	Nonfatal	Public Use
Preliminary	Preliminary	7/15/2007		Eden Prairie, MN	Monney M20J	N4785H	Nonfatal	Part 91: General Aviation
Preliminary	Preliminary	7/15/2007		Osceola, IN	AirTractor AT-301	N3158W	Fatal(1)	Part 137: Agricultural
Preliminary	Preliminary	7/15/2007		Camarillo, CA	North American F-51D	N51TK	Fatal(1)	Part 91: General Aviation

Exhibit 13-6   NTSB—Accident Database Query

Source: http://www.ntsb.gov/ntsb/query.asp

New York State Department of Motor Vehicles   MV-198C (11/06)

REQUEST FOR COPY OF ACCIDENT REPORT

Use only for accidents that happen in New York State.

Please choose one of the following:

☐ I am named in this accident report, or I am the authorized representative of a person named in this report.

☐ I am, or may be, a party to a civil action arising out of the conduct described in this accident report.

☐ I am the authorized representative of a person who is, or who may be, a party to a civil action arising out of the conduct described in this accident report.

☐ I am a representative of New York State or of a political subdivision of New York State, and will use this accident report ONLY for statistics or research relating to highway safety.

☐ Other reason: _____

Please Print Requester's Name and Address:

_____

_____

_____

Requester's Signature ▸ _____

Date of Signature _____

To Knowingly make a false statement or conceal a material fact in this written statement is a criminal offense, punishable under Penal Law Section 210.45.

Provide as much information as you can about the accident:

Accident Date: _____

Accident Location (County): _____

If more than 3 motorists were involved, please attach an additional MV-198C.

Fatal Accident: ☐ YES

Responding Police Agency:

☐ NYC Precinct # _____ Accident # _____

☐ NYS Police _____

☐ Local _____

Plate No.		Driver License ID No. or No. from Non-Driver ID Card	
NAME			Date of Birth
Address			Apt. No.
City		State	Zip Code

Plate No.	Driver License ID No. or No. from Non-Driver ID Card	Plate No.	Driver License ID No. or No. from Non-Driver ID Card
NAME	Date of Birth	NAME	Date of Birth
Address	Apt. No.	Address	Apt. No.
City	State Zip Code	City	State Zip Code

Check boxes below for all reports you are requesting:

☐ Police Report _____

☐ Motorist Report (NAME) _____

☐ Motorist Report (NAME) _____

☐ Motorist Report (NAME) _____

Mail completed form and payment to: NYSDMV, MV-198C Processing, PO Box 2086, Albany NY 12220-00860.

Non-refundable search fee $10.00

No. of reports requested _____ x $15 .... $ _____

Total Amount Enclosed .... $ _____

Please select payment method *(Do Not Send Cash)*:

☐ **DMV account number** | | | | | | | |

☐ **Check/Money Order** - Payable to *Commissioner of Motor Vehicles*

☐ **Exempt**

Print name and address where the accident report(s) should be mailed:

_____
_____
_____

Optional - Your reference number:

_____

DMV USE ONLY

Date: _____

Transaction #: _____

Operator: _____

☐ Records Found   ☐ No Records Found

Search fee (non-refundable) .... $10.00 _____

No. of Reports _____ x $15 ..... $ _____

Total .... $ _____

Amount Received .... $ _____

Refund .... $ _____

MV-198C (11/06)   **www.nysdmv.com**

EXHIBIT 13-7 NYS DMV request for a copy of accident report
Source: http://www.nydmv.state.ny.us/forms/mv198c.pdf

Alaska Department of Labor and Workforce Development
Alaska Workers' Compensation Board
P.O. Box 115512, Juneau, AK 99811-5512

REPORT OF OCCUPATIONAL INJURY OR ILLNESS

AWCB Case Number
6098

EMPLOYEE:	Answer ALL questions 1-20, sign, and give to your employer immediately.

1. Last Name Scott	First Name Mary	Initial B.	2. Telephone Number	3. Date of Birth 02/11/70	4. Sex ☐ M ☒ F	5. Social Security Number

6a. Mailing Address 24TH AVE	7a. Residence Address 24 TH AVE

6b. City ANCHORAGE	State AK	ZIP Code 99517	7b. City ANCHORAGE	State AK	ZIP Code 99517

8. Place (city/town/village/camp) where injury/occupational illness happened ANCHORAGE	9. Date of Injury or Exposure to Disease 01 / 15 / 2009 Time 03:25	☒ AM ☐ PM	10. On Employer's Premises? ☒ Yes ☐ No

11. Name and Address of Attending Physician PROVIDENCE PO BOX 196	12. Hospitalized In-Patient? ☒ Yes ☐ No	13. Name of Hospital N/A

City ANCHORAGE	State AK	ZIP Code 99519	Hospital Address	State	ZIP Code

14. Describe Part(s) of Body Injured / Nature of Occupational Illness ☐ Left ☐ Right BI-LATERAL PAIN & SWELLING, WRIST	15a. Describe How the Injury or Illness Happened STATES HER HANDS SLIPPED WHILE TRYING TO MOVE A FILE CABINET

15b.

15c.

16. To all health care providers:
You are authorized to provide my employer (named in box 18), its workers' compensation liability insurance company (box 21), and its claims adjuster (box 22), information concerning any health care advice, testing, treatment, or supplies provided to me for the injury or illness described above in box 14. This information will be used to evaluate my entitlement to receive benefits, including payment of medical benefits, under the Alaska Workers' Compensation Act. This authorization is valid for a one-year period from the date of my signature (box 17a). I know I have a right to receive a copy of this authorization and agree a photographic copy of this authorization is as valid as the

Employee/Patient's signature: **SIGNATURE ON FILE**

17. If Employee Unavailable for Signature, explain circumstances in this space:	17a. Date Signed 1 / 15 / 2009

EMPLOYER:	Review employee 18-20, answer questions 21-49.

18. Employer's Name SECURITY SERVICES	19. Employer' s Alaska Address (If different from mailing) 2909 ARCTIC BLVD ANCHORAGE AK 99503

20. Employer's Mailing Address (street and number) ARCTIC BLVD.,	21. Name of Insurer: IS Portland WC Office

20a. City ANCHORAGE	State AK	ZIP Code 99503	20b. Telephone	22. Full Name of Adjusting Company IS Portland WC Office

23. Date Employer First Knew of Injury 01 / 15 / 2009	24. Date/Time (a.m./p.m.) Employee Left Work Date / / Time 04:00 ☒ AM ☐ PM	22a. Mailing Address (street and number) 68TH PKWY

25. Off work after Injury or Illness? ☐ Yes ☒ No ☐ 3 or more days	26. Date Returned to Work 01 /15 / 2009	27. Death (Y/N) Date	22b. City Portland	State OR	ZIP 97223	22c. Telephone

28. Location Where Injury or Illness Happened: ARCTIC BLVD.,	29. Employee's Occupation DISPATCHER	30. Date Hired by Employer 05 / 19 / 2007

31. Earnings Calculated By: ☒ Hr. ☐ Day ☐ Output ☐ Wk. ☐ Mo. ☐ Year 05 / 19 / 2007	32. Rate of Pay $ 10.00 per ☒ Hr.	33. Days Employee Works per Week ☐ 3 or Less ☐ 4 ☒ 5 ☐ 6 ☐ 7	34. Describe Scheduled Days Off TH / FRI

35. Workday Began: ☐ AM ☒ PM 12:00	36. Employee Paid for day injured or ill? ☒ Yes ☐ No	37. Employer EIN # N/A	38. Give Details of How Injury or Illness Happened EMPLOYEE TRIED TO LIFT A FILE CABINET WHEN HER

38a. HAND SLIPPED, CAUSING PAIN & SWELLING TO BOTH WRISTS.

39. Injury/Illness Due to Machine Product Failure? ☐ Yes ☒ No	40. Mechanical Guard/Safeguards Provided? ☐ Yes ☐ No	41. List any machine/substance/object causing injury FILE CABINET	42. If Machine, What Part? N/A

43. Names and Addresses of Witnesses NONE	44. If Injury/Illness Caused by Anyone Besides Employee, Give Name/Address N/A
	45. Dependents (in Case of death), Names/Addresses N/A

46. If you Doubt Validity of Injury or Illness, State Reason

FORWARD INQUIRY TO: LEEN ELSEN

47. Signature of Authorized Employer Representative SIGNATURE ON FILE	48. Title DISTRICT ADMIN	49. Date Signed 01 / 15 / 2009

WARNING TO EMPLOYEES AND EMPLOYERS: AS23.30.250 imposes civil penalties for fraud as well as certain false or misleading statements or acts. Criminal penalties for theft by deception (including fines and incarceration) apply to knowingly made false statements, claims, or employee misclassifications.

Distribution: **Original – Workers' Compensation Division; Copy – Adjuster; Copy – Employer; Copy – Employee**

EXHIBIT 13-8   Report of occupational injury or illness
Source: http://labor.state.ak.us/wc/form/07-6101.pdf

Tax returns and affidavits from the client's employer are commonly used to document lost wages and the client's wage-earning capacity. The paralegal will also want to gather information from the client's W-2 forms, pay stubs for hourly or salaried workers, and, in some instances, documentation of employment contracts or fringe benefits.

The trial team may plan to have an economist, actuary, or accountant prepare an evaluation of economic damages. Most economic experts will request tax returns for at least three years preceding the date of injury, to make a determination as to future economic loss, when there has been impairment of future earning capacity.

Expenses Related to the Injury

The client should provide documentation of all expenses paid in relation to the injury and medical treatment. This includes receipts for equipment and supplies, such as:

- X-rays and radiologist
- Canes, braces, crutches, and wheelchair
- Heating pads or ice packs
- Hospital
- Ambulance
- Doctor
- Physical therapy/occupational therapy
- Bandages
- Prescription medicines
- Over-the-counter medicines
- Acupuncture
- Chiropractor
- MRI/CAT scan
- Special mattresses or recuperative furniture or equipment
- Bills from housekeeper, cook, visiting nurses, medical transport, or other assistance needed during recuperation.

The client should also document mileage and parking fees for trips to the doctor, hospital, and for any other therapy sessions. The paralegal should follow up to make sure the client is keeping records of this information.

Insurance Coverage and Other Benefits

The trial team will need to know how much of the client's medical and related expenses were paid by insurance policies, workers' compensation benefits, or other sources. The paralegal should also find out if the client is covered by or receiving any assistance from Social Security, Medicare, Medicaid, or any other governmental or private program.

The client should provide the paralegal with copies of any documentation about insurance coverage or possible assistance through governmental agencies. If the client is unable to produce such documentation, it may be necessary for the paralegal to contact the various agencies and request the information with an authorization signed by the client. The defendants may also be entitled to some information regarding the insurance payments and government or other benefits, even if such information is not admissible at trial. Depending on your jurisdiction, the fact that some of the plaintiff's bills have been paid may affect the defendant's responsibility to reimburse for expenses.

No-Fault Automobile Insurance. A major part of many negligence practices involves the handling of car accidents for clients. Accordingly, it is important to be aware of the insurance laws in your state, and whether your state has no-fault legislation. Thirteen states have no-fault legislation where parties can collect against their own policies of insurance, regardless of fault, for medical bills and lost wages from personal injuries. There is no recovery for pain and suffering. Generally, one cannot bring a lawsuit for personal injuries unless one meets a certain threshold and has a "serious injury." Some states have hybrid-type laws, and allow people to elect whether they will proceed with suit under traditional tort law or the no-fault statutes. No-fault does not pay for property damage; this is covered by another part of automobile insurance.

Police Accident Report. No matter what state you work in, when a client calls with a potential automobile claim, the first thing you must do is ask the client to bring in a copy of the police accident report. Also, you want to instruct the client not to discuss the case with anyone without first consulting the attorney who will be representing him or her. Oftentimes, people are very shook up after an accident and their version of what happened is very different from the police accident report. Also, clients may get confused and mistakenly speak with opposing counsel or the insurance representative for the other driver, before receiving advice from their own attorney.

Policy Limits. The attorney handling the case is going to want to know how much insurance each person in the accident carries. The potential client can have a seemingly great case, but if the driver who caused the accident has very little or no insurance, there may not be much your firm can do for the potential client. Some clients in some states will have extra insurance for just this eventuality. States vary as to the kind of insurance drivers are offered and required to have. For example, the minimum automobile insurance requirements in Minnesota are 30/60/10. This means that there is a total of $60,000 of insurance available for all persons injured in an accident, with a limit of $30,000 for one person, and there is $10,000 for property damage. The amount of insurance premiums will increase based upon the amount of coverage above the minimum a driver wishes to purchase.

See Table 13-1 listing the types of no-fault insurance available in certain states.

State	No-Fault Automobile Insurance
California	No—It's a tort system state. Drivers are responsible for damage they cause.
Florida	Yes—Partial no-fault. Each person pays own medical expenses.
Kansas	Yes
Kentucky	Choice: Drivers can select either tort system or no-fault system.
Massachusetts	Yes
Minnesota	Yes
New Jersey	Choice: Drivers can select either tort system or no-fault system.
New York	Yes
Ohio	No—Parties are financially responsible for damage they cause.
Pennsylvania	Choice: Drivers select either tort system or no-fault system called "limited tort."
Texas	No—It's a tort system state.
Utah	Yes

TABLE 13-1
Types of no-fault automobile insurance available by state

Previous Claims or Lawsuits of Plaintiff

It is necessary to know about any previous claims or lawsuits in which the client has been involved and how they were resolved. The trial team will determine the information to which the defendant is entitled if defense counsel inquires about this subject matter during discovery. Defendants usually ask for this type of information so as to use it against the plaintiff, to discredit the plaintiff, or to reduce the amount of damages in a lawsuit.

Clients will not always be able or willing to provide all the information concerning prior claims or lawsuits in which they have been involved. Some clients discard legal documents once a legal action is completed. The paralegal may have to visit the court clerk's offices or perform an on-line search to obtain the relevant documents concerning any past lawsuits.

---

practical **application**

Some people are "professional plaintiffs"; that is, they sue people for a living for injuries that are contrived or exaggerated. These people are not usually honest with their attorneys. Other clients are just injury-prone and seem to incur more than their share of injuries. A thorough interview and study of current and past medical records often help to determine whether a client's claims ring true. Note that the occasional malingerer is the exception and not the rule!

Previous Injuries to Plaintiff

As a general rule, "one takes the victim (plaintiff) as one finds him." However, it is important to determine if the part of the plaintiff's body that was injured in the accident and is the basis of the current lawsuit was ever injured in the past. It is vital to review medical records carefully to determine whether there are any references to similar injuries or other problems relating to the same part of the body, or whether there is evidence of any preexisting injuries.

For instance, if a plaintiff who has a stiff back from an earlier car accident slips and falls on a slippery floor at the grocery store and reinjures her back, the injured plaintiff may only bring a claim against the grocery store for the portion of injuries and expenses that result from aggravation of the existing condition. There can be no recovery against the grocery store for the stiff back that the plaintiff already had. The plaintiff's claim might be that her back is stiff more often, or that it gives her more pain than she previously experienced. An award against the grocery store for aggravation of an existing condition may be much less than the award for the preexisting stiff-back condition.

In this example, the paralegal should be sure to have all the medical information to evaluate and let trial-team members know that there was more than one injury to the plaintiff's back. The trial team will probably want to follow up with additional questions to the client regarding the previous back problem to ascertain if it is related to the pain attributed to the slip and fall. One's trial team may also want to follow up with the client's doctor.

Health Insurance Portability and Accountability Act (HIPAA).

The United States Department of Health and Human Services (HHS) issued a health information privacy rule to carry out the requirements of the Health

Insurance Portability and Accountability Act of 1996 (HIPAA). The health information of "individuals" is protected from certain "covered entities" (i.e., health care providers, insurance companies, Medicare and Medicaid providers) use. Basically, safeguards were put in place to protect the privacy rights of individuals concerning their personal health information, and how that information is used or transmitted, with certain exceptions. Rules (particularly regarding consent) must be followed before health information can be distributed to others. Violation of this law carries strict fines and penalties.

The importance of this law to the paralegal is that he or she must obtain the necessary signed authorization before making any attempt to obtain health information. Further, the paralegal is required to keep this information confidential and in a safe place, where it cannot be accessed by others without the necessary authorization. Likewise, the paralegal cannot give this information to others without the necessary signed authorization.

The Parties' Criminal Histories

Information on the parties' criminal histories is relevant for both defendants and plaintiffs in some cases. The trial team needs to know anything regarding the parties' arrests, convictions, and/or time spent in jail or prison, although this data might not be admissible at trial in your particular case.

Driving Records

Driving records may be particularly relevant in the investigation of an automobile accident, and can also be utilized to determine other information regarding the parties, such as alcohol use. If any party has been ticketed or arrested for an offense such as driving under the influence of alcohol or drugs, the trial team will want to know about it.

Having considered various investigatory techniques, it would be useful to apply these methods to specific types of tort cases. These applications are discussed in the next section.

▌ INVESTIGATING DIFFERENT TYPES OF TORT CASES

Various types of tort cases require specialized methods of investigation. Paralegals and attorneys learn the "right" techniques primarily through experience. This section provides some basic guidelines for investigating some typical tort cases encountered in private law practice.

In Exhibit 13-9 is a portion of some of the pages of a traffic collision report prepared by the police officer arriving at the scene of a four-car accident. The driver of the first car stopped his Lexus in the left lane because he had a flat tire

TRAFFIC COLLISION REPORT

CHP 555 Page 1 (Rev. 8-97) OPI 042

SPECIAL CONDITIONS	NUMBER INJURED ○	HIT & RUN FELONY ☐	CITY: LA		JUDICIAL DISTRICT LA Superior	LOCAL REPORT NUMBER
	NUMBER KILLED ○	HIT & RUN MISDEMEANOR ☐	COUNTY LA	REPORTING DISTRICT 734	BEAT 60	61204

LOCATION

COLLISION OCCURRED ON			MO DAY YEAR	TIME(2400)	NCIC #	OFFICER I.D.
I-10 E/B (SANTA MONICA FREEWAY)			12 / 20 / 2009	2100	90	219

MILEPOST INFORMATION 100 ☒ ☐ FEET/MILES E OF 10LA R9.74	DAY OF WEEK S M T ☒W T F S	TOW AWAY ☐ YES ☒ NO	PHOTOGRAPHS BY: ☒ NONE
☐ AT INTERSECTION WITH ☒ OR 100 ☐ ☐ FEET/MILES E OF HAUSER BLVD		STATE HWY REL ☒ YES ☐ NO	NONE

PARTY 1

DRIVER'S LICENSE NUMBER 53048212	STATE CA	CLASS CA	AIR BAG M	SAFETY EQUIP. G	VEH YEAR 04	MAKE/MODEL/COLOR LEXUS / 15300 / SLV	LICENSE NUMBER 189644	STATE CA

☒ DRIVER ☐ PEDESTRIAN ☐ PARKED VEHICLE ☐ BICYCLIST ☐ OTHER

NAME (FIRST, MIDDLE, LAST): **David Edward**
STREET ADDRESS: **611 Cash Rd.**
CITY/STATE/ZIP: **La Canada Flt, CA 91011**

OWNER'S NAME ☐ SAME AS DRIVER: **SOPHIA ANN**
OWNER'S ADDRESS ☐ SAME AS DRIVER: **47 Yarrow St Rose Hill, CA 91770**

SEX M	HAIR BRN	EYES BRN	HEIGHT 6'0	WEIGHT 250	BIRTHDATE MO DAY YEAR 08 / 12 / 69	RACE W

DISPOSITION OF VEHICLE ON ORDERS OF: ☐ OFFICER ☒ DRIVER ☐ OTHER **Driver**
PRIOR MECHANICAL DEFECTS: ☒ NONE APPARENT ☐ REFER TO NARRATIVE

HOME PHONE **(818) 555-1311**   BUSINESS PHONE **(818) 555-3055**

VEHICLE IDENTIFICATION NUMBER

INSURANCE CARRIER **AAA**   POLICY NUMBER **G8611053**

CHIP USE ONLY VEHICLE TYPE **01**

DESCRIBE VEHICLE DAMAGE: ☒ UNK ☐ NONE ☐ MINOR | ☒ MOD ☐ MAJOR ☐ ROLL-OVER

DIR OF TRAVEL E	ON STREET OR HIGHWAY I-10 E/B (SMF)	SPEED LIMIT 65

CA _____ DOT _____
CAL-T _____ TCP/PSC _____ MC/MX _____

PARTY 2

DRIVER'S LICENSE NUMBER D623456	STATE CA	CLASS CA	AIR BAG M	SAFETY EQUIP. G	VEH YEAR 99	MAKE/MODEL/COLOR Toyota / Camry / Gry	LICENSE NUMBER 40YP	STATE CA

☒ DRIVER ☐ PEDESTRIAN ☐ PARKED VEHICLE ☐ BICYCLIST ☐ OTHER

NAME (FIRST, MIDDLE, LAST): **Lisa Bethiwy**
STREET ADDRESS: **24 Stonesle CT**
CITY/STATE/ZIP: **Westlake Vlg, CA 91361**

OWNER'S NAME ☐ SAME AS DRIVER: **Jay Bethiwy**
OWNER'S ADDRESS ☒ SAME AS DRIVER

SEX F	HAIR BRN	EYES BRN	HEIGHT 5'0	WEIGHT 105	BIRTHDATE MO DAY YEAR 03 / 03 / 78	RACE W

DISPOSITION OF VEHICLE ON ORDERS OF: ☐ OFFICER ☒ DRIVER ☐ OTHER **Driver**
PRIOR MECHANICAL DEFECTS: ☒ NONE APPARENT ☐ REFER TO NARRATIVE

HOME PHONE **(805) 555-7828**   BUSINESS PHONE **(805) 555-1735**

VEHICLE IDENTIFICATION NUMBER

INSURANCE CARRIER **Farmers**   POLICY NUMBER **A151935649**

CHIP USE ONLY VEHICLE TYPE **01**

DESCRIBE VEHICLE DAMAGE: ☐ UNK ☐ NONE ☐ MINOR | ☒ MOD ☐ MAJOR ☐ ROLL-OVER

DIR OF TRAVEL E	ON STREET OR HIGHWAY I-10 E/B (SMF)	SPEED LIMIT 65

CA _____ DOT _____
CAL-T _____ TCP/PSC _____ MC/MX _____

PARTY 3

DRIVER LICENSE NUMBER 56011293	STATE CA	CLASS CA	AIR BAG M	SAFETY EQUIP. G	VEH YEAR 01	MAKE/MODEL/COLOR Ford/F-150/Gold	LICENSE NUMBER 9427550	STATE CA

☒ DRIVER ☐ PEDESTRIAN ☐ PARKED VEHICLE ☐ BICYCLIST ☐ OTHER

NAME (FIRST, MIDDLE, LAST): **Jose Alfredol**
STREET ADDRESS: **808 Gent St.**
CITY/STATE/ZIP: **La Puente, CA 91744**

OWNER'S NAME ☒ SAME AS DRIVER
OWNER'S ADDRESS ☒ SAME AS DRIVER

SEX M	HAIR BRN	EYES BRN	HEIGHT 5'11	WEIGHT 250	BIRTHDATE MO DAY YEAR 01 / 04 / 76	RACE H

DISPOSITION OF VEHICLE ON ORDERS OF: ☐ OFFICER ☒ DRIVER ☐ OTHER **Driver**
PRIOR MECHANICAL DEFECTS: ☒ NONE APPARENT ☐ REFER TO NARRATIVE

HOME PHONE **(626) 555-3421**   BUSINESS PHONE **(626) 555-0505**

VEHICLE IDENTIFICATION NUMBER

INSURANCE CARRIER **Mercury**   POLICY NUMBER **6A5313247**

CHIP USE ONLY VEHICLE TYPE **22**

DESCRIBE VEHICLE DAMAGE: ☐ UNK ☐ NONE ☐ MINOR | ☒ MOD ☐ MAJOR ☐ ROLL-OVER

DIR OF TRAVEL E	ON STREET OR HIGHWAY I-10 E/B (SMF)	SPEED LIMIT 65

CA _____ DOT _____
CAL-T _____ TCP/PSC _____ MC/MX _____

PREPARER'S NAME W. Line 219	DISPATCH NOTIFIED ☐ YES ☐ NO ☒ N/A	REVIEWER'S NAME PW 558	DATA REVIEWED 02 / 25 / 09

EXHIBIT 13-9   Traffic collision report
Source: http://www.actar.org/pdf/ca-rep1.pdf

DATE OF COLLISION (NO. DAY YEAR)	TIME (2400)	NCK	OFFICER ID.	NUMBER	
2/20/2009	2100	90	219		

PROPERTY DAMAGE	OWNER'S NAME		OWNER'S ADDRESS		NOTIFIED ☐ YES ☐ NO
	DESCRIPTION OF DAMAGE				

SEATING POSITION

1 - DRIVER
2 TO 6 - PASSENGERS
7 - STATION WAGON REAR
8 - REAR OCC. TRK. OR VAN
9 - POSMON UNKNOWN
0 - OTHER

(seating diagram: 1 2 3 / 4 5 6 / 7)

OCCUPANTS
A - NONE IN VEHICLE
B - UNKNOWN
C - LAP BELT USED
D - LAP BELT NOT USED
E - SHOULDER HARNESS USED
F - SHOULDER HARNESS NOT USED
G - LAP/SHOULDER HARNESS USED
H - LAP/SHOULDER HARNESS NOT USED
J - PASSIVE RESTRAINT USED
K - PASSIVE RESTRAINT NOT USED

SAFETY EQUIPMENT
L - AIR BAG DEPLOYED
M - AIR BAG NOT DEPLOYED
N - OTHER
P - NOT REQUIRED

CHILD RESTRAINT
Q - IN VEHICLE USED
R - IN VEHICLE NOT USED
S - IN VEHICLE USE UNKNOWN
T - IN VEHICLE IMPROPER USE
U - NONE IN VEHICLE

M / C BICYCLE- HELMET
DRIVER   PASSEMGER
V - NO   X - NO
W - YES   Y - YES

EJECTED FROM VEHICLE
0 - NOT EJECTED
1 - FULLY EJECTED
2 - PARTIALLY EJECTED
3 - UNKNOWN

INATTENTION CODES
A - CELLPHONE HANDHELD
B - CELLPHONE HANDSFREE
C - ELECTRONIC EQUIPMENT
D - RADIO / CD
E - SMOKING
F - EATING
G - CHILDREN
H - ANIMALS
I - PERSONAL HYGIENE
J - READING
K - OTHER

ITEMS MARKED BELOW FOLLOWED BY AN ASTERISK (*) SHOULD BE EXPLAINED IN THE NARRATIVE.

PRIMARY COLLISION FACTOR	TRAFFIC CONTROL DEVICES	1	2	3	SPECIAL INFORMATION	1	2	3	MOVEMENT PRECEDING COLLISION
LIST NUMBER (#) OF PARTY AT FAULT: 2									
A. VC SECTION VIOLATED: 22350 VC CITED ☐YES ☒NO	A CONTROLS FUNCTIONING				A HAZARDOUS MATERIAL	X			A STOPPED
	B CONTROLS NOT FUNCTIONING*				B CELL PHONE HANDHELD IN USE				B PROCEEDING STRAIGHT
B OTHER IMPROPER DRIVING*	C CONTROLS OBSCURES				C CELL PHONE HANDSFREE IN USE				C RAN OFF ROAD
	X D NO CONTROLS PRESENT / FACT0R	X	X	X	D CELL PHONE NOT IN USE				D MAKING RIGHT TURN
C OTHER THAN DRIVER*	TYPE OF COLLISION				E SCHOOL BUS RELATED				E MAKING LEFT TURN
D UNKNOWN*	A HEAD - ON				F 75 FT MOTORTRUCK COMBO				F MAKING U TURN
	B SIDE SWIPE				G 32 FT TRAILER COMBO				G BACKING
	X C REAR END				H		X	X	H SLOWING / STOPPING
WEATHER (MARK 1 TO 2 ITEMS)	D BROADSIDE				I				I PASSING OTHER VEHICLE
X A CLEAR	E HIT OBJECT				J				J CHANGING LANES
B CLOUDY	F OVERTURNED				K				K PARKING MANEUVER
C RAINING	G VEHICLE / PEDESTRIAN				L				L ENTERING TRAFFIC
D SNOWING	H OTHER				M				M OTHER UNSAFE TURNING
E FOG / VISIBILITY ___ FT.					N				N XING INTO OPPOSING LANE
F OTHER	MOTOR VEHICLE INVOLVED WITH				O				O PARKED
G WIND	A NON - COLLISION								P MERGING
LIGHTING	B PEDESTRIAN								Q TRAVELING WRONG WAY
A DAYLIGHT	X C OTHER MOTOR VEHICLE				OTHER ASSOCIATED FACTOR(S)	1	2	3	R OTHER
B DUSK - DAWN	D MOTOR VEHICLE ON OTHER ROADWAY	1	2	3	(MARK 1 TO 2 ITEMS)				
X C DARK - STREET LIGHTS	E PARKED MOTOR VEHICLE				A VC SECTION VIOLATION CITED ☐YES ☐NO				
D DARK - NO STREET LIGHTS	F TRAIN				B VC SECTION VIOLATION CITED ☐YES ☐NO				
E DARK - STREET LIGHTS NOT FUNCTIONING*	G BICYCLE				C VC SECTION VIOLATION CITED ☐YES ☒NO 22350 VC	1	2	3	SOBRIEYT - DRUG PHYSICAL (MARK 1 TO 2 ITEMS)
	H ANIMAL	X							
ROADWAY SURFACE					D	X	X	X	A HAD NOT BEEN DRINKING:
X A DRY	I FIXED OBJECT:				E VISION OBSCUREMENT:				B HBD - UNDER INFLUENCE
B WET					F INATTENTION				C HBD - NOT UNDER INFLUENCE*
C SNOWY - ICY					G STOP & GO TRAFFIC				D HBD - IMPAIRMENT UNKNOWN*
D SLIPPERY (MUDDY, OILY, ETC.)	J OTHER OBJECT:				H ENTERING / LEAVING RAMP				E UNDER DRUG INFLUENCE*
ROADWAY CONDITION(S) (MARK 1 TO 2 ITEMS)					I PREVIOUS COLLISION				F IMPAIRMENT - PHYSICAL*
A HOLES, DEEP RUT*	PEDESTRIANS ACTIONS				J UNFAMILIAR WITH ROAD				G IMPAIRMENT NOT KNOWN
B LOOSE MATERIAL ON ROADWAY*	X A NO PEDESTRIANS INVOLVED				K DEFECTIVE VEH. EQUIP: CITED ☐YES ☐NO				H NOT APPLICABLE
C OBSTRUSTION ON ROADWAY*	B CROSSING IN CROSSWALK - AT INTERSECTION								I SLEEPY / FATIGUED
D CONSTRUCTION - REPAIR ZONE	C CROSSING IN CROSSWALK - NOT AT INTERSECTION				L UNINVOLED VEHICLE				
E REDUCED ROADWAY WIDTH	D CROSSING - NOT IN CROSSWALK				M OTHER				
F FLOODED*	E IN ROAD - INCLUDES SHOULDER				N NONE APPARENT				
G OTHER*	F NOT IN ROAD	X	X		O RUNAWAY VEHICLE				
X H NO UNUSUAL CONDITIONS	G APPROACHING / LEAVING SCHOOL BUS								

SKETCH

HAUSER BLVD
CENTER MEDIAN
CENTER DIVIDER WALL
INDICATE NORTH
SOLID YELLOW LINE — 12'
DASHED WHITE LINES — 12' 12' 12'
SOLID WHITE LINE — 12'
6'
V-1, V-2, V-3, V-4, ①, ②, ③
#1 #2 #3 #4 #5
I-10 E/B (SANTA MONICA FREEWAY)
SHOULDER
RAISED CURB

MISCELLANEOUS

OSP 03 79147

Exhibit 13-9   Traffic collision report *(continued)*

399

NARRATIVE/SUPPLEMENTAL
CHP 556 (Rev. 7-90) OPI 061   page 5

DATE OF INCIDENT/OCCURRENCE 2/20/2009	TIME (2400) 2100	NCIC NUMBER 90	OFFICER I.D. NUMBER 219	NUMBER

"X" ONE	"X" ONE	TYPE SUPPLEMENTAL ("X" APPLICABLE)		
☒ Narrative	☒ Collision Report	☐ BA Update	☐ Fatal	☐ Hit and Run Update
☐ Supplemental	☐ Other: _____	☐ Hazardous Materials	☐ School Bus	☐ Other: _____

CITY/COUNTY/JUDICIAL DISTRICT	BEAT 60	CITATION NUMBER

LOCATION/SUBJECT	STATE HIGHWAY RELATED ☒ Yes ☐ No

1. NOTIFICATION:
2.
3. I RECEIVED A RADIO CALL FROM CHP DISPATCH OF A TRAFFIC COLLISION
4. WITH NO DETAILS. AT APPROXIMATELY 2100 HOURS.
5. I RESPONDED FROM THE VICINITY OF SRF110 NYB AND STADIUM
6. WAY AND ARRIVED ON SCENE AT APPROXIMATELY 2110 HOURS.
7. ALL TIMES, SPEEDS AND MEASUREMENTS ARE APPROXIMATE.
8. MEASUREMENTS WERE OBTAINED BY VISUAL ESTIMATION AND
9. ROLL-A-TAPE.
10.
11. STATEMENTS:
12.
13. PARTY #1 (EDWARD) WAS LOCATED AT THE SCENE AND RELATED THE FOLLOWING
14. INFORMATION IN ESSENCE: I WAS STOPPED IN THE #1 LANE AND CENTER MEDIAN
15. AS CLOSE TO THE WALL AS POSSIBLE DUE TO A FLAT TIRE WHEN I WAS STRUCK FROM BEHIND
16.
17. PARTY #2 (BETHIWY) WAS LOCATED AT THE SCENE AND RELATED THE
18. FOLLOWING INFORMATION IN ESSENCE: I WAS TRAVELING IN THE #1 LANE
19. AT APPROXIMATELY 65 MPH WHEN I NOTICED THE STOPPED
20. VEHICLE AHEAD I HIT THE BRAKES AND SWERVED TO THE
21. RIGHT, BUT IT WAS TOO LATE AND I HIT THE CAR IN
22. FRONT OF ME. AFTER THAT, THE TRUCK HIT ME FROM THE
23. RIGHT SIDE.
24.
25. PARTY #3 (ALFREDOL) WAS LOCATED AT THE SCENE AND RELATED THE
26. FOLLOWING INFORMATION IN ESSENCE: I WAS TRAVELING IN THE
27. #1 LANE AT APPROXIMATELY 70 MPH WHEN I NOTICED THE
28. TWO CARS STOPPED AHEAD OF ME. I HIT THE BRAKES AND
29. TRIED TO SWERVE TO THE RIGHT, BUT I ENDED UP HITTING
30. THE CARS ON BOTH MY LEFT AND RIGHT SIDE.
31. ☐ Continued

PREPARER'S NAME AND I.D. NUMBER W. LINE 219	DATE 2/20/2009	REVIEWER'S NAME	DATE

Use previous editions until depleted.   OSP 04 82787

EXHIBIT 13-9   Traffic collision report (continued)

DATE OF INCIDENT/OCCURRENCE 2/20/2009	TIME (2400) 2100	NCIC NUMBER 90	OFFICER I.D. NUMBER 219	NUMBER

"X" ONE	"X" ONE	TYPE SUPPLEMENTAL ("X" APPLICABLE)		
☒ Narrative	☒ Collision Report	☐ BA Update	☐ Fatal	☐ Hit and Run Update
☐ Supplemental	☐ Other: _____	☐ Hazardous Materials	☐ School Bus	☐ Other: _____

CITY/COUNTY/JUDICIAL DISTRICT		BEAT 60	CITATION NUMBER

LOCATION/SUBJECT	STATE HIGHWAY RELATED ☒ Yes ☐ No

1. STATEMENTS (CONTINUED):

2.

3.   PARTY #4 (MAGAB) WAS LOCATED AT THE SCENE AND RELATED

4.   THE FOLLOWING INFORMATION IN ESSENCE: I WAS TRAVELING IN THE #2 LANE AT

5.   APPROXIMATELY 65 MPH WHEN I HEARD SCREECHING TIRES AND

6.   THE TRUCK HIT ME FROM THE LEFT SIDE.

7.

8. SUMMARY:

9.

10.   THIS COLLISION OCCURRED IN THE #1 AND #2 LANES OF I-10

11.   E/B (SMF) EAST OF HAUSER BLVD P-1 WAS STOPPED IN THE #1 LANE

12.   AND CENTER MEDIAN DUE TO A FLAT TIRE. P-2 WAS TRAVELING IN THE

13.   #1 LANE AT APPROXIMATELY 65 MPH DIRECTLY TO THE REAR

14.   OF V-1. P-3 WAS TRAVELING IN THE #1 LANE AT APPROXIMATELY

15.   70 MPH BEHIND V-2 P-4 WAS TRAVELING IN THE #2 LANE AT

16.   APPROXIMATELY 65 MPH TO THE RIGHT OF V-1 AND V-2. P-2

17.   FAILED TO NOTICE V-1 STOPPED AHEAD UNTIL THE LAST MINUTE,

18.   APPLIED V-2'S BRAKES, AND SWERVED TO THE RIGHT, BUT

19.   IT WAS TOO LATE. THE LEFT FRONT OF V-2 STRUCK

20.   THE RIGHT REAR OF V-1. P-3 FAILED TO

21.   NOTICE THE TWO STOPPED CARS AHEAD AND APPLIED V-3'S BRAKES

22.   AND SWERVED TO THE RIGHT, BUT IT WAS TOO LATE. THE

23.   LEFT FRONT OF V-3 STRUCK THE RIGHT SIDE OF V-2, AND THEN

24.   THE RIGHT FRONT OF V-3 STRUCK THE LEFT SIDE OF V-4.

25.   AFTER THIS COLLISION, V-1 AND V-2 REMAINED AT THEIR

26.   POINTS OF REST AND P-3 AND P-4 MOVED FORWARD AND INTO

27.   THE #1 LANE AND AWAITED CHP ARRIVAL.

28.

29.

30.

31.

☐ Continued

PREPARER'S NAME AND I.D. NUMBER W. LINE 219	DATE 2/20/2009	REVIEWER'S NAME	DATE

Use previous editions until depleted.

OSP 04 82787

EXHIBIT 13-9 Traffic collision report *(continued)*

NARRATIVE/SUPPLEMENTAL
CHP 556 (Rev. 7-90) OPI 061   Page 7

DATE OF INCIDENT/OCCURRENCE 2/20/2009	TIME (2400) 2100	NCIC NUMBER 90	OFFICER I.D. NUMBER 219	NUMBER

"X" ONE	"X" ONE	TYPE SUPPLEMENTAL ("X" APPLICABLE)		
☒ Narrative	☒ Collision Report	☐ BA Update	☐ Fatal	☐ Hit and Run Update
☐ Supplemental	☐ Other: _____	☐ Hazardous Materials	☐ School Bus	☐ Other: _____

CITY/COUNTY/JUDICIAL DISTRICT	BEAT 60	CITATION NUMBER

LOCATION/SUBJECT	STATE HIGHWAY RELATED ☒ Yes ☐ No

1. AREAS OF IMPACT:
2.
3. AOI # 1 (V-2 VS. V-1) WAS LOCATED APPROXIMATELY 6 FEET SOUTH OF
4. THE NORTH ROADWAY EDGE OF I-10 E/B (SMF) AND APPROXIMATELY
5. 100 FEET EAST OF THE WEST EDGE OF HAUSER BLVD.
6.
7. AOI #2 (V-3 VS. V-2) WAS LOCATED APPROXIMATELY 10 FEET SOUTH
8. OF THE NORTH ROADWAY EDGE OF I-10 E/B (SMF) AND APPROXIMATELY
9. 90 FEET EAST OF THE WEST EDGE OF HAUSER BLVD.
10.
11. AOI #3 (V-3 VS. V-4) WAS LOCATED APPROXIMATELY 17 FEET SOUTH
12. OF THE NORTH ROADWAY EDGE OF I-10 E/B (SMF) AND
13. APPROXIMATELY 95 FEET EAST OF THE WEST EDGE OF HAUSER BLVD.
14.
15. THE AREAS OF IMPACT WERE DETERMINED BY DRIVERS'
16. STATEMENTS AND VEHICLE DAMAGE.
17.
18. CAUSE:
19.
20. P-2 CAUSED THIS COLLISION BY DRIVING IN VIOLATION OF
21. 22350 VC (UNSAFE SPEED FOR CONDITIONS). P-2 WAS
22. DRIVING TOO FAST TO SAFELY STOP AND AVOID A
23. COLLISION WITH P-1.
24.
25. P-3 CONTRIBUTED TO THIS COLLISION BY DRIVING IN
26. VIOLATION OF 22350 VC (UNSAFE SPEED FOR CONDITIONS).
27. P-3 WAS DRIVING TOO FAST TO SAFELY STOP AND AVOID
28. A COLLISION WITH P-2 AND P-4.
29.
30. THE CAUSE OF THIS COLLISION WAS DETERMINED BY DRIVERS'
31. STATEMENTS AND VEHICLE DAMAGE.

☐ Continued

PREPARER'S NAME and I.D. NUMBER W. LINE 219	DATE 2/20/2009	REVIEWER'S NAME	DATE

Use previous editions until depleted.

OSP 04 82787

EXHIBIT 13-9   Traffic collision report (continued)

and did not want to drive on the tire and ruin the tire or the rim. Ironically, the first thing the officer did was have driver number 1 drive his Lexus off the road, which he did with no problem. Had the driver done this to begin with, arguably, there might not have been the collision with driver 2 rear-ending the Lexus, and driver 3 hitting the right side of car 2 to the left of him, and the left side of car 4 to the right of him.

The officer took narrative statements from all four parties and concluded that the accident was caused by car 2 going too fast for conditions, striking car 1, which started the collision. Driver 2 claimed to be driving 65 mph (the speed limit), and driver 3 claimed to be driving 70 mph when he did not see the stopped car until right before the accident. Would you have reached the same conclusion as the officer as to the cause of the collision?

Automobile Accident Cases

An automobile accident causing injury usually entails a relatively straightforward investigation. The trial team needs to know who and what caused the accident and what damages the parties suffered. A typical general investigation includes the following steps:

- The client is interviewed for information as to how the accident happened, injuries, who was at fault, and any witnesses.
- Police accident reports are obtained for information such as:
  - Witness names and addresses
  - The exact location of the accident
  - The disposition of each party to the accident and each vehicle (i.e., what parties were taken to which hospital, what vehicles had to be towed and where they were taken)
  - Injury and property damage to vehicle and contents
  - Any tickets issued by police at the scene
  - Any comments in the report as to fault or factors that contributed to the accident (such as eating, drinking, falling asleep, or other activities)
  - Weather conditions.
- Photographs should be taken of the vehicle or vehicles and the parties' injuries, if necessary.
- Medical records should be ordered and particular attention paid to any tests for alcohol or drugs.
- If there is a question regarding a mechanical malfunction, an expert may be called in to inspect the vehicle or vehicles involved.
- If there are allegations of dangerous street design or street conditions, additional investigation may be required.

In addition to the preceding, when the trial team represents the defendant, it will be interested in investigating the following:

- Names of other possible defendants (owner of street, entity responsible for street maintenance)
- Defenses to the plaintiff's claims
- Acts of the plaintiff that contributed to the accident
- Prior lawsuits by the plaintiff
- Preexisting injuries of the plaintiff
- The plaintiff's prior accidents or claims
- Reputation and standing of the plaintiff's treating physician (who may be relied on by the plaintiff as an expert at trial).

Mechanical Malfunction. If there is a question about possible mechanical malfunction, the trial team probably will find itself going beyond a simple investigation and into the more extensive inquiry necessary in a products liability case. The client should be consulted regarding projected future expenses for which the client would be responsible before the investigation proceeds, as such lawsuits can be quite costly.

Dangerous Street Conditions. If there are indications of dangerous street conditions, the paralegal should watch for scenarios such as:

- Debris that fell from a truck or other vehicle that might have contributed to the accident
- Vegetation affecting visibility
- A street being repaired or under construction or allegations that lanes were not properly marked, equipment or machinery were left in the street, visibility was obscured, and so on
- A dangerous intersection or design of the street
- A street sign, such as a stop sign or one-way sign, that is obscured or missing
- Possible involvement of a municipality, and whether it is entitled by law to notice of the condition claimed before suit can be brought
- Other accidents at same location.

Construction Sites. If the site of the accident was under construction or repair at the time of the incident, an inquiry as to the conditions may be undertaken. Likewise, if there are allegations of debris on the road, that should be followed up, as any of these scenarios may indicate additional defendants.

Freedom of Information Act (FOIA) Requests. Under the Freedom of Information Act, 5 U.S.C. § 552, you can request many different kinds of federal agency records or information. Agencies are required to disclose information from records after receiving a written request. There is usually a photocopying charge for these requests. It is to be noted there are exceptions to this rule for national security and certain privacy interests.

State Public Records Laws. Requests for state and local agency records must be sent to the appropriate state or local agency. All fifty states have public records laws allowing the public to obtain certain documents and public records from state and local agencies. These records laws are similar to but not the same as the federal Freedom of Information Act. Accordingly, be sure to check your state provisions before making an information request.

Medical Negligence Cases

In a case involving possible medical negligence or malpractice, investigation can be quite complex and costly. Consider a hypothetical, but not unrealistic, example. A patient goes into a hospital to have his appendix removed. The doctor fails to remove a clamp from the patient before suturing him up. One week after being discharged from the hospital, the patient experiences severe pain and a high fever. The patient goes to the emergency room and is admitted for emergency exploratory surgery. The clamp is found and removed. Potential areas of investigation in such a case would include:

- What was the cause of injury or death?
    - Was it a result of medical treatment or lack thereof?
    - Was it a result of negligence on the part of the hospital staff or doctors?
    - Was it a result of something that was done or not done prior to admission to the facility?
    - Did the patient follow prescribed treatment?
- What do the medical records or autopsy records indicate as the cause of injury or death? (See Exhibits 13-10, 13-11, and 13-12.)
- What was the plaintiff's condition upon arriving at the emergency room?
- What diagnosis had been rendered during the previous hospital admission? (See Exhibit 13-10.)
- What types of consent forms and releases for treatment were signed, and who signed them (the victim, his or her guardian, and so forth)?
- Did the surgeon follow the standard of care that other surgeons performing appendectomies would have followed?

If the initial evaluation indicates a potential case, additional investigation will be warranted. Paralegals will want to find out about any doctors involved, their qualifications and training, and whether they have been the subject of previous lawsuits or complaints. One will also want to find out the same information about the hospital and its personnel.

Exhibit 13-10
Sample medical report (radiology)

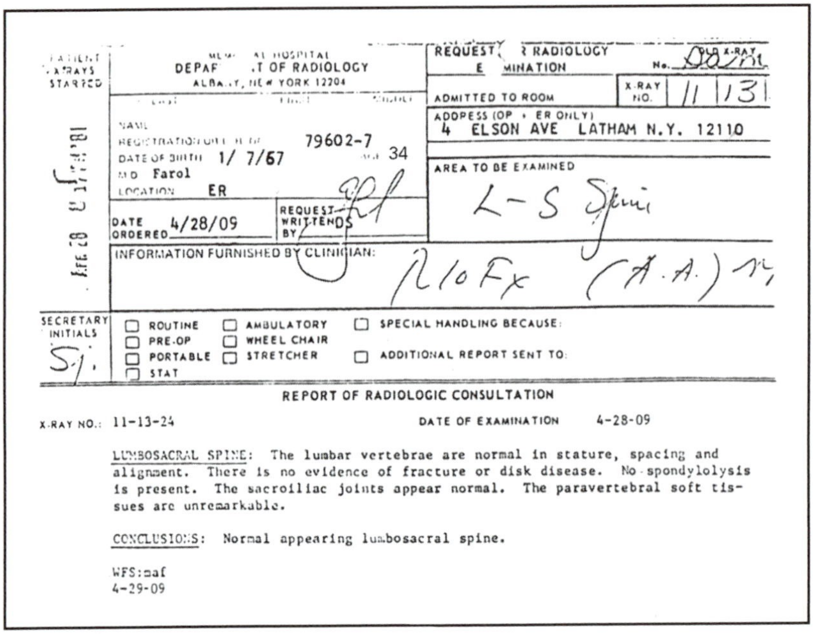

DEPAR . T OF RADIOLOGY
ALBA . Y, NEW YORK 12204

REQUEST FOR RADIOLOGY EXAMINATION

ADMITTED TO ROOM | X-RAY NO. 11 13 1

ADDRESS (OP + ER ONLY) 4 ELSON AVE LATHAM N.Y. 12110

REGISTRATION 79602-7

DATE OF BIRTH 1/ 7/67 34

MD Farol

LOCATION ER

AREA TO BE EXAMINED L-S Spine

DATE ORDERED 4/28/09

REQUEST WRITTEN BY

INFORMATION FURNISHED BY CLINICIAN: R/O Fx (A.A.)

SECRETARY INITIALS

☐ ROUTINE ☐ AMBULATORY ☐ SPECIAL HANDLING BECAUSE:
☐ PRE-OP ☐ WHEEL CHAIR
☐ PORTABLE ☐ STRETCHER ☐ ADDITIONAL REPORT SENT TO:
☐ STAT

REPORT OF RADIOLOGIC CONSULTATION

X-RAY NO.: 11-13-24 DATE OF EXAMINATION 4-28-09

LUMBOSACRAL SPINE: The lumbar vertebrae are normal in stature, spacing and alignment. There is no evidence of fracture or disk disease. No spondylolysis is present. The sacroiliac joints appear normal. The paravertebral soft tissues are unremarkable.

CONCLUSIONS: Normal appearing lumbosacral spine.

WFS:maf
4-29-09

Obtaining Information about Health Care Providers

Health care facilities, such as hospitals, nursing homes, retirement centers, and rehabilitation hospitals, are overseen by various governmental and private agencies and licensing organizations. For instance, if a paralegal has a case involving someone who contracted a disease from a blood transfusion, he or she should know that all blood banks are overseen by the American Association of Blood Banks. That association sets out standards and requirements, as well as inspection criteria.

Various specifications and standards for health care providers are set by governmental agencies, professional organizations, and licensing boards. They keep records regarding:

- Current addresses
- Schools attended and grades earned
- Professional credentials
- Honors and awards
- Continuing education requirements
- Licensure status and board certification
- Past and present complaints against the provider.

Therefore, these organizations are excellent resources for gathering information on defendant doctors, nurses, and other health care professionals. This information can also be utilized to evaluate health care professionals who have been designated as expert witnesses by defendants and those one might want to use as experts. Some states allow access to some of this information on-line.

SHANIKA THOMAS, M.D., P.C.
STAN HOFF, M.D., D.M.D., P.C.
65 Western Avenue, Albany, New York 12203
Telephone 438-4400

March 12, 2009

Cathy J. Okrent, Esq.
Washington Square
Box 1501
Albany, New York 12212

Re: Wanda Powers
d/a: 5/2/08

Dear Ms. Okrent:

Wanda Powers was in the office on March 12, 2009 concerning scars of the right lower leg. According to the history on May 2, 2008 she was apparently attacked by four dogs, receiving bites on the right lower leg. One bite required three sutures and one puncture wound required one suture. The wounds healed without infection.

Examination disclosed a white, soft scar 3 × 1.5 cms. on the lateral part of the mid calf of the right lower leg. This scar is permanent and no treatment is indicated. There are two puncture scars, each measuring 0.6 cms., on the upper and lower lateral leg. These scars are permanent and no treatment is indicated.

If I can be of any further help to you please do not hesitate to let me know.

Sincerely,

_____
SHANIKA THOMAS, M.D.

ST: mk

EXHIBIT 13-11
Sample medical report
(doctor's evaluation)

practical **application**

If the health care professional is a specialist, the paralegal should keep in mind that there are additional qualifications for each specialty area. A separate licensing board or organization typically oversees each specialty. For example, a surgeon might be certified to operate by the American Board of Surgery.

Exhibit 13-13 shows OSHA Form 301, an injury and illness incident report.

Exhibit 13-12
Sample medical report
(discharge form)

MEDICAL CENTER HOSPITAL
DISCHARGE INSTRUCTIONS & SUMMARY FORM

Patient Identification

I. FINAL DIAGNOSES: (list in order of importance; do not abbreviate)

Condition on discharge:

1. _____ ☐ Recovered ☒ Improved ☐ Not Improved
                    ☐ Diagnosis Only ☐ Not Treated
                    ☐ Other _____

2. _____ ☐ Recovered ☐ Improved ☐ Not Improved
                    ☐ Diagnosis Only ☐ Not Treated
                    ☐ Other _____

3. _____ ☐ Recovered ☐ Improved ☐ Not Improved
                    ☒ Diagnosis Only ☐ Not Treated
                    ☐ Other _____

4. _____ ☐ Recovered ☒ Improved ☐ Not Improved
                    ☐ Diagnosis Only ☐ Not Treated
                    ☐ Other _____

(Complete additional forms as necessary)

II. OPERATIONS AND/OR PROCEDURES

III. DISCHARGE INSTRUCTIONS AND MEDICATIONS WITH DOSAGE. If no medication check here ☑

IV. SUMMARY:

1. Reason for Admission:

2. Pertinent physical, psychological, x-ray and laboratory findings:

3. Course in hospital (medical, psychiatric, and/or surgical therapy):

(OVER)

Health Care Facilities That Receive Governmental Funding

If a health care facility receives government funds (such as Medicare), it is inspected by the state health department for compliance with regulations. Such

EXHIBIT 13-12
Sample medical report
(discharge form)
(continued)

3. Course in hospital, continued:

V. LIMIT OF DISABILITY:

Patient may return to work: □ YES   □ NO

Patient is essentially home bound: □ YES   □ NO

VI. PAP SMEAR INFORMATION FOR FEMALE PATIENTS:

Pap Smear done during this admission   □ YES □ NO □ WITHIN LAST 3 YEARS
□ REFUSED BY PATIENT

VII. PATIENT OR RESPONSIBLE OTHER VERBALIZES, DEMONSTRATES, OR EXHIBITS KNOWLEDGE OF:

		Completed by	
1. Nature of Illness	□ YES □ NO □ N/A	□ M.D.	□ RN □ Other _____ (Sign & Date)
2. Diet	□ YES □ NO □ N/A	□ M.D.	□ RN □ Other _____ (Sign & Date)
3. Wound care	□ YES □ NO □ N/A	□ M.D.	□ RN □ Other _____ (Sign & Date)
4. Medications	□ YES □ NO □ N/A	□ M.D.	□ RN □ Other _____ (Sign & Date)
5. Special health teaching (colostomy care, casts, diabetic care, etc.)	□ YES □ NO □ N/A	□ M.D.	□ RN □ Other _____ (Sign & Date)
6. Activity	□ YES □ NO □ N/A	□ M.D.	□ RN □ Other _____ (Sign & Date)
7. Follow-up appointments and referrals	□ YES □ NO □ N/A	□ M.D.	□ RN □ Other _____ (Sign & Date)

COMMENTS _____

_____

VIII. SIGNATURE OF PHYSICIAN RESPONSIBLE FOR DISCHARGE OF PATIENT:

_____ M.D.   □ Intern   □ Resident
□ Acting Intern
□ Fellow   □ Attending

TO BE COMPLETED BY THE NURSING DIVISION AT THE TIME THE PATIENT LEAVES THE HOSPITAL:

Date ___/___   Time ___ 11:10   Mode: □ Wheelchair □ Stretcher □ Walked out

Discharge to: □ Nursing Home of Extended Care Facility
□ Home
□ Other (Specify) _____

Belongings to _____   Accompanied by _____
Signature   □ Floor Clerk □ Nurse □ Other

state inspections, along with any compliance and deficiency reports, are public records. As such, they can be obtained for review under the Freedom of Information Act and through discovery. Exhibit 13-14 shows a supervisor's workplace accident investigation report.

OSHA'S Form 301
Injury and Illness Incident Report

U.S. Department of Labor
Occupational Safety and Health Administration

Attention: This form contains information relating to employee health and must be used in a manner that protects the confidentiality of employees to the extent possible while the information is being used for occupational safety and health purposes.

This Injury and Illness Incident Report is one of the first forms you must fill out when a recordable work-related injury or illness has occured. Together with the Log of Work-Related Injuries and Illness and the accompanying Summary, these forms help the employer and OSHA develop a picture of the extent and severity of work-related incidents.

Within 7 calendar days after you receive information that a recordable work-related injury or illness has occurred, you must fill out this form or an equivalent form. Some state workers' compensation, insurance, or other reports may be acceptable substitutes. To be considered an equivalent form, any substitute must contain all the information asked for on this form.

According to Public Law 91-596 and 29 CFR 1904, OSHA's recordkeeping rule, you must keep this form on file for 5 years following the year to which it pertains.

If you need additional copies of this form, you may photocopy and use as many as you need.

Information about the employee

1) Full name　Henry Joseph

2) Street　PO Box 3452
City　ANCHOR Manor　State　AL　Zip　99524

3) Date of birth　02 / 11 / 80

4) Date hired　05 / 19 / 06

5) ☒ Male　☐ Female

Information about the physician or other health care professional

6) Name of physician or other health care professional
DR. Miriam Schwartz

7) If treatment was given away from the worksite, where was it given?
Facility　Meadowviews Medical Center
Street　410 5th Street
City　ANCHOR Manor　State　AL　Zip　99519

8) Was employee treated in an emergency room?
☒ Yes
☐ No

9) Was employee hospitalized overnight as an in-patient?
☐ Yes
☒ No

Information about the case

10) Case number from the Log　1　(Transfer the case number from the Log after you record the case.)

11) Date of injury or illness　9 / 15 / 08

12) Time employee began work　0000　AM/PM

13) Time of event　0325　AM/PM　☐ Check if time cannot be determined

14) *What was the employee doing just before the incident occurred?* Describe the activity, as well as the tools, equipment, or material the employee was using. Be specific. *Examples:* "climbing a ladder while carrying roofing materials"; "spraying chlorine from hand sprayer"; "daily computer key-entry."

Attempting to lower a filing cabinet from a desktop to the floor.

15) *What happened?* Tell us how the injury occurred. *Examples:* "When ladder slipped on wet floor, worker fell 20 feet"; "Worker was sprayed with chlorine when gasket broke during replacement"; "Worker developed soreness in wrist over time."

Gripped sides of cabinet and attempted to lift. Felt immediate pain in wrists at that time.

16) *What was the injury or illness?* Tell us the part of the body that was affected and how it was affected; be more specific than "hurt," "Pain," or sore."*Examples:* "strained back"; "chemical burn, hand"; "carpal tunnel syndrome."

Pain & swelling in both wrists.

17) *What object or substance directly harmed the employee? Examples:* "concrete floor"; "chlorine"; "radial arm saw."*If this question does not apply to the incident , leave it blank.*

Filing cabinet.

18) *If the employee died, when did death occur?* Date of death_____ / _____ /

Completed by　Joy Wong

Title　DA

Phone　(348)562-4811　Date　9/15/08

Public reporting burden for this collection of information is estimated to average 22 minutes per response, including time for reviewing instructions, searching existing data sources, gathering and maintaining the data needed, and completing and reviewing the collection of information. Persons are not required to respond to the collection of information unless it displays a current valid OMB control number. If you have any comments about this estimate or any other aspects of this data collection, including suggestions for reducing this burden. contact: US Department of Labor; OSHA Office of Statistics. Room N-3644, 200 Constitution Avenue, NW, Washington, DC 20210. Do not send the completed forms to this office.

EXHIBIT 13-13　OSHA Form 301, injury and illness incident report
Source: http://www.dir.ca.gov/dosh/dosh-publications/CalOSHAform301.pdf

SUPERVISOR'S ACCIDENT INVESTIGATION REPORT

Send Completed Report to Risk   within Five (5) days of Date of Injury

Office Name: Governor's Hospital   No.: ___.___   Date of this Report: 12 · 18 · 09

EMPLOYEE INFORMATION

Name of Injured (F, MI, L): Alex A. Lizzuski   SSN: 135 - 06 - 9999   Hire Date: 02 · 03 · 96

Dept. Name: Nursing   Post Held at time of injury: 4 West   How long at this job: 13 yrs

Describe injuries sustained by employee: Laceration / Abrasion Shin Area

---

Has the employee lost any work time? ☐ Yes ☒ No   Were they kept overnight in a hospital? ☐ Yes ☒ No

Did the employee receive prompt and appropriate medical care? ☒ Yes ☐ No If no, briefly explain: ___

Treating Physician: Frances Teika, M.D.

Treating Facility: Governor's Hospital

Address: 410 Fifth Street   Tele: (203) 369-1410

ACCIDENT INFORMATION

Date of Injury: 12 · 18 · 09   Time of Injury: 4 · 10 · ___ AM (PM)   ☐ Daylight ☒ Dusk/Dawn ☐ Night

Type of Accident: ☐ Slip, ☐ Fall, ☐ Sprain, ☐ Strain, ☐ Lifting, ☐ Vehicle, ☐ Firearms, ☒ Other, please explain: Assisting other nurses with a combative patient, hit shin on oak bed rail

Type of Location (e.g. shopping mall, parking lot, city street, etc.): Hospital room

Accident Location: _____ , _____ , _____ , _____

Street Address   _City_   _State_   _ZIP_

Relevant Weather Conditions: ___

Type of Lighting at Time of Accident: ___

Client site? ☐ No ☒ Yes Client Name: Governor's Hospital

Any witnesses? ☐ No ☒ Yes Witness Names & Contact Info.(e.g. telephone numbers and/or addresses):

Bill Wittier   518 734 - 0002

Victor Roberge   518 734 - 0950

If vehicle related, has the _Auto. Loss Notice_ been properly filed? ☐ Yes ☐ No If no, briefly explain: ___

Based upon your investigation, briefly describe what took place (WHO, WHAT, WHEN, WHERE, HOW and WHY):

Patient Lavelle Chingere, didn't want to take medication from a needle, at 4:05 PM, Bpt Hosp, patient became combative, when officer Lix Lizos went to grab his legs, he was pulled into the oak rail and caused laceration/abrasion to Alex A. Lizuski's shin, left side. This is a pyhic wing, and each case is different

What can be done to avoid a recurrence of this type of accident? This type of injury just can't be avoided. This is one of two pyshic wings

What actions have been taken by you or the client to remedy any risk associated with this type of accident? ___

If applicable, has the client been notified of any related hazard or unsafe condition? ☒ Yes ☐ No If no, please explain: ___

If yes, has the condition been corrected? ☐ Yes ☒ No If no, have they committed to remedying the problem? Please explain: ___

as explained above

Investigator's Name: Jane Leppize, R.N.   Title: Shift Supervisor

Investigator's Signature: ☒ Jane Leppe

Reviewed by: _____ ☒ _____   Date: 12 · 18 · 09

EXHIBIT 13-14   Supervisor's workplace accident investigation report

▮ SUMMARY

Fact gathering is a significant paralegal role in tort investigations. Paralegals investigate and document the tort scene and interview the client, eyewitnesses, and other persons with pertinent information. Attorneys and law firms often have specialized techniques for conducting investigations. Some use in-house personnel; others hire outside investigative services. Paralegals should customize their investigations to fit the type and size of tort case involved. Details are critical. In part, factual investigations are designed to determine liability and damages. It is important to interview witnesses as soon as possible to obtain the best recollected information. Witnesses explain how the tort occurred according to their observational perspectives.

Defendants are usually determined in-house. It may be difficult to identify or locate potential defendants and witnesses, especially if they are business entities or transient individuals. One should exercise extreme caution when naming parties in lawsuits. The client and/or attorney or law firm could be liable or disciplined for suing the wrong business or person. Potential defendants can be identified in many ways: scrutinizing documents to glean names, addresses, and telephone numbers; making telephone calls to businesses or individuals involved; performing on-line searches; checking with the secretary of state's corporation or partnership divisions or the county or city offices in which assumed names of businesses are registered; and searching company records and documents. Special difficulties arise with ambulance and fire departments as defendants. These entities are often owned or supervised by local governmental agencies, or they may be volunteer services working under governmental contract. Information concerning licensed or regulated businesses can be obtained through the federal or state regulatory agencies.

Paralegals use photographs, videos, and traditional pencil-and-paper methods of documenting tort scenes. The events in a tort case and their sequence are documented and reconstructed under the same conditions in which the tort originally occurred. Paralegals must know their jurisdiction's evidentiary rules if they are to recognize the types of evidence that will be useful in the tort case. It is important to collect evidence in the proper evidentiary form so that it may be used at trial. Hearsay problems should be anticipated and overcome. Most litigation firms now use computer and video technologies to assist in documenting and reconstructing tort cases.

Local governmental agencies may possess a wealth of information concerning some parties involved in the tort case. Archives contain vital statistics, marriage licenses, property ownership records, police records, and civil suit or criminal records. Newspapers, television, and radio can also provide valuable information about the events that occurred when the tort happened. Databases can also furnish considerable information about the persons or businesses involved in the case.

Paralegals investigate employment and lost wages to help determine the client's damages. Tax, wage, and income records should be obtained. Injury expenses are carefully documented and investigated. It is important to know whether the injured party has received insurance or governmental benefits as a result of the tort. It is also necessary to know whether the plaintiff has previously been involved in claims or lawsuits, as well as preexisting injuries, involving the same factual circumstances as the present tort case. The parties' driving or criminal records may be critical to the current case.

Investigations are tailored to fit the specific aspects of each tort case. Cases involving automobile accidents or medical negligence and health care providers each require specialized questions that paralegals use to gather the information necessary for the trial team to successfully conclude the case.

KEY TERMS

business directory
discovery
fictitious name

freedom of information law
  (FOIL)
hearsay

investigation
service of process (process service)

PROBLEMS

Assume the following actual cases were actually assigned to you for investigation. As the senior paralegal for the law firm, you performed the preliminary interview of each of the named plaintiffs. Identify what kind of investigation you would conduct and the different sources you would consult to further your investigation. Be sure to consider each of the facts of the case, as well as all the potential defendants.

1. Ms. Santiago was admitted to the Glenwood hospital through the emergency room with severe pain to the abdomen. After an exploratory operation by Dr. Inexperienced, an infected appendix was discovered and removed. Ms. Santiago was released four days later. She continued to have increasingly severe pain and was readmitted to the hospital three weeks later. The same surgeon performed another operative procedure, recovered a surgical sponge left in her during the initial operation, and removed it.

2. Suzie Woo is seven months pregnant. While crossing the grounds of the Gentle Breeze Country Club with her friend Dewanna Stevens, she stepped on a circular manhole cover, which unbeknownst to her was slightly ajar. The manhole tipped open and she fell in the hole, with her stomach preventing her from falling completely down the open pit. Just minutes before, a Quick Rooter Plumbing truck was spotted driving off the grounds of the club.

3. Josh Tyler is walking up the hill on State Street when a car without a driver comes rolling out of a private parking lot, down the street, and pins him against an office building, breaking four of his ribs and his left leg. A store employee who sees the accident happen calls an ambulance. Josh is taken to the nearest hospital. He later learns that the car had recently been serviced by Jenelle's Auto Repair.

4. Arnold Rubitkowitz is playing bingo at the local Grand Tigers Club fundraiser at the Hotel Luxe. Just when his cards are finally starting to look promising, the five-foot-long fluorescent light fixture drops from the ceiling above his head, rendering him momentarily unconscious. The bingo caller stops the game long enough to summon the local fire department, the police, and the town paramedics, who take Arnold to the local emergency room for treatment.

5. Trevor Vincent is taking a Sunday ride on his motorcycle through a new development by Sherman Oaks Builders in the town of Leewood, Texas. As he approaches a sharp curve in the road, he comes upon some construction debris, is unable to complete the sharp turn, is thrown twenty feet from his motorcycle, lands on his head, and dies. Trevor was not wearing a helmet at the time of the accident.

REVIEW QUESTIONS

1. What are the basic components of a tort case investigation? Who conducts these investigations? How are investigations customized? What types of questions are witnesses asked in tort investigations?

2. Why is it important to identify the correct defendant(s) in a tort case? What could happen if incorrect persons or businesses are sued as defendants?

3. How can a client's documents and the telephone help locate potential defendants? Who should a paralegal contact to obtain information about corporations, partnerships, or sole proprietorships that are prospective defendants?

4. What special problems are associated with ambulance and fire departments that are defendants?

5. Who should a paralegal contact to investigate licensed or regulated businesses?

6. How should a paralegal document an accident scene? What conditions should be prevalent when the scene is investigated? What items should be included on the investigation checklist?

7. Why is it important to tort investigations to know the evidentiary rules from one's jurisdiction?

8. How can local governmental agencies, newspapers, television, radio, and computer databases be helpful in researching a tort case?

9. Why are criminal and driving records pertinent to tort investigations? What can this information reveal about the case being investigated?

10. What additional areas should a tort paralegal investigate?

11. What are some of the kinds of information that can be obtained on-line to assist in an investigation?

▌HELPFUL WEBSITES

This chapter focuses on tort investigation. To learn more about tort investigation, the following sites can be accessed:

West Legal Directory

http://www.lawoffice.com

Guide to Litigation Law

http://www.hg.org

American Arbitration Association

http://www.adr.org

Federal Rules of Civil Procedure

http://www.law.cornell.edu

Agencies That Gather Information Related to Tort Law

http://www.findlaw.com
http://www.statelocal.gov

Kelly Blue Book to Evaluate Property Damage

http://www.kbb.com

Locate People

http://www.switchboard.com

Annual Reports for Public Companies

http://www.investquest.com

Public Records

http://www.knowx.com

HIPAA

http://www.hhs.gov

Federation of Defense and Corporate Counsel

http://www.thefederation.org

Legal Research

http://www.kentlaw.edu
http://www.law.indiana.edu
http://www.lawlibrary.rutgers.edu

FOIA

http://www.usdoj.gov

STUDENT CD-ROM™
For additional materials, please go to the CD in this book.

ONLINE COMPANION™
For additional resources, please go to
http://www.paralegal.delmar.cengage.com

Appendices

Confidential Client

Information Form

CONFIDENTIAL CLIENT INFORMATION FORM

This questionnaire is a *confidential* questionnaire for the use of our office only in preparing your claim for personal injuries. The information you furnish us will not be released and will be held strictly confidential. When your claim has been concluded, we will return this questionnaire to you if you wish. Please answer every question fully and accurately because, as your attorneys, we must know all about you and your case. One surprise because of an incorrect or incomplete answer could cause you to lose your case. All of the questions are important even though they may not appear to have anything to do with your case.

   Please type or print all answers. Use additional sheets of paper or the reverse side of this form if needed.

Your name: _____

Your address: _____ E-mail: _____

Your telephone number: _____ Date of accident: _____

Cell phone number: _____ Fax number: _____

Insurance company: _____

Workers' compensation number, if any: _____

Birthplace: _____

Social Security number: _____ Age: _____ Birthdate: _____

Married: _____ Single: _____ Divorced: _____ Separated: _____ Widower: _____ Widow: _____

If divorced, date and place: _____

Names, ages, and addresses of all those (including children) who are dependent upon you for support, and your relationship to each:

Name	Address	Age	Relationship

List the addresses where you have resided during the past ten years and give the period of time at each residence, including dates:

Residence	From	To

Have you ever used any other name? _____ Where? _____

Why? _____

Are you married at the present time? _____ Date of marriage: _____

Place: _____

WORK BACKGROUND

Cell phone: _____

Present job: _____ Phone: _____

Name and address of employer: _____

E-mail address: _____ Fax number: _____

Present job title and duties: _____

How long have you worked at this job? _____ Your present pay: $ _____

When you first began working for this employer: _____

List prior employment for past five years:

Name	Address	Date Employed	Job

EDUCATION

How many years did you complete in school? _____ College? _____

Is your spouse employed? _____ Employer's name and address: _____

Wages: $ _____ per _____ Average income entire year for spouse: $ _____

How long employed? _____ Prior employment: _____

Are you living in your employer's household or premises? _____

If related to employer, state relationship: _____

Occupation when injured: _____ Were you doing your regular work? _____

On whose payroll when injured? _____

Wages when injured (per day, per week): _____ Work days per week: _____

Were you a temporary or steady employee? _____

If under 18 years of age, give name and address of your guardian or parent: _____

_____

ACCIDENT

Date of the injury (hour): _____

Date you were forced to leave work because of your injury (hour): _____

Place where injury was sustained (no., street, city or town): _____

_____

Were you on employer's premises? _____ Was injury caused by another person? _____

Name of other person: _____

Who is he/she employed by? _____

Have you claimed or received settlement for this injury? _____ From whom? _____

_____

Name and address of eyewitnesses: _____

_____

Telephone number: _____ Cell phone number: _____

When did you first report your injury? _____

To whom did you first report your injury? _____

Have you returned to work? _____ If so, on what date? _____

Describe your injury and how the accident happened: _____

_____

_____

MEDICAL HISTORY BEFORE ACCIDENT

Were you hospitalized at any time before the accident in this case? _____ If so, list below all hospitalizations:

Date	Hospital	Doctor	Duration	Nature of Illness

Have you had any physical examinations before this accident? If so, list all physical examinations for five years before the accident:

Date	Place	Name of Doctor	Purpose

Have you had any accidents or injuries before this accident? _____ If so, list below every such accident or injury, whether there was a claim for damages or not:

Date	Place	Nature of Accident or Injury	Treated By

Have you had any illnesses or diseases before this accident? _____ If so, list every such illness or disease suffered in the five years before this accident:

Date	Nature of Illness	Duration	Treated By

Have you had any chronic health problems? _____ If so, list them: _____

_____

Did you use any drugs regularly before the accident? _____ If so, list the type and reason why you used them: _____

_____

Have you ever had any insurance of any kind declined or cancelled? _____ If so, give reason:

_____

Have you ever had any broken bones? _____ If so, give date and circumstances: _____

List below what normal activities, including sports, hobbies, or other activities, you enjoyed before this accident: _____

STATEMENTS MADE

Have you told any police officer, investigator, insurance adjustor, or any other person about the accident? _____

Have you given any written statement to any person about the accident? _____ If so, answer the following:

Name of person to whom statement was given: _____

Date given: _____ If written, do you have a copy? _____ Was the statement recorded? _____

Persons present at time: _____ Did you sign the statement? _____

Please give us any statement you know the employer made about the accident, or that you understand he/she may have made: _____

_____

When and where made: _____

Name and address of person who heard it: _____

DAMAGES FROM ACCIDENT

State in full detail, all injuries you received as a result of this accident: _____

_____

State your physical condition—scars, deformities, headaches, pains, etc.—due to injuries received in this accident: _____

_____

Have you missed any time from work as a result of your injury? _____ If so, list the inclusive dates you were unable to work: From: _____ To: _____

From: _____ To: _____

Did you lose wages for the periods of time missed from work due to this accident? _____ If so, state the total wages lost to date and the dates: _____

Have you had any increases or decreases in your pay since the accident? _____ If so, explain: _____

List all hospitals in which you were examined or treated, or to which you were admitted as a patient as a result of the injuries sustained in the accident and the dates:

Hospital   Address   Dates

_____

_____

List the full name, address, and telephone number of each physician or surgeon who has examined or treated you for your injuries as a result of the accident:

Name   Address   Telephone No.

_____

_____

Have you used any of the following in connection with the treatment?

Back or neck brace? _____ Dates: _____

Crutches? _____ Dates: _____

Traction? _____ Dates: _____

Physiotherapy? _____ Dates: _____

Other? _____ Dates: _____

List here all of your usual employment activities that you have NOT been able to perform, or can perform only with difficulty, since the accident: _____

_____

Time lost from school (if you are a pupil): _____

Please summarize your out-of-pocket expenses, and if you have not previously given us the name and address, indicate to whom they are owed, as well as the amounts and whether they have been paid.

_____

_____

_____

_____

<u>CONCLUSION</u>

In completing this questionnaire, have you thought of any information for which we have not asked that might be of some assistance to us in serving you? _____ If so, please state it here, no matter how silly, trivial, or embarrassing it may seem. _____

_____

_____

_____

_____

Dated this _____ day of _____, 20___.

I have read the above statement and the statements contained therein are true and correct.

_____

Client

Understanding Appellate Court Opinions

Legal analysis consists of understanding appellate court opinions and applying rules of law to different factual situations. This section addresses legal analysis, a critical aspect of legal study.

Briefing Cases

Many of the chapters in this book include reprinted portions of appellate court opinions to illustrate various tort principles. At first glance, court decisions may appear garbled or unfocused. A structured formula applied to each case helps organize the ideas that the courts express. There are several such methods, but the most popular is explained here.

Structured Analysis

A structured analysis breaks an opinion into several components: facts, procedural history, issues on appeal, rationale, and ruling(s). This approach represents the standard analytical framework used by law school and paralegal students.

Facts From the court opinion, the reader gleans the *facts* that underlie or are necessary to the appellate court's final determination of the case. These are sometimes called the *legally significant facts*. Many facts in the case provide mere background information; these are called *background facts*. Although background facts are not critical to the court's decision, they must be noted to comprehend the complete circumstances involved in the litigation. Sometimes appellate opinions include irrelevant facts that have no real bearing on the outcome of the appeal.

Procedural History The *procedural history*, or *judicial history* as it is sometimes called, is the appellate court's summary of the previous events in the lawsuit: who sued whom, what legal claims were involved, and (most importantly) how the trial court decided the case (if a bench trial) or in whose favor the jury returned its verdict. Procedural history may include a summary of a lower appellate court's decision rendered before the case was appealed to the court that wrote the opinion being studied. Procedural information is critical to grasp the importance of the appellate court's ruling.

Issues The *issues* include the questions appealed from the trial court's judgment. Every appeal has at least one issue being reviewed by the appellate court, although more often several issues are involved. Issues are normally phrased in terms of a question: Did the trial court err in admitting certain evidence? Given the facts proven during trial, did the defendant commit a certain tort against the plaintiff?

Rationale The *rationale* is the appellate court's reasoning behind its ruling. It is the process through which the court applies the rules of law to the facts of the case. This application is accomplished by linking a series of arguments that appear to lead to a single logical conclusion (which, conveniently, happens to be the court's decision). Consider the following example. Suppose a state statute requires owners of agricultural vehicles used to haul grain to obtain a special commercial license. Charles sells his old twin-axle grain truck to Donny, who plans to use it in a furniture delivery business. Donny purchases ordinary truck license plates. Has Donny violated the statute? In its rationale, an appellate court would first explain the statutory language (i.e., rule of law) and then apply it to the facts of the case. Thus, although Donny bought a vehicle formerly used to haul grain, its present function is entirely nonagricultural (i.e., conveying furniture). Because the truck is not being used to carry grain, Donny would not be required to purchase the special licenses and thus has not violated the statute.

Ruling The *ruling* is the appellate court's decision in the case. This decree is directed toward the trial (or lower appellate) court's ruling. If the appellate court agrees that the trial court was correct in deciding the issue on appeal, then the appellate court *affirms* the trial court's judgment. If the appellate court disagrees with the trial court's determination of the appealed issue, then the appellate court *reverses* or *vacates* the trial court's decree. Often reversal or vacation is accompanied by a *remand*, or return, of the case to the trial court with instructions from the appellate court. These instructions may be simply that judgment should be entered for the plaintiff or the defendant (depending, of course, upon which side the appellate court thinks should prevail), or they may include directions that certain factual questions be retried by the trial court.

Briefing an Appellate Court Opinion

As mentioned previously, law school and paralegal students most often use this briefing formula to analyze appellate court opinions. To illustrate how this is done in practice, an actual appellate court opinion has been reproduced here, followed by a suggested case brief that summarizes the elements of the opinion using the briefing formula. To assist in reading opinions reprinted in this book, certain tangential matters and terminology are summarized or explained in brackets: "[ ]." Any parts of the original opinion that have been omitted are indicated in bracketed comments or by bracketed ellipses: "[...]."

EDWARDS V. TERRYVILLE MEAT CO.

577 N.Y.S.2d 477 (App. Div. 1991)
N.Y. Supreme Court, Appellate Division
December 23, 1991
Before MANGANO, P.J., and KUNZEMAN, EIBER and BALLETTA, J.J.

MEMORANDUM BY THE COURT.

In a negligence action to recover damages for personal injuries, the plaintiffs appeal [. . .] from [. . .] an order and judgment [. . .] of the Supreme Court, Suffolk County (Cannavo, J.), entered September 11, 1989, as granted the defendant's motion for summary judgment dismissing the complaint [. . .].

ORDERED that the order and judgment entered September 11, 1989, is affirmed [. . .].

In this slip-and-fall case, it was incumbent upon the plaintiffs to come forth with evidence showing that the defendant had either created the allegedly dangerous condition or that it had actual or constructive notice of the condition (see, *Eddy v. Tops Friendly Markets*, 91 A.D.2d 1203, 459 N.Y.S.2d 196, *aff'd*, 59 N.Y.2d 692, 463 N.Y.S. 2d 437, 450 N.E.2d 243[1983]).

To constitute constructive notice, a defect must be visible and apparent and it must exist for a sufficient length of time prior to the accident to permit defendant's employees to discover and remedy it" (*Gordon v. American Museum of Natural History*, 67 N.Y.2d 836, 837, 501 N.Y.S. 2d 646, 492 N.E.2d 774 [1986]). The injured plaintiff was in the defendant's store for only about 10 minutes before she allegedly slipped and fell on an unknown milky-colored substance which she concededly did not see until after she fell. There is no evidence that the defendant caused the substance to be on the floor, nor is there sufficient evidence to establish that the defendant had either actual or constructive notice of the substance [citations omitted]. Accordingly, the Supreme Court properly granted the defendant's motion for summary judgment.

A Suggested Case Brief

CITATION: *Edwards v. Terryville Meat Co.*, 577 N.Y.S.2d 477 (App. Div. 1991).

FACTS: Injured plaintiff was in defendant's store 10 minutes when she slipped and fell on unknown milky substance on floor. Plaintiff did not see substance until after falling. No evidence that defendant caused substance to be on floor.

PROCEDURAL HISTORY: Injured plaintiff and spouse sued defendant for negligence. Supreme Court of Suffolk County granted defendant's motion for summary judgment dismissing plaintiffs' complaint.

ISSUE: Did trial court err in granting defendant's motion for summary judgment?
    (*Implied Issue*) Did plaintiffs present sufficient evidence to establish defendant's liability for negligently causing plaintiff's injuries?

RATIONALE: This is a slip-and-fall negligence case. To establish defendant's negligence, plaintiffs must prove either that (1) defendant caused slippery substance to be on floor, or (2) defendant knew (or had constructive notice) that substance was on floor. Constructive notice requires that substance be present on floor for sufficient length of time prior to accident to permit defendant's employees to discover and remedy it. In this case, there was no evidence that defendant had created the hazard that injured plaintiff. Further, there was insufficient evidence that defendant had actual or constructive notice of substance, given the short time (10 minutes) that plaintiff was in store before she slipped and fell. Thus, trial court correctly granted defendant's motion for summary judgment.

RULING: Appellate Division affirmed supreme court's decision.

Glossary

A

abatement Reduction or decrease . . . [or] complete elimination.

abnormally dangerous (ultrahazardous) instrumentalities Activities or objects that are, by their very nature, extremely hazardous to persons or property. These are relevant to strict (absolute) liability cases.

absolute (strict) liability The legal responsibility for damage or injury, even if you are not at fault or negligent.

abuse of process Using the legal system unfairly; for example, prosecuting a person for writing a "bad check" simply to pressure him or her to pay.

alternate dispute resolution (ADR) Ways to resolve a legal problem without a court decision.

answer The first pleading by the defendant in a lawsuit. This pleading responds to the charges and demands of the plaintiff's complaint.

apprehension Fear or anxiety.

appropriation Taking something wrongfully.

arbitration Resolution of a dispute by a person whose decision is binding. This person is called an *arbitrator*. Submission of the dispute for decision is often the result of an agreement (an *arbitration clause*) in a contract.

assault An intentional threat, show of force, or movement that could reasonably make a person feel in danger of physical attack or harmful physical contact.

assembly defect A theory in products liability concerning whether a defective product is unreasonably dangerous. Errors in production manufacture or assembly may render a product unreasonably hazardous despite safe design.

assumption of risk Knowingly and willingly exposing yourself (or your property) to the possibility of harm.

In most states, a person who assumes a risk of harm cannot win a negligence lawsuit against the person responsible for the harm.

attachment Formally seizing property (or a person) in order to bring it under control of the court. This is usually done by getting a court order to have a law enforcement officer take control of the property.

attractive nuisance Any item that is dangerous to young children but that is so interesting and alluring as to attract them.

attractive nuisance doctrine A legal principle, used in some states, that if a person keeps dangerous property in a way that children might be attracted to it, then that person is responsible when they get hurt.

B

bad faith Dishonesty or other failure to deal fairly with another person.

battery An intentional, unconsented-to, physical contact by one person (or an object controlled by that person) with another person.

breach of warranty The violation of either an express or implied warranty.

burden of rejoinder The defendant's burden of proof to refute the plaintiff's evidence in a lawsuit.

business directory A listing of corporations and other business organizations by name, geographic location, product or service, brand name, advertising, and other subject headings.

but-for causation But for the defendant's acts, the plaintiff's injury would not have happened.

C

castle doctrine The principle that you can use any force necessary to protect your own home or its inhabitants from attack. Also called *dwelling defense doctrine*.

cause-in-fact Cause of injury in negligence cases. If the tortfeasor's actions resulted in the victim's injuries, then the tortfeasor was the cause-in-fact of the victim's harm.

chattel Item of personal property. Any property other than land.

class action A lawsuit brought for yourself and other persons in the same situation. To bring a *class action,* you must convince the court that there are too many persons in the class (group) to make them all individually a part of a lawsuit and that your interests are the same as theirs, so that you can adequately represent their needs.

coming and going rule Rule used when employees commit torts while coming to or going from work. In respondeat superior cases, this rule helps decide whether an employee's actions fall outside the scope of employment.

coming to the nuisance defense A defense to private nuisance lawsuits that may be used successfully when a plaintiff owns or uses land at a location in which the alleged nuisance activity was previously occurring. The plaintiff is said to have "come to the nuisance" and thus cannot recover against the defendant.

commercial disparagement An intentional tort that occurs when a tortfeasor communicates false statements to third parties about a person's goods, services, or business enterprise. The tortfeasor must intend to harm the victim's ability to use goods, furnish services, or conduct business.

common law 1. Either all caselaw or the caselaw that is made by judges in the absence of relevant statutes. 2. The legal system that originated in England and is composed of caselaw and statutes that grow and change, influenced by ever-changing custom and tradition.

common usage (use) principle Doctrine in strict liability cases that defines abnormally dangerous activities and substances as those not commonly undertaken or used in everyday life.

community 1. Neighborhood, locality, etc. A vague term that can include very large or very small areas. 2. A group with common interests. 3. Shared.

comparative negligence A legal rule, used in many states, by which the amount of "fault" on each side of an accident is measured and the side with less fault

is given damages according to the difference between the magnitude of each side's fault.

compensatory damages Damages awarded for the actual loss suffered by a plaintiff.

complainant 1. A person who makes an official complaint. 2. A person who starts a lawsuit.

complaint The first pleading filed in a civil lawsuit. It includes a statement of the wrong or harm done to the plaintiff by the defendant.

consent Voluntary and active agreement.

consortium The rights and duties resulting from marriage. They include companionship, love, affection, assistance, cooperation, and sexual relations.

consumer contemplation test If a reasonable person would not have anticipated the danger created by the fault in the product, then the product is unreasonably dangerous.

contempt 1. An act that obstructs a court's work or lessens the dignity of the court. . . . . 2. A willful disobeying of a judge's command or official court order.

contribution 1. The sharing of payment for a debt (or judgment) among persons who are all liable for the debt. 2. The right of a person who has paid an entire debt (or judgment) to get back a fair share of the payment from another person who is also responsible for the debt.

contributory negligence The plaintiff's own negligence that contributed to his or her injuries. In some jurisdictions this bars any recovery by a plaintiff.

control The power or authority to direct or oversee.

conversion Any act that deprives an owner of property without that owner's permission and without just cause.

culpability factoring (liability apportionment) A defense to negligence. When the plaintiff's negligence contributed to his or her injuries, comparative negligence calculates the percentage of the defendant's and the plaintiff's negligence and adjusts the plaintiff's damages according to the numbers.

D

damages Money that a court orders paid to a person who has suffered damage (a loss or harm) by the person who caused the injury.

danger/utility test A theory in products liability design that makes a product unreasonably dangerous. Under this test, a product is unreasonably dangerous if the danger created by its design outweighs the benefits derived from its use.

deep pocket The one person (or organization) among many possible defendants best able to pay a judgment . . . the one a plaintiff is most likely to sue.

defamation Transmission to others of false statements that harm the reputation, business, or property rights of a person. Spoken defamation is *slander* and written defamation is *libel.*

defamation by computer An intentional tort that occurs when the tortfeasor includes false information about a person's credit or credit rating in a computer database. This false information must be communicated to third parties and must injure the victim's ability to obtain credit.

defendant A person against whom an action is brought.

defense 1. The sum of the facts, law, and arguments presented by the side against whom legal action is brought. 2. Any counter-argument or counter-force. A defense can relieve a defendant of the liability of a tort.

defense of persons A defense to the intentional torts of assault, battery, and false imprisonment. Its elements include the use of reasonable force to defend or protect a third party from injury when the third party is threatened by an attacking force.

defense of property A defense to the intentional torts of assault and battery. Its elements include the use of reasonable force to protect property from damage or dispossession when another person, called the *invader,* attempts to injure or wrongfully take possession of the property.

discovery 1. The formal and informal exchange of information between sides in a lawsuit. . . . 2. Finding out something previously unknown.

dispossession Wrongfully taking away a person's property by force, trick, or misuse of the law.

dominion Legal ownership plus full actual control over something.

domitae naturae (Latin) "Domesticated nature." Tame, domestic animals.

due (reasonable) care That degree of care a person of ordinary prudence (the so-called *reasonable person*) would exercise in similar circumstances.

duty 1. An obligation to obey a law. 2. A legal obligation to another person, who has a corresponding right.

E

ejectment The name for an old type of lawsuit to get back land taken away wrongfully.

elements The essential parts or components of something.

emotional distress Mental anguish. Nonphysical harm that may be compensated for by damages in some types of lawsuits. *Mental anguish* may be as limited as the immediate mental feelings during an injury or as broad as prolonged grief, shame, humiliation, despair, etc.

entry The act of entering [as upon real property].

equitable relief (remedy) A remedy available in equity; generally non-monetary relief.

exclusive right A right granted to no one else.

exclusive right of possession A land owner's right to use his or her property without interference from other persons.

execution sale A public sale held by a sheriff or other public official of property seized under a writ of execution.

F

false imprisonment An unlawful restraint or deprivation of a person's liberty, usually by a public official.

false light in the public eye One type of the intentional tort of invasion of privacy. Occurs when the tortfeasor publicly attributes to another individual false opinions, statements, or actions.

family relationships rule Doctrine used in negligent infliction of emotional distress cases. A bystander may recover damages if he or she witnesses the tortfeasor injuring one or more of the bystander's relatives.

fee standard A test courts use in applying the governmental/proprietary distinction. If a governmental agency assesses a fee for an activity, the activity is considered proprietary; if not, it is considered governmental.

ferae naturae (Latin) "Of wild nature." Naturally wild animals.

fictitious name A trade or assumed name used by corporations for the purpose of conducting business.

foreseeability The notion that a specific action, under particular circumstances, would produce an anticipated result. In negligence law, if it were reasonably foreseeable that the plaintiff would be harmed by the defendant's actions, then the scope of duty includes the plaintiff. Foreseeability of injury is another aspect of negligence theory, which falls within proximate cause. Foreseeability is defined in terms of reasonableness.

foreseeable injury An injury that a reasonably prudent person should have anticipated.

foreseeable plaintiffs theory Under this theory, if it were reasonably foreseeable that the injured victim would be harmed as a consequence of the tortfeasor's actions, then the tortfeasor's scope of duty includes the victim.

fraud (deceit) Any kind of trickery used to cheat another of money or property.

freedom of information law (FOIL) A law requiring (or assisting) public access to government records.

frolic and detour rule Conduct of an employee that falls outside of the scope of employment that is purely for the benefit of said employee. An employer is not responsible for the negligence of an employee on a "frolic of his/her own."

G

governmental function An action performed for the general public good by a governmental agency . . . or by a private organization closely tied to the government. . . . These functions are state actions.

gross negligence Recklessly or willfully acting with a deliberate indifference to the effect the action will have on others.

H

hearsay A statement about what someone else said (or wrote or otherwise communicated).

hot (fresh) pursuit The right of a person who has had property taken to use reasonable force to get it back after a chase that takes place immediately after it was taken.

I

imminent danger exception A nineteenth- and early twentieth-century exception to the privity of contract requirement in defective product cases.

immunity An exemption from a legally imposed duty, freedom from a duty, or freedom from a penalty.

impact rule The rule (used today in very few states) that damages for emotional distress cannot be had in a negligence lawsuit unless there is some physical contact or impact.

indemnity A contract to reimburse another for actual loss suffered.

independent contractor A person who contracts with an "employer" to do a particular piece of work by his or her own methods and under his or her own control.

informed consent A person's agreement to allow something to happen (such as surgery) that is based on a full disclosure or full knowledge of the facts needed to make the decision intelligently.

injunction A judge's order to a person to do or to refrain from doing a particular thing.

intent The resolve or purpose to use a particular means to reach a particular result. *Intent* usually explains *how* a person wants to do something and *what* that person wants to get done.

intentional infliction of emotional distress An intentional tort that occurs when the tortfeasor's outrageous conduct, which is intended to cause severe emotional anguish in the victim, actually causes the victim such emotional suffering as a result of the tortfeasor's actions.

intentional tort An injury *designed* to injure a person or that person's property.

invasion of privacy A violation of the right to be left alone.

investigation A systematic examination, especially an official inquiry.

invitee A person who is at a place by invitation.

J

joint and several liability When two or more persons who jointly commit a tort can be held liable both together and individually.

judge The person who runs a courtroom, decides all legal questions, and sometimes decides entire cases by also deciding factual questions.

L

last clear chance doctrine Even though the plaintiff was at fault in causing his or her own injuries, the defendant had the last opportunity to avert harm and failed to do so; therefore, the plaintiff can still recover.

libel Written defamation. Publicly communicated, false written statements that injure a person's reputation, business, or property rights.

licensee A person who is on property with permission, but without any enticement by the owner and with no financial advantage to the owner.

loss of consortium The loss of one or more of a spouse's services (i.e., companionship, or ability to have sexual relations).

M

maintenance defect A theory in products liability concerning whether a defective product is unreasonably dangerous. If a seller fails to maintain a product properly, and the product later causes injury to the ultimate user, then the product was unreasonably dangerous.

malice 1. Ill will. 2. Intentionally harming someone. 3. In defamation law, with knowledge of falsity or with reckless disregard for whether or not something is false.

malicious prosecution A tort committed by bringing charges against someone in order to harm that person and with no legal justification for doing it.

mandamus (Latin) "We command." A *writ of mandamus* is a court order that directs a public official or government department to do something.

mass tort When large groups of people are injured as a result of a single tortious act. A mass tort typically involves thousands of claimants, years of litigation, and millions of dollars in attorneys' fees and costs. Generally, a smaller number of defendants are involved.

material Significant or important.

mediation Outside help in settling a dispute. The person who does this is called a *mediator*. This is different from arbitration in that a mediator can only persuade people into a settlement.

minitrial Alternate dispute resolution by a panel of executives from two companies engaged in a complex dispute. A neutral moderator helps the two sides reach a voluntary settlement.

minor A person who is under the age of full legal rights and duties.

misrepresentation 1. *Innocent misrepresentation* is a false statement that is not known to be false. 2. *Negligent misrepresentation* is a false statement made when [the one making the statement] should have known better. 3. *Fraudulent misrepresentation* is a false statement known to be false and meant to be misleading.

mistake An unintentional error or act.

mixed nuisance A nuisance that is both public and private.

motive The reason why a person does something.

N

national standard A standard applied throughout the nation.

necessary force That degree of force reasonably perceived as required to repel an attack or resist confinement. It is an aspect of self-defense.

necessity Often refers to a situation that requires an action that would otherwise be illegal or expose a person to tort liability. Competing harms.

negligence The failure to exercise a reasonable amount of care in a situation that causes harm to someone or something. It can involve doing something carelessly or failing to do something that should have been done.

negligence per se Negligence that cannot be debated due to a law that establishes a duty of care that the defendant has violated, thus causing injury to another.

negligent infliction of emotional distress Outrageous conduct by the tortfeasor that the tortfeasor reasonably should have anticipated would produce significant and reasonably foreseeable emotional injury to the victim. By his or her actions, the tortfeasor must breach the duty of reasonable care, and the victim must be a reasonably foreseeable plaintiff.

nominal damages Small or symbolic damages awarded in situations in which no actual damages have occurred, or the right has not been proven even though a right has been violated in an intentional tort action.

nuisance 1. Anything that annoys or disturbs unreasonably, hurts a person's use of his or her property, or violates the public health, safety, or decency. 2. Use of land that does anything in definition 1.

nuisance per se That which is considered a nuisance at all times and no matter the circumstances, regardless of location or surroundings.

O

occupier An individual who does not own but who uses real estate; includes tenants (lessees).

P

patient dumping Denial of treatment to emergency patients or women in labor, or transferring them to another hospital while in an unstable condition.

permanent injunction Abatement orders instructing a defendant to permanently stop doing a nuisance activity. Usually issued after a full hearing.

physical manifestations rule Doctrine applied in negligent infliction of emotional distress cases. The plaintiff may recover damages if physical symptoms accompanied his or her mental anguish.

plaintiff A person who brings a lawsuit.

police power The government's right and power to set up and enforce laws to provide for the safety, health, and general welfare of the people.

post-trial procedures The procedures that occur after a trial, such as an appeal or the steps taken to collect on an award.

preponderance of the evidence The greater weight of the evidence. A standard of proof generally used in civil lawsuits. It is not as high a standard as *clear and convincing evidence* or *beyond a reasonable doubt.*

pretrial procedures Any procedure that immediately precedes trial; for example, the settlement conference.

prima facie case A case that will be won unless the other side comes forward with evidence to disprove it.

private nuisance A tort that requires a showing of special harm to you or your property and allows the recovery of damages for the harm as well as an injunction.

privilege 1. An advantage; a right to preferential treatment. 2. An exemption from a duty others like you must perform. 3. The right to speak or write defamatory words because the law allows them in certain circumstances. 4. A basic right, such as *privileges and immunities.* 5. A special advantage, as opposed to a right; an advantage that can be taken away. 6. As a defense against an intentional tort, *privilege* is a legal justification to engage in otherwise tortious conduct in order to accomplish a compelling social goal.

privity of contract A legal relationship that exists between parties to a contract. In some cases privity must exist in order for an individual to make a claim against another.

probable cause A reasonable belief that the accused is guilty of the alleged crime.

process A court's ordering a defendant to show up in court or risk losing a lawsuit; a summons.

process serving The method by which a defendant in a lawsuit is notified that the plaintiff has filed suit against the defendant. Also called *service of process.*

product manufacturer The maker of a product that, if defective, gives rise to product liability.

product(s) liability The responsibility of manufacturers (and sometimes sellers) of goods to pay for harm to purchasers (and sometimes other users and even bystanders) caused by a defective product.

profession An occupation that requires specialized advanced education, training, and knowledge. The skill involved is mostly intellectual rather than manual.

professional community standard of care The standard of reasonable care used in negligence cases involving defendants with special skills and knowledge.

proprietary actions Certain business-like activities performed by governmental bodies that are usually associated with the private sector, and are not given immunity from tort liability.

prosecutor A public official who represents the government's case against a person accused of a crime.

proximate cause The "legal cause" of an accident or other injury (which may have several actual causes). The proximate cause of an injury is not necessarily the closest thing in time or space to the injury.

public disclosure of private facts One type of the intentional tort of invasion of privacy. Occurs when the tortfeasor communicates purely private information about a person to the public without permission, and a reasonable person would find this disclosure extremely objectionable.

public nuisance Activity by the tortfeasor that unreasonably and substantially interferes with the public's use and enjoyment of legal rights common to the public.

public policy The law should be applied in a way that promotes the good and welfare of the people.

publication Making public; communicating defamatory information to a person other than the person defamed.

punitive (exemplary) damages Extra money [over and above compensatory damages] given to a plaintiff to punish the defendant and to keep a particularly bad act from happening again.

purchaser One who acquires property through the purchase of said property.

R

reasonable force Force that is reasonable, limited to that which is necessary to dispel the attacking force for self-defense.

reasonable person test (standard) What a reasonable person would have done in the same or similar circumstances.

reckless infliction of emotional distress An intentional tort that occurs when the tortfeasor's outrageous conduct causes the victim to suffer severe mental anguish. Intent to produce the emotional suffering is not necessary. Instead, it is sufficient that the tortfeasor knew, or reasonably should have known, that his or her misbehavior would produce emotional distress. The tortfeasor's conduct is wanton, with no apparent regard for the victim's suffering.

remedy The means by which a right is enforced or satisfaction is gained for a harm done.

rent-a-judge Alternate dispute resolution in which two sides in a dispute choose a person to decide the dispute. The two sides may agree to make the procedure informal or formal.

replevin A legal action to get back property wrongfully held by another person.

res ipsa loquitur (Latin) "The thing speaks for itself." A rebuttable presumption (a conclusion that can be changed if contrary evidence is introduced) that a person is negligent.

respondeat superior (Latin) "Let the master answer." Describes the principle that an employer is responsible for most harm caused by an employee acting within the scope of employment. In such a case, the employer is said to have vicarious liability.

retailer One who makes retail sales of goods.

rightful repossession A defense to trespass to land, trespass to chattel, conversion, assault, and battery. Its elements include the use of reasonable force to retake possession of personal property of which the owner has been wrongfully disposed, or denied possession.

S

scope of duty In negligence law, defined in terms of those individuals who might foreseeably be injured as a result of the tortfeasor's actions.

scope of employment The range of actions within which an employee is considered to be doing work for the employer.

self-defense Physical force used against a person who is threatening physical force or using physical force. This is a right if your own family, property, or body is in danger, but sometimes only if the danger was not provoked. Also, deadly force may (usually) only be used against deadly force.

seller One who sells property, either its own or through contract with the actual owner.

sensibilities In nuisance law, ways in which people's physical and emotional senses are affected.

sensory perception rule Doctrine used in negligent infliction of emotional distress cases. A bystander may recover damages if he or she witnesses a tortfeasor injuring another person, so long as the bystander perceives the event directly through his or her own senses.

service of process The delivery (or its legal equivalent, such as publication in a newspaper in some cases) of a legal paper by an authorized person.

sexual harassment Unwelcome sexual advances, requests for sexual favors, and other verbal or physical conduct of a sexual nature, when this conduct affects an individual's employment, unreasonably interferes with an individual's work performance, or creates an intimidating, hostile, or offensive work environment.

sheriff's sale A sale [of property] held by a sheriff to pay a court judgment against the owner of the property.

shopkeeper's privilege A shopkeeper is allowed to detain a suspected shoplifter on store property for a reasonable period of time, so long as he or she has cause to believe that the person detained in fact committed, or attempted to commit, theft of store property.

slander Oral defamation. The speaking of false words that injure another person's reputation, business, or property rights.

slander of title Occurs when a tortfeasor makes false statements about an individual's ownership of property.

sovereign (governmental) immunity The government's freedom from being sued. In many cases, the United States government has waived immunity by a statute such as the Federal Tort Claims Act.

spoliation of evidence Withholding, hiding, or destruction of evidence relevant to a legal proceeding. This is a new tort.

statutes of limitations Laws that set a maximum amount of time after something happens for it to be taken to court, such as a "three-year statute" for lawsuits based on a contract, or a "six-year statute" for a criminal prosecution.

strict (absolute) liability The legal responsibility for damage or injury, even if you are not at fault or negligent.

substantial factor analysis A test for indirect causation in negligence cases. The tortfeasor is liable for injuries to the victim when the tortfeasor's conduct was a substantial factor in producing the harm.

summary jury trial Alternate dispute resolution in which the judge orders the two sides in a complex case to present their case to a small jury. The parties may agree in advance not to be bound by the verdict.

survival statute A state law that allows a lawsuit to be brought by a relative for a person who just died. The lawsuit is based on the cause of action that the dead person would have had.

T

"taking the victim as you find him" A theory in negligence cases that states that the victim's injuries were reasonably foreseeable even if the tortfeasor was unaware of the victim's peculiar physical, health, or other preexisting conditions.

temporary restraining order (TRO) A judge's order to a person to not take a certain action during the period prior to a full hearing on the rightness of the action.

tender years Minors; usually those under the age of seven.

tort A civil (as opposed to a criminal) wrong, other than a breach of contract. For an act to be a tort, there must be: a legal duty owed by one person to another, a breach (breaking) of that duty, and harm done as a direct result of the action. Examples of torts are negligence, battery, and libel.

tortfeasor A person who commits a tort.

toxic tort actions Actions involving toxic chemicals, pollution, hazardous waste disposal and transportation, and other environmentally sensitive issues. Many tort theories, including trespass to land, negligence, absolute liability for ultrahazardous substances, products liability, and nuisance apply.

transferred intent In tort law, the principle that if a person intended to hit another but hits a third person instead, he or she legally *intended* to hit the third person. This "legal fiction" sometimes allows the third person to sue the hitter for an intentional tort.

trespass A wrongful entry onto another person's property.

trespass to chattel Occurs when the tortfeasor intentionally deprives or interferes with the chattel owner's possession or exclusive use of personal property. The tortfeasor's possession or interference must be unauthorized, which means that the owner cannot have consented.

trial The process of deciding a case (giving evidence, making arguments, deciding by a judge and jury, etc.).

U

ultimate user In products liability law, a person who is injured by a defective product. It must have been reasonably foreseeable that the injured party would use the defective product.

unforeseeable plaintiffs Persons whose injuries the tortfeasor could not reasonably have anticipated as a result of the tortfeasor's actions.

unreasonable intrusion One type of the intentional tort of invasion of privacy. Occurs when the tortfeasor engages in an excessive and highly offensive invasion upon another person's seclusion or solitude.

V

vicarious liability Legal responsibility for the acts of another person because of some special relationship with that person; for example, the liability of an employer for certain acts of an employee.

vicious propensity rule Doctrine in absolute liability cases involving domestic animals. Normally owners are not strictly liable for injuries caused by their domestic animals. However, if the animals display vicious propensities and hurt someone or their property, then the owner is absolutely liable.

W

warranty Any promise (or a presumed promise, called an *implied warranty*) that certain facts are true. . . . In consumer law, . . . any obligations imposed by law on a seller that benefit a buyer; for example, the warranty that goods are merchantable and the warranty that goods sold as fit for a particular purpose are fit for that purpose.

wholesaler One who sells goods wholesale, rather than retail.

wrongful birth The birth of a child having serious defects that results from a doctor's failure to provide proper information (to advise, diagnose, or test properly).

wrongful death statute [Statute that allows] a lawsuit [to be] brought by the dependents of a dead person against the person who caused the death. Damages will be given to compensate the dependents for their loss if the killing was negligent or willful.

Z

zone of danger rule The rule in some states that a plaintiff must be in danger of physical harm, and frightened by the danger, to collect damages for the negligent infliction of emotional distress that results from seeing another person injured by the plaintiff.

Index

CENGAGE LEARNING HAS PROVIDED YOU WITH THIS PRODUCT FOR YOUR REVIEW AND, TO THE EXTENT THAT YOU ADOPT THE ASSOCIATED TEXTBOOK FOR USE IN CONNECTION WITH YOUR COURSE, YOU AND YOUR STUDENTS WHO PURCHASE THE TEXTBOOK MAY USE THE MATERIALS AS DESCRIBED BELOW.

IMPORTANT! READ CAREFULLY: This End User License Agreement ("Agreement") sets forth the conditions by which Cengage Learning will make electronic access to the Cengage Learning-owned licensed content and associated media, software, documentation, printed materials, and electronic documentation contained in this package and/or made available to you via this product (the "Licensed Content"), available to you (the "End User"). BY CLICKING THE "I ACCEPT" BUTTON AND/OR OPENING THIS PACKAGE, YOU ACKNOWLEDGE THAT YOU HAVE READ ALL OF THE TERMS AND CONDITIONS, AND THAT YOU AGREE TO BE BOUND BY ITS TERMS, CONDITIONS, AND ALL APPLICABLE LAWS AND REGULATIONS GOVERNING THE USE OF THE LICENSED CONTENT.

1.0 SCOPE OF LICENSE

1.1 Licensed Content. The Licensed Content may contain portions of modifiable content ("Modifiable Content") and content which may not be modified or otherwise altered by the End User ("Non-Modifiable Content"). For purposes of this Agreement, Modifiable Content and Non-Modifiable Content may be collectively referred to herein as the "Licensed Content." All Licensed Content shall be considered Non-Modifiable Content, unless such Licensed Content is presented to the End User in a modifiable format and it is clearly indicated that modification of the Licensed Content is permitted.

1.2 Subject to the End User's compliance with the terms and conditions of this Agreement, Cengage Learning hereby grants the End User, a nontransferable, nonexclusive, limited right to access and view a single copy of the Licensed Content on a single personal computer system for non-commercial, internal, personal use only, and, to the extent that End User adopts the associated textbook for use in connection with a course, the limited right to provide, distribute, and display the Modifiable Content to course students who purchase the textbook, for use in connection with the course only. The End User shall not (i) reproduce, copy, modify (except in the case of Modifiable Content), distribute, display, transfer, sublicense, prepare derivative work(s) based on, sell, exchange, barter or transfer, rent, lease, loan, resell, or in any other manner exploit the Licensed Content; (ii) remove, obscure, or alter any notice of Cengage Learning's intellectual property rights present on or in the Licensed Content, including, but not limited to, copyright, trademark, and/or patent notices; or (iii) disassemble, decompile, translate, reverse engineer, or

otherwise reduce the Licensed Content. Cengage reserves the right to use a hardware lock device, license administration software, and/or a license authorization key to control access or password protection technology to the Licensed Content. The End User may not take any steps to avoid or defeat the purpose of such measures. Use of the Licensed Content without the relevant required lock device or authorization key is prohibited. UNDER NO CIRCUMSTANCES MAY NON-SALEABLE ITEMS PROVIDED TO YOU BY CENGAGE (INCLUDING, WITHOUT LIMITATION, ANNOTATED INSTRUCTOR'S EDITIONS, SOLUTIONS MANUALS, INSTRUCTOR'S RESOURCE MATERIALS AND/OR TEST MATERIALS) BE SOLD, AUCTIONED, LICENSED OR OTHERWISE REDISTRIBUTED BY THE END USER.

2.0 TERMINATION

2.1 Cengage Learning may at any time (without prejudice to its other rights or remedies) immediately terminate this Agreement and/or suspend access to some or all of the Licensed Content, in the event that the End User does not comply with any of the terms and conditions of this Agreement. In the event of such termination by Cengage Learning, the End User shall immediately return any and all copies of the Licensed Content to Cengage Learning.

3.0 PROPRIETARY RIGHTS

3.1 The End User acknowledges that Cengage Learning owns all rights, title and interest, including, but not limited to all copyright rights therein, in and to the Licensed Content, and that the End User shall not take any action inconsistent with such ownership. The Licensed Content is protected by U.S., Canadian and other applicable copyright laws and by international treaties, including the Berne Convention and the Universal Copyright Convention. Nothing contained in this Agreement shall be construed as granting the End User any ownership rights in or to the Licensed Content.

3.2 Cengage Learning reserves the right at any time to withdraw from the Licensed Content any item or part of an item for which it no longer retains the right to publish, or which it has reasonable grounds to believe infringes copyright or is defamatory, unlawful, or otherwise objectionable.

4.0 PROTECTION AND SECURITY

4.1 The End User shall use its best efforts and take all reasonable steps to safeguard its copy of the Licensed Content to ensure that no unauthorized reproduction, publication, disclosure, modification, or distribution of the Licensed Content, in whole or in part, is made. To the extent that the End User becomes aware of any such unauthorized use of the Licensed Content, the End User shall immediately notify Cengage Learning. Notification of such violations may be made by sending an e-mail to infringement@cengage.com.

5.0 MISUSE OF THE LICENSED PRODUCT

5.1 In the event that the End User uses the Licensed Content in violation of this Agreement, Cengage Learning shall have the option of electing liquidated damages, which shall include all profits generated by the End User's use of the Licensed Content plus interest computed at the maximum rate permitted by law and all legal fees and other expenses incurred by Cengage Learning in enforcing its rights, plus penalties.

6.0 FEDERAL GOVERNMENT CLIENTS

6.1 Except as expressly authorized by Cengage Learning, Federal Government clients obtain only the rights specified in this Agreement and no other rights. The Government acknowledges that (i) all software and related documentation incorporated in the Licensed Content is existing commercial computer software within the meaning of FAR 27.405(b)(2); and (2) all other data delivered in whatever form, is limited rights data within the meaning of FAR 27.401. The restrictions in this section are acceptable as consistent with the Government's need for software and other data under this Agreement.

7.0 DISCLAIMER OF WARRANTIES AND LIABILITIES

7.1 Although Cengage Learning believes the Licensed Content to be reliable, Cengage Learning does not guarantee or warrant (i) any information or materials contained in or produced by the Licensed Content, (ii) the accuracy, completeness or reliability of the Licensed Content, or (iii) that the Licensed Content is free from errors or other material defects. THE LICENSED PRODUCT IS PROVIDED "AS IS," WITHOUT ANY WARRANTY OF ANY KIND AND CENGAGE LEARNING DISCLAIMS ANY AND ALL WARRANTIES, EXPRESSED OR IMPLIED, INCLUDING, WITHOUT LIMITATION, WARRANTIES OF MERCHANTABILITY OR FITNESS FOR A PARTICULAR PURPOSE. IN NO EVENT SHALL CENGAGE LEARNING BE LIABLE FOR: INDIRECT, SPECIAL, PUNITIVE OR CONSEQUENTIAL DAMAGES INCLUDING FOR LOST PROFITS, LOST DATA, OR OTHERWISE. IN NO EVENT SHALL CENGAGE LEARNING'S AGGREGATE LIABILITY HEREUNDER, WHETHER ARISING IN CONTRACT, TORT, STRICT LIABILITY OR OTHERWISE, EXCEED THE AMOUNT OF FEES PAID BY THE END USER HEREUNDER FOR THE LICENSE OF THE LICENSED CONTENT.

8.0 GENERAL

8.1 Entire Agreement. This Agreement shall constitute the entire Agreement between the Parties and supercedes all prior Agreements and understandings oral or written relating to the subject matter hereof.

8.2 Enhancements/Modifications of Licensed Content. From time to time, and in Cengage Learning's sole discretion, Cengage Learning may advise the End User of updates, upgrades, enhancements and/or improvements to the Licensed Content, and may permit the End User to access and use, subject to the terms and conditions of this Agreement, such modifications, upon payment of prices as may be established by Cengage Learning.

8.3 No Export. The End User shall use the Licensed Content solely in the United States and shall not transfer or export, directly or indirectly, the Licensed Content outside the United States.

8.4 Severability. If any provision of this Agreement is invalid, illegal, or unenforceable under any applicable statute or rule of law, the provision shall be deemed omitted to the extent that it is invalid, illegal, or unenforceable. In such a case, the remainder of the Agreement shall be construed in a manner as to give greatest effect to the original intention of the parties hereto.

8.5 Waiver. The waiver of any right or failure of either party to exercise in any respect any right provided in this Agreement in any instance shall not be deemed to be a waiver of such right in the future or a waiver of any other right under this Agreement.

8.6 Choice of Law/Venue. This Agreement shall be interpreted, construed, and governed by and in accordance with the laws of the State of New York, applicable to contracts executed and to be wholly preformed therein, without regard to its principles governing conflicts of law. Each party agrees that any proceeding arising out of or relating to this Agreement or the breach or threatened breach of this Agreement may be commenced and prosecuted in a court in the State and County of New York. Each party consents and submits to the nonexclusive personal jurisdiction of any court in the State and County of New York in respect of any such proceeding.

8.7 Acknowledgment. By opening this package and/or by accessing the Licensed Content on this Web site, THE END USER ACKNOWLEDGES THAT IT HAS READ THIS AGREEMENT, UNDERSTANDS IT, AND AGREES TO BE BOUND BY ITS TERMS AND CONDITIONS. IF YOU DO NOT ACCEPT THESE TERMS AND CONDITIONS, YOU MUST NOT ACCESS THE LICENSED CONTENT AND RETURN THE LICENSED PRODUCT TO CENGAGE LEARNING (WITHIN 30 CALENDAR DAYS OF THE END USER'S PURCHASE) WITH PROOF OF PAYMENT ACCEPTABLE TO CENGAGE LEARNING, FOR A CREDIT OR A REFUND. Should the End User have any questions/comments regarding this Agreement, please contact Cengage Learning at Delmar.help@cengage.com.